Ivosic

GB

W9-BBM-075

Management

R. WAYNE MONDY
Northeast Louisiana University

ARTHUR SHARPLIN
Northeast Louisiana University

ROBERT E. HOLMES
James Madison University

EDWIN B. FLIPPO
The University of Arizona

ALLYN AND BACON, INC.
Boston • London • Sydney • Toronto

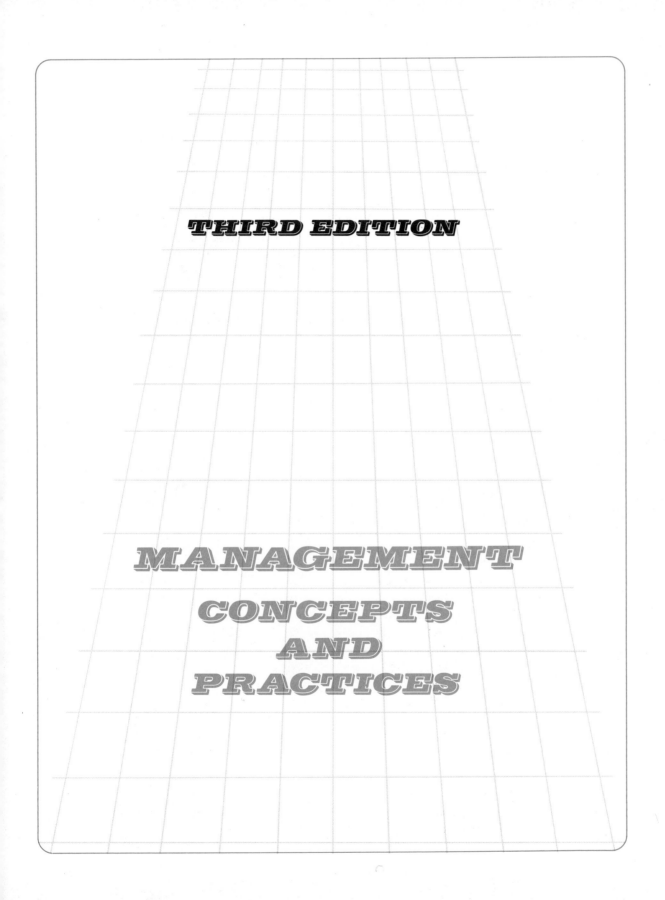

THIRD EDITION

MANAGEMENT
CONCEPTS
AND
PRACTICES

LIBRARY OF CONGRESS CATALOGING-IN-PUBLICATION DATA

Main entry under title:

Management, concepts and practices.

    Rev. ed. of: Management, concepts and practices/
R. Wayne Mondy, Robert E. Holmes, Edwin B. Flippo.
2nd ed. c1983.
    Bibliography: p.
    Includes index.
    1. Management. I. Mondy, R. Wayne,
II. Mondy, R. Wayne,   Management, concepts
and practices.
HD31.M29183 1986   658.4   85–11164
ISBN 0–205–08525–3
ISBN 0–205–08686–1 (International)

Series editor: Jack Peters

Developmental editor: Wendy Ritger

Production administrator: Rowena Dores

Manufacturing buyer: Ellen Glisker

Text designer: Karen Mason

Cover coordinator: Linda Dickinson

Photo researcher: Laurel Anderson/Picture Research Consultants
                    of Salem, Massachusetts

Editorial-Production Service: Winifred B. Hodges/Bywater Production
Services

All photos in table of contents by Robert Frerck/Odyssey
Productions, Chicago

To Frank and Alvora Edens,
*whose friendship, patience, and understanding
have been invaluable*

RWM

To the late J.C. Collier,
whose memory we cherish

ADS

To Diane McKnight Holmes
*for her encouragement,
love, and faith in me*

REH

To my family

EBF

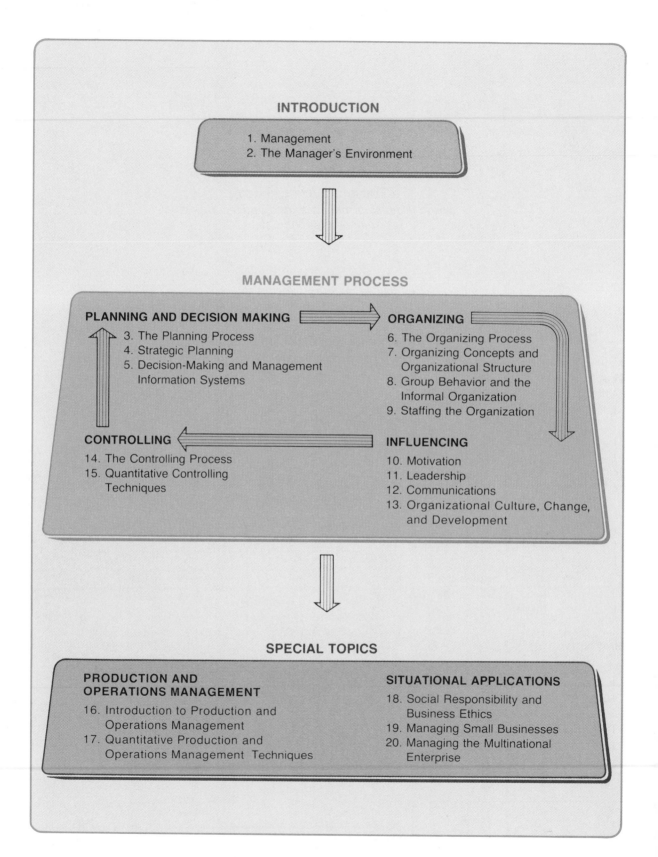

INTRODUCTION

1. Management
2. The Manager's Environment

MANAGEMENT PROCESS

PLANNING AND DECISION MAKING

3. The Planning Process
4. Strategic Planning
5. Decision-Making and Management Information Systems

ORGANIZING

6. The Organizing Process
7. Organizing Concepts and Organizational Structure
8. Group Behavior and the Informal Organization
9. Staffing the Organization

CONTROLLING

14. The Controlling Process
15. Quantitative Controlling Techniques

INFLUENCING

10. Motivation
11. Leadership
12. Communications
13. Organizational Culture, Change, and Development

SPECIAL TOPICS

PRODUCTION AND OPERATIONS MANAGEMENT

16. Introduction to Production and Operations Management
17. Quantitative Production and Operations Management Techniques

SITUATIONAL APPLICATIONS

18. Social Responsibility and Business Ethics
19. Managing Small Businesses
20. Managing the Multinational Enterprise

Contents

Preface

Like the two previous editions, the third edition of *Management: Concepts and Practices* is written for an audience that expects management theory to be linked with actual management practice. A major feature of the third edition is the inclusion of introductory company vignettes for each chapter. Each tells a story about a particular high-profile company, most of which both professors and students will recognize. The vignettes are integrated throughout the chapter to give the discussion coherence and add interest. In addition, each chapter includes a company or an executive profile. The following companies are featured:

Chrysler Corporation
Wendy's International Inc.
Pan American World Airways, Inc.
Nucor Corporation
Holiday Corporation
G. D. Searle & Company
General Electric Company
General Mills, Inc.
Atari, Inc.
Murphy Oil Corporation
Wal-Mart Stores, Inc.
Freeport Firestone
Sears, Roebuck and Co.
National Aeronautics and Space Administration
Derek Garment Factory
Formfit Rogers, Inc.
Lincoln Electric Company
Delta Air Lines, Inc.
Nissan Motor Corporation—USA
People Express Airlines, Inc.
Wickes Companies, Inc.
International Business Machines Corporation
State Farm Mutual Automobile Insurance Company
Adolph Coors Company
7-Eleven Stores Division, The Southland Corporation
The Chase Manhattan Bank, N.A.
General Motors Corporation
Apple Computer, Inc.
Deere & Company
Briggs & Stratton Corporation
Phillips Petroleum Company

Johnson & Johnson
Union Carbide Corporation
Wall Drug Store, Inc.
Sharpco, Inc.
American Motors Corporation
ITT Corporation

Every chapter has been significantly revised and updated. In addition, three new chapters have been added:

- *Strategic Planning:* This topic is receiving increased emphasis in schools of business and is included in the third edition to provide a top management focus for the planning process.
- *Organizational Culture, Change, and Development:* With the publication of *In Search of Excellence, Theory Z,* and *Corporation Cultures,* the concept of organizational culture has captured the fancy of U.S. managers and educators. This topic is blended with a traditional treatment of organizational change and development.
- *Quantitative Controlling Techniques:* The information revolution has brought the capability of handling ever-increasing quantities of data and manipulating those data for management purposes. This chapter segregates the quantitative controlling techniques in use today, giving them additional emphasis and allowing the previous chapter, which examines the controlling process, to be less quantitative.

The third edition offers the features listed below in addition to those mentioned earlier. Some of these did not appear in earlier editions; the ones that have have been refined.

- Chapter outlines appear at the beginning of each chapter to allow readers to see the flow of the chapter in advance.
- A list of key terms is provided at the start of each chapter. Considerable attention has been given to ensuring that each key term is explicitly defined in the text material. Each key term is highlighted in the margin for easy and quick reference.
- Learning objectives are listed at the beginning of each chapter to provide students with an understanding of the purpose of the chapter.
- In the test bank that has been developed to accompany this text, a number of test items are related to each learning objective.
- A large number of easy-to-read figures and tables help describe the concepts and practices that are discussed.
- Review questions are provided for each chapter.
- End-of-chapter exercises permit students to relate the concepts discussed in the text to practical situations.
- A comprehensive list of references permits students to expand study of selected topics.
- Two true-to-life case studies at the conclusion of each chapter allow for class discussions that develop clearer understanding of the practical application of subject matter.
- A longer case is provided at the end of each part to allow an extensive discussion that encompasses the concepts from several chapters.
- Four experiential exercises are included in the instructor's resource manual to give students additional insights, new knowledge, and skills in solving problems and dealing with people in a variety of situations.

Instructors may wish to supplement this text with the study guide prepared by Kathryn W. Hegar and Robert N. Lussier. We believe that it will be of significant value to students.

In summary, we believe the third edition keeps the features of earlier editions that have made them such outstanding successes while adding new information to help students and professors adapt to the changing world of management. The managerial experience of the authors hopefully adds realism to the book. Our sincere desire is that readers be both stimulated and equipped to go into one of the most challenging and rewarding careers, Management.

ACKNOWLEDGMENTS

The writing of a book cannot be accomplished without the assistance of many people. This is especially true for *Management: Concepts and Practices.* Although it would be impossible to list each person who assisted in this project, we feel that certain people must be given credit due to the magnitude of their contributions.

Frank N. Edens of Louisiana Tech University, Jerry M. DeHay of Tarleton State University, along with Robert M. Noe III and James R. Young, both of East Texas State University, all dear and close friends of ours, provided the inspiration and moral support we needed to see the project through to completion. A sincere note of appreciation also goes to the faculty and staff of the College of Business at Northeast Louisiana University for their support and encouragement throughout the preparation of the text. In addition, President Dwight Vines, Dean Van McGraw, and David Loudon, our department head, were with us all the way. Perhaps most important, we had the good fortune of having available to us the services of Barbara Duncan Pace, an author in her own right and certainly the most expert manuscript development specialist we have known.

We would like to thank our wives for their tangible contribution in the preparation of the manuscript. Without their patience, understanding, encouragement, and creative editing, the project would not have been completed. They willingly made a number of sacrifices during the long writing process.

We would also like to acknowledge the many contributions of our editors, Jack Peters and Wendy Ritger, for their thoughtfulness and assistance throughout the project. Finally, we would like to thank our reviewers for their many excellent suggestions during the preparation of the third edition of *Management: Concepts and Practices:*

Yohannan T. Abraham, Southwest Missouri State University; Jerry W. Anderson, Xavier University; Allen Bluedorn, University of Missouri at Columbia; Ralph F. Catalanello, Northern Illinois University, DeKalb; John T. Haller, Jr., Slippery Rock University of Pennsylvania; Edson G. Hammer, University of Tennessee at Chattanooga; Paul Harmon, University of Utah; Dean Headley, Kansas Newman College; Harvey Hoag, San Antonio College; Charles P. Leo, California State University at Northridge; Richard S. Linton, California State University, Longbeach;

Daniel E. Lockhart, Eastern Kentucky University; Richard D. McAfoose, Indiana University of Pennsylvania; Daniel McNamara, College of St. Thomas; Micol R. C. Maughan, University of Northern Iowa; Kenneth Newgren, Illinois State University; William A. Nowlin, Rochester Institute of Technology; Victor G. Panico, California State University, Fresno; Robert Rosen, University of South Carolina; Mary Schmiesing, South Dakota State University; Joseph B. Stulberg, Baruch College, CUNY; Ellen West, Portland State University; Burl Worley, Allan Hancock College; Carl Zeithaml, Texas A & M University.

Management

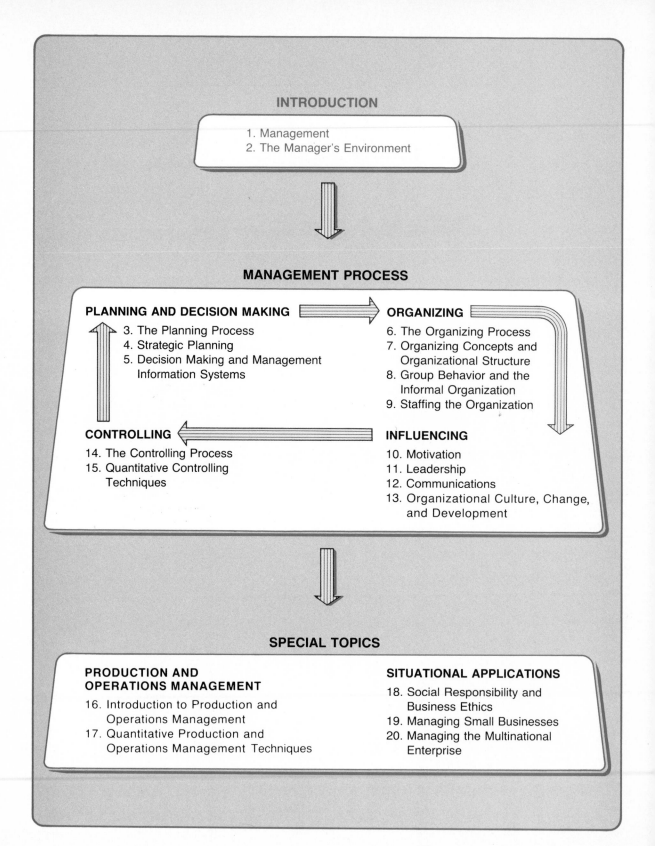

INTRODUCTION

1. Management
2. The Manager's Environment

MANAGEMENT PROCESS

PLANNING AND DECISION MAKING

3. The Planning Process
4. Strategic Planning
5. Decision Making and Management Information Systems

ORGANIZING

6. The Organizing Process
7. Organizing Concepts and Organizational Structure
8. Group Behavior and the Informal Organization
9. Staffing the Organization

CONTROLLING

14. The Controlling Process
15. Quantitative Controlling Techniques

INFLUENCING

10. Motivation
11. Leadership
12. Communications
13. Organizational Culture, Change, and Development

SPECIAL TOPICS

PRODUCTION AND OPERATIONS MANAGEMENT

16. Introduction to Production and Operations Management
17. Quantitative Production and Operations Management Techniques

SITUATIONAL APPLICATIONS

18. Social Responsibility and Business Ethics
19. Managing Small Businesses
20. Managing the Multinational Enterprise

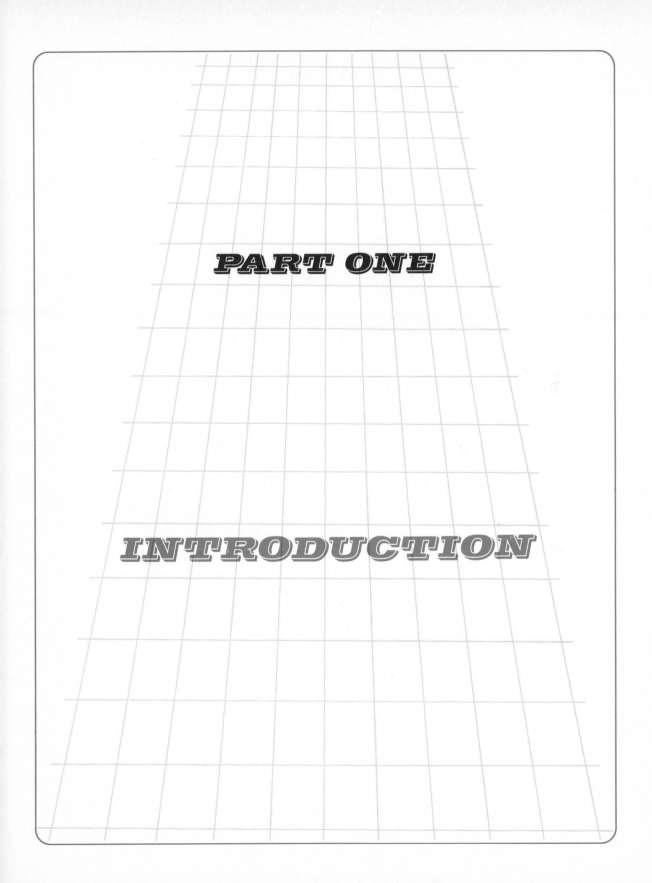

PART ONE

INTRODUCTION

management	decision making	classical school of
function	supervisory managers	management
planning	middle managers	scientific management
organizing	top managers	behavioral school of
influencing	conceptual skill	management
motivation	technical skill	human relations
leadership	human skill	movement
communication	productivity	Hawthorne effect
controlling		modern behaviorism

LEARNING OBJECTIVES

After completing this chapter you should be able to

1. Define *management* and explain the work of managers.
2. Explain the management functions of planning, organizing, influencing, and controlling.
3. Describe the work of managers at different organizational levels.
4. Discuss the importance of conceptual, technical, and human managerial skills.
5. Define productivity and state why it is important to managers.
6. Describe the classical and behavioral schools of management.

1

Management

CHAPTER OUTLINE

What Is Management?
The Management Functions
Management at Different Levels
Managerial Skills
The Productivity Challenge
Basic Schools of Management Thought
Purposes and Organization of This Text
Appendix: Careers in Management

CHRYSLER
CORPORATION

When Lee Iacocca assumed the presidency of Chrysler in 1979, the company had just suffered its worst one-quarter loss in history. The U.S. auto industry was beset by foreign competition. The country was entering a lengthy recession. Interest rates were at all-time highs, depressing demand for autos and other durable consumer goods. Actual and threatened auto industry layoffs, along with wage and benefit cuts, had produced a difficult labor relations climate. Iacocca had his work cut out for him.

Iacocca brought with him impressive credentials. He also brought along a number of able lieutenants, most former Ford executives. As a Ford Motor Company executive himself, he had been credited with developing the Mustang and had risen rapidly through the ranks to become second in command to Henry Ford, II. Many thought Iacocca had an uncanny knack for sensing market needs and creating products to meet those needs. He had a reputation for getting the most out of his subordinates, for creating enthusiasm, for making difficult decisions, and for working harder than anyone else.

At Chrysler, Iacocca tried to live up to his billing. He visited factories, jawboned the union, cut television commercials, and at all times maintained the appearance of a vibrant, forceful, in-charge—though kindly—executive.

Behind the glamour, though, there were hard decisions to be made and great personal risks for Iacocca. Chrysler's factory employment was cut in half. One-third of the company's plants were closed. A number of Chrysler's cars were redesigned to reuse parts of older models and to use fewer parts overall. The dissatisfaction Iacocca's actions created was immediate, although the benefits were significantly delayed, and the company was still losing hundreds of millions in 1981.

But Chrysler was on its way to recovery. The company's market share increased from 7.8 percent in 1980 to 12.5 percent in 1984. Billion-dollar losses in 1979 and 1980 became billion-dollar profits by 1984. Chrysler moved up eight spots on the Fortune 500 list of companies, to number 21. Government-guaranteed loans, made to help Chrysler survive, were completely repaid. And Chrysler's breakeven point, the number of cars that the company must sell to keep from losing money, was reduced from 2.3 million units to less than half that figure.

As so often happens, the benefits of effective management were widely distributed at Chrysler. Stockholders saw their share prices more than double in a three-year period. The management team that saw Chrysler through its crisis received millions of dollars in bonuses. And the employees, who had agreed to wage and benefit cuts in the beginning, ended up substantial owners of the corporation because of shares contributed to their retirement plan.[1]

What accounts for Chrysler's remarkable success? Most would agree that effective management played a major part. This book is about management. The topic is not a simple one. At Chrysler, management involved negotiations with government and with unions. It required laying off employees, closing plants, and forecasting future opportunities and preparing to take advantage of them. An executive team had to be developed. An organization of 80,000 men and women had to be given a boost, made to pull together toward common goals, or at least compatible ones. A complex organization, involving a dozen levels of management, had to be administered and improved.

Most managerial situations are not as exciting as that which Iacocca faced. And not all business adventures end in success. Half of all new businesses fail within the first two years of operation, and 70 percent fail within five years. In over 90 percent of the cases, the cause of failure is said to be ineffective management. Despite Iacocca's reputation, few gave him much chance of salvaging Chrysler, let alone making it a leader. The costs of poor management to individuals and to society are great. Not only are financial and physical resources wasted, but individuals often suffer psychological damage from a business failure. It is not fun to say you have failed. Many business failures can be avoided through good management practices.

We live in a society of large and small organizations. In these organizations people work together to accomplish goals that are too challenging to be achieved by a single individual. Throughout life we have experiences with a variety of organizations—hospitals, schools, churches, the military, businesses, colleges, government agencies, and other types of institutions. More and more, it is being recognized that the most significant factor in determining the performance and success of any organization is the quality of its management.

Why are some managers successful and others not? The reasons are as diverse as individual personalities. Elton H. Rule, president of American Broadcasting Companies, was asked his formula for managerial success. He replied:

> Intelligence, integrity, imagination, and energy: these are qualities essential to any manager anywhere. Here, though, two other qualities are equally important. A successful manager must be responsive; we serve many communities, not least among them the public at large. A manager too devoted to a single community or a single approach will rapidly become unable to function effectively. And a successful manager must be people-oriented, because human judgment and creativity are by a wide margin the most productive assets of our industry.

As Rule's comments suggest, managers must work through others. In this book we are concerned with providing you with knowledge about the fundamental concepts and techniques used by good managers like Rule and Iacocca. We will present ideas, concepts, and practices that can serve as aids to effective management. Many actual examples will be presented. Although our primary focus will be on the management of business organizations, most of what we write will also apply to nonbusiness organizations such as hospitals, churches, government agencies, and schools or universities.

In this first chapter we discuss the concept of management and then describe the four management functions. Next, we show how management differs at various levels in the organization. Then, the skills managers need are categorized, and the productivity challenge management faces is discussed. The chapter ends with a brief discussion of the basic schools of management thought.

WHAT IS MANAGEMENT?

Unless you inherit a fortune, you will probably choose to be employed by some type of organization. Many of you will become managers, and those who are not managers are likely to be professional and technical personnel such as engineers, salespersons, systems analysts, accountants, market researchers, or computer programmers. In any case, all of you will manage others and be managed at various times in your lives. Thus, it is important to address the question, "What is management?"

management

We define **management** as *the process of getting things done through the efforts of other people.* This often involves the allocation and control of money and physical resources. Lee Iacocca's position as president of Chrysler Corporation gave him extraordinary power over those with whom he worked. He could hire and fire managers and others. He could fund or not fund the activities his subordinates favored. He could shut down plants, replace workers with robots, and carry out his purposes at Chrysler in dozens of other ways. Our definition of management includes all of these ideas. What is excluded is the action of an individual working alone. A person is not a manager unless involved in the process of getting things done through others.

THE MANAGEMENT FUNCTIONS

By general agreement, the management process is thought of as consisting of four functions: planning, organizing, influencing, and controlling. A

function

function is *a type of work activity that can be identified and distinguished from other work.* Each of the next four parts of this book is devoted to one of the management functions; a brief discussion of them is presented here.

Planning

planning

Planning is *the process of determining in advance what should be accomplished and how to do it.* Ideally plans should be stated in specific terms so that they provide clear guidance for managers and workers. For example, when Chrysler Corporation decided to gain market share by developing new products, management had to make specific decisions about both the types of new cars and the numbers to make. Partly as a result of introduction of the K-car and the minivan, Chrysler's market share climbed by more than 30 percent. Chrysler's plans were specific not only about the number of cars to be produced but about the market share improvement sought as well.

The Chrysler story is a well-known example of top-level planning; however, the planning process is similar no matter what the level of the organization. Suppose at the first of the week a supervisor is given a production list for completion by Friday. This list tells the supervisor what should be accomplished. Part of the planning has already occurred; however, the supervisor may have to determine how the required production can be completed. Perhaps the supervisor will schedule one-fifth of the output for Monday, one-fifth for Tuesday, and so forth. Analyzing the information available and making decisions are major aspects of the planning process. Planning is the subject of Chapters 3 and 4.

Organizing

Organizing is *the process of prescribing formal relationships among people and resources to accomplish goals.* For Chrysler Corporation in 1979, organizing required determining the new relationships that would exist among thousands of workers and managers. It also required determining work flows among the remaining plants. At lower levels, workers were assigned to different supervisors, assembly lines were rearranged, and many activities previously performed by Chrysler employees were contracted out. Chapters 6 and 7 discuss organizing as a formal process. Of course, the formal organization must take into account the informal relationships and group behavior patterns that exist among organization members. These are the subject of Chapter 8.

A most important aspect of organizing is ensuring that the right people with the right qualifications are available at the right places and times to accomplish the purposes of the organization. This is called staffing and is the subject of Chapter 9.

Influencing

Influencing is *the process of determining or affecting the behavior of others.* This involves motivation, leadership, and communication. **Motivation** is defined as *the willingness to put forth effort in the pursuit of goals.* Motivating workers often means simply creating an environment that makes them want to work. Part of this environment is the direction provided by the manager. Each worker may require a different means of motivation. A manager cannot motivate a worker to produce unless the worker chooses to respond. But managers can often create a situation where workers will want to produce more (be motivated). We discuss motivation in greater detail in Chapter 10.

Leadership is *getting others to do what the leader wants them to do.* A good leader is one who motivates others to put forth their best efforts. As will be seen in Chapter 11, leaders may depend in part on charisma or other outstanding personal characteristics. For example, many believe that

organizing

influencing
motivation

leadership

The leadership style that works best will vary.   Christian Delbert/The Picture Cube

much of Lee Iacocca's success is his ability to inspire others. However, good leadership more often results from learning what motivates individual workers and using this knowledge to direct their activities. The leadership style that works best will vary depending on the characteristics of the leader, the led, and the situation. Zoltan Merszei, chairman of Dow Chemical Company, summed up the appropriate philosophy of leadership when he said, "A leader must *lead*, not drive. People are unpredictable, different from one another, often irascible, frequently petty, sometimes vain, but always magnificent if they are properly motivated."

communication   **Communication** is *the transfer of information, ideas, understanding, or feelings between people.* Much of a manager's day is spent communicating. Supervisors, for example, tell workers what needs to be done. They also report to upper-level management, summarizing their unit's activities, seeking support and guidance, and representing subordinates. Communication will be discussed further in Chapter 12.

The way in which managers motivate and lead workers and communicate with superiors and subordinates affects and is affected by corporate culture. The culture can be one of openness and support, as the authors of the landmark book *In Search of Excellence* said is the case at IBM and Xerox. It also may be one of autocracy and fear that some say exists at Manville Corporation, the huge asbestos maker that obtained bankruptcy court protection in 1982 from thousands of asbestos victims who sought recompense. Corporate culture—the system of shared values, beliefs, and habits within an organization—is discussed in Chapter 13.

Controlling

Controlling is *the process of comparing actual performance with standards and taking any necessary corrective action.* The purpose of establishing controls is to ensure proper performance in accordance with plans. In the event of unsatisfactory performance, corrective action can be taken. For instance, if a company's costs for producing a product are higher than planned, management must have some means to recognize the problem and take the appropriate action to correct the situation. Controls can also work on the positive side. When sales of Chrysler's minivans exceeded expectations in 1982, shifts were added at existing plants, and plans were made to reopen a factory that had been closed.

controlling

An aspect of the controlling function that relates uniquely to the human resource is disciplinary action. This is action taken to correct undesired behavior and ranges from a verbal warning to outright dismissal. The control function is discussed in Chapter 14.

Decision Making and the Management Functions

A task that managers perform in carrying out each of the management functions is decision making. **Decision making** is *the process of generating and evaluating alternatives and making choices among them.* Perhaps no other attribute so frequently distinguishes the excellent manager from mediocre ones as does decision-making skills.

decision making

Lee Iacocca is certainly an effective decision maker. When plans were made to produce the minivan, it was necessary to decide how many to make and where to make them. Decisions also had to be made as to how the new, more flexible organization at Chrysler would function. Upon arriving at Chrysler, Iacocca found an unmotivated, listless work force. Among the hard decisions made to change this was the decision to give much of Chrysler's stock to the employee stock ownership plan. Finally, Iacocca and his management team had to decide what kinds of controls to impose. Quality control especially was important in the light of the threat represented by high-quality Japanese imports. As the Chrysler story indicates, decision making is of the very essence of management and is involved in each of the management functions.

 "Where's the Beef?™" rasped the old lady, launching one of the most widely acclaimed advertising campaigns in history. The ads caught the fancy of America, and the slogan became a household phrase. Wendy's had won another skirmish in the "Great Burger War" among the top three hamburger marketers, Wendy's, McDonald's, and Burger King. Founded in 1969, Wendy's is the new kid on the block. But it was the first fast service chain to surpass $1 billion in annual sales within ten years, and total revenue has recently exceeded $2 billion.

Wendy's Has the Beef

No matter how excellent Wendy's advertising program, the funds necessary to finance the company's rapid expansion would not have been available without profits. And Wendy's is said to have the most efficient production system of any other quick service company. The founder, R. David Thomas, who named the chain after his daughter, said, "Quality is our Recipe.®" A number of Wendy's policies support this motto. Wendy's uses only fresh, locally purchased beef. There are no heating lamps, microwave ovens, or steam cabinets to keep food hot, and every hamburger is produced to order when ordered. If a meat patty is not sold within two minutes, it is put into the chili pot.

The Wendy's System stresses not only quality but also productivity. The hamburgers are produced on a hamburger assembly line, similar to those at Detroit. Each worker has a specific job. Speed and efficiency are stressed. A recent survey indicates that on average Wendy's serves customers twice as fast as do competitors.

As the hamburger market has become more and more competitive, Wendy's has had to diversify its product line, making the production process more complicated. A salad bar was added, followed by a chicken sandwich, taco salad and then baked potatoes.

Maintaining efficiency in the face of this increasing complexity presents a major challenge. To help meet the challenge, Wendy's has boosted its research and development expenditures to five times the 1980 level. The company has invested in computerized cash registers, which compile data for sales analysis, inventory projections, cash control, and even labor scheduling. Customer count and product mix data are rapidly communicated to regional and corporate offices so that no opportunity is missed to improve the system. With over 3000 restaurants, Wendy's has been able to save millions through new building designs, resulting in better operations control and lower energy costs.

With its large competitors using similar sophisticated techniques, Wendy's must continually innovate, seeking ever more efficient ways to make and market hamburgers and related products. As the "Great Burger War" goes on, no one doubts that Wendy's has the beef to remain a major combatant.[2]

MANAGEMENT AT DIFFERENT LEVELS

We sometimes think of managers only in terms of top-level positions within large organizations. Certainly Chrysler's Lee Iacocca is a manager. But most managers do not have responsibility for an entire company. Although the distinctions are by no means clear, it is useful to think of managers as being divided into three groups. These groups are shown in Figure 1–1, and we will refer to them as the levels of management.

supervisory managers   **Supervisory managers** are *persons who directly oversee the efforts of those who actually perform the work.* Most supervisory managers have titles like supervisor, foreman, leadman, or office manager. Department heads at universities are typically considered to be supervisory managers because they oversee the activities of professors, who actually do the jobs of

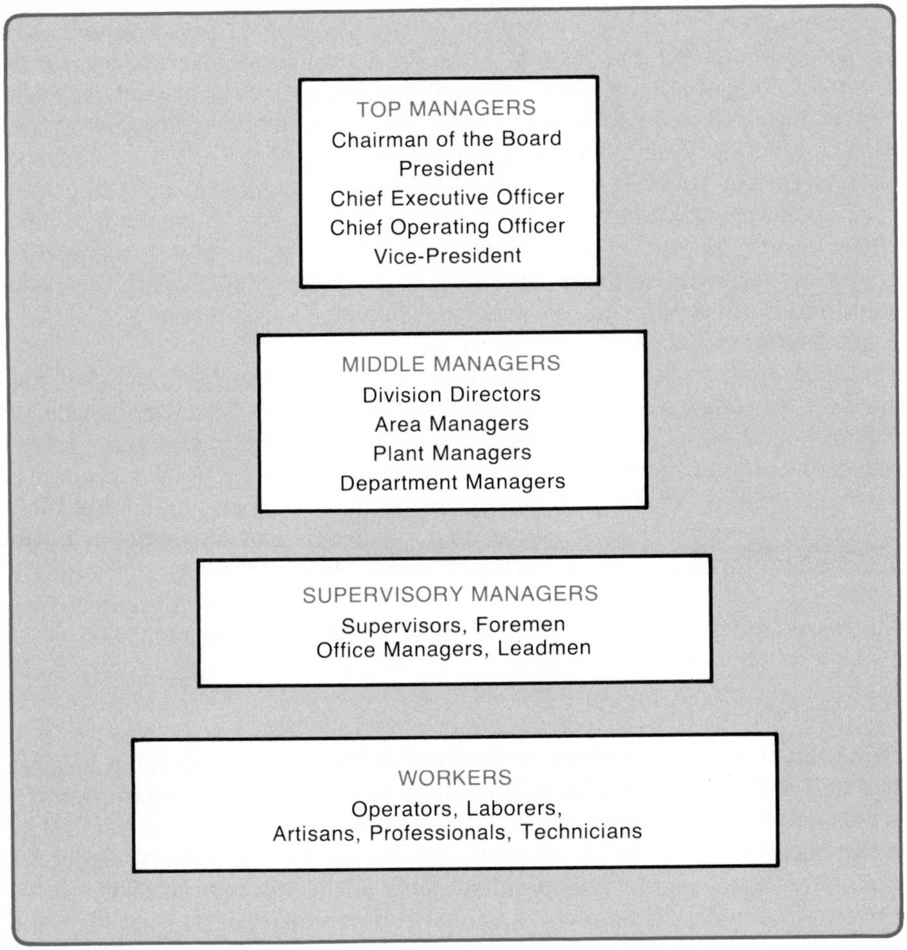

```
┌─────────────────────────────────────────┐
│        ┌──────────────────────┐          │
│        │     TOP MANAGERS     │          │
│        │ Chairman of the Board│          │
│        │      President       │          │
│        │Chief Executive Officer│         │
│        │Chief Operating Officer│         │
│        │    Vice-President    │          │
│        └──────────────────────┘          │
│                                          │
│      ┌──────────────────────────┐        │
│      │      MIDDLE MANAGERS     │        │
│      │    Division Directors    │        │
│      │       Area Managers      │        │
│      │      Plant Managers      │        │
│      │   Department Managers    │        │
│      └──────────────────────────┘        │
│                                          │
│    ┌──────────────────────────────┐      │
│    │     SUPERVISORY MANAGERS     │      │
│    │     Supervisors, Foremen     │      │
│    │   Office Managers, Leadmen   │      │
│    └──────────────────────────────┘      │
│                                          │
│  ┌──────────────────────────────────┐    │
│  │             WORKERS              │    │
│  │        Operators, Laborers,      │    │
│  │ Artisans, Professionals, Technicians│ │
│  └──────────────────────────────────┘    │
└─────────────────────────────────────────┘
```

Figure 1–1

Managerial Levels

research and teaching. At Wendy's the person responsible for a particular store is a supervisory manager.

Middle managers are *managers above the supervisory level but subordinate to the firm's most senior executives.* These persons might be department managers, division directors, area managers, or plant managers. Wendy's has a number of levels of middle managers; for example, a district manager may have charge of ten restaurants. Division or area managers may be responsible for a number of district managers.

middle managers

Top managers are *the organization's most senior executives.* They usually include the chairman of the board and the president, along with vice-presidents who are responsible for major subdivisions of the organization. Top managers are responsible for providing the overall direction of the firm.

top managers

Top management at Wendy's includes at least the top two or three levels of officials, the chairman of the board, the president, and the vice-presidents in charge of various operations. The legendary founder of Wendy's, R. David Thomas, was for many years the most senior of Wendy's top managers. He gave Wendy's its unique character, and his influence will be felt for many years.

In summary, a *manager is anyone, at any level of the organization, who directs the efforts of other people.* Wherever a group of people work together to achieve results, a manager is usually present. School principals, meat market supervisors, and service station operators are managers, just as are the presidents of General Motors, Prudential Insurance, Gulf Oil, and Bank of America. The president of the United States is a manager, too, along with government agency heads and college deans. *A manager is the catalyst who makes things happen.* The manager establishes goals, plans operations, organizes various resources—personnel, materials, equipment, capital— leads and motivates people to perform, evaluates actual results against the goals, and develops people for the organization.

Unfortunately, in many organizations, the success of a particular manager is judged exclusively on short-run output. In other words, a manager may be said to be effective if his or her unit is earning a profit, reducing costs, or increasing the market share for the company's products. Naturally, these accomplishments are very important to a business organization; however, a major added challenge and obligation of any manager is the development of subordinates. More than any other single variable, it is perhaps the quality of a manager's subordinates that determines the long-term success and effectiveness for that manager.

MANAGERIAL SKILLS

To be effective, a manager must possess and continually develop several essential skills. Figure 1–2 illustrates three categories of skills important to a manager's overall effectiveness. The relative significance of each skill varies according to level of management, but the best managers recognize that they must develop and practice each of the managerial skills to be effective in accomplishing organizational and personal goals. They dare not concentrate their efforts on only one of these skills, even though it may be the most important one at their level in the organization. It is the combination of skills that is vital to managerial success. With this clearly in mind, let us now consider the three categories of skills separately.

Conceptual Skills

conceptual skill

The ability to comprehend abstract or general ideas and apply them to specific situations is **conceptual skill**. It is through the exercise of conceptual skills that the manager understands the complexities of the overall organization, including how each subunit contributes to the accomplishment of the firm's purposes. These skills are crucial to the success of top-level executives. They must be concerned with the big picture—assessing opportunities and deciding how to take advantage of them. For instance, the "Great Burger War" might be equated to a chess game in which Wendy's must not only plan its own action but anticipate the initiatives of McDonald's and Burger King. A mistake here can mean disaster. The further down in the organization one looks, the less vital conceptual skills are. Middle managers need moderate conceptual skills but not as much as top managers. Supervisors typically have the least need for conceptual skills because they usually are given fairly specific guidelines. Supervisors are primarily

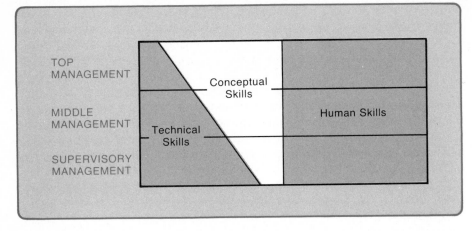

Figure 1–2

*Skills at Various
Levels of Management*

concerned with their department and other closely related departments, and these relationships are more clearly defined. A Wendy's restaurant manager, for example, does not have to consider the restaurant design. That complex matter has been decided at higher levels.

Technical Skill

Technical skill is *the ability to use specific knowledge, methods, or techniques in performing work.* This category of skills is very important to job success for supervisors. They need technical skills partly because they must train new workers. Also, knowing how the job should be performed helps the supervisor monitor daily work activities. If corrections are needed, the technically skilled supervisor is much better qualified to make them. Managers at every level in the Wendy's organization are concerned with how to make the perfect hamburger, but it is the store manager who must answer the customer's question, "Where's the beef?"

    As one moves to higher levels of management within the organization, the importance of technical skills usually diminishes because managers at those levels have less direct contact with day-to-day problems and activities. Top management has perhaps the least need for technical skills. Many upper-level managers have technical backgrounds, but, unlike supervisors, they seldom use their technical skills on a day-to-day basis. For instance, the president of an engineering firm, although trained as an engineer, is not likely to design a new machine personally. We do not wish to overstate the case. Some chief executives, including Chrysler's Lee Iacocca and Wendy's R. David Thomas, are highly respected by subordinates for their technical expertise. Undoubtedly this makes them better managers.

technical skill

Human Skills

The ability to understand, motivate, and get along with other people is **human skill.** Human skills are about equally important at all levels of management. Activities requiring human skills include communicating, leading, and motivating. For example, a Wendy's store manager must interact with workers, customers, and suppliers. And Chairman R. David Thomas

human skill

must communicate with and influence other executives and directors in the company and persons outside the organization such as investment bankers.

THE PRODUCTIVITY CHALLENGE

The development of managerial skills is not an end in itself. Most people would agree that these skills are useless unless applied toward increasing the quality and quantity of goods and services produced in the economy. For society, and for the individual, high standards of living are obtained by producing goods and services efficiently. Historically, the United States has

productivity   had the highest levels of productivity of all major countries. **Productivity** is *a measure of the relationship between inputs (labor, capital, natural*

Figure 1–3   Relative Levels in Real Gross Domestic Product per Employed Person, Selected Countries and Years, 1960–1981   Source: Bureau of Labor Statistics, 1983.

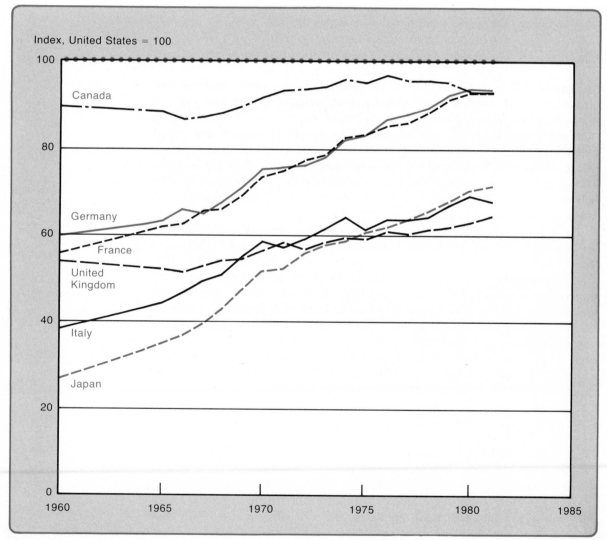

resources, energy, and so forth) and the quality and quantity of outputs (goods and services). Note from this definition that outputs must be measured in terms of both quality and quantity. For example, although the Chevrolet Vega was produced in the United States at a cost approximating that of the Toyota Corolla, made in Japan, the U.S. auto industry productivity was not as high as that of Japan. The output in terms of quantity may have been the same but the Corolla was clearly superior in terms of quality.

Productivity is usually expressed only in terms of output per person hour or output per employed person. What causes it to be high or low? Productivity is a result not only of the capability and motivation of workers but also of technology, capital investment, capacity utilization, scale of production, and many other factors.

How does productivity in the United States compare with that in other countries? Figure 1–3 shows the relative levels of productivity in terms of output per employed person in the major industrial countries over two decades. Note that although the United States has a commanding lead over most of these other countries, that lead is narrowing in a relative sense. Even in 1982, however, the United States held about an 8 percent productivity advantage over its nearest competitor nation.

In the 1980s there is much concern in the United States because the rate of growth in productivity is less than that for other industrial nations. Table 1–1 illustrates this for the countries represented in Figure 1–3. Remember, Table 1–1 does not show productivity levels but the rates of growth in productivity. Note that for the first period shown, productivity in the United States grew more slowly than that for any of the other countries. During the second period, only Canada's productivity growth was lower than that of the United States. This is not a recent phenomenon, however, and it exists in part because the United States started from a higher base. For example, in 1960, when Japanese productivity was less than one-fourth that in the United States, an increase in productivity by the same absolute amount for both countries would have been four times as high a percentage increase for Japan. Still, the major challenge facing American management during the 1980s and 1990s will be to attain levels of productivity growth that will ensure that the United States remains, as it has always been, the most productive major nation in the world. This can be accomplished through improvements in all of the factors of production. If management has a single societal goal, increasing productivity has to be it. Remember,

TABLE 1–1   Rates of Growth in Productivity (average annual percent change)

Country	Real gross domestic product per employed person	
	1965–1973	1973–1981
United States	1.6	0.2
Canada	2.4	0.1
France	4.6	2.4
Germany	4.3	2.5
Japan	8.2	2.9
United Kingdom	3.2	1.3

Source: U.S. Department of Commerce.

Technical expertise is often a needed managerial skill.

David Aronson/Stock, Boston Inc.

as we have defined the term *productivity,* it includes a measure of both the quality and the quantity of output.

Several authorities—such as John Naisbitt, who wrote *Megatrends,* and Thomas Peters and Robert Waterman, authors of *In Search of Excellence*— have noted the shift in the United States from an industrial economy to a service and information one. As this occurs, productivity becomes more difficult to measure. For example, it is harder to calculate the output of a computer programmer or a financial adviser than that of a person who works on an assembly line at General Motors. Nevertheless, productivity remains the control objective of organized human activity.

BASIC SCHOOLS OF MANAGEMENT THOUGHT

The emphasis in this book is on the current state of management thinking. But just as political science students cannot fail to consider the history of government, management students must have at least a passing familiarity with what has gone before in the field of management. The history of management obviously extends several thousand years into the past. Moses, for example, is credited with having employed the first management consultant (his father-in-law) to help design the organization through which Moses governed the Hebrews. But it was not until the late nineteenth century that management began to be considered a formal discipline. To place the recent history of management thought in some perspective, although at the risk of oversimplification, we will discuss two schools of management thought in terms of the historical development of the field. Then we will show how one expert has categorized the modern theories of management without regard to their connection to history.

Classical School of Management

The oldest and perhaps most widely accepted school among practitioners has been called the **classical school of management** thought. This is *the approach to management thought that arose mainly from efforts between 1900 and 1940 to provide a rational and scientific basis for the management of organizations.* This is sometimes referred to as the traditional school of management.

classical school of management

As a result of the Industrial Revolution, people were brought together to work in factories. This system was in marked contrast to the handicraft system whereby people worked separately in small shops or in their own homes. Thus industrialization created a need for the effective management of people and other resources in the emerging organizations. In other words, there was a need for efficient planning, organizing, influencing, and controlling of work activities.

In response to the growth of large organizations in the late nineteenth century and during the early twentieth century, there was an intensified interest in management as a process and as a science. It was apparent to many that management could be made more effective and efficient. The primary contributions of the classical school of management include the following:

1. The application of science to the practice of management
2. The development of the basic management functions: planning, organizing, influencing, and controlling
3. The articulation and application of specific principles of management

Classical management concepts have significantly improved the practice of management, leading to substantial improvements in performance within organizations.

Scientific Management

Frederick Taylor, who made major contributions to management thinking around the turn of this century, is often called the Father of Scientific Management. Taylor was supported in his efforts by Henry Gantt, Frank and Lillian Gilbreth, and Harrington Emerson. All of these Taylor disciples became famous in their own rights. Together with Taylor they revolutionized management thinking. **Scientific management** is *the name given to the principles and practices that grew out of the work of Frederick Taylor and his followers and that are characterized by concern for efficiency and systematization in management.* Taylor was convinced that the scientific method should apply to the management process. The scientific method provides a logical framework for the analysis of problems. It basically consists of defining the problem, gathering data, analyzing the data, developing alternatives, and selecting the best alternative. Taylor believed that following the scientific method would provide a way to determine the most efficient way to perform work. Instead of abdicating responsibility for establishing standards, for example, management would scientifically study all facets of an operation and carefully set a logical and rational standard. Instead of guessing or relying solely on trial and error, management would

scientific management

go through the time-consuming process of logical study and scientific research to develop answers to business problems. Taylor's philosophy can be summarized in the following four principles:

1. Developing and using the scientific method in the practice of management (finding the "one best way" to perform work)
2. Using scientific approaches to select employees who are best suited to perform a given job
3. Providing employees with scientific education, training, and development
4. Encouraging friendly interaction and cooperation between management and employees but with a separation of duties between managers and workers

Taylor stated many times that scientific management would require a revolution in thinking by both the manager and the subordinate. His purpose was not solely to advance the interests of the manager and the enterprise. He believed sincerely that scientific management practices would benefit both the employee and the employer through the creation of a larger surplus. The organization would achieve higher output, and the worker would receive more income.

The greater part of Taylor's work was oriented toward improving management of production operations. The classic case of the pig iron experiment at the Bethlehem Steel Company illustrates his approach.[3] The task he studied at Bethlehem was so simple most managers would tend to ignore it. Laborers would pick up 92-pound pigs (chunks of iron) from a storage yard, walk up a plank onto a railroad car, and place the pigs in the car. In a group of seventy-five laborers, the average output was about 12.5 tons per man per day. In applying the scientific method of study to this problem of getting work done through others, Taylor developed (1) an improved method of work, (2) a prescribed amount of rest on the job, (3) a specific standard of output, and (4) payment by the unit of output. Using this approach, the average output per worker rose from 12.5 tons to 48 tons. Under the incentive system, the daily pay rose from $1.15 to $1.85, an amount substantially higher than the going rate.

Taylor's dedication to systematic planning and study of all kinds of process pervaded his entire life. With a specially designed tennis racket, he became part of the National Doubles Tennis Championship team. When he played golf, he used uniquely designed clubs for any predictable type of lie. When he used a particular putter, his friends refused to play because of its accuracy. A famed novelist reported that Taylor died of pneumonia in a hospital, probably with his stopwatch in his hand.

Frank and Lillian Gilbreth concentrated on motion study to develop more efficient ways to pour concrete, lay bricks, and perform many other repetitive tasks. After Frank's death, Lillian became a professor of management at Purdue University. Until her death in 1972, she was considered the First Lady of Management.

H. L. Gantt developed a control chart that is used to this day in production operations. The Gantt chart is considered by many to have been the forerunner of modern PERT (program evaluation and review technique) analysis to be discussed in detail in Chapter 17.

Harrington Emerson set forth "twelve principles of efficiency" in a 1913 book of that title. Certain of Emerson's principles state that a manager should carefully define objectives, use the scientific method of analysis, develop and use standardized procedures, and reward employees for good work. His book remains a recognized management classic.

General Management Theory

In contrast to Taylor, Emerson, Gantt, and the Gilbreths, Henri Fayol and C. I. Barnard attempted to develop a broader theory concerned with general management. (Although Frederick Taylor and Henri Fayol were contemporaries, the two apparently never knew of one another's work. Fayol's major contribution to management literature, *Industrial and General Management,* was not translated into English until long after Taylor died and, in fact, after Fayol himself had died.) Fayol's thesis was that the fundamental functions of any manager consist of planning, organizing, commanding, coordinating, and controlling. He attempted to develop a number of general principles designed to improve the practice of general management.

Chester Barnard's ideas, expressed in his classic book, *The Functions of the Executive,* have significantly influenced the theory and practice of management for nearly half a century.[4] For years, Barnard was president of New Jersey Bell Telephone and also held a number of important public service posts. Barnard believed that the most important function of a manager is to promote cooperative effort toward goals of the organization. He believed that cooperation depends on effective communications and a balance between rewards to, and contributions by, each employee.

Behavioral School of Management

In the 1920s and 1930s, some observers of organizations became convinced that scientific management was shortsighted and incomplete. In particular, Elton Mayo and F. J. Roethlisberger began to point out that the approaches advanced by scientific management were not necessarily the most efficient, nor did they always work as intended. These researchers believed the human aspects of business organizations had been largely ignored. The **behavioral school of management** is *the approach to management thought that is primarily concerned with human psychology, motivation, and leadership as distinct from simple mechanical efficiency.* The behavioral school of management thought includes what has come to be called the human relations movement, as well as modern behaviorism.

behavioral school of management

Human Relations

The field of human relations emerged from the work of Elton Mayo, who has become recognized as the Father of the Human Relations Movement. The **human relations movement** is the name given *the trend that began in the 1920s and that reached its apogee in the 1940s and 1950s toward treating satisfaction of psychological needs as the primary management concern.* The project that had the most to do with the beginning of the concern for human relations in business was the Hawthorne experiments, conducted in the Chicago Western Electric Company plant (the Hawthorne works) between 1927 and 1932. In these experiments, researchers attempted to prove the validity of certain accepted management ideas. Several of the

human relations movement

experiments attempted to determine the relationship between working conditions and productivity.

In one study, the researchers set up *test groups,* for which changes were made in lighting, frequency of rest periods, and working hours, and *control groups,* for which no changes were made. When rest periods and other improvements in working conditions were introduced, productivity of the test groups increased, as expected; however, the researchers were surprised when output increased again when the various improvements in working conditions, such as rest periods, were removed.

Mayo and the other researchers concluded that their presence had influenced the behavior of the workers being studied. *The influence of behavioral researchers on the people they study* has come to be called the **Hawthorne effect**. A management corollary is that when employees are given special attention, output is likely to increase regardless of the actual changes in the working conditions. Mayo and Roethlisberger followed up the early experiments at the Hawthorne plant with (1) an investigation of cliques, work groups, and other information relationships in organizations, and (2) an intensive interviewing program. The basic conclusions reached as a result of the interviewing program were that the psychological needs of individuals have a significant impact on group performance and that employees often misstate their concerns.

Hawthorne effect

Much behavioral research supports the thesis that reasonable satisfaction of the needs and desires of employees will lead to greater output. This suggests that any management approach that ignores or deemphasizes the human element may result in only partly accomplished objectives.

Modern Behaviorism

Since the early experiments at the Hawthorne plant, there has been an increased interest in and application of behavioral science in management. The human relations approach has evolved into modern behaviorism. The term **modern behaviorism** refers to *the current stage of evolution of the behavioral school of management, which gives primacy to psychological considerations but treats fulfillment of emotional needs mainly as a means of achieving other, primarily economic, goals.*

modern behaviorism

In recent years, there has been renewed interest in developing techniques to utilize people more effectively in organizations. The contributions of such well-known behavioral scientists as Abraham Maslow, Douglas McGregor, Chris Argyris, Frederick Herzberg, and Rensis Likert have provided considerable insight into ways to achieve managerial effectiveness. We will discuss the contributions of each of these behavioral scientists in considerable detail in Chapters 10 and 11. At this point, brief mention of the basic precepts of modern behaviorism will suffice.

Behavioral scientists have often criticized classical management theory and scientific management as not being responsive enough to the human needs. The behaviorists' specific criticisms include the following:

- Jobs have been overly specialized.
- People are underutilized.
- Managers have exercised too much control and have prevented employees from making decisions they are competent to make.

- Managers have shown too little concern about subordinates' needs for recognition and self-fulfillment.

Behavioral scientists argue that the design of work has not changed to keep pace with changes in the needs of today's employees. In today's complex, affluent, and rapidly changing society, they say, employees cannot be treated *like interchangeable parts*. Today's worker has a higher level of education and tends to possess higher expectations for the working environment than did workers of the past. Modern behaviorists say employees of the 1980s desire diverse and challenging work. This desire has placed increased pressure on management to be responsive to change and to provide an environment designed to meet human needs.

Classifying Management Theories

Although the discussion thus far has focused on the classical and behavioral schools of management, it should not be concluded that these two basic schools encompass all possible approaches or theories of management. Harold Koontz, in attempting to clarify what he has described as a "management theory jungle," identified eleven schools or approaches to the study of management.[5] The Koontz classification system is briefly described in Table 1–2.

Although Koontz's classification system has not been widely accepted, it represents one of the few efforts to make sense of what Koontz called the "management theory jungle." We believe that of the theories listed, the operational approach comes closest to capturing the essence of modern management thinking. Still, we do not confine ourselves to any single concept of management. Rather, we will draw on all of the management approaches Koontz identified and others as well.

PURPOSES AND ORGANIZATION OF THIS TEXT

In this text we hope to provide you with the following:

- A greater knowledge of and insight into the responsibilities of managing people and other resources
- A better understanding of the problems of operating a business organization
- An opportunity to learn the skills essential to effective managerial decision making
- An understanding of basic principles of management
- Increased knowledge about production and operations management techniques
- The ability to identify and cope with internal and external forces in the environment that affect performance
- The skills and attitudes to continue your professional development

This book is organized into seven parts, as illustrated in Figure 1–4. We believe we present fundamental management concepts and practices in a readable and interesting format. We provide examples that have a high degree of applicability among different types of enterprises, including business firms, public sector firms such as government agencies, and not-for-profit organizations such as hospitals, schools, and universities.

TABLE 1–2   Koontz's Classification of the Theories of Management

Empirical or Case Approach	In this school, management is studied through case examples of the successes and failures of practicing managers. This approach can assist managers in developing basic generalizations to support theories or principles of management. However, this method of learning about management may create illusions for current managers because the future is quite likely to be considerably different from the past. An analysis of past experiences of managers may not prove to be very helpful in solving current managerial problems.
Interpersonal Behavior Approach	According to this school of thought, management is concerned with accomplishing results through others. Therefore, the study of management should concentrate on interpersonal behavior and the study of psychology. This school focuses on the study of motivation and leadership. While the study of human behavior in organizations is important, a manager's knowledge of management is incomplete if that's all a person understands.
Group Behavior Approach	By applying research findings of sociology, anthropology, and social psychology, this approach explains management in terms of group behavior. According to this view, effective management requires a thorough understanding of behavioral patterns of group members within the organization. However, rigid adherence to this approach may cause managers to place more emphasis on organization behavior and not on other equally fundamental concepts of management.
Cooperative Social Systems Approach	An outgrowth of the interpersonal and group behavior approaches, the cooperative social systems school of management has often been referred to as the "organization theory" approach. While all managers perform in a cooperative social system, this approach does not explain complexities of modern management. Social systems is a broader concept than management, and it overlooks a number of principles, techniques, and factors that are important to effective management.
Sociotechnical Systems Approach	The sociotechnical systems approach is based on the work at the Tavistock Institute in England. It was discovered that the technical system—the machines and methods used—has a strong influence on the social system within the working environment. Personal attitudes of group members were strongly influenced by the technical system of the workplace. A major task of management is to make sure that the social and technical systems are harmonious. While closely related to industrial engineering, the approach has made a significant contribution to the practice of management. It does not, however, provide an overall theory of management.
Decision Theory Approach	The major responsibility of managers is to make decisions, according to the decision theory approach to management. While many who study and/or practice management agree that decision making is an essential skill, the approach overlooks other skills and requirements of management. In some cases, the actual making of the decision may be relatively straightforward.
Systems Approach	The systems approach to management concentrates on the effective and efficient use of resources in order to produce desirable products and/or services. The systems approach requires that the physical, human, and capital resources be interrelated and coordinated within the external and internal environment of an organization.
Mathematical or Management Science Approach	This school or approach to management uses mathematical models, concepts, and symbols in solving managerial problems, particularly those requiring decisions. Advocates of the school argue that management can be made more scientific through the use of mathematical and simulation models. Many advocates argue that the mathematical or management science approach offers a complete school of management. Other theorists and practitioners believe that mathematical models are tools of analysis, not a separate school of thought.
Contingency or Situational Management	Contingency or situational management refers to managers' abilities to adapt to meet particular circumstances and restraints a firm may encounter. In other words, managerial action depends upon circumstances within the situation. That is, "no one best approach" will work in all situations. Applying a situational approach requires that managers diagnose a given situation and adapt to meet the conditions present. The difficulty with this approach is that few management writers have prescribed precisely what a manager should do in a given situation.
Managerial Roles Approach	Henry Mintzberg observed and studied what managers actually do in managing and identified the primary roles of managers.[a] He concluded that executives do not always perform the traditional managerial functions of planning, organizing, directing, controlling, but instead perform a variety of other activities. According to Mintzberg, managers have three dominant roles: interpersonal, informational, and decision making. In the interpersonal role, a manager acts as a figurehead, leader, and liaison person. In the informational role, a manager serves as a monitor,

TABLE 1–2 (continued)

	disseminator, and spokesperson. In the decision-making role, a manager acts as entrepreneur, disturbance handler, resource allocator, and negotiator. A difficulty that arises is that roles Mintzberg identifies inadequately describe managerial activities and functions. Such important roles as those of goal setting, strategy identification and implementation, developing the organization, and selecting and developing managers are not included.
Operational Approach	The operational approach to management indicates that the foundations for management science and theory are drawn from a number of other schools and approaches. The operational approach recognizes that there are significant concepts, principles, theories, and techniques that comprise the effective practice of management. This approach draws on pertinent knowledge from other fields of study including political science, sociology, social psychology, psychology, mathematics, economics, decision theory, general systems theory, and industrial engineering. We believe that the operational approach provides a logical framework for the study of management theory and practice.

Source: Harold Koontz, ''The Management Theory Jungle Revisited,'' *Academy of Management Review* 5, no. 2 (April 1980). Reprinted with permission of the author and *Academy of Management Review*.

[a]Henry Mintzberg, ''The Manager's Job: Folklore and Fact,'' *Harvard Business Review* 53, no. 4 (1975):49–61.

Figure 1–4

Organization of the Book

PART I   INTRODUCTION
Chapter 1   Management
Chapter 2   The Manager's Environment

PART II   PLANNING AND DECISION MAKING
Chapter 3   The Planning Process
Chapter 4   Strategic Planning
Chapter 5   Decision Making and Management Information Systems

PART III   ORGANIZING
Chapter 6   The Organizing Process
Chapter 7   Organizing Concepts and Organizational Structure
Chapter 8   Group Behavior and the Informal Organization
Chapter 9   Staffing the Organization

PART IV   INFLUENCING
Chapter 10   Motivation
Chapter 11   Leadership
Chapter 12   Communication
Chapter 13   Organizational Culture, Change, and Development

PART V   CONTROLLING
Chapter 14   The Controlling Process
Chapter 15   Quantitative Controlling Techniques

PART VI   PRODUCTION AND OPERATIONS MANAGEMENT
Chapter 16   Introduction to Production and Operations Management
Chapter 17   Quantitative Production and Operations Management
                    Techniques

PART VII   SITUATIONAL APPLICATIONS
Chapter 18   Social Responsibility and Business Ethics
Chapter 19   Managing Small Businesses
Chapter 20   Managing the Multinational Enterprise

SUMMARY

We live in a society dominated by large organizations in which people must work together effectively to accomplish goals. The degree of success of all organizations—business and nonbusiness—is determined to a great extent by the quality of management they receive. Management is the process of getting things done through the efforts of other people. Managers perform the functions of planning, organizing, influencing, and controlling. Planning is determining in advance what should be accomplished and how it should be done. Organizing is acquiring human, material, and financial resources and specifying their relationships to each other in order to get things done. Influencing means determining or affecting the behavior of others. This involves motivation, leadership, and communication. Controlling is comparing what is happening with what should be happening and taking corrective action if necessary. A task that managers perform in carrying out each of the management functions is decision making: identifying and evaluating alternatives and making choices among them.

Although the distinctions are by no means clear, it is useful to think of managers as being divided into three groups. Supervisory managers are persons who directly oversee the efforts of those who actually perform the work. Middle managers are above the supervisory level but subordinate to the firm's most senior executives. Top managers are the organization's most senior executives, such as chairman of the board or president.

To be effective, a manager must possess and continually develop several essential skills. The ability to comprehend abstract or general ideas and apply them to specific situations is conceptual skill. Technical skill is the ability to use specific knowledge, methods, or techniques in performing work. The ability to understand, work with, and get along with other people is human skill.

Historically, the United States has had the highest levels of productivity of all major countries. Productivity is a measure of the relationship between inputs—labor, capital, natural resources, energy, and so forth—and the quality and quantity of outputs—goods and services. In 1982, the United States held about an 8 percent advantage over its nearest competitor nation in terms of productivity.

Although the history of management obviously extends several thousand years into the past, it was not until the late nineteenth century that management began to be considered a formal discipline. There are two basic schools of management thought in terms of historical development of the field. The classical school of management developed from the turn of the century through the 1930s and sought to provide a rational and scientific basis for the management of organizations. Key figures in this school of thought include Frederick Taylor, Harrington Emerson, H. L. Gantt, Frank and Lillian Gilbreth, Henri Fayol, and Chester Barnard.

The behavioral school of management is the approach to management thought that is primarily concerned with principles of human relations, motivation, and leadership, as distinct from simple mechanical efficiency. The human relations movement is the name given the trend toward treating satisfaction of psychological needs as the primary management concern. Modern behaviorism refers to the current stage of evolution of the behavioral school of management. It gives primary consideration to psychological concerns but treats fulfillment of emotional needs mainly as a means of achieving other, mainly economic, goals.

REVIEW QUESTIONS

1. Define management. Why does the definition of management exclude the action of an individual working alone?

2. What are the functions of management? Briefly describe each function.

3. Distinguish by definition and example among supervisory managers, middle managers, and top managers.

4. List and briefly define the types of skills important to managerial effectiveness.

5. Define the term *productivity*. How does the United States rank among industrial nations

with regard to levels of productivity? Productivity growth?

6. What is the classical school of management? Identify the major contributors to this school of management.

7. Discuss the behavioral school of management. What specific criticisms did behavioral scientists have of traditional or classical organizations?

EXERCISES

1. Interview three managers from different types of organizations (for example, talk to managers in a bank, a retail store, a manufacturing plant, or a college). Have a list of prepared questions such as the following:
   a. How did you become a manager?
   b. What does your job as a manager entail? Describe your on-the-job activities.
   c. Why are you a manager?
   d. What skills do you believe are necessary for success as a manager?
   e. What advice would you give a person interested in a career in management?
   f. Is management a profession?
   g. Can one learn or be taught to be a better manager? If so, how?

2. Review the employment ads in *The Wall Street Journal* and a Sunday edition of a large city newspaper. Make a list of the types of managerial jobs shown, the companies offering employment, and the qualifications needed to obtain the positions. What are your basic conclusions after this review in terms of the availability of managerial positions and the necessary qualifications for obtaining a position?

CASE STUDY

From Operator to Manager

Brenda Sidoli had been working as a machine operator at Parma Cycle Company's Cleveland, Ohio, plant for three years when she got her chance to become a manager. The supervisor in the frame-painting department quit, and Brenda had applied and got the job. The promotion did not mean a pay raise, but Brenda saw it as an opportunity to advance. She also liked the idea of wearing nicer clothes than the overalls machine operators had to wear. Brenda thought she was selected primarily because of her good record. She had missed only one day in attendance in the last two years. She also had one of the highest records of quality and quantity in the plant, and her supervisor had always marked her "excellent" in cooperativeness on her performance evaluations.

Brenda had expected a few days of training, but the old supervisor was already gone when she reported for work that first day, and her new boss, the assistant plant manager, was away on a week-long trip. Brenda went to see the plant manager, Mr. Roberson, and asked him what she was to do. He said, "Just move into your office, study the procedures manuals for the paint department, and try to get to know your people." The plant manager seemed to be in a rush, so Brenda didn't take any more of his time. Her office was an 8-foot-square room next to the frame-painting line with windows from about waist high to the ceiling. Brenda found the procedures manuals and began to look through them while watching the operators on the paint line.

QUESTIONS

1. Discuss the pros and cons of Brenda's accepting the job as a manager.

2. How and when would you recommend that Brenda approach her new subordinates? Explain.

3. Explain how Brenda might expect to be involved in performance of the four management functions. How will this differ from the way the plant manager is involved?

CASE STUDY

The New President

As Gloria Phillips seated herself behind her new executive desk on her first day as president at Wharton Products Company, she decided to allow herself a moment of nostalgia. She had come to work early that morning with the intention of getting a running start at the day. But she was a full two hours early and thought that she could afford a well-deserved few minutes of relaxation.

Wharton Products is a New Brunswick, New Jersey, maker of high-quality control mechanisms for the petrochemical industry. Gloria had known that she was the likely choice for president when the previous president resigned. She had worked hard over the years and was respected for her competence in the field and for her ability to work with employees at all levels. As she sipped her coffee that morning, her thoughts raced back over the twenty years she had been with Wharton.

Gloria had come to Wharton as a young college graduate with a degree in industrial management but no business experience. She was hired as an assistant supervisor and was immediately placed on the production line. "I don't see how I got by," she thought. "I knew so little about the operations and even less about management. It seemed that every day was filled with one brush fire after another." Thanks to procedures manuals and a patient superior, Gloria was able to stay out of trouble. In fact, she was soon competent to handle the supervisor's job alone.

She didn't get to do that, though. After just six months on the job, she had a chance to become production manager, and the supervisor who had been her boss became one of her subordinates. As a supervisor, Gloria had been primarily concerned with daily operations. As production manager, she found it necessary to plan weeks and even months in advance. She also had to complete more reports and attend more meetings, and she found herself with less time for the technical responsibilities she had enjoyed carrying out as a supervisor.

She chuckled as she thought about the time, just after she took over as production manager, when she discovered that the operating procedures manuals were grossly out of date and inadequate. Several new machines had been installed, and one whole production line had been added since the last revision to the procedures manuals. It took Gloria more than a year to get them in order. In the process, she learned a lot about how the production division fitted into the overall plant operations. She also visited several other plants and discovered a number of new and better ways of doing things, which she incorporated into the procedures manuals.

Because the company was growing and changes in the manufacturing technology Wharton used occurred frequently, the procedures manuals had to be modified often. Soon Gloria was able to turn this work over to an assistant and spend more time on planning and assisting her subordinates in doing their jobs better. She also spent a good deal of time in meetings and discussions with superiors and in reviewing and completing reports.

When Gloria was twenty-eight, just five years after she had become production manager, Wharton lost its vice-president for planning to a competitor. Gloria applied for the job and, in competition with five other well-qualified applicants, got the promotion. Gloria had thought herself to be well qualified, but the complexities of her new position were overwhelming at first. It was difficult enough to forecast production requirements a year in advance, but the typical lead time for a new plant or even a new production line was several years. Also, in the new job, Gloria had to consider the interrelationships among marketing, finance, personnel, and production. The higher Gloria rose in the organization, the less she was able to depend on standard operating procedures.

From the planning job, Gloria was promoted to senior vice-president, manufacturing, and later to chief operating officer before her recent advancement to president.

"Surely," thought Gloria, "at some point one begins to feel fully competent to handle any situation that might arise." Gloria knew that she had not reached that point, however. She felt nervous and apprehensive about how things would go over the next few months.

QUESTIONS

1. What specific skills will be most important to Gloria's success as president of Wharton Products? Do you feel that she possesses these skills? Explain.
2. How do managerial responsibilities change as one progresses up the hierarchy in an organization?
3. Explain how Gloria's progression to the top management position in her company might be similar to or differ from that which is typical.

NOTES

1. This case is a composite of a number of published accounts, among them: Jill Bettner, "What's Good for GM Isn't Good for the Country," *Forbes,* November 7, 1983; "Blue Collars in the Board Room," *Time,* May 19, 1980; "Cooperation, UAW-Style," *Business Week,* November 21, 1983; Edwin Diamond, "Driving Ambition: A Man with the Pedal to the Floor," *Family Weekly,* May 27, 1984, pp. 4–9; John Hoerr, "Auto Workers Inch toward the Driver's Seat," *Business Week,* February 9, 1981; Michael Moritz and Barrett Seaman, *Going for Broke: The Chrysler Story* (Garden City, N.Y.: Doubleday, 1981); James K. Glassman, "The Iacocca Mystique," *New Republic,* July 23, 1984, pp. 20–23; numerous articles in *The Wall Street Journal;* and Chrysler Corporation, *Annual Reports* (various years).

2. "Wendy's International Inc.," *Standard & Poors Corporate Daily News,* August 5, 1983, p. 7039; "The Fast-Food War, Big Mac under Attack," *Business Week,* January 30, 1984, pp. 44–46; "Burger Wars: Round 3," *Marketing and Media Decisions* (July 1983): 42; Verne Gay, "Brand Report 59: Fast Foods," *Marketing and Media Decisions* (November 1980): 137–150; Hume Scott, "Major Fast Fooders Locking Horns Again," *Advertising Age,* September 12, 1983, p. 94; Richard Greene, "Specialty Retailers," *Forbes,* January 3, 1983, pp. 208–209.

3. Frederick W. Taylor, *The Principles of Scientific Management* (New York: Harper, 1911), pp. 41–47.

4. Chester I. Barnard, *The Functions of the Executive* (Cambridge: Harvard University Press, 1938).

5. Harold Koontz, "The Management Theory Jungle Revisited," *Academy of Management Review* 5, no. 2 (April 1980).

REFERENCES

Boone, Louis E., and James C. Johnson. "Profiles of the 801 Men and 1 Woman at the Top." *Business Horizons* 23, no. 1 (February 1980): 47–53.

Cetron, Marvin, and Thomas O'Toole. *Encounters with the Future: A Forecast of Life into the 21st Century.* New York: McGraw-Hill, 1982.

Cook, Curtis .W. "Guidelines for Managing Motivation." *Business Horizons* 23, no. 2 (April 1980): 61–70.

Drucker, Peter F. *Management: Tasks, Responsibilities and Practices.* New York: Harper, 1974.

Fayol, Henri. *General and Industrial Management.* New York: Pitman, 1949.

George, Claude, Jr. *The History of Management Thought.* Englewood Cliffs, N.J.: Prentice-Hall, 1972.

Hay, Christine D. "Women in Management: The Obstacles and Opportunities They Face." *Personnel Administrator* 25, no. 4 (April 1980): 25–31.

Kantrow, Alen M. "Why Read Peter Drucker?" *Harvard Business Review* 58, no. 1 (January–February 1980): 74–83.

Koontz, Harold. "The Management Theory Jungle Revisited." *Academy of Management Review* 5, no. 2 (April 1980): 175–189.

McGregor, Douglas. *The Professional Manager.* New York: McGraw-Hill, 1967.

Mintzberg, Henry. "The Manager's Job: Folklore and Fact." *Harvard Business Review* (July–August 1975): 49–61.

———. *The Nature of Managerial Work.* New York: Harper, 1973.

Naisbitt, John. *Megatrends.* New York: Warner Books, 1982.

Newman, William H., ed. *Managers for the Year 2000.* Englewood Cliffs, N.J.: Prentice-Hall, 1978.

Oliva, Terence A., and Christel M. Capdevielle. "Can Systems Really Be Taught? (A Socratic Dialogue)." *Academy of Management Review* 5, no. 2 (April 1980): 277–281.

Peters, Thomas J., and Robert H. Waterman, Jr. *In Search of Excellence.* New York: Harper & Row, 1982.

Roethlisberger, F. J., and W. J. Dickson. *Management and the Worker: An Account of a Research Program Conducted by the Western Electric Company Hawthorne Works, Chicago.* Cambridge: Harvard University Press, 1939.

APPENDIX

Careers in Management

People need to know much more than that they desire a career in management. The number and types of managerial positions are many. If people are to be happy in a chosen career, the best position that meets their specific needs must be obtained. This is precisely what this appendix is about—finding the right job that will lead to a career in management.

In order to do this a person should progress through a series of important steps. This appendix begins by showing how to gain valuable insight into what a person desires from a career. It is followed by a discussion of how to identify career objectives. Next, the types of careers available in management are presented, after which the actual sequence for searching for the right job is discussed. Finally, we present some job realisms. The overall purpose of this appendix is to identify what entry-level management positions are available and how a person can obtain the best match with the firm.

GAINING INSIGHT INTO YOURSELF

Successful managers come from a wide variety of experiences. Some know immediately that they want to be managers. Others believe that they want to be in management and learn later on that management is not their cup of tea. There are individuals who may be extremely successful as a manager in one situation and a dismal failure in another environment.

The number of students who graduate from college without a clear understanding of their career goals is astounding. It is difficult to achieve a goal if you do not know what you want to accomplish. Statements such as "I want to be a manager," or "I want to be in a job where I can work with people," are not sufficient. You must be willing to go into much greater depth to gain a realistic appreciation of what you desire to accomplish in a career.

People must develop a realistic understanding of themselves. Once this has been accomplished, it is likely that individuals will be in a much better position to identify what they desire as a career. The following discussion is directed primarily toward college students who have little or no business experience and are unsure of their career goals. You need to gain critical insight into who you are and what you desire out of life.

Just as no two personalities are exactly alike, each of us has different strengths and weaknesses. People who are serious about an attempt to gain better insight into their career objectives will need to know their strengths or weaknesses. It is through the recognition of your strengths that you are encouraged toward a particular career. A knowledge of weaknesses shows a person what cannot be accomplished unless the deficiencies are removed.

Talk to Professionals

People who have gained success in their jobs are a valuable resource from which to uncover career information. It is likely that you, your parents, or close friends know individuals who would be willing to share career information with you. Most likely these people would be willing to talk to you about the demands of a particular job. Prior to setting up an interview with such a person, it would be wise to identify some questions you would like answered. To get your mind working, some potential questions are provided below:

1. What type of entry-level position would be available to a person with my education and experience?
2. If I didn't start off in a managerial position, typically how long would it take to progress to a first-level managerial position?
3. What type of training does your firm regularly provide management personnel?
4. What is the typical salary range for a person like myself starting with your firm?
5. What would be the typical duties a new employee would be expected to perform?
6. How supportive is your firm when an employee makes a mistake?
7. Whom should I contact if I am interested in a position similar to yours?
8. What's your firm's policy regarding promotion from within?
9. What type of preparation or qualifications does a person need for a career with your firm?

The list could go on and on. The point to be stressed is that you should ask the professionals questions that concern you the most. The benefits are numerous. You are now in a position to discover if a particular job might be interesting. The professional is not under the pressure of conducting an interview and will answer questions candidly. Also, if this type of job proves interesting, you have gained valuable information that can be used in future job interviews. Confidence is built up because you can now talk intelligently about the position you are applying for. You are also able to learn the typical salary range for a specific position. This information is important because a recent college graduate can be realistic about salary expectations by not asking for too much or too little.

University Testing Center

A resource that often goes unused by most college students is the university testing center. You might say, "Why should I use the testing service? There is nothing wrong with me." Perhaps this myth has been built up because it has been assumed that only people who are really "messed up" should use the university testing service. Nothing could be further from the truth. The unique feature of the testing center is that you can discover many things about yourself prior to going for an interview. You can be absolutely honest because only you and your counselor will see the results. Since many companies give similar tests to their job applicants, it is likely individuals will discover that they feel much more relaxed when these tests are administered. If you wait until after graduation to utilize a similar service, it may be quite expensive. Fees up to over $5,000 are sometimes charged for these services.

The purpose of using the testing services is to gain an insight into yourself that may prove beneficial when seeking a job. Some of the topics you may desire to explore in greater detail relate to interests, aptitude, personality, and intelligence. Each will be briefly discussed from the standpoint of how the tests can be beneficial in selecting the best job.

Interest Tests

One would be surprised at the number of college students who do not know what they want to do once they graduate. One of the authors of this book in fact changed majors five times! In the "old days," he did not have the opportunity to use a modern university testing service. *Interest tests* are designed to help a person identify career fields. If the test interpretation supports the person's belief in what is desired in a career, there is a good chance that the situation has been properly assessed. A person is reinforced in the belief that the proper decision has been made. On the other hand, the individual may discover that there are other areas that were not initially recognized. Knowledge of these additional interests can provide a person with the stimulus to evaluate other alternatives.

Aptitude Tests

At times our abilities and our interests do not match up. A person may have an interest in being a brain surgeon but not the aptitude for the career. *Aptitude tests* assist individuals in determining if they have the natural inclination or talent needed for a particular job. These tests are valuable in determining a person's probability for success in a selected job.

Personality Tests

There are jobs for which certain personalities have proved to be more useful than others. *Personality tests* assist a person in determining if he or she possesses the proper personality for a particular job. Although it is difficult to generalize about which qualities may be beneficial on a particular job, a person should benefit from the interpretation of the test results. Corporations, like individuals, have distinctive personalities. People tend to be attracted to organizations that provide the means for meeting their goals and aspirations. A person may be quite successful in one firm and a failure in another merely because of personality differences.

Intelligence Tests

If a career field requires a certain level of intelligence, it is best to find out if you meet the minimum levels before pursuing this career. Through hard work a person may meet the entry requirements, but what will the results be in the long run? Instead, a more realistic job, with just as much challenge, may need to be considered. We cannot all be Albert Einsteins! *Intelligence tests* assist in this endeavor.

The testing service should not be expected to provide all the answers. Test results should be viewed only as indicators and should never be thought of as providing the final decision concerning the entry into a profession. However, if the results of the tests suggest an alternate career path would be warranted, it may be beneficial to reevaluate personal goals. A conference with a respected instructor may provide some assistance. You will do well to remember that we are often *pushed* into careers not of our choosing because of well-intending, but perhaps misinformed, friends.

CAREER OBJECTIVES

Once you have a thorough understanding of yourself, you are in a much better position to develop realistic career objectives. It is at this juncture that a person either enhances or diminishes his or her chances to obtain a position that will lead to a career of his or her choice. Take for instance these two career objectives, which were found on resumes of recent college graduates:

I. *Career Objective:* To obtain a position where I can work with people, perhaps in management.

II. *Career Objective:* To obtain an entry-level position in personnel management that provides the opportunities for ultimately progressing into a middle-management position.

The personnel director who showed these career objectives to one of the authors was amazed at how many college seniors are not capable of identifying what they desire in their first job. Two general guidelines are provided:

1. Be as specific as possible in identifying the type of job you would like. This point becomes quite obvious when comparing career objective I and career objective II. The company needs to know the type of job you are interested in if it is to be capable of evaluating your credentials. The personnel director is also in a position to see whether a person has given serious consideration to the type of job he or she would prefer.

2. In the objective statement provide an indication of your goals during the next five years. Most personnel directors recognize that a person does not want to stay forever in an entry-level position. But they also want to know if prospective employees are realistic in their expectations.

Once you have clearly thought out your career objectives, you are, for the first time, in a position to evaluate the firms that have the potential for satisfying these goals. It is not a task that is accomplished overnight. Often this is the most agonizing part of the job search, but it is likely one of the most important.

ENTRY-LEVEL POSITIONS IN MANAGEMENT

Now that you have decided that you ultimately want to be a manager, the decision must be made as to what avenues are available to accomplish this goal. But now a problem arises. What types of managerial positions are available? Few first-level managerial positions are available for recent college graduates with minimal work experience. The discussion of possible entry-level positions in management will begin by gaining an appreciation of the risk factor as it applies to determining whether a person has an opportunity to secure a particular job. Next, four of the many possible avenues for obtaining entry-level management positions will be discussed. As each type of entry-level position is presented, you should consider the significance of the risk factor.

The Risk Factor

A major factor in determining the type of managerial positions that may be available to recent college graduates relates heavily to the risk factor that a company places on a particular position. *Risk* will be defined as the probability of a particular decision(s) having an adverse effect on the company. A low-risk managerial job is one in which if a mistake is made, there is a minimal potential loss for the firm. A high-risk managerial job is one in which a mistake by the manager may have a major impact on the organization. The types of managerial positions that are available may be viewed as a continuum that goes from low risk to high risk.

Typically, the lower the risk, the greater the opportunities available for a recent graduate with minimal work experience. A person who desires to enter management after graduation must usually search for these low-risk positions. It will do little good to set your sights on a job that is associated with high risk; these positions are likely reserved for individuals who have already proved themselves in lower-risk jobs.

The risk continuum might be viewed as a thermometer. The better the impression a person makes on the individual(s) doing the hiring in a firm, the higher the temperature rises. For many management positions you may want, however, there will be no movement on the thermometer. This means that there is no chance for that particular job. But if you have done your *homework,* it is likely that the *temperature* will rise at least enough to permit you to get an entry-level position. It may not mean that you will go immediately into management.

The concept of risk as it applies to different firms is often not consistent. There are organizations that rapidly place inexperienced new employees in positions of responsibility. One manufacturing firm may hire recent industrial management graduates and place them immediately into first-level supervisory positions. Another firm that manufactures a similar product may have a policy of placing only experienced individuals into first-line managerial positions. It is necessary for the graduate to study the risk factor as it applies to specific firms.

Risk should also be considered from the standpoint of how much security a person desires from his or her job. There is a common myth currently circulating among some college seniors that their risk of failure will be less in a major corporation as opposed to a smaller one. They reason that a large firm will take the time to train a person on a job prior to placing the employee in a position of responsibility. Job security is therefore enhanced. This myth should be dispelled. A firm, no matter what size, is in business to make money. If economic conditions do not warrant keeping an employee, the large firms as well as the small ones reduce the number of personnel. This fact was vividly illustrated to one of the authors when he began his business career. One of his first jobs was with General Electric in computer sales. GE decided to get out of the computer business and terminated a vast number of personnel. His next position was with a "big eight" CPA firm as a systems analyst. A recession reduced the staff from fifty consultants to ten within one month. Risk is associated with any position, whether the company is large or small.

Entry-Level Management

As we discussed above, there are instances where a person with limited work experience can progress immediately into management. The risk factor will have to be low, but there are entry-level management positions. Many of these positions carry the title of assistant manager. Decisions typically are made under the supervision of a manager with experience. These jobs offer young graduates the opportunity to get their feet wet without fear of making that one wrong decision that could be detrimental to a career. Many of these positions are in retail management with titles such as assistant manager of a department or grocery store.

Management Training Programs

A smaller number of the entry-level management positions involve a formal *management training program* (MTP). In an MTP, a college graduate is provided formal training for from three months to two years in the job that he or she ultimately will be filling. The trainee is often exposed to both classroom and experiential training so as to get the overall "big picture" of operations within the firm. Along with the formal classroom training, an individual may work in production one month, marketing the next, and accounting the following month. A person is exposed to the many different aspects of the firm that could affect performance. Once the training program is completed, the individual is placed in a managerial position.

A point that should be remembered is that formal management training programs are often quite expensive for a firm. The firm does not receive benefits from the employee until the training is complete. Thus, it is likely that a highly competitive screening process will be used. The company must feel that the individual will become a productive long-term employee before the employee is permitted to enter the training program. If an MTP is desired, young graduates must thoroughly convince the company representatives of their potential and that the risk factor is not excessive.

From Professional to Management

Many people graduate in a technical field such as accounting, computer science, or engineering. Perhaps management was not their initial goal, but they later see their future in management. It is likely that a person must first prove ability in the technical aspect of the job before being considered for a managerial position.

There are times when this path to a managerial position can be a delicate transition. A person who has always been associated with the technical aspect of a job has been known to have difficulty in moving into a managerial position. A good engineer or accountant will not always become an effective manager. But since many firms believe that their first-level supervisors must have technical ability, managers must come from the ranks of technical and professional staff members.

Jerry Wayne Box, manager for the Rocky Mountain District of Sunmark Exploration Company, progressed from a technical job to a managerial position. On receiving the M.S. in geology, Jerry went to work for Sunmark. After being with the firm four years, Jerry was identified as a *high potential* individual, meaning that he had impressed his supervisors as possessing certain managerial qualities. In preparation for moving Jerry into management, he was placed in assignments outside the geology department and moved to other locations in the firm for training. He worked for several months in the human resources department, supervising a task force of three people in developing a management by objectives program. Jerry was then moved to the organization and systems development department where he again directed a task force in reorganizing a geology department. Finally, after approximately eighteen months, Jerry was transferred back into geology as a manager. Sunmark views the additional corporate exposure as vital in the career progression of a manager.

From Sales to Management

An avenue that is being used increasingly by college graduates is to progress to a management position through an entry-level sales job. A person who is in sales is in a position to learn the operations of the entire company. Thus, many college graduates have found that the quickest path to a managerial position is through sales. It is likely this situation has occurred because approximately 50 percent of all entry-level positions open to college graduates are in sales.

Some firms make it mandatory to progress through sales before any of their employees can enter management. For instance, one large insurance company has initiated a program to attract bright college graduates into their management ranks. In this program new employees spend three months at the home office working in various departments and another three months observing in the field. They are then required to produce as a salesperson for one year. At this point they have the option of going into management or remaining in sales.

The point that should be clearly understood is that a sales position can lead to managerial positions other than in sales management. Many people have been able to go from sales to other departments, such as production. Because salespeople have been dealing with the customer who purchases the product, it is reasoned that they provide valuable input if placed in the production area of the business.

THE SEARCH FOR THE RIGHT INDUSTRY

A good starting point in a job search is to identify the growth industries. Industries that are projected to grow rapidly in the future would be the target for further analysis to identify several of the *best* companies operating within the industry.

Examples of *fast-growth* industries might include: computer products, health-care products and services, electronics, energy-related, banking and financial services, various leisure-time industries, and various types of service industries. *Slow-growth* industries might include education, transportation (particularly railroads), and steel.

Thus, an individual should follow this recommended procedure:

1. Identify growth industries.
2. Pinpoint or select for further study and analysis the industries that would seem to fit your goals, needs, or interests.
3. Determine the three or four "leading" firms in the industry. These firms may not be the largest, but they may be growing or predicted to grow at a rapid rate over the next several years.
4. Seek interviews with the companies you select from your analysis as described above. The procedure to be followed will be discussed in the following section, "The Search for the Right Company."
5. Finally, be concerned about the specific entry-level position, fully recognizing that if you perform well, you won't be in this position long—probably not more than one or two years.

Naturally, there are excellent opportunities available in some industries that are identified as slow growth. This discussion should not be taken to mean that a person should not apply to firms in the slow-growth industries. The authors merely suggest that considerable thought should be given to the selection of which industry should be pursued.

THE SEARCH FOR THE RIGHT COMPANY

You have now accomplished a thorough self-assessment, developed an appreciation of your career goals, determined companies in growth industries, and obtained an overview of the types of jobs that are available to begin a career in management. But you cannot start your career until a job offer is obtained (a truism if there has ever been one). Thus, this section will concentrate on the remaining sequence of events that should be accomplished in order to obtain the management position of your choice. The importance of preparing a resume will first be presented. This will be followed by the steps necessary to match yourself with the right company.

The Resume

In many instances the first contact that a prospective employee has with the person in charge of hiring is through a resume. As such, the resume becomes an extension of an individual's personality. The resume *sells* in a person's absence. It should be designed to present an individual in the best possible perspective.

An intensive evaluation must be made by college seniors preparing themselves to enter the job market. It must be remembered that the resume must be developed to present *you* in the best possible image. Any deficiencies can be explained during the interview, but it is difficult to accomplish this task if the opportunity to participate in the interview is not available.

Through experience and through contacts with numerous personnel directors, some guidelines have been developed that may prove to be beneficial in the preparation of a resume. They are:

1. Present your most significant accomplishments and attributes. If it is the truth, it is not bragging.

2. The order of the presentation of items on a resume is dictated by your strengths. If you have high grades, stress your grades; if you have a significant amount of work experience, it is possible that this item should receive top priority.

3. Companies are placing additional emphasis on activities outside the classroom such as membership and offices held in social and business organizations. If you have been particularly active in various campus organizations, highlight these endeavors.

4. The amount of college expenses that you personally paid is also receiving additional attention. A statement such as "paid 50 percent of college expenses" is often quite helpful.

5. If you are willing to be mobile, this should be stressed. For a company that is located in cities throughout the United States, a statement of geographical preference of "None" would likely receive higher attention than one that said "Butte, Montana." Naturally, if geographical preference is truly a restriction, it should be stated as such.

6. A person who has had work experience while in college should stress this fact. A firm recognizes that individuals who are working to finance their way through college will not likely have fancy titles. They are interested in determining how you performed while employed. It is highly satisfying for a recruiter to call one of your past employers and receive statements such as "He is a hard worker" or "She did not constantly watch the clock."

7. A person who has work experience should describe the functions that were performed while working. Merely listing the position titles does not give the recruiter significant insight into what type of work was actually performed. Action phrases such as "was responsible for," "coordinated the activities of," and "in charge of" are much more descriptive.

8. If references are to be placed on a resume, permission should be requested even though the reference is a good friend. References can assist you by tailoring their comments to meet the requirements of the job that you are seeking.

The next step in searching for the right company is to identify the firms that can afford a person the greatest opportunity to achieve career objectives. However, remember what the old philosopher said: "You can never turn down a job until an offer has been made." Identification of these firms is a task that often proves quite difficult for students seeking their first job. But it is one that must be done. Here you will be attempting to identify firms that might meet your specific needs.

There are numerous sources from which to obtain the names of the firms that will match your specific needs. A great deal of information can be found in *trade journals* that apply to the particular firm in which you are interested. Also, a large amount of useful data may be found in *Standard and Poors, Fortune, Forbes,* and *The Wall Street Journal.* You should select only the firms that have the potential for fulfilling specific needs. For instance, if your goal is to be employed by a medium-sized firm headquartered in the Southwest, Coca-Cola would not be on the list (headquartered in Atlanta). Dr Pepper (headquartered in Texas and much smaller) might meet the requirements. The authors have found it beneficial to select a maximum of twenty-five companies representing several industries from which to continue the job search.

Once a list of prospective companies has been developed, you still are not in a position to send out a resume. A certain amount of research remains. Data concerning each company should be obtained so as to send a personal cover letter to each firm. This also includes obtaining the name of a person to be addressed. In the cover letter state the reason for wanting a job with this company. Remember that the *only* reason a firm will consider a person for employment is that they expect the services rendered will make money for the company.

The job search does not stop here. The waiting process begins. This also is quite difficult. But because you have done your homework, it will now be assumed that an invitation has been received to visit a company. Before leaving on a trip, additional research, or at least a review of your previous research, may be necessary. Much more information than last year's sales is necessary. In addition, it may be wise to develop a list of questions that you as a prospective employee would like to know about the company. The interview is a two-way street; the interviewee is attempting to determine if this particular company is a good place to work, and the firm is evaluating the individual for potential to fit into the organization.

If the interview goes well and you believe that the company has the potential to satisfy your career objectives, it is customary to write a letter expressing your sincere interest. In this letter you should also tell precisely why you feel qualified to take a position with the company—A comment such as, "The work that a quality control inspector with your firm performs appears extremely interesting and challenging. I am confident that I possess the type of personality to be capable of working with the people on the line, my supervisor, and top management." On the other hand, if you discover after your visit that the position is not what you expected, a courteous letter should be written thanking them for their interest but telling the company representative that you do not believe a proper match exists.

A technique that has been quite successful in enhancing the chances of obtaining the desired position is the follow-up phone call. Approximately one day after the follow-up letter has been received by the company, place a phone call to the person who interviewed you. During this call, you should ask intelligent, searching questions as well as again express interest in the firm. Once the call has been completed, you have had the opportunity to visit with the company representatives four times: by resume, in person, by letter, and by phone.

Once an offer has been tendered, the decision must be made as to whether it should be accepted or rejected. This usually poses no problem unless several offers are received. Hopefully, since your homework has been done, this will be the case. In making a decision as to which job to take, a major point should be remembered: the job with the greatest long-run potential should be selected. Try to pick a company you can be comfortable with, including its head office location. This job is not necessarily the one with the highest starting salary. It is often tempting to take the highest salary offer without considering all other factors. But success on the first job after graduation can have a tremendous impact upon an entire career. It should be chosen with care.

INITIAL JOB THREATS

Recent college graduates have conquered a major hurdle in their lives. The world's problems are now going to be solved. But from a realistic viewpoint, certain cautions should be observed. This section is not inserted to frighten or disillusion a person, but it is felt that it is needed so that the first job will be approached from a realistic appreciation of the work environment. Although a job has been secured, there are numerous initial *job threats* that a person should be aware of if long-term success is to be achieved.

The Young Brat Syndrome

Not all employees of a firm will always welcome with open arms a new college graduate. Although top management may realize that it is important to bring bright, young, college-educated people into the firm, this enthusiasm may not be shared by all. Graduates may find themselves working either with or for people without a college degree. The starting salary of college graduates may be more than that of employees who have been with the firm for a long time. Some may even perceive a new college graduate as a threat. Graduates have found that out of necessity their college degree may need to be *played down.* In time people will discover that you have your degree and will likely respect you more for not bringing it to their attention.

Making Changes

After graduation, a college graduate's mind is filled with new ideas or approaches that have been learned in the classroom. But the company may have been successfully accomplishing a task in a certain manner for many years. To the graduate it may be obvious that changes need to be made, and it may come as quite a shock when your ideas are not immediately accepted. Although a person's first inclination may be to start making changes, it may be best to first establish a good working relationship with members of the department and gradually bring forth new ideas.

Politics

The hardest lesson a young person must learn is that hard work and long hours do not guarantee advancement. In school, most likely students were told that salary increases and promotions were a direct result of productivity. In reality, obtaining a promotion or raise may depend on whom one knows and with whom a person plays golf or tennis. While this policy is certainly not advocated, it does at times occur and an individual should be alert to the different power groups at work within the organization.

The Free Spirit

Just as each of us has different personalities, companies are also different in their attitudes toward what is an acceptable standard of appearance. If a graduate goes to work for a firm in which all of the company's managerial personnel wear suits, conformity will likely be the order of the day. Resistance to this image can only result in difficulties. If a person wants to be less conventional, there are firms that likely accept this attitude.

The Boss

Some graduates often feel that their superior is not as intellectually enlightened or supportive as they believe a person in that position should be. Assuming that you desire to maintain that position (a reasonable alternative might be to quit or request a transfer), you must realize that the supervisor is still the boss. If an individual desires to progress in that firm, an overt effort must be made to support the activities of the department. Expressing doubt concerning the superior's abilities to other employees can only hurt the chances for advancement. If a person wishes to make changes, they must be accomplished within the system.

systems approach   stockholders   efficiency

open system   informal organization   effectiveness

union

After completing this chapter you should be able to

1. Describe the major factors in the external environment that can affect an organization.

2. Explain the major environmental factors that can affect middle and lower managers.

3. Describe the basic transformation process that may occur in any organization.

2

The Manager's Environment

Pan American World Airways, Inc., or Pan Am, has been a leader in U.S. aviation for more than fifty years. In the early 1980s, Pan Am's operating routes served cities throughout the U.S. and in forty-four foreign countries. The 1978 deregulation of the airline industry had brought new challenges to all of the major airlines. At about the same time, a major recession began and airline travel was hit particularly hard. International travel was dampened by unfavorable exchange rates. Through 1981, fuel prices, a major part of air carrier costs, continued the upward trend that had begun in 1973 with the Arab oil embargo. To make matters worse, in 1982 the air traffic controllers walked out, resulting in a lengthy strike and eventually in a decision by President Ronald Reagan to fire all the striking controllers. Civil Aeronautics Board chairman Dan McKinnen was provoked to remark, "Nobody in his wildest imagination could dream of such negative factors all coming together at once."

In an attempt to strengthen its position, Pan Am acquired National Airlines and hoped to use it to build a major domestic hub. But stung by $700 million in losses in 1981–1982, Pan Am gutted most of National's domestic system, using what was left mainly to feed passengers to Pan Am's international flights. Pan Am restructured its routes and introduced a discount fare program that undercut competition by 17 to 53 percent. To keep operating, Pan Am had to sell its profitable Intercontinental Hotels Corporation subsidiary and some of its planes. Ten vice presidents and 112 management-level staffers were fired, and the overall workforce was cut by 5,000 employees.

Although Pan Am was able to keep 60 percent of its seats filled in 1983, the company was barely profitable. Pan Am's problems were made worse by foreign exchange losses of $11.5 million for the 1984 second quarter—more than a third of the company's revenues are paid in foreign currencies. Pan Am spent another $8 million to pay overtime to its crews and to provide free drinks to passengers during air traffic control delays at major airports. Finally, the company's Worldpass program, under which passengers obtain free travel credits, cost Pan Am significantly. Eleven percent of the company's second quarter 1984 air travel represented free rides. Pan Am had set June 30 as the last date to use the credits and there was a rush to use them before they expired. Still, Pan Am did better than Braniff International and Continental Airlines, which sought protection under the federal bankruptcy laws. Even high-flying Delta saw losses in 1983, and Eastern Airlines survived only by threatening bankruptcy and compensating its employees in part with company stock.

In late 1984, Pan Am seemed to have weathered the storm. In the words of a Shearson Lehman/American Express analyst, "Pan Am certainly has built enough strength to eliminate any concern that they may be in dire circumstances." But stockholders were not at all confident of the company's survival. Pan Am's stock was down to 7-1/4 in October 1983, a fraction of its historical value. By August 1984, the price was bumping 4—and still tending downward.

Even if the great old names like Pan Am survive, it will be in a new, more competitive environment. Upstart companies like People Express, providing no-frills services and with nonunionized workers, are sure to keep downward pressure on prices. In August 1984, People Express announced sharply reduced fares on the New York to Miami run, one of Pan Am's strongest routes. Pan Am posted a loss of $49.8 million for its 1984 second quarter, while several other major carriers showed profit increases. The company had sold 15 of its DC-10s and accumulated $400 million in cash by August 1984. But the large cash balance was not expected to help Pan Am in its labor negotiations. The company set a goal of increasing productivity by one-fourth through relaxed work rules and longer working hours. Management sought approval for the planned measures from the company's five major unions, but workers were threatening to strike.[1]

Managers at Pan Am could well have been shellshocked because of the wide diversity of environmental situations that the company recently has faced. From the security of a federally regulated industry to the ruthlessly competitive environment, Pan Am has staggered, then righted itself, only to be struck by renewed negative forces. Under government regulation, the airlines did not have to be particularly efficient. Prices were set by bureaucrats to provide a reasonable profit to any competent competitor. Winning concessions from government was easier than fighting unionization, and practically every major airline was unionized—from the pilots down to the workers who repaired the engines. Before the 1970s, economic recessions had barely affected airline travel. Persons who could afford to travel by airplane did not change their travel plans when the economy turned up or down.

By the start of the 1979–1983 recession, however, most Americans, from lower middle income to the very wealthy, flew from time to time, so that recession hit the airlines harder than any other industry. Management at Pan Am had to scramble to cut costs, and some managers lost their jobs. The company had to turn from a pattern of trying to influence government regulators to one of trying to influence its employees to work harder and the public to buy its tickets. The Pan Am story illustrates aptly how the environment of management influences the practice of management.

This chapter begins with an overview of the components of a business system. Next, some of the major external factors that can affect managers will be described. Then, the major internal variables that affect managers will be discussed, and it will be shown how these variables differ at various management levels. Finally, the way in which inputs are converted to outputs within the business systems will be described.

THE BUSINESS SYSTEM: AN OVERVIEW

systems approach

open system

The Pan Am story illustrates the necessity for considering the interrelationships between the firm and its environment. Middle and lower managers at Pan Am have to think of the external environmental factors and of the way their subunits interact inside the organization. The systems approach offers a handy way of thinking about these interactions. The **systems approach** is *the viewing of any organization or entity as an arrangement of interrelated parts that interact in ways that can be specified and to some extent predicted.* The vital features of the systems approach are interrelatedness and interdependency. When the systems approach is taken, one is inevitably led to the conclusion that every organization, indeed every system, is an open system. An **open system** is *an organization or assemblage of things that affects and is affected by outside events.* If the managers of Pan Am had not seen the company as an open system, the company would probably have failed. In fact, when competitors cut fares and government regulations changed, outside factors were forcibly brought to Pan Am's attention.

Figure 2–1 illustrates the business system. Note that the organization's environment consists of a number of external forces, such as competitors, stockholders, and customers. Managers within the organization, especially those at lower levels, confront an internal environment markedly different from that of the organization. This internal environment consists of such factors as the management style of the boss, written guidelines, employees, organizational structure, the informal organization, other departments, and the union. Within these environments, inputs are converted to outputs through a transformation process directed and controlled by managers. Figure 2–1 will provide a framework for the remainder of the chapter.

THE EXTERNAL ENVIRONMENT

The manager's job is not accomplished in a vacuum. Many interacting external factors can affect managerial performance. As you can see from Figure 2–1, the external environment is comprised of a variety of factors: legal considerations, competitors, the labor force, unions, stockholders, suppliers, customers, and society. Each of these, separately or in combination with others, can constrain today's managers. A better way of looking at environmental changes, however, is that they can provide immense opportunities. For example, the deregulation that forced Pan Am to make difficult decisions in order to survive, allowed the upstart People Express and a number of other smaller airlines to compete. Let us now consider individually the separate factors that make up the external environment.

Legal Considerations

Legal considerations in the environment include laws and regulations applicable to organizations, along with the courts and government officials who interpret and enforce them. Table 2–1 shows some of the federal laws that affect managers. Note from the table that a number of the laws that have had the greatest impact on business date from the 1930s and before. This includes the Social Security Act, the National Labor Relations Act, the

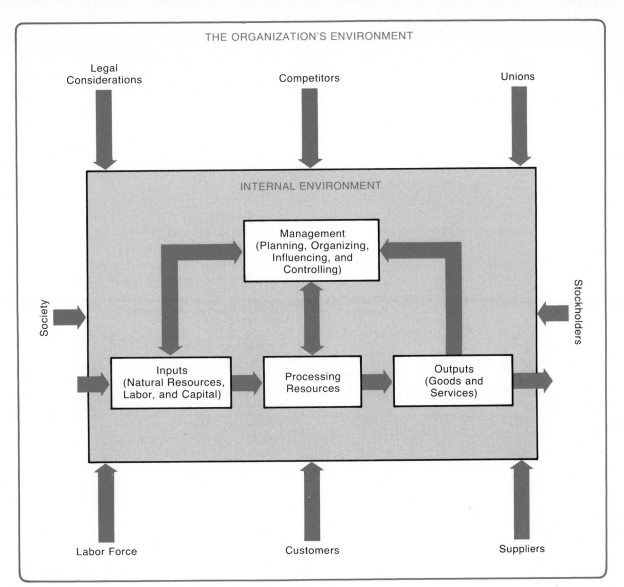

THE ORGANIZATION'S ENVIRONMENT

Legal Considerations

Competitors

Unions

INTERNAL ENVIRONMENT

Management
(Planning, Organizing, Influencing, and Controlling)

Society

Stockholders

Inputs
(Natural Resources, Labor, and Capital)

Processing Resources

Outputs
(Goods and Services)

Labor Force

Customers

Suppliers

Figure 2–1 The Business System

Pure Food and Drug Act, and the Sherman Act. Legislation that particularly affects human resource management will be discussed in greater detail in Chapter 9.

Among the laws that have been passed in the last several decades, perhaps the Civil Rights Act of 1964, as amended, has affected business managers most extensively. This act has been responsible for bringing many more women and minorities into the work force and for giving them opportunities for advancement. The civil rights sword cuts both ways, of course. In *Diaz* v. *Pan American* (1971), Pan Am argued that stewardess jobs should be available only to women. Pan Am lost the case. Today there are many male flight attendants at Pan Am and every other major airline.

TABLE 2–1 Samples of Federal Laws Affecting Business

Laws	Major Provision
Sherman Act of 1890	The federal government's first large-scale intervention in private business; aimed at controlling trusts and preventing monopolies
Pure Food and Drug Act of 1906 as amended	Designed to protect consumers by requiring inspection of food and drug products
Clayton Act and the Federal Trade Commission Act of 1914	Clayton Act made tying contracts, exclusive trading, and price discrimination illegal; Federal Trade Commission Act established the Federal Trade Commission to enforce the Clayton Act
Security Exchange Commission Act of 1934	Protects investors from fraud and swindling and regulates securities markets
National Labor Relations Act of 1935	Protects rights of employees to form unions and levies bargaining responsibilities on management
Social Security Act of 1935	Established a federal insurance program to provide retirement survivor benefits, disability payments, medicare, and unemployment insurance
Fair Labor Standards Act of 1938	Requires firms to pay minimum wages and extra compensation for overtime
Air Pollution Control Act of 1962 as amended by the Clean Air Acts of 1970 and 1977	Established air quality standards to promote the public health and welfare and the productive capacity of the nation
Equal Pay Act of 1963	Requires that males and females on the same job get equal pay
Civil Rights Act of 1964 as amended in 1972 by the Equal Employment Opportunity Act	Prohibits discrimination in hiring, training, promotion, and pay on the basis of race, color, religion, nationality, and sex
Age Discrimination Act of 1967 as amended in 1978	Prohibits discrimination against older employees
Occupational Safety and Health Act of 1970	Sets safety and health standards and enforces them through surprise inspections and fines
Consumer Products Safety Act of 1972	Sets safety standards for consumer products and bans products that create undue risk of injury
Employee Retirement Income Security Act of 1974	Protects employee rights in private pension plans

Competitors

Unless an organization is in the unusual position of monopolizing the market it serves, other firms will be producing similar products or services. A decision made by one firm may affect the competition, and vice-versa. A decision to raise or lower prices must take into consideration the effect that it will have on the competition. For many years AT&T, through its Bell System subsidiaries, had a virtual monopoly on telephone service in the United States. Under government pressure, AT&T was broken up, and now its former subsidiaries compete against one another.

More and more, when a company thinks of competitors, it must look beyond national boundaries. Pan Am flies to a number of foreign countries. It must compete on its international routes with companies such as Qantas (Australia) and British Caledonian, in addition to domestic carriers like Eastern and American. In a number of industries, particularly steel and autos, the strongest competitors of U.S. companies are based outside the United States.

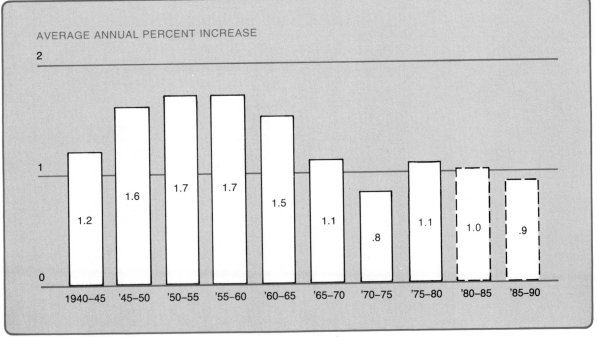

AVERAGE ANNUAL PERCENT INCREASE

1.2	1.6	1.7	1.7	1.5	1.1	.8	1.1	1.0	.9
1940–45	'45–50	'50–55	'55–60	'60–65	'65–70	'70–75	'75–80	'80–85	'85–90

Figure 2–2 Rate of Population Growth   Source: Bureau of the Census.

The Labor Force

The number and characteristics of individuals in the labor force represent another major external factor. By 1990, there will be approximately 119 million persons in the civilian labor force.[2] This estimate represents an 18.5 percent increase over the 1978 figure of 100 million. Figure 2–2 shows actual and expected labor force growth rates through 1990. The drop in expected growth between 1985 and 1990 is because of lower numbers of young people entering the work force, a less rapid growth in the participation rate for women, and a decrease in the rate of population growth since the 1950s and 1960s.

The figures do not tell the entire story because the labor force composition is also changing. Although the participation rate for men continues to decline, that for women is rising (Figure 2–3). Women are moving into traditionally male-dominated jobs, such as computer sales, public accounting, and management in increasing numbers. In addition, members of minority groups are gaining increased acceptance in higher-level jobs. These changes in the labor force will likely require attitude changes on the part of managers of the future.

The industries that will be capable of absorbing these additional employees will also likely be different from those of today. The goods-producing industries, such as agriculture, construction, mining, and manufacturing, are expected to remain relatively stable in terms of employment. But job opportunities in service industries, such as health care, trade, repair and maintenance, government, transportation, banking, and insurance, will increase (Figure 2–4). By 1990, employment in the

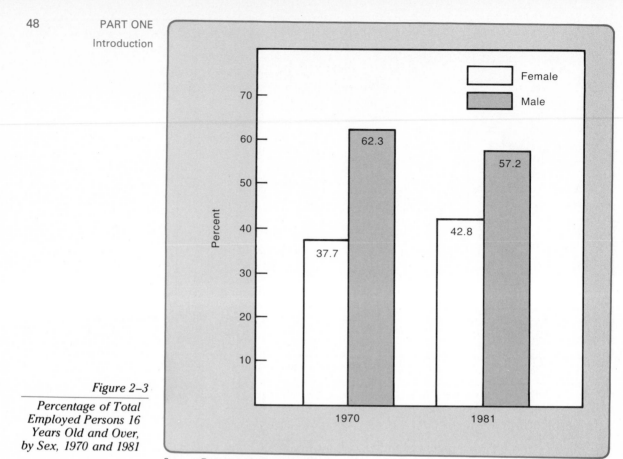

Figure 2–3

*Percentage of Total
Employed Persons 16
Years Old and Over,
by Sex, 1970 and 1981*

Source: Bureau of Labor Statistics.

service industries is expected to expand by 30 percent over 1978 figures. In goods-producing industries, employment is projected to increase by only 13 percent. Recent employment growth by occupation is presented in Figure 2–5.

The number of white-collar workers is expected to increase through 1990, while the number of blue-collar workers should remain relatively stable. Farm workers are expected to decline 14 percent by 1990 (Figure 2–6).

Unions

union

Wage levels, fringe benefits, and working conditions for millions of employees now reflect decisions made jointly by unions and management. A **union** is *a group of employees who have joined together for the purpose of dealing with their employer.* Unions are treated as an environmental factor because they essentially become a third party when dealing with the company. It is the union rather than the individual employee that negotiates an agreement with the firm. This tends to increase labor costs but often improves the lot of the employees. Pan Am confronts a unionized work force and thus has less flexibility and higher labor costs than nonunionized airlines such as

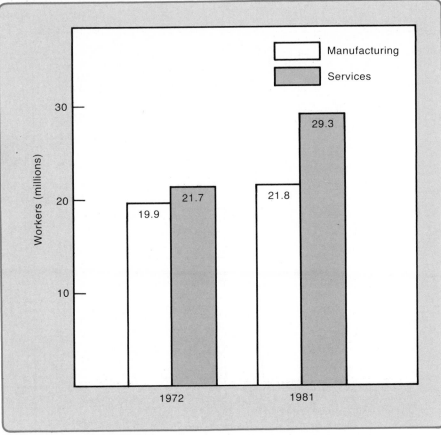

Figure 2–4

*Number of Workers in
the Manufacturing and
Service Industries,
1972 and 1981*

Source: Bureau of Labor Statistics.

Delta. There are approximately 20 million union members in the United States.[3] The existence of this huge union power base threatens many nonunion firms that strive to maintain their nonunion status.

Although unions remain a powerful force, union membership as a percentage of the nonagricultural work force slipped from 33 percent in 1955 to about 20 percent in 1984. This trend is likely to continue for a number of reasons. Young women who become blue-collar workers are reluctant to join unions because they think unions are dominated by men. In addition, an increasing percentage of the work force is involved in service rather than manufacturing. Service employees, such as clerical workers and computer programmers, have traditionally resisted unionization.

Stockholders

The owners of a corporation are called **stockholders**. There are two major classes of stockholders: those who own common shares and those who own preferred shares. By general agreement and to some extent because of court decisions, it is the common shareholder to whom corporate management owes primary responsibility.

stockholders

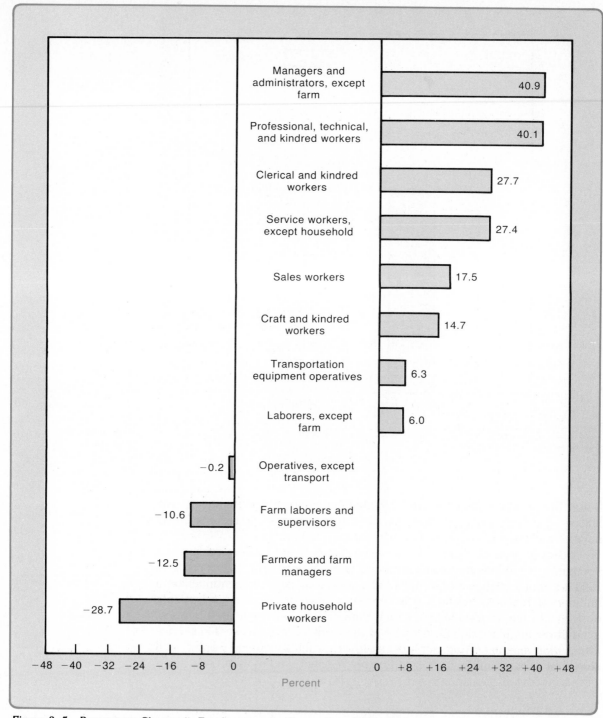

Figure 2–5 Percentage Change in Employment, by Occupation, 1972–1981   Source: Bureau of the Census.

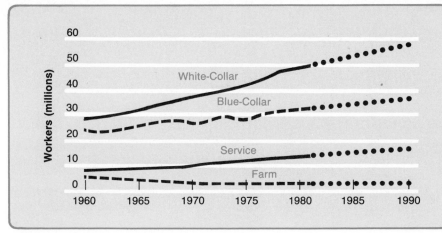

Source: Bureau of Labor Statistics.

Figure 2–6

Projected Growth of White-collar, Blue-collar, Service, and Farm Workers through the 1980s

As a legal matter, common shareholders have the right to elect the board of directors, who in turn typically appoint or elect company top management and make other major decisions regarding company operations. In practice, however, stockholders of major companies do not actively vote their shares but usually assign their voting rights to the board of directors. For the typical publicly held company, stockholders are primarily interested in the stock price and the dividends they receive and do not become involved in company management.

In a sense shareholders do "vote," by selling their shares or buying additional ones. This drives share price down or up and is a matter of significant concern to corporate managers. Shareholder disapproval of management action is why Pan Am's stock was selling for such a low price in 1984. Many managers are compensated through stock options and bonuses paid in the form of common shares. Others, especially small business managers, may own a large percentage of the company stock by virtue of having founded the company. For closely held companies (those owned by one or just a few stockholders), the owners usually are the managers.

Because stockholders have a monetary investment in the firm, they may at times challenge programs considered by management to be beneficial to the organization. Managers may be forced to justify the merits of a particular program in terms of how it will affect future profits. For instance, if it is recommended that equipment be bought that will make the environment better, the purchase will likely have to be justified with regard to how it affects the profitability of the firm. Stockholders are concerned with how expenditure decisions will increase revenues or decrease costs.

Another means by which stockholders can influence a company is through stockholder activism. Such activism was virtually unheard of in 1960, but now management has become extremely sensitive to its public image. A very small number of socially concerned stockholders may force a corporation to change to avoid bad public relations. The last thing most corporations want is criticism of the firm's performance on the front page of a major newspaper.[4]

More and more, when a company thinks of competitors it must look beyond national boundaries. Michael Hayman/Stock, Boston Inc.

Suppliers

Except for the relationship with customers, perhaps no other external environmental consideration is more important than a firm's association with its suppliers. Every organization must get materials, supplies, and capital goods in adequate quantities, at reasonable prices, and at the appropriate times. Pan Am planes consume millions of gallons of fuel each year. When most of the world's suppliers of fuel oil banded together to set prices and restrict supply in the 1970s, the increased cost had to be passed on to passengers, resulting in a decrease in airline travel. Because fuel costs then represented a large proportion of total expenses, the airlines began shopping for more fuel-efficient planes. The three major U.S. suppliers of airplanes—Boeing, Lockheed, and McDonnell-Douglas—all tried to respond to this new demand. Boeing, for example, produced the new fuel-efficient 737s and 767s. Firms that were more financially able to buy these planes, like Delta Airlines, gained an advantage.

Because of the need to decrease the cost and improve the quality of automobiles, U.S. car companies began in 1984 to do more outpurchasing. This meant that parts that had previously been produced in-house would be purchased from a variety of suppliers, both in the United States and abroad. In this case, the relationship with these suppliers had to be carefully negotiated because of the need for just-in-time delivery of components.

Customers

The people who purchase a firm's products and services must be considered part of the organization's environment. For Pan Am, airline passengers are

*A union is a group of
employees who have
joined together for the
purpose of dealing with
their employer.*
Ellis Herwig/The Picture Cube

the major customers. Other customers include those who ship parcels and freight on Pan Am planes. The modern concept of marketing requires that every manager, whether in production, personnel, or finance, focus on fulfilling customer needs as a primary goal of the organization. Certainly no company can long exist unless it serves customers effectively. It is not enough, however, just to fill customer needs. To succeed, Pan Am, or any other company, must do this about as well as competitors. This requires continually improving the quality of customer service. To be content with the status quo is a sure way to fail.

Until recently, most U.S. companies had to serve customers only as well as their U.S. competitors. With the continued internationalization of business, however, U.S. citizens are viewed as customers by many foreign companies. A construction company, for example, can choose U.S., Belgian, or Japanese steel for a construction project. At the same time, U.S. companies are enlarging the customer base abroad.

Society

A major concern of every manager should be to ensure that the organization responds appropriately to society's needs. For example, when airport congestion occurred during periods at major cities in 1984, Pan Am and other airlines negotiated schedule changes to decrease delays and improve safety. Because of public concern about chemical waste dumps, a number of U.S. companies spent millions cleaning up inactive disposal sites in the mid-1980s. And a federal Superfund was established to clean up those for which individual company responsibility could not be determined.

Partly because of such events as the poison gas disaster at Bhopal, India, involving Union Carbide Corporation, and the Three Mile Island nuclear disaster, the U.S. public is less willing than in the past to accept the actions of business without question. The public has found that the

Because stockholders have a monetary investment in the firm, they may at times challenge programs.

ASG/Stock, Boston Inc.

pressure of voices and votes can bring about change. Societal influence is obvious in the large number of regulations and laws that have become effective since the early 1960s (refer to Table 2–1). Recent surveys have indicated that the general public does not have a favorable perception of business; as many as 50 percent of persons surveyed have expressed displeasure with the actions and intentions of business.

The public also has an exaggerated view of overall business profitability. When asked what a typical business firm earns on each dollar of sales, many people estimate that profits are almost thirty cents (30 percent) per dollar of sales. In reality, profits decreased from a median of 5.2 cents on each sales dollar in 1979 to 4.8 cents in 1980.[5]

The general public includes the firm's employees. The influence of these employees may be substantial. For instance, if an organization has 10,000 employees, these individuals will have an influence over a larger number of people who are not connected with the firm, perhaps friends or members of an employee's family. Assume that each of Pan Am's 27,000 workers communicates regularly with 10 friends and that each of these communicates with 5 other persons. If this is true, information about internal company affairs will be transmitted to over 1.3 million Americans. Therefore a firm should maintain clear communications with its employees so that the firm's side of any story is told.

NUCOR   As steel producers go, Nucor Steel has recently been a high flyer. While giants like U.S. Steel and Bethlehem suffered huge losses in the early 1980s, Nucor entered an era of prosperity. More than a hundred thousand steel workers were out of work in 1984, but Nucor had not laid off a single hourly employee.

*Winning in
A Losing Game*

Things were not always so rosy for this relatively small (if a half-billion dollars in sales can be called small by any measure) steel producer. Nucor started off during the depression as Reo Motors Inc., a corporate spinoff of the R. E. Olds Company. In 1938, the company even filed for reorganization under the bankruptcy laws. It was briefly revived by World War II and then lingered until 1954, when liquidation seemed to have ended its suffering.

The only remnant that survived was Nuclear Corporation of America, the shares of which had been distributed to the former shareholders of Reo Motors. Nuclear Corporation was a hodgepodge of small, unrelated businesses, one of which was a steel bar joist maker. Bar joists are light steel beams made of angle iron and rods and used to support elevated floors and roofs in commercial buildings. Nuclear Corporation struggled along until 1965, posting a $2.2 million loss in that year alone.

In the depths of Nuclear's despair, Kenneth Iverson took over as president and chief executive officer. Things began to change. By 1971 sales were $64.8 million and profits $2.7 million, healthy in comparison with the company's past performance. By 1980, sales had grown 600 percent, to $482.4 million. Profits had increased even more markedly, to $45.1 million.

When the recession of the early 1980s decimated the rest of the steel industry, Nucor barely flinched. What accounts for the success of Nucor while the rest of the steel industry stagnates? Opinions differ, but there are a number of possibilities. First, the company produces a narrow product line, using modern and highly efficient mini-mills to melt scrap steel and shape it into angles, channels, and bars. This is in contrast to operations of the large integrated companies like U.S. Steel, Bethlehem, and Armco, which mine iron ore and attempt to produce every kind of steel plate and shape.

In the early 1970s, Nucor's business was making steel bar joists from rods and angles purchased from others. By making its own steel, Nucor has been able to decrease the costs of its finished joists.

Probably the most significant single factor in Nucor's success has been the productivity of its work force and the company's ability to avoid unionization. In the rural areas where Nucor located its mini-mills, the work ethic is strong, and there is little pro-union sentiment. President Ken Iverson believes two things are very important to most people: "One is, what am I going to be paid, and the other is, am I going to have a job tomorrow?" Two fundamental Nucor policies grow out of this line of thinking: First, compensation is based on individual and group productivity and company profitability. Second, Nucor has not laid off an hourly employee in the past twelve years. "We had some short weeks last summer," when the recession put 70,000 unionized steel workers out of work, Mr. Iverson said. "But nobody has ever lost a job here because business was bad."

Nucor also emphasizes communication with employees. There are only three layers of management. John Savage, manager of personnel services, said that in communicating with employees you should "tell them everything or tell them nothing." He continued, "We definitely believe in telling employees everything about the company—about its successes, its failures, its mistakes and its good *and* bad decisions." In summary, Mr. Savage said, "It has been Nucor's experience that the American worker is willing to work. Too many times, management gets in their way. Our employees take a great deal of pride in being as productive as we are."[6]

THE MANAGER'S ENVIRONMENT VERSUS THE ORGANIZATION'S ENVIRONMENT

The organization's environment both constrains and creates opportunities for the organization. For example, Nucor Steel found great opportunities in a market where the major steel companies were unable to compete with foreign manufacturers. These kinds of problems and opportunities are certainly primary concerns of top management.

To place this in perspective, just as the overall organization is surrounded by an environment made up of stockholders, customers, society, and so forth, each subunit of the organization, right down to the six-person section, is surrounded by a relevant environment, much of it internal to the overall organization. It is important for the subunit manager to understand that environment.

Supervisory managers are only indirectly exposed to the organization's external environment. Let us consider how seven factors in the internal environment affect lower-level managers.

Management Style of the Boss

The attitudes and preferences of middle and top management constrain supervisory managers in much the same way that the attitudes and preferences of stockholders constrain top managers. This is why it is important for an organization like Nucor Steel to have a consistent policy about the degree of openness and participation that is appropriate. For Nucor Steel, this is simplified by the fact that the company has so few management levels. Even in a firm like Nucor, some conflict among managerial personnel is unavoidable. Therefore subordinate managers must be prepared to work with their supervisors, whatever their managerial styles.

At times, the managerial style of the boss is different from that of a subordinate manager. For example, a middle manager may believe in simply giving orders and having them followed. A supervisor who works for that manager may prefer to involve employees in decision making and give them a larger amount of freedom. This may create conflict, especially if the boss views the supervisor's approach as indicating a lack of grit or decisiveness.

Written Guidelines

Much of what lower and middle managers do is regulated by written guidelines from upper management. Some find these guidelines restrictive. Others rely heavily on them and tend to operate strictly by the book. Guidelines are necessary to maintain consistency in the organization, as well as to promote productivity. Upper managers have a right to expect written guidelines to be followed. Other managers should try to constructively apply the guidelines that exist. For example, some Nucor supervisors may object to informing their subordinates about failures and mistakes of the firm; however, since top management has clearly established this as a guideline, supervisors should exercise little discretion about the matter. If they feel the guidelines are inappropriate, they should try to get them changed.

Employees

"Hire good people and let them do their thing" is the philosophy toward personnel held by many effective managers. But it may be best to avoid viewing persons as simply good or bad. Because we are all different in terms of goals, aspirations, backgrounds, experiences, and personalities, some persons are a better match with one organization than another. It has been found that employees tend to move toward a firm that possesses an environment closely compatible with their goals and needs. To some degree, Nucor Steel ensures a match between the company and its workers by locating plants in rural areas where the work ethic is strong and there is little pro-union sentiment.

Managers must consider individual differences among their subordinates while at the same time managing them as a group. For an individual supervisor at Nucor, there is probably less diversity among workers than there would be in a typical urban factory. In other organizations, the fact that individual employees are so different makes it difficult for the supervisor to manage them as a group. However, there are always some identifiable similarities among any group of subordinates. Understanding how individuals are alike helps the supervisor determine where to focus attention. For instance, supervisors who direct a group of experienced workers may give less attention to the technical details of the job and more to encouraging cooperation.

Organizational Structure

As used here, organizational structure means the manner in which the firm is organized or arranged. Organizational structures may be rigid or flexible depending on how rapidly the environment is changing. Another aspect of structure is the determination of where major decisions are made. In some companies, all important decisions are made by top managers. In other firms, lower-level managers are permitted to make significant decisions. Lincoln Electric Company, a Cleveland, Ohio, welding products maker, lets lower-level employees make important decisions. Richard Sabo, an executive with Lincoln, says, "Around here we give a high school graduate more authority than some companies give their mid-level managers." Yet another important characteristic of organizational structure is the number of managerial levels—whether the structure is tall (many managerial levels) or flat (few managerial levels). Nucor Steel has an extremely flat organizational structure, with only three levels of management. Organizational structure will be discussed in greater detail in Chapters 6 and 7. At this point, it is adequate to note that the manager's job is very different in a flexible and flat organization than where the reverse is true.

The Informal Organization

A new manager soon learns that there are two organizations within the firm: the formal and the informal. The formal organization is more visible because people can see their place on the company's organizational chart. In addition, their job descriptions tell what they are to do and to whom they report.

informal organization   Existing within every formal organization is an informal one, and it is often quite powerful. The **informal organization** is *the set of relationships among organizational members that are not formally prescribed.* It can significantly affect the manager's ability to accomplish the job. For instance, an older worker may have considerable influence over the crew and even over workers and supervisors in other departments. How managers deal with the informal organization can determine their success or failure. A manager may have the formal right to command, but high productivity requires cooperation as well as obedience. Smart managers understand the informal system and work with it to accomplish their jobs. The informal organization is described in Chapter 8.

Other Departments

The actions of one department affect others. Some of the possible relationships among departments may be seen in Figure 2–7. The personnel department helps maintain a competent work force. The purchasing department buys materials and parts. One department precedes another in the work flow. And one department's output becomes an input to another department. At Nucor Steel, for example, the output of the melting furnace department flows continuously to the various rolling mills.

Managers must be keenly aware of such interrelationships. Most soon discover that cooperation with other departments is necessary if the job is to get done. If they make enemies of other managers, they may find that their department's productivity is lowered. An otherwise great department might be a failure because another department does not cooperate.

The Union

We discussed the union earlier as part of the external environment because the union organization is a separate entity; however, union members and representatives interact daily with managers inside the organization, particularly supervisory managers. Upper management negotiates the labor-management agreement, but supervisors must live with it. In most instances, the agreement places restrictions on actions managers can take. For example, a supervisor may want to fire a worker for being late two days in a row. If the union-management agreement states that workers must be given a written warning before firing, the supervisor must adhere to this. Promotion procedures are usually stated in the agreement. Seniority is often the major factor. Supervisors may become frustrated when they would like

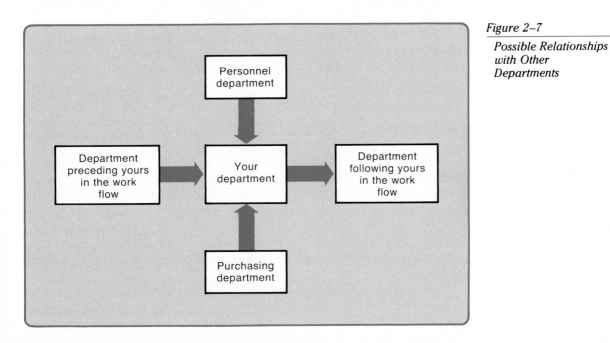

Figure 2–7

Possible Relationships with Other Departments

to promote highly qualified workers but find that less productive persons with more seniority must be given the jobs.

Of course, the union is not a major internal environmental factor for companies like Nucor, which have no union. Only about one in every five U.S. workers is a union member. But managers who value the freedom nonunion status gives them must be continuously on guard to avoid actions that invite unionization. This is why some nonunion companies are careful to pay wages as high as their unionized competitors.

THE TRANSFORMATION PROCESS

In any organization, management's job is to use resources (inputs) in an efficient manner to produce desirable products and/or services (outputs). The basic transformation process components are illustrated in the highlighted portion of Figure 2–8 and discussed below.

Inputs

First, let us consider the inputs to the transformation process. Just as humans cannot live long without food and water, a dynamic business system cannot survive without resources that keep it alive. These items are categorized as natural resources, labor, and capital. The inputs needed vary according to the type of business the firm is in and its particular goals. If, for example, a watch manufacturer emphasizes high-quality watches, the inputs needed are likely to be highly trained craftspersons and quality equipment and materials. A manufacturer of low-quality watches may need different inputs, such as equipment capable of mass production and perhaps less skilled employees.

efficiency

effectiveness

The proportional relationship between the quality and quantity of inputs and the quality and quantity of outputs produced is referred to as **efficiency**. *The degree to which the process produces the intended outputs* is called **effectiveness**. In managing the transformation process, the objective of the manager is to obtain high effectiveness and to do so efficiently.

Processing Resources

Inputs are processed within the organization to create desired output in the form of goods or services. Goods may be processed according to three kinds of operations. First, inputs may be *combined* to form significantly different outputs. This occurs when sand, gravel, and Portland cement are mixed in a concrete plant to make concrete. Another type of production process is *extraction* of something that is useful. An example is the iron smeltering process, whereby usable iron is removed from natural iron ore. The third type of production process is *changing the form* of inputs. Rolling iron into sheets, cutting logs into boards, and spinning glass into fiberglass are examples.

The process for service industries is not as easy to understand as that for manufacturing industries because service firms do not produce a tangible product. Rather, they create, produce, and distribute services. The growing importance of the service industry is illustrated by the fact that

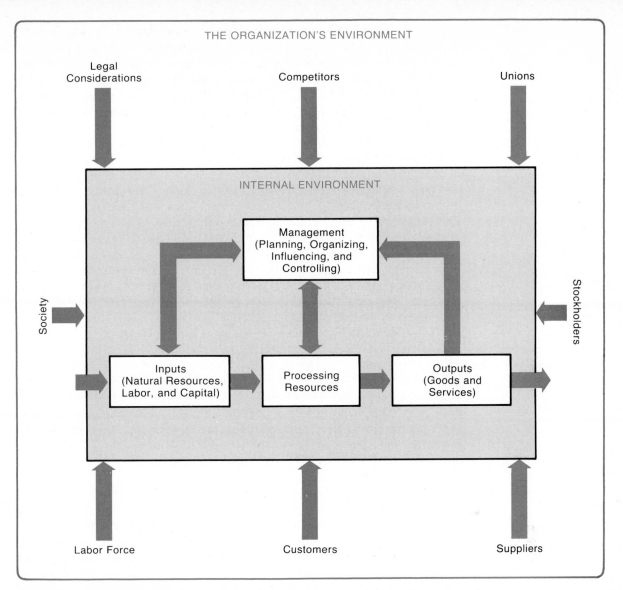

Figure 2–8 The Business System

approximately two of every three working Americans are employed in this area. Examples of service industries are banking, insurance, transportation, real estate, medical care, beauty, education, and government agencies. Still, the similarities between service and manufacturing are greater than the differences. Hospitals transform ill patients into healthy ones; schools change uninformed students into knowledgeable ones; and beauty salons transform individuals into more attractive ones.

The Transformation Process at Nucor Steel

The physical aspect of the transformation process at Nucor Steel is relatively simple. Scrapped steel is melted and converted to billets, which are then rolled out into various plates and shapes. In actual practice, however, the process is far more complex. Nucor managers have to consider the many factors in the organization's external environment. Major external factors for Nucor include competitors, the labor force, customers, and suppliers. For example, foreign competitors continually try to undercut Nucor prices. Domestic producers try to suggest that the quality of Nucor steel is lower than their own higher-priced steel. The labor force accessible to Nucor's rural plants shows a strong work ethic, but the number of workers available near a plant is often limited. Nucor attempts to produce standard products in order to keep costs low, but customers often demand steel of nonstandard composition, shape, or size. A major input to Nucor's transformation process is the electricity used to melt the scrap iron. Thus, when the utility company that supplies that electricity changes its pricing structure, Nucor must either pass any increased costs along or find offsetting cost reductions elsewhere.

Clearly the external environment has a great impact on the internal environment. For example, it is from the labor force (an external factor) that Nucor must obtain its employees (an internal factor). And it is to meet customer demands that Nucor determines the appropriate organizational structure and written guidelines to place in effect.

The transformation process at Nucor is directly subject to the internal environmental factors but is directed by managers. A purchasing manager, for example, may be responsible for making sure that the materials and supplies are of adequate quality and are obtained at the appropriate times and at the lowest possible cost. The manager of the furnace crew must not only ensure that the furnaces operate efficiently but must interact with other managers to keep them advised and respond to their needs. The marketing manager must direct the sale and distribution of Nucor's output and keep the production department aware of the quality and quantity of products that can be sold.

Top management is responsible for the overall transformation process and must be concerned not only with the interrelationships among departments involved in the process but also with those among internal and external environmental factors. The foregoing analysis of Figure 2–3 suggests the complexity of the job faced by top management. In actuality, Figure 2–3 is a gross simplification designed to help us understand the infinite complexities of the business system.

Outputs

Goods and services are the end result of the transformation process. Once inputs are converted to outputs, they return to the environment. The output of IBM is largely information processing, while Consolidated Edison produces energy. A different transformation system will be required for each firm.

Management

The operation of the business system, as illustrated in Figure 2–8, is the responsibility of management. Management must plan, organize, influence, and control. As the arrows indicate, management receives feedback from the output of the production process and monitors the inputs and the process itself. Inputs are then controlled or changed and the production process adjusted to provide the desired results in the form of outputs.

SUMMARY

The systems approach is viewing any organization or entity as an arrangement of interrelated parts that interact in ways that can be specified and to some extent predicted. When this systems approach is taken, one is inevitably led to the conclusion that every organization is an open system. An open system is an organization or assemblage of things that affects and is affected by outside events.

The organization's environment consists of a number of external forces. One of the most relevant forces relates to federal, state, and local legislation and regulations. These laws range from legislation devoted to protecting the environment to a law prohibiting discrimination in employment based on race, color, sex, religion, or national origin. Regarding competition, a manager must remember that a decision made by another firm may also affect the competition, and vice-versa.

The nature of the labor force will be quite different in the future as more women and minorities enter the work force. The union must be considered an external environmental factor because it essentially becomes a third party when dealing with the company. Stockholders own the company. Stockholders are vitally interested in the firm's operating effectiveness, and managers must be sensitive to stockholders' needs.

Lack of adequate supplies can cause the manufacturing process to be reduced or cause cessation of operation even though the firm has sufficient machinery and employees. Also, the people who actually use a firm's products and services—the customers—must be considered part of the external environment. Finally, society exerts considerable pressure on management because the public has found that changes can be made through their voices and votes.

Supervisory managers are only indirectly exposed to the organization's external environment. There are several factors in the internal environment that affect middle and lower managers: (1) the management style of the boss, (2) written guidelines, (3) employees, (4) organizational structure, (5) the informal organization, (6) other departments, and (7) the union.

In any organization, management's job is to use resources (inputs) in an efficient manner to produce or achieve desirable products and/or services (outputs). Inputs are categorized as natural resources, labor, and capital. The inputs or resources needed by the system vary according to the type of business the firm is in. Inputs are processed within the organization to create desired outputs. Goods and services are the end results of the transformation process. Once inputs are converted to outputs, they return to the environment. A different transformation system will be required for each firm.

The operation of the business system is the responsibility of management. This includes planning, organizing, influencing, and controlling. Management receives feedback from the output of the production process and monitors the inputs and the process itself. Inputs are then controlled or changed and the production process adjusted to provide the desired results.

REVIEW QUESTIONS

1. Define a system. Why does a manager need to understand the systems approach?
2. Identify and describe the major external environmental factors that can affect top managers.
3. How is the work force expected to change by the year 1990?
4. How does the environment differ for top managers as opposed to supervisory managers?
5. What are the components of an organization's transformation process?

1. Consider the following objectives from two different firms:

   Firm A: Our goal is to be an innovator in the creation of new products and services.

   Firm B: Our goal is to mass produce products that have a proven record of success.

   Given these different objectives, how might the transformation processes involved be different? Are there factors from the external environment that would be different for each firm?

2. Listed below are three different managerial positions. Describe and discuss the major environmental factors that would likely affect these positions.

   a. President of General Motors

   b. President of a regional college or university

   c. Owner and operator of Bob's Convenience Store located in a small rural community

CASE STUDY

A Tough Decision

As the largest employer in Ouachita County, Arkansas, International Forest Products Company (IFP) is an important part of the local economy. Ouachita County is in a mostly rural area of south-central Arkansas. IFP employs almost 10 percent of the local work force, and there are few alternative job opportunities available.

Scott Wheeler, the personnel director at IFP, tells of a difficult decision he had to make in December 1982:

> Everything was going along pretty well despite the economic recession, but I knew that sooner or later we would be affected. I got the word at a private meeting with the president, Mr. Deason, that we would have to cut employment by 30 percent on a crash basis. I was to get back to him within a week with a suggested plan. I knew that my plan would not be the final one, since the move was so major. But I knew that Mr. Deason was depending on me to provide at least a workable approach.
>
> First of all, I thought about how the union would react. Certainly, workers would have to be let go in order of seniority. The union would try to protect as many jobs as possible. I also knew that all management's actions during this period would be intensely scrutinized. We had to make sure that we had our act together.
>
> Then there was the matter of the impact on the surrounding community. The economy of Ouachita County had not been in good shape recently. Aside from the impact on individual workers who were laid off, I knew that our cutbacks would further depress the area's economy. I knew that there would be a number of government officials and civic leaders who would want to know how we were trying to minimize the harm done to the public in that area.
>
> We really had no choice but to make the cuts, I believed. First of all, I had no choice because Mr. Deason said that we were going to do it. Also, I had recently read a news account that one of our competitors, Johns Manville Corporation in West Monroe, Louisiana, had laid off several hundred workers in a cost-cutting move. To keep our sales from being further depressed, we had to ensure that our costs were just as low as those of our competitors. The wood products market is very competitive, and a cost advantage of even 2 or 3 percent would allow competitors to take many of our customers.
>
> Finally, a major reason for the cutbacks was to protect the interests of our shareholders. A few years ago we had a shareholder group that disrupted the

annual meeting to insist that IFP make certain antipollution changes. In general, though, the shareholders seem to be more concerned with the return on their investment than with social responsibility. At our meeting, the president reminded me that, just like every other manager in the company, I should place the shareholders' interest foremost. I really was quite overwhelmed as I began to work on a personnel plan that would balance all of the conflicting interests that I knew about.

QUESTIONS

1. List the elements in the company's environment that will affect Scott's suggested plan. How legitimate is the interest of each of these?

2. Is it true that Scott should be concerned first and foremost with protecting the interests of the shareholders? Discuss.

CASE STUDY

Getting by on a Shoestring

As the personnel director for KBH Stores in St. Louis, Missouri, Virginia Knickerbocker knew that she had her work cut out for her. Company management had just announced a goal of opening ten new stores during the next twelve months. KBH employed 480 people in the thirty-five stores they then had in operation. Virginia knew that staffing the new stores would require hiring and training about 150 people. She felt that her own small office was inadequately funded and staffed to handle such a level of operations.

Virginia found out about the expansion plans from a friend who knew the president's secretary. Although she didn't like being kept in the dark, she was not surprised that she had not been told. Glenn Sullivan, the president of KBH, was noted for his autocratic leadership style. He tended to tell subordinates what he wanted them to know. He expected everyone who worked for him to follow orders without question. He wasn't an unkind person, though, and Virginia had always gotten along with him pretty well. She had never confronted Mr. Sullivan about anything, so it was with some concern that she approached his office that day.

"Mr. Sullivan," she began, "I hear that we are going to be opening ten new stores next year." "That's right, Virginia," said Mr. Sullivan. "We've already arranged the credit lines and have picked out several of the sites." "What about staffing?" asked Virginia. "Well, I presume that you will take care of that, Virginia, when we get to that point," replied Mr. Sullivan.

"What about my own staff?" asked Virginia, "I think I am going to need at least three or four more people. We are crowded already, too, so I hope you plan to expand the personnel office." "Not really," said Mr. Sullivan. "You will have to get by with what you have for at least a year or so. It's going to be hard enough to afford the new stores and the people we need to staff them."

QUESTIONS

1. How does the environment Virginia faces differ from that confronting top executives?

2. How does the internal environment affect Virginia's ability to do her job?

NOTES

1. This discussion is a composite from a number of popular articles appearing between 1981 and 1984, among them: John Greenwald, "Turbulence in the Skies," *Time,* February 21, 1983, pp. 52–53; "Can Pan Am Weather Another Storm?" *Newsweek,* February 14, 1983, pp. 69–70; Louis Kraas, "Putting Pan Am Back Together Again," *Fortune,* December 28, 1981, pp. 42–47; "Lenders Ease Pan Am Debt/Equity Need," *Aviation Week and Space Technology,* January 3, 1983, p. 25; and "The Surgery Pan Am Hopes Will Save It," *Business Week,* June 15, 1981, pp. 36–37.

2. *Occupational Outlook Handbook,* 1980–81 ed., U.S. Government Bulletin, Number 2075.

3. "The Rise and Fall of Big Labor," *Newsweek,* September 5, 1983, p. 51.

4. David Vogel, "Ralph Nader's All Over the Place: Citizens vs. the Corporation," *Across the Board* 1 (April 1979): 26–31.

5. Ford S. Worthy, "The Fortune Directory of the Largest U.S. Industrial Corporations," *Fortune,* May 4, 1981, p. 322.

6. John Savage, "Incentive Programs at Nucor Corporation," *Personnel Administrator* (August 1981): 33–49; Richard I. Kirkland, "Petguims Profits at Nucor," *Fortune,* April 6, 1981, pp. 43–46; Don Bedwell, "Nucor's Lean, Mean Management Team," *South Magazine* (August 1980): 50–56; Thomas M. Rohan, "The 'Other' U.S. Steel Industry Is Booming," *Industry Week,* July 13, 1981, pp. 56–62; and George J. McManus, "Steel Industry Breaking Ranks," *Iron Age,* June 15, 1983, pp. 23–25.

REFERENCES

Appley, Lawrence A. "New Directions for Management." *Supervisory Management* 26 (February 1981): 9–12.

Dam, Andre va. "The Future of Management." *Management World* (January 1978): 3–6.

Fram, Eugene H., and Andrew Deubrin. "Time Span Orientation: A Key Factor of Contingency Management." *Personnel Journal* 60 (January 1981): 46–48.

Gest, Ted. "Battle of the Sexes over Comparable Worth." *U.S. News & World Report,* February 20, 1984, pp. 73–74.

Grayson, C. Jackson. "Productivity's Impact on Our Economic Future." *Personnel Administrator* 24 (December 1979): 21, 23.

Hammer, Nancy R. "Companies Must Communicate Their Commitment to Promoting Women." *Personnel Administrator* (June 1983): 95.

Holmes, Sandra L. "Adapting Corporate Structure for Social Responsiveness." *California Management Review* 21 (Fall 1978): 47–54.

Lanier, Linda K. "Florida Finds a High-Tech Fountain of Youth." *U.S. News & World Report,* April 25, 1983, pp. 58–59.

Leslie, C. E. "Critical Issues Confronting Managers in the '80's." *Training and Development Journal* 34 (January 1980): 14–17.

Luthans, Fred, and Todd I. Stewart. "A General Contingency Theory of Management." *Academy of Management Review* 2 (April 1977): 181–195.

Marsh, Robert M., and Hiroshi Minnari. "Technology and Size as Determinants of Organizational Structure of Japanese Factories." *Administrative Science Quarterly* 26 (March 1981): 33–57.

Mills, D. Quinn. "Reforming the U.S. System of Collective Bargaining." *Monthly Labor Review* (March 1983): 18–22.

Mintzberg, Henry. "The Manager's Job: Folklore and Fact." *Harvard Business Review* (July–August 1975): 49–51.

Nicholson, Joan, Toby Cooper, Russell Peterson, Hazel Henderson, and James Densen. "How Business Treats Its Environment." *Business and Society Review* 33 (Spring 1980): 56–65.

Rieder, George A. "The Role of Tomorrow's Manager." *Personnel Administrator* 24 (December 1979): 27–31.

"The Rise and Fall of Big Labor." *Newsweek,* September 5, 1983, pp. 50–53.

Skrzycki, Cindy. "Will Robots Bring More Jobs—or Less?" *U.S. News & World Report,* September 5, 1983, p. 25.

Wooten, Leland M. "The Mixed Blessings of Contingency Management." *Academy of Management Review* (July 1977): 431–441.

TENNCO MANUFACTURING COMPANY

John Meyer's big opportunity had finally arrived. In September 1985 he was appointed plant manager at his company's tubular products facility near Memphis, Tennessee. The plant employed 175 workers at that time and was responsible for rolling stainless steel strip into tubing, welding up the seam, and drawing it down to various shapes and wall thicknesses. The process was a moderately complex one, but most of it was done by heavy machines. The workers, all hired from the local area, required only one or two weeks of training.

John had been with his employer, Tennco Manufacturing Corporation, for ten years, having joined the company as an engineer just out of college. He had worked at several Tennco plants, first as a draftsman, then as a design engineer, and most recently as plant engineer at a Tennco chemical plant in Texas. The tubing plant was far different from anywhere John had worked before, but he was confident that the job of managing was about the same regardless of the organization or management level.

WORK FORCE

At John's previous job, most workers were highly trained technicians, most with at least some college. Here the rank and file was generally young and unskilled. There was a larger percentage of blacks and far more women workers than John had seen at his previous plants. In discussions with the personnel director, John had learned that employee turnover averaged about 50 percent a year. Almost none of the workers and few of the supervisors had been with Tennco for more than five years.

The work force was not unionized, but an organizing drive the year before had almost succeeded. When John took the job as plant manager, he was told by the company president, "The Memphis plant hasn't lived up to our expectations. That's why you're being sent down there. Any major reversals—if the plant goes union, for example—and we'll have no choice but to go out of the tubing business."

MANAGEMENT TEAM

John had reviewed the personnel records of each of his immediate subordinates and had questioned his predecessor about them. During the first few days on the job, he met with each of them individually. His purposes were to try to get to know them better, to learn about any problems they had, and to set the right tone for future relationships.

The personnel director was a twenty-eight-year-old college graduate accountant. He had moved into the personnel job because he "wanted to work with people" and because the previous personnel director had quit unexpectedly and no one else wanted the job. There were only two clerks who worked in personnel. During their conversation, the personnel director complained to John, "I've never had any authority around here. I'm really just a glorified record keeper. The production manager does most of the hiring and firing."

The chief accountant, who was also responsible for financial planning and quality control, was on temporary assignment from the home office in Knoxville. He seemed to John to be very competent, but John knew that he would have to move back to his regular job as soon as a replacement could be found. There were three clerks in the bookkeeping department.

The production manager was the only "old salt" at the plant. He had been with Tennco for twenty-five years, the last fifteen at Memphis. He told John that although he didn't have a college degree, he knew more about this business than anybody else in the company. "I learned manufacturing in the school of hard knocks," he said, "and when you learn there it stays with you."

In discussions with each of the managers, John explained what he expected of them. "Our purpose here is to make as much standard-quality, stainless steel tubing as we can at the lowest possible cost" is the way he put it. "Each manager should focus on helping me to accomplish that goal." John got no argument from anyone except the production manager, who simply said, "There is only so much you can do with the kind of lazy hoodlums you can hire for $4 an hour." John let that comment pass, but it was disturbing to him.

A TRUSTY SECRETARY

John felt that the most positive aspect of his new job was his secretary, Anne Bourne. Anne was nearly fifty, had retired from the U.S. civil service at a nearby navy base, and had good typing and shorthand skills. After a few days, Anne asked if she could talk frankly with John. Assured that she could, Anne confided, "I really want to see this plant do well. For many of the people around here, it's the best job they could get, and they really need it. But you have your work cut out for you." John asked, "What do you see as the major problem?" Anne replied, "I don't know that there is any one major problem. This is the only tubing plant Tennco has, and I'm not sure they place much importance on it. I don't know what it will take to change that, but I want you to know that I'll do everything in my power to help you do it."

SUPPORT FROM THE TOP

At the end of that first week on the job, John called his boss, Noah Livingston. After the usual pleasantries, John said, "Mr. Livingston, I think I'm going to have to make some major changes down here, and some of our people are going to be pretty upset." "What kind of changes are you talking about?" asked Mr. Livingston. "Well," said John, "for one thing, I think I may have to hire a new production manager and let Sam go. Also, we're going to have to start paying decent wages here so we can get people with a higher skill level and keep them longer." Mr. Livingston answered, "Well, John, you know what your budget is, and you're much closer to that situation than I am. All I'm asking you to do is make it work. Whatever you need from me, except more money, you'll get. I've watched you for a long time and I have great confidence in your ability. Don't let me down. But more important than that, don't let yourself down." As John hung up the phone, he had the uneasy feeling that he was out on a limb and everybody around him had a saw.

QUESTIONS

1. What management function should John pay most attention to first? Justify your answer.

2. Do you agree with John that management is similar regardless of the organization or management level? Why or why not?

3. What environmental forces are likely to affect John in his new job? What should be his attitude toward people and things outside the plant?

4. Should John terminate the production manager? Defend your answer.

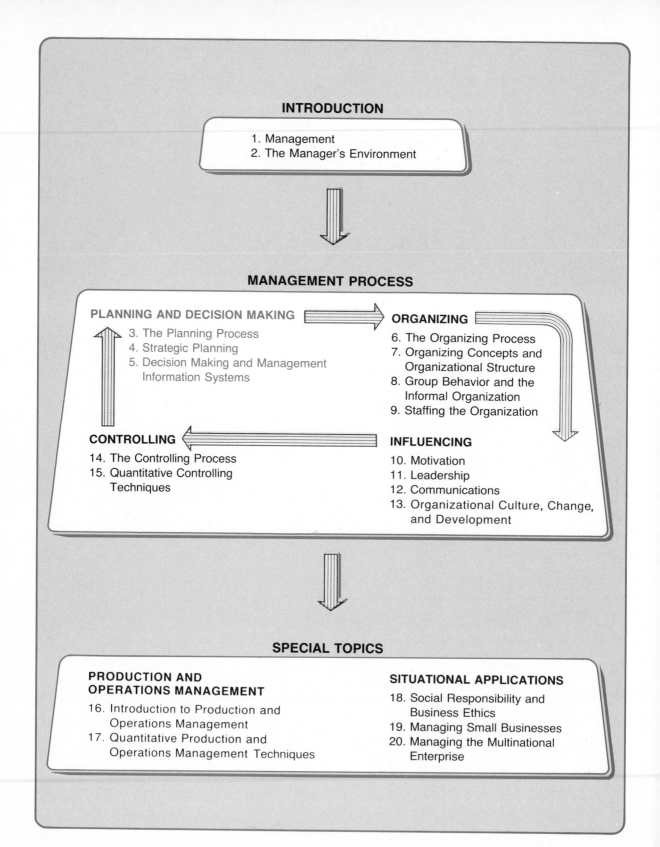

INTRODUCTION

1. Management
2. The Manager's Environment

MANAGEMENT PROCESS

PLANNING AND DECISION MAKING

3. The Planning Process
4. Strategic Planning
5. Decision Making and Management Information Systems

ORGANIZING

6. The Organizing Process
7. Organizing Concepts and Organizational Structure
8. Group Behavior and the Informal Organization
9. Staffing the Organization

CONTROLLING

14. The Controlling Process
15. Quantitative Controlling Techniques

INFLUENCING

10. Motivation
11. Leadership
12. Communications
13. Organizational Culture, Change, and Development

SPECIAL TOPICS

PRODUCTION AND OPERATIONS MANAGEMENT

16. Introduction to Production and Operations Management
17. Quantitative Production and Operations Management Techniques

SITUATIONAL APPLICATIONS

18. Social Responsibility and Business Ethics
19. Managing Small Businesses
20. Managing the Multinational Enterprise

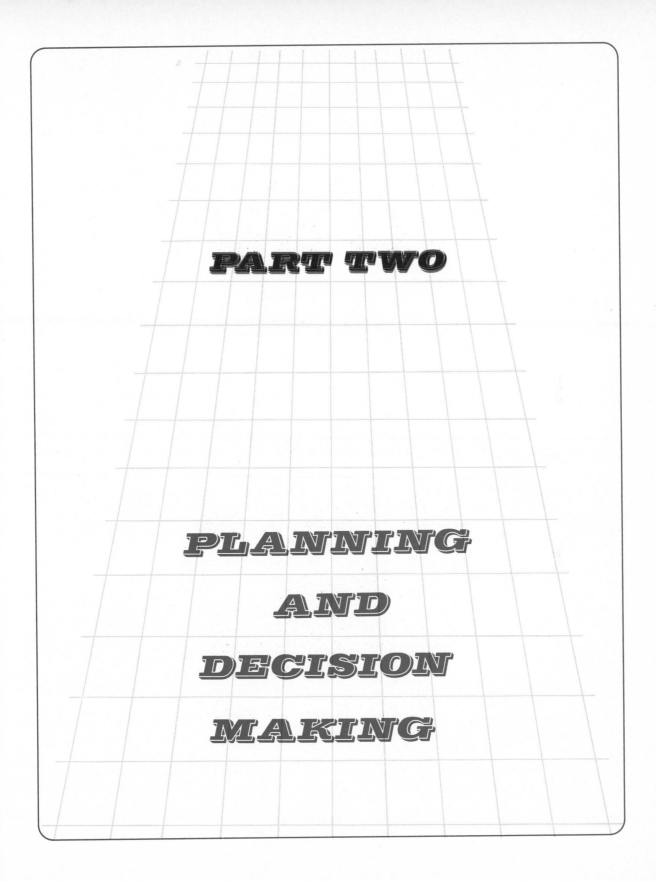

PART TWO

PLANNING

AND

DECISION

MAKING

LEARNING OBJECTIVES

After completing this chapter you should be able to

1. Describe the planning process and explain the function of a mission statement.

2. Define the term *objective* and identify the characteristics of good objectives.

3. Describe the main types of objectives and state some problems encountered in establishing objectives.

4. Identify the questions that planning should answer and distinguish among a policy, a procedure, and a rule.

5. Explain contingency planning.

6. Describe management by objectives (MBO) and explain the essential elements of the MBO process.

7. List and briefly describe the primary benefits and potential problems with MBO programs.

3

The Planning Process

*Planning
to Remain the
World's Innkeeper*

HOLIDAY
CORPORATION

For many years Holiday Inns (recently renamed Holiday Corporation) called itself the "Nation's Innkeeper." But with almost 2,000 hotels in fifty-three countries, a more apt title is now the "World's Innkeeper." Holiday Inns did not attain its position of supremacy by standing still. Kemmons Wilson, the founder and long-time chief executive officer, was well known for his devotion to effective planning.

By 1984, the business of Holiday Inns had expanded quite beyond the provision of lodging services. Then the company billed itself as the "world's largest hospitality company." In addition to its flagship chain of Holiday Inn hotels, the company had opened three new hotel chains: one to appeal to upscale business travelers, a suite-type hotel chain aimed at persons who planned to stay several days in one location, and another directed at economy-minded travelers. Holiday Inns was also in the process of expanding its gaming business. The company's Harrahs Casinos were located in Las Vegas and Atlantic City.

Although in a number of businesses, Holiday Inns management recognized the company's reliance on its traditional main business. Efforts were made to upgrade the Holiday Inns chain. It was determined how many hotels were to be closed and how many new ones were to be built. Specific goals were set in terms of the frequency of guests' complaints. Emphasis on the human aspect of Holiday Inns's business was of central concern. Confident of success, Holiday Inns management issued a remarkable guarantee, "Your room will be right . . . or we'll make it right . . . or you stay that night free."[1]

Planning is central to the success of any company. As the Holiday Corporation story suggests, it involves far more than just deciding what to do on a given day. Company management at Holiday Corporation has a clear picture of the business they are in and of what they intend to accomplish. This is communicated throughout the organization. Specific goals are established in a wide range of areas. Because goals and plans are specific and well thought out, management is justified in being confident of success. This is why the company was able to issue such a strong guarantee. This is also why few doubt that Holiday Inns will continue to be the nation's leading hotelier.

This chapter begins with a brief overview of the planning process. Next, the parts of the planning process—mission, objectives, and plans—are discussed in detail. The remainder of the chapter is devoted to discussion of the following planning topics: standing plans, the planning process for supervisors, contingency planning, and management by objectives. Throughout the chapter we will attempt to provide students with an appreciation of the importance of effective planning, regardless of whether the planner is a company president, a supervisor, or a manager of a small business.

THE PLANNING PROCESS: AN OVERVIEW

Effective planning can have a major impact on the productivity of managers at all levels in an organization. **Planning** is *the process of determining in advance what should be accomplished and how it should be done.* The planning process presented in Figure 3–1 serves as a guide for the entire chapter. This process is appropriate whether planning is done by upper- or lower-level management

planning

Tex Schramm, president and general manager of the Dallas Cowboys, recognizes the value of planning. He states, "My team's objective is to win, and win consistently." His long-range plan involves creating an environment

Planning is central to the success of any company.

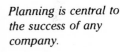

Ellis Herwig/Stock, Boston Inc.

to accomplish this objective. Management stability is emphasized as part of the plan. Apparently this approach has worked; the Cowboys have been in the National Football League playoffs most years, and since their beginning in 1960, there has been but one coach, Tom Landry. The player personnel director and many of the assistant coaches also have been with the team for a long period. Tex says about the Cowboys, "It is our policy to allow people to work in their area of expertise and use their initiative to gain not only team and organizational success but individual recognition." Coach Landry provides each player with a team play book that covers offensive

Figure 3–1   The Planning Process

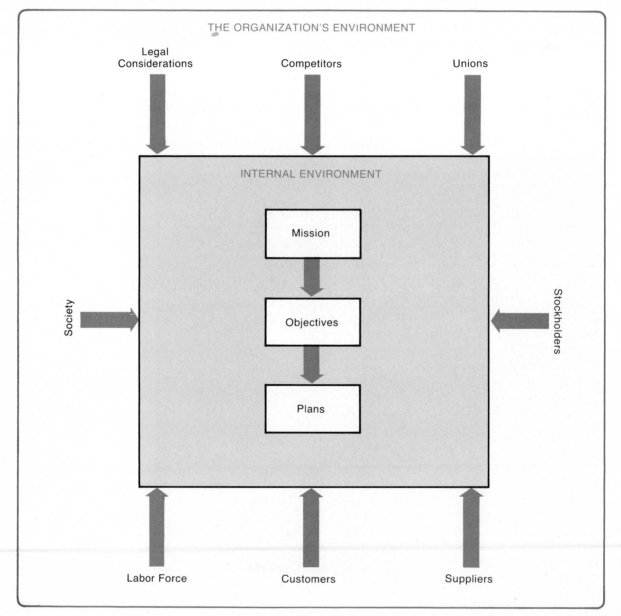

and defensive formations, as well as individual assignments in detail. All phases of the planning process for the Dallas Cowboys relate to the objective of winning.

The process begins with a mission statement. From the mission statement specific goals or objectives can be established. Then plans can be developed to accomplish those objectives. The planning process is dynamic and should be carefully evaluated and modified to conform to the current and anticipated situation.

MISSION

Mission is *the organization's continuing purpose or reason for being.* The expressed mission statement of Holiday Inns, for example, is "Making people feel welcome—all over the world." Holiday Corporation calls itself the world's largest hospitality company and not just a motel chain. Holiday Corporation's managers know that, "and to make a profit doing this" is an implied continuation of the mission statement. Obviously the company must make a profit serving hospitality needs, but the published mission statement still serves to guide employees throughout the organization.

mission

Each unit within the organization should have a clearly understood mission.

Tyrone Hall/Stock, Boston Inc.

Each management level in the organization should conduct its operation with a clear understanding of the overall mission of the firm. In fact, each unit within the organization (division, plant, department) should have a clearly understood mission that coincides with the organizational mission.

OBJECTIVES OR GOALS

objectives

Specific objectives, or goals, can be established once the mission is understood. **Objectives** are *the desired end results of any activity*. Objectives should be set at each managerial level in the organization; however, lower-level objectives must be consistent with upper-level objectives.

Characteristics of Good Objectives

Objectives should have four basic characteristics: (1) they should be expressed in writing; (2) they should be measurable; (3) they should be specific as to time; and (4) they should be challenging but attainable. Placing the goals in written form increases understanding and commitment. Confusion as to what the goals actually are is less likely to occur when they are written.

Measurability suggests that the goals should be quantified whenever possible. It would be much better to have a goal of increasing profits by 10 percent during a certain period instead of just saying, "We want to increase profits." A 1 percent increase would meet the latter goal.

Objectives should be specific as to time. Individuals need and want to know when an objective should be accomplished. Also, a goal that is set without a time limit cannot be challenging. In the above example, are the profits to be increased by 10 percent this year or by the end of the century?

Finally, an objective that is too easily accomplished provides little satisfaction when completed. On the other hand, an unattainable goal is more likely to frustrate workers than to encourage them. The corporate goals for Robertshaw Controls are shown in Table 3–1.

Objectives are established at each level of management. Objectives set by top management should be consistent with the overall mission of the firm. And goals of lower-level management must be in line with those of upper-level management.

The persons charged with the responsibility of establishing corporate objectives vary from business to business. At times, the president or chairman of the board provides the major thrust in goal creation. At other times, a group of top-level executives are consulted. Whatever the source, these objectives provide the course toward which future energies of the firm will be directed and set the tone for objective setting throughout the organization.

Types of Objectives

The creation of specific organizational and subunit objectives is no simple task. Numerous external factors exert their influence on a firm. An organization usually has a number of objectives, and the emphasis each receives may change depending on the impact of a particular environmental

TABLE 3-1   Robertshaw Controls Company Corporate Goals, 198-

1. Minimize historical trends in sales and profits.
   (Objective: 10 percent profit before tax is necessary to assure adequate stockholder return and reinvestment in corporate growth.)

2. Increase Robertshaw's sales and profits in the international market.
   (Objective: 10 percent minimum annual profit growth assures compounding profitability and established positive trend line.)

3. Increase utilization of stockholders' equity through return on assets and return on investment justification.
   (Objective: 10–15 percent annual sales growth is required to double the sales of the corporation every five to eight years.)

4. Review all product lines and products that cannot justify continuance based on ROA.
   (Objective: Within the broad parameters of sensors and associated controls, Robertshaw can develop adequate diversification and maximize in-house abilities and expertise.

5. Establish corporate and divisional financial standards.
   (Objective: To evaluate and justify investments in new or old areas of opportunity to verify the potential for the corporation to achieve an industry position of no less than third.)

6. Develop improved consumer awareness and recognition of Robertshaw.
   (Objective: The criteria for growth must include favorable corporate identity at the consumer and investor levels.)

Source: Y. K. Shetty, "New Look at Corporate Goals." © 1979 by the Regents of the University of California. Reprinted from *California Management Review,* vol. 22, no. 2, p. 72, by permission of the Regents and the Company. Used also with permission of Robertshaw Controls Company.

factor or group of factors. At least three main types of objectives can be identified:

- *Economic objectives*—survival, profit, and growth.
- *Service objectives*—creation of benefit for society.
- *Personal objectives*—goals of individuals and groups within the organization.

Economic Objectives

Survival is a basic objective of all organizations. Whether an organization is producing a desired economic value or not seems to take second place to just staying alive. It is difficult for a firm to take into account higher social objectives when it is not known whether the next payroll can be met. As an anonymous statesman once said, "It is extremely difficult to think that your initial objective was to drain the swamp when you are up to your neck in alligators."

In order to survive, a firm must at least break even—that is, it must generate enough revenues to cover costs. But business firms want more than mere survival; they are in business to make a profit. Profit provides a vital incentive for the continued, successful operation of the business enterprise. An adequate profit primarily depends on the industry and the specific needs of an organization. For many companies, it depends on how much profit is possible.

Growth—in sales, number of employees, or number of facilities—may also be a major objective of a firm. Growth may set the stage for long-term survival. A company may seek unrestricted growth, and sometimes this growth can become an end in itself. When this happens, the company may fail to give proper emphasis to profitability. There are, of course, certain economic advantages that come with size, and many companies see growth as a way of competing more effectively.

Service Objectives

Profit alone is often viewed as the primary motive for being in business. While it is true a firm cannot survive for long without making a profit, many managers recognize an obligation to society. Even those who feel no such responsibility know that if a firm cannot consistently create economic value for society, it will not stay in business long enough to make a profit. Many firms have gone out of existence when they ceased to produce goods and services that were desired by society. Manville Corporation, the well-known maker of asbestos, became unprofitable after the public learned how dangerous asbestos is, a fact the company suppressed for many years.

Personal Objectives

Organizations are made up of people who have different personalities, backgrounds, experiences, and goals. Personal goals are seldom identical to the objectives of the organization. If personal and organizational goals are incompatible, the employee concerned may choose to withdraw from the firm. But an employee may not feel financially able to leave the firm. A conflict between the employee's goals and the organization's goals can result in minimum work effort, absenteeism, and even sabotage. Employees are not the only ones whose goals, when they differ from those of the organization, can affect that organization. For instance, a stockholder can cease to provide support for the organization in such a case by selling stock.

Personal goals also include the objectives of groups. If an organization is to survive, grow, and earn a profit, it must provide a reasonable match between its goals and the goals of powerful groups. Table 3–2 shows how the objectives of a business might differ from those of related groups. It is not unusual for particular groups or members to experience actual or imagined conflict between their personal goals and the goals of the organization. For instance, some customers may believe that higher wages will make the price of products higher, while the union may believe that

---

TABLE 3–2　Possible Goals of the Organization and Related Groups

Groups	Possible Goal
Organization	Maximize profits
Management	Promotions, higher salaries, or bonuses
Employees	Increased wages and bonuses
Government	Adherence of firm to all government legislation, laws, and regulations
Competition	Attain a greater share of the market
Customers	Quality product at lowest price
Stockholders/owners	Higher dividends
Society	Protection of the environment
Unions	Greater influence for union members

stockholders' profits are too high. Management has the difficult task of reconciling these conflicts, whether or not they are based on factual information.

Problems Encountered in Establishing Objectives

Goal conflict can result from many sources. Three potential causes are the existence of real goals that are different from the stated ones, the use of multiple objectives, and the application of quantitative and nonquantitative goals.

Real versus Stated Objectives

The *real* goals may be at odds with the *stated* goals. Objectives are often the result of power plays and pressures that come from circumstances in the marketplace or from internal tensions. The personal goals of the board of directors, outside creditors, lower-level managers, employees, stockholders, and labor unions are bound to be different. Goals are often significantly altered by individuals and groups who seek to adapt the organization to their narrower purposes. Because of these differences, the stated goals are at times different from the actual goals.

To determine the real goals, one must look at the actual decisions and actions that occur from day to day. A manager's actions speak louder than words. What functions or groups actually receive the major share of the resources? What type of behavior is accorded the greatest rewards by management? If the administration of a prison, for example, specifies its major goal as rehabilitation of prisoners but has only two counselors on its payroll while it employs five hundred guards, the facts belie the stated goal. And if Holiday Corporation were to fail to train its employees to serve customers well, its service objective would be called into question.

Multiple Objectives

All organizations have multiple goals that must be recognized by management. For instance, what is the major goal of a university? Is it to provide education for students, to conduct research to advance the state of knowledge, or to provide community service? In some universities, research is given the first priority in money, personnel, and privilege. In others, the teaching goal is dominant. In still others, an attempt is made to be all things to all people. Given limited funds, however, priorities must be established. One can debate the priority of goals for such institutions as a mental hospital (therapy or confinement); a church (religion or social relationships); a prison (rehabilitation or confinement); a vocational high school (skill development, general education, or keeping young people off the streets); a medical school (training medical students for clinical practice, basic research, or academic medicine); and an aerospace firm (research information or usable hardware).

Seemingly conflicting goals may not be mutually exclusive, but choices must be made as to how much emphasis each is to receive. At Holiday Corporation, for example, decisions frequently are made to forgo short-term profit so that the company can maintain its reputation for quality hotel service.

Quantitative versus Nonquantitative Objectives

In general, the more quantitative a goal, the greater the attention and pressure for its accomplishment. The feasibility of quantifying goals varies throughout the organization. Production managers, for example, often have specific quotas and schedules. It is easy to tell if either quantity or quality declines. Personnel managers, on the other hand, often have more subjective goals. The fact that the personnel manager's goals are more subjective does not mean that they are less important.

If the most important goal is also the most measurable, as with the goal of winning with a professional sports team, then little distortion will take place. If the reverse is true, the organization is likely to be pushed in the direction of more quantitative, but perhaps less important, goals. In universities, research and publication are far easier to measure precisely than excellence in teaching. The primary goal of excellence in education may be replaced with the research emphasis.

PLANS

plans   Objectives are concerned with the end results desired. **Plans** are *statements of how objectives are to be accomplished.* Planning is a task that every manager, whether a top-level executive or a first-line supervisor, must perform. Stating an objective does not guarantee its accomplishment. A plan must be developed to tell people what to do in order to fulfill the goal. There are usually more ways than one to accomplish a goal. The plan states which approach is to be taken. Specifically, planning should answer the following questions:

1. What activities are required to accomplish the objectives?
2. When should these activities be carried out?
3. Who is responsible for doing what?
4. Where should the activities be carried out?
5. When should the action be completed?

When Walter Mondale decided to challenge Ronald Reagan for the presidency in the 1984 election, he had to answer each of these questions. His intermediate objective was to get a majority of the delegates at the Democratic convention. First, though, he had to build a campaign organization in each state; obtain funds; and win caucuses, presidential preference primaries, and other kinds of elections.

This could not all be done at once, nor could it be done in random order. So it was necessary to determine a time schedule. Some of the times when things had to be accomplished were determined by election dates and other factors over which Mondale had no control. With regard to other scheduling questions, however, he had flexibility.

Responsibilities had to be assigned to members of the campaign organization. Mondale had to appoint a chairman and assign responsibility to many others further down in the campaign organization.

The question of where the activities should be carried out was a dominant one throughout the campaign. Emphasis had to shift to California, for example, when that large state was approaching its election. And the candidate himself had to plan to be in certain states at opportune times.

Finally, Mondale wanted to lock up the nomination early in the campaign, so a goal was set to sweep the early primaries and convince everyone that he was the choice. It did not work out that way; Gary Hart won several of the early primaries, and Walter Mondale had to modify his goal. It was not until the results were in on the California primary, in June 1984, that Walter Mondale could say with authority that he was the nominee. Then he looked toward a later goal, winning the general elections. This required new plans, plans that would prove unsuccessful.

STANDING PLANS

Plans that remain roughly the same for long periods of time are referred to as **standing plans**. The most common kinds of standing plans are policies, procedures, and rules.

standing plans

Policies

A **policy** is *a predetermined guide established to provide direction in decision making.* As such, policies should be based on a thorough analysis of corporate objectives. Separate policies cover the important areas of a firm such as personnel, marketing, research and development, production, and finance.

policy

To formulate policies, the manager must have knowledge and skill in the area for which the policy is being created; however, there are certain generalizations that apply to the establishment of policies. The most important has already been stated: policies must be based on a thorough analysis of objectives. Several other general principles can help the manager create appropriate policies:

1. *Policies should be based on factual information.* It is a fact, for example, that Holiday Corporation is in the hotel business; it is an opinion that the corporation is the world's best hotelier.

2. *Subordinate and superior policies should be complementary, not contradictory.* A policy for an individual Holiday Corporation hotel should not directly conflict with the company's corporate policy.

3. *Policies of different divisions or departments should be coordinated.* They should be directed toward overall organizational optimization instead of optimizing a particular department such as sales, engineering, purchasing, or production, to the detriment of the whole.

4. *Policies should be definite, understandable, and preferably in writing.* If a policy is to guide actions, persons concerned must be aware of its existence, and this requires creating understandable directives in a definitive written form. In effect, policies are the memory of the organization, which it uses to help cope with future events.

5. *Policies should be flexible and stable.* The requirements of policy stability and flexibility are not contradictory; one is a prerequisite to the other. Stable policies change only in response to fundamental and basic changes in conditions. Government regulations can represent such a basic change in conditions that they can have a major impact on a firm's employment policies. The higher the organizational level, the more stable the policy must be. Changing the direction of the enterprise is a much more complex and time-consuming task than changing the direction of a department or section. The

TABLE 3–3 Armco Policies

Ethics	To do business guided and governed by the highest standards of conduct so the end result of action taken makes a good reputation an invaluable and permanent asset.
Square deal	To insist on a square deal always. To make sure people are listened to and treated fairly, so that men and women really do right for right's sake and not just to achieve a desired result. For everyone to go beyond narrowness, littleness, and selfishness in order to get the job done.
Organization	To develop and maintain an efficient, loyal, aggressive organization, who believe in their company, to whom work is a challenge, and to whom extraordinary accomplishment is a personal goal.
Working conditions	To create and maintain good working conditions . . . to provide the best possible equipment and facilities . . . and plants and offices that are clean, orderly, and safe.
Quality and service	To adopt "Quality and Service" as an everyday practice. Quality will be the highest attainable in products, organization, plant, property, and equipment. Service will be the best possible to customers, to shareholders, to city, state, and nation.
Opportunity	To employ people without regard to race, sex, religion, or national origin. To encourage employees to improve their skills by participating in available educational or training programs. To provide every possible opportunity for advancement so that each individual may reach his or her highest potential.
Compensation	To provide not only fair remuneration, but the best compensation for service rendered that it is possible to pay under the changing economic, commercial, and other competitive conditions that exist from time to time. It is Armco's ambition to develop an organization of such spirit, loyalty, and efficiency that can and will secure results which will make it possible for individual members to earn and receive better compensation than would be possible if performing a similar service in other fields of effort.
Incentive	To provide realistic and practical incentive as a means of encouraging the highest standard of individual performance and to assure increased quantity and quality of performance.
Cooperation	To recognize cooperation as the medium through which great accomplishments are attained. Success depends more on a spirit of helpful cooperation than on any other one factor.
Objectivity	To always consider what is right and best for the business as a whole, rather than what may be expedient in dealing with a single, separate situation.
Conflict of interest	To prohibit employees from becoming financially interested in any company with which Armco does business, if such financial interest might possibly influence decisions employees must make in their areas of responsibility. The above policy does not apply to ownership in publicly owned companies. This is not considered a conflict of interest but, rather, is encouraged as part of the free enterprise system.
Citizenship	To create and maintain a working partnership between industry and community in this country and throughout the world. To support constructive agencies in communities where Armco people live and work in an effort to create civic conditions that respond to the highest needs of the citizens.

Used with permission from the Armco Steel Corporation.

higher the organizational level, the more policy resembles principle. The Armco Steel Corporation provides an excellent example of a firm whose policies have been remarkably stable. First formulated in 1919, these policies, outlined in Table 3–3, are still applicable today.

6. *Policies should be reasonably comprehensive in scope.* Policies conserve the executive's time by making available a previously determined decision. The manager should organize the work in such a way that subordinate personnel can handle the routine and predictable work in conformity with established policies, while the manager's time is devoted to exceptional events and problems. If the body of policies is reasonably comprehensive, few cases arise that are not covered by policy.

Procedures and Rules

Procedures and rules might be thought of as further restrictions on the actions of lower-level personnel. They are usually established to ensure adherence to a particular policy.

TABLE 3-4 Examples of Policies, Procedures, and Rules

Policy:

It is the policy of the company that every employee is entitled to a safe and healthful place in which to work, and to prevent accidents from occurring in any phase of its operation. Toward this end the full cooperation of all employees will be required.

Management will view neglect of safety policy or program as just cause for disciplinary action.

Procedure:

The purpose of this procedure is to prevent injury to personnel or damage to equipment by inadvertent starting, energizing, or pressurizing equipment that has been shut down for maintenance, overhaul, lubrication, or setup.

1. Maintenance persons assigned to work on a job will lock out the machine at the proper disconnect with their own safety lock and keep the key in their possession.
2. If the job is not finished before shift change, the maintenance person will remove the lock and put a seal on the disconnect. A danger tag will be hung on the control station stating why the equipment is shut down.
3. The maintenance person who will be coming on the following shift will place his or her lock on the disconnect along with seal.
4. Upon completion of the repairs, the area supervisor will be notified by maintenance that work is completed.
5. The supervisor and the maintenance person will check the equipment to see that all guards and safety devices are securely in place and operable. Then the supervisor will break the seal and remove the danger tag from the machine.

Rules:

The following rules are intended to promote employee safety.

1. The company and each employee are required to comply with provisions of the Occupational Safety and Health Act (OSHA). You will be informed by your supervisor on specific OSHA rules not covered here that apply to your job or area.
2. Report all accidents promptly that occur on the job or on company premises—this should be done whether or not any injury or damage resulted from the incident.
3. Horseplay, practical jokes, wrestling, throwing things, running in the plant, and similar actions will not be tolerated as they can cause serious accidents.
4. Observe all warning signs, such as "No Smoking," "Stop," etc. They are there for your protection.
5. Keep your mind on the work being performed.
6. Familiarize yourself with the specific safety rules and precautions that relate to your work area.
7. Approved eye protection must be worn in all factory and research lab areas during scheduled working hours or at any other time work is being performed.
8. Hearing protection is required when the noise level in an area reaches limits established by OSHA.
9. Adequate hand protection should be worn while working with solvents or other materials that might be harmful to hands.
10. Wearing rings or other jewelry that could cause injury is not allowed for persons performing work in the factory area.
11. Good housekeeping is important to accident prevention. Keep your immediate work area, machinery, and equipment clean. Keep tools and materials neatly and securely stored so that they will not cause injury to you or others.
12. Aisles, fire equipment access, and other designated "clear" areas must not be blocked.
13. Learn the correct way to lift. Get help if the material to be lifted is too heavy to be lifted alone. Avoid an effort that is likely to injure you.
14. Only authorized employees are allowed to operate forklifts and company vehicles. Passengers are not allowed on lift equipment or other material-handling equipment except as required in the performance of a job.
15. Learn the right way to do your job. If you are not sure you thoroughly understand a job, ask for assistance. This will often contribute to your job performance as well as your job safety.
16. Observe safe and courteous driving habits in the parking lot.

Procedure

procedure

A **procedure** is *a series of steps established for the accomplishment of some specific project or endeavor.* Many organizations have extensive procedures manuals and instructions designed to provide guidelines for those managers and workers lower in the organization. *The stable body of policies and procedures, written and unwritten, that governs an organization* is called **standard operating procedures (SOP)**. For most policies, there are accompanying procedures to indicate how that policy should be carried out.

standard operating procedures (SOP)

Rule

rule

A **rule** is *a specific and detailed guide to action set up to direct or restrict action in a fairly narrow manner.* There may be a rule that requires hard hats be worn in a certain work area, for example.

An illustration of the differences among policies, procedures, and rules is shown in Table 3–4. As may be seen from the illustration, procedures and rules may overlap as a definition. Taken out of sequence, a step in a procedure may actually become a rule.

Policies, procedures, and rules are designed to direct action toward the accomplishment of objectives. If we could be assured that the persons doing the work were thoroughly in agreement with and completely understood basic objectives, there would be less need for policies, procedures, and rules. Moreover, it is apparent that objectives at times are unclear and even controversial. Thus, all organizations have a need for policies, procedures, and rules. They should be more definitive and understandable than the objectives on which they are based.

LEVELS OF PLANNING

Planning occurs at every level in the organization. At the top management level, the primary concern is with strategic planning, relating to overall organizational purposes. This is the subject of Chapter 4. Strategic plans must be broken down into less generalized operating or tactical plans. In essence, these are plans designed to implement or carry out the broader-based plans of top management. They often relate to limited functional areas such as sales, finance, production, and personnel. Operating plans also encompass a shorter time frame than strategic plans. Finally, the managers responsible for implementing operating plans tend to be middle and lower managers, rather than top managers.

THE PLANNING PROCESS FOR SUPERVISORS

All too often, a discussion of planning is limited to the benefits top management may derive from proper planning. Sometimes we forget that all effective managers engage in planning. The planning process for top-level and lower-level managers is quite similar; however, the environment of lower-level managers is comprised largely of company factors. A lower-level manager is constrained by overall company objectives and strategies, but the importance of planning remains. For example, no matter how grandiose Holiday Corporation's corporate planning, the company would fail without effective planning by thousands of hotel managers, maintenance supervisors, and bell captains.

The amount of time spent in the planning function at lower levels of management may not be as great as at higher levels. For instance, as compared to a corporate executive, a hotel manager may devote a much larger percentage of time to influencing or controlling than to planning; however, this does not diminish the importance of planning for the hotel manager. Also, the time frame for planning may be shorter for lower-level managers than for senior executives. To be successful, top-level management must make decisions affecting operations far into the future. But to ask a lower-level manager to plan five years ahead may be unrealistic. Daily, weekly, monthly, and annual quotas must be met.

It is quite possible that long-range planning for some supervisors may encompass a relatively short time span; however, the shorter time span does not diminish the importance of long-range planning. Consider some of the types of plans that supervisors typically make:

- *Production plans*—The goal might be to meet a daily, weekly, or monthly production schedule. The production plan at the supervisor's level would involve scheduling jobs and assigning workers to do them.
- *Methods improvement plans*—The goal could be to find the best way to do a certain task. The plan might consist of a simple listing of the steps necessary to obtain the improvements.
- *Absences plans*—The goal might be to ensure that the work continues to get done when some of the workers are absent. Scheduling vacation time is an example of this form of planning.
- *Budget plans*—A budget is a statement of desired results expressed in financial or numerical terms. Although the budget itself is a plan, the supervisor's goal might be to stay within the budget. Therefore, the supervisor's budget plan would describe what is considered the most effective way to expend budgeted funds.

SEARLE Although G. D. Searle and Company spends millions on research and development, the company's most exciting product, NutraSweet, was discovered by accident. The Searle scientist who is credited with developing NutraSweet in 1965 was working on a product for ulcer treatment. By 1984, NutraSweet accounted for nearly half of Searle's billion-dollar annual sales. NutraSweet is used in hundreds of products today. Customers range from Coca-Cola and Pepsi, General Foods, Procter and Gamble, Heinz, and Wrigley to the millions of consumers who have made the NutraSweet-based diet sweetener Equal an instant best seller.

How Sweet It Is

The path from the development of the product in 1965 to its domination of the artificial sweetener market in 1985 was not an easy one, though. Exceptional management skill was required. First, the Food and Drug Administration (FDA) had to be convinced that the product was safe. Partial FDA approval came in 1981, sixteen years after the product was developed. It was not until 1983 that the government allowed carbonated soft drinks to be sweetened with NutraSweet.

Searle created a new division for NutraSweet in 1983. Donald Rumsfeld, Searle's chief executive, chose Robert Shapiro, the company's general counsel, to head this division. Shapiro had no previous management experience. "Don Rumsfeld felt that since this was an unprecedented thing, he might as well give it to someone who doesn't start with any preconceptions," says Shapiro. "I certainly had the virtue of ignorance going in," he adds. The multimillion dollar marketing effort Shapiro initiated was aimed mainly at consumers, although NutraSweet was not sold to them directly. The slogan was, "You can't buy it, but you're gonna love it." A million packages of NutraSweetened gumballs were mailed to consumers. And every product that contains NutraSweet has that fact prominently mentioned on the container label.

Because of the exceptional success of the advertising program, Shapiro faced another challenge. How could the company produce 3 million pounds and be ready for the growth that was sure to come? Two European companies were engaged to help make NutraSweet. A new $160 million plant was begun in Augusta, Georgia. Still, demand outstripped supply, and Searle had to refuse new customers.

A number of groups inevitably questioned NutraSweet's safety. While Shapiro was fighting off adverse publicity, he had to build a new organization involving thousands of workers and hundreds of managers and sales personnel.

Competitors in West Germany and the United States had already patented innovative new sweeteners, and others were on the verge of doing so. So Shapiro had to intensify research and development efforts. "Our objective is to make sure that we're the people who make NutraSweet obsolete," he said.

Also, Shapiro knows that, at $90 a pound—compared to $4 for saccharin—NutraSweet will face continuing cost pressure. Efforts are underway to increase the productivity at NutraSweet plants in University Park, Illinois, and Harbor Beach, Michigan, and to make the Georgia plant as efficient as it can be.[2]

CONTINGENCY PLANNING

contingency planning

Robert Burns's line, "The best laid plans of mice and men often go astray," is certainly applicable in today's business world. Events can occur so rapidly that plans may be useless before they can be fully implemented. External and internal disturbances often occur that can result in the necessity for a change in plans. **Contingency planning** is *the development of different plans to be placed in effect if certain events occur.* For instance, G. D. Searle undoubtedly has a plan to confront competition if and when another company begins to market any of the new sweeteners now under development.

Clearly contingency planning entails a recognition that unforeseen events can and will occur to alter the results of initial plans. Contingency planning makes it unnecessary for a firm to wait for a situation to occur before it prepares to respond. Naturally not all situations can be anticipated, but the manager who tries to anticipate reasonably probable occurrences will stand a much better chance of coping with the future.

A disaster recovery plan for a computer installation is a common example of a contingency plan. Organizations that use computers become very dependent on them. This is true for practically every modern company. But what happens when the system fails? Sabotage and vandalism are human-made disasters to which computer systems may be vulnerable. Fires, floods, rainstorms, tornadoes, and hurricanes are natural threats that often disable computer systems. Holiday Corporation hotels in coastal areas of Florida are especially susceptible to hurricanes.

The plan for recovery typically involves provisions for backups (not only for the information contained in the computer but also for the functions the computer performs). Think what the cost might have been if G. D. Searle had lost the data from the years of testing NutraSweet. The data processing personnel for a large firm like Searle may make daily or weekly copies of master files and place them in a secure location. Contingency plans are made to obtain these files if and when they are needed. Some other aspects of a data processing contingency plan might be site evacuation, damage assessment, emergency processing, and methods to keep system users informed about restoration efforts. Reciprocal emergency processing agreements and mutual aid pacts between firms are often the subject of contingency plans. Contingency planning is increasingly important in the field of data processing, but it applies to most other aspects of the organization as well.

PLANNING THROUGH MANAGEMENT BY OBJECTIVES

During the past two decades, few other developments in the theory and practice of management have received as much attention and application as MBO. Effective management practice concentrates on establishing and attaining measurable goals. **Management by objectives (MBO)** is *a philosophy of management that emphasizes the setting of agreed-on objectives by superior and subordinate managers and the use of these objectives as the primary basis of motivation, evaluation, and control efforts.* Above all else, MBO represents a way of thinking that concentrates on achieving results. It forces management to plan explicitly as opposed to simply responding or reacting on the basis of guesses or hunches. It provides a more systematic and rational approach to management and helps prevent "management by crisis," "firefighting," or "seat-of-the-pants" methods. MBO emphasizes measurable achievements and results and may lead to improvements in both organizational and individual effectiveness.[3] The approach depends heavily on active participation in objective setting at all levels of management.

management by objectives (MBO)

BACKGROUND AND EVALUATION OF MBO

Peter Drucker first described management by objectives in 1954 in *The Practice of Management.*[4] According to Drucker, management's primary responsibility is to balance conflicting demands in all areas where performance and results directly affect the survival, profits, and growth of the business. Drucker stated that specific objectives should be established in the following areas:

- Market standing
- Innovation
- Productivity
- Worker performance and attitude
- Physical and financial resources
- Profitability
- Managerial performance and development
- Public responsibility

Drucker argued that the first requirement of managing any enterprise is "management by objectives and self-control." As originally described, an MBO system was designed to satisfy three managerial needs.

First, *MBO should provide a basis for more effective planning.* Drucker had in mind what might be called the systems approach to planning—that of integrating objectives and plans for every level within the organization. The basic concept of planning should consist of *making it happen* as opposed to *just letting things happen.* According to Drucker, MBO is a planning system requiring each manager to be involved in the total planning process by participating in establishing the objectives for his or her own department and for higher levels in the organization.

Second, *MBO improves communications within the firm by requiring that managers and employees discuss and reach agreement on performance objectives.* In the process, there is frequent review and discussion of the goals and plans of action at all levels within the firm.

Finally, *Drucker thought that the implementation of an MBO system would encourage the acceptance of a behavioral or more participative approach to management.* By participating in the process of setting objectives, managers and employees develop a better understanding of the broader objectives of the organization and how their goals relate to those of the total organization.[5]

activity trap

One of the foremost advocates of MBO contends that special efforts must be undertaken to avoid the **activity trap**.[6] This is *the tendency described by George Odiorne of some managers and employees to become so enmeshed in carrying out activities that they lose sight of the reasons for what they are doing.* As a result, such persons often justify their existence by the energy and sweat expended and avoid questioning whether they have accomplished any result necessary to organizational effectiveness. Successful managers like Searle's Donald Rumsfeld recognize the threat to efficiency imposed by the activity trap and take pains to avoid it.

-

THE MBO PROCESS

The dynamics of an MBO system are illustrated in Figure 3–2. Notice that MBO requires top management support and commitment and involves four steps. These aspects of MBO are discussed below.

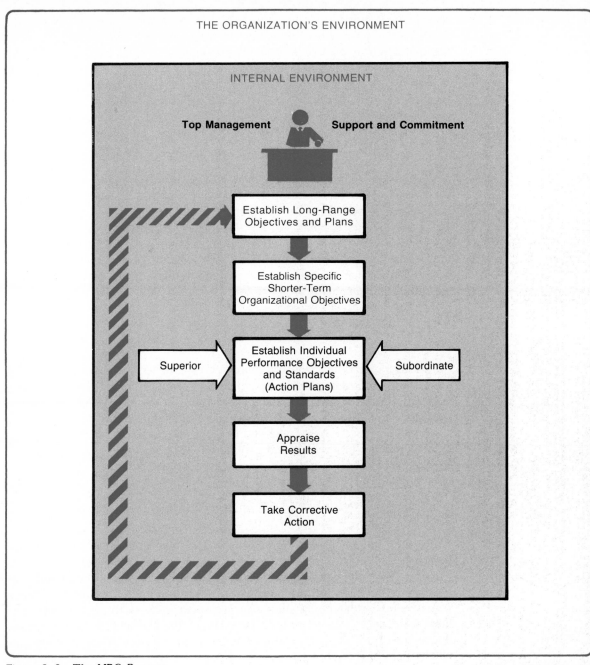

INTERNAL ENVIRONMENT

Top Management   Support and Commitment

Establish Long-Range
Objectives and Plans

Establish Specific
Shorter-Term
Organizational Objectives

Superior → Establish Individual
Performance Objectives
and Standards
(Action Plans) ← Subordinate

Appraise
Results

Take Corrective
Action

Figure 3–2   The MBO Process

Top Management's Support and Commitment

An effective MBO program requires the enthusiastic support of top management. It is because of the lack of top-level commitment that many MBO programs fail. For MBO to be effective, the philosophy of top management must be consistent with its principles. MBO relies on the participative approach to management, requiring the active involvement of the managers at all levels. The chief executive should trust subordinates and be personally committed to a participative style of management. Top management cannot introduce MBO by simply giving an order or a directive. Lower-level managers, too, must be convinced of the merits of the system and desire meaningful participation in the process.

Establish Long-range Objectives and Plans

A vital element of MBO is the development of long-range goals and plans. Long-term plans are developed through thoughtful consideration of the basic purpose or mission of the organization.

G. D. Searle expects to be the major competitor in the artificial sweetener market even after NutraSweet becomes obsolete. Specific, though undisclosed, goals have been set in order to accomplish these long-term goals. Shapiro has intensified research and development efforts and rapidly expanded Searle's customer base for NutraSweet.

Establish Specific Short-term Organizational Objectives

After long-range objectives and plans are established, management must be concerned with determining specific objectives to be attained within a shorter time period. These objectives must be supportive of the overall purpose, as well as the long-range goals and plans. Usually shorter-term goals are expressed as specific and quantifiable targets covering such areas as productivity, marketing, and profitability. At Searle, these would include the sales goal and the production cost goal for the current year.

Establish Individual Performance Objectives and Standards (Action Plans)

action planning

The establishment of performance objectives and standards for individuals is known as **action planning**. The crucial phase of the MBO process requires that challenging but attainable objectives and standards be established through an interaction with superiors and subordinates. Action plans require clear delineation of *what* specifically is to be accomplished and *when* it is to be completed. For example, the NutraSweet sales manager whose territory includes Boston might have an individual performance objective of increasing sales in that area by 38 percent next year. The action plan might include the employment of three experienced salespersons, six calls a week by the sales manager on major customers, and assignment of appropriate sales quotas to all the salespersons.

Appraise Results

The next step in the MBO process is to measure and evaluate the actual performance based on progress toward goal attainment. Having specific performance goals provides management with an objective basis for comparison. When goals are agreed on by the manager and the subordinate, self-evaluation and control become possible. In fact, with MBO, performance appraisal can be a joint effort based on mutual agreement.

Take Corrective Action

Although an MBO system provides a good management framework, it is left up to the managers themselves to take corrective action when results are not as planned. Such action may take the form of changes in personnel, the organization, or even the goals themselves. Other forms of corrective action may include providing additional training and development of individual managers or employees to enable them to achieve the desired results better. Corrective action should not necessarily have negative connotations. Under MBO, objectives can be renegotiated downward without any penalty or fear of loss of job.

CHARACTERISTICS OF OBJECTIVES FOR THE INDIVIDUAL

In order for MBO to achieve maximum results, objectives for each individual should be carefully developed. They should be limited in number, highly specific, challenging, and attainable. The number of objectives for each manager should range from four to eight. Each objective should be assigned a priority, perhaps ranging from 1 to 3. Should time and resources prove to be more limited than anticipated, this ranking gives the individual a basis for deciding which objective to pursue.

Perhaps the most important characteristic of good objectives is that they should be stated in specific terms. In most instances, this means quantification. For example, goals may have little impact when stated in such terms as "improve the effectiveness of the unit," "keep costs to a minimum," or "be alert to market changes." At the performance review, one should be able to answer definitely the question, "Did I do it or not?" A goal stating that production will be increased by 1,000 units during a given period is clear. Thus, in writing objectives, a special attempt should be made to state them in such terms as volume, costs, frequency, ratios, percentages, indexes, degrees, and phases. It is particularly important to place time limits on each objective. In ten of eleven studies that examined the impact of such specific goals on performance, evidence supported the contention that specifically stated goals will increase the level of accomplishment.[7]

Developing challenging and attainable objectives requires a delicate balance. Obviously the superior desires that objectives be set at such a level that special efforts on the part of the subordinate must be made. Some researchers have pointed out that if promotion and salary are related to success in attaining objectives, as they should be, the participatory approach may well be asking the subordinate to construct a "do-it-yourself hangman's kit."[8] For instance, Dean Bishop, a hospital supply sales representative, might optimistically indicate to his sales manager that he plans to sell $1 million in surgical instruments and supplies during the next three months. Since no one else in the company had ever accomplished this level of sales in a three-month period and since Dean sold only $1 million in supplies the previous year, it is highly unlikely that he will attain his goal. It is much more likely that Dean has just hung himself because his goal is unrealistic and probably unattainable.

In the initial phases of new MBO programs, one of the more common errors is the establishment of objectives that are unattainable. This is particularly the case if the time period for review is six months to a year. Anything seems possible with that much time. The superior must not allow excessively high goals to be set. Specific attention must be given to obstacles that affect accomplishment, particularly the availability of resources. The impact of other personnel on the subordinate's performance must be recognized and discussed.

Research indicates that challenging objectives lead to greater accomplishment only if the subordinate truly accepts the goals as reasonable and only if goal accomplishment actually leads to rewards. Challenging goals with a history of past success will lead to continued success. A series of failures creates a mental set that makes attainment increasingly less likely. The subordinates' assessment of the probability of success should be that they at least have a fifty-fifty chance of achieving each objective.

CHARACTERISTICS OF TEAM OBJECTIVES

The accomplishment of most goals requires that individuals cooperate as a team. Many factors can affect the attainment of group or team objectives. For instance, it should be apparent that if the sales manager sets a specific objective of selling 50,000 units by March 1, the goal cannot be met if production does not manufacture that number of units. One of the recommended approaches to overall goal setting involves team meetings to establish group goals. Team goal setting requires an open and supportive organizational climate. The following is a suggested sequence in an MBO team approach: (1) team meetings of top executives to set overall organizational objectives; (2) team meetings at unit level; (3) individual person-to-person goal-setting sessions; (4) individual reviews of accomplishments; (5) team meetings at unit level to review progress and accomplishment; and (6) review at the top level to determine the degree of overall organizational success.[9]

In one instance, "a medium-size service company experimented with the team approach and decided to ignore individual objectives altogether, reasoning that too much interlinking support and cooperation are required to blame or reward any individual for the production of any single end result."[10] If team goal-setting sessions are to be used, some training in group processes most likely is necessary. It is difficult enough for a manager to establish an open and participatory climate with an employee, but it is far more complex and challenging to try the same thing in a group. Programs of training directed toward this end go under the title of *organizational development,* a subject discussed at length in Chapter 13.

BENEFITS OF MBO PROGRAMS

Proponents of MBO have claimed the following benefits:

1. *Results in better overall management and the achievement of higher performance levels.* MBO systems encourage a results-oriented philosophy of

management that requires managers to do specific planning. Managers are required to develop action plans and consider the resources needed.

2. *Provides an effective overall planning system.* MBO helps the manager avoid management by crisis and firefighting.

3. *Forces managers to establish priorities and measurable targets or standards of performance.* MBO programs sharpen the planning process. Rather than just saying "do your best" or "give it your best shot," specific goals tend to force specific planning. Such planning is typically more realistic because the program calls for a scheduled review at a designated future date. Subordinates make sure that they can obtain the resources necessary for goal accomplishment and that obstacles to performance are discussed and removed. MBO forces planning a logical sequence of activities before action begins.

4. *Clarifies the specific role, responsibilities, and authority of personnel.* Objectives must be set in key areas, and individuals responsible must be given adequate authority to accomplish them. A production plant superintendent who has a goal of producing 10,000 units a day must be given the authority to organize and direct resources to achieve the desired level of production.

5. *Encourages the participation of individual employees and managers in establishing objectives.* If the process of MBO has been undertaken on a joint and participatory basis, the chances are that increased commitment will be obtained.

6. *MBO facilitates the process of control.* Periodic reviews of performance results are scheduled, and information collected is classified by specific objectives. Subordinates are forced to report what was accomplished rather than concentrate on descriptions of what they did or how hard they worked. MBO also stimulates improvement in the performance of superiors, who are forced to clarify their own thinking and to communicate this to subordinates.

7. *MBO provides a golden opportunity for career development for managers and employees.* Personal development goals are often part of the set of objectives developed in joint sessions. MBO results identify the areas where employees need additional training. Establishment of priorities provides realistic guides for effort, as well as enabling the concrete demonstration of goal accomplishment. This, in turn, makes possible a more realistic and specific annual performance review, which is crucial in deciding on promotions, pay increases, and other organizational rewards.

8. *Other specific strengths of an MBO system* might include:
   a. Lets individuals know what is expected of them.
   b. Provides a more objective and tangible basis for performance appraisal and salary decisions.
   c. Improves communications within the organization.
   d. Helps identify promotable managers and employees.
   e. Facilitates the enterprise's ability to change.
   f. Increases motivation and commitment to employees.[11]

MBO: ASSESSING ITS OVERALL EFFECTIVENESS

In a review of 185 studies, Jack N. Kondrasuk found that there are numerous arguments pro and con as to the effectiveness of MBO.[12] Many organizations have adopted MBO on faith, often as a result of questionable case studies or unsubstantiated testimonies. One researcher concluded, "There is relatively little empirical evidence to demonstrate the impact of MBO on any aspect of organizational or individual behavior, including job performance."[13]

TABLE 3–5   MBO Effectiveness as Applied in 185 Organizations

Research Approach	Positive	Mixed	Not Positive	Ratio Positive: Not Positive
Case Studies	123	8	10	12:1
Surveys	9	2	1	9:1
Quasi-experiments	20	3	4	5:1
True experiments	1	2	2	1:2
Totals/average	153	15	17	9:1

Source: From Jack N. Kondrasuk, "Studies in MBO Effectiveness," *Academy of Management Review* 6, no. 3 (1981): 425. Used with permission.

As illustrated in Table 3–5, MBO did achieve positive results in 153 organizations—a ratio of 9 to 1, positive to not positive. Case studies and surveys show a much higher level of effectiveness for MBO than do experiments. "Positive results" does not necessarily mean that respondents thought MBO to be worth the effort. According to the researcher, "There are tendencies for MBO to be more effective in the short term [less than two years], in the private sector, and in organizations removed from direct contacts with the customer. We may conclude that MBO can be effective, but questions remain about the circumstances under which it is effective."

POTENTIAL PROBLEMS WITH MBO

Although there are numerous benefits attributed to MBO, certain problems may be encountered, such as the following:

1. MBO programs often lack the support and commitment of top management.
2. Goals are often difficult to establish.
3. The implementation of an MBO system can create excessive paperwork if it is not closely monitored.
4. There is a tendency to concentrate too much on the short run at the expense of long-range planning.
5. Some managers believe that MBO programs may be excessively time-consuming.

Although there is strong evidence that MBO has not generally worked out well as a complete system, it still provides a good model for planning. The central principles of MBO have been incorporated into all kinds of organizations and continue to have a major impact. These principles include specific, verifiable objectives; evaluation of performance on the basis of goal accomplishment; and integration of individual objectives with organizational objectives. When these are established as part of a rigid MBO structure, they have not tended to work out too successfully. But individually, they are sound concepts.

SUMMARY

Effective planning can have a major impact on the productivity of managers at all levels in an organization. Planning is determining in advance what should be accomplished and how to do it.

The planning process begins with a mission statement. Mission is the organization's continuing purpose or reason for being. Specific objectives, or goals, can be established once the mission is understood. Objectives are the end results desired. Objectives should have four basic characteristics: (1) they should be expressed in writing, (2) they should be measurable, (3) they should be specific as to time, and (4) they should be challenging but attainable. At least three main types of objectives can be identified: economic, service, and personal. Some problems encountered in establishing objectives include: real versus stated objectives, multiple objectives, and quantitative versus nonquantitative objectives.

Objectives are concerned with the end results desired. Plans are statements of how objectives are to be accomplished.

Plans that remain roughly the same for long periods of time are referred to as standing plans. The most common kinds of standing plans are policies, procedures, and rules. A policy is a predetermined general course or guide established to provide direction in decision making. A procedure is a series of steps established for the accomplishment of some specific project or endeavor. A rule is a very specific and detailed guide to action, which is set up to direct or restrict action in a fairly narrow manner.

Events can occur so rapidly that plans may be useless before they can be fully implemented. Contingency planning is developing different plans to be placed in effect if certain events occur. Contingency planning makes it unnecessary for a firm to wait for a situation to occur before it prepares to respond.

Management by objectives (MBO) is a systematic approach to planning that focuses on achieving goals. The steps in the MBO process are to: (1) gain management's support and commitment, (2) establish long-range goals and strategies, (3) establish specific organizational objectives, (4) establish individual performance objectives and standards (action plans), (5) appraise results, and (6) take corrective action.

In order for MBO to achieve maximum results, objectives for each individual should be carefully developed. They should be limited in number, highly specific, challenging, and attainable. The accomplishment of most goals requires that individuals cooperate as a team.

REVIEW QUESTIONS

1. What are the steps involved in the planning process?
2. What is the purpose of a mission statement?
3. Describe the characteristics of good objectives. What are the three main types of objectives?
4. What are the specific questions that planning should answer?
5. Distinguish by definition and example among policies, procedures, and rules.
6. What is meant by the term *contingency planning?*
7. What is management by objectives (MBO)? Describe the basic steps in the MBO process.
8. Briefly discuss the benefits and problems with MBO.

EXERCISES

1. What do you believe would be the missions of the following firms?
   a. Ford Motor Company
   b. American Airlines
   c. Peat, Marwick, Mitchell & Co. (a "big eight" CPA firm)
   d. New York Yankees
   e. Girl Scouts of America
   f. Internal Revenue Service
2. Assume that your objective is to obtain a 4.0 grade point average next semester. Develop a plan stating policies, procedures, and rules that could help you achieve this goal.
3. Apply the management by objectives concepts discussed in this chapter by developing clear-cut personal goals for yourself for next year. Be sure to include specific goal statements and completion times for routine, problem solving, and innovation goals and for personal development. Also include specific action plans to ensure goal accomplishment.

Certified Department Stores' MBO Program

Parker Neilson was irritated and confused after his meeting with Dale Simpson. Parker was the manager of the Kansas City Certified store and Dale the district manager for the company, in charge of stores in Missouri, Kansas, and Oklahoma. Three weeks earlier, Parker had received a letter from Dale explaining that top management had decided on an MBO program to help Certified Stores in improving efficiency and increasing profit contributions. In that letter, Dale had said that the objectives established would be used to measure performance of store managers and that salary increases and promotion would be directly related to performance. The accompanying instructions required managers to list the objectives they felt were appropriate for their store and then stand by for the district manager's review visit.

Parker had done just what he was instructed to do. In a meeting with his five department managers, Parker had chosen objectives that they all agreed were appropriate. All of the objectives represented performance levels that were improvements from the past year and were reasonably attainable. The objectives they established were:

- Increase selling efficiency, as measured by the ratio of sales salaries to sales, by 10 percent.
- Reduce inventory losses to 2 percent of sales.
- Reduce cash register shortages to 0.05 of sales.
- Improve customer service to the extent that 20 percent fewer complaint letters will be mailed to the home office.

Dale Simpson arrived late for the MBO review visit and stressed that there was little time. Dale quickly scanned the written statement of objectives Parker gave him. He then explained that profit improvement was really what the home office was interested in rather than trying to monitor multiple objectives from each store. Senior management had decided that a 12 percent increase in profit would be a reasonable objective for Parker's store. This single objective, Dale said, would facilitate the monitoring of performance by the home office and would also reduce the amount of information the store would have to submit. The visit was cut short because the district manager had to attend a meeting on the advertising budget back at the home office.

QUESTIONS

1. Did the MBO system at Certified meet the criteria for an effective program as discussed in the chapter? Why or why not?
2. Evaluate Parker's approach to goal setting.
3. Discuss the quality of communication that occurred in the case.
4. If you were Parker, what would be your approach to Certified's MBO program? Defend your answer.

The Peach Farmer

Buford Coenen was up early that June morning. When the sun began to peek over the horizon, he was already at his peach orchard thinking about how to accomplish the day's work. Within an hour, he would have thirty workers in the field picking his bumper crop of peaches. Buford needed to be there early to think about how the pickers were to be kept supplied with baskets and the trucks efficiently scheduled to deliver the peaches to the broker's warehouse with a minimum of handling.

There were many other matters to attend to. The pickers were paid according to the amount they picked, so careful records had to be kept. The peaches had to be picked at just the right ripeness or Buford would be docked a certain percentage when they were inspected at the warehouse. Even simple details like not having drinking water available to the pickers could significantly slow down the harvest.

Buford thought about how complicated peach farming was. He and his father had planted the trees twelve years earlier. They had spent what then seemed to be a lot of extra money to get the finest strain of hybrid trees that were available. These trees produced 50 percent more than ordinary peach trees and had a longer bearing life. It was necessary to prune and spray the trees every year, to irrigate them during dry periods, and to cultivate and fertilize the area covered by the root systems. It was also useful to treat the ground to eliminate bore worms and to supply "blossom fast" liquid to each tree to decrease the likelihood that it would shed its blooms before the fruit buds were properly formed.

Buford was the third generation of Coenens to be in the peach farming business, and this orchard was the best ever. It would not be the best for long though. The previous fall Buford had planted 300 acres with a new type of tree that was expected to do even better. Buford had become moderately wealthy raising peaches, but he knew his success had not happened by accident. He hoped to pass on to his son, then twelve, not only the finest peach orchard in Georgia but also a legacy of scientific farming and disciplined hard work.

Even as the first pickers were arriving that morning, Buford was looking forward to the fall. He thought of how he would prune and trim his peach trees so that they could withstand a cold winter, in case one occurred, and produce an even larger crop the following year.

QUESTIONS

1. How is the planning process Buford should follow similar to that followed by a manager of a modern office or factory?

2. What kinds of contingency plans would you recommend that Buford make? Why?

3. In what areas of Buford's agribusiness should plans be made, and over what time frames should those plans extend?

NOTES

1. This discussion is a composite from a number of published accounts, among them: "For Hotels, an Era of Change," *New York Times,* June 24, 1983, pp. 41–43; "Holiday Inns Opens Doors for the Upscale Traveler," *Business Week,* April 25, 1983, pp. 101–104; Geoffrey, Smith, "Holiday Inns—the Middle Year," *Forbes,* August 15, 1983, pp. 42–43; Scott Hume, "Hotels Go Upscale for Business Travelers," *Advertising Age,* May 9, 1983, p. 58; "Holiday Inns: Refining Its Focus to Food, Lodging—and More Casinos," *Business Week,* July 21, 1980, pp. 100–104; and numerous articles from *The Wall Street Journal.*

2. Jennifer Alter, "Something Old, Something New Sweeten Searle's Sales Picture," *Advertising Age,* February 14, 1983; Gene Bylinsky, "The Battle for America's Sweet Tooth," *Fortune,* July 26, 1982; Matt Clark and Mary Hager, "A Sweet Sugar Substitute," *Newsweek,* July 27, 1981, p. 63; Jay Gissen, "Beginners Luck," *Forbes,* May 21, 1984, p. 240; "NutraSweet Business Unit," *Searle Annual Report,* 1983, pp. 2–11; Robert Shapiro, "Masterminding Searle's Sweet Taste of Success," *S&MM,* January 16, 1984; and numerous articles from *The Wall Street Journal.*

3. Anthony P. Raia, *Managing by Objectives* (Glenview, Ill.: Scott, Foresman, 1974), pp. 10–12.

4. Peter F. Drucker, *The Practice of Management* (New York: Harper, 1954).

5. ———, *Management: Tasks, Responsibilities, Practices* (New York: Harper, 1974).

6. See George S. Odiorne, *Management by Objectives* (Belmont, Calif.: Pitman, 1965), and *Management Decisions* (Englewood Cliffs, N.J.: Prentice-Hall, 1969).

7. Raia, *Managing,* pp. 14–15.

8. Gary P. Latham and Gary A. Yuki, "A Review of Research on the Application of Goal Setting in Organizations," *Academy of Management Journal* 18, no. 4 (December 1975): 829.

9. Richard E. Byrd and John Cowan, "MBO: A Behavioral Science Approach," *Personnel* 51, no. 2 (March–April 1974): 48.

10. W. J. Reddin, *Effective Management by Objectives* (New York: McGraw-Hill, 1971), p. 16.

11. Harold Koontz, "Making MBO Effective," *California Management Review* 20 (Fall 1977): 5–7.

12. Jack N. Kondrasuk, "Studies in MBO Effectiveness," *Academy of Management Review* 6, no. 3 (1981): 419–430.

13. Ibid.

REFERENCES

Allen, David. "Establishing a Financial Objective—A Practical Approach." *Long Range Planning* 12 (December 1979): 11–16.

Allen, L. A. "Managerial Planning: Back to the Basics." *Management Review* 70 (April 1981): 15–20.

Babcock, R., and P. F. Sorensen, Jr. "MBO Checklist: Are Conditions Right for Implementation?" *Management Review* 68 (June 1979): 59–62.

Bologna, J. "Why MBO Programs Don't Meet Their Goals." *Management Review* 69 (December 1980): 32.

Camillus, John C., and John H. Grant. "Operational Planning: The Integration of Programming and Budgeting." *Academy of Management Review* 5 (July 1980): 369–379.

Denny, W. A. "Ten Rules for Managing by Objectives." *Business Horizons* 22 (October 1979): 66–68.

Dowst, S. "Classify Your Objectives." *Purchasing,* April 25, 1979, p. 38.

Ford, C. H. "MBO: An Idea Whose Time Has Gone?" *Business Horizons* 22 (December 1979): 48–55.

Ford, R. C. "MBO: Seven Strategies for Success." *SAM Advanced Management Journal* 42 (Winter 1977): 4–13.

———, et al. "Ten Questions about MBO." *California Management Review* 23 (Winter 1980): 48-55.

Goldstein, S. G. Mike. "Involving Managers in System-Improvement Planning." *Long Range Planning* 14 (February 1981): 93–99.

Haines, W. R. "Corporate Planning and Management by Objectives." *Long Range Planning* 10 (August 1977): 13–20.

Jackson, J. H. "Using Management by Objectives: Case Studies of Four Attempts." *Personnel Administrator* 26 (February 1981): 78–81.

Kahalas, Harvey. "Planning Types and Approaches: A Necessary Function." *Managerial Planning* 28 (May–June 1980): 22–27.

Kelly, Charles M. "Remedial MBO," *Business Horizons* (September–October 1983): 62–67.

Koontz, H. "Making MBO Effective." *California Management Review* 20 (Fall 1977): 13–15.

Linsay, W. M., and L. W. Rue. "Impact of the Organization Environment on the Long Range Planning Process: A Contingency View." *Academy of Management Journal* 23 (September 1980): 385–404.

Lopata, R. "Key Indicators: Simpler Way to Manage." *Iron Age,* January 26, 1981, pp. 41–44.

McCaskey, Michael B. "A Contingency Approach to Planning: Planning with Goals and Planning without Goals." *Academy of Management Journal* 17 (June 1974): 281–291.

Michael, Steven R. "Feedforward versus Feedback Controls in Planning." *Managerial Planning* 29 (November–December 1980): 34–38.

———. "Tailor Made Planning: Making Planning Fit the Firm." *Long Range Planning* 13 (December 1980): 74–79.

Migliore, R. Henry. *MBO: Blue Collar to Top Executives.* Washington, D.C.: Bureau of National Affairs, 1977.

Muczyk, J. P. "Dynamics and Hazards of MBO Application." *Personnel Administrator* 24 (May 1979): 51–61.

O'Donnell, Merle, and Robert J. O'Donnel. "MBO—Is It Passé?" *Hospital and Health Services Administration* (September–October 1983): 46–58.

Pack, R. J., and W. M. Vicars. "MBO—Today and Tomorrow." *Personnel* 56 (May 1979): 68–77.

Pekar, Peter P. "Planning: A Guide to Implementation." *Managerial Planning* 29 (July–August 1980): 3–6.

Ratcliffe, Thomas A., and D. J. Logsdon. "Business Planning Process—A Behavioral Perspective." *Managerial Planning* 28 (March 1980): 32–38.

Schaeffer, Dorothy. "MBO Pitfalls," *Supervision* (August 1983): 9–10.

Schneier, C. E., and R. W. Beatty. "Combining BARS and MBO: Using an Appraisal System to Diagnose Performance Problems." *Personnel Administrator* 24 (September 1979): 51–60.

Simmons, William W. "Future of Planning." *Managerial Planning* 29 (January–February 1981): 2–3.

Snyder, N., and W. F. Glueck. "How Managers Plan the Analysis of Manager's Activities." *Long Range Planning* 18 (February 1980): 70–76.

Stephenson, E. "Assessing Operational Policies." *Omega* 6 (1976): 437–446.

Tosi, H., et al. "How Real Are Changes Induced by Management by Objectives?" *Administrative Science Quarterly* (June 1976): 276–306.

Townsend, Robert. *Up the Organization.* Greenwich, Conn.: Fawcett, 1971.

Weitzul, J. B. "Pros and Cons of an MBO Program." *Best's Review* 81 (January 1981): 72–73.

Wiehrich, H. "TAMBO: Team Approach to MBO." *University of Michigan Business Review* 31 (May 1979): 12–17.

Word, E. Peter. "Focussing Innovative Effort through a Convergent Dialogue." *Long Range Planning* 13 (December 1980): 32–41.

Wright, Phillip C. "Management by Objectives—One More Time." *Supervision* (January 1984): 3–5.

KEY TERMS

strategic planning

corporate-level
strategic planning

organizational mission

strategic business unit

SBU-level strategic
planning

functional-level
strategic planning

strategic planning staff
specialists

organizational
strategists

product life cycle

corporate culture

integration

forward integration

backward integration

horizontal integration

diversification

conglomerate
diversification

concentric
diversification

retrenchment

LEARNING OBJECTIVES

After completing this chapter you should be able to

1. Describe the various levels of strategic planning.
2. Explain the strategic planning process.
3. Relate the impact of the environment on strategic planning.
4. Describe the tools used in strategic management.
5. Identify several grand strategies that may grow out of the strategic planning process.

4

Strategic Planning

**GENERAL
ELECTRIC**

General Electric is primarily identified with major appliances, electric motors, and lighting. But the company also makes jet engines, electronics items, and medical equipment and even provides financial services. In 1984 GE was engaged in about forty businesses.

When Jack Welch took over as chairman and chief executive officer of GE in 1981, he identified this diversity as a major problem. He reasoned that it was impossible for a company to be a leader in so many different kinds of activities.

Sixteen of the businesses accounted for 92 percent of GE's 1983 profits and 87 percent of sales. In each of these businesses, GE was one of the dominant competitors. In the other twenty or so business areas, GE was not dominant, although some were growing rapidly.

Top managers of the laggard businesses were put on notice: either become a dominant player or be sold or closed. Jack Welch's plan was clear: to strip the corporation of its low performers and concentrate management talent and financial resources on the others. By 1984, the small appliance division and the subunit that makes central air-conditioning systems had been sold. A number of unrelated businesses, such as broadcasting, were up for sale.

Within the individual businesses, Welch and his staff were trying to make sure resources were applied where they would do the most good. New plant investment was at $1.9 billion in 1983, up 20 percent from the year before, and the company spent a whopping $2 billion on research and development.

Largely because of its divestitures, GE began 1984 with $3 billion in cash and expected that to grow to $5 billion by year end. But with interest rates near record levels, there was no rush to reinvest the cash in plant and equipment. While GE continues to look for companies to buy, it is interested only if they are exceptional bargains. And once in the GE family, they will be subject to the same mandate to performance that guides GE's existing businesses.

At forty-eight, Jack Welch has been at the helm for three years. He claims to have accomplished only 15 percent of what he intends to do at GE. Welch states the company's goal this way: "We were a company that was identified with safety. Now it is safety with up-side potential."[1]

In Chapter 3, we discussed the planning process. That process remains essentially the same at each level in the organization; however, managers today have access to a number of concepts and techniques related

Strategic planning is the determination of overall organizational purposes and objectives and how they are to be achieved. Ellis Herwig/Stock, Boston Inc.

specifically to strategic planning. **Strategic planning** is *the determination of overall organizational purposes and objectives and how they are to be achieved.* *strategic planning*

General Electric has long been a leader in strategic planning. Jack Welch recognizes that GE's common stock has typically been considered a safe investment but one with little upside potential. He expects to improve the common shareholders' opportunity for gain without decreasing the security of the stock. Part of his strategic plan for doing this is to concentrate on those businesses where GE is a market leader and to eliminate weak divisions.

In this chapter, we will first discuss the levels of strategic planning, identify the organizational strategists, and briefly describe the process. Next, a number of environmental considerations will be explained. This will be followed by a description of four of the tools strategic planners use. Finally, four grand strategies, which may relate to any organization, will be discussed.

THE LEVELS OF STRATEGIC PLANNING

It is important to consider the levels of strategic planning in organizations, particularly in the light of the growth in recent decades of complex organizations such as General Electric, United Technologies, Allied Corporation, and Textron. Figure 4–1 illustrates the organizational levels for a typical complex corporation, with the corresponding levels of strategic planning. The tools and processes that are useful at the three levels differ.

Corporate-level Strategic Planning

Corporate-level strategic planning is *the process of defining the overall character and purpose of the organization, the businesses it will enter and* *corporate-level strategic planning*

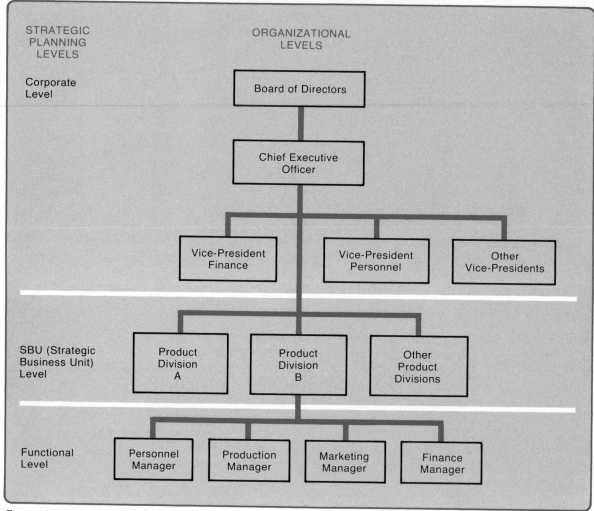

Figure 4–1   The Levels of Strategic Planning

leave, and how resources will be distributed among those businesses. Corporate-level planners seek to answer such questions as the following:

- What are the purposes of the organization?
- What image should the organization project?
- What are the ideals and philosophies the organization desires its members to possess?
- What is the organization's business or businesses?
- How can the organization's resources best be used to fulfill corporate purposes?

Referring again to Figure 4–1, corporate-level strategic planning is primarily the responsibility of the organization's top executives, like Jack Welch and his immediate subordinates at GE. The major focus here is on formulating *organizational mission* strategies to accomplish the organization's mission. **Organizational mission** is *the organization's continuing purposes—in short, what is to be accomplished for whom.* This will be discussed in detail later.

SBU-level Strategic Planning

To facilitate management of large organizations, they are usually divided into strategic business units (SBUs). A **strategic business unit** is *any part of a business organization that is treated separately for strategic planning purposes.* In general, an SBU engages in just one line of business. For example, GE's jet engine division is an SBU. Many companies set up SBUs as separate profit centers, sometimes giving them virtual autonomy. Other companies have tight control over their SBUs, enforcing corporate policies and standards down to very low levels in the organization.

strategic business unit

SBU-level strategic planning is *the process of determining how an SBU will compete in a particular line of business.* At the SBU level, strategic questions include the following:

SBU-level strategic planning

- What specific products or services does the SBU produce?
- Who are the SBU's customers or clients?
- How can the SBU best compete in its particular product or service segments?
- How can the SBU best conform to the total organization's ideals and philosophies and support organizational purposes?

In general, SBU-level strategic planning is the responsibility of vice-presidents or division heads. In single-SBU organizations, senior executives have both corporate-level and SBU-level responsibilities.

Functional-level Strategic Planning

Practically every important organization is divided into functional subdivisions. Most businesses define the functions of production, marketing, finance, and personnel. Military installations have supply, police, and maintenance departments, among others. Churches have preaching, education, and music ministries. Each of these functional subdivisions is typically vital to the success of the organization. **Functional-level strategic planning** is *the process of determining policies and procedures for relatively narrow areas of activity that are critical to the success of the organization.* For example, strategic planning for the finance function at GE involves establishing budgeting, accounting, and investment policies and the allocation of SBU cash flows. In the personnel area, policies for compensation, hiring and firing, training, and personnel planning are of strategic concern. Strategic planning is not concerned with day-to-day supervision; it mainly involves providing general, longer-range direction and guidance.

functional-level strategic planning

THE ORGANIZATIONAL STRATEGISTS

For most organizations, it is difficult to identify the organizational strategists. In ancient Greece, where the concept of strategy originated, perhaps strategy was determined by the general. For some companies today, strategy clearly comes from the top. Lee Iacocca, chairman of Chrysler Corporation, Robert Goizueta, president and chief executive officer (CEO) of Coca-Cola, and Frank Borman, president and chairman of Eastern Airlines, seem to call the shots. Many companies use in-house **strategic planning staff specialists**, *specialists who assist and advise managers in strategic planning.* Strategic

strategic planning staff specialists

management involves planning and doing. Staff strategic management specialists are especially involved in planning. At GE, the corporate planning staff includes over one hundred persons.

Many organizations retain consultants to assist in designing and implementing strategy. Consultants are particularly useful for performing marketing and other research to provide an informational base for strategic decisions. Consultants can play an effective part in strategic planning, even for small firms.[2] In fact, most small firms cannot afford full-time staff specialists. For these companies, using consultants may be the most economical approach to strategic planning.

At least to a limited extent, every manager is an organizational strategist.[3] This is because every manager is responsible for activities related to continuing and vital corporate objectives. It should be recognized, however, that what is an overwhelming matter to the personnel director—such as the size of the annual personnel department budget—might be relatively incidental from the standpoint of the total organization. It is not a question of whether a matter is important to any one individual that determines whether it is strategic. The question is how important is it to the organization as a whole and the degree to which it has continuing significance. So **organizational strategists** are generally considered to be *those persons who spend a large portion of their time on matters of vital or far-ranging importance to the organization as a whole.* In general, this includes the top two levels of management, in-house staff specialists in strategic management, and retained consultants in the area.

*organizational
strategists*

THE STRATEGIC PLANNING PROCESS

Strategic planning is broken into four steps: (1) determination of organizational mission, (2) assessment of the organization and its environment, (3) setting of specific objectives or direction, and (4) determination of strategies to accomplish those objectives. The second phase, strategy implementation, is the process of doing what has been planned; however, this chapter is concerned only with strategic planning, even though effective plans cannot be made without considering how to implement them.

Note that the strategic planning process is essentially the same as the basic planning process discussed in Chapter 3. In strategic planning, of course, more emphasis is given to the mission of the organization as a whole and to environmental considerations.

Figure 4–2 illustrates a simple sequential process. Diagrams like this help us to understand complex processes; however, no drawing can accurately represent real-world complexity.[4] In most organizations, all of the steps are occurring at any one time. Emphasis at GE, for example, may be on analyzing the environment. This does not mean that the organizational strategists, like Jack Welch, can avoid considering the company's existing objectives and possible changes to them. It is also important to remember that the steps do not always occur in the order shown, and the process—or parts of it—is repeated a number of times. Still, it is useful to think of strategic planning in a systematic way. Let us look at the individual steps as if they follow one another.

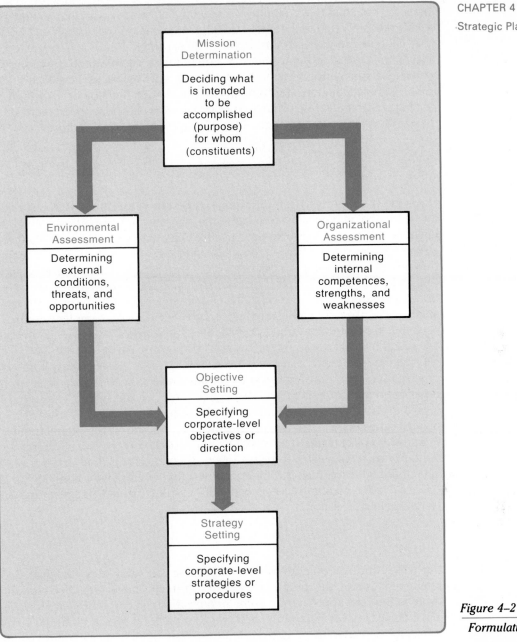

Mission
Determination

Deciding what
is intended
to be
accomplished
(purpose)
for whom
(constituents)

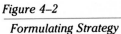

Figure 4–2

Formulating Strategy

Mission Determination

The first step is to determine the corporate mission. As mentioned in Chapter 3, mission is the organization's continuing purpose. Arriving at a mission statement should involve answering the question, "What are we, in management, attempting to do for whom?" Should we maximize profit so that shareholders can receive higher dividends or so that share price will increase? Or should we emphasize stability of earnings so that employees remain secure? Remember that GE had previously emphasized safety but now is more concerned with growth in earnings. There are many other possibilities. Mission determination also requires deciding the principles on which management decisions will be based. Will the corporation be honorable or dishonorable, ruthless or considerate, devious or forthright, in dealing with its various publics? The answers to these questions, once arrived at, tend to become embedded in an organizational culture.

Organizational and Environmental Assessment

Once the mission has been determined, the organization must be assessed for strengths and weaknesses, and the threats and opportunities in the environment must be evaluated. Specific objectives can be established and strategies developed for accomplishing those objectives. For example, through environmental assessment BIC Corporation discovered an opportunity during the early 1980s to market disposable safety razors. Organizational assessment revealed that BIC had greater capability to mass produce small, plastic-based items than almost any other U.S. company. The company set sales, production, and profit objectives, designed strategies, and quickly became the world's leading marketer of disposable safety razors.

Making strategic plans involves information flows from both the organization and the environment. From inside comes information about organizational competencies, strengths, and weaknesses. Scanning the environment allows the organizational strategists to identify threats and opportunities, as well as constraints. In brief, the job in the planning phase is to develop strategies that take advantage of the company's strengths and minimize its weaknesses in order to grasp opportunities and avoid threats. One of the opportunities BIC identified was that of employing John McEnroe, the "bad boy" of tennis, to promote its 29-cent razors. The resulting ads were highly successful.

Objective or Direction Setting

Explicitly stating objectives and directing all activities toward their attainment is not the only approach to strategic management; it may not even be the best approach for some organizations at certain times. However, since Peter Drucker coined the term *management by objectives* in the 1950s, it has been generally accepted that the use of objectives improves the process of management. This is no less true at the corporate level of strategic management than it is for the miler who wishes to better the existing world record.

Characteristics of Strategic Objectives

Objectives should be challenging but attainable. If the miler mentioned above were capable of running near world-record speed but were to set an objective of a five minute mile, it could be easily achieved; however, the miler would probably not run at maximum speed. On the other hand, if the objective were set at three minutes, no one in the world could come close.

Anyone who attempted it would be frustrated. Corporate goals, too, should offer a reasonable opportunity for accomplishment. To avoid frustration, the probability of accomplishment should not be zero, and to avoid suboptimum performance, it should not be nearly 100 percent.

Remember, too, that objectives should be specific, preferably quantifiable, and measurable. An objective to "maximize profits" offers little specific guidance. To earn $1.2 million in profits or to increase profits by 5 percent over last year's level is specific. The more specific objectives are, the more definite can be the strategies designed to accomplish them.

Satisficing

Herbert Simon has suggested that managers in general do not attempt to optimize or maximize corporate results.[5] He believes that the term *satisficing* more correctly describes what managers do. According to Simon's theory, managers typically accept the first satisfactory outcome they are offered. For example, one who believes that 10 percent is a reasonable return on invested funds is likely to approve any ROI (return on investment) objective that exceeds that amount.

If Simon is right, many corporate strategists may be more concerned with establishing direction than with setting specific objectives. As long as this year's sales and profits are above last year's, that may be acceptable because the direction is upward. Many effective organizations have never set specific objectives. In fact, some have only a vague understanding of the direction in which they are headed. It appears likely, however, that any organization can improve its performance by setting objectives that are challenging but attainable and specific, preferably quantified.

Strategy Setting

Once objectives are established or direction is determined, strategies can be determined. The acquisition strategy at GE is to maintain large cash balances so that the company can take advantage of exceptional bargains immediately rather than having to go into the financial markets, a time-consuming process. It is important that this strategy be understood by the financial vice-president and other managers so that everyone will cooperate to generate the needed funds and to keep them in reserve rather than committing them to other purposes.

In contrast to GE, many organizations limit their written strategic plans to financial budgets. And some do not even have budgets. Most authorities, however, consider it worthwhile to reduce strategies to writing. Whether strategies are written or not, it is the task of organizational strategists to clearly communicate how the organization intends to accomplish its goals. The remainder of this chapter is devoted to a discussion of how environmental considerations affect the strategic process, a description of a number of tools used in setting strategies, and a description of several grand strategies.

ENVIRONMENTAL CONSIDERATIONS

In earlier chapters, the organization's environment was seen as consisting of various groups—customers, suppliers, unions, and others—that affect the organization from without. In this chapter, the same environmental groups are recognized but in terms of the types of forces they bring to bear: social, political, technological, and economic. Let us consider each of them individually.

The social aspect involves ethical and moral considerations and the responsibilities strategic managers have to persons because of their humanity and not because of any legal, economic, or political forces they may bring to bear. Some would have the strategic manager be completely rational, perhaps even self-serving. However, every manager, indeed every human, experiences the emotions of friendship, love, pity, admiration, and so forth. These emotions properly influence the behavior of organizational strategists and therefore of organizations.

The political facet of the environment is concerned with laws and regulations and the courts and government officials who interpret and enforce them. It also involves other groups and institutions in society that wield power. The increasing burden of laws and regulations is of concern to every manager. An early goal of the Reagan presidency was to reduce government regulation of business. Still, thousands of government agencies, many with overlapping areas of responsibility, restrict organizational activity. To the extent that the laws are objectively stated and uniformly enforced, they simply limit the activities of organizational strategists. Inconsistently applied, as they often are, they impart uncertainty. For example, because of the inconsistency in the way nuclear plant construction is regulated by the federal government, the Washington Public Power System, later nicknamed WHOOPS, saw billions in cost overruns and eventually failed.

In addition to government, many other groups and institutions in society hold power. Organizational strategists both are influenced by and seek to influence these groups and institutions. For example, contributions to the Republican or Democratic party might be made to strengthen this power center because corporate strategists might agree with the ideologies it supports. Of course, such contributions might also be made to influence the powerful group in question.

The technological side of the environment is the sum total of machines, materials, and knowledge that go into the production of goods and services. Technology should not be confused with high-tech, which is the *advanced, mostly electronic, technology involved in computers, robotics, space travel, and so on.* The technological facet includes these, of course, but it also includes all kinds of machines and systems for accomplishing practical purposes. Technological innovations account for many of the success stories in business and are a proper concern for corporate strategists. Henry Ford built Ford Motor Company on the assembly-line method of manufacture. Steven Jobs and Steve Wozniak created the first Apple Computer in Wozniak's garage and became millionaires.

Economic forces are considered by many to be the most important aspect of the organization's environment. For example, Nobel Laureate economist Milton Friedman once said, "The only social responsibility of business is to earn a profit within the rules of the game."[6] In what has been called the "capitalist manifesto," Adam Smith suggested that if entrepreneurs pursue their own economic interests, society will benefit.[7] Whether one agrees with these conservative ideas or not, economic considerations are at the center of the strategic planning process. Every organization that fails, fails economically, and every one that succeeds, succeeds economically.

CHAPTER 4   113
Strategic Planning

James F. Olson

As manager of corporate strategic planning for General Mills, Inc., James Olson is responsible for coordinating the various elements of the annual five-year corporate plan. This includes developing planning assumptions, instructions, financial aggregation, issue identification, and strategic analysis. James reports to the vice-president and director of corporate growth and planning and works closely with division general managers and subsidiary presidents of more than forty business planning units. Mr. Olson obtained his B.A. from the University of Minnesota in 1962, with a degree in industrial psychology. In 1965, he received his MBA from Kansas University.

When asked, "What is planning?" James replied, "Most managers at General Mills would agree that there are several dimensions to planning and that any definition of planning would include a combination of these factors. First, it is a philosophy. GMI management firmly believes that planning is a continuous management function. Second, planning deals with the future impact of current decisions. Managers examine the current business climate and select a course of action depending upon their perception of the future environment. Third, planning is a process. The process begins with the development of objectives, defines the strategies to achieve the objectives, and develops plans to make sure that the strategies are carried out to accomplish the objectives. Fourth, it is a structure of plans. It is a structure that integrates strategic plans from areas of corporate responsibility with plans from business units, industry areas, and with the corporation as a whole."

He also says, "The fundamental purpose of GMI's strategic planning process is to provide the framework for developing a common understanding and agreement among all levels of management on basic objectives and broad strategies for each planning entity within the corporation and for the corporation as a whole. This purpose is accomplished when corporate management has achieved a relative degree of comfort with the proposed plans of the managers and when it has come to grips with such issues as:

1. Whether proper goals have been developed.
2. Whether the corporation is properly organized for achieving its goals.
3. Whether major areas of longer-term concern or opportunity have been identified and are being properly addressed."

When asked what he believed had to have contributed to the development of an effective planning process and to quality planning within General Mills, James identified these ten aspects of strategic planning, which he regards as fundamental to effective long-term management:

1. Match planning with the organizational structure.
2. Plan continuously.
3. Identify key issues.
4. Include competitive developments.
5. Keep it simple.

6. Secure the full involvement of top decision makers.
7. Review every plan.
8. Compose the review group of top decision makers.
9. Use contingency planning.
10. Know the purpose of planning.

SOME TOOLS OF STRATEGIC MANAGEMENT

There are a number of tools and techniques especially useful for strategic planning. Referring to the profile of James F. Olson, companies like General Mills that employ strategic planning professionals make use of most of the tools available. Among the more popular of these are the BCG matrix, product life cycle theory, and what is called the PIMS data base and the Seven S Framework. Let us discuss each of these.

The BCG Matrix

During the 1970s, there were a number of attempts to make sense of the process of corporate-level strategic management. Recent research shows that half or more of America's largest corporations practice some kind of formal business portfolio planning.[8] Most of them use a two-dimensional diagram to display various attributes of a diversified corporation's group of businesses (or SBUs) in a concise way. The best-known way of doing this was developed by the Boston Consulting Group (BCG). The BCG matrix is illustrated in Figure 4–3. Each circle on the BCG matrix represents a different SBU. Although the BCG matrix greatly simplifies the strategic planning process, showing the SBUs of a complex company like General Mills (40 SBUs) still produces a rather cluttered diagram.

Placing SBUs on the BCG Matrix

The matrix shows three things about each SBU. First, the area of each circle is proportional to the sales revenue of the respective business. For example, SBU–A is the largest in sales among those illustrated. SBU–E has the lowest contribution to the firm's total sales.

The relative position of a circle along the horizontal axis is determined by the respective SBU's market share as compared to that of the largest rival firm. For example, in the personal computer business, Apple is very large, having sold over 500,000 units. As compared to IBM, its major competitor, however, Apple sells fewer than half as many PCs. So IBM would place its personal computer business at the extreme left of the BCG matrix, with Apple shown farther to the right.

The vertical axis of the BCG matrix measures market growth rate, not the growth rate in sales of the individual business. A business that is gaining market share will be growing more rapidly than the market in general. The rate of growth of IBM's personal computer business has recently exceeded 30 percent a year. Still, this business would be shown on the BCG matrix according to the growth of the personal computer business in general, about 20 percent a year.

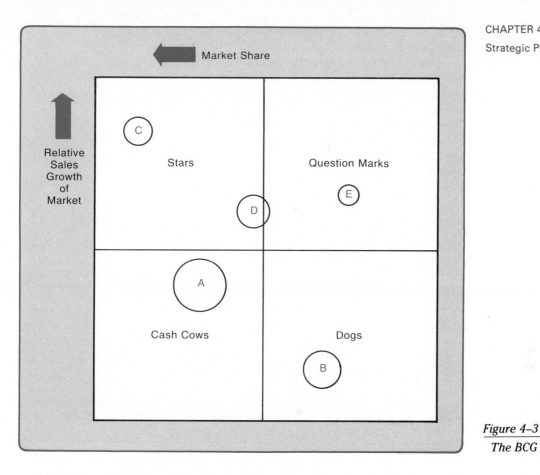

Figure 4–3

The BCG Matrix

Stars, Question Marks, Cows, and Dogs

An implicit assumption of the BCG analysis is that market share in a given business signifies strength and that market growth rate signifies opportunity. This is why GE demands that each division of the company be, or become, dominant in its field. Referring again to Figure 4–3, businesses with high market shares in high-growth-rate industries are given the favorable designation, "Stars." Theoretically they offer the best profit and growth opportunities for the company. SBUs with low market shares in low-growth industries are called "Dogs" because their market shares suggest competitive weakness and because the slow industry growth rates suggest approaching market saturation. The steel industry, for example, is considered by many to be saturated.

The major focus of the BCG analysis is cash flows. SBUs that hold high market shares in low-growth industries should not be expanding investment rapidly (because there are better investments available). Still, the high market shares should allow those business to earn profits. Research suggests that profitability of such companies depends mostly on employee productivity, capital utilization, and pricing policies, not added investment.[9] Since there is no need for added investment in the business, the profits can be used to finance the corporation's other businesses, particularly Stars. So businesses that plot in the lower left-hand quadrant of the BCG matrix are called "Cash Cows."

Usually when a company enters a new business, it will at first have a low market share. If the business segment is growing rapidly, like the home computer industry recently has, any new entry faces an uncertain future. So low market share businesses in high-growth industries are called "Question Marks" on the BCG matrix. Typically they require large amounts of cash in order to develop them into Stars. Sometimes, however, a Question Mark business is so rapidly growing and profitable that it can generate the cash flows required for its own growth.

Implications of the BCG Analysis

The corporate-level strategist who uses the BCG approach must ask, "What are the strategic implications for the corporation as a whole? What does BCG analysis say about resource allocation and about disposition of the various SBUs?" First, BCG proponents argue, the corporation's overall cash flow must be balanced. There should be enough Cash Cows in the business portfolio to fund the cash needs of the Stars and Question Marks, which offer the greatest promise. Second, BCG clearly feels that positions on the BCG matrix imply certain strategies. Sale or liquidation is recommended for Dogs and perhaps weak Cash Cows. Growth is the right path for Question Marks and Stars. Efforts should be made to get back the investment from Cash Cows.

Some researchers feel that resource allocation is an important but often ignored use of the BCG matrix.[10] In other words, BCG analysis, they feel, should not be limited to buy-sell and invest-disinvest decisions but should also be used to distribute funds within the corporation.

Product Life Cycle

product life cycle

The pattern of sales volume that all products follow and that includes the stages of introduction, growth, maturity, and decline is referred to as **product life cycle**. Corporate strategists who value stability in sales and earnings will tend to diversify among businesses, of course. But to gain maximum benefit from diversification, they will also tend to promote a balance of products and services across product life cycle stages. Figure 4–4 illustrates the product life cycle curve. Certainly every product must go through the life cycle stages; however, some products get a new lease on life. For example, a few years ago, Arm & Hammer baking soda, well into the decline phase of the product life cycle, saw renewed growth in response to a national advertising campaign touting its multiple uses.

Still, for most products, the cycle is rather consistent with variation only in the length of the various stages and the amount of sales and profits earned in each stage. Because of this, many companies, especially consumer goods companies such as Procter & Gamble, try to have a certain number of products or services in each stage of the product life cycle at all times. As one product goes into the decline stage, another is experiencing sales growth, and the company has a stable source of profits from those products in the mature stage.

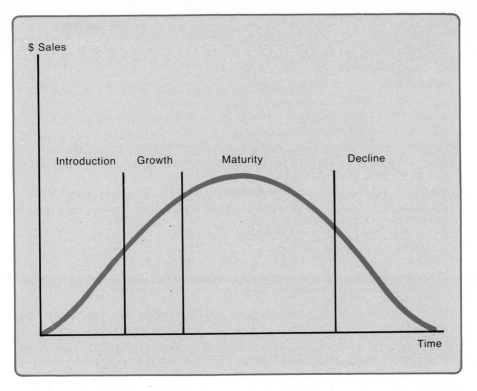

Figure 4–4

The Product Life Cycle

The PIMS Project

Started by GE, but now under the nonprofit Strategic Planning Institute, the PIMS (profit impact of market strategies) project is perhaps the most comprehensive study of strategic factors ever conducted. The project is an ongoing one. It has built up a huge array of data from over 1,500 product and service businesses, or SBUs, representing 200 corporations. Early results indicated that return on investment (ROI) was most significantly affected by market share, investment intensity, and corporate diversity.[11]

Investment intensity and corporate diversity are difficult concepts and will not be discussed further here; however, market share usually can be objectively determined. There may be disagreement about whether market share determines profitability, as BCG says, or management competence determines both profitability and market share. Still, most companies seek high market shares in those businesses in which they are earning their highest profits. PIMS data suggest a number of other conclusions relevant to corporate strategists but which are beyond the scope of an introductory management text.

The McKinsey Seven S Framework and Corporate Culture

Originally developed in 1977 but publicized only in the 1980s, the McKinsey Seven S Framework is a powerful addition to the arsenal of organizational strategies. The Seven Ss are illustrated in Table 4–1. In their best-selling

TABLE 4–1	The McKinsey Seven Ss
1. *Structure:*	Those attributes of the organization that can be expressed through an organizational chart (span of control, centralization versus decentralization, etc.).
2. *Strategy:*	Actions the organization plans or undertakes in response to or in anticipation of the external environment.
3. *Systems:*	Procedures and processes regularly followed by an organization.
4. *Staff:*	The kinds of specialties or professions represented in an organization ("engineering types," "used car salesmen," "MBAs," "computer jocks").
5. *Skills:*	Distinctive attributes and capabilities of the organization and its key people in comparison with its competition.
6. *Style:*	Patterns of behavior and managerial style of senior managers.
7. *Shared values:*	Spiritual or philosophical principles and concepts that an organization is able to instill in its members.

Source: Adapted from Anthony G. Athos and Richard T. Pascale, *The Art of Japanese Management: Applications for American Executives* (New York: Simon & Schuster, 1981).

book, *In Search of Excellence,* Peters and Waterman say that corporate strategists have tended to rely on the hardware of organization—structure, strategy, and systems—and have ignored the softer elements.[12] Two other well-known authors, Athos and Pascale, argue that "the four 'soft' elements can no longer be regarded as frosting on the corporate cake. They are indispensable parts of any corporate commitment to long time success."[13] Proponents of the Seven S Framework believe a balanced emphasis on all of the Seven Ss is more likely to be successful.

corporate culture   **Corporate culture** has been defined as *the system of shared values, beliefs, and habits within an organization that interacts with formal structure to produce behavioral norms.* The McKinsey Seven S framework offers a concise way of viewing corporate culture.

The Seven S model is useful for three purposes:

1. It helps managers and analysts understand the corporate culture in their organizations.
2. It helps strategists compare their organizations with others along each of the seven dimensions, thereby identifying organizational strengths and weaknesses.
3. As a tool of strategy implementation, the Seven S model can help managers change the attributes of the corporate culture that they consider vital to success and to do so in a systematic way.

Arguing eloquently for the Seven S model, Peters and Waterman say:

> It has enabled us to say, in effect, "All that stuff you have been dismissing for so long as the intractable, irrational, intuitive, informal organization *can* be managed. Clearly, it has as much or more to do with the way things work (or don't) around your companies as the formal structures and strategies do. Not only are you foolish to ignore it, but here's a way to think about it. Here are some tools for managing it. Here, really, is the way to develop a new skill."[14]

The difficulty of changing corporate culture and the time required to do so should not be underestimated. When Frederick W. Taylor, the Father of Scientific Management, argued that what was needed in 1898 was a "mental revolution," he expressed the opinion that accomplishing this might take as much as five years.[15] The time required for cultural change has not diminished since Taylor's day. Under the guidance of such consulting firms as the Management Analysis Center of Cambridge, Massachusetts, a number of modern U.S. corporations, including Chase Manhattan Bank, American Telephone & Telegraph, and First Chicago Corporation, have attempted to extensively change their corporate cultures. The efforts have not been altogether successful. One researcher, who analyzed ten cases of attempted cultural change, was provoked to say that "it cost a fortune and takes forever."[16] *Fortune* magazine's Bro Uttal says, "Executives who have succeeded in fundamentally transforming a culture put a more precise estimate on how long the process requires: '6 to 15 years.' "[17] Still, if culture is a major determinant of corporate success—as it clearly is—strategists will, and should, continue to search for ways to manipulate it.

SEVERAL GRAND STRATEGIES

We have described in general terms much of the nature of the strategic planning process. Let us now consider several grand or master strategies that often grow out of that process.

Integration

A commonly used term among organizational strategists is **integration**, *the unified control of a number of successive or similar operations.* When companies combine, this is integration. Integration also includes a company's taking over a portion of the industrial or commercial process that previously was accomplished by other firms. Integration need not involve ownership, only control. Thus, supply and marketing contracts are forms of integration. *Integration toward the final users of a company's product or service,* as when Tandy Corporation opened its Radio Shack stores, is **forward integration**. *A company's taking control of any of the sources of its inputs, including raw materials and labor,* is **backward integration.** Southland Corporation's 1983 purchase of a petroleum refinery that supplies gasoline to the company's Seven-Eleven stores is an example of backward integration. *Buying or taking control of competitors at the same level in the production and marketing process* is **horizontal integration.** For example, when Firestone, already in the auto service business, recently took over J. C. Penney's auto service centers, that was horizontal integration.

integration

forward integration

backward integration

horizontal integration

While recognizing its possible disadvantages, Harrigan lists the following competitive advantages of integration:[18]

- Improved marketing and technological intelligence.
- Superior control of the firm's economic environment.
- Product differentiation advantages.

Each type of integration can be a strategy for accomplishing different objectives. For example, if the objective is to decrease costs of inputs, one possible way to do this would be to buy out suppliers that earn profits producing the inputs. If the strategic objective is to obtain additional market share, horizontal integration might accomplish this. This was done when Southland Corporation bought the Pak-A-Sak convenience store chain. Southland Corporation provides an example of a single company that was involved in both backward and horizontal integration.

Backward and forward integration are usually designed to accomplish one or both of two purposes: capturing additional profits or obtaining better control. Backward integration does this for the supply channels. Forward integration does this for distribution channels. Obviously if a supplier or an intermediate customer is making exorbitant profits, vertical integration may be justified on this basis alone. Vertical integration may also be justified when a company can perform the functions of suppliers or intermediate customers effectively and efficiently. If better control of sources of supply or distribution channels is the only objective, it may be better not to buy the business. There may be better ways to ensure control, such as making franchise agreements with intermediate customers and long-term supply agreements with suppliers. Besides, taking over customers or suppliers is costly and often involves a company in businesses with which its managers are unfamiliar.

Diversification

diversification
conglomerate
diversification

concentric
diversification

Diversification is *increasing the variety of products or services made or sold.* Diversification may be conglomerate or concentric. **Conglomerate diversification** simply means *the development of businesses unrelated to the firm's current businesses.* **Concentric diversification** means *the development of businesses related to the firm's current businesses.*[19] As a grand strategy, diversification usually has reduction of risk as its purpose. A company that is involved in a number of different businesses avoids

Diversification is increasing the variety of products or services made or sold.

Kirk Williamson

having all its eggs in one basket. Ideally, when some of a conglomerate firm's businesses decline, others will be on the increase.

Countercyclical firms are those that tend to see increasing sales while the economy in general is declining. Such businesses are hard to find. The do-it-yourselfer hand tool market is one of the rare exceptions. When times are tough, people tend to repair their own automobiles and need tools in order to do so.

About the best that can be hoped for, in general, is a group of SBUs whose valleys and peaks occur at different times in the business cycle. Of course, diversification into related businesses may not appear to serve the risk reduction objective as well as conglomerate diversification; however, concentric diversification tends to be more successful in improving profitability.[20] This is probably because the managers of the concentrically diversifying firm know something about the business they are buying.

Diversification often occurs as a by-product of bargain hunting by corporate strategists. Even if the preference is for a related merger candidate, corporate-level strategists may opt for acquiring an SBU in an entirely different business because it is deemed to be greatly underpriced. Diversification can also be a product of a desire for growth. During the growth fever of the 1970s, many companies, including Textron, Beatrice Foods, and United Technologies, acquired unrelated, though rapidly growing, subsidiaries.

Retrenchment

Another grand strategy, usually applied only when failure is imminent, is retrenchment. **Retrenchment** means *the reduction of the size or scope of a firm's activities.* Most corporate managements resist this strategy. Although growth is often an objective, retrenchment seldom is. When a retrenchment strategy is followed, the goal is often survival. For example, Braniff Airlines emerged from bankruptcy reorganization in 1983 a fraction of its former size; however, it was not until late 1984, when there was virtually no hope of survival, that the company decided to retrench further and agreed to sell off twenty of its thirty remaining planes.

retrenchment

When Sanford Sigiloff took over Wickes Companies in 1981, it was in similar dire straits. Sigiloff immediately began to sell off unproductive assets, lay off employees, and guide the company through a lengthy retrenchment process. By 1984, Wickes had again become a profitable, though somewhat smaller, company. The Wickes example suggests that retrenchment should be considered as viable an option as growth. Prompt elimination of losing businesses has been the hallmark of a number of successful corporate managers.

SUMMARY

Strategic planning is the determination of overall organizational purposes and objectives and how they are to be achieved. A strategic business unit (SBU) is any part of a business organization that is treated separately for strategic planning purposes. In general, an SBU engages in just one line of business.

There are three basic levels of strategic

planning. Corporate-level strategic planning is defining the overall character and purpose of the organization, the businesses it will enter and leave, and how resources will be distributed among these businesses. SBU-level strategic planning is determining how an SBU will compete in a particular line of business. Functional-level strategic planning is determining policies and procedures for relatively narrow areas of activity critical to success of the organization.

Strategic planning is broken into four steps: (1) determination of organizational mission, (2) assessment of the organization and its environment, (3) setting of specific objectives of direction, and (4) determination of strategies to accomplish these objectives. In most organizations, all of the steps are occurring at any one time. The environment for strategic planning can be viewed as consisting of four major elements: social, political, technological, and economic.

There are a number of planning tools and techniques especially useful at the strategic level. More than half of America's largest corporations use some kind of formal business portfolio planning. The best-known way of doing this was developed by the Boston Consulting Group (BCG). Another technique is the product life cycle

approach. The necessity for all products to go through the stages of introduction, growth, maturity, and decline is referred to as product life cycle. To gain maximum benefit from diversification, companies need to promote a balance of products and services across product life cycle stages.

The profit impact of market strategies (PIMS) project is perhaps the most comprehensive study of strategic factors ever conducted. Early results indicated that return on investment (ROI) was most significantly affected by market share, investment intensity, and corporate diversity. The McKinsey Seven S Framework is another powerful addition to the arsenal of organizational strategies. In their best-selling book, *In Search of Excellence,* Peters and Waterman say that corporate strategists have tended to rely on the "hardware" of organizations—structure, strategy, and systems—and have ignored the softer elements.

There are several grand or master strategies. Integration is the unified control of a number of successive or similar operations. Diversification is increasing the variety of products or services made or sold. Retrenchment means reducing the size or scope of a firm's activities.

REVIEW QUESTIONS

1. Define strategic planning. What is a strategic business unit?

2. Distinguish among corporate-level strategic planning, SBU-level strategic planning, and functional-level strategic planning.

3. Who are the organizational strategists?

4. List and briefly describe each step in the strategic planning process.

5. Describe the concept of satisficing as suggested by Herbert Simon.

6. What are the major environmental elements

that affect strategic management? Briefly describe each.

7. Briefly identify the major elements of the following tools of strategic management:
   a. Boston Consulting Group Matrix
   b. Product Life Cycle
   c. PIMS Project
   d. McKinsey Seven S Framework

8. Identify and briefly describe the grand or master strategies that grow out of the strategic planning process.

EXERCISES

1. Write an appropriate mission statement for each of the following:
   a. Chrysler Corporation
   b. Procter and Gamble (major consumer goods merchandiser)

   c. Harvard University
   d. A small grocery store

2. Using the Boston Consulting Group model, draw the following businesses in their correct positions:

a. General Motors' automobile business

b. Tandy Corporation's Radio Shack computer business

c. AT&T's new robot manufacturing division

d. General Electric's small appliance division

CASE STUDY

Master Hardware

Master Hardware stores is a chain of twelve retail outlets located in small towns in northern Kentucky and southern Ohio. The parent corporation, Master Merchandisers, Inc., is a Kentucky corporation owned by the Booker family of Louisville. The Bookers, led by Beatrice, who was eighty-three years old in 1985, have steadfastly refused to vary from the plan that Beatrice found successful when the first Master Hardware stores were opened during the 1940s. The plan is simple: only one store is opened in each town, and the towns must be between 8,000 and 15,000 population at the time. Inventories are tightly controlled, and no item is stocked unless it turns at least four times a year. Each store is managed by a carefully selected local citizen who is paid 50 percent of the profits the store generates. All purchasing is done by the central office in Louisville, although most items are shipped directly from hardware wholesalers and manufacturers to the individual stores. The store buildings are rented. After an initial infusion of capital, each store is required to pay its own way. If it does not, it is closed.

Master Merchandisers had opened no new stores for several years, although the existing stores were quite profitable. The company had never done much borrowing, so the high profits resulted in increasing cash balances, even after paying family members director's fees, salaries, and so forth.

Until 1984, the excess funds were invested in U.S. Treasury securities, which are safe but yield low returns. That year, Beatrice Booker agreed with the board of directors—made up of two of her sons, a nephew, and a niece—that the company should go into the restaurant business. The Bookers decided that Master Merchandisers would invest $3 million and build at least five new seafood restaurants. They would feature pond-raised catfish and would be located in towns similar to those where the Master Hardware stores were.

The restaurant business was separately incorporated as Catfish Master Restaurants, Inc. By mid-1985 three Catfish Master Restaurants were opened. The system was patterned as much as possible after the Master Hardware chain. Restaurant managers were paid on a percentage of the profit basis. Purchasing was done centrally, and each restaurant was required to support itself after the initial investment. It became clear within a year, however, that the first two restaurants would have to be closed unless additional funds were provided.

QUESTIONS

1. As clearly as you can, state what you believe to be the corporate mission of Master Merchandisers, Inc.

2. List the strategies discussed in the case that you would consider SBU-level strategies and the ones that are corporate-level strategies. Explain your answer.

3. What kind of integration occurred when Master Merchandisers went into the restaurant business? Discuss.

4. Do you believe that the Booker family is likely to be successful in the restaurant business? Why or why not?

A Strategic Management Consultant

On a late evening flight from Seattle to Phoenix, I had the good fortune of sitting beside a gentleman who introduced himself as "a management consultant who helps companies develop strategies for overcoming personnel problems." His name was Joe Zuber. Joe said that most of his clients were banks, although he had been employed by businesses as diverse as hospitals, contractors, and computer firms.

I asked him to describe a typical consulting situation for me. He said that he was a member of a three-person firm headquartered in Denver that advertised nationally in *The Wall Street Journal* and several other business publications. When his office in Denver was contacted by a potential client, one of the three principals would make an initial sales pitch by telephone asking the client simply to defray expenses involved in preparing a proposal.

In a recent case, Joe had worked with a large savings and loan company in Phoenix. In fact, he was on his way back there at the time to submit his final report. What he had done for the bank was conduct a series of interviews with the bank's fourteen managers, starting with the chief executive and working on down. Each manager was asked to identify any problems or opportunities and to suggest how the company might go about addressing them.

Before talking to anyone other than the chief executive, Joe asked that a memorandum be prepared saying that he had been retained to help the company seek ways to improve its operations. After an initial series of interviews, each taking about an hour, Joe prepared an interim report. With the president's permission, he met with the managers as a group and discussed the conflicts and frustrations that had been mentioned without identifying the managers involved. He also discussed each opportunity that had been stated by as many as two of the managers.

I asked Joe to give me an example of an opportunity and a problem. He said, "The major problem, which came up time and again, was that the chief executive was too involved in the details of the operation and didn't give his subordinates as much authority as their abilities justified." There was no consensus about the opportunities. Four of the fifteen managers said that they should move into commercial banking, that is, short- and intermediate-term business loans and business checking accounts. The banking industry had recently been deregulated, and banks and savings and loan companies were often crossing over onto one another's turf.

Joe said that after the initial series of interviews and the interim report, he visited again with several of the managers whom he considered to be especially well informed. They again went over the problems and opportunities that had received some agreement. After that, he had gone back to the main office in Denver to prepare his final report. His intention, he said, was to clear the report with the chief executive and then ask for another meeting of all the managers. This meeting would preferably be held in the evening, and a meal would be served. He expected the meeting to last for several hours.

There was much more that I wanted to ask Joe, but we were interrupted by the flight attendant telling us we were about to land in Phoenix. It was not until then that Joe asked me what my business was. Upon learning that I was a management professor, he asked if we might keep in touch. I assured him that I would like that.

QUESTIONS

1. Explain why you think a bank might hire a consultant like Joe Zuber when it has fifteen managers on the permanent payroll.

2. What do you believe is likely to happen when the chief executive receives the final report highlighting his own tendency to get too much involved in detail and to withhold authority from his subordinates?

NOTES

1. This discussion is a composite from a number of popular articles appearing in 1983 and 1984, among them: Howard Banks, "General Electric—Going with the Winners," *Forbes,* March 26, 1984, pp. 97–106; N. Nelson-Horchtes, "GE Builds a High-Tech Arsenel," *Industry Week,* October 3, 1983, pp. 49–50; N. Snyderman, "GE Is Doing the Things the U.S. Must Do to Be Competitive," *Electronic News,* suppl. B, October 3, 1983; and "A New P/E for the New GE," *Fortune,* January 9, 1984, p. 114.

2. Richard B. Robinson, Jr., "The Importance of 'Outsiders' in Small Firm Strategic Planning," *Academy of Management Journal* 25 (March 1982): 80–93.

3. James J. Polyczynski and Jason Leniski, "Inviting Front-Line Managers into the Strategic Planning and Decision Making Process," *Appalachian Business Review* 9 (1982): 2–5.

4. Frederick Gluck, Stephen Kaufman, and A. Steven Walleck, "The Four Phases of Strategic Management," *Journal of Business Strategy* 2 (Winter 1982): 11–12.

5. Herbert A. Simon, *The New Science of Management Decision* (New York: Harper & Row, 1960).

6. Milton Friedman, *Capitalism and Freedom* (Chicago: University of Chicago Press, 1962).

7. Adam Smith, *The Wealth of Nations* (1776; New York: Modern Library, 1937).

8. Philippe Haspeslagh, "Portfolio Planning: Uses and Limits," *Harvard Business Review* 60 (January–February 1982): 58–73.

9. Ian C. MacMillan, Donald C. Hambrick, and Diana L. Day, "The Product Portfolio and Profitability: A PIMS-based Analysis of Industrial-Product Businesses," *Academy of Management Journal* 25 (December 1982): 733–755.

10. Frederick Gluck, "The Dilemmas of Resource Allocation," *Journal of Business Strategy* (Fall 1981): 67–71; and Philippe Haspeslagh, "Portfolio Planning: Uses and Limits," *Harvard Business Review* 60 (January–February 1982): 58–73.

11. S. Schoeffler, R. D. Buzzell, and D. F. Haney, "Impact of Strategic Planning on Profit Performance," *Harvard Business Review* (March 1974): 137–145.

12. Thomas J. Peters and Robert H. Waterman, Jr., *In Search of Excellence* (New York: Harper & Row, 1982).

13. Anthony G. Athos and Richard T. Pascale, *The Art of Japanese Management: Applications for American Executives* (New York: Simon & Schuster, 1981), pp. 83–84.

14. Peters and Waterman, *In Search,* p. 11.

15. Daniel A. Wren, *The Evolution of Management Thought,* 2d ed. (New York: John Wiley, 1979), p. 156.

16. Bro Uttal, "The Corporate Culture Vultures," *Fortune,* 108, October 17, 1983, p. 70.

17. Ibid., p. 72.

18. Kathryn Rudie Harrigan, "A Framework for Looking at Vertical Integration," *Journal of Business Strategy* 3 (Winter 1983): 30–37.

19. In a technical sense, the term *related diversification* is better than *concentric diversification,* but the latter has found more widespread use.

20. Richard A. Bettis, "Performance Differences in Related and Unrelated Diversified Firms," *Strategic Management Journal* 2 (October–December 1981): 379–393.

REFERENCES

Anderson, Carl R., and Frank T. Paine. "Managerial Perceptions and Strategic Behavior." *Academy of Management Journal* 18 (December 1975): 811–823.

Athos, Anthony G., and Richard T. Pascale. *The Art of Japanese Management: Applications for American Executives.* New York: Simon & Schuster, 1981.

Bettis, Richard A. "Performance Differences in Related and Unrelated Diversified Firms." *Strategic Management Journal* 2 (October–December 1981): 379–393.

Bowman, Edward H. "Risk/Return Paradox for Strategic Management." *Sloan Management Review* 21 (Spring 1980): 17–31.

Fox, H. W. "Frontiers of Strategic Planning: Intuition or Formal Models." *Management Review* 70 (April 1981): 44–50.

Friedman, Milton. *Capitalism and Freedom.* Chicago: University of Chicago Press, 1962.

Gluck, Frederick. "The Dilemmas of Resource Allocation." *Journal of Business Strategy* (Fall 1981): 67–71.

Gluck, Frederick, Stephen Kaufman, and A. Steven Walleck. "The Four Phases of Strategic Management." *Journal of Business Strategy* 2 (Winter 1982): 11–12.

Gup, Benton E. "Begin Strategic Planning by Asking Three Questions." *Managerial Planning* 28 (November

1979): 28–31.

Harrigan, Kathryn Rudie. "A Framework for Looking at Vertical Integration." *Journal of Business Strategy* 3 (Winter 1983): 30–37.

Haspeslagh, Philippe. "Portfolio Planning: Uses and Limits." *Harvard Business Review* 60 (January–February 1982): 58–73.

Judla, R. J. "Elements of Effective Corporate Planning." *Long Range Planning* 9 (August 1976): 82–93.

MacMillan, Ian C., Donald C. Hambrick, and Diana L. Day. "The Product Portfolio and Profitability: A PIMS-based Analysis of Industrial-Product Businesses." *Academy of Management Journal* 25 (December 1982): 733–755.

Martin, John. "Business Planning: The Gap between Theory and Practice." *Long Range Planning* 12 (December 1979): 2–10.

Naylon, T. H. "Organizing for Strategic Planning." *Managerial Planning* 28 (July 1979): 3–9.

Pearson, G. J. "Setting Corporate Objectives as a Basis for Action." *Long Range Planning* 12 (August 1979): 13–19.

Peters, Thomas J., and Robert H. Waterman, Jr. *In Search of Excellence.* New York: Harper & Row, 1982.

Polyczynski, James J., and Jason Leniski. "Inviting Front-Line Managers into the Strategic Planning and Decision Making Process." *Appalachian Business Review* 9 (1982): 2–5.

Robinson, Richard B., Jr. "The Importance of 'Outsiders' in Small Firm Strategic Planning." *Academy of Management Journal* 25 (March 1982): 80–93.

Schoeffler, S., R. D. Buzzell, and D. F. Haney. "Impact of Strategic Planning on Profit Performance." *Harvard Business Review* (March 1974): 137–145.

Simon, Herbert A. *The New Science of Management Decision.* New York: Harper & Row, 1960.

Smith, Adam. *The Wealth of Nations.* 1776; New York: Modern Library, 1937.

Taylor, Bernard. "Strategies for Planning." *Long Range Planning* (August 1975): 437–446.

Thune, Stanley S., and Robert J. House. "Where Long-Range Planning Pays Off." *Business Horizons* 13 (August 1970): 81–87.

Uttal, Bro. "The Corporate Culture Vultures." *Fortune,* (October 17, 1983): 66–72.

Vancil, Richard F., and Peter Lorange. "Strategic Planning in Diversified Companies." *Harvard Business Review* 53 (January–February 1975): 81–90.

Vesper, Volker D. "Strategic Mapping—A Tool for Corporate Planners." *Long Range Planning* 12 (December 1979): 75–92.

Wren, Daniel A. *The Evolution of Management Thought.* 2d ed. New York: John Wiley, 1979.

LEARNING OBJECTIVES

After completing this chapter you should be able to

1. Define decision making and identify the steps in the decision-making process.

2. Identify major factors that can have an impact on the manager's decision making.

3. Explain the scientific method.

4. Describe group methods used in decision making.

5. Relate the importance of management information systems to decision making.

6. Identify and briefly describe several important trends in the use of computers.

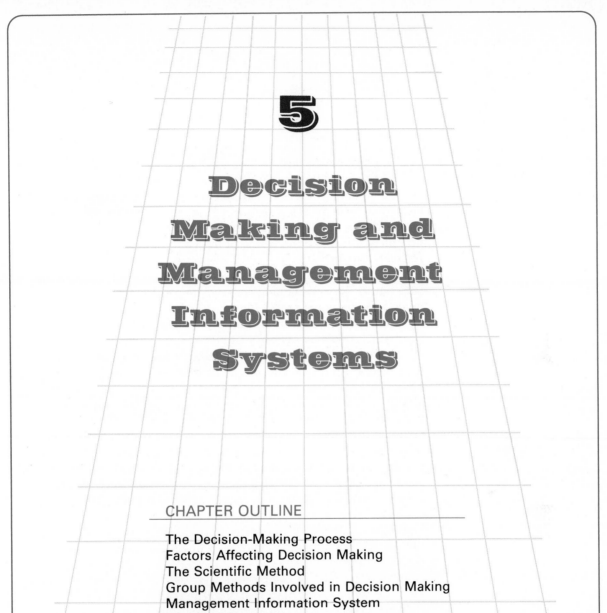

5

Decision Making and Management Information Systems

The Rise and Fall of Atari

ATARI® Nolan Bushnell founded Atari, Inc., in 1972 in California's Silicon Valley. By 1974 the company was producing and selling about 10,000 per year of Bushnell's Pong electronic table tennis games. But Bushnell could not finance the operation, so he made an agreement with Sears, Roebuck and Company to expand marketing of the game, and together they sold 100,000 units in 1975.

The company outgrew Bushnell's ability to manage it, and he sold out to Warner Communications, Inc., in October 1976 for $28 million. With annual sales of more than $3 billion and a wide array of high-technology businesses, Warner could provide the needed financing, as well as research and development capabilities.

Shortly after the acquisition, Warner's management began to intervene in Atari's operations. In 1978, Bushnell was replaced by Raymond Kassar. Kassar made many management changes, set specific sales and marketing goals, and established formal reporting procedures and financial controls. By this time, Atari's product line included the Video Computer System (VCS). Buyers of this system could play a number of games simply by changing a cassette. Under Kassar's guidance, the company expanded sales and production and developed dozens of different game cartridges for the VCS. Space Invader cartridges alone sold over 1 million units in 1980.

Later Atari introduced home computers. By September 1982, over 5 million U.S. households owned Atari video games. Atari marketers saw the VCS owners, especially, as a huge, untapped market for home computers.

By 1982 a host of competitors were selling video game cartridges for their own and for Atari systems. The leading challengers were Coleco's ColecoVision and Mattel's Intellivision. To reduce costs and increase capacity, Atari moved much of its production to Hong Kong and Taiwan. Some competitors publicized their own efforts to preserve American jobs by manufacturing only in the United States.

In late 1982, Atari reported significantly reduced sales and earnings prospects. Instead of doubling and tripling, as sales and profits had done for several years, they were to increase only slightly for 1982. Because of this news, Warner Communications' stock fell by 25 percent the day of the announcement, wiping out $1.2 billion in market value. Through 1983 and 1984, Atari's fortunes—and Warner Communications' stock—failed to recover. To make matters worse, Coleco started airing a series of television advertisements comparing

Coleco's video game systems with Atari's supposedly inferior ones. As if to rub salt into Atari's wounds, Coleco ended each advertisement, "Sorry, Atari."

Atari's problems continued, and by 1984 Warner was ready to give up on what had been its star performer. The unit was sold to Jack Tramiel, former president of Commodore International Ltd., in July 1984. Because Warner management had confidence that Tramiel could turn Atari around and because it had few other options, Warner accepted $240 million in promissory notes in partial payment. There was no certainty, however, that the notes would be paid because Atari continued to lose money throughout the year. What had been Warner Communication's crown jewel was threatening to become a liability.[1]

The Atari story suggests the extensive need for decision making in business. **Decision making** is *the process of generating and evaluating alternatives and making choices among them.* When Bushnell invented the video game, he had to decide whether to market it himself or to sell the idea to others. Even after forming Atari, he found that each year brought new decisions: Get help in marketing the product or go it alone? Sell out to Warner Communications or cut back on growth? Expand the product line or stay with the video game? After Bushnell was replaced, Atari had to decide whether to manufacture overseas, how to go about restoring its respectability in the stock market, and how to combat increasingly aggressive competitors.

decision making

The need for decision making is so pervasive that decision making may be considered synonymous with managing. It is a large portion of the manager's job. Every employed person is required to engage in decision-making activities as part of the work performed. College professors make decisions about the nature of the information they will present to their students. Physicians diagnose problems and prescribe treatments. Scientists formulate hypotheses and select experiments for testing them.

Decisions made by professional managers may be no more or less crucial than those of the physicians or scientists. A managerial decision typically affects a great number of people—customers, stockholders, employees, and the general public. The professional manager sees the results of decisions reflected in the firm's earnings report, the welfare of employees, and the economic health of the community and the country. As Levitt contends, unlike lawyers, scientists, or physicians, "the manager is judged not for what he knows about the work that is done in his field, but by how well he actually does the work."[2] To survive and prosper, the manager must be able to make professional decisions.

In this chapter, we will describe the decision-making process and discuss several important factors which affect decision making. Next, we will describe the scientific method and group methods of decision making. The final sections of the chapter are devoted to management information systems, types of computers, and trends in the use of computers.

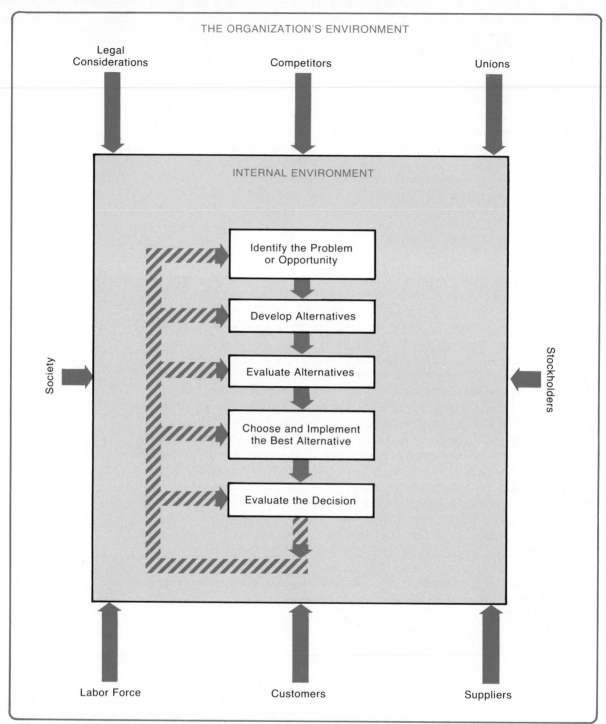

Figure 5–1   The Decision-Making Process

THE DECISION-MAKING PROCESS

Companies do not want dynamic failures; they want individuals who are properly equipped to make correct decisions. This does not mean that the managers must be right 100 percent of the time; no one is perfect. It does suggest that successful managers have a higher batting average than less successful managers.

There is a growing tendency to evaluate managers primarily on the results of their decisions. Some apparently successful executives follow an intuitive approach to decision making, basing their decisions on hunches and gut feelings. We believe, however, a more formalized approach to decision making, such as that illustrated in Figure 5–1, can usually increase a manager's batting average.

The implementation of a decision does not complete the decision-making process. The arrows in the decision-making process model indicate that there is constant reevaluation and feedback to every phase of decision making. The outcome—whether good or bad—provides information that can contribute to future decisions. After the disastrous result of the Atari earnings report in 1982, Warner learned not to disclose such shocking news suddenly but to keep investors more informed from day to day. The environment of decision making and the steps in the process are discussed below.

Environmental Factors

Decision making does not occur in a vacuum. Notice from Figure 5–1 that the elements of the environment remain the same as those identified in Chapter 2. Variations in any of these factors can affect decision making. For example, it was because of intense competition that a decision had to be made by Warner Communications concerning what to do with its Atari unit. Also, dissident stockholders may have had a part in determining the nature of the decision made, that is, divestiture.

In a similar manner, the internal environment confronted by a particular manager helps to determine what decisions are made and who makes them. At most companies, for example, individual supervisors make the final hiring decisions. Because of the complexities of labor laws, however, personnel departments at other firms are heavily involved in the hiring and firing of employees. This is true at AT&T (American Telephone and Telegraph Corporation). In fact, AT&T has agreed to a federal consent decree that requires that the personnel department tightly control hiring and firing.

Identify the Problem or Opportunity

Some people view decision making only as problem solving; however, problems are usually better treated as opportunities. The first step in the decision-making process should be to look more for decision-making opportunities rather than for problems. Eventually problems make themselves evident. Atari's worsening competitive position became clear in 1982 when the company's financial statement showed a drop in profits. Opportunities, however, usually must be sought out. In purchasing a company like Atari for $28 million, Warner was taking advantage of an opportunity. Within a few years after the purchase, Atari had earned over $1 billion. Often the distinction between a problem and an opportunity is not clear. For example, the environment of the steel industry in the early 1980s was seen as a problem by U.S. Steel and the other integrated producers. As was pointed out in Chapter 2, that same environment provided great opportunity for Nucor Steel Company, which used nonunion employees and participative management techniques to keep costs low.

In defining a problem (or opportunity), it is important to consider not just the problem itself but the underlying causes. For example, the problem may be an increased number of defects coming off a production line. Untrained workers may have been assigned to the department. Maintenance people may have been doing a poor job of servicing the equipment. Or defective material may have been received because of sloppy purchasing practices. The causes of a problem must be understood before they can be corrected.

Often, solving a problem or taking advantage of an opportunity requires working with other departments. Defining the problem or opportunity in terms of what caused it will help identify the persons and groups who need to be involved. If the problem was caused by poor maintenance, for instance, it may be necessary to involve the maintenance supervisor in deciding how to correct it.

Develop Alternatives

A problem can usually be "solved" in any of a number of ways. The only alternative that really counts, of course, is the one judged best among those considered. At this point in the decision-making process, however, it is important to consider all of the feasible ways in which a problem can be solved. Naturally, the number of alternatives generated is limited by the amount of time available for the decision, as well as by the importance of the decision itself. Obviously, however, the best alternate cannot be chosen if no one thinks of it.

Until the alternatives have been evaluated, it is best not to eliminate any from consideration. After Atari's earnings began to decline, it was necessary to consider ways to cut costs. Among the various alternatives proposed, one of the most distasteful was moving production overseas, thus costing American jobs. Yet after evaluation, this alternative seemed to Atari management the best among those considered.

Evaluate Alternatives

Usually advantages and disadvantages can be found in every possible solution. One alternative may be clearly superior, but it may also have some weak points. The alternative of making Atari video games overseas carried with it the risk of alienating Americans concerned about the high unemployment rates that existed then.

It is essential that managers realistically appraise arguments for or against a particular alternative. Sometimes an idea sounds good on first hearing. But taking time to weigh the pros and cons of alternatives usually pays off and prevents the manager's having to say, "I wish I had put more effort into making that decision."

There are a number of ways of evaluating alternatives. One way is to list the pros and cons of each alternative. Doing this often results in one alternative's being identified as clearly superior. Care should be taken, however, not to place too much emphasis on the number of pros and cons but rather to consider the overall importance of those relating to each alternative.

Another way to evaluate alternatives is to determine the expected payoff associated with each alternative. This requires consideration of both costs and benefits. It is also necessary to consider the probability that a certain payoff will occur if the respective alternative is chosen. For example, an alternative that offers a 50 percent probability of a $1 million payoff generally will be chosen over one with a 10 percent probability of a $2 million payoff. There are mathematical techniques available to calculate expected payoffs, but these are beyond the scope of this chapter.

Choose and Implement the Best Alternative

The ability to select the best course of action from several possible alternatives often separates successful managers from less successful ones. The alternative offering the highest promise of attaining the objective, taking into consideration the overall situation, should be selected. This step may sound easy, but for managers it is the toughest part of their job. However sophisticated the evaluation technique followed, a manager can never be sure that the results of a decision will be favorable. Perhaps the decision Atari made to manufacture overseas was the best that could have been made under the circumstances; nevertheless, the company's fortunes continued to worsen.

Fear of making a "wrong" decision sometimes causes a manager to make no decision at all. It is no wonder that relatively high salaries are paid to managers who have a reputation for having the fortitude to make decisions and for making correct ones most of the time. It is easy to be a "Monday morning quarterback" and criticize the coach's decisions. The coach, however, has to make decisions on the football field and never has the luxury of knowing how those decisions will turn out. Many thought it wrong when Chrysler managers received large bonuses after having seen their company through its recent crisis, but the bonuses may have been justified by the difficulty of the decisions these managers had to make. If those decisions had been wrong, the company might have failed, and Lee Iacocca, along with his faithful lieutenants, would have been out on the street.

It is easy to see how the managers of Chrysler felt a responsibility not only to make correct decisions but to ensure that they were implemented properly. Although most decision making is not done in such crisis situations as that which faced Chrysler, the responsibility for implementation can never be avoided. No matter how technically correct the decision and how faithfully a manager has followed the recommended process, a decision has no value except through its implementation.

Evaluate the Decision

No decision-making process is complete until the decision has been exposed to the realities of the business environment. Evaluation requires an objective assessment of how the decision has solved the problem. This is particularly important for firms that stress decentralized management. In these companies, lower-level managers are provided the opportunity to become more involved in decision making. This provides junior managers with decision-making experience, improving their intuition and judgment.

FACTORS AFFECTING DECISION MAKING

Many factors can have an impact on the manager's decision making. Some of the more important factors are described below. All of these factors influence managers as they make decisions, though some are more important at higher levels than at lower levels, and vice-versa.

Routine versus Nonroutine Decision Making

Management decisions may range from such major ones as whether to build a new plant or to enter a new business all the way to the rather routine decisions such as deciding on a supplier of bathroom tissue. Decisions may be viewed as routine or nonroutine.

Routine Decisions

Most managers make numerous routine decisions in the performance of their jobs. Routine decisions made by managers are governed by the policies, procedures, and rules of the organization, as well as the personal habits and preferences of the managers. Managers certainly should not devote as much time to making routine decisions as they would to making more serious ones. It would be silly, for example, to follow a formal procedure in deciding who to assign to a certain machine on a given day. Managers should be flexible in their decision making, just as in any other aspect of their job.

Policies, procedures, and rules provide a framework for decision making, thus freeing managers for more challenging and difficult problem solving. Managers are little more than clerks, however, if they simply adhere to the rule book and do not exercise some personal judgment.

Nonroutine Decisions

While routine decisions may take up a considerable portion of a manager's time, individuals succeed or fail as managers on the basis of their nonroutine decisions. **Nonroutine decisions** are *decisions designed to deal with unusual problems or situations.* The decision to expand to foreign markets, build a new production plant, or buy a more advanced computer system are examples of nonroutine decision situations. Warner Communications' decision to sell its Atari unit was a nonroutine decision. Managers at all levels in the organization make nonroutine decisions. Nonroutine decisions made by a first-line supervisor might include firing an employee or changing the layout or procedures in the department.

nonroutine decisions

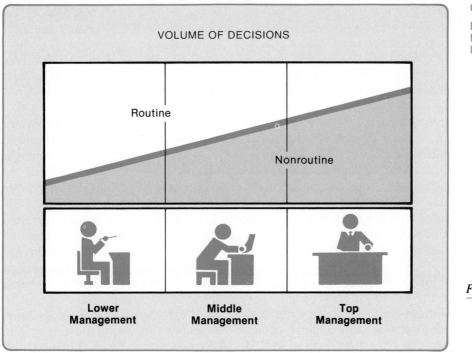

VOLUME OF DECISIONS

Routine

Nonroutine

**Lower
Management**

**Middle
Management**

**Top
Management**

Figure 5–2

*Managerial Levels and
the Amount of Routine
versus Nonroutine
Decisions*

Figure 5–2 illustrates the relationship among three levels of management and the time devoted to routine and nonroutine decisions. As a manager progresses to higher levels, the number of nonroutine decisions increases. Nonroutine decisions require that managers exercise creativeness, good judgment, and even intuition.

Time Available

The amount of time that can be devoted to decision making is often a critical factor. Managers would prefer to have sufficient time to evaluate and analyze thoroughly all alternatives prior to making a decision, but few have this luxury. Decisions frequently must be made in time-pressure situations. When Coleco began to air its "Sorry, Atari" ads, Atari could not wait to see what effect they would have before intensifying its own advertising program. As another example, assume that a customer of yours offers to make a large purchase at a low, though profitable, price. Assume further that the order must be accepted today or the buyer will go to another supplier. Even if you have good reasons to prefer taking your time with such decisions, you dare not do so.

MURPHY
OIL CORPORATION

When Robert Sweeney graduated from college at the age of twenty, he did not realize that one day he would be president of a company with over 4,400 employees and annual sales of $2.57 billion. His success did not happen overnight. On his way to the top, Mr. Sweeney served as a reservoir engineer, chief reservoir

*Robert J.
Sweeney*

engineer, chief engineer, assistant manager of production and exploration, president of Murphy Eastern Oil Company, and in 1972 became president and chief operating officer.

When questioned regarding any critical events in his life, Mr. Sweeney said that a change of employment decision was one. "The decision to leave Arkansas Natural Companies and join Murphy Oil in 1952 was a major one," he said. "As I recall, the Arkansas Natural Companies were subject to a consent decree negotiated by Cities Service, the majority stockholder, and the Justice Department. Under the terms of the consent decree, the utility businesses were to be divested and the oil and pipeline businesses merged into Cities Service. Because of this situation I think it fair to say that the Arkansas Natural Companies had been forced into a holding pattern pending implementation of the consent decree. In any event, I knew I was dissatisfied with the trend of things, but coming to Murphy was a soul-searching decision. I wanted to work for a large corporation, and Murphy at the time was a family-owned enterprise with assets perhaps around $50 million and thirty-five or forty employees. I also knew that it was difficult to move from a small company to a larger one. In general, companies tend to promote from within or hire outside people from larger companies, not smaller companies. To the extent this was true, my chances of ever regaining employment with a large company appeared minimal if I accepted the Murphy offer. After talking with Mr. Murphy, however, I was convinced that he fully intended to build a large company. I simply placed my bets on his ability and took the job."

Being too young nearly caused him some problems. Sweeney commented, "Because I graduated from college at a relatively early age (twenty) and was lucky in the sense of having a knack of being in the right place at the right time, I usually found myself to be quite young for the position I held at any given time. Further, my bosses were always relatively young; therefore I could never see any clear-cut path of progression during most of my career with Murphy. In the end, though, I always decided against alternative employment because I was happy with my work; I was comfortable with the high ethical standards of the Murphy enterprise; and, in fact, history had proved me wrong over and over again as regards my being 'boxed in.' In short the good things associated with working for the Murphy enterprise always outweighed the increased income that might be realized through a change."

Finally, Mr. Sweeney said, "I will never know, of course, whether I made the proper decision at any of these critical moments, but I do know that I am reasonably pleased with the way it turned out and have no desire to turn back the clock and run the 'gauntlet' again."

Risk Associated with the Decision

decision risk

Decision risk is *exposure to the probability that an incorrect decision will have an adverse effect on the organization.* It is a factor that all managers consider, consciously or unconsciously, in decision making. For instance, Betty Harris, president of a small book publishing company, is considering paying $100,000 to a well-known author to write a book. If the book sells well, the firm could make $500,000, but if the book does not, Harris's company will lose the $100,000 plus an additional $75,000 in developmental and promotional cost. She may decide not to take the risk if the loss of $175,000 could put her company out of business.

On the other hand, the purchasing manager for General Motors often signs contracts for automobile parts that greatly exceed $1 million. The risk in such decisions is low because of the size of the organization. Even the loss of $1 million for General Motors would not have a disastrous effect on the firm. As the decision risk increases, more time and effort are often devoted to individual decisions.

Degree of Acceptance and Support by Equals and Superiors

At times new managers are not immediately accepted. Perhaps the manager is in a division where most of the other managers are much older. One of Robert J. Sweeney's concerns was his youthfulness in comparison with others who held similar positions. A similar concern exists for a manager who is a female in a male-dominated organization. If the acceptance and support by other managers is lacking, it is up to the individual to overcome the problem. Think of how Cathy Martin, a supervisor of computer programmers for a major store operation, got support for her decisions. Talking about her first few weeks on the job, Cathy said:

> When I took the job, I really didn't realize what I was getting into. Everybody seemed to hate the programming department. The previous chief programmer had just rammed things down the throats of other managers. Top management was committed to putting everything on the computer. So, the chief programmer was given free rein. I knew that if I made many mistakes, my job would be difficult. Unlike the previous supervisor, I was younger than most of the managers that I had to work with. They thought that I was a "whiz kid." I tried to dispel that impression by seeking their advice before I made changes that affected their departments. I became a politician. Although I was overwhelmed by the workload, I made it a point to have coffee or visit with at least one other manager every day. It took a while, but now I believe we have an excellent working relationship with everyone, from accounting to purchasing.

Cathy was able to overcome her problem by establishing a good working relationship with other managers. She realized that gaining the acceptance of other managers was an important aspect of getting the job done.

A lack of acceptance on the part of subordinates can also limit a manager's ability to make decisions and get them implemented. Solutions requiring close cooperation may not even be feasible if subordinate acceptance is lacking. Perhaps the best way for a manager to gain acceptance is to earn subordinates' respect. Making an effort to improve communication and involve workers in the decision-making process helps develop a feeling of mutual respect. When Lee Iacocca came to Chrysler, he kept his reputation for working harder than anyone else, coming to work early and staying late. It was also clear that he knew his job and was willing to put out extra effort to get the job done. Any manager who wishes to gain subordinate acceptance may have to work hard to get it.

There is another side to the matter of gaining the support of subordinates. Lee Iacocca had to make drastic changes at Chrysler and

*Management involves
establishing good
working relationships
with other managers.*

Ellis Herwig/The Picture Cube

knew that many managers would resist his efforts. He simply replaced a number of these with faithful subordinates he had known in his previous position at Ford Motor Company. This, coupled with his charismatic leadership qualities, undoubtedly improved the cooperativeness of others.

Perhaps the most important factor affecting decision making is a manager's own ability and attitude. While Harry Truman was president of the United States, he kept a plaque on his desk that stated, "The buck stops here." He was the person responsible, and he was always willing to make the final decision. Still, no matter how willing a person is to make decisions and be responsible for them, they need the ability to make correct decisions. To some degree, this is dependent on following an appropriate decision-making process.

A manager's own experiences and level of understanding also help determine the quality of that manager's decisions. Experience tends to be a good teacher, as evidenced by the fact that many college recruiters place major emphasis on the experience a student has gained from business and extracurricular activities. They believe the learning process for a particular job may be shortened if a student has been active in other endeavors while in college. But decision makers who rely only on experience may base a judgment mainly on their feel for the situation. If such decision makers confront situations to which they have not been previously exposed, faulty decisions often result. For instance, when Nolan Bushnell decided to sell Atari for $28 million, his feeling probably was that he was getting a fair price. Within a few years, however, the price Warner paid seemed to have been far too low. Basing decisions only on experience has several obvious shortcomings, among them:

1. Learning from experience is usually random.
2. Although we may have experience, there is no guarantee we learned from it.
3. What we learn from experience is necessarily circumscribed by the limits of our experience.
4. Conditions change, and the past may not be a good indicator of current or future conditions.[3]

The question may be asked, "Do you have twenty years of experience, or do you have one year of experience twenty times?" Ralph C. Davis's classic statement summarizes the need for a bond between experience and intellect for a professional decision maker:

A man who has nothing but background is a theorist. A man who has nothing but practical experience is a business mechanic. A professionally trained executive is one in whom there is an effective integration of these two general types of experiences, combined with adequate intelligence regarding the types of problems with which he must deal.[4]

THE SCIENTIFIC METHOD

A widely used approach to carrying out individual phases of the decision-making process is the scientific method. **The scientific method** is *a formal way of doing research that comprises observation of events, hypothesis formulation, experimentation, and acceptance or rejection of hypothesis.*

the scientific method

Observation of Events

The scientific method requires that a person has the desire to explore fully the relationships among the elements of a system and a curiosity to know how and why they produce a particular outcome. The process usually begins with the discovery that something is not as it should be. For example, several years ago Ram, Inc., an Omaha, Nebraska, parts distributor, was experiencing a high level of employee turnover. This problem was forcibly brought to the attention of Geri Hodges, Ram's personnel manager, when she had to recruit seven new workers in a single week.

Hypothesis Formulation

hypothesis

The second step in the scientific method is the creation of one or more possible explanations of the causes of the problem. A **hypothesis** is *a tentative statement of the nature of the relationships that exist.* A hypothesis provides an explanation of the cause that brought about the observed effect. For instance, after some study, Geri Hodges decided that a possible cause of the high turnover was the perception of low pay by employees.

Experimentation

After the hypothesis has been clearly stated, it should be subjected to one or a series of tests to determine whether the tentatively stated relationship does in fact exist. Tests confirm or support the hypothesis or prove it to be unsound. Geri Hodges decided to do a simple survey to determine if her initial hypothesis was correct. In the survey, she asked employees to offer suggestions for improvements at Ram.

Acceptance or Rejection of Hypothesis

The final step in the scientific method is the acceptance or rejection of the hypothesis. Upon studying the results of her survey, Geri Hodges noted that seven out of ten of the employees surveyed listed higher pay first or second among the ways suggested to improve conditions. This convinced her that her initial hypothesis was correct.

GROUP METHODS INVOLVED IN DECISION MAKING

Up to this point we have discussed decision making as if it were a process carried out by the individual manager. In most organizations, individuals are responsible for the outcomes of decisions under their control. However, there are several ways that groups can be involved in any stage of the process. Three of these are brainstorming, nominal grouping, and the Delphi technique.

Brainstorming

brainstorming

Brainstorming is *an idea-generating technique wherein a number of persons present alternatives without regard to questions of feasibility or practicality.* Through brainstorming, individuals are encouraged to identify a wide range of ideas. Usually one individual is assigned to record the ideas on a chalkboard or writing pad. Brainstorming may be used at any stage of the decision-making process but is most useful as a means of generating alternatives once a problem has been stated. Sometimes the alternatives produced through brainstorming may be rather bizarre. For example, if a brainstorming group were to consider how Atari might respond to Coleco's advertising program, one of the ideas might be to buy out Coleco. Building on this, another participant might suggest selling out to Coleco. No criticism is allowed because the purpose is to come up with innovative possibilities. Evaluation can wait until later and is not part of brainstorming.

Nominal Grouping

Nominal grouping represents an attempt to move away from the unstructured approach of brainstorming and yet to encourage individual creativity.[5] **Nominal grouping** is *an approach to decision making that involves idea generation by group members, group interaction only to clarify the ideas, member rankings of ideas presented, and alternative selection by summing ranks.* The steps are as follows:

nominal grouping

1. *Statement of the problem.* After the nominal group is assembled, the group leader states the decision problem clearly but succinctly. No discussion is allowed, although group members may ask questions to clarify the problem.
2. *Idea generation.* Group members silently record and number their ideas for solving the problem.
3. *Round-robin recording.* The group members alternatively present their ideas while the group leader lists the ideas presented on a flip chart or chalkboard. The process continues without discussion until all of the ideas have been recorded.
4. *Clarification of ideas.* Under the leader's guidance, group members question one another to clear up any confusion about what each idea means. No evaluation is allowed yet.
5. *Preliminary voting.* Each group member independently ranks what are considered the best several of the decisions presented. The ideas that receive the lowest average ranks are eliminated from further consideration.
6. *Discussion of revised list.* Individual group members question one another to clarify the ideas that remain. The purpose is not to persuade but to understand.
7. *Final ranking.* Group members rank all of the ideas. The one with the highest total ranking is adopted.

This technique is called *nominal grouping* because members act independently. Thus, they form a group in name only, or nominally. An important feature of this technique is that it allows the members to meet face to face but does not restrict individual creativity as traditional group discussions often do.

Delphi Technique

The **Delphi technique** is *a formal procedure for obtaining consensus among a number of experts through the use of a series of questionnaires.* The procedure is similar to nominal grouping but participants do not meet.

Delphi technique

In fact, ideally the experts do not know who else is involved. The steps in the Delphi technique are as follows:

1. The problem is presented to group members through means of a questionnaire that asks them to provide potential solutions.
2. Each expert completes and returns the questionnaire.
3. Results are compiled and provided to the experts, along with a revised and more specific questionnaire.
4. The experts complete the second questionnaire. The process continues until a consensus emerges.

Although the Delphi technique prevents the respondents from being influenced by the personalities of the other participants, it does make provision for the sharing of ideas. Unlike nominal grouping, the end result is a consensus decision. This method was conceived by the Rand Corporation to forecast how seriously a nuclear attack would affect the United States. It is expensive and time consuming and generally has been limited to important and futuristic ideas.

MANAGEMENT INFORMATION SYSTEM

*management
information system
(MIS)*

No attribute of an organization is as important to decision making as the management information system. A **management information system (MIS)** is *any organized approach for obtaining information on which to base management decisions.* The MIS should be designed to provide information with the following characteristics:

- Timely—up to date.
- Accurate—correct.
- Concise—only important data are presented.
- Relevant—provides information that the manager needs to know.
- Complete—information that is needed to make a decision is provided.

The absence of even one of these characteristics creates difficulty in decision making. Modern MISs typically use computers, word processors, and other sophisticated technologies. Because computers are so important to decision making today, we have reserved the last two main sections of this chapter for a discussion of computers and the trends in their use.

The MIS draws information from an organization's functional areas, such as marketing, production, and finance, and integrates this information. Thus, a unified body of knowledge is provided for decision making. The MIS should provide a means of processing business transactions to reflect the day-to-day operations of an organization and providing management with useful information in time to assist in decision making.

Each level of management makes unique demands on the MIS. Top managers require the most information from the external environment. For example, they need to know about government legislation, economic trends and forecasts, and competitors' activities. Lower-level managers depend primarily on internal data. These managers focus on such things as when inventory items should be reordered and the number of workers to assign to a specific project. Top-level managers usually will want only product data that is summarized, perhaps by quarter. Lower-level managers may need production data on a daily or even hourly basis.

A successful MIS must produce several types of output. These are:

- *Routine reports*. Business data are summarized on a scheduled basis.
- *Exception reports*. Major variations requiring management's attention are highlighted.
- *On-demand reports*. Information is provided in response to specific requests.
- *Forecasts*. The outputs of predictive models are reported.

Let us consider four recommended steps in designing an MIS that will provide these kinds of output in conformity with the criteria mentioned earlier.

Study the Present System

In assessing the existing MIS, we might ask these questions: (1) What is the present flow of information? (2) How is the information used? (3) How valuable is this information in terms of decision making? At one stage in his career, Wayne Mondy was a team member in charge of developing one of the first integrated state highway information systems. Detailed analysis was done of all discernible information flows and uses. One of the agencies involved was the state highway patrol. In conversations with local troop members, Wayne discovered that only the weekly report to headquarters caused special difficulty. For each troop (there were thirteen) it took one officer about four hours to prepare the report. Wayne went to headquarters to determine how the data were used in the decision-making process. He found that the reports were neatly filed by a secretary, and the data were never used. When one of the reports was not submitted on time, however, the secretary was directed to prepare a letter of reprimand to the unit commander. Identifying this kind of deficiency is the reason for asking the third question above.

Develop a Priority of Information that Managers Need

Once the current system is thoroughly understood, it is used to develop a priority of information that managers need. There is certain information a manager must have if proper decisions are to be made, but some are merely nice to have—not critical to the manager's job performance. The MIS design must ensure provision of the high-priority information. Data lower in the priority list should be generated only if their benefits exceed the costs of producing them. The weekly report described above should not have had the priority it was accorded.

One approach to prioritizing information needs is to have individual managers develop their own priority lists and to integrate them into a list for the entire organization. Certain departments may discover that the information they identify as top priority will be far down the organization's list. The needs of the entire organization must be the controlling factor.

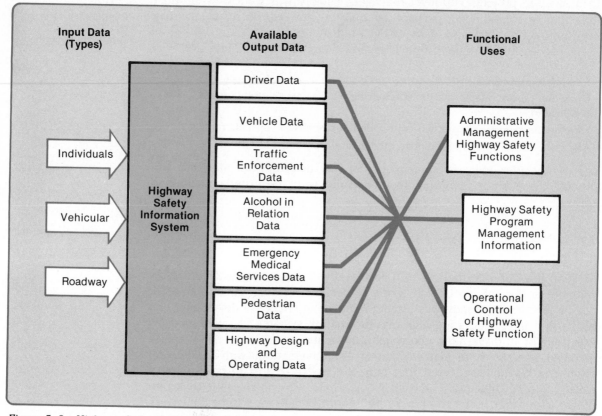

Figure 5–3   Highway Safety Information System

Develop the New Information System

The organization's information needs priority list should govern the design of the new MIS. A system of required reports should be developed and diagrammed. Treating the whole organization as a unit allows the elimination of duplicated information. At a certain point on the priority list, the information is not worth the cost of providing it and should not be included.

After a thorough study of the existing highway information system discussed above and setting of priorities, the diagram shown in Figure 5–3 was prepared to show how the system should function. The summary diagram was supported by many detailed reports and procedures. As can be seen, there are several types of necessary input data. On the output side, the system provides various types of information for both administration and operations. All departments are tied together. Data that come in from one department of the state can provide the information used in another department. If a person has a car wreck and is given a ticket, this information not only is used by law enforcement agencies but also forms a data base to identify high-accident locations. When an MIS is properly designed, the important information an organization needs in the decision-making process is available.

Choose a Computer

Today it is reasonable to assume that the MIS for any significant-sized organization will make use of a computer. Because of the ever-expanding use of computers, it is becoming increasingly important for managers to be "computer literate"; however, managers need not be data-processing experts, just as they do not need to be skilled accountants. Of course, managers do need some accounting knowledge to understand and interpret financial reports. They also need to know what computers can and cannot do. Managers need to know enough to make good decisions regarding the use of computers. Computers certainly should not be feared. Their use is far too pervasive and their usefulness far too great.

A mistake many firms make is to purchase or lease a computer and then attempt to design the information system around the computer. If a computer is needed to provide accurate, timely, and useful information, the computer chosen should provide the best capability of processing the data that management needs. There are many sizes and capabilities of computers from which to choose.

TYPES OF COMPUTERS

Traditionally, computers have been classified as micros, minis, and mainframes, but the boundary lines have recently become fuzzy. One way of distinguishing among types of computers is according to price. A micro is said to be any computer that costs $5,000 or less. A mini is said to sell for up to $50,000 and a mainframe far more than that. A problem in using cost as a distinguishing feature is that for the same amounts of money, you can buy a much more capable computer today than you could a few years ago. Recognizing that the distinction among types of computers is not clear, let us use them to describe how computers are used today.

Microcomputers/Desktop Computers

Microcomputers are not just for small businesses. Large corporations use thousands of them. Because of their flexibility, micros make the job of management much simpler. The microcomputer can be a stand-alone tool for the busy executive. It can show financial trends, answer "what if" questions, and even keep the executive's calendar. Some managers who previously wrote memoranda in longhand now zip them out on the keyboard. Micros may give executives access to corporate data bases or sophisticated programs when the microcomputer serves as a terminal to a mainframe system. They are used in research and development laboratories, on shop floors, and in hospitals. Microcomputers acquire data, take measurements, and control all kinds of processes in ways that greatly simplify manufacturing and production. They can be used in remote locations such as offshore oil well platforms. They also work well in adverse environments, such as on ships and airplanes. Micros can automatically change the settings of valves and other control devices in responses to changes in physical conditions such as pressures and temperatures. Industrial robots often depend on

*Computers are more
important to the
workplace than ever
before.*

Ellis Herwig/Stock, Boston Inc.

microcomputers to help them do factory assembly operations formerly too complex for mechanization.

Many engineering firms today specialize in computer-aided design and computer-aided manufacturing (CAD/CAM). The cost of CAD/CAM has been greatly reduced through the use of powerful microcomputers, some of which even small engineering and machine shops can afford. Because of their application to every stage of the product development cycle, microcomputers have made major contributions toward meeting the productivity challenge, which was discussed in Chapter 1.

In every kind of organization and at every level, microcomputers simplify the job of administration. Traditional office paperwork is created and processed with computer help. Because microcomputers can communicate with one another, many written reports and other documentation have even been eliminated. Word processing software is available to assist in entering, arranging, correcting, retrieving, and printing all types of business information and correspondence.

Minicomputers

Between the mainframe computer and the microcomputer is the minicomputer. A mini may look much like a micro. Minis have faster internal processing speeds and larger memories. They are also likely to have a larger number of terminals and other peripheral devices. Minis were developed because they could meet particular needs at significantly lower costs than could large computer systems. They are also much easier to install and have fewer environmental restrictions.

Mainframe Computers

At the upper end of the spectrum are computers costing millions of dollars and capable of handling vast amounts of data. Included within this category are the IBM Model 158 and 168 and the Burroughs B7800 and B7900. Amdahl Corporation, Cray Research, and Control Data Corporation have developed huge "supercomputers" to meet the information-processing needs of such organizations as national laboratories, university research centers, financial service companies, and service bureaus. Many of these systems can do millions of computations per second. Simulation, design and engineering work, and applications requiring large data bases can be handled effectively when large-computer capabilities are available.

TRENDS IN THE USE OF COMPUTERS

Changes in computer technology are occurring virtually daily. It is impossible to foresee all the new uses for computers that will occur. The only certainty is that managers must be alert to these innovations if they are to remain competitive in this rapidly changing world. Some trends are discussed below.

Videotex

The remote display on a TV-type screen (cathode ray tube or CRT) of information from computer files and data bases is referred to as **videotex**. The growth of videotex is expected to be dramatic. It is expected to change the way many firms do business. Banking at home is already possible in some cities. Some stores allow customers to order from television displays of merchandise. And some major newspapers are planning to transmit their contents to videotex subscribers.

videotex

Teleconferencing

Partly because of the high cost, in both time and money, of business travel, teleconferencing is becoming increasingly popular. **Teleconferencing** is *the method of conducting or participating in discussions by telephone or videophone.* One or more of the participants in a teleconference may be able to see the others. Teleconferencing may become a major means of not only improving managerial communications and productivity but of lowering cost as well.

teleconferencing

Voice Mail

Voice mail is *spoken messages transmitted electronically and stored for delivery to the recipient at a later time.* When a voice mail system is used,

voice mail

an individual gains access by dialing a special number and stating or dialing a password and user identification number. The user may then listen to any new messages, listen again to old messages, eliminate messages, and record messages for others.

Robotic Systems

robot

The use of robots in industry is increasing at a dramatic pace. A **robot** is *an automatically controlled machine that can perform mechanical tasks.* To date, robotic systems have had the greatest impact on the automobile, steel, and aerospace industries. General Motors has been a leader in using robotics and plans to have about 14,000 industrial robots in use by 1990. Other automakers are following suit because the use of robots has promoted high product quality and uniformity, as well as increased production efficiency.

The most advanced robots have touch sensors (allowing them to "feel") and optical scanners (allowing them to "see"). Some robots "learn" new patterns of movement by being led through an operating cycle only once. For example, a certain robotized paint sprayer will paint a series of identical automobiles after an experienced painter controls the painting the first time.

Costs of robotic systems vary widely, ranging from under $8,000 to more than $170,000. Even costs near the high end are easy to justify because robots can work around the clock and demand no fringe benefits. Since modern robots are electronically controlled, they can be made to generate data for management reports and for diagnostic purposes.

Artificial Intelligence

artificial intelligence (AI)

The successes in computer technology during the 1950s led many to believe it possible to develop computers that "think." Although the debate continues as to whether that has or even can come about, researchers have been working for more than two decades in an area they call **artificial intelligence (AI)**. This is *the field of information technology that attempts to simulate human cognitive processes, such as learning, reasoning, problem solving, and natural language communication.* A leader in the field is Artificial Intelligence Corporation of Waltham, Massachusetts. That company markets software that allows computer users to question the computer in ordinary English. If the computer does not understand any of the words used, it will so inform the user, ask for a definition, and add the new word to its vocabulary; thus, the computer can "learn" just as the robot described in the previous section "learns."

In terms of human thinking, reasoning is perhaps a step beyond learning, but a number of systems currently in use simulate human reasoning processes. At Stanford University, a computer-directed analyzer diagnoses certain blood infections. SRI International employs a system called "Prospector," which reads seismographic information and identifies possible mineral deposits. Of course, computers do not actually reason in the sense that we normally think of the term, but many of the tasks that require reasoning on the part of humans can be done by computers. As the definition above suggests, developing computer systems that do such tasks comes under the heading of artificial intelligence.

A related area of AI research concerns communication using ordinary language. This was mentioned above in connection with the systems that answer queries typed in at the keyboard. It also includes voice synthesizers, which create a voice output from computers, and speech recognition programs, which translate voice inputs into language the machine understands. Voice synthesizers have already received wide usage, notably at many grocery store check-out counters, where a voice announces the prices as the checker sweeps the product across an optical scanning device. Voice recognition, on the other hand, has proved more difficult to develop. Although a number of systems accept voice commands, the vocabularies of those systems typically consist of just a few hundred words. Clearly this technology will move along, and voice recognition will see increasing use. AI is a truly exciting field that promises great benefits in terms of productivity and the quality of life.

SUMMARY

Decision making is the process of generating and evaluating alternatives and making choices among them. The decision-making process consists of the following steps: (1) identifying the problem or opportunity, (2) developing alternatives, (3) evaluating alternatives, (4) choosing and implementing the best alternative, and (5) evaluating the decision.

Several factors can affect decision making. Routine decisions made by managers are governed by the policies, procedures, and rules of the organization, as well as the personal habits of the managers. Nonroutine decisions are those decisions that are designed to deal with unusual problems or situations. Another factor to be considered is the amount of time that can be devoted to decision making. Decision risk, the third factor, is exposure to the probability that an incorrect decision will have an adverse effect on the organization. The fourth major concern is the degree of acceptance and support by equals and superiors. Finally, perhaps the most important factor affecting decision making is the decision maker's own ability and attitude.

A widely used approach to carrying out individual phases of the decision-making process is the scientific method. The process begins with the recognition that something is not as it should be. The second step is the creation of one or more possible explanations of the causes of the problem. Next, the hypothesis should be subjected to one or a series of tests to determine whether the

tentatively stated relationship does in fact exist. The final step in the scientific method is the acceptance or rejection of the hypothesis.

Groups can be involved in any stage of the decision-making process in several ways. Brainstorming is an idea-generating technique whereby a number of persons present alternatives without regard to questions of feasibility or practicality. Nominal grouping is an approach to decision making that involves unrestrained idea generation by individual group members and alternating presentation of those ideas, without discussion, followed by group discussion to clarify and evaluate the ideas and group decision making through individual ranking of the ideas. The Delphi technique is a formal procedure for obtaining consensus among a number of experts through the use of a series of questionnaires.

A management information system (MIS) is an organized approach for obtaining information on which to base management decisions. The MIS should be designed to provide information with the following characteristics: timely, accurate, available, concise, relevant, and complete. The general steps that should facilitate the development of a useful MIS include: (1) study the present system, (2) develop a priority of information, (3) develop the information system, and (4) choose a computer. Some trends in the use of computers include videotex, teleconferencing, voice mail, robotic systems, and artificial intelligence.

1. Define decision making and identify the steps in the decision-making process. How important do you feel it is to a manager?

2. What is meant by the following statement: "The ability to select the best course of action from several possible alternatives often separates successful managers from less successful ones"?

3. This text identifies several factors that can have an impact on the manager's decision making. Identify and briefly discuss each.

4. What are the steps involved in the scientific method?

5. Define each of the following terms:

   a. Brainstorming
   b. Nominal grouping
   c. Delphi technique

6. Define a management information system (MIS) and list the characteristics of a properly designed MIS.

7. List the steps involved in developing an MIS.

8. Describe each of the following trends in the use of computers:

   a. Videotex
   b. Teleconferencing
   c. Voice mail
   d. Robotic systems
   e. Artificial intelligence

EXERCISES

1. Assume that you are CEO of Warner Communications (see the story at the beginning of the chapter). As Atari's fortunes are worsening, explain the alternatives you believe Warner has and describe how you would select among them.

2. Apply the scientific method to a decision you have recently made. Would this have changed your decision? Explain.

CASE STUDY

A Request for Special Favors

"My husband has made plans for us to go, and he says we are going," said Barbara Kener. Barbara was a payroll clerk at Wellingham Corporation, a Brockton, Massachusetts shoe manufacturer. Barbara had just asked Jerry Wall, the payroll department manager, if she could take a week of vacation the first week of January to visit her husband's family. Jerry had tried to talk her out of it because of the heavy work load during that period, but Barbara clearly felt strongly about taking the time off.

It had been customary for payroll department clerical personnel to schedule their vacations at times other than during January because it was then that the payroll department had the most to do. All of the individual payroll records had to be finished, and a wide range of reports, including the employee W-2 forms for 2,000 employees, had to be completed. Jerry was not even sure that he would be able to meet the deadlines for preparation of the reports without Barbara's help. Barbara was an especially efficient worker and, although she had been employed only since March, Jerry had come to depend on her.

Jerry recalled that when Barbara was hired, he had failed to discuss the need for avoiding January vacations, telling her only that she would be eligible for one week of vacation for each six months of employment. Jerry felt somewhat responsible for the misunderstanding. But he knew that letting Barbara take her vacation as requested might hurt morale in the department, even if the work load could be handled. Not only would the others have to work harder, but Jerry remembered having turned down two special requests for January vacations in the past.

1. What should Jerry do about Barbara's request? In answering this question, use the decision-making process developed in the chapter.
2. What situational factors should Jerry consider in making the decision? Why?

CASE STUDY

At Odds over a Computer

In March 1985, Leon and Roy Sivils were hotly debating whether their small company ought to buy a computer. For the third time in as many years, Roy had brought up the subject. "I think we have a pretty good system now," said Leon. "Look, Leon," replied Roy, "I don't know of any other company the size of ours which doesn't have a computer. Besides, the cost has gotten so low, an Apple or a Radio Shack or a Kaypro costs only a little more than a typewriter. I don't think we can afford not to computerize."

Roy and Leon are the owners of the TAC Agency, Inc., which owns and operates a number of residential sewer and water systems around Fort Wayne, Indiana. The TAC Agency had about 2,500 customers in 1985. Each customer was billed every month for sewer or water service, or both. Until then the bills had been prepared by hand. Cash receipts were manually recorded on individual ledger cards. The work was done by part-time employees hired at minimum wage.

Going back over the records for the previous year, Roy had found eighty posting errors in customer account records. Some payments had been credited to the wrong accounts, and other customers had been credited with payments that had not been made. Most of the mistakes made in the company's favor had been pointed out by customers and corrected. The ones that Roy found in the customer's favor had generally remained undiscovered.

After Roy explained this to Leon, Leon agreed that TAC needed a computer. "I wonder if we can use it to help us to decide how much to pay for water and sewer systems?" asked Leon. Roy answered, "I don't know, but I know how to find out. I'll call Mike Freeman, a programmer I know, and ask him to visit with us about it."

QUESTIONS

1. Should Roy and Leon buy a computer? Explain the pros and cons of that decision.
2. From the little you know about the TAC Agency, what uses might be found for a microcomputer, if the company buys one?

NOTES

1. This story is a composite of a number of published accounts, among them: Robert Gerson, "Atari's Falcon and Other Scrambled News," *Video Review* (May 1983): 134; Paul Trachtman, "A Generation Meets Computer on the Playing Fields of Atari," *Smithsonian* (September 1981): 50–61; B. Anne Pillsbury, "Warner's Fall from Grace," *Fortune,* January 10, 1983, pp. 82–83; "Atari's Struggle to Stay Ahead," *Business Week,* September 13, 1982; "Atari: The Problem Child That Warner Can't Get Rid Of," *Business Week,* September 24, 1984, p. 110; and numerous articles in the *Wall Street Journal.*

2. Theodore Levitt, "The Managerial Merry-Go-Round," *Harvard Business Review* 52 (July–August 1974): 120.

3. Adapted from Alvar O. Elbing, *Behavioral Decision in Organizations* (Glenview, Ill.: Scott, Foresman, 1970), p. 14.

4. Ralph C. Davis, *The Fundamentals of Top Management* (New York: Harper, 1951), p. 55.

5. A. L. Delbecq and A. H. Van de Ven, "A Group Process Model for Problem Identification and Program Planning," *Journal of Applied Behavioral Science* 7 (1971): 466–492.

REFERENCES

Archer, Ernest R. "How to Make a Business Decision: An Analysis of Theory and Practice." *Management Review* 69 (February 1980): 54–61.

Brown, Rex V. "Do Managers Find Decision Theory Useful?" *Harvard Business Review* 51 (May–June 1970): 78–89.

Daniel, D. W. "What Influences a Decision? Some Results from a Highly Controlled Defense Game." *Omega* 8 (November 1980): 409–419.

Davis, Ralph C. *The Fundamentals of Top Management.* New York: Harper, 1951.

Delbecq, A. L., and A. H. Van de Ven. "A Group Process Model for Problem Identification and Program Planning." *Journal of Applied Behavioral Science* 7 (1971): 466–492.

Dutton, J. E., L. Fayey, and V. K. Narayanan. "Toward Understanding Strategic Issue Diagnosis." *Strategic Management Journal* 4 (October–December 1983): 307–324.

Elbing, Alvar O. *Behavioral Decision in Organizations.* Glenview, Ill.: Scott, Foresman, 1970.

Grayson, C. Jackson, Jr. "Management Science and Business Practice." *Harvard Business Review* 51 (July–August 1973): 41–48.

Hagarth, Robin M., and Spyors Mankridaks. "Value of Decision Making in a Complex Environment—An Experimental Approach." *Management Science* 27 (January 1981): 93–107.

Henderson, John C. "Influence of Decision Style on Decision Making Behavior." *Management Science* 26 (April 1980): 371–386.

Hughes, Robard Y. "A Realistic Look at Decision Making." *Supervisory Management* 25, no. 1 (January 1980): 2–8.

Kirby, Peter G. "Quality Decisions Start with Good Questions." *Supervisory Management* 25, no. 8 (August 1980): 2–7.

Levitt, Theodore. "The Managerial Merry-Go-Round." *Harvard Business Review* 52 (July–August 1974): 120.

McKenny, J. L., and P. G. W. Keen. "How Managers' Minds Work." *Harvard Business Review* 52, no. 3 (May–June 1974): 79–90.

Mangrum, Claude T. "Determining the Right Regimen of Managerial Exercises." *Supervisory Management* 26, no. 2 (February 1981): 26-30.

Meyer, Alan D. "Mingling Decision-Making Metaphors." *Academy of Management Review* 9 (January 1984): 6–17.

Nitzan, Shmuel, and Jacob Paroush. "Small Panels of Experts in Dichotomous Choice Situations." *Decision Sciences* 14 (July 1983): 314–325.

Pitz, Gordon F., Natalie J. Sachs, and Joel Heerboth. "Procedures for Eliciting Choices in the Analysis of Individual Decisions." *Organizational Behavior and Human Performance* 26, no. 3 (December 1980): 396–408.

Roy, Delwin A., and Claude A. Simpson. "Expert Attitudes of Business Executives in a Smaller Manufacturing Firm." *Journal of Small Business Management* 19 (April 1981): 16–22.

Sherman, Stratford P. "Microsoft's Drive to Dominate Software." *Fortune,* January 23, 1984, pp. 82, 84, 88, 90.

Simon, Herbert A. *The New Science of Management Decision.* Rev. ed. Englewood Cliffs, N.J.: Prentice-Hall, 1977.

———. "Rational Decision Making in Business Organization." *American Economic Review* 69, no. 4 (September 1979): 493–513.

Tjosvold, Dean. "Effects of Crisis Orientation on Managers' Approach to Controversy in Decision Making." *Academy of Management Journal* 27 (March 1984): 130–138.

Vroom, Victor H. "A New Look at Managerial Decision Making." *Organizational Dynamics* 1, no. 4 (Spring 1973): 66–80.

Wright, Peter. "The Harassed Decision Maker: Time Pressures, Distractions and the Use of Evidence." *Journal of Applied Psychology* 59, no. 5 (October 1974): 555–561.

AIROMATIC TOOL, INC. (ATCO)

On a cold December morning James Holt got into his 1962 Thunderbird to go to work at Custom Valve Manufacturing Company, a firm that he and his brother, Brad, started six months previously. The only thing different about this particular morning was that the old, reliable T-Bird would not back out of James's garage. The reverse gear band had snapped in the transmission, and James was stranded in his garage. Being mechanically inclined, James proceeded to repair the car himself after calling his office to tell them that he would be late. He changed clothes, grabbed some wrenches, and slipped under the car to make what he thought would be an easy adjustment. After four hours of frustration, James finally emerged from under the T-Bird. He had succeeded in repairing the car, but his hands were sore and battered, and he was muttering to himself—"There must be a better way."

This experience remained in James's mind along with the need for a tool that would have prevented the battering of his knuckles and fingers, as well as his psyche. Stimulated by this experience, in addition to his background in plumbing, carpentry, air-conditioning and heating, and television repair, he began attempting to develop a concept of a power wrench. After a year of research and design, trial and error, he produced a prototype of the first "pneumatic ratchet wrench." After about six months, he and his brother, Brad, had invested considerable time and almost $12,000 of Custom Value's very limited capital in this project. About a year from his experience in his garage trying to repair his car, James and Brad had successfully developed what they thought would be a highly useful power tool.

The Holts now had a new product with seemingly great potential, but no market research had been conducted to estimate the demand for the product. A patent attorney was employed, and a U.S. patent was acquired on the new wrench. Several of the prototypes were loaned to mechanics for the purpose of "testing" the product to see if it would perform what the mechanic needed when repairing an automobile. Without exception, the mechanics indicated that they were very impressed with the pneumatic wrench and greatly encouraged the Holts to produce and market it. Encouraged and excited by the mechanics' reactions, James and Brad Holt decided to form a new company, Airomatic Tool, Inc., which would manufacture the tool. Shortly after forming the new company, the brand name ATCO was adopted, and the officers of the firm were James Holt, president; Brad Holt, vice-president; and Danny Jones, secretary-treasurer. All three men were excellent mechanics, and while none were graduate engineers or designers, all three possessed strong technical expertise. Each of the three had only limited management experience and none had any prior background in marketing.

ATCO's first problem was that of acquiring needed developmental capital. Commercial lenders were not willing to risk the needed capital with so little collateral on a new product venture. Finally, the U.S. Small Business Administration, through the Security Bank of Cato, Texas, provided a $120,000 loan to ATCO to purchase equipment and build a 5,600-square-feet building. A condition of this loan was that ATCO would be moved to Cato, a small town of about 600 located approximately sixty-five miles from Dallas.

The new facilities were developed and ATCO started producing the air-powered ratchets. Sales were initially slow, and working capital was soon exhausted. In December 1970, another Small Business Administration loan through the Security Bank of Cato was granted for the amount of $76,000.

James had continued to be very active in the research and development area. He had developed three additional models of the "air ratchets," an air drill, an impact wrench, swivel hose assemblies, and a twin connector for air hoses. He acquired patent rights to all these products except the twin connector.

With the additional working capital, the corporation started producing all of these products. However, the basic pneumatic ratchet accounted for about 75 percent of sales.

COMPETITION

The attributes of the pneumatic ratchet wrench and the market potential of the product were very apparent and immediately drew attention from domestic and foreign tool manufacturers. Within two years after ATCO had introduced the new tool concept, two large domestic producers and one Japanese manufacturer had comparable tools on the market. These firms had discovered weaknesses in the patents and engineered around the ATCO products. The exclusive rights to the swivel hose connector was considered one of the greatest losses to the firm since it was becoming a universal accessory used with all pneumatic hose products. ATCO believed these competitive products were outright infringements on its patent rights but did not have the money to get involved in lengthy court battles with these large firms.

The larger competitors had established channels of distribution available for the new products along with huge promotional budgets. They were able to price their products lower than ATCO due to lower operating costs and the acceptance of lower margins. These firms had other successful products to spread costs over and their total volume was much greater than ATCO's, thus permitting lower unit margins. One competitor rapidly moved into private branding of its pneumatic ratchet with several large retailers.

MARKETING

Initially ATCO sales were brisk, and it was difficult for the company to keep pace with demand for the new pneumatic ratchet. By the end of the first year of being on the market, pneumatic tools sales reached 300 units per month. Barely into the second year of operation, the company accepted a contract from a large distributor for 1,000 units per month. ATCO did not have the production capacity to meet this demand, but in an effort to try, the company either dropped or significantly limited its supply to other clients. This, naturally, greatly irritated ATCO's other purchasers who were forced to obtain their wrenches from ATCO's competitors. The contract with the large distributor was dropped the next year, and ATCO was left "holding the bag." This event created considerable misfortune for ATCO, making it difficult for them to continue in business. Since competition had increased significantly, most of ATCO's older clients had shifted their business to other suppliers. Suddenly, ATCO was faced with virtually no market demand and more plant capacity and labor than was needed. After the large distributor cancelled its contract for 1,000 pneumatic ratchets per month, demand for ATCO's products was at fewer than 300 units per month.

ATCO utilized industrial distributors as the primary element of its distribution system. The company had no full-time sales staff of its own, although James Holt attempted to make personal calls on all corporate distributors. James indicated that this was most difficult, and he was not able to consistently accomplish these sales calls. Despite James Holt's personal sales calls, management had very limited feedback from the final users of the wrenches. The Holts did very limited advertising, but ATCO did conduct a direct mail campaign directed at all independent garage owners in Texas. This campaign involved a series of three mail-outs describing ATCO's products. However, the firm received only very limited response to the mail-outs. A survey of competitive products indicated that ATCO's prices were higher than most of the other companies in the industry.

FINANCES

Sales of ATCO had peaked at just over $1 million three years after the firm began operations but had recently declined to about $500,000. After earning a profit after taxes of $76,000 the second year in business, ATCO sustained a net loss of $124,500 in their most recent year.

Pondering the financial results of the past year, James and Brad Holt were wondering if ATCO could survive. And if the firm was to survive, what actions would be necessary?

QUESTIONS

1. Identify the problems at ATCO. What were the causes of these problems?
2. Could the problems have been avoided? If so, how?
3. Would the concept of strategic planning, or other elements of planning, have helped ATCO management? Discuss.
4. Describe the backgrounds and experiences of the managers at ATCO. Were they capable of adjusting to increasing competition?

This case was prepared by R. Dean Lewis formerly of Sam Houston State University and Robert E. Holmes of James Madison University as a basis for class discussion rather than to illustrate either effective or ineffective handling of an administrative situation. Presented at a Case Research Association Workshop and distributed by the Intercollegiate Case Clearing House, Soldiers Field, Boston, Mass. 02163. All rights reserved to the authors.

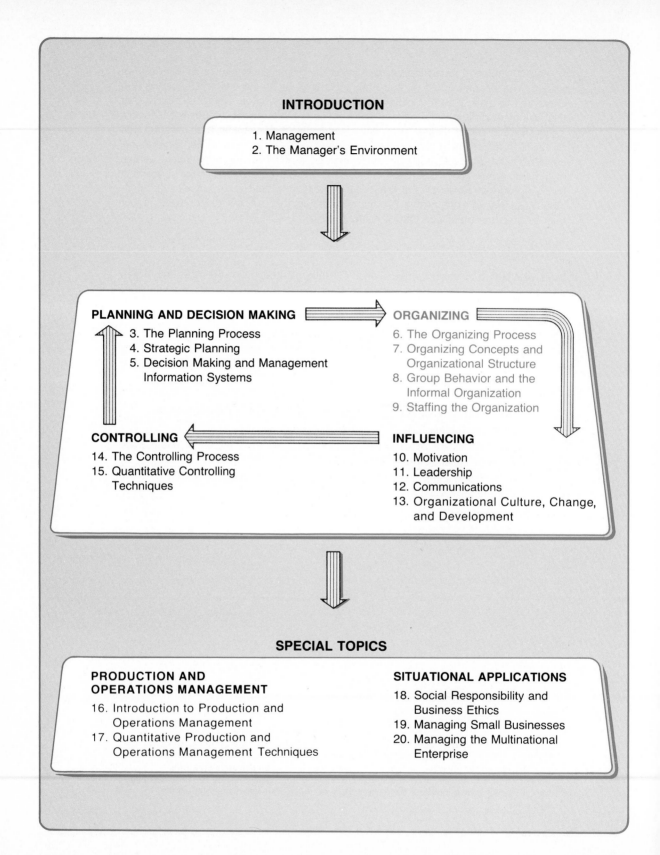

INTRODUCTION

1. Management
2. The Manager's Environment

PLANNING AND DECISION MAKING

3. The Planning Process
4. Strategic Planning
5. Decision Making and Management Information Systems

ORGANIZING

6. The Organizing Process
7. Organizing Concepts and Organizational Structure
8. Group Behavior and the Informal Organization
9. Staffing the Organization

CONTROLLING

14. The Controlling Process
15. Quantitative Controlling Techniques

INFLUENCING

10. Motivation
11. Leadership
12. Communications
13. Organizational Culture, Change, and Development

SPECIAL TOPICS

PRODUCTION AND OPERATIONS MANAGEMENT

16. Introduction to Production and Operations Management
17. Quantitative Production and Operations Management Techniques

SITUATIONAL APPLICATIONS

18. Social Responsibility and Business Ethics
19. Managing Small Businesses
20. Managing the Multinational Enterprise

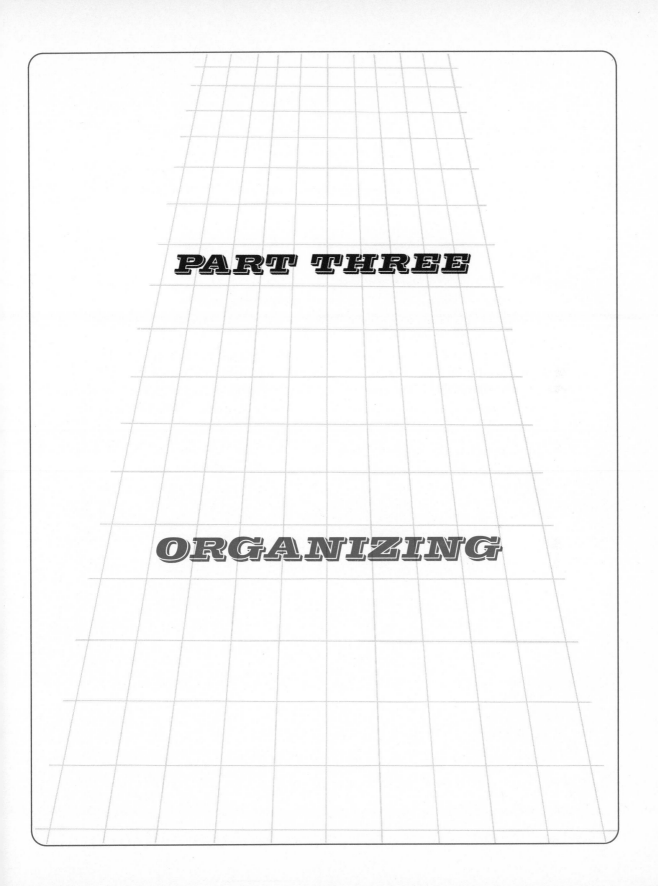

PART THREE

ORGANIZING

KEY TERMS

organization
organizing
function
specialization of labor
departmentation
vertical differentiation
horizontal differentiation
coordination

LEARNING OBJECTIVES

After completing this chapter you should be able to

1. Define organization and describe the organizing process.
2. Define function and specialization of labor and identify the benefits and limits of specialization of labor.
3. Identify and describe the primary means of departmentation.
4. Identify and describe the factors that determine the extent to which functions should be grouped in an organization.
5. Describe and give examples of vertical and horizontal differentiation.

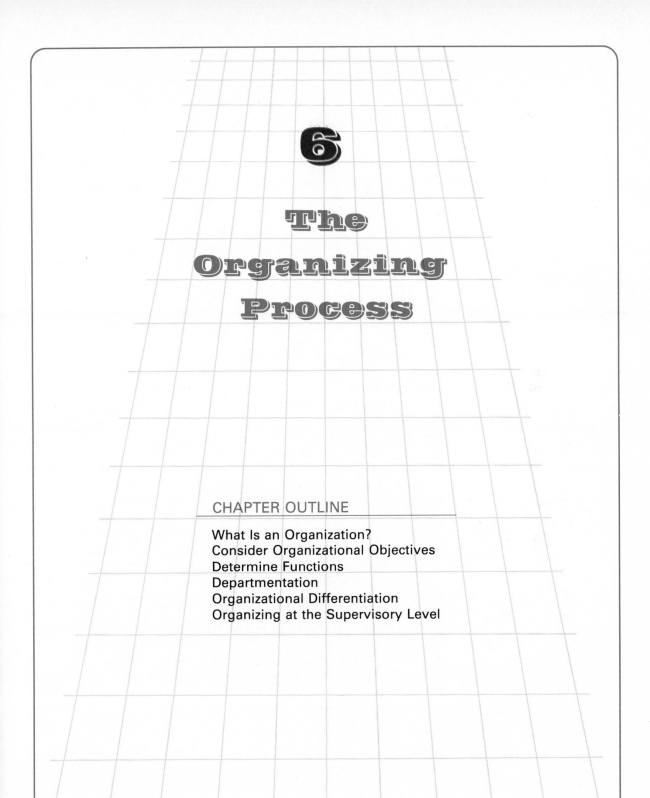

6

The Organizing Process

CHAPTER OUTLINE

WAL-MART With over $4.7 billion in sales, Wal-Mart stores is the nation's seventeenth largest retailing company. The company has about 700 stores, most of them in the South and Southwest. Wal-Mart is headquartered in the tiny town of Bentonville, Arkansas, where the Wal-Mart saga began with a single store twenty years ago. In terms of sales and profit growth, Wal-Mart has recently been consistently first among the top 100 retailers, clocking gains as high as 50 percent per year in both categories.

The man credited with Wal-Mart's success is its affable chairman, Sam Walton. Walton and the other senior managers still spend several days a week going from store to store visiting with store managers and employees—who are called "associates"—about ways to improve the operation. Walton calls this the "grass-roots management style."

The company stresses participation. Not only are managers expected to interact with their people on a daily basis, but there is a mandatory meeting once a year to gather suggestions that will be passed on to top management. The view of employees as associates is more than window dressing. It is not uncommon to see a store manager or department chief cleaning up a spill or cleaning handprints off the store's glass doors, and every employee is encouraged to own stock in the company.

Although management at Wal-Mart emphasizes individual initiative and autonomy, managers are accountable for results. Every store manager must prepare a monthly financial statement listing each expenditure, from taxes and rent to paper clips and telephone charges. District managers are required to review each report and discuss ways to reduce expenses.

Rex Chase, who oversees ten Wal-Mart stores in Texas, says that his group of store managers and associates is "like family." He continues, "The hardest part of my job is when I have to demote someone. If I can go an extra mile with him—and some people fault me because I go the extra mile—I can save that man. I've done him a favor and I've done the company a favor."[1]

By all accounts, Sam Walton is a master of organization. He has to be to manage a $4 billion home-grown enterprise with over 600 separate units. The managerial function of organizing is similar whether one is concerned with managing a university, a hospital, a government organization, or a large company like Wal-Mart.

In this chapter, we will define organization and then provide an overview of the organizing process. Next, a section of the chapter is devoted to each component of the process. Then, the organizational differentiation that results from growth will be discussed. Finally, organizing at the supervisory level will be described.

WHAT IS AN ORGANIZATION?

The term *organization* is widely used; most of us are reminded of it each day as we read newspapers, walk about the university campus, watch television programs, or listen to the radio. When some of us hear the word *organization,* we think of large companies such as Sears, General Motors, and U.S. Steel. Few of us are reminded of the local grocery store, service station, fast food restaurant, or nursery school. Each of these, however, is an organization too.

Organizations, large or small, have at least these three common characteristics:

1. They are composed of people.
2. They exist to achieve goals.
3. They require some degree of limitation on member behavior.

Thus, an **organization** is defined as *two or more people working together in a coordinated manner to achieve group results.* Since most of us spend a considerable part of our lives working in organizations, it is important to understand fully how organizations function and how organizations can be managed effectively. To be effective, a manager must be capable of organizing *human resources, physical factors,* and *functions*—production, marketing, finance, personnel—in a manner designed to ensure the achievement of the goals of the firm. This process is crucial to the success of every organization where people work together as a group.

organization

Organizing is *the process of prescribing formal relationships among people and resources to accomplish goals.* The organizing process is illustrated in Figure 6–1.

organizing

External Environment

As we discussed in Chapter 2, the external environment affects the organizing process. For instance, laws and public concern about clean water and air may create the need to add personnel to monitor any substances a company discharges.

The necessity to deal with a wide range of suppliers and to buy in large volumes requires a sophisticated purchasing department at company headquarters. Differences in legislation from state to state require that someone be responsible for helping individual store managers stay within the law.

More than in the past, rapidly changing technology influences the organizing process. For example, new automotive technology has required U.S. automobile manufacturers to make major changes in assembly lines, which had changed little from those developed by Henry Ford before 1920. Robots now do repetitive tasks previously done by humans. In some plants,

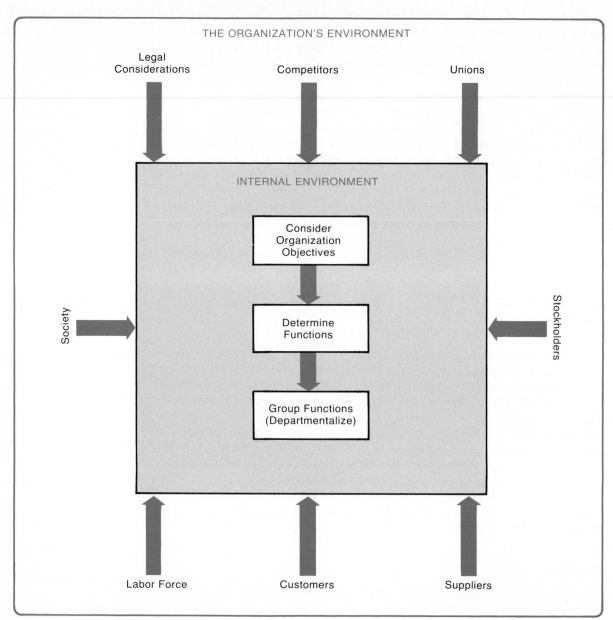

Figure 6–1   The Organizing Process

cars are assembled at work stations rather than on mile-long assembly lines. Similar rapid technological change is occurring in virtually every industry segment. As changes in the manufacturing process occur, organizations must be able to respond with new and more flexible ways of assigning persons and machines to jobs.

Internal Environment

The organizing process is also influenced by the internal environment that the individual manager faces. As we pointed out in Chapter 2, the internal environment consists of such factors as the management style of the boss, written guidelines, and the informal organization. The approach to organizing that an individual manager uses must be compatible with the internal environment. For example, the company's procedure manual may specify the manner in which machinery can be rearranged and personnel regulations may restrict reassignment of workers.

The boss's view of the company's strategic and operating plans will limit the way a manager can organize resources to carry out those plans. At Chrysler Corporation, for example, it is well known that Lee Iacocca places emphasis on product quality as well as on low cost. Therefore, managers at Chrysler must create organization units that tightly control quality *and* contain no "fat" in the form of additional management levels or positions.

Let us now consider the organizing process that exists within such environmental constraints. As Figure 6–1 illustrates, it is first necessary to consider organizational objectives before attempting to determine the kind of organization needed to accomplish those objectives. Next, management must determine the functions, or activities, that will be required. Finally, a number of departments or separate organizational units are set up, each designed to carry out a separate function or group of functions.

CONSIDER ORGANIZATIONAL OBJECTIVES

Everything the manager does should be directed toward goal accomplishment. Organizing is no exception. It should have as its purpose arranging people and resources in the best way possible to support the organization's objectives. At Wal-Mart, a major purpose is to earn high profits through discount merchandising. This purpose dictates that the Wal-Mart organization be able to respond quickly to moves of competitors while keeping costs at a minimum inside the company. There is no room, for example, for four or five levels of highly paid managers at Wal-Mart. A typical store manager directs a number of moderately paid department supervisors who not only manage groups of workers but do work themselves. It is important that every phase of the organizing sequence be directed at goal accomplishment.

DETERMINE FUNCTIONS

Once objectives have been established, it is necessary to determine the types of functions or work that must be performed within the organization. A **function** is *a type of work activity that can be identified and distinguished from other work.*

function

On a typical baseball team, players perform the basic functions of fielding, hitting, and pitching. A good team must develop specialists capable of each of these activities. The pitching function can be further broken down into the necessity for starters, long-term relievers, and short-term relievers. The team also has infielders who specialize in playing third base, shortstop, second base, and first base.

As in the baseball example, basic functions or work activities can be defined in any business, government, or educational organization. The major

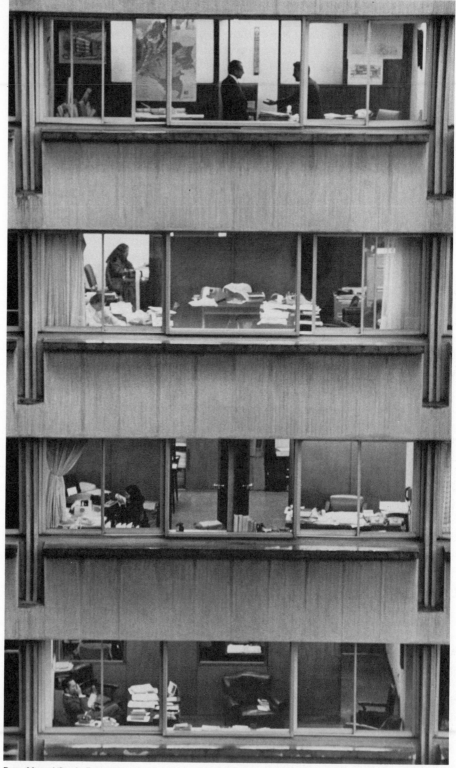

*Most of us spend a
considerable part of
our lives working in
organizations.*

Peter Menzel/Stock, Boston Inc.

functions of a manufacturer are production, marketing, and finance. For a retailing company, like Wal-Mart, the basic functions are buying and selling of merchandise and extending credit. The major activities in a bank include depositing or receiving a customer's money and making loans to borrowers. In a university, teaching, research, and service are the main functions that must be performed.

Saying that the primary functions at Wal-Mart are buying and selling does not provide an adequate basis for organizing a store. Selling sporting goods is certainly different from selling lingerie. It is appropriate to consider these as two separate functions. There are also a number of supporting functions that require special skills. For example, store buildings must be maintained. Shelves must be stocked, money must be collected from the cash registers, and someone must approve checks. The point of all this is that, as part of the organizing process, functions must be described in great detail. Generalities will not suffice.

Specialization of Labor

In his 1776 book, *The Wealth of Nations,* Adam Smith explained how he was able to increase the productivity of a group of pin makers by more than a thousand-fold through specialization (division) of labor. **Specialization of labor** means *the division of a complex job into simpler tasks so that one person or group may carry out only identical or related activities.* A purpose of organizing, like everything else the manager does, is to improve productivity. Through specialization of labor, it is possible for a member of the organization to specialize, resulting in increased output. Specialization is especially essential for the achievement of efficiency in mass-production industries. In fact, most work activities performed in nearly all organizations are of a specialized nature. For example, a stocker in a Wal-Mart store normally would not be expected to operate a cash register.

specialization of labor

Organizations have endless options as to the degree of specialization associated with each job. For instance, if a company produces small transistor radios, several different approaches might be available, such as:

1. Each employee assembles the entire radio (low specialization).
2. Each employee assembles one component of the radio (moderate specialization).
3. Each employee performs a few routine operations such as putting the knobs on for tuner and volume control (high specialization).

Advantages of Specialization

Specialization may offer five specific benefits. First, specialization often increases productivity. A worker who is able to concentrate skill and effort on a small number of tasks can usually achieve a high level of output. In manufacturing electronic components, output per worker tends to be much higher in situations where employees perform highly specialized work activities. Similarly, high performance results are apparent in many fast food restaurants such as McDonalds where employees perform specialized functions, for example, cooking hamburgers or french fries.[2] This is in contrast to more traditional restaurants where employees may perform a wide variety of jobs.

Second, specialization may permit a manager to supervise a large number of employees. A manager may be able to supervise effectively thirty to fifty workers who are performing the same specialized tasks. If workers are performing a number of diverse tasks, the number of employees that a manager can effectively supervise is fewer.

Third, it decreases training time. A more specialized job can be learned more quickly than a job with numerous work activities. When training time is reduced, the workers become productive at a faster rate. For instance, the time required to train a worker to cook french fries or prepare milk shakes would be minimal when compared with the time required to learn all the jobs performed in a fast food restaurant.

Fourth, specialization contributes to consistently higher-quality products and services. It has been said that we live in an age of specialization, one in which most people are employed as specialists. Many students who choose to pursue a degree in business administration specialize in accounting, computer information systems, finance, management, or marketing. Few other professions demonstrate the move to specialization more than medicine. As more is learned about each phase of medicine, entire careers emerge concentrating on a specific part of the body or a specific symptom. Forty or fifty years ago, most medical doctors treated all ailments of each member of the family. Now most physicians specialize, becoming pediatricians, cardiologists, ophthalmologists, proctologists, and so forth. By specializing in a narrow range of the medical profession, a physician is able to offer the best diagnosis and treatment the current research and technology of that field has available.

Finally, specialization facilitates the achievement of complex goals. The successful completion of any complex project usually requires a number of specialists. The United States' successful space program would not have been possible without the contributions of thousands of specialists. The National Aeronautics and Space Administration assembled a team of specialists, each knowledgeable regarding a particular phase of the project. Similarly, the design and construction of airplanes or the construction of large buildings often requires the contributions of many specialists.

Disadvantages of Specialization

Despite the advantages of the specialization of labor, its application may not always be desirable. In some organizations, certain jobs have become oversimplified. Too much specialization in the design of jobs may create boredom and fatigue among employees. For example, some people find it very difficult to perform an assembly-line job requiring the tightening of a bolt 1,000 times a day. Typically the highest degree of specialization is found in assembly-line work. Boredom on assembly lines sometimes causes employee turnover, absenteeism, and a deteriorating quality of output. These negative consequences of specialization may offset its advantages and increase costs.

A number of companies have established programs to overcome the disadvantages of specialization. Others have actually reduced the degree of specialization. General Motors is experimenting with using work teams, with team monitors assigned on a rotating basis. This gives each worker a feeling of involvement in the effort to improve the quality and quantity of output. Shaklee Corporation has installed a unique management philosophy at its new plant in Norman, Oklahoma. There, small groups of employees make, inspect, and package a diverse array of products. The teams establish their own production schedules and working hours. They select new workers from a pool approved by the personnel department and can even initiate discharges.[3]

Efforts to overcome the detrimental effects of specialization were intensified in the 1980s with the publication of such books as *Theory Z* and *In Search of Excellence,* which touted what has come to be called "Japanese management." The result was the institution of quality circles and other participative devices, especially in industries that compete directly with the Japanese.

DEPARTMENTATION

The process of grouping related functions or major work activities into manageable units is known as **departmentation**. The purpose of departmentation is to contribute to more effective and efficient use of organization resources. In this section we will first discuss how functions should be grouped in an organization. Then common types of departments will be described.

departmentation

Grouping Similar Functions

Ideally, each department or division in the organization should be made up of people performing similar tasks. This is the concept of functional similarity. This principle guides us in the creation of sections, departments, and divisions. Jobs with similar objectives and requirements are grouped to form a section. A person with the background necessary to supervise these functions effectively should be assigned as the manager. For example, a construction company might employ a plumbing crew, an electrical crew, and so forth. Each different crew performs a group of related functions. At Wal-Mart, the data processing section performs only tasks involving computers and does not become involved in other functions, like managing the in-store restaurants.

As important as functional similarity is, there are a number of factors that affect our ability to achieve it throughout the organization. Several of these are discussed below.

Sufficient Volume of Work

Sometimes the volume of work is inadequate to allow specialization. In small firms, personnel have to cope with a wide assortment of jobs. But with increases in volume, the concept of functional similarity can be applied more rigorously. For example, let us compare the operations of a small grocery store with those of a large supermarket. In the small store, one person might perform such functions as stocking shelves, working in the produce section, checking, and bagging groceries. In the large supermarket, personnel will tend to specialize in one or only a few of the basic functions. It is common to have individual managers of the produce section and the stocking, checking, and bagging functions.

Tradition, Preferences, and Work Rules

Although the tasks may be similar, traditions, work rules, and personal preferences may prevent their assignment to a certain individual. For example, installing electrical conduit (the steel pipe that protects electrical wire) is quite similar to running water piping; however, few plumbers would be willing to run conduit, and electricians would usually object to installing water pipes. This is because of the set of behavioral expectations, duties, and responsibilities that individuals associate with a given position.[4] In unionized organizations, formal work rules often prohibit the assignment of plumbers to electrical work or electricians to plumbing and other such violations of tradition.

Functions Similar to Others in the Organization

A third complicating factor is that the particular function in question is often similar to other functions. For example, inventory control would appear to fit logically with the purchasing function. The purchasing department buys the material and thus has need for records of inventory levels; however, production uses these materials and in scheduling must work with these same inventory records. Inventory control could be placed in either section.

Separation of Functions to Prevent Conflicts of Interest

Sometimes similar functions are not combined because doing so might create conflicts of interest. Quality control is intimately involved in production; inspectors frequently work side by side with production employees. The inspector, however, should not be unduly influenced by the production manager's interest in quantity and costs. Thus, inspection, although similar to production, should be separate from production to protect its independence.

Combining Dissimilar Functions to Allow Coordination

Finally, there are occasions when two dissimilar functions must be combined for purposes of effective action and control. Although purchasing is clearly differentiated from selling in a factory organization, buying and selling are so interdependent in department stores that one person is often made responsible for both. The theory is that a well-bought dress or hat is half-sold.

Kinds of Departments

There is no standard way to divide an organization into departments. Even companies in the same industry often have vastly different kinds of departments; however, it is possible to identify five bases on which departmentation normally occurs. The resulting kinds of departments are: (1) functional, (2) product, (3) customer, (4) geographic territory, and (5) project.

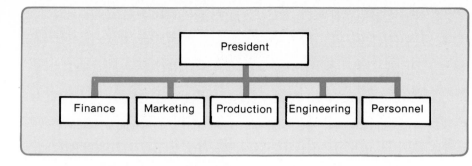

Figure 6–2

*Departmentation by
Function*

Departmentation by Function

Departmentation by function is perhaps the most common means of grouping related functions. Under this approach departments are formed on the basis of specialized functions, such as production, marketing, engineering, finance, and personnel (Figure 6–2). This has the advantage of allowing specialists to be grouped together so that they can become more efficient. Departmentation by function is especially useful in stable environments where technical efficiency and quality are important.[5] Undoubtedly, functional specialists also feel more comfortable working with others of similar background and experiences. Departmentation by function may create certain problems for management, however. Employees in specialized departments may become more concerned with their own department than with the overall company. Because of the sometimes conflicting purposes of various departments, upper management must ensure that an effective means of coordination exists.

An example of interdepartmental conflict occurred at Tennco Products Company's Tubular Products facility near Memphis, Tennessee. The personnel director asked the production manager to hire more women machine operators, thinking that this would be a simple task. The production manager argued that qualified women were not available and top management demands for increasing efficiency made taking time to train women impractical. In the end, more women were hired, but only after the president became involved and encouraged production and personnel to settle their differences.

Departmentation by Product

Product departmentation is concerned with organizing according to the type of product being produced and/or sold by the firm. This enhances the application of specialized knowledge of particular products or services and is often used by rather large, diversified companies. Figure 6–3 shows the organization of a large electronics firm divided into three product divisions. Firms manufacturing and selling technologically complex products are often set up in this way.[6]

Until 1983, General Motors was divided into five product divisions: Chevrolet, Pontiac, Oldsmobile, Buick, and Cadillac. Because of what GM executives call "creeping complexity," the company has recently been reorganized, resulting in only two product divisions: the Chevrolet, Pontiac, and GM Canada division and the Buick, Cadillac, and Oldsmobile division. Small cars will be designed and manufactured by the first group and intermediate and large cars by the latter.[7]

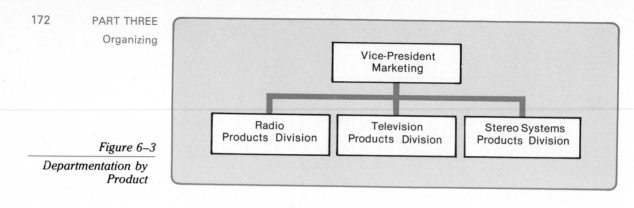

Figure 6–3

Departmentation by Product

Departmentation by Customer

Departmentation by type of customer is used by organizations that have a special need to provide better service to different types of customers. As illustrated in Figure 6–4, a diversified manufacturing company may have industrial, government, and consumer sales divisions. A U.S. Steel salesperson who deals with obtaining government contracts simply maintains good relations with purchasing agencies and makes sure that U.S. Steel has opportunities to bid. Selling to industrial customers, in contrast, requires greater emphasis on personal persuasion and long-standing relationships. A person who does well in one area may be a failure in the other. Banks also use departmentation along customer lines. For example, commercial loan officers deal only with business customers, while consumer lending specialists make personal loans. When client satisfaction is the main competitive issue, especially in an uncertain environment, customer departmentation is often appropriate.[8]

Departmentation by Geographic Territory

Grouping activities according to geographic territory is used by organizations that have physically dispersed and/or noninterdependent operations or markets to serve. The marketing function of the company shown in Figure 6–5 is organized into the southern, western, and eastern regional divisions. Geographic departmentation offers the advantages of better services with local or regional personnel, often at less cost. Division by geography is the single most common scheme for international

Figure 6–4

Departmentation by Customer

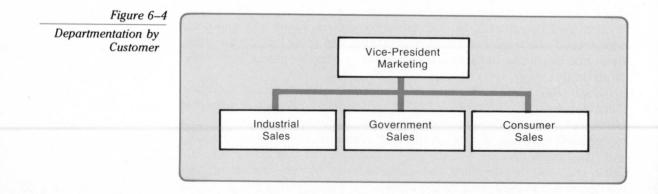

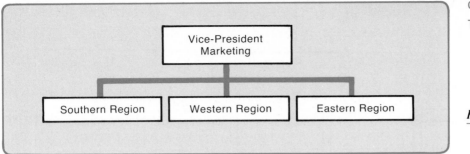

Figure 6–5

Departmentation by Geographic Territory

companies. For example, when Wendy's hamburgers decided to expand into Europe, it faced a very different competitive and legal environment from that in the United States. Therefore, a separate division was established for the European operations. Geographic departmentation is most effective when the corporation's activities are widespread and there are few product lines.[9]

Departmentation by Project

When the work of an organization consists of a continuing series of major projects, departmentation by project normally occurs. This is especially common in the construction industry. Figure 6–6 shows how a typical construction operation might be departmentalized. In this example, each project superintendent is responsible for a separate contract under the direction of the general superintendent. Such an organization changes frequently as projects are completed and new ones started. The superintendent who is now in charge of Project A may transfer to a new project or back to headquarters or be laid off when Project A is finished. In addition,

Figure 6–6   Departmentation by Project

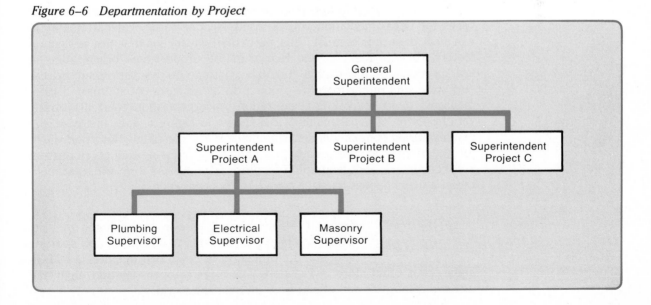

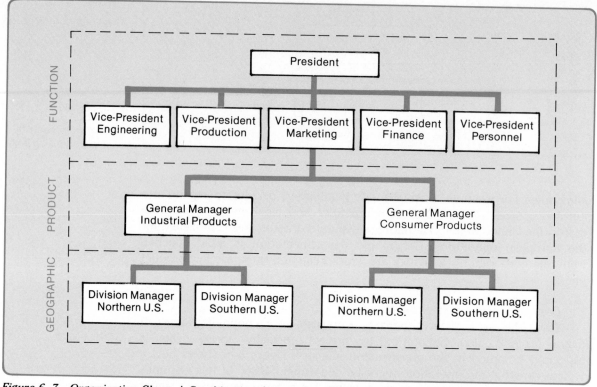

Figure 6–7   Organization Chart: A Combination Approach to Illustrating Departmentation

the plumbing supervisor currently working on Project A may move to Project C when the plumbing on Project A is complete.

Departmentation: A Combination Approach

Unless the organization is quite small, it is likely that several different bases for departmentation will be used. No one form of departmentation can meet the needs of most firms, particularly in such companies as General Motors, General Electric, and Exxon. In the product-type organization at GM, portions of the design function continue to be performed by the corporate staff rather than the product divisions. Also, GM still uses district managers in its marketing organization. An organization chart illustrating various forms of departmentation is shown in Figure 6–7. In this case, the manufacturing company is departmentalized by type of functions performed (engineering, production, marketing, and so on), type of products (industrial and consumer), and geographic territory. The precise form of departmentation a firm chooses must be based on its own needs.

Freeport Firestone: Branching Out

≡FREEPORT
≡FIRESTONE

Freeport, Maine, is well known as the home of L. L. Bean Company, a catalog merchandiser of sporting goods and clothing. L. L. Bean also operates a 50,000-square-foot retail store in Freeport. The store is open day and night and attracts celebrities and others from all over the world.

Woodrow Shepherd, who now owns Freeport Firestone, started out as an L. L. Bean employee in 1969. The owner of the only Gulf Oil station in Freeport died in 1974, and the service station came up for sale. Woodrow quit his job with L. L. Bean and invested his life savings plus $20,000 in borrowed funds in the service station. At first, Woodrow worked from daylight to dark six days a week. He employed only one helper, Joe Gross, who pumped gas, fixed flats, and did whatever else Woodrow needed him to do. As Freeport grew over the next ten years, Woodrow's business did also. It was not long before the bookkeeping was too much for him, so he asked Mrs. Shepherd to start coming in half days to take care of that.

Woodrow added on to his service station and got the Firestone tire franchise in 1976. The tire business was especially profitable, so Woodrow spent most of his time in the tire department selling, installing, and repairing tires. By that time, Joe Gross had become a seasoned and dependable attendant. So Woodrow hired another man to help Joe take care of the service island. He also hired a helper in the tire department.

By 1980, Woodrow found it necessary to replace Mrs. Shepherd with a full-time bookkeeper. He also employed an additional worker and a supervisor in the tire department. This freed Woodrow to keep a watch on the work Joe was doing at the service islands and spend a little more time keeping track of bookkeeping and financial matters.

Until 1981, Woodrow called the place simply "Shepherd's Gulf Station." That year, he had a nice sign painted and changed the name to Freeport Firestone.

Business continued to expand, and by 1984 Woodrow had installed another service island and added a tire and battery showroom next to the tire service bays. Since the L. L. Bean store was open all night and generated significant traffic, Woodrow had hired a night manager to keep the service islands open until midnight. At that time, Freeport Firestone employed fourteen persons full time and two part time.

The town of Freeport had grown to about 25,000 in population, and Woodrow thought about opening a smaller service station and tire center at the opposite end of Main Street. He missed waiting on customers himself and realized that if he opened another outlet, he would have to hire managers for both stores and would probably have to spend all his time solving problems and coordinating the activities of his subordinates. He decided to do it anyway, and by 1985 ground had been broken for the new branch of Freeport Firestone.

ORGANIZATIONAL DIFFERENTIATION

In a newly formed small organization, an owner-manager performs all the major functions of the business, such as providing the necessary financing, procuring materials, designing the product, and making and selling the product. This was the case with Woodrow Shepherd of Freeport Firestone when he first opened his service station. As the volume of business grows, the work required will increase beyond the capacities of one person. With the employment of additional personnel, vertical and horizontal differentiation must occur. When Woodrow Shepherd decided to hire Joe Gross, he had to describe the tasks Joe would perform, that is, differentiate them from other tasks. Joe has to pump gas and fix flats, among other duties. A new

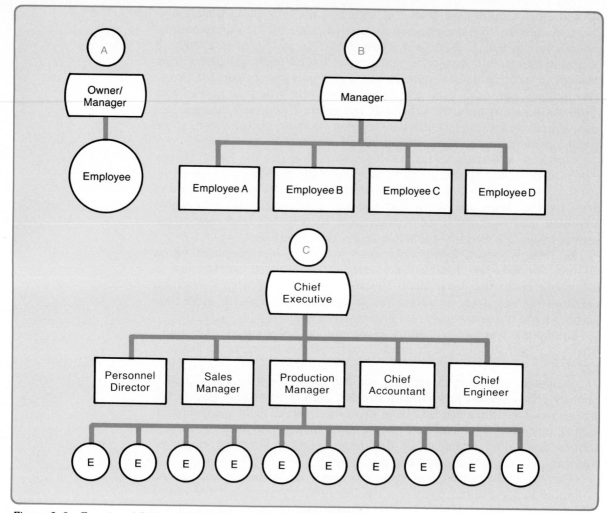

Figure 6–8   *Functional Differentiation Downward and Outward*

level in the organization had been created, even though Freeport Firestone was only a two-person firm (Section A of Figure 6–8).

vertical differentiation

The process of creating additional levels in the organization is defined as **vertical differentiation**. Initially there are just two levels, managerial and operative. But managers like Woodrow Shepherd usually do not assign all the operative work to a subordinate. Woodrow continued to wait on customers and often worked alongside Joe Gross in addition to supervising him. In the early stages of organizational growth, functions considered vital to success and that require special expertise, like sales and finance, often continue to be done by the manager.

horizontal differentiation

As the volume of business continues to grow, additional personnel will be added and more operative functions differentiated and allocated. *The process of forming additional units at the same level in the organization* is called **horizontal differentiation**. The result is shown in section B of Figure 6–8. For Freeport Firestone, this occurred when Woodrow hired a person to help Joe on the service island and a helper for the tire department. Although Woodrow continued to do operative work for a time, he knew that the management job would soon become too demanding for him to continue doing so. Woodrow Shepherd employed horizontal differentiation because the work load became too great. Another reason for adding additional workers or departments at a given level is because the original manager may find that certain functions can be more effectively and economically performed by a specialist. For example, a manager may find sales a weak area because of ineffective or inadequate training programs. Therefore, a sales trainer would be employed to take over that phase of the business so the manager can devote more time to other areas. As in the case of Freeport Firestone, horizontal growth usually occurs at lower levels as additional workers are required. When the number of workers exceeds that which one manager can supervise, additional supervisors must be added. As the organization grows, horizontal differentiation usually results in functions being split off that are most complex and least similar to other functions of the firm.

As shown in section C of Figure 6–8, horizontal differentiation usually results in several functional departments being created. If the organization continues to grow, further vertical and horizontal differentiation will be needed. Figure 6–8 shows how personnel, production, and engineering might be further subdivided, resulting in an additional level of managers. When differentiation occurs, coordination is required. **Coordination** is *the process of ensuring that persons who perform interdependent activities work together in a way that contributes to overall goal attainment.* Coordination assumes a greater importance as the organization becomes more complex. For example, the manager of the company illustrated in Figure 6–9 would have to be much more concerned with coordination than was Woodrow Shepherd when his only employee was Joe Gross.

coordination

ORGANIZING AT THE SUPERVISORY LEVEL

Thus far we have viewed organizing as if it were strictly the province of top-level management. Organizing is important for any manager, even first-line supervisors. Organizing decisions at this level might include determining who will work on a particular project this week, how the workplace will be arranged, and the like.

Numerous factors can have a major influence on the supervisor's ability to organize. First, supervisors may find it difficult to reassign workers if there is a union. In some nonunion firms, people can be readily moved to respond to the needs of the situation. Delta Airlines attributes much of its success to workers' willingness to perform a multitude of tasks; for example, a Delta ticket agent may sometimes load baggage.

Second, in some firms, virtually every aspect of the supervisor's job is controlled by standard operating procedures. The supervisor may have little discretion in rearranging people or tasks except as prescribed by the procedure manual.

Third, some bosses are willing to give supervisors considerable flexibility. Others tell the supervisors exactly what to do. If the boss is inflexible, it may be a waste of time for the supervisor to try to reorganize.

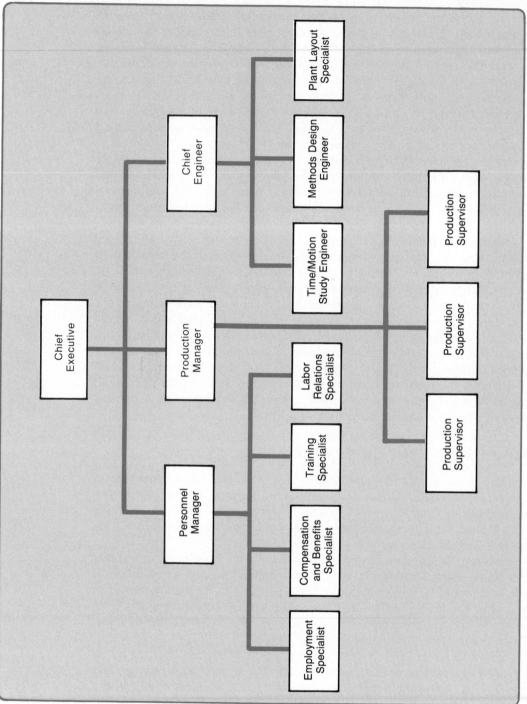

Figure 6–9 Horizontal Differentiation of Functional Departments

Coordination assumes a greater importance as the organization becomes more complex.   Jim Steere/Nawrocki Stock Photo, Courtesy of the Chicago Symphony Orchestra

Fourth, if workers are qualified in a variety of tasks, organizing flexibility is increased. For instance, a punch press operator may also be qualified on a drill press. This worker can be assigned to either job.

Finally, supervisors who have considerable influence within the organization are usually in a much better position to make changes. These supervisors can also arrange human and physical resources with little interference.

SUMMARY

An organization is defined as two or more people working together in a coordinated manner to achieve group results. Organizing is prescribing formal relationships among people and resources to accomplish goals. In organizing, it is first necessary to consider organizational objectives before attempting to determine the kind of organization needed to accomplish those objectives. Next, management must determine the functions, or activities, that will be required. Finally, a number of departments, or separate organizational units, are set up, each designed to carry out a separate function or group of functions.

Specialization of labor means breaking a complex job into simple tasks so that one person or group may carry out only identical or related activities. Through specialization of labor, it is possible for a member of the organization to specialize, resulting in increased output. Specialization is especially essential for the achievement of efficiency in mass-production industries.

The process of grouping related functions or major work activities into manageable units is known as departmentation. Functions should be grouped according to the following guidelines: (1) similar functions; (2) sufficient volume of work; (3) tradition, preferences, and work rules; (4) functions similar to others in the organization; (5) separation of functions to prevent conflicts of interest; and (6) combining dissimilar functions to allow coordination.

It is possible to identify five bases on which departmentation normally occurs. Departmentation by function is formed on the basis of specialized functions, such as production, marketing, engineering, finance, and personnel. Departmentation by product is concerned with organizing according to the type of product being produced and/or sold by the firm. Departmentation by customers is used by organizations that have a special need to provide better service to different types of customers. Departmentation by geographic territory is used by organizations that have physically dispersed and/or independent operations or markets to serve. When the work of an organization consists of a continuing series of major projects, departmentation by project normally occurs. Unless the organization is quite small, however, it is likely that several different bases for departmentation will be used.

The process of creating additional levels in the organization is defined as vertical differentiation. Initially there are just two levels, managerial and operative. As the volume of business continues to grow, additional personnel will be added and more operative functions differentiated and allocated. The process of forming additional units at the same level in the organization is called horizontal differentiation. When differentiation occurs, coordination is required. Coordination is ensuring that persons who perform interdependent activities work together in a way that contributes to overall goal attainment.

Numerous factors have a major influence on the supervisor's ability to organize. First, supervisors may find it difficult to reassign workers if there is a union. Second, in some firms, virtually every aspect of the supervisor's job is controlled by standard operating procedures. Third, some bosses are willing to give supervisors considerable flexibility, while others are not. Fourth, if workers are qualified in a variety of tasks, organizing flexibility is increased. Finally, supervisors who have considerable influence within the organization usually are in a much better position to make changes.

REVIEW QUESTIONS

1. Define organization. What are the three common characteristics of an organization?
2. Describe the process of organizing. What tasks must managers perform in the organizing process?
3. In terms of the organizing process, define a function. What types of functions are needed on a baseball team? a football team? a fast foods restaurant? a small-appliance assembly plant?
4. Define specialization of labor. What are the advantages and disadvantages?
5. What guidelines should be used in grouping functions?
6. Define *departmentation*. What are the primary means of departmentation?
7. Distinguish by example and definition between horizontal and vertical differentiation.
8. What are the factors that can have a major influence on the supervisor's ability to organize?

EXERCISES

1. Specialization has both advantages and disadvantages. List the specialized education and training required for the following professions. Which profession(s) is possible with your present level of education and training? Which could you achieve?

a. Electrical draftsman
b. Neurosurgeon
c. Machine operator
d. College president
e. Personnel manager

2. Assume that you are production manager for a small firm. The firm currently is experiencing much growth and success with its product line, and sales have tripled in the past year. As a result, you have hired forty new employees over the last six months to keep up with production demands. Describe the horizontal and vertical differentiation that you would implement in the company for maximum efficiency as the organization continues to grow.

CASE STUDY

The Organization of Quality Control

Shelton Lewis is production manager for Memorand, Inc., a company that manufactures small component parts for the hydraulics industry. Shel, as his employees call him, came to Memorand fifteen years ago as a production foreman. He believes the company has been good to him, and, though he has had a number of offers of better-paying jobs with competing firms, he has chosen not to leave.

Gloria Honeycutt is in charge of the quality control section at Memorand and reports directly to Shelton. Gloria started as Shelton's secretary five years ago. With his encouragement she attended college and recently obtained a degree in industrial management with a concentration in quality control. She then was reassigned to the quality control job but continued to report directly to Shelton. Like Shelton, Gloria is intensely loyal to Memorand.

Yesterday a delicate situation arose, creating a strain on the usually excellent relationship between Shelton and Gloria. The problem began with the following conversation:

Gloria: "Shel, I'm finding a large number of imperfections in the cylinders we're making for Ingersol Rand. I know you're facing a deadline, but I believe we should slow down and inspect all the cylinder parts before they are assembled."

Shelton: "Have you found more than the standard number of defectives?"

Gloria: "No, but a number of the cylinders just passed the leakage tests, and many of the mounting holes are just within specs. If you don't slow down, we may miss a chance at future orders from Ingersol Rand. You know how quality conscious they are."

Shelton: "If we do slow down, we won't make the scheduled delivery date. If we don't do that, Memorand may not even be considered for future contracts. I don't expect you, of all people, to stand in the way of getting the order out on time."

Gloria didn't know what to do, so she just left the office. She still felt she was right. The contract with Ingersol Rand was a lucrative one, and it had been given to Memorand only because Shelton had guaranteed quick delivery. Pleasing Ingersol Rand could easily result in a 10 percent sales increase for the company as a whole. Ingersol Rand has a reputation for selecting suppliers carefully and sticking with them as long as delivery and quality are up to par.

QUESTIONS

1. Is there anything amiss with the organizational relationship between Gloria and Shelton? If so, what? How would you change it? Defend your answer.

2. What do you believe Gloria should do at this point? Explain.

Materials Organization at Newco Manufacturing

Tom Johnson, the new materials manager for the Newco Manufacturing Company, was concerned about the lack of organization in his department. Newco had 250 employees and manufactured small electrical motors. Tom reported to the vice-president of manufacturing, Charles McDowell. His fifteen subordinates performed such functions as stocking, receiving, inventory control, purchasing, and outside sales.

Partly because the work flow was unpredictable, the previous materials manager had allowed the department's personnel to do whatever they thought necessary. They often shifted from job to job—working the parts issue window while mechanics were ordering parts, stocking the parts bin when time permitted, receiving parts when deliveries were made, and shipping orders to customers. The same employees answered the phone and handled outside sales as required. Employee complaints had been frequent regarding such matters as inadequate pay, unclear work assignments, and lack of competent leadership.

Tom was given a rather detailed account of the past performance of the materials operation by his boss. McDowell described the materials department as performing very poorly and attributed this to a lack of overall direction, ineffective organization, and incompetent personnel. McDowell described several of the department's personnel as "dope heads" or "long hairs" who did as little work as possible. The turnover rate had been in excess of 200 percent per year for the past three years. McDowell suggested that Johnson "clean house" by firing most of the employees in the department and starting with a fresh crew.

Johnson was obviously shaken by the comments made by Mr. McDowell and the complaints of the personnel and considered finding a new position; however, he chose not to leave the company before giving the assignment his best efforts for at least a few months.

QUESTIONS

1. Using concepts and principles discussed in this chapter, how would you recommend that Tom Johnson improve the materials department?
2. What type of organization chart would you recommend Tom develop?
3. Should Tom clean house as suggested by Mr. McDowell?

NOTES

1. This is a composite of a number of published accounts, among them: Bette Hendrix, "Wal-Mart Stock History," *Wal-Mart World* 13, no. 1 (January 1983): 19; "Wal-Mart Discounts Everything But People," *Retailing* (January 18, 1982): 32, 52; Howard Rudnitsky, "How Sam Walton Does It," *Forbes* (August 16, 1982): 42–44; "Wal-Mart Reigns, Jamesway Second," *Chain Store Age* (June 1983): 51, 53; "Rex Chase—Pure Wal-Mart Lore," *Chain Store Age* (March 1983): 35; "The Service 500," *Fortune* (June 11, 1984): 170; and a number of articles from *The Wall Street Journal.*

2. "The Fast-Food War: Big Mac under Attack," *Business Week* (January 30, 1984): 45.

3. "The New Industrial Relations," *Business Week* (May 11, 1981): 85–98.

4. W. G. Astley and A. H. Van de Ven, "Central Perspectives and Debates in Organization Theory," *Administrative Science Quarterly* (June 1983): 248.

5. R. L. Daft, *Organization Theory and Design.* St. Paul, Minn.: West Publishing Company, 1983, p. 227.

6. Theodore T. Herbert, "Strategy and Multinational Organization Structure: An International Relationships Perspective," *Academy of Management Review* (April 1984): 263.

7. "Can GM Solve Its Identity Crisis?" *Business Week* (January 23, 1984): 32–33.

8. Daft, *Organization Theory,* p. 23.

9. Herbert, "Strategy," p. 263.

REFERENCES

Alexander, E. R. "Design of Alternatives in Organizational Contexts: A Pilot Study." *Administrative Science Quarterly* 24 (September 1979): 382–404.

Astley, W. G., and A. H. Van de Ven. "Central Perspectives and Debates in Organization Theory." *Administrative Science Quarterly* (June 1983): 248.

Bobbitt, H. R., Jr., and J. D. Ford. "Decision-Maker Choice as a Determinant of Organizational Structure." *Academy of Management Review* 5 (January 1980): 13–23.

"Can GM Solve Its Identity Crisis?" *Business Week* (January 23, 1984): 32–33.

Cherman, C. "Organizing for Strength." *Personnel Journal* 58 (July 1979): 437–438.

Daft, R. L. *Organization Theory and Design.* St. Paul, Minn.: West Publishing Company, 1983.

Dalton, D. R., W. D. Todor, J. Spendelini, J. Fielding, and L. W. Porter. "Organization Structure and Performance: A Critical Review." *Academy of Management Review* 5 (January 1980): 61–64.

"The Fast-Food War: Big Mac under Attack." *Business Week* (January 30, 1984): 45.

Gerwin, D. "Relationships between Structure and Technology at the Organizational and Job Levels." *Journal of Management Studies* 16 (February 1979): 70–79.

Handy, C. "Shape of Organizations to Come." *Personnel Management* 11 (June 1979): 24–27.

———. "Through the Organizational Looking Glass." *Harvard Business Review* 58, no. 1 (January–February 1980): 115–121.

Herbert, Theodore T. "Strategy and Multinational Organization Structure: An International Relationships Perspective." *Academy of Management Review* (April 1984).

Huber, G. P., et al. "Optimum Organization Design: An Analytic Adoptive Approach." *Academy of Management Review* 4 (October 1979): 567–578.

Naylor, T. H. "Organizing for Strategic Planning." *Managerial Planning* 28 (July 1979): 3–9.

"The New Industrial Relations." *Business Week* (May 11, 1981): 85–98.

Scanlan, K. "Maintaining Organizational Effectiveness— A Prescription for Good Health." *Personnel Journal* 58, no. 5 (May 1980): 381–386.

Slocum, J. W., Jr., and D. Hellriegel. "Using Organizational Designs to Cope with Change." *Business Horizons* 22 (December 1979): 65–76.

KEY TERMS

responsibility

authority

delegation

accountability

unity of command
principle

scalar principle

chain of command

span of management

centralization

organizational
structure

line organizations

line departments

line and staff
organizations

staff departments

functional organization

functional authority

project organization

matrix organization

committee

LEARNING OBJECTIVES

After completing this chapter you should be able to

1. Describe the concepts of responsibility, authority, delegation, and accountability.
2. List several important organizing principles.
3. Identify the advantages of centralization versus those of decentralization.
4. Identify the basic types of organizational structures and the advantages and disadvantages of each.

7

Organizing Concepts and Organizational Structure

 In 1886, Richard Sears opened his mail-order business in Minnesota. A hundred years later, the company is the world's largest merchandising organization, selling not only the watches Richard Sears started with, but the broadest array of products imaginable and a large number of services— insurance, real estate, and stockbrokering—as well. And today the mail-order business, while much larger than that of its nearest competitor, is dwarfed by Sears's department store retailing. Sears sells its products through nearly eight hundred retail stores and its services through thousands of other outlets.

In consumer circles, Sears is known for its size (approaching $40 billion in sales), its dependability (satisfaction guaranteed), and the quality and diversity of its products. In management circles, Sears is recognized as one of the world's leaders in enlightened, aggressive, and responsible management. When Sears was primarily a catalog business, the company had a highly centralized management system. But the need for farflung department stores to respond to local customers and the increasing diversity of the organization made centralized management impractical. Decisions could no longer be made at headquarters and simply passed down the line.

Over the years from 1930 to 1950, a new pattern of management evolved and has been the model for many other U.S. companies since that time. Each major aspect of Sears's business—merchandising, financial services, real estate, insurance, and world trade—is directed by a chief executive officer (CEO) who reports to the corporate chairman. These five CEOs and the chairman, along with the corporate vice-president of planning, make up the strategic planning committee, but each subsidiary operates in a relatively autonomous manner.

Even within the divisions, power is decentralized. For instance, Sears store managers are able to decide what items to stock in their stores within very broad limitations. There are, of course, certain "basic basics" that must be stocked by all Sears stores, but the main job of central management is to offer assistance to the store manager. Never a company to rest on its laurels, Sears proudly states in a recent annual report, "We have the economic strength and the resolve to make the Sears family of companies a truly significant global trading company."[1]

In Chapter 6 we discussed the organizing process, showed how departmentation occurs as organizations grow, and described how the supervisor is involved in the process. Sears, Roebuck and Company provides an example of effective application of organizing principles. For example, managers at Sears are typically given charge of their units and expected to perform with limited supervision. There are few levels of managers at Sears so that even workers do not feel too distant from company management.

In this chapter, we first discuss responsibility, authority, delegation, and accountability. Then, several principles or guidelines important to a manager's performance of the organizing function are reviewed. Next, trade-off between the needs of centralization and decentralization is discussed. In the final section of the chapter, we describe the common types of organizational structures.

RESPONSIBILITY

In accepting a certain job, a person takes responsibility for performing the tasks involved. **Responsibility** is *an obligation to perform work activities.* For example, if we say that Joan Lewis, a manager with Sears, is responsible for the data processing center, we mean that she should plan, organize, influence, and control the work of computer operators and analysts. And that is not all. She must also provide for maintenance of the computer equipment and programs, plus numerous other activities essential to the success of the data processing department.

responsibility

One reason for Sears's success has undoubtedly been the fact that Sears managers take their responsibilities seriously. In this regard, responsibility is a felt obligation. We can enhance the degree to which a manager feels the obligation to perform by making sure that responsibilities are clearly defined. Nothing is more frustrating to a manager or a worker than to be confused about the nature, scope, and details of specific job responsibilities. For instance, suppose that Susan James, a first-line supervisor for a large insurance company, has the following conversation with her boss, Phil Williams:

Susan: Am I responsible for processing the new commercial fire insurance policies, or should Joe Davis's unit handle them?

Phil: I don't think it really matters too much which unit handles these policies so long as it's done correctly and thoroughly.

Susan: But what do you expect me to do?

Phil: I'll get back to you later on this—I'm busy at the moment.

Obviously Phil's comments leave Susan unsure of her responsibility. In fact, in cases such as this, managers often assume that someone else will do what needs to be done. Therefore, Phil should not be surprised if the new policies do not get processed at all. When this occurs, he may be upset with Susan, but the real fault is his own.

Ambiguous instructions can be dangerous. An example of this occurred when Metropolitan Edison's nuclear plant at Three Mile Island in Pennsylvania overheated in 1979. Public safety in the area was endangered. There was fear that the clouds of radioactive gas released in the incident would expose citizens to high levels of radioactivity and that radiation would later show up in cows' milk and other food products. A study of the Three Mile Island nuclear incident showed that job-related tension brought on by confusion about what was expected contributed to the accident.[2] Apparently the reactor operators were not sure who had responsibility for taking various safety measures, so some important steps were omitted.

AUTHORITY

A common complaint of managers is that while they have unlimited responsibility, their authority is often inadequate. **Authority** is *the right to decide, to direct others to take action, or to perform certain duties in achieving organizational goals.* Sears is well known for assigning challenging responsibilities to its managers and giving them considerable authority to carry out their jobs. The definition suggests that authority has at least three key characteristics.

1. Authority is a *right.*
2. Exercising authority involves *making decisions,* taking actions, or performing duties.
3. Authority is granted for the purpose of achieving *organizational goals.*

Every manager must have some authority in order to organize and direct the use of resources to attain the goals of the organization.

At any level in the organization, various degrees of authority may be given to a manager. For example, a supervisor made responsible for staffing a department can be given any one of the following levels of authority:

- Rights to recruit, screen, and hire all personnel.
- Rights to recruit, screen, and hire, subject to prior approval from a higher-level manager.
- No rights to recruit and screen. This function has been given to the personnel department, but the supervisor can accept or reject candidates.
- No rights to hire. The supervisor must take whomever the personnel department sends.

In the last instance, the supervisor may feel a lack of authority to perform the job adequately; however, many large companies maintain tight control of the personnel function to ensure compliance with civil rights legislation and to protect the interest of employees.

DELEGATION

The process of assigning responsibility along with the needed authority is referred to as **delegation**. Delegation is one of the most significant concepts or practices affecting a manager's ability to get the job done. It creates a risk for managers, however, for they are ultimately responsible for the success or failure of an operation. When a manager delegates a responsibility to a subordinate, a relationship based on an obligation exists between the two. Managers should remember an important point: *one cannot relieve oneself of any portion of the original responsibility; delegation allows only for someone else to do the work.* As a result, some managers have attempted to reduce the risk by avoiding delegation and doing everything themselves. Yet delegation of responsibility and authority is essential if the manager is to provide opportunities for the development of people. Also, few managers have the capability of personally performing all the duties for which they are responsible. One of the most frequent causes of failure is the unwillingness or inability of some managers to delegate responsibility and authority.

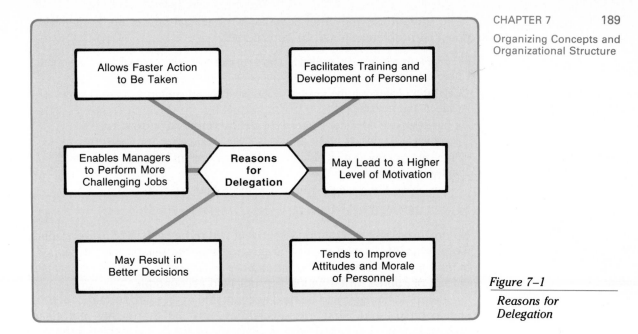

Figure 7–1

*Reasons for
Delegation*

Some of the more significant reasons why delegation is important are illustrated in Figure 7–1. First, delegation of authority often leads to quicker action and faster, better decisions. Action can be taken much faster if we can avoid going to a higher level in the organization for a decision. For example, Sears's store managers can decide within very broad limitations what items to stock. In general, when routine matters are handled at a level higher than necessary, work output will likely be less than optimum.

Second, delegation tends to be an important factor in training and developing personnel in the organization. Managers cannot learn to perform a certain function or make decisions unless given the opportunity. Delegation of responsibility and authority is essential if the firm is concerned about the development of personnel to assume more challenging and demanding jobs in the future.

Third, delegation may lead to higher levels of motivation. Persons who are given authority and responsibility by their superiors often see this as a reflection of trust in their abilities. This may become a self-fulfilling prophecy as subordinates try to live up to that trust.

Fourth, closely related to improved motivation is the attitudes and morale of employees. Persons who are given responsibility and authority tend to have a better attitude toward their superiors. They are often easier to manage and more cooperative, and their morale is also higher.

Fifth, delegation may result in better decisions. The person who is closest to the job being done is often the one who knows how to do it best.

Finally, it is through delegation that managers are able to perform especially challenging jobs. Delegation can be thought of as the way of extending the manager's capabilities. Evidence suggests that managers recognize this. A recent study of graduating MBAs and practicing managers revealed that the ability to perform a wide variety of tasks tends to be associated with increasing delegation.[3]

Despite these and other advantages of delegation, certain limitations or potential problems should be considered:

- If improper feedback is provided, the manager may lose control and may not have the time to correct the situation should a problem occur.
- Delegation can fail if the level of responsibility and authority is not clearly defined and understood.
- If the delegatee does not possess the ability, skills, and/or experience to accomplish the job or make decisions, delegation can prove disastrous.
- Problems can result if an employee is given a responsibility but insufficient authority to perform the task.

ACCOUNTABILITY

accountability

No organization can function effectively without a system of accountability. **Accountability** is *any means of ensuring that the person who is supposed to do a task actually performs it and does so correctly.* Situations can rapidly get out of control when people are not held accountable.

Before a manager can be held accountable for results, certain conditions should be present. First, responsibilities must be thoroughly and clearly understood. An individual who is unaware of what is expected cannot be properly held accountable. Second, the person must be qualified and capable of fulfilling the obligation. It would be inconceivable to assign the responsibility and authority for performing engineering or accounting functions to individuals having no previous educational background and/or experience in these areas. Finally, sufficient authority to accomplish the task must be delegated. Assigning a manager the total profit responsibility for a department but no authority to hire or fire employees might mean that insufficient authority has been delegated. This manager probably would object to being held accountable for results.

Since it is so closely related to responsibility, a manager's accountability cannot be delegated to someone else. Managers are usually accountable not only for their own actions and decisions but also for the actions of their subordinates. An extreme case of this is the naval tradition that the captain must go down with the ship.

Accountability can be established in several ways. The first method is through personal inspection by the manager. After assigning a person to do the task, the manager observes to see that it is done properly. The second method is to have the subordinate complete reports and give them to the manager. However, because it is human nature to want to be seen in the best possible light, such reports might be biased in favor of the subordinate. A third method is through reporting done by others. A quality control inspector might report the number of defective units for each worker to the manager. Customers may report poor service or faulty products. This method of accountability is not in the hands of the person held accountable and is therefore reasonably free of bias. For example, customers who have complaints about the service they receive at Sears can contact managers at Sears Tower in Chicago or the manager of the local Sears store or work the problem out with the salesperson involved. Sears managers are trained not to take offense when they are bypassed by irate customers. Finally, accountability may be obtained through a machine with a counter or other measuring device. In a grocery store, a cash register tape of all sales does this. Most modern retailers like Sears use point-of-sale accounting systems, where most mistakes are immediately logged for correction.

ORGANIZING PRINCIPLES

Several important organizing principles exist. These principles are briefly discussed below and are summarized in Table 7–1.

Unity of Command

The **unity of command principle** is *the belief that each person should answer to only one immediate superior; each employee has only one boss.* Unity of command enables better coordination and understanding of what is required and improves discipline. An employee with two or more bosses can receive contradictory orders.

unity of command principle

Although unity of command is a sound concept, it does have certain limitations. In large organizations especially, a person may be accountable to more than one boss. At Sears, for example, store managers are expected to follow the directives from the central personnel office.

Equal Authority and Responsibility

An important principle of management is that authority should equal responsibility. Following this principle ensures that work will be performed

TABLE 7–1   Organizing Principles

Principle	Definition of	Reason for	Possible Causes of Violation	Possible Results of Violation
Unity of command	A person should report to only *one* boss ("one boss")	Clarity and understanding, to ensure unity of effort and direction, and to avoid conflicts	Unclear definition of authority	Dissatisfaction or frustration of employees and perhaps lower efficiency
Equal authority and responsibility	The amount of authority and responsibility should be equal (Responsibility = authority)	Allows work to be accomplished more efficiently, develops people, and reduces frustration	Fear on the part of some managers that subordinates might "take over"	Waste of energies and dissatisfaction of employees, thereby reducing effectiveness
Scalar Principle	There should be a clear definition of authority in the organization ("to go through channels")	Clarity of relationship avoids confusion and improves decision making and performance	Uncertainty on the part of the employee or a direct effort by the employee to avoid chain of command	Poor performance, confusion, and/or dissatisfaction
Span of management	There is a limit to the number of employees a manager can effectively supervise	Increased effectiveness in direction and control of a manager	Overloading a manager due to growth in number of personnel	Lack of efficiency and control, resulting in poor performance

more efficiently and with a minimum amount of frustration on the part of personnel. By not delegating an adequate amount of authority, energies and resources are wasted, and employee dissatisfaction often results. Many managers continue to give their subordinates more responsibility than authority, however.

The Scalar Principle and the Chain of Command

scalar principle

chain of command

The **scalar principle** is *the philosophy that authority and responsibility should flow from top management downward in a clear, unbroken line.* If the scalar principle is followed, there is a clear chain of command for every person in the organization. The **chain of command** is *the line along which authority flows from the top of the organization to any individual.* A clear chain of command clarifies relationships, avoids confusion, and tends to improve decision making, thus often leading to more effective performance. When the scalar principle is followed, superiors and subordinates communicate by going through channels.

Span of Management

span of management

The number of direct subordinates reporting to any manager is referred to as the **span of management** (control). Although the span of management may vary greatly, there is a maximum number of employees a manager can effectively supervise in a given circumstance. Efficient use of managerial talent also dictates that at least a minimum number of subordinates be assigned to each manager. Organizations like Sears, which values a flat structure, with few levels of management, can achieve this only by having large spans of management.

Although it is not appropriate to attempt to specify the correct span of management for every situation, it is useful to think about how relationships increase when a manager has more than about eight direct subordinates. This was the subject of research by V. A. Graicunas, a management consultant of the 1930s. Graicunas derived a formula to determine the potential interactions or relationships that were possible when a manager had a given number of employees.[4] Graicunas's formula is as follows: $R = n + n(n - 1) + n(2^{n-1} - 1)$, where R represents the number of relationships or interactions and n is the number of subordinates reporting to the manager.

According to the Graicunas formula, a manager with two employees would have six potential relationships. For example, if Ed Bishop has two subordinates, John and Susan, Table 7–2 would illustrate the six possible interactions. As Table 7–3 shows, each additional employee whom a manager supervises creates a substantial number of additional relationships.

Accepted spans of management have historically been relatively narrow, usually ranging from six to fifteen. Short spans of management permit closer supervision of personnel but tend to create tall organizational structures with a large number of levels. This may cause difficulties in communications and result in managers and workers at lower levels feeling isolated. Wide

TABLE 7–2   Possible Relationships with Two Employees

Number of Relationships

2	Ed may meet and talk with John Ed may meet and talk with Susan	*These are direct relationships.*
2	Ed may meet and talk with John with Susan present, and vice-versa	*These are group relationships.*
2	John may interact with Susan without Ed being present or Susan may meet with John without Ed being present	*These are cross-relationships.*
6		

spans result in relatively fewer levels, or flat organizations, and greater freedom for the individual employee.

A number of factors affect the span of management:

1. In general, the more complex the work, the shorter the optimum span of management.
2. The span can be longer if the manager is supervising employees performing similar jobs.
3. If jobs are closely interlocked and interdependent, the manager may have greater problems with coordination, creating the need for a rather limited span of management.
4. If the organization is operating in an unstable environment, a narrow span may prove to be more effective.
5. The establishment of numerous standards increases predictability and provides the basis for effective control, thereby resulting in a wider effective span.
6. Managers and employees who are highly skilled, experienced, and motivated generally can operate with wider spans of management and with less supervision.
7. Where high commitment to the organization is as important as technical efficiency, such commitment can be enhanced through wider spans of management.[5]

TABLE 7–3   Possible Relationships with Different Number of Employees

Number of Employees	Potential Number of Relationships
1	1
2	6
3	18
4	44
5	100
6	222

In addition, technology can have a significant impact on the span of management. Joan Woodward, a British researcher who conducted studies in 100 English manufacturing firms, discovered that the type of technology had a significant impact on the spans of management actually used in business organizations. Woodward classified production technology on the basis of the following categories:

- Unit or small batch processing (for example, made-to-order goods such as custom-tailored clothing).
- Mass production (assembly-line operations).
- Process production with continuous long runs of a standardized product such as oil, chemicals, or pharmaceuticals.

She discovered that spans of management were widest in firms using mass-production technology. The jobs in a mass-production situation tend to be more routine and similar to one another, thereby leading to wider appropriate spans of management.[6] On the other hand, unit and process production were marked by smaller spans of management.

CENTRALIZATION VERSUS DECENTRALIZATION

centralization

It is important that management determine the appropriate levels of responsibility and authority to be delegated. **Centralization** is *the degree to which authority is retained by higher-level managers within an organization rather than being delegated.* If a limited amount of authority is delegated, the organization is usually characterized as being centralized. If a significant amount of authority is delegated to lower levels, the enterprise is described as being decentralized. There are many degrees of centralization. The real question is not whether a company should decentralize but what degree of decentralization is appropriate.

In a highly centralized structure, individual managers and workers at lower levels in the organization have a rather narrow range of decisions or actions they can initiate. By contrast, the scope of authority to make decisions and take actions is rather broad for lower-level managers and employees in decentralized organizations. In a highly centralized organizational structure, upper management makes all decisions regarding the hiring or firing of personnel, approval of purchasing of equipment and supplies, and similar activities. In a decentralized structure, lower-level management may make these decisions.

Decentralization is advocated by many who believe that a greater share in management decision making should be given to lower organizational levels. Decentralization tends to create a climate for more rapid growth and development of personnel. If virtually all decisions and orders come from one central source, organization members tend to act as robots and unthinking executors of someone else's commands. On the other hand, there are exceptionally competent managers in high positions, like Lee Iacocca at Chrysler, who are better able to make valid decisions than are their subordinates. When this is the case, a reasonable tendency is to lean toward centralization. In addition, many employees and lower-level managers do not wish to be involved at high levels in the organization. For them, life is complicated enough when top management makes the major decisions.

In addition to the human behavior implications of decentralization and centralization, several other factors affect a manager's decision in this regard. Centralization

1. produces uniformity of policy and action.
2. results in few risks of errors by subordinates who lack either information or skill.
3. utilizes the skills of central and specialized experts.
4. enables closer control of operations.

On the other hand, decentralization

1. tends to make for speedier decisions and actions on the spot without consulting higher levels.
2. results in decisions that are more likely to be adapted to local conditions.
3. results in greater interest and enthusiasm on the part of the subordinate to whom the authority has been entrusted (these expanded jobs provide excellent training experiences for possible promotion to higher levels).
4. allows top management to utilize time for more study and consideration of the basic goals, plans, and policies of the enterprise.

Additional factors to be taken into account concerning the degree of centralization are discussed below.

Size and Complexity of the Organization

The larger the enterprise, the more authority the central manager is forced to delegate. If the firm is engaged in many separate businesses, the limitations of expertise will usually lead to decentralization of authority to the heads of these units. Each major product group is likely to have different product problems, varying kinds of customers, and varied marketing channels. If speed and adaptability to change are necessary to success, decentralization is a must.

Dispersion of the Organization

When the difficulties of size are compounded by geographic dispersion, it is evident that a greater degree of decentralization must occur. General Motors Company is a prime example of decentralization because of size and geographic dispersion. Not every decision or every function must be decentralized, however. Control of operations may have to be pushed down to lower levels in the organization, while control of financing may still be centralized. Because of the increasing complexity of federal and state legislation affecting employment practices and unionization, centralization of labor relations is often established for purposes of uniformity throughout the company.

Competency of Personnel Available

A major limiting factor in many organizations is the adequacy or inadequacy of present personnel. If the enterprise has grown up under centralized

*Decentralization of
authority requires
competent personnel.*

Cary Wolinsky/Stock, Boston Inc.

decision making and control, past experience has often equipped subordinate personnel poorly to start making major decisions. They were hired and trained to be followers, not leaders and decision makers. In some convenience store chains, this has developed into a major problem. Store managers are promoted to supervisor because they are able to perform basic store functions, not because of their decision-making ability but because they can ensure that store managers follow standard operating procedures. In such a situation, a person who eventually makes it to the top may not be equipped to cope with the large number of decisions to be made that are not based on established practices and procedures. Those who were inclined toward more independent thought and action may be driven away from the centralized firm.

Adequacy of Communications System

Size, complexity, and geographic dispersion lead to the delegation of larger amounts of authority for decision making to lower levels in the organization. The manager can seek to avoid decentralization through the development of a communication system that provides for speed, accuracy, and capacity of information needed for top management to exercise centralized control. In effect, although size and geography may preclude being on the spot, one can attempt to control subordinates by detailing standards of performance and process and by ensuring that information flows quickly and accurately to the central authoritative position.

Computer Technology

The widespread use of computers in business gives managers more flexibility in deciding whether to decentralize. Today computers or terminals are available at virtually all site locations. Thus, information can be supplied to headquarters virtually instantaneously. In the past, an organization might have decided to decentralize because of the time delay involved in getting decision-making information to top-level managers. Today this is less of a problem.

Even when it is not feasible to centralize all aspects of management, certain functions can be handled at headquarters. Thus, most major companies have centralized accounting and finance functions to some degree.

TYPES OF ORGANIZATIONAL STRUCTURES

The formal relationships among groups and individuals in the organization are called **organizational structure**. The organizational structure provides guidelines essential for effective employee performance and overall organizational success. The structure clarifies and communicates the lines of responsibility and authority within the firm and assists management in coordinating the overall operation.

organizational structure

Although we usually think of large companies when we discuss organizational structures, every firm, large or small, has a structure. It may or may not have an organizational chart. Small businesses may have simple structures that are easily understood. In fact, the organizational structure may be informal and highly changeable in a small, uncomplicated business. By contrast, large, diverse, and complex organizations usually have a highly formalized structure, but that does not mean the structure is so rigid as not to change, perhaps even frequently. Determining the most appropriate organizational design or structure is not a simple matter if one considers the frequency of reorganization to be an indication. Newly formed high-technology companies are most likely to restructure or reorganize frequently, but even some of the largest Fortune 500 industrial firms often experience a major reorganization.

Although many variations of organizational structures are used today, we will discuss line, line and staff, functional, project, and matrix structures.

Line Organization

line organizations

line departments

Line organizations are *those organizations that have only direct, vertical relationships between different levels within the firm.* They include only line departments. **Line departments** are *those departments directly involved in accomplishing the primary purpose of the organization.* In a typical company, line departments include production and marketing. In a line organization, authority follows the chain of command. Figure 7–2 is an illustration of a simple line organizational structure.

Several advantages are quite often associated with the pure line organization structure.

1. A line structure tends to simplify and clarify responsibility, authority, and accountability relationships within the organization. The levels of responsibility and authority of personnel operating within a line organization are likely to be precise and understandable.

2. A line structure promotes fast decision making and allows the organization to change directions more rapidly since there are few people to consult when problems arise.

3. Since pure line organizations are small, there are the advantages of greater feelings of closeness of management to the employees, and all personnel usually have an opportunity to know what is going on in the firm.

There are also certain disadvantages to the line structure. The major disadvantage is the increasing lack of effectiveness as the firm grows larger.

Figure 7–2

A Line Organization Structure

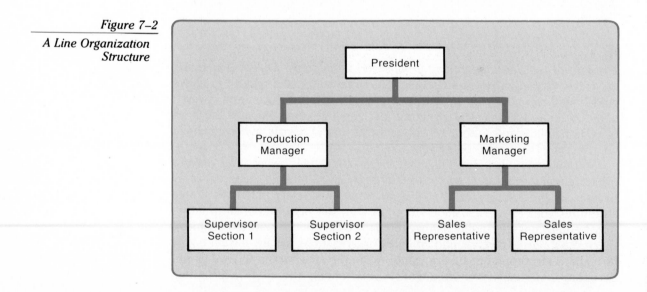

At some point, improving speed and flexibility do not offset the lack of specialized knowledge and skills. This occurs long before a company reaches the size of Sears. In other words, a line structure may force managers to be experts in too many fields and thereby possibly reduce their effectiveness. In a line organization, the firm may have a tendency to become overly dependent on one or a few key people who can perform numerous jobs. If the organization is to remain purely line, one solution is for management to seek help by creating additional levels to share the managerial load. This, however, will result in a lengthening of the chain of command and a consequent loss of some of the values of speed, flexibility, and central control. Therefore, there are few pure line organizations of any substantial size.

Line and Staff Organization

Most large organizations are of the line and staff type. **Line and staff organizations** are *those organizations that have direct, vertical relationships between different levels and also specialists responsible for advising and assisting other managers.* Such organizations have both line and staff departments. **Staff departments** are *departments that provide line people with advice and assistance in specialized areas.*

As shown in the line and staff organization chart in Figure 7–3, staff functions under the president typically include personnel, research,

line and staff organizations

staff departments

Figure 7–3   Line and Staff Structure of a Typical Manufacturing Company

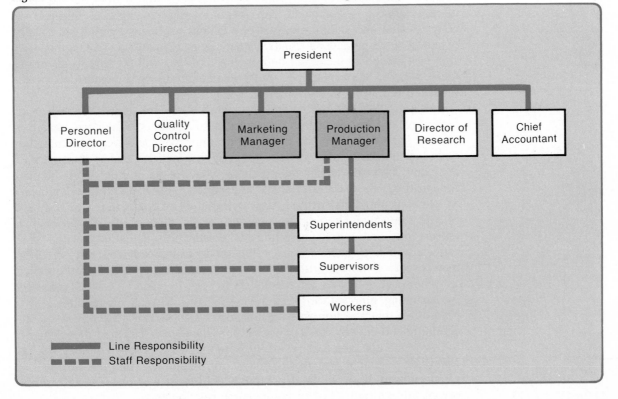

Line Responsibility
Staff Responsibility

accounting, and quality control. The line functions, marketing and production, are highlighted. Each of the staff managers has responsibilities to persons at every level within the organization. For simplicity, however, only the staff relationships between the personnel directors and persons in the production department are shown. Notice the dotted lines from personnel to superintendents, supervisors, and workers. The personnel director also has staff responsibilities to the other department heads. While personnel, research, accounting, and quality control are staff functions in the firm, there is a direct-line reporting relationship between the managers of these functions and the president.

Three separate types of specialized staffs can be identified: (1) advisory, (2) service, and (3) control. It is possible for one unit to perform all three functions. For example, the personnel manager may advise line managers on the appropriateness of recognizing a particular labor union. The department simultaneously provides a service by procuring and training needed production and sales personnel. A control orientation enters when the personnel manager audits salaries actually paid to ensure conformity to line-approved pay ranges. Some staffs are predominantly one or the other in character. For example, a staff economist advises the establishment of long-range plans, and a quality control staff unit enforces authorized product standards. It is apparent that the potential for conflicts in coordination between line and staff tends to grow as one moves from advice to service to control. One can possibly ignore advice, but service is needed, and control is often unavoidable.

There are both advantages and disadvantages of a line and staff organization structure. The primary advantage is that it uses the expertise of specialists. A manager can become more scientific because of concentrated and skillful analysis of business problems by staff specialists. In addition, the manager's effective span of management can be lengthened— that is, relieved of technical details, the manager will be able to supervise more people. Some staff personnel even operate as an extension of the manager and assist in coordination and control.

Despite the fact that a line and staff structure allows for increased flexibility and specialization, it may create conflicts. When we introduce various specialists into the organization, line managers may feel that they have lost authority over certain specialized functions. These managers do not want staff specialists telling them what to do or how to do it even though they recognize specialists' knowledge and expertise. It is important to use staff personnel without destroying unity of command. The authority of line managers should be preserved while their ability to produce is enhanced. Some staff personnel have difficulty adjusting to the role, especially if line managers are reluctant to accept advice. Staff personnel may resent not having authority, and this may cause line and staff conflict.

There is a tendency for specialists to seek to enlarge personal influence by assuming line authority in their specialty. This is compounded by a realization that the fundamental purpose of all staff is to produce greater economy and effectiveness of operation. This means that staff must attempt to introduce changes that result in more efficiency. These changes will not always be welcomed with open arms by line personnel. Thus, the introduction of specialized, noncommand personnel into what was once a fairly simple organization structure often complicates relationships.

Functional Organization

The **functional organization** is *a modification of the line and staff organization whereby staff departments are given authority over line personnel in narrow areas of specialization.* In a pure line organization, there is limited use of specialists by management. In the line and staff organization, specialization of particular functions characterizes the structure, but the specialists only advise and assist. In the functional structure, however, specialists are given **functional authority**. This is *the right of staff specialists to issue orders in their own names in designated areas.*

functional organization

functional authority

The principle of unity of command (having one boss) is violated when functional authority exists. Even though few, if any, organizations give all of their staff managers functional authority, it is quite common to do so for one or two specialists. If a function is considered to be of crucial importance, it may be necessary for the specialist to exercise direct rather than advisory authority. The violation of unity of command is intentional. The possible losses resulting from confusion and conflicting orders from multiple sources may be more than offset by increased effectiveness.

Examples of specialists often given functional authority are the managers of quality control, safety, and labor relations. Figure 7–4 shows a functional organization. Notice that this is quite similar to the line and staff organization shown in Figure 7–3 except for the nature of the relationship between the staff specialist and other managers. Quality control is a very important function in most manufacturing firms, and its level of authority and status

Figure 7–4   Functional Organizational Structure

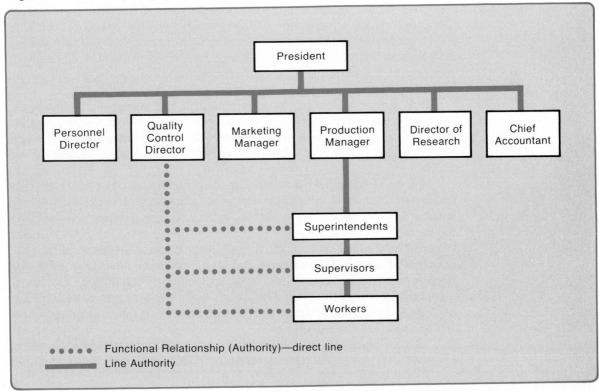

Functional Relationship (Authority)—direct line
Line Authority

within the organization has increased over the years. A traditional staff department would merely advise. Because of the critical nature of its work, however, a quality control department often directs as well as advises.

Safety and labor relations specialists may exercise functional authority over personnel in other areas throughout the organization but only in relation to their specific specialties. A safety manager may issue compliance guidelines and give direct interpretations of the Occupational Safety and Health Act (OSHA) throughout the organization. The labor relations specialist often will have complete authority in contract negotiations with the union. In each of the above illustrations—quality control, safety, and labor relations—the traditional chain of command has been split. As long as this splitting process is restricted, coordination and unity of action are not in excessive danger. Many organizations that utilize functional relationships attempt to confine the impact to managerial rather than operative levels. Thus, a department supervisor may have to account to more than one boss, but the employees are protected from this possible confusion.

The major disadvantages of a functional organization are: (1) the potential conflicts resulting from the violation of the principle of unity of command and (2) the tendency to keep authority centralized at higher levels in the organization. If the functionalized structure is used extensively, there may be a tendency for the line department supervisor to become little more than a figurehead. The structure can become very complicated when there are functional specialists on various levels in the organization.

The Vision of Apollo

NASA

"One small step for man, one giant leap for mankind"— the words of Neil Armstrong in July 1969 as he stepped onto the surface of the moon had become part of the American legend. They represent the realization of the dream to explore space and walk on the moon. More than that, though, landing on the moon was the culmination of a determined ten-year effort initiated by President John F. Kennedy. It was one of the most highly organized and technically complex endeavors ever undertaken.

The "Vision of Apollo," which resulted in Neil Armstrong's moonwalk, has hardly been characteristic of the support given the U.S. space program. The funding for NASA in 1985, as a percentage of the federal budget, is less than one-half that which characterized the Apollo yearly budgets of the 1960s.

Still, NASA has moved forward with challenging goals. The space shuttles *Columbia, Challenger,* and *Discovery* were immensely complex to build and launch. Just to process the shuttle orbiter, external tank, and boosters required 6,027 contractor employees. Not only must NASA be well organized to coordinate such complex activities, but the participant corporations, like Lockheed, Rockwell International, and Martin Marietta, must align their own organizations to accomplish the tasks at hand. For example, at Lockheed, competing teams were established, each including a former astronaut, and each team formed an alliance with a major airline to take advantage of the airline's operational experience.

Just the proposals on the shuttle processing contracts are expected to run over 500 pages. Organizing and coordinating the extremely complex

The Bettmann Archive

*The space program was
one of the most highly
organized ever
undertaken.*

technology, the diverse and highly trained personnel, and the contributions
of hundreds of subcontractors has been a monumental task. The future
presents even greater challenges. President Reagan has charged NASA with
developing "more visionary, long-term space program goals." Among the
ideas being seriously promoted are a lunar base and a systematic exploration
of the solar system.

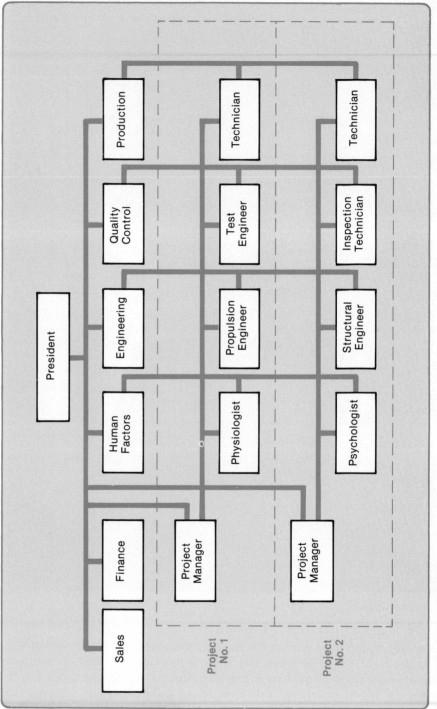

Figure 7–5 Project Structure

Project and Matrix Organization Structures

The line, line and staff, and functional organization structures have been the traditional approaches to organization. The primary goal of these forms of organizations has been the establishment and distribution of authority to coordinate and control the firm by emphasizing vertical, rather than horizontal, relationships. In major aerospace projects like Apollo, however, work processes may flow horizontally, diagonally, up, or down. The direction of work flow depends on the distribution of talents and abilities in the organization and the need to apply them to the problem that exists. The organizations that have emerged to cope with this challenge have been referred to as project and matrix organizations.

A **project organization** is *a temporary organization designed to achieve specific results by using teams of specialists from different functional areas within the organization.* The team focuses all of its energies and skills on the assigned project. Once the specific project has been completed, the project team is broken up, and personnel are reassigned to their regular positions in the organization or to other projects. Many business organizations and government agencies make use of project teams or task forces to concentrate their efforts on a specific project assignment like the development of a new product or new technology or on the construction of a new plant.

project organization

Perhaps the most famous example of the successful use of the project form of organization has been by NASA. The significant space achievements of the United States have been due in part to the project organization structures used by NASA. For each major space goal, a project team was assigned. Neil Armstrong was a member of such a team. The terms used to describe our missions in space, such as *Gemini* and *Apollo,* are familiar to millions of people. Each of these was a distinct project at NASA.

Project organization structures are probably most valuable when the work is:

1. definable in terms of a specific goal and target date for completion that have been established,
2. somewhat unique and unfamiliar to the existing organization,
3. complex with respect to interdependence of activities and specialized skills necessary for accomplishment,
4. critical in terms of possible gain or loss, and
5. temporary with respect to duration of need.

Figure 7–5 illustrates a highly simplified project organization that is attached to an existing organization. Personnel are assigned to the project from the existing permanent organization and are under the direction and control of the project manager. The project manager specifies what effort is needed and when work will be performed, while the concerned department managers may decide who in their unit is to do the work and how it is to be accomplished. Home base for most personnel is the existing department—engineering, production, purchasing, personnel, or research and development.

The authority over the four project members is shared by both the project manager and the function managers in the permanent organization.

The specialists are temporarily on loan and spend only a portion of their time on the project assignment. It is apparent that authority is one of the crucial questions of the project structure. A deliberate conflict has been established between the project manager and managers within the permanent organization. The authority relationships are overlapping, presumably in the interest of ensuring that all problems will be covered.

Project managers and department heads are often forced into using means other than formal authority to accomplish results. Informal relationships become more important than formal prescriptions of authority. In the event of conflict and dispute, discussion and consensus are required rather than the forcing of compliance by threat or punishment. Full and free communication, regardless of formal rank, is required among those working on the project. More attention is allocated to roles and competencies in relation to the project than to formal levels of authority.

Project structures are temporary attachments to existing organizations. When the concept is introduced in a permanent form, the result is a matrix

matrix organization

organization. A **matrix organization** is *a permanent organization designed to achieve specific results by using teams of specialists from different functional areas within the organization.* They are often used when it is essential for the firm to be highly responsive to a rapidly changing external environment. For example, an electronics firm might find that the matrix structure facilitates quick response by the company to its environment. Matrix organization structures have been used successfully in such industries as banking, chemicals, computers, and electronics. However, matrix organizations require the use of an effective coordinating mechanism to offset the negative effect of dual authority.[7]

In matrix organizations, there are functional managers and product (or project) managers. Functional managers are in charge of specialized resources such as production, quality control, inventories, scheduling, and selling. Product managers are in charge of one or more products and are authorized to prepare product strategies and call on the various functional managers for the necessary resources. When a firm moves to a matrix structure, functional managers must realize that they will lose some of their authority and will have to take some direction from the product managers, who have the budgets to purchase internal resources.

Despite limitations, the effectiveness of the project and matrix management concepts demonstrates that people can work for two or more managers and that managers can effectively influence those over whom they have only partial authority. There is the possibility of conflict and frustration, but the opportunity for prompt, efficient accomplishment is great.

COMMITTEES

committee

Committees have been the brunt of many harsh jokes. For example, we have heard that a camel is a horse designed by a committee. A **committee** is *a group of people assigned to work together to do something not included in their regular jobs.* Other names used to designate committees include *board, council,* and *task force.* A permanent committee is referred to as a standing committee. Committees are necessary for several reasons. They can bring together experts from various areas to handle difficult problems. At least in theory, two heads are better than one. Even if the decisions that committees make are technically no better than those made by individuals, such decisions are often more readily accepted. In fact, it is common practice to make sure that persons likely to oppose an expected decision be placed on the committee responsible for making it.

Committees also have weaknesses. Often the decision process is slow. One person can make decisions faster than can a group. Committees are also costly. If five people are on a committee and the average cost of each is $25 an hour, it costs $250 to have a two hour meeting. Another weakness of committees is that they often encourage compromise, even though the best decision is at one extreme or the other.

The shortcomings of committees can be minimized if a few simple rules are followed:

1. The purpose of the committee should be clearly stated in writing.
2. The size of the committee should be just adequate to obtain the representation and intellectual input required.
3. There should be an odd number of members so that the committee will not deadlock on important issues.
4. Every committee meeting should have a specific written agenda.
5. The committee should be immediately disbanded when it has accomplished its purpose.

SUMMARY

In accepting a certain job, a worker takes responsibility for performing the tasks involved. Responsibility is an obligation to perform work activities. On the other hand, authority is the right to decide, to direct others to take action, or to perform certain duties in achieving organizational goals. The process of assigning responsibility along with the needed authority is referred to as delegation. Any means of ensuring that the person who is supposed to do a task actually performs it and does so correctly is referred to as accountability.

There are several important organizing principles. The principle of unity of command states that each person should answer to only one immediate superior. Another principle is that there should be equal authority and responsibility. The scalar principle is the philosophy that authority and responsibility should flow from top management downward in a clear, unbroken line. Finally, the number of direct subordinates reporting to any manager is referred to as the span of management.

Centralization is the degree to which authority

is retained by higher-level managers within an organization rather than being delegated. If a significant amount of authority is delegated to lower levels, the enterprise is described as being decentralized. There are many degrees of centralization. The real question is not whether a company should decentralize but what degree of decentralization is appropriate.

The formal relationships among individuals in the organization are called organizational structure. Line organizations are those organizations that have only direct, vertical relationships between different levels within the firm. Line departments are those departments directly involved in accomplishing the primary purpose of the organization. Line and staff organizations are those organizations that have direct, vertical relationships between different levels within the firm and also specialists responsible for advising and assisting other managers. Staff departments are departments that provide line people with advice and assistance in specialized areas. The functional organization is a modification of the line and staff organization where staff departments are given authority over line departments in a narrow area of specialization. A project organization is a temporary organization designed to achieve specific results by using a team of specialists from different functional areas within the organization. A matrix organization is a permanent organization designed to achieve specific results by using teams of specialists from different function areas within the organization. A special kind of organizational unit is the committee. A committee is a group of people assigned to work together to do something not included in their regular jobs.

REVIEW QUESTIONS

1. Distinguish by definition among the following terms:
   a. Responsibility
   b. Authority
   c. Delegation
   d. Accountability
2. Describe each of the following organizing principles:
   a. Unity of command
   b. Equal authority and responsibility
   c. Scalar principle
3. Distinguish between centralization and decentralization. Briefly describe the primary factors to be considered in determining the degree of centralization that is appropriate for an organization.
4. What are the basic forms of organizational structure? Briefly describe each.
5. Under what circumstances are project and matrix structures most appropriate?
6. Discuss the merits of this statement: "A camel is a horse designed by a committee."

EXERCISES

1. Analyze the organization charts of a local retail store (for example, Sears), a bank, a manufacturing company, and your college or university. How are these firms organized? What changes, if any, would you suggest to the managers of these organizations? Draw new charts if necessary.

CASE STUDY

An Opportunity in Disguise

It was only seven months after Glen Frost took over as postmaster at Norman, Oklahoma, when he received notice of a 20 percent RIF (reduction in force) to take effect at the end of the next pay period. Glen was really worried. He was not sure he could do the job with eight people, which would be the number remaining after the RIF.

Glen finally decided that this might really be an opportunity in disguise. He had tried to rearrange the work area several times in the past, but to no avail. Even though he had suggested a number of layouts, any of which would have improved efficiency, one worker or another—or several—always objected. The postal workers were comfortable with the arrangement of the stamp machine, the sorting boxes, and the counters just where they had been for years.

Glen seized on the opportunity created by the reduction in force. He asked the remaining workers to help him select the best work space arrangement. Within a few days, there was a consensus about how the work stations, machines, and counters should be arranged for maximum efficiency. Glen was also able to reassign some of the work and to eliminate several operations that did not need to be performed at all. As soon as the postal workers became accustomed to the new organization, the post office provided better service than it ever had and the workers actually had an easier time. Although Glen had already lost two people, he decided not to hire a replacement when the next one quit or retired.

QUESTIONS

1. Explain why you believe the postal workers cooperated with Glen after the RIF.
2. Do you approve of Glen's failure to impose a new arrangement of the work flow prior to the RIF? How would you have handled the situation? Defend your answer.
3. Do you believe that Glen's authority was equal to his responsibility? Explain.

CASE STUDY

Misco Paper Converters

When Dick Valladao and George Smeltzer, owners of Misco Paper Converters, began their business, it was only a part-time operation. The operation involved buying rolls of brown kraft paper, such as that used for grocery bags, cutting it into various shapes and sizes, bundling the sheets together, and shipping the bundles to industrial customers. The pieces of paper were used for various purposes: as vapor barriers in electronic equipment, to place between glass or china plates and bowls prior to shipping, and as a protective wrapping for many small manufactured items.

As the business grew and became more profitable, Dick and George decided to leave their jobs and work at Misco full time. They had been doing the work in a small metal building behind George's house, but when they went into the business full time they rented a 6,000-square-foot warehouse. They also purchased a shear press and a stripper in addition to the press and stripper they already owned, as well as a truck to pick up the raw paper at the paper mill and to make some deliveries. Usually the bundles of paper were shipped by common carrier to customers, some of which were as much as 600 miles distant.

Dick and George found it necessary to hire six operators. The operation was simple. The paper was fed off the large rolls through a stripper, which cut it to the appropriate widths. The stripping machine was set to clip the paper off every fifty feet or so. Then the strips were stacked on top of one another on a set of rollers that allowed the paper to be fed back into one of the shear presses. When a stack of strips was fifty layers thick, it was fed into the shear press, which clipped it to the appropriate length. The resulting rectangular stacks of brown paper were tied with twine and stacked onto shipping pallets. When a pallet was full, it was set aside to wait for shipment.

At first, George and Dick worked with the operators as a team, with each worker doing whatever needed to be done. Each person soon learned to operate the forklift, the strippers, and the shear presses and tie bundles as well. Dick and George felt themselves to be relative equals, so neither attempted to exercise authority over the other. As time went on, however, Dick began to think that the whole operation could be accomplished more efficiently if some kind of structure were imposed.

QUESTIONS

1. Do you believe that anything is to be gained at Misco by establishing an organizational structure, including specialization and lines of authority and responsibility? Explain your answer.

2. Assuming that George and Dick decided to set up a typical kind of organization, how should they decide who is to be chief executive? Should they have to decide that at all? Explain.

NOTES

1. "The New Sears," *Business Week,* (November 16, 1981): 140–144; "Financial Services at the Checkout Counter," *Chain Store Age Executive Edition* (December 1982): 31–32; "Sears Biz Centers: Far Ahead of Plan," *Chain Store Age General Merchandising Edition* 60 (February 1984): 63–66; "New Look for the Top Retailer," *Time* (December 5, 1983): 66–68; Sears, Roebuck & Co., *Annual Report;* and numerous articles from *The Wall Street Journal.*

2. R. F. Chisholm and S. V. Kasl, "The Nature and Predictors of Job Related Tension in a Crisis Situation: Reactions of Nuclear Workers to the Three Mile Island Accident," *Academy of Management Journal* (September 1983): 401.

3. J. D. Ford and W. H. Hegarty, "Decision Makers' Beliefs about the Causes and Effects of Structure: An Exploratory Study," *Academy of Management Journal* (June 1984): 281.

4. V. A. Graicunas, "Relationships of Organizations," in *Papers on the Science of Administration,* ed. L. Gulick and L. Urwick (New York: Columbia University Press, 1947).

5. L. W. Fry and J. W. Slocum, Jr., "Technology, Structure, and Workgroup Effectiveness: A Test of a Contingency Model," *Academy of Management Journal* (June 1984): 236.

6. Joan Woodward, *Industrial Organization: Theory and Practice* (London: Oxford University Press, 1965): 52–62.

7. J. L. C. Cheng, "Interdependence and Coordination in Organizations: A Role-System Analysis," *Academy of Management Journal* (March 1983): 160–161.

REFERENCES

Arnold, John D. "The Why, When, and How of Changing Organizational Structures." *Management Review* (March 1981): 17–20.

Cheng, J. L. C. "Interdependence and Coordination in Organizations: A Role-System Analysis." *Academy of Management Journal* (March 1983): 156–162.

Chisholm, R. F., and S. V. Kasl. "The Nature and Predictors of Job Related Tension in a Crisis Situation: Reactions of Nuclear Workers to the Three Mile Island Accident." *Academy of Management Journal* (September 1983): 385–405.

Daft, R. L. *Organization Theory and Design.* St. Paul, Minn.: West Publishing Company, 1983.

Ford, J. D., and W. H. Hegarty. "Decision Makers' Beliefs about the Causes and Effects of Structure: An Exploratory Study." *Academy of Management Journal* (June 1984): 271–291.

Fry, L. W., and J. W. Slocum, Jr. "Technology, Structure, and Workgroup Effectiveness: A Test of a Contingency Model." *Academy of Management Journal* (June 1984): 221–246.

Gibson, James L., John M. Ivancevich, and James H.

Donnelley, Jr. *Organizations: Behavior Structure and Processes.* Dallas: Business Publications, 1981.

Haynes, M. E. "Delegation: There's More to It Than Letting Someone Else Do It." *Supervisory Management* 25 (January 1980): 9–15.

Karasek, R. A., Jr. "Job Demands, Job Decision Latitude for Job Redesign." *Administrative Science Quarterly* 24 (June 1979): 285–308.

Logges, J. G. "Role of Delegation in Improving Productivity." *Personnel Journal* 58 (November 1979): 776–779.

Nicholson, P. J., Jr., and S. C. Goh. "The Relationship of Organization Structure and Interpersonal Attitudes to Role Conflict and Ambiguity in Different Work Environments." *Academy of Management Journal* (March 1983): 148–155.

Ouchi, W. G. "Relationship between Organizational Structure and Organizational Control." *Administrative Science Quarterly* 22 (March 1977): 206–216.

Peters, T. J. "Beyond the Matrix Organization." *Business Horizons* 22 (October 1979): 15–27.

Potter, B. A. "Speaking with Authority: How to Give Directions." *Supervisory Management* 25 (March 1980): 2–11.

Rousseau, D. M. "Assessment of Technology in Organizations: Closed versus Open Systems Approaches." *Academy of Management Review* 4 (October 1979): 531–542.

Waterman, H., Jr., J. Peters, and R. Phillips. "Structure Is Not Organization." *Business Horizons* 23, no. 3 (June 1980): 14–26.

LEARNING OBJECTIVES

After completing this chapter you should be able to

1. Describe the numerous factors that affect group behavior.
2. Explain the characteristics of the informal organization.
3. List the positive and negative aspects of the informal organization.
4. Explain the concepts of status, status sources, and status symbols.
5. Relate the importance of understanding power and politics.

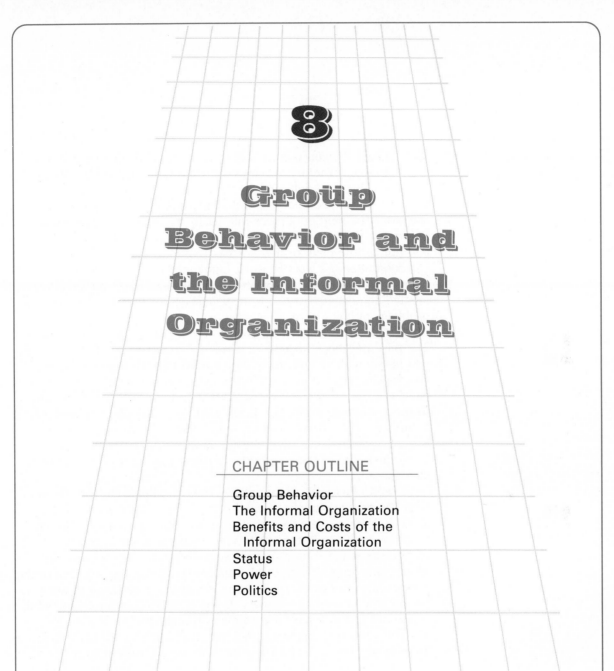

8

Group Behavior and the Informal Organization

Linda Watson was excited to have her new job at the Derek Garment Factory in Barnwell, South Carolina. She had been looking for a job for nearly six months, and her employment compensation had expired. Linda was especially pleased that she would be paid on a piece-rate basis. Wherever she had worked before, she found herself doing more work than most other people and not getting paid for it.

Soon after she went to work, Linda made several new friends, most of them women. During coffee breaks and lunch periods they chatted about their husbands or ex-husbands, their children, and the problems of being working women.

Within two weeks, Linda was exceeding the production standard. The third paycheck included a piece-rate bonus of nearly $50. Linda was barely making ends meet and needed the extra money. As she was walking toward the plant entrance, happily looking at her paycheck, she noticed Charissa Gorman, one of the more experienced workers, walking beside her. Linda said, "Hi, Charissa. I made a $50 bonus this week. It sure will come in handy." Charissa answered, "I know it will, Linda. It would for any of us. But if you keep it up, they'll just change the piece rate. Anyway, you're making the rest of us look bad."

Despite Charissa's disapproval, Linda continued to work faster. Over the next few weeks, several more of her friends spoke to her about it. Within a few days she began to notice a coolness. No one would sit with her in the lunchroom. Even when she joined the others, she found it hard to start a conversation. A couple of times when Linda approached a table, the conversation stopped. One of the women, who had never really been friendly, said to Linda as she was leaving the lunchroom one day, "If you don't stop trying to show off, you're not going to have a friend left around here."

The next week Linda allowed her production to fall back to just a little above standard. She knew that this would make the other workers feel better toward her. Within a few days, the other workers were being friendly again.

Linda's problem did not result from formal rules or regulations but from pressure put on her by her coworkers. Although she needed more money, she changed her behavior because of the pressure. This is not an unusual occurrence. Informal relationships often have considerable influence over workers' behavior on the job. Managers who do not recognize this or who try to prevent such informal relationships from existing may have difficulty.

Many managers are proud of the formal organizational structure that has been developed. It is logical and orderly. Everyone knows exactly who the boss is and what tasks are expected of them. Some managers believe they can sit back in their executive suites and the company will run itself because of the structure that has been developed.

As in Linda's case, inserting the human element into an organization confuses the clear, logically designed official structure desired so much by some managers. In fact, the behavior suggested by the formal organization and the way the employees actually interact to accomplish the task may be completely different. Employees develop friendships and relationships with individuals in other departments. They also choose their own informal leaders, who may or may not be the same as those selected by the formal organization.

In this chapter, we first examine some characteristics of group behavior. Then we study the informal organization and identify its benefits and costs. Finally, status, power, and politics are discussed as these topics relate to both the formal and informal organization.

GROUP BEHAVIOR

A **group** is *the joining of two or more people together to accomplish a desired goal.* All of us belong to many groups. Within a company, many different groups can exist. There are formal work groups, of course, made up of managers and subordinates. Linda was assigned to a certain supervisor at Derek Garment Factory as part of a formal work group. Our concern here, though, is primarily informal groups. An **informal group** is defined as *two or more persons associated with one another in ways not prescribed by the formal organization.* At first, Linda was becoming a member of an informal group based on such common interests as husbands or ex-husbands and the problems of working women. The informal group includes workers who are especially close friends and have their own cliques. Two or three people might belong to the same church or baseball team, or they might go fishing or have parties together. There are job-related groups, too, within work groups. If you work close to a person who does similar work, you will probably communicate with that person much more than with others. Managers need to understand all of these kinds of groups if they are to accomplish their jobs effectively.

group

informal group

Norms

The formal organization has its performance standards, and the informal organization has its norms. A **norm** is *a standard of behavior expected of informal group members.* Those who violate group norms are helped to see the errors of their ways. Informal pressures to conform to group norms are often more powerful than the official sanctions used by managers to enforce conformance to organizational standards. Workers who are high producers (very acceptable to the formal organization) may be sanctioned by the informal organization until their production falls back in line with the informal group's norms. In the example at the beginning of the chapter, Linda Watson was influenced to conform to the group norm of expected

norm

Managers need to understand both the formal and informal organization.   Janice Fullman/The Picture Cube

output. Group norms are unwritten rules that new members, if they are to remain members, gradually learn. Norms are frequently established concerning how hard one should work, whether one should be friendly, the degree to which one should cooperate with management, and whether one should be innovative.

Role

role   The concept of role is broader than that of its counterpart in the formal organization—the job. A **role** consists of *the total pattern of expected behavior of an individual.* In the formal organization, it includes, but goes beyond, the official content of the job description. If a person is officially designated a supervisor, pressure may be exerted to dress, talk, and act similar to other managers in the organization. If managers in a particular firm typically dress formally, the manager who fails to wear the proper "uniform" is not fulfilling the expected role.

Individuals who are members of an informal group also are presented with an expected role to act out. Whether the informal group is supportive of management has a major impact on the roles of the group members. If the group decides they should not support a decision made by top management, the pattern of their behavior (role) may reflect indifference or slowing down on the job. Failure to conform to the expected role may result in a member's being cast out of the informal group. This may harm the formal organization as well as the individual.[1]

A person may have many roles that he or she must constantly play. For instance, when working toward a doctorate, one of the authors was a student, a teacher, a consultant, and a military officer in the reserves. For each of these activities, there was a different role, and failure to change roles immediately at the proper time often resulted in difficulties. Being a military officer on the weekend with considerable authority, followed on Monday morning by playing the humble role of a doctoral student, was sometimes not easy. Students who go back to school part time while working as a supervisor in a firm often encounter the same difficulties.

Leadership

In the formal organization, leaders (managers) are placed in their position of authority by top management. By filling a particular supervisory position, the individual is designated the leader. An entirely different procedure is at work in selecting a leader for the informal organization. The informal leader is usually chosen in one of two ways. People may appoint themselves. A leadership vacuum may have existed, and the first person who takes charge may be automatically followed. Or the informal leader may be chosen through consensus. In this case, the person who is closest to the norms of the group often becomes the leader. Charissa Gorman may have been such a leader at Derek Garment Factory. There is no formal title attached to this individual. This person is the one who is looked to for guidance in achieving the group's goal. Should the leader begin to deviate from group norms, another leader who is closer to the group norm will take his or her place. For example, if Charissa began to increase her own output, she would probably lose her influence with the group.

Cohesiveness

The degree of attraction that the group has for each of its members is referred to as **cohesiveness**. It has importance to both the formal and informal organization. It is identified by such attitudes as loyalty to the group, friendliness, congeniality, a feeling of responsibility for group effort, and defending against outside attack. Cohesive informal work groups are powerful instruments that can work for or against the formal organization. For instance, a highly cohesive group whose goals are in agreement with organizational objectives can use this strength to assist the firm in increasing productivity. On the other hand, a highly cohesive group that is not in agreement with organizational objectives can have an extremely negative effect on the accomplishment of the firm's goals. Because of this potential problem, some managers attempt to reduce cohesion in order to maintain control. The informal work group at Derek Garments is both highly cohesive and has goals that conflict with company goals.

Several factors will affect the degree of cohesiveness group members have for each other. First, a group that works under dangerous conditions often develops great cohesiveness. The manager who is seen as a threat by

cohesiveness

workers can cause them to band together in opposition. Second, groups whose members work alongside each other are likely to be more cohesive. Group members who seldom see each other are not likely to be as cohesive. Third, groups consisting of workers of one sex, race, or age are usually more cohesive than mixed groups. That is one of the reasons why women or minorities are often not readily accepted into a work group that consists of white males. The fact that most of the garment workers at Derek were women probably made the informal work group more cohesive. Group cohesiveness may break down as characteristics of group members become more diverse. Fourth, if being a member of the group satisfies members' needs, they will have a stronger desire to stay with the group. Finally, smaller groups tend to be more cohesive. Large groups have so many different relationships that cohesiveness is reduced.

Size

The informal group tends to be small so that its members may interact frequently. But when groups get too small, difficulties arise. The dyad, or two-person group, is a perfect example. When a decision is required and there is not a consensus, one group member must lose.

There has been considerable research devoted to determining the most effective group size. This research has led to the following conclusions:

- When quality of a complex group decision is important, the use of seven to twelve members under a formal leader is most appropriate.
- When consensus in a conflict situation is important, the use of three to five members with no formal leader will ensure that each member's view will be discussed.
- When both quality and consensus are important, five to seven members seems most appropriate.[2]

There tends to be greater group conflict in even-sized groups, and there is more conflict in groups of two and four members than there is in those of six members. In seating arrangements, members who sit across from each other tend to engage in more frequent and often argumentative communication. If consensus is the goal, members with high conflict potential should be seated alongside each other.

Thus, when dealing with the subject of effective work groups, we are primarily concerned with small ones. Obviously, many organizations consist of thousands of members. The initial approach to organization must therefore be formal in nature, resulting in the design of official units, jobs, and formal relationships of authority, responsibility, and accountability. Within this formal organization, a limitless number of small, informal work groups will be spontaneously established and, it is hoped, will be aligned with overall organizational objectives.

Synergism

synergism   **Synergism** is *the potential for two or more persons working together to accomplish more than they could working separately.* It implies the possibility of accomplishing tasks that could not have been done by two people working alone.[3] The concept of synergism has implications for both formal and informal groups. Managers need to recognize that greater effect may be achieved when two workers are placed together. However, through the synergistic effect, the informal group may become more powerful. People in groups often have much more influence than each individual has alone.

Applying Knowledge of Group Behavior

There would be no need to concern ourselves with informal groups if managers could just tell subordinates what to do and it would be done, but this is seldom the case. Few managers know everything their subordinates need to do. In addition, humans are not only rational beings; they are also emotional ones, with feelings and sentiments. Managers who ignore these feelings and sentiments are only doing part of their job. An understanding of group behavior is a valuable tool of management. All of the informal relationships and small informal groups combine together to constitute what is called the informal organization.

THE INFORMAL ORGANIZATION

The manager of the formal organization establishes what employees should do through organizational charts and job descriptions. Traditional managers tend to emphasize the values of organizational and personal loyalty. They often can tolerate incompetence more readily than disloyalty. The official organization attempts to specify the way things should be accomplished in the various sections, departments, and divisions of the firm.

The official structure is only a portion of the story. There emerges another structure, existing alongside the formal one and sometimes extending beyond it, consisting of informal relationships, created not by officially designated managers but by organizational members at every level. This structure is called the *informal organization.*

Because of the impact of the informal organization, increasing numbers of firms are training their managers to be able to cope with the informal group. Gerritt Starke, director of corporate personnel for Kemper Insurance Company, says, "We teach our managers/supervisors to be alert to the formation of 'informal work groups' and that such groups can be either a positive or a negative influence on a department or company objective." Corning Glass Works also has an extensive management development program devoted to both understanding how the informal group functions and designing ways to have the informal group work in a positive manner. In light of the influence the informal organization exerts at Derek Garment, it might be useful for management there to build on the informal relationships in attempting to increase productivity.

The informal organization has certain characteristics. First, its members are joined together to satisfy needs. They may, however, be seeking to satisfy completely different needs. One worker may want to make friends, and another may be seeking advancement. Second, the informal organization is continuously changing. Relationships that exist one day may be gone the next. Third, members of various organizational levels may be involved. The

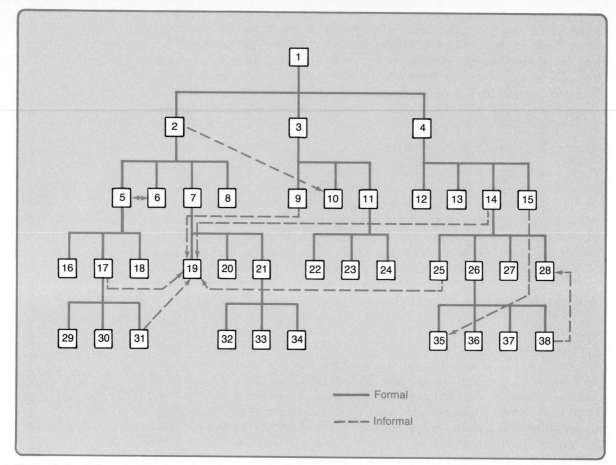

Figure 8–1   A Contact Chart

informal organization does not adhere to the boundaries established by the formal one. A manager in one area may have close ties to a worker in another. Fourth, the informal organization is affected by relationships outside the firm. A top-level manager and a supervisor may associate with each other because they are members of the same golf club. Finally, the informal organization has a pecking order: certain people are assigned greater importance than others by the informal group. Workers who adhere more closely to the group norms tend to be given greater respect.

Although not capable of being placed into a formal organizational chart, the informal organization has its own structure. As with the formal structure, informal groups may also have different levels in the chain of command. It may even be charted by management, but the members themselves have not drawn up a formal structure. Gerritt Starke of Kemper Insurance Company states, "We should recognize that 'informal work groups' exist at all levels of the organization. A formal organization chart can be very misleading in terms of who has 'real' authority and influence."

The dynamic nature of the informal structure constantly changes. As different members enter into and exit from the group, the structure is modified. The structure is heavily based on the communication patterns that develop among group members. If many people attempt to gain the advice of one individual, this individual is often the informal leader, and the structure develops around this individual. Just as formal organizations have vice-presidents, the informal group may have an equivalent counterpart. The structure evolves rather than being formally laid out but often it is more effective than the formal organizational structure.

One means by which the organizational structure of the informal work group may be studied is through the use of a contact chart. A **contact chart** is *a diagram showing various individuals in the organization and the numbers of interactions they have with others.* These charts are developed to identify the connections that an individual has with other members of the organization. As may be seen from the contact chart in Figure 8–1, all contacts do not follow the formal organizational chart. In various instances, certain levels of management are bypassed; others show cross-contact from one chain of command to another. Based on the number of workers contacting the employee, individual 19 appears to be very popular. A similar analysis done for Derek Garments would have to show that Linda was building relationships at first. A later contact chart would have revealed her isolation. Still later, as her productivity dropped, the earlier contacts were restored and perhaps increased.

contact chart

A difficulty with a contact chart is that it does not show the reasons for relationships. Also, it is never clear whether contacts shown will work for or against the organization. Individual 19 could be assisting other employees accomplish their tasks. On the other hand, this individual could be talking down the organization and promoting disharmony among company employees. Once managers have identified the major contact points, they are in a position either to encourage or discourage the individual within the work group.

BENEFITS AND COSTS OF THE INFORMAL ORGANIZATION

Managers often have mixed emotions about the informal organization. Although it is capable of contributing to greater organizational effectiveness, it is not without drawbacks; there are certain costs. If management is properly trained to understand and work with the informal organization, however, the benefits should exceed the costs, as Figure 8–2 suggests. But if management is not careful, the reverse may be true.

Benefits of the Informal Organization

It is fortunate that management cannot destroy the informal organization because it is capable of providing significant benefits to an organization's effectiveness. Most would consider the informal organization at Derek Garment Factory to have been detrimental to productivity; however, it probably provided at least one or two of the benefits of the informal organization discussed below.

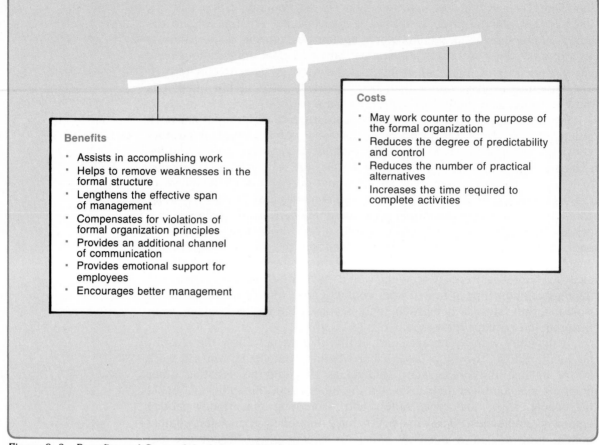

Benefits

* Assists in accomplishing work
* Helps to remove weaknesses in the formal structure
* Lengthens the effective span of management
* Compensates for violations of formal organization principles
* Provides an additional channel of communication
* Provides emotional support for employees
* Encourages better management

Costs

* May work counter to the purpose of the formal organization
* Reduces the degree of predictability and control
* Reduces the number of practical alternatives
* Increases the time required to complete activities

Figure 8–2   Benefits and Costs of the Informal Work Group

Assists in Accomplishing Work

For managers to be effective, their subordinates must be permitted a certain degree of flexibility in accomplishing assigned tasks. Advance approval of every move is detrimental to achieving success. If people in an organization acted only when they were told to act, followed standard instructions to the letter at all times, and contacted others only when duly authorized, a business would have to cease operations. However, the traditionalist tends to rely more heavily on formal decisions based on a scientific study of business problems.

There are also occasions when the formal command is wrong or inadequate for the situation. If the atmosphere is heavily traditional, subordinates may exhibit malicious obedience by executing a command faithfully despite personal knowledge that their action will ultimately result in failure. Many managers have discovered that a subordinate can agree with them all day, follow every directive to the letter, and yet will fail miserably. If more faith is placed in informal relationships, subordinates may voluntarily adapt the formal order to the requirements of the actual situation. When loosely structured, groups are often able to achieve organizational objectives more effectively in an informal manner.

Helps to Remove Weaknesses in the Formal Structure

The formal organization often has a number of gaps that the informal group can fill. Let us consider a person who is promoted to a position that exceeds his or her current capabilities. This is not an unusual occurrence in the armed services, for instance, where a young officer is appointed unit commander. Without the advice and assistance of an experienced sergeant, young officers might not survive their first assignment. In fact, most likely there are many officers who have been unsuccessful in the military because they have failed to recognize the power of the informal organization. The formal orders and regulations say that the person is the commander, with certain responsibilities and authorities. By admitting one's temporary weaknesses, help may be obtained from other officers and enlisted personnel. In effect, deficiencies in the formal structure have been removed by sharing decision making with others. In time, the informal group may resemble the formal organization more closely.

Lengthens the Effective Span of Management

As we indicated in Chapter 7, the number of people a manager can effectively supervise is referred to as the span of management. As individuals and small groups learn to interact more effectively and are permitted to do so by their supervisors, the manager should be able to devote less time to each individual worker. This could well contribute to a broadening of a manager's effective span of management.

Compensates for Violations of Formal Organization Principles

The development of informal relationships also influences the effectiveness of certain traditional principles of formal organizations. For example, it has been pointed out that even though authority should equal responsibility, the principle is often violated. As a result, the employee tries to develop informal contacts with personnel over whom he or she has no formal authority. Favors are traded and friendships formed. One quickly learns that the formal prescription of authority often is not a sufficient base for operation. Yet this still does not negate the desirability of having responsibility equal authority.

Provides an Additional Channel of Communication

The informal means by which information is transmitted in an organization is referred to as the **grapevine**. To some traditional managers, the grapevine constitutes an obstacle to be destroyed. They seek to channel and control most, if not all, communications through the official chain of command. However, the grapevine can add to organizational effectiveness if the manager will use it. The grapevine is fast and usually accurate in the information it transmits.

The use of the grapevine does not decrease the importance of the official channel of communication and command. Although it can spread much information in a short period, it cannot provide the authority that is necessary for much of the action that will take place.

Provides Emotional Support for Employees

Over half of all voluntary resignations in many organizations occur within the first six months of employment. This is often due to poor

grapevine

induction procedures, when little help is provided the new employee in joining and being accepted within the group. Friendships, or at least speaking acquaintances, are highly essential to a satisfactory working environment for most people. In one hospital where the termination rate among janitorial personnel was high, the formation of cleanup teams reduced turnover considerably. Such personnel felt isolated and uncomfortable when working alone among physicians, nurses, and patients.

Encourages Better Management

Awareness of the nature and impact of the informal organization often leads to better management decisions. The acceptance of the fact that

Managers should realize that organizational performance can be affected by the workers who grant or withhold cooperation and enthusiasm.

Owen Franken/Stock, Boston Inc.

formal relationships will not enable full accomplishment of organizational tasks stimulates management to seek other means of motivation. If most of the work is done informally, managers will seek to improve their knowledge of the nature of the people in general and subordinates in particular. Managers should realize that organizational performance can be affected by the workers who grant or withhold cooperation and enthusiasm. Means other than formal authority must be sought to develop attitudes that support effective performance.

Costs of the Informal Organization

The informal organization is not without its drawbacks. Here are some possible costs of informal work groups.

May Work Counter to the Purposes of the Formal Organization

It is apparent to most managers that individuals and groups can and sometimes do work contrary to the formal goals of an enterprise. If the goals of the informal group could always be the same as those of the organization, few would object to the encouragement of its formation; however, there are results such as work restriction, pressuring other workers to exhibit disinterest in company requirements, disloyalty, insubordination, and unauthorized actions that work at cross-purposes with other functions in the organization.

Reduces the Degree of Predictability and Control

The supervisor of Linda Watson and Charissa Gorman is not in control of Linda's productivity. A basic purpose of an organization is to ensure predictability and control of individual behavior so that the individual will work effectively toward organizational goals. This depends, however, on people interpreting and executing the formal guidelines. If we recognize and accept the possibility of a good outcome from permitted flexibility, we also must accept the risks that accompany this lesser degree of control. The human element can and does add much to an organization's effectiveness; it also can and does add much to the degree of uncertainty.

Reduces the Number of Practical Alternatives

A study of the U.S. Army during World War II concluded that the natural unit of personal commitment was the informal group, not the total formal organization.[4] For example, the soldiers reported that one of the major reasons for moving forward in combat was to avoid letting the other fellow down. In all organizations, business or military, the solidarity of the informal group is a major constraint to management actions.

This solidarity may create problems in the reassigning of personnel. If informal groups are broken up by moving individual members in and out of them, members may feel insecure and show decreased motivation and cooperation. This may suggest that management should think in terms of moving groups around, rather than individuals. If management wishes to capitalize on the considerable values issuing from the development of informal relationships in work groups, it must be willing to accept the loss of some flexibility in decision making.

Increases the Time Required to Complete Activities

If the cooperative efforts of the informal work groups can be aligned with the objectives of the firm, management has the best of both worlds. The collective power generated can be phenomenal. Informal work group activities such as gossiping, betting pools, long coffee breaks, and general horseplay are time-consuming and may be detrimental to efficient operations. These are acts that will tax the patience of rigid, rational managers. Yet if an effective work group is to be established, some of these activities will have to be permitted and should even be encouraged. Managers must realize that, despite concern for goal accomplishment, they must allow the group time and opportunity to maintain itself in good working order. People can usually sustain action for a longer period of time under an informal atmosphere than they can when the situation is highly rigid, controlled, and formal.

Dorothy Tivis Pollack

From her first job on her home-town newspaper in Fargo, North Dakota, to her current position as vice-president for retail merchandising and fashion director at Formfit, Dorothy Pollack's career has been one big love affair—with people.

"My big love always has been meeting and talking with people," she says, and when she left Fargo for the lure of New York City, she used people-to-people contact as the basis for romantic fiction and advice to the lovelorn, which she turned out regularly for McFadden and Fawcett Publications. Jobs followed on several New York papers including the *New York Post* and, after a stint in the foreign department of United Press International, she abandoned journalism for a career as a successful fashion model. Weary of that tiresome role ("You work like a truck horse!") and anxious to use the fashion expertise she'd gained by working before the cameras, Dorothy launched still a third career as the advertising director for an intimate apparel manufacturer. Later, at Formfit she added promotion and fashion merchandising, but "the best was yet to come," says Vice-President Pollack.

Retailers, and most particularly large department stores, she explains, found themselves in trouble during the 1970s as consumers turned to mass merchandisers to satisfy their needs. The big stores, feeling the pinch, needed help, especially in certain soft goods areas where marketing and merchandising efforts were lacking. Formfit already was busy establishing itself as a leader in the industry with plans to introduce a unique new product: YOU panties made of Lita, a fabric that breathes, which alone was five years in developing. Under the leadership of a bright new management team, the company employed every conceivable marketing tool to bring the concept to consumers successfully.

"As a result," Dorothy continues, "a brand new division of retail merchandising was formed and I leaped at the chance to head it." Ms. Pollack all along had been polishing her skills in people-to-people contact through networking, a technique of giving and gleaning information and education from one's peers, which women new to the business world find especially helpful in getting ahead. No slouch in helping others herself, Dorothy has headed THE FASHION GROUP's Women in Management and Job Counseling Committees for several years and has been a seminar leader since the inception of conferences held by the American Woman's Economic Development Corp. (AWED).

Of her travels introducing new fashion concepts at stores around the country, she speaks enthusiastically: "When I prove to a sports-minded woman that a bra from Formfit's *Active Woman Collection* will give her necessary support and comfort, or watch a full-figured woman's face light up when she sees our *A Cut Above Collection,* I know that we're all on the right track." Although the division is still in its infancy, she adds, "It's booming, which is proof to us that retailers and manufacturers must join hands to make it all work."

STATUS

Status is involved in both the formal and informal organization. *A person's rank or position in a group* is called **status**. It is an important relationship that has considerable effect on the morale and efficiency of any organization. Status is an inevitable component of human relationships in all aspects of life, business and nonbusiness. In this section, we examine the sources of status in business organizations, the symbols that denote status levels, and the functions of a status system.

status

Status Sources

The sources of status, or social rank, can be of both an informal and a formal nature. Examples of these sources are as follows:

Formal Organizational Sources	Personal Sources
Occupation or job	Education
Organizational level	Age
	Seniority
	Race
	Religion
	Parentage
	Sex
	Competence
	Associates

It is apparent that certain occupations are accorded more prestige than others. For example, white-collar jobs are usually more highly esteemed than blue-collar jobs. Dorothy Pollack's job as fashion model in some respects carried more status than her first management job as advertising director. Within particular companies, management has discovered, often with great surprise, the following status differentials: long-distance telephone operators have higher social rank than operators handling local calls; cooks who work on white meat have higher status than those who work on dark; and cafeteria personnel who handle fish dishes have less prestige than those who serve beef. As can be seen, the status of one's occupation depends on the rank accorded it by one's peers, and not by management alone. The job assigned to a person and the level of organization in which it is placed are significant sources of status; in general, the higher the organizational level, the higher the level of prestige.

Finally, there is status that comes from one's associates. This is social rank that comes from friendship, kinship, or social organizations. Membership in a certain fraternity or club and graduation from certain schools are examples of status being assigned to a person on the basis of the status accorded the larger group. Membership in these groups is often based on possession of some of the other personal sources of status.

Status Symbols

status symbol *A visible, external sign of one's social position* is referred to as a **status symbol**. A stranger can enter an organization and, if aware of status hierarchies, is able to obtain a social fix quickly by reading the various symbols. Status symbols often vary from firm to firm. For example, one would usually expect that higher-status positions are accompanied by more elaborate office furnishings. In one organization, however, the high-status positions were given antique roll-top desks, whereas the lower jobs were equipped with new, shiny, modern furniture. Symbols sometimes change with the times. Some typical status symbols in business are the following:

- Job titles
- Pay
- Bonus/stock plans
- Size and location of desk or office
- Location of parking space or reserved parking
- Type of company car assigned
- Secretaries

TABLE 8-1   Status Symbols

Visible Appurtenances	Top Dogs	V.I.P.'s	Brass
Brief cases	None—they ask the questions	Use backs of envelopes	Someone goes along to carry theirs
Desks, office	Custom made (to order)	Executive style (to order)	Type A, "Director"
Tables, office	Coffee tables	End tables or decorative wall tables	Matching tables, type A
Carpeting	Nylon—1-inch pile	Nylon—1-inch pile	Wool-twist (with pad)
Plant stands	Several—kept filled with strange exotic plants		Two—repotted whenever they take a trip
Vacuum water bottles	Silver	Silver	Chromium
Library	Private collection	Autographed or complimentary books and reports	Selected references
Shoe shine service	Every morning at 10:00	Every morning at 10:15	Every day at 9:00 or 11:00
Parking space	Private—in front of office	In plant garage	In company garage—if enough seniority

- Privacy
- Use of executive clubs
- Cocktail party invitations
- Furnishings, including rugs, pictures, tables, and similar items
- Privileges, including freedom to move about, not punching the time clock, and freedom to set own working hours and to regulate coffee break
- Ceremonies of induction
- Number of windows in office

Within the company, however, many of the symbols are within the control of management and constitute the basis for many conflicts. Executives have gotten down on their hands and knees to measure and compare the sizes of offices. Windows are counted, steps from the president's office are paced off, secretaries who can use a word processor are sought, parking space is fought for, and company cars are wangled. In some organizations, having a window office is a major status symbol. A humorous treatment of status symbols is presented in Table 8–1. Some reflection on this table leads one to believe that there is more truth than fiction here.

Some managements have sought to abolish the whole problem of awarding status symbols by attempting to equalize all privileges, offices, and furnishings. For instance, NCR has eliminated the executive dining rooms and uses open-landscaped offices. In some universities the department head position is rotated among the department members, thereby reducing the status attached to the position. Windowless buildings have been constructed, office sizes are completely standardized, and only one type of company car is available. However, as long as there are differences in status, some type of symbol will be worked out by the group.

No. 2s	Eager Beavers	Hoi Polloi
Carry their own—empty	Daily—carry their own—filled with work	Too poor to own one
Type B, "Manager"	Castoffs from No. 2s	Yellow Oak—or castoff from Eager Beavers
Matching tables, type B	Plain work table	None—lucky to have own desk
Wool-twist (without pad)	Used wool pieces—sewed	Asphalt tile
One medium-sized—repotted annually during vacation	Small—repotted when plant dies	May have one in the department or bring their own from home
Plain painted	Coke machine	Water fountains
Impressive titles on covers	Books everywhere	Dictionary
Every other day	Once a week	Shine their own
In company properties—somewhere	On the parking lot	Anywhere they can find a space—if they can afford a car

Status Functions

Status produces several desirable values such as the following:

- *Assisting in meeting the needs of the individual.* Most people wish to be accorded some degree of respect by others. They want to have their abilities and accomplishments recognized, and status symbols constitute tangible evidence of this respect.

- *Facilitating the process of communication.* We receive many messages daily from people we do not know personally. The status title of the person or position helps us to evaluate the worth of the message. For example, if a medical doctor tells you something about your backache, the information will likely have more meaning than if the service station attendant diagnosed the problem.

- *Serving as a motivational device for management.* Management has discovered that employees will strive for prestige and prestige symbols as well as for money. Therefore, nonfinancial incentives can be worked into a more comprehensive incentive system. A job title change is often as satisfying as more money. A change to a job of lesser pay but more prestige is often a change a particular person will find satisfying, providing that the pay is still sufficient. Thus, status as a motivating tool has its greatest use in situations where monetary requirements have been met to a reasonable degree. If management is aware of status systems and the symbols it can control, more comprehensive and coordinated incentives can be developed.

POWER

power

The ability of one person to influence the behavior of another person is referred to as **power**. Like status, power is neither completely informal nor formal in nature. The concept of power goes well beyond the capacities provided by the formal organization. Therefore, it is included in this section of the text.

Power is an emotionally laden term, particularly in cultures that emphasize individuality and equality. To label a manager as a *power seeker* is to cast doubt on that manager's motives and actions. Some of these negative views issue from older analyses that have suggested that power is evil, that it corrupts people, that it is largely comprised of naked force, and that the amount is limited in supply. Certainly, the modern business corporation constitutes a major concentration of economic power that has materially improved the standard of living of millions of people. When such concentrations lead to abuse, control rather than its elimination would appear to be the more desirable course of action. Power can be a highly effective instrument for the good of the people.

Sources of Power

The sources of power are many and varied and are not all under the control of management. A popular listing of the sources of power is presented below.

Legitimate Power

This type of power results from a person's being placed in a formal position of authority. It results from a person's occupying a certain position in the organizational structure and being granted legitimate authority. Individuals feel obligated to do what their manager says. The fact that Dorothy Pollack holds the office of vice-president at Formfit Rogers gives her this kind of power.

Reward Power

Reward power is derived from a person's ability to reward another individual. Reward power may be formal or informal. Formal reward power might depend on the manager's ability to obtain a promotion or a pay raise for a worker. The informal group might reward a person through acceptance by coworkers. In the story at the beginning of the chapter, Linda was rewarded by the informal group for decreasing her output.

Coercive Power

This type of power is derived from the ability to punish or to recommend punishment. From a formal standpoint, the manager might fire a worker. The informal group might punish an individual by imposing the silent treatment, as happened to Linda Watson when she started doing too much work.

Referent Power

This form of power is based on a liking for or a desire to be like the power holder. The particular personality and characteristics of an individual will affect the degree to which other persons wish to identify and be associated with that person. President John F. Kennedy is known to have possessed this form of power to a remarkable degree. His admonition, "Ask not what your country can do for you but what you can do for your country," resulted in thousands of volunteers for the Peace Corps.

Expert Power

This form of power comes from a person's possessing special knowledge or skill. It is often the most effective type. Even though an individual has limited formal authority, expertise in a particular area will give that person considerable influence. Famed oil well firefighting expert "Red" Adair is well known by roughnecks (oil field workers) the world over for his knowledge of how to put out oil well fires. This expertise gives him the ability to go aboard an oil drilling platform anywhere in the world and immediately start to issue orders that will be obeyed without question.

Expert power possessed by subordinates is often difficult for management to accept. For example, if a computer programmer becomes so knowledgeable and competent as to be considered indispensable to the organization, problems can result. The supervisor may feel unable to even reprimand the programmer for fear that person will quit or sabotage the supervisor.

This brings to light a potential problem with line and staff organizations: the line has the legitimate power, whereas the staff depends on expert power. The formal right to manage a firm remains with line managers, but the capacity to manage it has been diluted and spread among a number of experts.

Power versus Formal Authority

The concept of power discussed above extends far beyond formal authority. A person's total power can be represented by the following formula:

$$\frac{\text{Total}}{\text{Power}} = \frac{\text{Legitimate}}{\text{Power}} \pm \frac{\text{Reward}}{\text{Power}} \pm \frac{\text{Coercive}}{\text{Power}} \pm \frac{\text{Referent}}{\text{Power}} \pm \frac{\text{Expert}}{\text{Power}}$$

A person's total power is the total of all these forms of power. The only power given by the manager's position in the organization is legitimate power. The formula shows that total power can be strengthened or weakened by reward, coercive, referent, or expert power. That is the reason for the plus or minus signs. For instance, a supervisor with little legitimate power might still be quite powerful because of being an expert in the field. On the other hand, a manager with considerable legitimate power might be virtually powerless because of a lack of job knowledge.

When President Reagan appointed Sandra Day O'Connor as a justice of the Supreme Court, she probably already had great referent and expert power. Afterward, however, this was supplemented by legitimate power based on the respect people have for her position and reward and coercive power, resulting from her ability to determine benefits and penalties in important cases.

Significance of Power to the Manager

Research has shown that a good manager must have a concern for acquiring and using power. In a number of studies, it was found that over 70 percent of managers have a higher need for power than does the general population.[5] And the better managers have a stronger need for power than a need to be liked by others. This need for power is not a desire to be dictatorial, nor is it necessarily a drive for personal enhancement. Rather, it is a concern for influencing others on behalf of the organization. It is a need for socialized power rather than for personal power. When managers feel a greater need to be liked than a need to influence others, they tend to be less effective in many organizations.

The control of situational factors, both in and out of the organization, is of significant concern to modern managers. It has been noted that when organizations grow so large and complex that no one individual has the capacity to manage all of the interdependencies, a dominant managing group will develop. This coalition is sometimes formalized into a presidential or executive office. It will exist, however, whether or not it is actually recorded on a chart. If the president of the firm heavily depends on the vice-president of finance to develop the crucial programs, that vice-president is likely to be a member of the dominant coalition and have actual power in excess of that suggested by the official chart. Within the organization, smaller and sometimes more temporary coalitions are formed so that a task involving significant interdependencies can be executed. The formation, use, and dissolution of such coalitions are sometimes called politics.

POLITICS

In everyday conversations with the general public, the politician would most likely receive low marks of approval. Political scandals have regularly hit the front page of the daily newspaper. Although the politician's image is low, politics and politicians are with us in all forms of organized society, and not just the politicians who are in government. Political action can and does provide positive values in promoting cooperation among individuals and groups with differing interests and objectives.

Politics can be described as *a "network of interaction by which power is acquired, transferred, and exercised upon others."*[6] Let us think about this definition in order to gain a thorough appreciation of what it means. The politician is working with and through many people. As such, politics transcend the traditional organizational structure boundaries. In the process of these interactions, the medium of exchange is power. Just as the dollar is used as the medium of exchange in our economic system, power provides virtually the same function in politics. The shrewd politician acquires power and transfers it to another person when it can *purchase* something of value. Politicians use this medium of exchange in the network that they establish to exert pressure on others in order to gain their desired end result. Just like the accountant, the politician has a balance sheet. When power is transferred, something is received in return. To the political, a favor given now is power to be extracted in the future. Thus, we are all politicians to a certain extent; some are better at it than others.

politics

Role of Politics in Business Organizations

If all actions could be foreseen and prescribed for with accuracy, perhaps there would be little need for politics. This would also assume that all conflicts could be resolved in some rational manner acceptable to all. Inasmuch as neither of these two circumstances is likely, the individual will be asked to adjust and accommodate to varying conditions and pressures. Perhaps *adjustments* and *accommodations* are more understandable terms for this political process. Although going exclusively by the rule book could under certain circumstances be construed as one form of politicking, accommodation usually requires additional interactions to be forthcoming. It sometimes involves a bending of the rules, an exchange of favors, and offers of reward for the cooperation. It often comes as a shock to some students of management to discover that merely doing the job as expected will not extract the expected rewards.

In instances where one has control over items or services that can be adapted to personal as well as organizational use, the power is even greater. There have been cases where personal furniture has been constructed on company time with company materials, as well as instances where personal cars have been repaired in company motor pools.

The degree of politicking is limited not only by the formal organization restrictions but also by one's personal code of ethics and conscience. The fact that at times politics may be unethical should not preclude a discussion of the subject. That such actions as the above do exist in various business organizations is undeniable. Few businesses are run completely and rigidly by the book, and such politicking cannot be condemned per se. Some accommodations are constructive, whereas others are perhaps destructive of both organized activity and individual morals.

Values of Political Action

It is apparent that some degree of politics is a fact of organized life regardless of the caliber of people involved or the degree of formalization of organization rules and regulations. No doubt some political maneuvering can make a net contribution toward organization effectiveness. Where there is head-on conflict and where interdependencies make some degree of cooperation essential, concessions worked out between the parties often involve some bending or reinterpretation of the rules. On many occasions, the various conflicting interests are all highly legitimate and rest on solid ground. Some type of informal accommodation, compromise, or exchange is essential for a degree of reconciliation that permits the basic work of the organization to continue. One is usually safe, personally, if one sticks to the rule book and the letter of the law. Unfortunately, one also becomes known as a pathological bureaucrat who is more interested in being right, according to the rules, than in accomplishing the objectives as revealed by the situation. On the other hand, organizations could evolve into complete chaos if everyone acted as a power politician above the law and the formal organization. It is clear that neither extreme is the answer.

SUMMARY

A group exists when two or more people join together to accomplish a desired goal. An informal group is defined as two or more persons associated with one another in ways not prescribed by the formal organization. There are several characteristics of group behavior. A norm is a standard of behavior expected of informal group members. A role consists of the total pattern of expected behavior. The informal leader is usually chosen in one of two ways. A leadership vacuum may have existed, and the first person who took charge was automatically followed. Or the informal leader may be chosen through consensus.

Another characteristic of groups is cohesiveness, the degree of attraction that the group has for each of its members. Also, size of the group is a major factor determining its effectiveness. Finally, synergism is the potential for two or more persons working together to accomplish more than they could working separately.

The informal organization consists of informal relationships, created not by officially designated managers but by organizational members of all levels. One means by which the organizational structure of the informal work group may be studied is through the use of a contact chart. The informal organization can have both positive and negative consequences for the manager. Benefits of the informal organization include the following: (1) assists in accomplishing work, (2) helps to remove weaknesses in the formal structure, (3) lengthens the effective span of management, (4) compensates for violations of formal organizational principles, (5) provides an additional channel of communication, (6) provides emotional support for employees, and (7) encourages better management. Costs of the informal organization are the following: (1) may work counter to the purposes of the formal organization, (2) reduces the degree of predictability and control, (3) reduces the number of practical alternatives, and (4) increases the time required to complete activities.

Status, power, and politics are concepts that all

managers constantly observe. A person's rank or position in a group is referred to as status. Status symbols are visible signs of a person's social position and have several important values of status. Status assists in meeting the needs of an individual, aids in the communication process, and serves as a motivational device for management.

Power, on the other hand, refers to the ability of one person to influence the behavior of another person. As with status, it is neither completely formal nor informal. The primary sources of power are: legitimate, reward, coercive, referent, and expert. Power is important to managers because it permits them to benefit others on behalf of the organization.

Politics in an organization provides positive values in promoting cooperation among individuals and groups with differing interests and objectives. Politics is a means by which power can be acquired, transferred, and exerted on others. Through politics, adjustments and accommodations are made to varying conditions and pressures. Some degree of political actions will occur in any organization regardless of the caliber of people involved or the degree of formalization or organization rules and regulations.

REVIEW QUESTIONS

1. Define *group* and state the factors involved in determining group behavior.
2. What are the identifiable characteristics of the informal organization?
3. In your own words, describe the values and losses that may be attributed to the informal work group.
4. What is the purpose of a contact chart?
5. Define: *status; power; politics.*
6. What are the three functions of status?
7. In your own words, describe the various sources of power. What is the significance of the understanding of power to a manager?
8. What is the role of politics in today's business organization?

EXERCISES

1. Develop a contact chart for an organization of which you are a member. Interpret the results.
2. Identify three groups of which you are a member. What are the various status symbols associated with each organization?
3. Using the formula for determining total power provided in this chapter, state the kind and how much total power each of the following individuals might possess:
   • Guard in a maximum security prison
   • President of Chrysler Corporation
   • College senior who has made an A in five computer information system courses

CASE STUDY

Who's in Charge Around Here?

When Doug Self came to work in the accounting department at Ritger Paper Products Company, James Norris considered it a personal victory. Doug had been the top business school graduate last year at nearby Wichita State College. He had also been president of the Student Government Association for two years and was active in every aspect of campus life. James was the comptroller at Ritger and supervised nine accountants and clerks. He was pleased to have attracted such an outstanding young man and made sure his superiors knew of the excellent recruiting job he had done.

Within a short while after Doug went to work, it was clear to everyone in the department that Doug was not only friendly, outgoing, and easy to talk to but well informed about accounting. Before long, Doug had made friends with everyone in the office, and James noticed that a number of the accountants began to take their questions and problems to Doug for solution. He always seemed to have the right answer and to enjoy taking time to help. He also did an excellent job on all his own work.

Doug's presence in the accounting department made James's job easier. In fact, most of the problem-solving duties James had handled in the past were soon being brought to Doug. Only when a decision was required from outside the department would James be consulted. In a way, James was pleased with the way things were turning out. But two things bothered him. First, the accountants and clerks began to consult with Doug even about personal matters. Because he was twenty years older than Doug, James felt himself to be more qualified in that respect. Second, Doug had developed a number of fast friendships outside the department, especially with two of the company's senior officials. James felt very insecure about this. He thought it would only be a matter of time until Doug began to bypass him on official matters.

James decided to take action. Although he was not really sure how to handle the situation, James began to look for chances to criticize Doug in front of his peers. He also began to check with anyone who took a problem or question to Doug, reminding them that he was their direct superior and looking for ways to change or demean the advice Doug had given. It was not long before the other employees got the signal. Ultimately, James's strategy worked; Doug quit. But within a week, three other of James's best accountants turned in their resignations, and the department was thrown into complete confusion.

QUESTIONS

1. Why did Doug become the informal leader?
2. To what extent was Doug a threat to James? Explain.
3. Discuss the impact of status, power, and politics on the accounting department.

CASE STUDY

Assuming the Worst

Springfield Products Company in Springfield, Missouri, is a medium-sized manufacturer of small outboard motors. The motors are supplied to major retailing chains, which sell them under their own brand names. For the past few years, sales at Springfield Products had been falling. The decline was industry wide. In fact, Springfield was faring better than its competitors and had actually been able to increase its share of the market slightly. While forecasts indicated that the demand for the company's outboards would improve in the future, Anne Goddard, the company's president, believed that something needed to be done immediately to help the company maintain its financial health through this temporary slump. As a first step, she employed a consulting firm to determine if a reorganization might be helpful.

A team of five consultants arrived at the firm. They told Goddard that they first had to gain a thorough understanding of the current situation before they could make any recommendations. She told them that the company was open to them. They could ask any questions that they thought appropriate.

The grapevine was full of rumors virtually from the day the consulting group arrived. One employee was heard to say, "If they shut down the company, I don't know if I could take care of my family." Another worker said, "If they try to move me away from my friends I'm going to quit."

When workers questioned their supervisors, they received no explanation. No one had told the supervisors what was going on either. The climate began to change to one of fear. Rather than being concerned about their daily work, employees worried about what was going to happen to the company and their jobs. Productivity dropped drastically as a result.

A month after the consultants left, an informational memorandum was circulated through the company. It stated that the consultants had recommended a slight modification in the top levels of the organization to achieve greater efficiency. No one would be terminated. Any reductions would be the result of normal attrition. By this time, however, some of the best workers had already found other jobs, and company operations were severely disrupted for several months.

QUESTIONS

1. What part did the informal organization play in what happened at Springfield Products?
2. Why do you believe the employees tended to assume the worst about what was happening?
3. How could this difficulty have been avoided?

NOTES

1. P. J. Nicholson, Jr., and S. C. Goh, "The Relationship of Organization Structure and Interpersonal Attitudes to Role Conflict and Ambiguity in Different Work Environments," *Academy of Management Journal* (March 1983): 148.

2. L. L. Cummings, George P. Huber, and Eugene Arendt, "Effects of Size and Spatial Arrangements in Group Decision Making," *Academy of Management Journal* 17 (September 1974): 473.

3. Arthur D. Sharplin, "Synergism In Action," Northeast Louisiana University, December 1981.

4. Samuel A. Stouffer et al., *The American Soldier* (Princeton: Princeton University Press, 1949), 2:1974.

5. David C. McClelland and David H. Burnham, "Power Is the Great Motivator," *Harvard Business Review* 54 (March–April 1976): 102.

6. John M. Pfiffner and Frank P. Sherwood, *Administrative Organization* (Englewood Cliffs, N.J.: Prentice-Hall, 1960), p. 311.

REFERENCES

Allen, R. W. et al. "Organizational Politics: Tactics and Characteristics of Its Actors." *California Management Review* 22 (Fall 1979): 77–83.

Briscoe, Dennis R. "Organizational Design: Dealing with the Human Constraint." *California Management Review* 23 (Fall 1980): 71–80.

Cummings, L. L., George P. Huber, and Eugene Arendt. "Effects of Size and Spatial Arrangements in Group Decision Making." *Academy of Management Journal* 17 (September 1974): 473.

Franklin, J. E. "Down the Organization: Influence Processes across Levels of Hierarchy." *Administrative Science Quarterly* 20 (June 1975): 153–164.

Hall, R. H. et al. "Patterns of Interorganizational Relationships." *Administrative Science Quarterly* 22 (September 1977): 457–474.

Herker, C., and H. Aldrich. "Boundary Spanning Roles and Organization Structure." *Academy of Management Review* 2 (April 1977): 217–230.

Hodge, John. "Getting Along with the Informal Leader." *Supervisory Management* 25 (October 1980): 41–43.

Lincoln, J. R., and J. Miller. "Work and Friendship Ties in Organizations: A Comparative Analysis of Relational Networks." *Administrative Science Quarterly* 24 (June 1979): 181–199.

Lucas, H. C., Jr. "MIS Affects Balance of Power." *Management Accounting* 61 (October 1979): 61–68.

McClelland, David C., and David H. Burnham. "Power Is the Great Motivator." *Harvard Business Review* 54 (March–April 1976): 102.

McKenna, R. F. "Blending the Formal with the Informal System." *Journal of System Management* 26 (June 1975): 38–41.

March, James G., and Martha S. Feldman. "Information

in Organizations as Signal and Symbol." *Administrative Science Quarterly* 26 (June 1981): 171–186.

Mayes, B. T., and R. W. Allen. "Toward a Definition of Organizational Politics." *Academy of Management Review* 2 (October 1977): 672–678.

Miles, R. H., and W. D. Perreault, Jr. "Organizational Role Conflict: Its Antecedents and Consequences." *Organizational Behavior and Human Performances* 17 (October 1976): 19–44.

Miller, J. "Isolation in Organizations: Alienation from Authority, Control, and Expressive Relations." *Administrative Science Quarterly* 20 (June 1975): 260–271.

Moschis, G. P. "Social Comparison and Informal Group Influence." *Journal of Marketing Research* 13 (August 1976): 237–244.

Nicholson, P. J., Jr., and S. C. Goh. "The Relationship of Organization Structure and Interpersonal Attitudes to Role Conflict and Ambiguity in Different Work Environments." *Academy of Management Journal* (March 1983): 148.

Pfiffner, John M., and Frank P. Sherwood. *Administrative Organization.* Englewood Cliffs, N.J.: Prentice-Hall, 1960.

Quick, J. C. "Dyadic Goal Setting and Role Stress: A Field Study." *Academy of Management Journal* 22 (June 1979): 241–252.

Quinn, R. E. "Coping with Cupid: The Formation, Impact, and Management of Romantic Relationships in Organizations." *Administrative Science Quarterly* 22 (March 1980): 57–71.

Roos, L. L., Jr., and R. I. Hall. "Influence Diagrams and Organizational Power." *Administrative Science Quarterly* 25 (March 1980): 57–71.

Schmidt, S. M., and T. A. Kochal. "Interorganizational Relationships: Patterns and Motivations." *Administrative Science Quarterly* 22 (June 1977): 230–234.

Schriensheim, C. A. "Similarity of Individually Directed and Group Directed Leader Behavior Description." *Academy of Management Journal* 22 (June 1979): 345–355.

Stouffer, Samuel A. et al. *The American Soldier.* Princeton: Princeton University Press, 1949.

staffing

training and
  development (T&D)

performance appraisal

compensation

health

safety

comparable worth

human resources
  planning

job analysis

job description

job specification

personnel demand
  analysis

labor supply analysis

recruitment

employment
  requisition

selection

preliminary interviews

orientation

LEARNING OBJECTIVES

After completing this chapter you should be able to

1. Identify and briefly describe the basic human-resources-related functions that must be accomplished if the firm's employment needs are to be met.

2. List the predominant laws that affect the staffing process.

3. Describe what is involved in human resources planning and recruitment.

4. Explain each phase of the selection process.

5. State some special considerations involved in selecting managerial personnel and identify some techniques for identifying managerial talent.

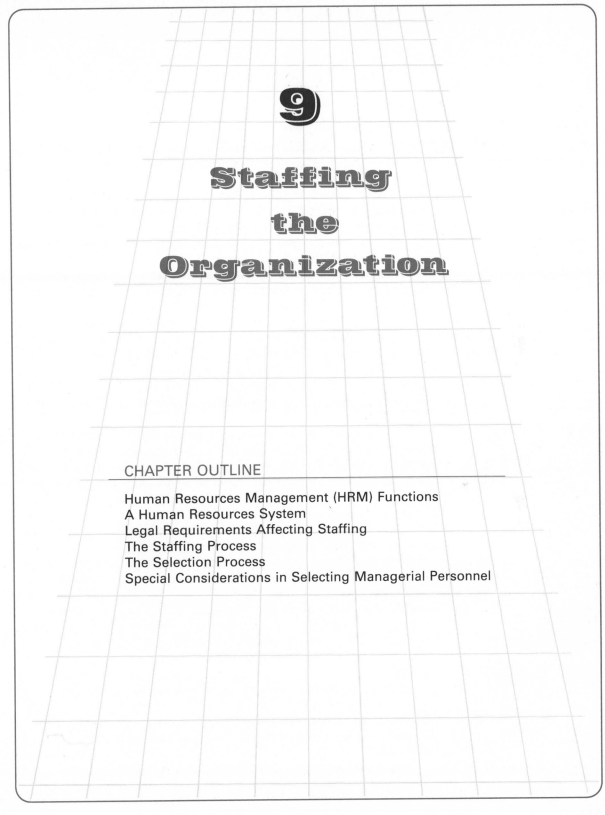

9

Staffing the Organization

CHAPTER OUTLINE

**LINCOLN
ELECTRIC**

The economic recession of 1979–1984 hit Cleveland, Ohio's Lincoln Electric Company especially hard. In 1982 alone, the firm's revenue dropped 30 percent. For most companies, this would have spelled disaster; in fact, for many it did, as business bankruptcies climbed to record highs. But Lincoln was ready. The company remained profitable; not a single worker was laid off; and at all times Lincoln was ready to meet the demand for its products that the inevitable recovery would bring.

How does Lincoln do it? In the opinions of many, credit should be given to the ability, loyalty, and enthusiasm of the Lincoln work force. This in turn undoubtedly springs in large measure from a number of unusual personnel policies. Workers at Lincoln are guaranteed lifetime employment. In exchange, they have to be willing to accept transfer to different jobs when changes in product demand occur. The company also promotes managers only from within. Every job opening is advertised internally, and any employee can apply. If workers are needed from outside, they are hired only at the entry level.

Almost every worker is paid on a piece-rate basis, so much per item produced. Part of the company profits, usually about half, is paid out as employee bonuses just before Christmas each year. These bonuses have averaged about the same as annual wages, and wages without the bonuses are on a par with those of other Cleveland workers.

New workers are placed on one year's probation. Those who are not attuned to the rapid pace at Lincoln normally leave on their own accord within the year. Outsiders who apply for Lincoln jobs are carefully screened—first by the personnel department, then by a committee of vice-presidents and supervisors—before being placed in the qualified applicant pool. Supervisors who have an unfilled vacancy at the entry level can hire whomever they please from this pool. There are no employment tests and no educational requirements, except for salespersons, who must be graduate engineers.

Significant credit must be given to Lincoln managers, who eschew executive perquisites. There are no reserved parking places. The executive offices are austere, purely functional, and carpetless. Even the company president eats in the cafeteria and pays for his own meals.

More important than self-effacement, however, is the management discipline practiced at Lincoln. The work force is expanded only reluctantly, and employees normally work several hours of overtime each week. That way, a significant sales decline can be absorbed without cutting anyone back below forty hours.

Managers at Lincoln responded quickly as the recession began, making the difficult decision to cut workers back to the guaranteed minimum thirty hours per week before that had to be done. Because the cutback occurred in a timely manner, though, it was possible to move back toward a normal work week sooner than might have been the case otherwise.

Some of the employees complained when their hours were cut back and their bonuses reduced; they had become accustomed to total compensation levels double those of other Cleveland workers. But no one was fired. And their employer remains economically sound and optimistic about the company's ability to take the good and the bad in stride.[1]

Lincoln Electric is known the world over as a leader in managing human resources. The Lincoln example illustrates that the personnel policies and practices a company follows must be integrated into a sound, overall management system.

A central focus of the organizing function is the people who work together in pursuit of organizational goals. Making sure that the organization has the right people in the right jobs at the right time is referred to as *staffing*.

In this chapter, we will first define the basic human-resources-related functions. Then, the major legislation affecting staffing will be identified. Next, the elements of the staffing process will be described. The remainder of the chapter will be devoted to some special considerations involved in selecting managerial personnel and the identification of some techniques for identifying managerial talent.

HUMAN RESOURCES MANAGEMENT (HRM) FUNCTIONS

Managers must work with the firm's human resources if organizational goals are to be accomplished. The firm must attract, select, train, and retain qualified people. Six basic HRM functions must be accomplished if the firm's human resources needs are to be met. These are staffing, training and development, compensation, health and safety, employee and labor relations, and personnel research.[2] Let us discuss each of these functions.

Staffing

Staffing is *the process of ensuring that the organization has qualified workers available at all levels in order to achieve company objectives.* The staffing process primarily involves human resources planning, recruitment, and selection—the focus of this chapter. These three tasks must be carefully coordinated if the firm is to satisfy its work force requirements.

staffing

Women are moving into responsible management positions in ever increasing numbers.

Lynne Jaeger Weinstein/Woodfin Camp & Associates

Training and Development

training and development (T&D)

Training and development (T&D) is the term applied to *programs designed to assist individuals, groups, and the entire organization to become more effective.* Training is needed because people, jobs, and organizations are always changing. T&D should begin at the time individuals join the firm and continue throughout their careers.

performance appraisal

Closely associated with T&D is performance appraisal. **Performance appraisal** is *the formal process of evaluating the activities of employees to determine how well they are performing their assigned tasks.* T&D programs are often aimed at overcoming deficiencies and maximizing performance.

Compensation

compensation

The question of what constitutes a fair day's pay has been a major concern for decades. Employees must be provided with adequate and equitable rewards for their contributions to organizational goals. **Compensation** includes *all rewards individuals receive as a result of their employment.* As such, it is more than monetary income. The reward may be one or a combination of the following:

- Pay: The money that a person receives for performing jobs. It is the cash that you can jingle in your pockets.
- Benefits: Additional financial rewards other than base pay such as paid holidays, medical insurance, and retirement programs.

- Nonfinancial: Nonmonetary rewards that an employee may receive, such as enjoyment of the work performed and a pleasant working environment.

Health and Safety

Health refers to *the employees' freedom from illness and their general physical and mental well-being.* **Safety** involves *the protection of employees from injuries due to work-related accidents.* These topics are important to management because employees who enjoy good health and work in a safe environment are more likely to be efficient. For this reason, forward-thinking managers have long advanced safety and health programs. Today, because of federal legislation, all organizations have become concerned with their employees' safety and health.

health
safety

Employee and Labor Relations

Over 20 million employees currently belong to labor unions and employee associations. Business firms are required by law to recognize unions and bargain with them in good faith, and this relationship has become an accepted way of life for many employers.

The vast majority of workers in the United States are not union members. In 1985, approximately 19 percent of the work force was unionized. However, nonunion organizations are often knowledgeable about the union goals and activities. These firms typically strive to satisfy the needs of their employees in every reasonable manner. They attempt to make it clear that a union is not necessary for individuals to achieve their personal goals.

Personnel Research

The personnel manager's research laboratory is the work environment. Research needs permeate every human resources management function. For instance, research may be conducted to determine the type of workers who will prove to be most successful in the firm. Or it may be directed toward determining the causes of certain work-related accidents. Personnel research is expected to be increasingly important to all forms of organizations in the future.

A HUMAN RESOURCES SYSTEM

In recent years, many organizations have developed comprehensive human resources systems such as the Kemper Insurance Company approach illustrated in Figure 9–1. At Kemper, the goal is "to have fully effective personnel at all levels of the organization to meet present and future need." Kemper's Human Resource System includes six major elements and twenty-six components. All twenty-six of the components are integrated into a coordinated management system.

A detailed study of each component in the Kemper Human Resource System is beyond the purpose of this chapter. However, it is important that managers and future managers recognize the scope of a total personnel system in today's complex business organization. Prior to discussing the

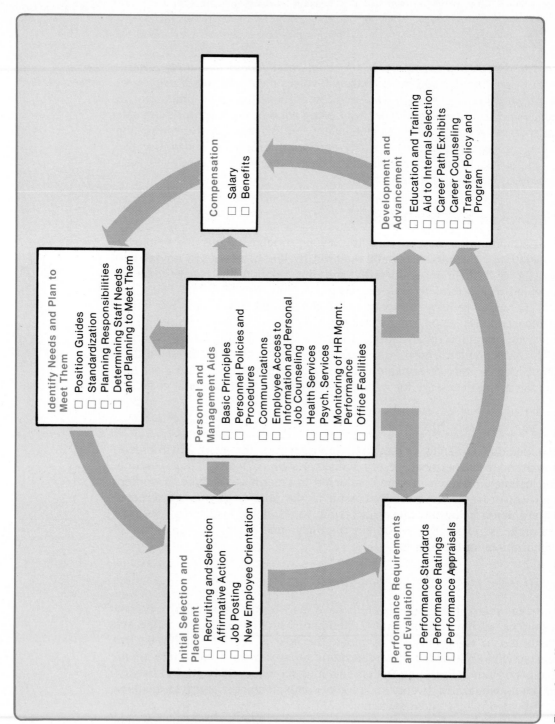

Figure 9–1 Kemper Human Resource System Used with the permission of Kemper Insurance Companies.

essential elements of staffing—personnel planning, recruitment, and selection of a firm's work force—managers should have an awareness of the major laws affecting personnel and human resources management.

LEGAL REQUIREMENTS AFFECTING STAFFING

The predominant external factor that managers must consider in performing the staffing function is legislation and court decisions. Every manager involved in selecting new employees must comply with federal, state, and local laws. This is no small task. The impact of recent federal laws is illustrated by the following comments of W. L. McMahon, vice-president of Corning Glass:

> Recruitment of personnel in today's organization requires careful consideration of federal laws. This has greatly increased the complexity of selecting qualified personnel at all levels in the company. We must comply with several equal employment opportunity laws often without a clear understanding of how to comply. Compliance is further complicated by the fact that guidelines may have been issued from different sources. The guidelines are often presented in different formats and may provide information that is inconsistent or difficult to implement.

Some of the most important federal laws are described below. The discussion focuses on laws passed since 1960. Some of the earlier federal legislation is summarized in Table 9–1.

Equal Pay Act of 1963—Amended 1972

The Equal Pay Act (an amendment to the Fair Labor Standards Act of 1938) prohibits wage discrimination on the basis of sex where the jobs require equal skills, effort, and responsibility and are performed under similar working conditions. Exceptions are permitted if the payment is made based on a seniority system, a merit system, or a system that measures earning by quality or quantity of production. Pay differentials are also permitted if they are based on factors other than sex. This act is applicable only to employers who are engaged in commerce or in the production of goods for commerce. The act is enforced by the Equal Employment Opportunity Commission (EEOC). In 1972, the act was extended to include executive, administrative, professional, and outside sales force categories, as well as employees in most state and local governments, hospitals, and schools.

Many groups and political leaders have attempted to extend the meaning of the Equal Pay Act to include the doctrine of comparable worth. **Comparable worth** refers to *the concept that pay for a given job should be determined by the amount of skill and effort required in the performance of a job.* Advocates of this idea believe that American women have been systematically—and illegally—underpaid for jobs that are just as demanding and just as important to the employer as higher-paying jobs done by men. Evidence cited in support of this argument includes the fact that in 1982 women averaged 63 cents for every dollar paid to men.[3]

comparable worth

TABLE 9–1   Selected Federal Legislation Affecting HRM Passed prior to 1960

Legislation	Major Provisions
Railway Labor Act of 1926	Provided procedures for collective bargaining and for settling disputes between labor and management within the railroad industry
Davis-Bacon Act of 1931	Required federal construction contractors to pay the prevailing wage for a particular geographical area
Anti-Injunction Act of 1932 (Norris-La Guardia Act)	Severely restricted the use of injunctions in labor disputes and made the "yellow dog" contract legally unenforceable
National Labor Relations Act of 1935 (Wagner Act)	Guaranteed employees the rights to self-organization and to bargain collectively with their employers, and specifically prohibited five unfair labor practices by management
Social Security Act of 1935	Established a federal tax to be placed on payrolls and provided for unemployment and retirement benefits
Walsh-Healey Act of 1936	Required firms doing business with the federal government to pay wages at least equivalent to the prevailing wages in the area where the firm is located. Overtime payments are required after eight hours in one day or forty hours in one week
Fair Labor Standards Act of 1938	Established minimum wages, overtime pay, and child-labor standards
Labor-Management Relations Act of 1947 (Taft-Hartley Act)	A major amendment to the Wagner Act. Gave employees the right to refrain from union activity. Denied supervisors protection of the law in obtaining union recognition. Enumerated six unfair labor practices by unions. Outlawed the closed shop and authorized state right-to-work laws
Labor Management Reporting and Disclosure Act of 1959 (Landrum-Griffin Act)	A major labor reform act aimed at regulating the internal affairs of unions (including their relationships with their members) and regulating certain managerial activities. Also contained important amendments to the Taft-Hartley Act

Source: R. Wayne Mondy and Robert M. Noe, III, *Personnel: The Management of Human Resources* (Boston: Allyn and Bacon, 1981), p. 34.

Civil Rights Act of 1964—Amended 1972

Title VII of the Civil Rights Act of 1964 as amended by the Equal Employment Opportunity Act of 1972 has had a significant impact on personnel selection. This legislation prohibits discrimination on the basis of race, color, religion, sex, or national origin in selection, promotion, and other areas of employment. The 1972 amendment extended coverage to state and municipal employees and to employees in educational institutions. It also reduced the number of employees necessary to bring an organization under Civil Rights Act jurisdiction from twenty-five to fifteen. This legislation is administered by the EEOC, which has the power to seek compliance with the law and to investigate alleged employment discrimination. The EEOC sometimes requires employers to develop and implement affirmative action programs designed to increase the number of minority and female employees.

The federal courts have had the primary responsibility for interpreting and enforcing the civil rights laws. Court decisions have significantly affected personnel selection policies and practices. Several court decisions have clarified and strengthened a strict interpretation of the Civil Rights Act. For example, in *Phillips* v. *Martin Marietta* (1971), the court ruled that the company had discriminated against a woman who was denied a job because she had young children. In a highly significant case, *Griggs et al.* v. *Duke Power Company* (1971), the U.S. Supreme Court ruled that preemployment requirements, including tests, must be job related.

Age Discrimination in Employment Act of 1967—Amended 1978

The Age Discrimination in Employment Act (ADEA) prohibits employers from discriminating against individuals between the ages of forty and seventy. The act pertains to employers with twenty or more employees. In

An organization must ensure that the right people with the right qualifications are available at the right places and times to accomplish the purpose of the organization.   Cary Wolinsky/Stock, Boston Inc.

contrast to Title VII, the ADEA provides for trial by jury. This is important in that the jury may have greater sympathy for older people who have possibly been discriminated against. Also, in addition to the trial-by-jury provision, the act provides that an employee may receive more than lost wages if discrimination is proved.

Occupational Safety and Health Act of 1970

Few federal laws have been as controversial or received as much widespread publicity as the Occupational Safety and Health Act (OSHA) of 1970. The act, enforced by the Occupational Safety and Health Administration, was designed to assure American workers of safe and healthy working conditions by requiring employers to comply with safety and health standards. OSHA has taken such a broad view of interpreting and applying safety and health standards that virtually all organizations must comply with the act.

Rehabilitation Act of 1973

This law covers government contractors or subcontractors or organizations that receive federal grants in excess of $2,500. All contractors or subcontractors that exceed the $2,500 base are required to post notices that they agree to take affirmative action to employ and promote qualified handicapped individuals. If the contract or subcontract exceeds $50,000 or if the contractor has fifty or more employees, an affirmative action program must be prepared. The Office of Federal Contract Compliance Programs administers the act. The contractor must indicate what reasonable accommodations are being made in hiring and promoting handicapped persons.

This act is expected to have even more impact in the future. The definition of what constitutes handicapped has not been thoroughly tested by the courts. In some courts, epilepsy and alcoholism have been considered handicaps.

Federal Privacy Act of 1974

The Privacy Act of 1974 was passed to "provide certain safeguards for an individual against an invasion of personal privacy." The act is limited to the federal government and its contractors. Any private business that has a contract with the government is covered for the duration of the contract. The purpose of the act is to limit federal agencies that maintain records about individuals and to control dissemination of information from one agency to another. Individuals must be permitted access to any personal records concerning them.

Employee Retirement Income Security Act of 1974

One of the most complex laws affecting employee benefit programs is the Employee Retirement Income Security Act (ERISA) of 1974. ERISA was designed to protect the interests of participants in employee benefit plans and their beneficiaries by establishing standards of conduct, responsibility, and obligations for fiduciaries of employee benefit plans. The purpose of ERISA was to "protect employees," not to force employers to create employee benefit plans. The law establishes standards in the areas of participation, vesting of benefits, and funding for existing and new retirement and pension plans. ERISA provides for appropriate remedies, sanctions, and access to the federal courts if provisions of the law are violated.

Pregnancy Discrimination Act of 1978

The Pregnancy Discrimination Act is an amendment to the 1964 Civil Rights Act. The act prohibits discrimination in employment based on pregnancy, childbirth, or complications arising from either. Pregnancy and childbirth must be treated like other disabilities covered by fringe benefits. Compliance may require changes to health insurance programs. Also, failing to hire or terminating a woman strictly because of pregnancy is prohibited. And, so-called pregnancy leaves, while permissible, cannot be mandatory.

Civil Service Reform Act of 1978

The Civil Service Reform Act had a great impact on the structure and practice of personnel management in federal government installations. The act, and two related agency reorganization plans, resulted in the abolishment of the U.S. Civil Service Commission, the creation of the Office of Personnel Management and the Merit System Protection Board, and an expanded affirmative action mission for the EEOC. It also included the first federal collective bargaining law enacted since 1955.

EEOC Guidelines—Sexual Harassment

It is anticipated that in the 1980s the most fervently pursued discrimination guidelines by the EEOC will relate to sexual harassment. Managers of profit and nonprofit organizations, in performing all human resources functions including staffing, should be particularly alert to the issue of sexual harassment. In November 1980, the EEOC defined sexual harassment as "unwelcome sexual advances, request for sexual favors, and other verbal or physical conduct of a sexual nature that occur under any of the following situations:

- "When submission to sexual advances is a condition of keeping or getting a job, whether expressed in explicit terms or not.
- "When a supervisor or boss makes a personnel decision based on an employee's submission to or rejection of sexual advances.
- "When sexual conduct unreasonably interferes with a person's work performance or creates an intimidating, hostile, or offensive environment."[4]

One of the major implications of the guidelines is that they "make the employer responsible for misbehavior by supervisory personnel, their assistants, coworkers, or outside personnel."[5]

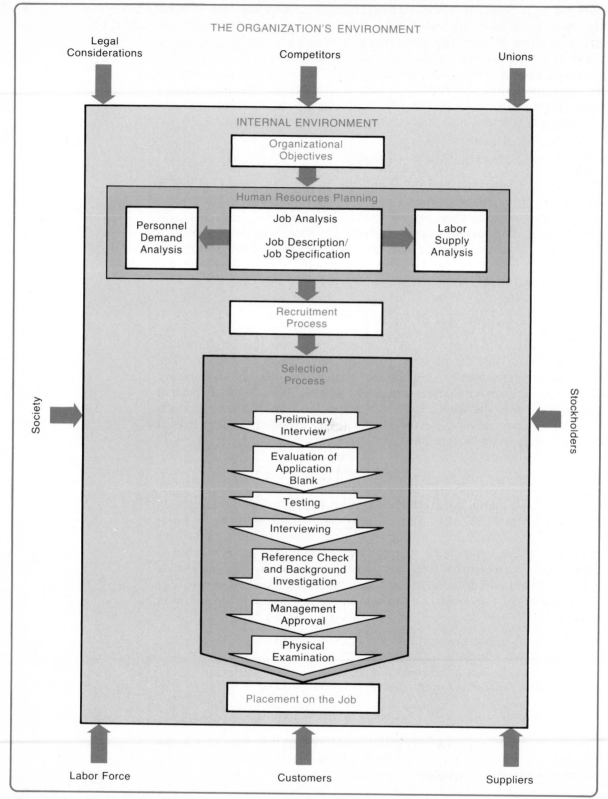

THE ORGANIZATION'S ENVIRONMENT

Legal
Considerations

Competitors

Unions

INTERNAL ENVIRONMENT

Organizational
Objectives

Human Resources Planning

Personnel
Demand
Analysis

Job Analysis

Job Description/
Job Specification

Labor
Supply
Analysis

Recruitment
Process

Selection
Process

Preliminary
Interview

Evaluation of
Application
Blank

Testing

Interviewing

Reference Check
and Background
Investigation

Management
Approval

Physical
Examination

Placement on the Job

Society

Stockholders

Labor Force

Customers

Suppliers

Figure 9–2   The Staffing Process

252

The staffing process involves planning for future personnel requirements, recruiting individuals, and selecting from among those recruited individuals employees who fulfill the needs of the firm. Figure 9–2 illustrates the basic elements of the staffing process. Each element is discussed below.

Human Resources Planning

Human resources planning is *the analysis of future personnel requirements*. When Lincoln Electric (see the case presented at the start of the chapter) made plans for its new factory in Mentor, Ohio, a major aspect of the plans was making sure that qualified people would be available. Human resources planning, when performed properly, can do the following:

human resources planning

- Enable management to anticipate shortages and surpluses of labor, allowing the development of plans for avoiding or correcting problems before they become serious.
- Permit forecasts of recruitment needs in terms of both the numbers and types of skills sought.
- Help in the analysis of sources of supply of labor in order to focus recruitment efforts on the most likely supply sources.
- Provide for identification of replacements or backup for present key managers from either inside or outside the organization.
- Integrate personnel plans with financial plans and forecasts.[6]

Components of human resources planning include job analysis, job description, job specialization, personnel demand analysis, and labor supply analysis.

Job Analysis

The process of determining the duties and skills required for performing jobs in the organization is referred to as **job analysis**. Job facts are gathered, analyzed, and recorded as the jobs exist. Job analysis is the most basic HRM tool. Without properly conducted job analyses, it would be difficult to perform the other HRM functions satisfactorily. Several techniques may be used in conducting job analysis, including the following:

job analysis

- Observations of and interviews with present employees performing the jobs
- Questionnaires completed by present employees or supervisors of the work
- Analysis by experts
- A diary of activities performed by present employees.

Job Description

The job description is a product of the job analysis process. As shown in Figure 9–3, a **job description** is *a summary of the purpose, principal duties, and responsibilities of a job*. Job descriptions are accurate, concise statements of what employees are expected to do on their jobs. A job description includes statements on the following items:

job description

1. Duties to be performed.
2. Supervision given and received.

<table>
<tr><td colspan="2">POSITION TITLE

SECRETARY II</td><td colspan="2">POSITION NUMBER
217</td></tr>
<tr><td colspan="2"></td><td colspan="2">APPROVAL
RHS</td></tr>
</table>

POSITION TITLE		POSITION NUMBER
SECRETARY II		217
		APPROVAL
		RHS

DIVISION OR STAFF DEPARTMENT	LOCATION	REPORTS TO	EFFECTIVE DATE
All	All		May, 1981

DEPARTMENT OR ACTIVITY	SECTION	POINTS	GRADE	REVISES
		165	6	

JOB SUMMARY

Performs clerical, stenographic, and administrative duties for a manager and often one or more staff members of a major function.

NATURE OF WORK

Performs a wide variety of office duties including most of the following:

a. Typing correspondence, reports, manuscripts, graphs, charts, etc., from shorthand notes, dictating machine tapes, and/or hand written drafts proficiently and with minimum direction and instructions.
b. Receiving telephone calls and visitors skillfully and handling incoming mail efficiently.
c. Originating routine correspondence and handling inquiries, and routing non-routine inquiries and correspondence to proper persons.
d. Establishing and maintaining department files and records.
e. Assuming responsibility for arranging appointments and meetings, screening calls, and handling personal and confidential matters for superior.
f. Assembling, organizing, processing, and evaluating data and reports; operating office machines needed for accomplishing this.
g. Performing administrative duties and special projects as directed, such as collecting and compiling general reference materials and information pertaining to company, division, or department practices and procedures.

Works independently, receiving a minimum of supervision and guidance on established office procedures. Relieves supervisor of minor administrative details. May have some light work direction over others in department. Structure is light and most work is not checked.

QUALIFICATIONS

High school education or its equivalent plus three years of clerical and stenographic experience, including one year with the Company, and a typing skill of at least 60 WPM. Demonstrated proficiency in English grammar, punctuation, spelling, and proper word usage. Must be able to anticipate problems and use sound judgment and tact in handling confidential matters, screening telephone calls and visitors, and scheduling superior's time. Must have the ability to acquire a thorough knowledge of the organization's policies, procedures, and personnel in order to relieve superior of specified administrative duties. A shorthand skill of at least 80 WPM is necessary if required in a specific position. A basic figure aptitude and/or a working knowledge of certain business machines may be necessary depending on the specific job.

Figure 9–3   A Nonexempt Job Description   Source: General Mills, Inc.

3. Relationships with other jobs.

4. Equipment and materials needed.

5. Physical working conditions.

Job descriptions are useful in virtually every HRM function. Job descriptions facilitate the recruitment process by clarifying the specific nature of objects and responsibilities of jobs. They are also a helpful tool in the orientation and training of new employees. While job descriptions exist in many large firms, managers sometimes do not understand or use them properly. For instance, some managers believe that having job descriptions restricts management's flexibility and creativity in staffing the organization. However, to be useful to the manager, job descriptions must be translated into a statement of human requirements.

Job Specifications

The statement of the minimum acceptable human qualities necessary to perform the job is the **job specification**. The job specification pinpoints such characteristics required for the job as education, experience, personality, and physical abilities.

job specification

Because of the legislation passed since 1960 with regard to discrimination concerning race, color, national origin, religion, sex, age, and handicaps, organizations need to be able to show that any standard included on the job specification is job related. The job specification is the standard to which the applicant is compared in each step of the selection process.

Personnel Demand Analysis

Personnel demand analysis is *the determination of the numbers and types of employees needed to achieve organizational goals.* It requires a firm to calculate the type and volume of work that needs to be done. When the analysis indicates a personnel shortage, the firm must initiate recruitment efforts. When demand analysis shows a personnel surplus, restricted hiring, reduced hours, early retirement, or layoffs may be required. When Lincoln's sales dropped in the early 1980s, that company chose to reduce working hours and reassign workers rather than lay anyone off.

personnel demand analysis

Labor Supply Analysis

Personnel demand analysis provides the manager with the means of estimating how many and what kind of employees will be required. But there is another side of the coin: managers must also determine if they will be able to secure employees with the necessary skills and the sources from which these individuals may be obtained. **Labor supply analysis** is *the process of determining the availability of needed employees.* The supply of employees may be met by obtaining people from within the company, or the firm may decide to go outside the organization to meet its needs. With a long waiting list of prospective workers, Lincoln Electric has less concern than most other companies about whether or not workers will be available.

labor supply analysis

Delta, the free world's sixth largest airline, has earned the respect of the airline industry and financial markets as well. Except for one year, the company has been continuously profitable since before World War II. Delta also claims the smallest number of passenger complaints to the Federal Aviation Administration of any major airline.

The Spirit of Delta

Delta began in Monroe, Louisiana, in 1924 as a crop dusting operation. C. E. Woolman, an entomologist (specialist in insects) by profession and an aviation enthusiast, is credited with growing what was then Huff Daland Dusters into the world's largest privately owned aircraft fleet. In addition to its internal growth, the company merged with Chicago and Southern Airlines in 1953 and with Northeast Airlines in 1972. Today, Delta serves nearly a hundred cities in the United States and six foreign countries, operating a fleet of more than 300 planes and employing nearly 40,000.

The airline industry was in a state of turmoil in the mid-1980s. A major recession had begun in 1979 and was to last for several years. The air traffic controllers' strike, which occurred in 1981, was never really settled, placing a great strain on the air traffic system. At the same time, the airline industry, like several other major industries, was deregulated, resulting in an intensification of competition. While companies like Braniff and Continental were failing, throwing thousands out of work, Delta's employees were optimistically buying the company its first Boeing 767 aircraft. They named the plane the *Spirit of Delta.* Delta's rank and file are nonunionized, but pay scales and employee benefits equal or surpass averages for the predominantly unionized industry.

An open door policy enables employees to air any grievances. Flexibility in work assignments—a ticket agent willingly shifts to baggage handling, for example—has helped to increase productivity. Guaranteed employment and a promotion from within policy are credited with giving employees a feeling of security. All of the company's top managers have been with the company for over two decades, and no one at Delta expects to be kept from a promotion by someone hired from outside.

While a number of major airlines were selling off planes in order to survive, Delta was modernizing its fleet with Boeing 767s. Delta has also improved its competitive edge in the unregulated market by developing its DATAS II computerized reservation system, expanding its hubs at Dallas and Cincinnati, and carefully managing its long-term debt. In 1984, the company put into effect a new flight planning system that is expected to save the company several million dollars a year, reduce fuel costs, and give a smoother ride.

Looking into the future, President David C. Garrett, Jr., says, "In the longer term, we have great confidence in the future of the company. Our aircraft and ground facilities are superior. Our family of Delta professionals is unexcelled in the industry. Our financial position is strong. We have virtually everything we need to maintain and extend our position as the leader in the airline industry."[7]

Recruitment

recruitment

Recruitment involves *the encouragement of individuals with the needed skills to make application for employment with the firm.* In most large organizations, this begins with an employment requisition. An **employment**

employment requisition

requisition is *a form issued to activate the recruitment process; it typically includes such information as the job title, starting date, pay scale, and a brief summary of principal duties.* Personnel recruitment can range from locating individuals within the firm who are qualified to a sophisticated and extensive search for a new president.

The usual means of internal recruiting is through the use of a job bidding and posting system. The purpose of job posting is to communicate the fact that job openings exist. Job bidding permits individuals in the organization who believe that they possess the required qualifications to apply (bid) for the job. At Lincoln, every job above the entry level is filled from within. Internal recruitment or promotion from within is an important source of personnel for positions above the entry level. Promotion from within has several advantages; it

1. increases morale of employees;
2. improves the quality of selection since an organization usually has a more complete evaluation of the strengths and weaknesses of internal applicants as opposed to those from outside the firm;
3. motivates present employees to prepare for more responsible positions;
4. attracts a better quality of external applicants if chances for promotion from within are good; and
5. assists the organization to utilize personnel more fully.

Despite the advantages of internal recruiting, there are several disadvantages to be considered. Two of these are the following:

1. There may be an inadequate supply of qualified applicants.
2. Internal sources may lead to inbreeding of ideas—current employees may lack new ideas on how to do a job more effectively.

Some well-known companies in addition to Lincoln that practice promotion from within are Delta Airlines, IBM, and Hewlett-Packard.

Even if a company is committed to promotion from within, external recruitment is required just to maintain a stable work force. It is particularly necessary in light of the change and growth most organizations experience. Some companies use outside recruitment to bring new skills into the firm and to prevent inbreeding. Possible external sources of recruitment include high schools and vocational schools, community colleges, colleges and universities, the competition and other firms, and unsolicited applicants. Some recruiting methods are advertising, employment agencies, recruiters, and employee referrals. Essentially the firm must first determine where potential employees may be found and then use the appropriate methods to encourage them to make application. Only when a firm has applicants for a job can the selection process begin.

THE SELECTION PROCESS

The ultimate objective of recruitment is to select individuals who are most capable of meeting the requirements of the job. **Selection** is *the process of identifying those recruited individuals who will best be able to assist the firm in achieving organizational goals.* The selection process is shown in Figure 9–4.

selection

Preliminary Interview

Preliminary interviews are *those interviews used to eliminate the obviously unqualified applicants.* Reasons for elimination may include excessive salary

preliminary interviews

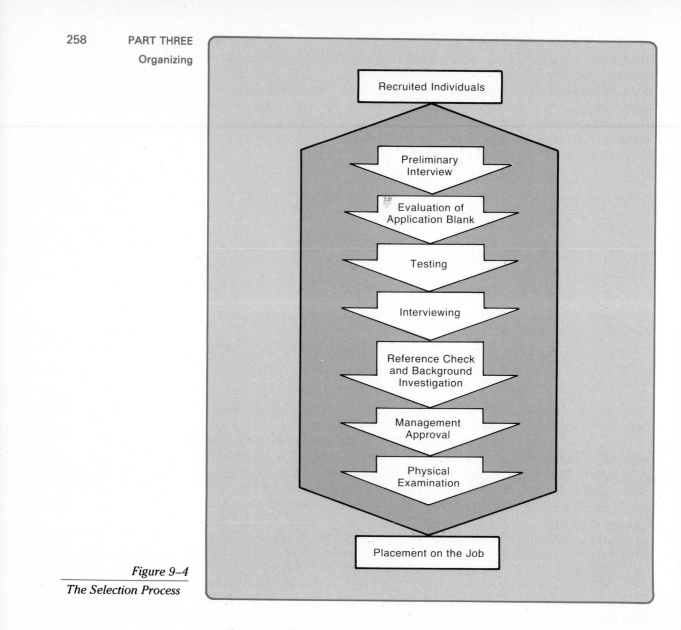

Figure 9–4
The Selection Process

requirements, inadequate training or education, or lack of job-related experience. An applicant who appears to qualify for a position is asked to complete the application blank.

Evaluation of Application Blank

The next step in the selection process is to have the prospective employee complete an application blank. The employer should evaluate the application with regard to whether there appears to be a match between the individual and the position. The specific type of information requested in an application blank may vary from firm to firm and by positions within the organization. Sections of an application typically include education, work experience, and other specific job-related data.

An application blank must fill the firm's informational needs while meeting legal requirements. An example of a properly designed application form is provided in Figure 9–5. As you can see, only questions that have job relevance are included. Notice that there are no questions related to sex, age, national origin, religion, color, or race. Answers to questions regarding criminal convictions may be considered only if job related. For jobs such as pilot positions at Delta Airlines, the application blank may ask for licensing information.

Testing

Traditionally, testing has been an integral component in the selection process. Tests have been used to screen applicants in terms of skills, abilities, aptitudes, interest, personality, and attitudes. The Civil Rights Act and interpretations by the federal courts have had the effect of reducing the use of selection tests. For instance, in *Griggs* v. *Duke Power Company,* the U.S. Supreme Court ruled that preemployment requirements, including tests, must be job related. It has proved to be very difficult to design tests consisting totally of job-related items.

Certain conditions should be met if tests are to be used for employee selection. First, a test should be reliable; that is, it should provide consistent results. If a person takes the same test a number of times, scores should be similar. Second, tests should be valid; they should measure what they are designed to measure. If a test is designed to predict job performance, prospective employees who score high on the test should prove to be high performers. Third, a selection test should be objective. When different scorers can interpret the results of the same test and arrive at similar results, the test is said to be objective. Finally, a test should be standardized. This requires that it be administered under standard conditions to a large group of persons who are representative of the individuals for whom it is intended. The purpose of standardization is to obtain norms in order that a specific test score can be meaningful when compared to other scores in the group.

Interviewing

The interview is the most widely used and probably the most important method of assessing the qualifications of job applicants. At Lincoln Electric, it is almost the only method used. The subjective judgments that are often made during employment interviews sometimes reduce their reliability, however. Interviews accomplish the following purposes:

1. Obtaining additional information about the applicant.
2. Providing information regarding the firm.
3. Selling the company.

Interviews may be distinguished by the amount of structure they possess. Probing, open-ended questions are asked in the nondirective interviews. Usually only highly trained interviewers use the nondirective technique because it requires a highly subjective appraisal of the job candidate. On the other hand, the patterned interview consists of

GENERAL ⊕ ELECTRIC
An Equal Opportunity Employer
Application For Employment

It is the policy of the General Electric Company to provide employment, training, compensation, promotion and other conditions of employment based on qualifications, without regard to race, color, religion, national origin, sex, age, veteran status or handicap.

Print

Name _____ _____ _____
Last   First   Middle

Date of Application _____

Address _____
Number and Street

_____ _____ _____
City   State   Zip Code

Telephone _____ Social Security No. _____
Area Code/Number

Job Interest

Position Desired _____

Wages or Salary Expected $ _____ Per Hr. ☐ Week ☐ Month ☐
(Please Check One)

Other Positions for Which you are Qualified _____

Date Available for Employment _____

Were you Ever Employed by GE? Yes ☐ No ☐

If Yes, Where? _____ Dates _____ _____
From   To

Education and Training

Circle Highest Grade Completed in Each School Category

	Grade School	High School	Tech School	College	Grad School
	1 2 3 4 5 6 7 8	9 10 11 12	1 2	1 2 3 4	1 2 3 4

	Name	Location	Course/Degree	Class Standing
Grade School				
High School				
College				
Graduate School				
Apprentice, Business, Technical, Military or Vocational School				

Other Training or Skills (Factory or Office Machines Operated, Special Courses, Military Training, etc.) _____

Other Job-Related Activities

List professional, trade, business or civic activities and offices held (exclude groups which indicate race, color, religion, sex or national origin). _____

To Be Detached By Employee Relations

Personal Data

Print

Name _____ _____ _____
Last   First   Middle

Address _____
Number and Street

_____ _____ _____
City   State   Zip Code

Telephone _____ Social Security No. _____
Area Code/Number

Is Your Age: Under 18 ? _____ Yes ☐ No ☐
(Please Check One)

Over 70 ? _____ Yes ☐ No ☐
(Please Check One)

Are you a citizen of USA? _____ Yes ☐ No ☐
(Please Check One)

If you are not a U.S. Citizen, have you a legal right to remain permanently in the U.S.? _____ Yes ☐ No ☐
(Please Check One)

Military

Were you in the U.S. Armed Forces? _____ Yes ☐ No ☐
(Please Check One)

If yes, what branch? _____

Date Entered _____ Date Discharged _____

Final Rank _____ Type of Discharge _____

Military experience should have been included in Employment History section on Page 2.

Convictions

Have you ever been convicted of a felony? _____ Yes ☐ No ☐
(Please Check One)

Have you been convicted of a misdemeanor committed within the past five years, or were you imprisoned for a misdemeanor which occurred more than five years ago? _____ Yes ☐ No ☐
(Please Check One)

If **Yes** to either of above questions, please explain fully. **This information will not necessarily bar an applicant from employment.**

_____

Additional Information

State any additional information you feel may be helpful to us in considering your application:

_____

Employment History

Please read carefully before starting. List all employment starting with present or most recent employer. Account for all periods, including unemployment and service with the Armed Forces. Also include relevant voluntary and/or part-time work experience. Use additional sheet if necessary.

	Dates		Hourly Rate/Salary	
Employer	From	Month / Year	Starting	$ per
Address	To	Month / Year	Final	$ per
Describe Major Duties				
Reason For Leaving				
Job Title				
Department				
Supervisor				

	Dates		Hourly Rate/Salary	
Employer	From	Month / Year	Starting	$ per
Address	To	Month / Year	Final	$ per
Describe Major Duties				
Reason For Leaving				
Job Title				
Department				
Supervisor				

	Dates		Hourly Rate/Salary	
Employer	From	Month / Year	Starting	$ per
Address	To	Month / Year	Final	$ per
Describe Major Duties				
Reason For Leaving				
Job Title				
Department				
Supervisor				

	Dates		Hourly Rate/Salary	
Employer	From	Month / Year	Starting	$ per
Address	To	Month / Year	Final	$ per
Describe Major Duties				
Reason For Leaving				
Job Title				
Department				
Supervisor				

Interviewer's Comments:

Interviewed By: _____ Date: _____

Affirmative Action

Special Employment Notice To Disabled Veterans, Vietnam Era Veterans And Individuals With Physical Or Mental Handicaps:

Government contractors are subject to Section 402 of the Vietnam Era Veterans Readjustment Act of 1974 which requires that they take affirmative action to employ and advance in employment qualified disabled veterans and veterans of the Vietnam Era (i.e., served more than 180 days between August 5, 1964 and May 7, 1975), and Section 503 of the Rehabilitation Act of 1973, as amended, which requires government contractors to take affirmative action to employ and advance in employment qualified handicapped individuals.

Please Check Below If You Are A:

☐ Vietnam Era Veteran

☐ Disabled Veteran

☐ Handicapped Individual

And wish to be considered under our Affirmative Action Program(s). **Submission of this information is voluntary.**

Please read this carefully before signing:

Employee Release and Privacy Statement

I understand that the General Electric Company requires certain information about me to evaluate my qualifications for employment and to conduct its business if I become an employee. Therefore, I authorize the Company to investigate my past employment, educational credentials and other employment-related activities. I agree to cooperate in such investigations, and release those parties supplying such information to the Company from all liability or responsibility with respect to information supplied.

I agree that the Company may use the information it obtains concerning me in the conduct of its business. I understand that such use may include disclosure outside the Company in those cases where its agents and contractors need such information to perform their functions, where the Company's legal interests and/or obligations are involved, or where there is a medical emergency involving me. I understand, however, that the Company intends to protect the confidentiality of personal information it obtains concerning me. Consequently, personal information in Company record-keeping systems, other than the fact and location of past or present Company employment, the dates of employment, or the job name or description of general duties, will not otherwise be disclosed outside the Company with a personal identifier without my consent. Further, the Company will require its agents and contractors to safeguard personal information disclosed to them by the Company.

I understand that any employment with the Company would not be for any fixed period of time and that, if employed, I may resign at any time for any reason or the Company may terminate my employment at any time for any reason in the absence of a specific written agreement to the contrary.

I understand that any false answers or statements made by me on this application or any supplement thereto or in connection with the above-mentioned investigations will be sufficient grounds for immediate discharge, if I am employed.

Applicant's Signature: _____ Date: _____

Figure 9–5 An Employment Application   Source: General Electric.

standardized questions that are asked of all applicants for a specific group of jobs. This standardization permits the candidates to be compared easily and greatly aids the validation process.

Interviews can be conducted in several ways. A majority of employment interviews consist of the applicant's meeting with an interviewer in a one-on-one situation. This form of interviewing is the least threatening type. Another form of interviewing is the group interview. Here several applicants interact in the presence of one or more company representatives. Or one candidate may be quizzed by several interviewers. This is called a board interview.

Sometimes the stress interview is used in the selection of managers and sales personnel. The stress interview attempts to make the applicant defensive by putting pressure on the person in order to observe his or her reactions to stress and tension.

One of the authors, in an early stage of his career, was exposed to a stress interview when he applied for a sales position. The initial interview for the job had gone well, so a second one was scheduled with the firm's sales manager. On meeting the sales manager, the author was bluntly told he was not qualified for the position. At that point, the author had no idea a stress interview was in progress. He was put on the defensive. But, being a rather confident person, he maintained that he was the best-qualified person for the job. At the end of the two-hour interview, the author was offered the job. Not until several months later was he made aware that a stress interview had been conducted. The job would not have been offered to the author if he had not responded to the stress with confidence.

Regardless of the type of method used, the interview is the most relied upon element in the selection of new personnel. Since most managers must rely on interviewing when selecting new employees and evaluating candidates for promotion, following sound practices is essential. The following guidelines have been found to be helpful in conducting effective interviews:

1. *Plan for the interview*—review job specification and description as well as the applications of candidates.
2. *Create a good climate for the interview*—try to establish a friendly, open rapport with the applicant.
3. *Allow sufficient time for an uninterrupted interview.*
4. *Conduct a goal-oriented interview*—seek the information needed to assist in the employment decision.
5. *Avoid certain types of questions*—try not to ask leading questions or questions that may imply discrimination.
6. *Seek answers to all questions and check for inconsistencies.*
7. *Record the results of the interview immediately on completion.*[8]

Over the years, the interview, much like testing, has received considerable criticism concerning its ability to predict success on the job. In interviewing an applicant for employment, many factors influence the decision of the interviewer. Interviews can be instruments of discrimination, and for this reason, they have received close scrutiny by the EEOC in recent years. Charges of possible discrimination have led to an increase in the use of the patterned interview since it has significantly higher reliability and validity than other methods of interviewing.

An effective means of assessing the success of an organization's interviewing process is to compare performance of employees with the evaluation of these same employees when they were interviewed for the job. In other words, how effective or valid is the interview in predicting job success?

Reference Check and Background Investigation

Once an applicant successfully clears the interviewing hurdles, the practice of many organizations is to conduct reference checks and background investigations. The purpose of the reference check is to provide additional insight regarding an applicant. A weakness of the reference check is that job applicants provide their own list of references. Therefore, the majority of references are biased in a positive manner. Also, since the passage of the Federal Privacy Act of 1974, persons who have been employed by the federal government have the legal right to review reference checks that have been made regarding their employment unless they waive this right.

Although a reference check often provides enough information to verify information on the application blank, there are many times when it does not. Often it is important to perform a background investigation into the applicant's past employment history. The background investigation may be helpful in determining if past work experience is related to the qualifications needed for the new position. Another reason for background investigations is that credential fraud has increased in recent years.[9] It has been found that between 7 and 10 percent of job applicants are not what they present themselves to be.[10] A frequently used but perhaps questionable way of verifying background information is the polygraph or lie detector.

Management Approval

In most large organizations, many of the above functions are performed by a personnel department. However, the personnel department does not usually make the final decision as to which person is selected for a particular position. Under most circumstances, the manager or supervisor who will be the immediate superior of the new employee will make the final hiring decision. The selection decision is usually made after interviewing the applicants and reviewing the recommendations of the personnel department. The immediate supervisor knows the needs of his or her unit or department and is in the best position to evaluate the qualifications and characteristics of prospective employees. The supervisor or manager should be able to identify factors in the applicant's background or work experience that would be helpful to the new employee in fitting into the work unit.

Physical Examination

Once a decision to make a job offer has been reached, a physical examination is often conducted. Typically, job offers are contingent on successful completion of physical examinations. Obviously, one reason for requiring a physical is to screen out individuals who have contagious diseases. The exam also assists in determining if an applicant is physically capable of performing the work. An often ignored purpose of physical examinations is to provide a record to protect the company against claims for previously existing medical conditions.

Placement on the Job: Orientation

orientation   **Orientation** is *a formal and informal process whereby new employees are introduced to their company, jobs, and members of the work group.* Once applicants have been selected and have joined the firm, several days may be spent in orientation. The purposes of orientation are the following:

1. to create a favorable impression on the new employee of the organization and its work,
2. to help ease the new employee's adjustment to the organization, and
3. to provide specific information concerning the task and performance expectations of the job.[11]

Every new employee goes through an orientation period regardless of whether the firm has a formal orientation program. New recruits must "learn the ropes" or "rules of the game" if they are to succeed. Much of the new employee orientation takes place on an informal basis—during coffee

Figure 9–6

Orientation Outline

1. History and nature of the business
2. Goals of the company
3. Basic products/services provided by the firm
4. Organizational structure
5. Policies, procedures, and rules covering such areas as:
   a. Work schedules
   b. Salaries and payment periods
   c. Physical facilities
   d. Attendance and absenteeism
   e. Working conditions and safety standards
   f. Lunch and coffee breaks
   g. Discipline and grievance
   h. Parking
6. Company benefits
   a. Insurance programs
   b. Pension and/or profit sharing plans
   c. Recreational programs—bowling, tennis, golf, etc.
   d. Vacations and holidays
7. Opportunities
   a. Advancement, promotion
   b. Suggestion systems
8. Specific departmental responsibilities
   a. Department functions
   b. Job duties/responsibilities/authority
   c. Introduction to other employees in work group

breaks, at lunch, or during work—by interactions with employees often referred to as old-timers. However, most organizations have formal orientation programs designed to acquaint new personnel with the areas as shown in Figure 9–6.

SPECIAL CONSIDERATIONS IN SELECTING MANAGERIAL PERSONNEL

In recruiting and selecting nonmanagerial personnel, it is usually possible to use objective factors in identifying potentially successful employees; more subjective judgment is often involved in selecting managerial personnel, however. Proper selection is even more important here. The actions of a senior manager at Delta, for example, might affect the lives of thousands of employees and others. In selecting managers, concern is typically focused on an evaluation of skills, abilities, attitudes, and characteristics, many of which are intangible. Some of these include:

• Planning skills
• Communication ability
• Decision-making skills
• Organizing ability
• Motivation and leadership skills
• Conceptual skills
• Adaptability to change
• Qualities such as self-confidence, aggressiveness, and empathy

The recruitment and development of high-quality managerial personnel is essential to the continuing success of every organization. Because of this, organizations must be concerned with determining needs for managerial personnel and identifying persons with managerial potential.

Techniques for Identifying Managerial Talent

Identifying individuals with potential executive talent has become an increasingly important activity in large organizations. In general, the activity has taken these two directions:

1. determining the significant personal characteristics or behaviors that seem to predict managerial success, and
2. establishing managerial talent assessment centers.

Personal Characteristics

Over the years, there has been considerable interest in determining the personal characteristics related to managerial success. Major companies such as AT&T, Sears, General Electric, Standard Oil, and many others have engaged in research within their firms to identify a series of traits or characteristics necessary for success. The studies related measures of job performance such as productivity, salary level, and quality of work of successful managers with personal characteristics and attitudes of these managers. Some of the characteristics of managers included in these studies were grades in college, level of self-confidence, organized and orderly thought, personal values of a practical and economic nature, intelligence, nonverbal reasoning, and general attitudes. Research at AT&T found a significant relationship between grades in college and salary level achieved. In a study of 10,000 managers in the Bell System, it was found that 51 percent of those in the top 10 percent of their college class were located in the top third of the salary levels in the company. For the most part, studies of personal characteristics of managers have not yielded accurate predictions of managerial success.

Assessment Center

In an effort to improve managerial selection, the use of the assessment center has become popular in recent years. The assessment center is designed to provide for the systematic evaluation of the potential of individuals for future management positions. The assessment center requires individuals to participate in a series of activities similar to what they might

Figure 9–7

Typical Assessment Center Schedule

Day 1	Orientation of dozen candidates
	Break-up into groups of four to play a *Management Game* (observe and assess organizing ability, financial acumen, quickness of thinking, efficiency under stress, adaptability, leadership)
	Psychological Testing (measure and assess verbal and numerical abilities, reasoning, interests, and attitudes) and/or *Depth Interviews* (assess motivation)
	Leaderless Group Discussion (observe and assess aggressiveness, persuasiveness, expository skill, energy, flexibility, self-confidence)
Day 2	*In-Basket Exercise* (observe and assess decision making under stress, organizing ability, memory and ability to interrelate events, preparation for decision making, ability to delegate, concern for others)
	Role-playing of Employment or Performance Appraisal Interview (observe and assess sensitivity to others, ability to probe for information, insight, empathy)
	Group Roles in preparation of a budget (observe and assess collaboration abilities, financial knowledge, expository skill, leadership, drive)
Day 3	*Individual Case Analyses* (observe expository skill, awareness of problems, background information possessed for problems, typically involving marketing, personnel, accounting, operations, and financial elements)
	Obtainment of *Peer Ratings* from all candidates.
	Staff assessors meet to discuss and rate all candidates
Weeks later	Manager with assessor experience meets with each candidate to discuss assessment with counseling concerning career guides and areas to develop

be expected to do in an actual job. Such activities typically include in-basket exercises, management games, leaderless group discussions, mock interviews, and tests. Assessors observe the employees over a period of time. Figure 9–7 illustrates a three-day schedule of an assessment center that uses a number of different bases on which to evaluate executive candidates. The assessment center approach was introduced to American business in the mid-1950s by the American Telephone and Telegraph Company and has grown in popularity since. More than 200 large companies now utilize assessment centers.

A survey of thirty-three companies reveals that the three most widely used assessment techniques are in-basket exercises (thirty-one firms), business games (thirty firms), and leaderless group discussion (thirty-one firms).[12] An in-basket consists of a set of notes, messages, telephone calls, letters, and reports that the candidate is expected to handle within a period of one or two hours. The candidate's decisions can be rated by assessors with respect to such abilities as willingness to take action and organizing of interrelated events.

A business game is a competitive simulation where teams are required to make decisions concerning production, marketing, purchasing, and finance in competition with each other. The leaderless group discussion assesses participant activities in taking the lead in discussion, influencing others, mediating arguments, speaking effectively, and summarizing and classifying issues. In addition, various other exercises are often designed to fit the firm's particular situation. For example, J. C. Penney utilizes the "Irate Customer Phone Call," made by an assessor, in order to rate the candidate's ability to control emotions, demonstrate tact, and satisfy the complaint.[13] Psychological tests and depth interviewing are frequently used techniques but generally show lower levels of accuracy in predicting future success. Personality tests, in particular, appear to be the weakest predictor.

In determining the predictive accuracy of the assessment center approach, the initial study at AT&T was most impressive. Assessor ratings were not communicated to company management for a period of eight years in order not to contaminate the results. In a sample of fifty-five candidates who achieved the middle-management ranks during that period, the center correctly predicted 78 percent of them.[14] Of seventy-three persons who did not progress beyond the first level of management, 95 percent were correctly predicted by the assessment staff. As a result, this company has maintained its centers, processing an average of 10,000 candidates a year. Reviewing ratings and actual progress of 5,943 personnel over a ten-year period demonstrated a high validity of assessment center predictions.

SUMMARY

People are the most important asset of any organization. Most firms today realize that acquiring and developing quality human resources is essential if the organization is to survive and grow. This statement provides an excellent summary of the significance of staffing to every organization. In most large firms, a human resources or personnel department is responsible for administering the organization's staffing function. However, every manager, regardless of function, must understand and participate in the staffing process.

The six basic human-resources-related

functions are staffing, training and development, compensation, health and safety, employee and labor relations, and personnel research. Staffing primarily involves human resources planning, recruitment, and selection. Training and development programs are designed to assist individuals, groups, and the entire organization to become more effective. Compensation includes all rewards individuals receive as a result of their employment. Health and safety programs are designed to enable workers to have a safe and healthy work environment. Employee and labor relations involves dealing with the union or developing an environment where employees believe the union is unnecessary. Personnel research is directed toward gaining a better understanding of human relations problems.

Every manager involved with human resources management is affected by government legislation. Some of the most important legislation passed during the last twenty years includes: Equal Pay Act of 1963, as amended in 1972; Civil Rights Act of 1964, as amended in 1972; Age Discrimination in Employment Act of 1967, as amended in 1978; Occupational Safety and Health Act of 1970; Rehabilitation Act of 1973; Federal Privacy Act of 1974; Employee Retirement Income Security Act of 1974; the Pregnancy Discrimination Act of 1978; and the Civil Service Reform Act of 1978.

The staffing process involves planning for future personnel requirements, recruiting individuals, and selecting from those recruited individuals employees who fulfill the needs of the firm. The process of determining the human qualifications required to perform the job is called job analysis. A job description summarizes the purpose, principal duties, and responsibilities of the job. The statement of the minimum acceptable human qualities necessary to perform the job is the job specification. Personnel demand analysis is the determination of the numbers and types of employees needed to achieve organizational goals. Labor supply analysis is the process of determining the availability of needed employees.

In most large organizations, an employee requisition is issued whenever a job becomes available. Recruitment may then begin. The ultimate objective of recruitment is to select individuals who are most capable of meeting the requirements of the job. Selection from among those recruited applicants is the next step. The steps in the selection process are: (1) preliminary interview, (2) evaluation of application blank, (3) testing, (4) interviewing, (5) reference check and background investigation, (6) management approval, and (7) physical examination. Once individuals have been selected, they need to receive an orientation to the organization.

REVIEW QUESTIONS

1. What are the basic components of human resources management? Briefly define each.
2. What are the major federal laws that affect the staffing process?
3. Distinguish between a job description and a job specification.
4. Describe the advantages and disadvantages of promotion from within.
5. List and discuss the two basic types of employment interviews.
6. What steps are involved in the personnel selection process?
7. What is the purpose of an assessment center? Discuss.

EXERCISES

1. Assume you are a personnel director for the following types of firms and have a vacancy that requires the skills identified below. What phase(s) of the personnel selection process do you believe would require special attention?

   a. Faculty member for a major university that stresses research
   b. General laborer for a construction firm
   c. Skilled welder for work on an assembly line
   d. Senior secretary who is required to take dictation and type 70 words per minute

e. Production supervisor

2. Consult the personnel wanted section of a major Sunday newspaper. Evaluate the positions that are available for the following career fields. Can you detect a general pattern of job requirements that are needed for an applicant?

a. Personnel manager
b. Computer specialist
c. Car salesperson
d. Production supervisor

CASE STUDY

Expansion Plans at Eagle Aircraft

David Johnson, personnel manager for Eagle Aircraft, was a little anxious as he checked through his in-basket that morning. He had just returned from a long weekend at Cozumel, Mexico. His friend Carl Edwards, vice-president of marketing, had called the night before to tell him about a meeting of the company's executive council. "It was a great meeting," Carl had said. "I don't think the future has ever looked brighter for Eagle."

Carl had gone on to tell about the president's decision to expand operations. He continued, "Everyone at the meeting seemed to be completely behind the president. Joe Davis, the controller, stressed our independent financial position; the production manager had done a complete work-up on the equipment we are going to need, including availability and cost information. And I have been pushing for this expansion for some time. So I was ready. I think it will be good for you too, David. The president said he expects employment to double in the next year."

David found nothing in his mail about the meeting. He decided not to worry about it. "I suppose they'll let me know when they need my help," he thought.

Just then he looked up to see Rex Scherer, a production supervisor, standing in the doorway. "David," said Rex, "the production manager jumped me Friday because maintenance doesn't have anybody qualified to work on the new digital lathe they are installing." "He's right," David replied, "we'd better get hot and see if we can find someone." David knew that it was going to be another busy Monday.

QUESTIONS

1. What deficiencies do you see in planning at Eagle Aircraft?
2. How might the planning situation at Eagle Aircraft be improved?
3. When should David start to work on finding the maintenance person for the digital lathe? Why?

CASE STUDY

A Question of Fairness

Five years ago when Bobby Bret joined Crystal Productions as a junior accountant, he felt that he was on his way up. He had just graduated from college with a B+ average and was well liked by both his peers and by the faculty. He had been an officer in several student organizations. Bobby had shown a natural ability to get along with people, as well as to get things done. He remembered what Roger Friedman, the controller at Crystal, had told him when he was hired, "I think you will do well here, Bobby. You've come highly recommended. You are the kind of guy that can expect to move right on up the ladder."

Bobby felt that he had done a good job at Crystal and everybody seemed to like him. In addition, his performance appraisals had been excellent. After five years, however, he was still a junior accountant. He had applied for two senior accountant positions that had come open, but both were filled by people hired from outside the firm. When the accounting supervisor's job came open two years ago, Bobby had not applied. Bobby had hoped that Ron Greene, a senior accountant he particularly respected, would get the job. Bobby was surprised when his new boss turned out to be a hot-shot graduate of State University whose only experience was three years with a "Big Eight" accounting firm.

On the fifth anniversary of his employment at Crystal, Bobby decided it was time to do something. He made an appointment with the controller. At that meeting Bobby explained to Mr. Friedman that he had worked hard to obtain a promotion and described his frustration about having stayed in the same job for so long. "Well," said Mr. Friedman, "you don't think that you were all that much better qualified than the people that we have hired, do you?" "No," said Bobby, "but I think I could have handled the senior accountant job. Of course, the people you have hired are doing a great job, too." The controller responded, "We just look at the qualifications of all the applicants for each job and, considering everything, try to make a reasonable decision."

QUESTIONS

1. Explain the pros and cons of having a promotion-from-within policy at Crystal.
2. Do you believe that Bobby has a legitimate complaint? Explain.

NOTES

1. Arthur Sharplin, "The Lincoln Electric Company," *Case Research Journal* (1982): 59–84; Arthur Sharplin, "Lincoln Electric's Unique Policies," *Personnel Administrator* (June 1983): 8–10; Arthur Sharplin, "Lincoln Electric Company, 1984," in Arthur Sharplin, *Strategic Management* (New York: McGraw-Hill, 1985).

2. Based on the discussion in R. Wayne Mondy and Robert M. Noe III, *Personnel: The Management of Human Resources,* 2d ed. (Newton, Mass.: Allyn and Bacon, 1984), pp. 8–10.

3. "Battle of the Sexes over 'Comparable Worth,'" *U.S. News & World Report* (February 20, 1984): 73.

4. Eliza G. C. Collins and Timothy Blodgett, "Sexual Harassment: Some See It—Some Won't," *Harvard Business Review* 59, no. 2 (March–April 1981): 79.

5. Ibid.

6. Lewis E. Albright, "Staffing Policies and Strategies," in *ASPA Handbook of Personnel and Industrial Relations,* ed. Dale Yoder and Herbert Heneman (Washington, D.C.: Bureau of National Affairs, 1974), pp. 4–21.

7. "A Bleak New Year for Airline Profits," *Business Week* (January 10, 1983): 38; James Ott, "Delta Expanding Route System with 737–200s," *Aviation Week and Space Technology* (April 2, 1984): 32–33; "Delta: The World's Most Profitable Airline," *Business Week* (August 31, 1981): 68–71; James Ott, "Delta Anticipates Savings in Flight Planning System," *Aviation Week and Space Technology* (April 30, 1984): 34–39; and numerous articles from *The Wall Street Journal.*

8. C. Harold Stone and Floyd L. Ruch, "Selection, Interviewing, and Testing," in Yoder and Heneman, *ASPA Handbook,* pp. 152–154.

9. Kenneth C. Cooper, "Those 'Qualified' Applicants and Their Phony Credentials," *Administrative Management* 38 (August 1977): 44.

10. Scott T. Rickard, "Effective Staff Selection," *Personnel Journal* (June 1981): 477.

11. Diana Reed-Mendenhall and C. W. Millard, "Orientation: A Training and Development Tool," *Personnel Administrator* 25 (August 1980): 40.

12. Joseph M. Bender, "What is 'Typical' of Assessment Centers?" *Personnel* 50 (July–August 1973): 51.

13. William C. Byham, "Assessment Centers for Spotting Future Managers," *Harvard Business Review* 48 (July–August 1970): 158.

14. Douglas W. Bray and Donald L. Grant, "The Assessment Center in the Measurement of Potential for Business Management," *Psychological Monographs* 80, no. 17 (1966): 24.

15. James R. Huck, "Assessment Centers: A Review of the External and Internal Validities," *Personnel Psychology* 26 (Summer 1973): 198.

REFERENCES

Breaugh, J. A. "Relationship between Recruiting Sources and Employee Performance, Absenteeism, and Work Attitudes." *Academy of Management Journal* 24 (March 1981): 142–147.

Bucalo, J. "Personnel Directors: What You Should Know before Recommending MBO." *Personnel Journal* 56 (April 1977): 176–178.

Byham, William C. "Assessment Centers for Spotting Future Managers." *Harvard Business Review* 40 (July–August 1970): 158.

Collins, E. G. C., and Timothy Blodgett. "Sexual Harassment: Some See It—Some Won't." *Harvard Business Review* 59, no. 2 (March–April 1981): 79.

Davies, G. S. "Consistent Recruitment in a Graded Manpower System." *Management Science* 22 (July 1976): 1215–1220.

Dhanens, T. P. "Implications of the New EEOC Guidelines." *Personnel* 56 (September 1979): 32–39.

Heflich, D. L. "Matching People and Jobs: Value Systems and Employee Selection." *Personnel Administration* 26 (January 1981): 77–85.

Henderson, J. A. "What the Chief Executive Expects of the Personnel Function." *Personnel Administration* 22 (May 1977): 40–45.

Higgins, James M. "A Manager's Guide to the Equal Employment Opportunity Laws." *Personnel Journal* 55 (August 1976): 406–412.

Hoffman, W. H., and L. L. Wyatt. "Human Resources Planning." *Personnel Administration* 22 (January 1977): 19–23.

Hollingsworth, A. T., and P. Preston. "Corporate Planning: A Challenge for Personnel Executives." *Personnel Journal* 55 (August 1976): 386–389.

Malinowski, F. A. "Job Selection Using Task Analysis." *Personnel Journal* 60 (April 1981): 288–291.

Marr, R., and J. Schneider. "Self-Assessment Test for the 1978 Uniform Guidelines on Employee Selection Procedures." *Personnel Administration* 26 (May 1981): 103–108.

PARMA CYCLE: THE NEW PLANT

Parma Cycle Company of Parma, Ohio, a Cleveland suburb, is one of only three firms that actually manufacture complete bicycles in the United States. Most of Parma's competitors import parts from other countries and simply assemble bicycles here. In 1985, Parma Cycle employed about 800 workers, mainly machine operators and assemblers. The main factory is laid out, coincidentally, like a bicycle wheel, with component manufacturing departments representing the tire and spoke area and assembly being done in the center of the factory, representing the hub.

Parma Cycle makes a line of bicycles and markets them under the Parma name; however, most of the bicycles are purchased by large national retailers and marketed under those retailers' house names. A few bicycles are exported to Europe and South America, but Parma has found it difficult to compete in the international markets with Japanese and Italian manufacturers.

Jesse Heard is the personnel director. He has been with Parma Cycle for twenty-three years. His first job was as a painter, when painting was done with a hand-held spray gun. He was later promoted to supervisor and worked in several departments at the plant. Because the company paid for college tuition and fees, as well as books, to encourage supervisors to advance their education, Jesse went to college. In 1970, he received the bachelor's degree in personnel administration from Case Western University in Cleveland. Jesse was immediately promoted to a job in the personnel department and three years later became the personnel director.

Parma's work force is unionized, with the local union being a member of the National Association of Machinists. Employee recruitment is done primarily through referrals from current workers. Selection is based on personal interviews, evaluation of job-related application forms, and, for certain jobs, a basic skills test conducted by the supervisor. The supervisor makes the final hiring decision. Workers must join the union before the end of a three-month probationary period. Over the years, the union has won wages and benefits about average for the Cleveland area.

In general, the working environment at Parma Cycle has been good. The company has a relatively flat organizational structure with few levels of managers. The organizational chart is shown on the next page.

In May 1983, the Equal Employment Opportunity Commission (EEOC) received a complaint about employment practices at Parma. It was alleged that while the proportion of blacks in the Cleveland area approached 25 percent, only 8 percent of the Parma Cycle work force were black. Further, the complaint alleged, there were only two black managers above the level of supervisor.

Jesse Heard felt that the company was doing everything that it should with regard to equal opportunity. The firm had an affirmative action plan and a practice of encouraging managers to employ blacks and other minority group members, as well as women. In fact, Jesse's efforts to encourage the employment of protected group members had provoked some managers to complain to the company president. The complaint was withdrawn in 1984 after a visit from an EEOC investigator.

One morning in late 1984, Gene Wilson, the corporate planner at Parma, visited Jesse Heard. He was ecstatic about word he had just received that the board of directors had approved a new southern plant, in Clarksdale, Mississippi. "I really

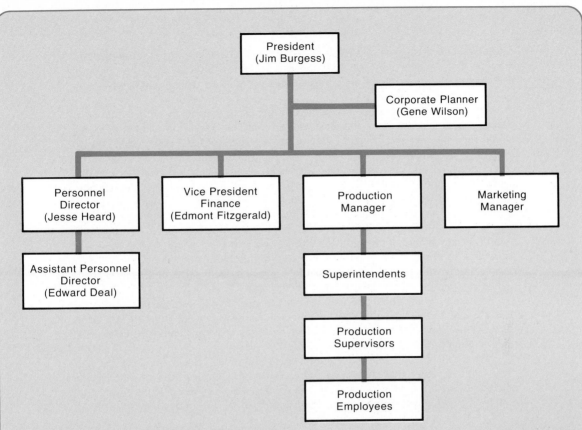

Para Cycle Company Organizational Chart

appreciate your help on this, Jesse," he said. "Without the research you did on the personnel needs for the new plant, I don't think that it would have been approved." "We still have a long way to go," said Jesse. "There is no doubt that we can construct the building and install the machinery. But getting skilled workers in Clarksdale may not be so easy." "Well," said Gene, "the results of the labor survey that you did there last year indicate that we'll be able to get by. Anyway, some of the people here at Parma will surely agree to transfer." "When is the new plant scheduled to open?" asked Jesse. Gene replied, "The building will be finished in February 1985. The machinery will be in by May. The goal is to be in production by September 1985." "Gosh," said Jesse, "I had better get to work."

A few minutes later, back in his office, Jesse considered what the future held at Parma Cycle. The company had been located at Parma, Ohio, a Cleveland suburb, since its founding. It had grown over the years to become the nation's fourth largest bicycle manufacturer. The decision to open the Clarksdale, Mississippi, plant had been made in hopes of achieving decreased production costs because of lower wages. Although no one ever came right out and said it, it was assumed that the southern plant would be nonunion. The elimination of union work rules was expected to be a benefit.

The state of Mississippi had offered a ten-year exemption from all property taxes, a significant advantage because tax rates for Cleveland-area industries were extremely high. Jesse was pleased that he had been involved in the discussions from the time that the new plant was first suggested. Even with the advanced preparation he had done, he knew that the coming months would be extremely difficult for him and his staff.

At that moment, Jesse's assistant, Edward Deal, walked in with a bundle of papers. "Hi, Ed," said Jesse, "I'm glad you're here. The Clarksdale plant is definitely on the way, and you and I need to get our act together." "That's great," said Edward. "It is quite a coincidence, too, because I had just been going over this stack of job descriptions, identifying which ones we might eliminate as we scale back at this plant." Jesse said, "Remember, Ed, we are not going to cut back very much here. Some jobs will be deleted and others added. But out of the 800 positions here, I'll bet that not more than 40 will be actually eliminated." "So, what you are saying is that we basically have to staff the plant with people we hire from the Clarksdale area?" Edward asked. Jesse replied, "No, Ed, we will have some people here who are willing to transfer even though their jobs are not being eliminated. We will then replace them with others we hire in the Cleveland area. Most of the workers at Clarksdale, though, will be recruited from that area."

Ed asked, "What about the management team?" "Well," said Jesse, "I think the boss already knows who the main people will be down there. They are managers we currently have on board plus a fellow we located at a defunct three-wheeler plant in Mound Bayou, Mississippi."

"What will be that plant's relationship to this one?" asked Ed. Jesse replied, "The plant manager there will work directly for Mr. Burgess [the president]. But personnel, marketing, and finance will be centralized, with just a supervisor and a couple of clerks for each function in Clarksdale."

QUESTIONS

1. Draw an organizational chart for Parma Cycle as it will exist after the new plant is open. Classify the organization in at least two ways and explain your classifications.

2. Explain the part the informal organization might play in determining who is willing to transfer to the southern plant.

3. Discuss how you believe Parma Cycle should staff the new plant.

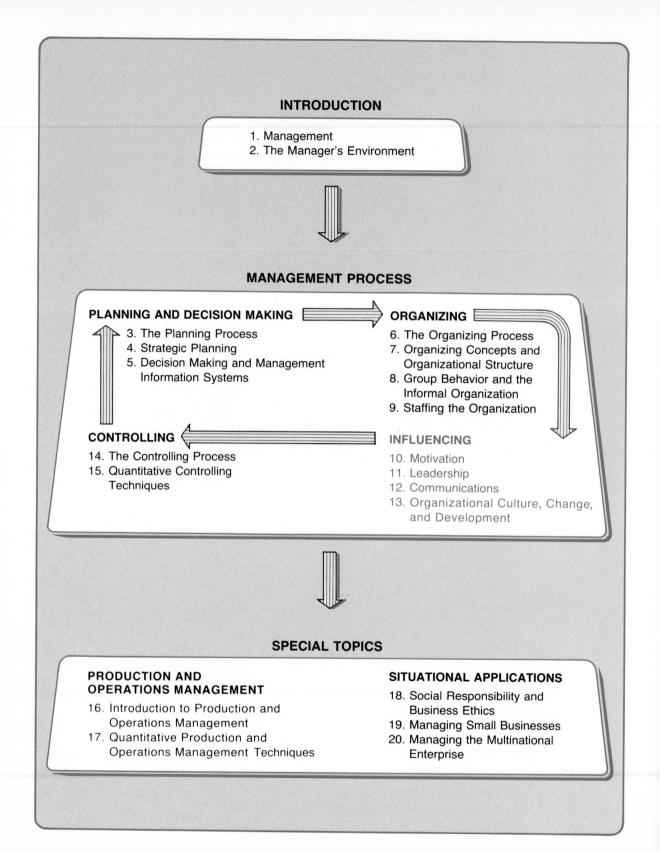

INTRODUCTION

1. Management
2. The Manager's Environment

MANAGEMENT PROCESS

PLANNING AND DECISION MAKING

3. The Planning Process
4. Strategic Planning
5. Decision Making and Management Information Systems

ORGANIZING

6. The Organizing Process
7. Organizing Concepts and Organizational Structure
8. Group Behavior and the Informal Organization
9. Staffing the Organization

CONTROLLING

14. The Controlling Process
15. Quantitative Controlling Techniques

INFLUENCING

10. Motivation
11. Leadership
12. Communications
13. Organizational Culture, Change, and Development

SPECIAL TOPICS

PRODUCTION AND OPERATIONS MANAGEMENT

16. Introduction to Production and Operations Management
17. Quantitative Production and Operations Management Techniques

SITUATIONAL APPLICATIONS

18. Social Responsibility and Business Ethics
19. Managing Small Businesses
20. Managing the Multinational Enterprise

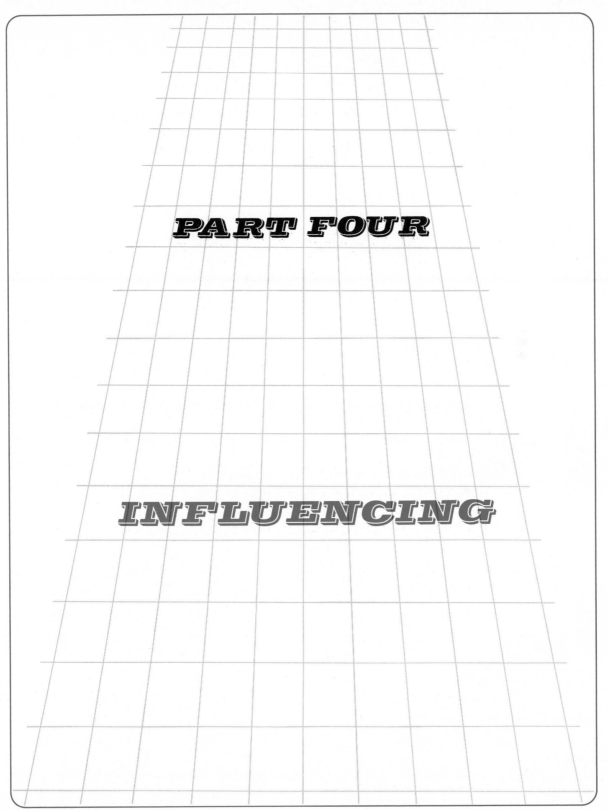

PART FOUR

INFLUENCING

motivation
Theory X
Theory Y
expectancy
valence

reinforcement theory
organizational
  behavior modification
  (OBM)
job enrichment

job enlargement
quality circles (QCs)
Theory Z

LEARNING OBJECTIVES

After completing this chapter you should be able to

1. Define motivation and explain some basic philosophies of human nature.
2. Distinguish between the motivation theories of Abraham Maslow and Frederick Herzberg.
3. Describe the work of David McClelland as it relates to motivation.
4. Explain the expectancy theory of motivation.
5. Explain how reinforcement theory and organizational behavior modification might be applied to business.
6. Explain job design and its relationship to job enrichment and job enlargement.
7. Describe equity theory and the self-fulfilling prophecy.
8. Explain quality circles and Theory Z management.

10

Motivation

NISSAN

"We're a U.S. corporation which builds trucks in the U.S. with American employees. We happen to be owned, like a lot of banks and hotels, by a foreign company," said Jerry Benefield. Jerry is vice president of manufacturing for Nissan Motor Manufacturing Corporation U.S.A. Nissan's light truck facility in Smyrna, Tennessee, had been announced in October 1980. The first truck rolled off the line in June 1983 and in March 1985 the first passenger car was produced. The plant is expected to reach full production capacity of 240,000 cars and light trucks by spring 1987.

The foreign company to which Jerry Benefield referred is Nissan Motor Company, Ltd. of Tokyo. With manufacturing operations in 24 countries and distribution centers in 130, Nissan is the world's fourth largest manufacturer of motor vehicles. Company officials say that Nissan was attracted to the United States by the large market. The company also has a corporate objective to produce vehicles in the countries where they are sold. Finally, the threat of import controls undoubtedly played a part in the decision.

To get the Nissan plant, Tennessee offered a number of the usual incentives—tax abatements, new roads, training funds, etc. But according to a Nissan spokesperson, "These had little to do with the location decision. Every state, and indeed every country, offers similar incentives." She continued, "If there is one single factor which distinguished Tennessee from other areas it was that Tennessee is very centrally located. When you are distributing something as large as cars and trucks, then transportation costs are a very big bill." According to Nissan, Smyrna, Tennessee is within 500 miles of perhaps half of the U.S. population.

But all that would have been irrelevant if Nissan had not been convinced that American employees could produce cars competitively. That had been brought into question by the well known inability of U.S. automakers to meet foreign competition in the early 1980s, resulting in layoffs for hundreds of thousands of auto workers.

Many blame the problems of the U.S. auto industry on unionization. The Nissan plant in Smyrna is not unionized, but a Bridgestone tire plant, just two miles away, has a United Rubber Workers local and a number of companies in nearby Nashville, such as Ford Motor Company's glass plant, have unions. Still, the rural farming area of Tennessee is hardly bedrock union country and Nissan clearly prefers to remain nonunion. Marvin T. Runyon, the former Ford executive who runs the Smyrna operation for Nissan, emphasizes that joining a union is "up to the employees and not up to the company." He adds that, "We like talking with our employees directly, without a third party being involved."

Runyon believes in a participative, "bottom-up" management style. "We want the person who is doing the job to have something to say about how the job gets done," Runyon explains. Jerry Benefield says, "Domestic manufacturing utilizes an autocratic management style which doesn't involve those who have to execute decisions in the decision-making process." "At Nissan," he continues, "we allow employees to participate in making all the decisions that affect their jobs."

Nissan claims a wage structure "comparable with the U.S. auto industry." The starting wage for a "technician," the title Nissan gives its hourly employees, is $10.35 an hour plus $1.35 an hour bonus. The bonus is paid twice a year, in June and December. A Nissan spokesperson says, "Perhaps some day the bonus will be connected to quality, productivity, and other such factors, but for now it is just a bonus paid for each hour for which employees are compensated."

There have been 180,000 applicants for the 3,000 jobs the plant will eventually provide. In a state where unemployment has recently approached 13 percent, job security was no small part of the attraction. Nissan does not promise lifetime job security, as is sometimes done in Japan, but the company says, "We will do everything we can to make sure jobs are preserved." One thing the firm has done is contract out certain auxiliary functions like security, grounds maintenance, and food service so that if things ever turn down it will be possible to release the contract personnel and fill the jobs with Nissan employees. Also, Nissan is committed to limiting production at the Tennessee plant to only the solid base of U.S. demand. The peaks and valleys in the market, according to the company, will be absorbed by imports from Japan.

The Smyrna plant is said to be one of the most technologically advanced automotive facilities in the world. Robots do many of the repetitive jobs. State-of-the-art computers and communications systems provide for energy management, preventive maintenance, and detailed control of the entire manufacturing process. Workers at Nissan are each taught a number of skills so that they can maintain as well as operate the plant's complex machinery. Nissan managers claim that multi-skilled workers are not only more productive but more contented than traditional assembly-line workers. Larry Seltz, Director of Personnel Development, says, "People want to do a total job. They don't want to stand in one spot and shoot screws all day." The managers are right, according to Lonnie Blitte, who is learning to operate a robotized paint sprayer. Lonnie says, "I feel responsible for this piece of equipment, as if it were my own."[1]

More than any other single factor, the encroachment of the Japanese into U.S. automobile markets has stimulated a renewed concern for productivity. The primary way that productivity can be achieved is probably through developing a motivated work force. **Motivation** is defined as *the willingness to put forth effort in the pursuit of organizational goals.* If Nissan is successful in making trucks in the United States, it will be because the workers at the plant are motivated.

Management traditionally has relied on the use of rewards, such as increased pay, job security, and good working conditions, or punishments, such as dismissal, demotions, or withholding rewards to motivate employees, to achieve high performance. Management in today's environment, however, cannot rely on the manipulation of pay, benefits, or working conditions to motivate personnel to perform effectively. Motivation is a much more complicated process.

The manager must seek to understand the forces that energize workers' behavior. The manager has the responsibility to develop an effective work environment or climate that will make use of the enormous energy that is within every person. In essence, then, a manager's major task in motivating personnel is to create and develop a climate or environment in which they will want to be productive, contributing members of the organization.

In this chapter, we will attempt to understand motivation. First, we will discuss two philosophies of human nature that suggest the need for a new way of thinking about motivation. Next, a number of popular theories of motivation are described. The final section presents several ideas that relate to motivation in practice.

PHILOSOPHIES OF HUMAN NATURE

In order to learn how to create an environment conducive to a high level of employee motivation, managers must develop an understanding of the philosophies of human nature.

The assumptions that managers have regarding other people are a major factor in determining the climate for motivation. For instance, Nissan assumes that workers desire responsibility and wish to work together cooperatively toward meaningful objectives. This is a far cry from the traditional confrontational attitudes of U.S. automobile workers and managers. The idea that the assumptions we make about others in large measure determine how they will behave is central to the following two philosophies of human nature.

McGregor's Theory X and Theory Y

Douglas McGregor stressed the importance of understanding the relationships between motivation and philosophies of human nature.[2] In observing the practices and approaches of traditional managers, McGregor believed that managers usually attempt to motivate employees by one of two basic approaches. He referred to these approaches as Theory X and Theory Y.

Theory X   **Theory X** is *the traditional view of management that suggests that managers are required to coerce, control, or threaten employees in order to motivate them.* In contrast, McGregor proposed an alternative philosophy of human

Theory Y   nature, which he referred to as Theory Y. **Theory Y** is *a view of management by which a manager believes people are capable of being responsible and mature.* Thus, employees do not require coercion or excessive control by

TABLE 10-1 A Comparison of McGregor's Theory X and Theory Y Assumptions about Human Nature

Theory X	Theory Y
The average person inherently dislikes work and will avoid it if possible.	The expenditure of physical and mental effort in work is as natural as play or rest.
Because of the dislike of work, most people must be coerced, controlled, directed, and threatened with punishment to get them to perform effectively.	People will exercise self-direction and self-control in the service of objectives to which they are committed.
The average person lacks ambition, avoids responsibility, and seeks security and economic rewards above all else.	Commitment to objectives is a function of the rewards associated with achievement.
Most people lack creative ability and are resistant to change.	The average person learns, under proper conditions, not only to accept but to seek responsibility.
Since most people are self-centered, they are not concerned with the goals of the organization.	The capacity to exercise a relatively high degree of imagination, ingenuity, and creativity in the solution of organizational problems is widely, not narrowly, distributed in the population.

Source: Based on Douglas McGregor, *The Human Side of Enterprise* (New York: McGraw-Hill, 1960).

the manager in order to perform effectively. McGregor's belief was that Theory Y is a more realistic assessment of people.

Table 10-1 illustrates the different assumptions of these two philosophies of human nature. The Theory Y assumptions represent the manager's high degree of faith in the capacity and potential of people. If one accepts the Theory Y philosophy of human nature, managerial practices such as the following will be seriously considered: (1) abandonment of time clocks, (2) flexible working hours on an individual basis, (3) job enrichment, (4) management by objectives, and (5) participative decision making. All are based on the beliefs that abilities are widespread in the population and each person is trusted to behave in a responsible manner. Thus, management would create an environment that will permit workers to be motivated to fully utilize their potential. However, one should not conclude that McGregor advocated Theory Y as the panacea for all managerial problems. The Theory Y philosophy is not utopia, but McGregor argued that it did provide a basis for improved management and organizational performance.

Argyris's Maturity Theory

The research of Chris Argyris has also aided managers in developing a more complete understanding of human behavior. Argyris emphasized the importance of the process of maturity. He suggests that there is a basic difference between the demands of the mature personality and the demands of the typical organization. Argyris concluded that if plans, policies, and methods/procedures are described in detail, an employee will need to be submissive and passive, which suggests a Theory X type of organization. The demand is for the subordinate to concentrate on the orders as given and not question or attempt to understand these orders in a broader perspective. In brief, such a detailed prescription may ask individuals to work in an environment where:

1. They have little control over their workaday world.
2. They are expected to be passive, dependent, and subordinate.

3. They are expected to have a short time perspective.

4. They are induced to perfect and value the frequent use of a few shallow abilities.

5. They are expected to produce under conditions leading to psychological failure.[3]

When the mature employee encounters the conditions described above, three reactions are possible:

1. *Escape.* An employee may escape by quitting the job, being absent from work, or attempting to climb to higher levels in the firm where the structure is less rigid.

2. *Fight.* A person can fight the system by exerting pressure on the organization by means of informal groups or through formally organized labor unions.

3. *Adapt.* The most typical reaction by employees is one of adaptation by developing an attitude of apathy or indifference. The employee "plays the game," and pay becomes the compensation for the penalty of working.

According to Argyris, adaptation is the least representative of good mental health. Many companies like Nissan have attempted to diminish the need for adaptation by workers by letting them participate in decisions that affect them.

Criticisms of McGregor and Argyris

Managers cannot assume that all employees are mature as defined by Argyris or Theory Y types as defined by McGregor. These assumptions may be valid when managers are dealing with highly educated professional, technical, and managerial employees, but to the industrial workers, security may mean more than a challenging job. The industrial worker may enjoy the highly structured and repetitive tasks that may be boring to others.

Argyris argues that a highly structured environment requires employees to act immaturely. One could argue as well that maturity involves the ability to adapt to any kind of environment, structured or not. Many people can and have adjusted to tightly regimented work situations that Argyris contends would demand immature behavior; one need only observe workers on an assembly line to recognize this. However, only a fraction of the jobs in U.S. business is of the highly structured, totally controlled type. Workers who prefer challenges can find them. To the degree that an open job market operates effectively, there will be matching of varying human needs and organizational demands.

The ideas of McGregor and Argyris have some relevance to the practice of management, of course. Managers probably have tended to make Theory X type assumptions about their subordinates, and the modern organization does restrict behavior somewhat. To suggest that either of these philosophies is an adequate guide for managers in all situations is erroneous, however.

MOTIVATION THEORIES

There are nearly as many theories of motivation as there are psychologists. Because of the vast amount of difference associated with the theories, the acceptance of one may actually mean that another theory will be rejected. None of the theories provides a universally accepted approach that explains all human behavior. Human beings are far too complex. However, a basic understanding of these theories can be useful to managers as they attempt to motivate people in their organizations. Our purpose in presenting different theories of human motivation is not to identify one as being superior. Rather, it is to develop a thought process that will ultimately lead managers to their own concept of motivation.

Maslow's Hierarchy of Needs

Many psychologists believe that there are certain patterns or configurations of human needs, although there obviously are individual differences. A common approach to establishing this need pattern is that of developing a universal need hierarchy. Abraham Maslow has proposed one widely accepted pattern, which is illustrated in Figure 10–1. Examples of how an organization might help to satisfy these basic needs are also presented. Maslow states that individuals are motivated to satisfy certain unsatisfied needs. His theory of human motivation is based on the following assumptions:

- Needs that are not satisfied motivate or influence behavior. Satisfied needs do not motivate behavior.
- Needs are arranged according to a hierarchy of importance.
- An individual's needs at any level on the hierarchy emerge only when the lower-level needs are reasonably well satisfied.[4]

According to Maslow's hierarchy of needs theory, an individual's needs are arranged in a hierarchy from the lower-level physiological needs to the higher-level needs for self-actualization. The physiological needs are the highest priority because until they are reasonably satisfied, other higher-level needs will not emerge to motivate behavior. One reason that some predict that Nissan will not be successful in its U.S. plant is because of the firm's emphasis on guaranteed employment, which appeals to safety needs. The suggestion is that U.S. workers are on a higher level of hierarchy than Japanese workers and thus are not as concerned with security.

A person is never completely satisfied on any need level, but a sufficient amount of gratification of lower-priority needs must be met if the individual is to seek to satisfy upper-level needs. Maslow suggests a hypothetical example for an average person who is 85 percent satisfied in physiological needs, 70 percent in safety needs, 50 percent in love needs, 40 percent in the self-esteem category, and 10 percent in self-actualization needs.

The use of the universal needs hierarchy by a manager in motivating employees is based on the concept that reasonably well-satisfied needs do not motivate. Therefore, if an individual's lower-level needs are fairly well satisfied, management cannot use these needs to motivate behavior.

While Maslow's theory of human needs is widely known and adopted by many practicing managers, some research studies have contradicted it.[5] These studies suggest that there are only two or three distinct categories of needs, not five as Maslow proposed. In addition, some critics question the *order* of the hierarchy of needs. It is argued that while considerable importance is placed on physiological needs if they have not been satisfied, a person does not move up the hierarchy in an orderly or predictable manner once the physiological needs are satisfied. A clear-cut pattern of

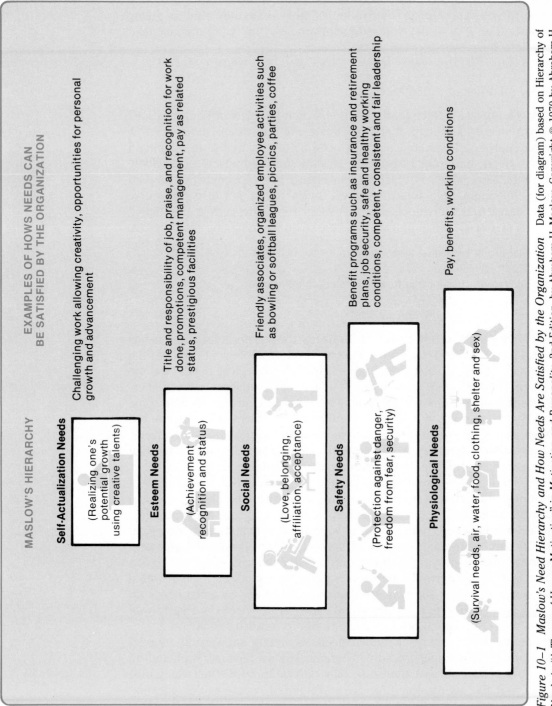

MASLOW'S HIERARCHY

EXAMPLES OF HOWS NEEDS CAN
BE SATISFIED BY THE ORGANIZATION

Self-Actualization Needs

(Realizing one's
potential growth
using creative talents)

Challenging work allowing creativity, opportunities for personal
growth and advancement

Esteem Needs

(Achievement
recognition and status)

Title and responsibility of job, praise, and recognition for work
done, promotions, competent management, pay as related
status, prestigious facilities

Social Needs

(Love, belonging,
affiliation, acceptance)

Friendly associates, organized employee activities such
as bowling or softball leagues, picnics, parties, coffee

Safety Needs

(Protection against danger,
freedom from fear, security)

Benefit programs such as insurance and retirement
plans, job security, safe and healthy working
conditions, competent, consistent and fair leadership

Physiological Needs

(Survival needs, air, water, food, clothing, shelter and sex)

Pay, benefits, working conditions

Figure 10–1 Maslow's Need Hierarchy and How Needs Are Satisfied by the Organization   Data (for diagram) based on Hierarchy of Needs in "A Theory of Human Motivation" in *Motivation and Personality*, 2nd Edition, by Abraham H. Maslow. Copyright © 1970 by Abraham H. Maslow. Reprinted by permission of Harper & Row, Publishers, Inc.

the progression of needs that require satisfaction has not emerged.
According to Maslow, a need that has been relatively well satisfied ceases
to motivate. This may well be the case for the physiological, security, and
social needs. But such a conclusion may not be warranted if we are talking
about the upper-level needs of esteem and self-actualization, achievement,
recognition, or acceptance of responsibility.

Herzberg's Motivation-Hygiene Theory

Maslow saw motivation as operating across a single continuum from
psychological needs to self-actualization needs. The Herzberg theory
proposes that there are in reality two significantly different classes of
factors and thus two different continuums. One class, referred to as *hygiene*
factors, operates across a continuum ranging from dissatisfaction to no
dissatisfaction.[6] As shown in Figure 10–2, hygiene factors relate to the
environment and are external to the job. Herzberg indicates that these
factors do not serve to promote job satisfaction; rather, their absence or
deficiency can create dissatisfaction. Hygiene factors maintain an employee;
they do not make a person healthy but rather prevent unhealthiness. An
organization that meets the hygiene needs of its employees will eliminate
dissatisfaction but will not motivate employees to work harder. The fact
that workers are paid less at Nissan than at other automobile plants could
create dissatisfaction if Herzberg is right; however, the emphasis on job
security, another hygiene factor, might offset this result.

The second class of factors or needs, referred to as *motivators,* makes
up a continuum leading from not motivated to highly motivated. As shown
in Figure 10–2, the work itself, recognition, achievement, possibility of
growth, and advancement are motivation needs. These are concerned with
the work itself rather than its surrounding physical, administrative, or social
environment. They are internal to the job, and if the worker is to be truly
motivated, the job is the major source of that motivation.

Herzberg's theory seems to suggest a clear delineation between

Figure 10–2   Motivation and Hygiene Factors

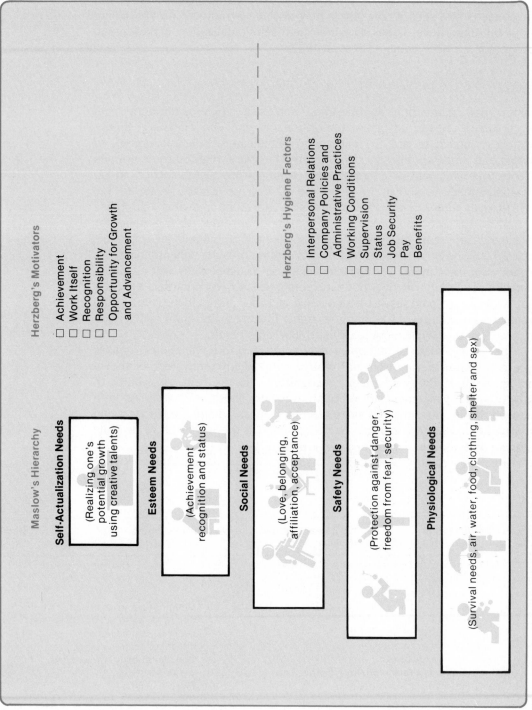

Figure 10–3 Maslow and Herzberg Related

motivators and hygiene in terms of absolute categories—pay is categorized as a hygiene factor for each individual. Pay may be a dissatisfier to some individuals and a satisfier to others. Thus, it can be argued that hygiene and motivation factors should not be considered as absolute categories.

Specific criticisms of Herzberg's theory include the following:

1. The research methodology using the critical incident technique of asking people to reflect back on experiences may cause people to recall only the most recent experiences. Also, analysis of the responses derived from this approach is highly subjective.
2. The theory is most applicable to knowledge workers—managers, engineers, accountants, and other professional-level personnel. Thus, it is not possible to say that the findings apply equally to other occupational groups. Most studies have shown that when the employees are professional or managerial-level employees, the theory is applicable. Studies of lower-level or manual workers are less supportive of the theory.
3. The theory focuses too much attention on satisfaction or dissatisfaction rather than on the performance level of the individual. Satisfaction may or may not be directly related to job performance.

Despite these criticisms, Herzberg's two-factor theory has made a significant contribution toward improving a manager's basic understanding of motivation. As a result, managers must be aware of the potentially successful application of the theory as the work force becomes increasingly better educated and develops higher expectations of management and as organizational life becomes more complex.

There is a fairly close relationship between Maslow's hierarchy of needs theory and Herzberg's motivation-hygiene theory (see Figure 10–3). Herzberg's *motivators* are most closely related to the esteem and self-actualization needs on Maslow's hierarchy. The hygiene factors closely correspond to the physiological, safety, and social needs. Herzberg's basic contention is that most organizations give inadequate attention to the *motivation factors* in the work environment. Most of the efforts of managers are concentrated on meeting the low-level needs, which are satisfied by the *hygiene factors*. But just because the hygiene or maintenance needs are satisfied—by good pay, benefits, or working conditions—this does not mean that the individual's performance will be positively influenced. To achieve effectiveness, the organization must satisfy both the hygiene and the motivation needs of its employees. Most organizations have given consideable attention to the hygiene needs but inadequate attention to the motivation needs of its personnel. This is understandable since hygiene needs can be met in a more tangible or specific manner than can the motivational needs. It may be easier to provide employees with improved pay, fringe benefits, or working conditions than a job that is more responsible or challenging.

Advocates of Herzberg's two-factor theory of motivation suggest that management can assist employees in meeting their motivational needs by providing employees with more challenging and responsible jobs. According to Herzberg, increasing the level of autonomy, skill variety, task significance, and feedback will lead to better job performance and more satisfied employees.

McClelland's Needs Theory

Whereas Maslow's theory stresses a universal hierarchy of needs, the research of David McClelland emphasizes that there are certain needs that are learned and socially acquired as the individual interacts with the environment. McClelland's needs theory is concerned with how individual needs and environmental factors combine to form three basic human motives: the need for achievement (*n Ach*), the need for power (*n Pow*), and the need for affiliation (*n Aff*). As previously discussed, motives explain behavior. McClelland conducted numerous studies attempting to define and measure basic human motives.

Need for Achievement

A person with a high *need for achievement* tends to be characterized as an individual who

- wants to take personal responsibility for finding solutions to problems.
- is goal oriented.
- seeks a challenge—and establishes moderate, realistic, and attainable goals that involve risk but are not impossible to attain.
- desires concrete feedback on performance.
- has a high level of energy and is willing to work hard.

People exhibiting a high *n Ach* have found the above pattern of behavior personally rewarding. For these people, the value of goal accomplishment is enhanced if the goals are at least moderately difficult to achieve and if there is a significant degree of risk involved.[7] McClelland's research has shown that a high *n Ach* is probably a strong or dominant need in only 10 percent of the U.S. population. Persons high in the need for achievement tend to gravitate toward entrepreneurial and sales positions. In these occupations, individuals are better able to "manage" themselves and satisfy the basic drive for achievement.

Need for Power

A high *need for power* means that an individual seeks to influence or control others. Such an individual tends to be characterized by the following types of behavior:

- Is concerned with acquiring, exercising, or retaining power or influence over others.
- Likes to compete with others in situations that allow him or her to be dominant.
- Enjoys confrontations with others.

McClelland says that there are two basic aspects of power: positive and negative. Positive use of power is essential of a manager is to accomplish results through the efforts of others. The negative face of power is when an individual seeks power for personal benefit, which may prove detrimental to the organization.[8]

Need for Affiliation

The *need for affiliation* is related to the desire for affection and establishing friendly relationships. A person with a high need for affiliation tends to be characterized as one who

- seeks to establish and maintain friendships and close emotional relationships with others.
- wants to be liked by others.
- enjoys parties, social activities, and "bull" sessions.
- seeks a sense of belonging by joining groups or organizations.

To varying degrees, each of us possesses these three motives; however, one of the needs will tend to be more characteristic of the individual than the other two.[9] People in a given culture may have the same needs, but the relative strength of those needs differs. For example, the strength of Japanese workers' need for affiliation may be stronger than that of U.S. workers. Therefore, the family feeling that Nissan promotes may have less appeal in the United States than in Japan.

Each of McClelland's three motives evokes a different type of feeling of satisfaction. For example, the achievement motive tends to evoke a sense of accomplishment, whereas a manager may have a feeling of being in control or influencing others when the power motive is prevalent. According to this theory, the probability that an individual will perform a job effectively and efficiently depends on a combination of:

- The strength of the motive or need relative to other needs.
- The possibility of success in performing the task.
- The strength value of the incentive or reward for performance.

The most effective mixture of these three motives depends on the situation. In studies of over 500 managers, it was concluded that the most effective managers have a high need for power, a moderate need for achievement, and a low need for affiliation. These managers tend to use their power in a participative manner for the good of the organization. The best managers have a moderate need for achievement but not strong enough to interfere with the management process. Persons with high needs for both power and achievement have high managerial motivation, but they may not make the best managers.[10] After all, management is getting work done through the efforts of others, not overpowering them.

Outstanding sales personnel tend to be high in the need for achievement and moderately high in the need for power. Entrepreneurs who develop ideas and promote specific enterprises tend to be high in achievement motivation. They delight in personally solving problems and getting immediate feedback on the degree of success. Entrepreneurs sometimes are unable to make the transition to top-level management positions. Their need for personal achievement gets in the way of the requirements for effectively influencing the organization's employees.

Expectancy Theories of Motivation

The approaches to motivation developed by Maslow, Herzberg, and McClelland do not adequately account for differences in individual employees or explain why people behave in certain ways. Victor Vroom developed an approach to motivation known as *expectancy theory* that attempts to explain behavior in terms of an individual's goals and choices and the expectations of achieving these goals.[11] It assumes that people can determine which outcomes they prefer and make realistic estimates of the chances of obtaining them. The key concepts of the expectancy theory are that motivation depends on:

- **expectancy**—*an individual's perception of the chances or probability that a particular outcome will occur as a result of certain behavior.*
- **valence**—*the value an individual places on a specific outcome.*

Expectancy theory can be stated mathematically as follows:

$$\text{Motivation} = \text{Expectancy} \times \text{Valence}.$$

Both factors must be present before a high level of motivation can occur. In other words, a high expectancy or a high valence alone will not ensure motivation. For example, if an employee had a low expectancy (perceived little chance) of receiving a pay increase but placed a high value on money, the employee would not be highly motivated to work hard to obtain the increase.

All employees in an organization do not share the same goals or values regarding pay, job security, promotions, benefits, or working conditions. For instance, assume Susan Johnson is a supervisor in the systems and programming division. She places a high value on receiving a promotion to a more challenging and responsible position. Susan perceives that excellent performance in her current supervisory position is essential to achieving her desired promotion. Susan's manager recognizes the value that Susan places on a promotion. Therefore, the manager attempts to let Susan know that there is a high probability of being promoted if she performs effectively in her current position. Thus, Susan will seek to perform in a superior manner in order to achieve the promotion. Another employee, Bill Thomas, an office supervisor, values stability and job security and is not interested in a promotion because he does not want more responsibility. Thus, Bill will not be motivated by an opportunity for a promotion.

A key factor in the expectancy model is what the employee perceives as important or of value, not what the manager believes the employee should seek or value. Thus, employees are motivated by what they perceive or expect in terms of rewards as a result of a given behavior. A manager's ability to motivate employees depends on a thorough knowledge of each individual employee as to background, goals, experiences, and other attributes. The manager needs to identify what sparks motivation in the employee.

A major contribution of expectancy theory is that it explains how the goals of employees influence their behavior on the job. The employees' behavior depends on their assessment of the probability that the behavior will actually lead to the attainment of the goal.

In summary, the manager who wishes to use the expectancy model of motivation should devote attention to the following:

1. Ensuring that employees have sufficient training to do the task assigned.
2. Removing organizational obstacles to proper performance.
3. Instilling in employees confidence concerning capacity to perform.
4. Selecting organizational rewards that will meet specific employee needs.
5. Communicating clearly the relationship between rewards and performance.
6. Administering the reward system in a consistent and equitable fashion so that

employees will perceive a relationship between performance and the rewards they receive.

CHAPTER 10   293

Motivation

Although expectancy theory is the most widely accepted theory of motivation, empirical support for it has not been strong. One reason may be the difficulty of measuring valence and expectancy consistently. For example, although a certain outcome may have the same degree of desirability (valence) for two persons, one may assign that outcome a valence of 9 (highly desired) and the other may assign it a valence of only 7.[12] For the manager, however, expectancy theory does provide a useful starting point for understanding motivation. In applying expectancy theory, the manager's goals should be to provide outcomes that subordinates highly value and to ensure that workers perceive a high probability of those outcomes occurring if they behave as desired.

Reinforcement Theory

Reinforcement theory is based primarily on the research of B. F. Skinner and has been increasingly applied in business situations. **Reinforcement theory** is *the idea that human behavior can be explained in terms of the previous positive or negative outcomes of that behavior.* People tend to repeat behaviors that they have learned will produce pleasant outcomes. Behavior that is reinforced will be repeated; behavior that is not reinforced will not be repeated.

reinforcement theory

Skinner contends that people's behavior can be controlled and shaped by rewarding (reinforcing) desired behavior while ignoring undesirable actions. Over time, the reinforced behavior will tend to be repeated, whereas the unrewarded behavior will tend to be extinguished and will disappear. Punishment of undesired behavior is to be avoided since it may contribute to feelings of restraint and actions of rebellion. Thus, over a period of years, the conditioner can control human behavior without the person becoming aware of being controlled. In his book, *Beyond Freedom and Dignity,* Skinner says that people can be controlled and shaped while at the same time feeling free.[13]

Skinner's theory of shaping behavior is useful to managers, but one should not assume that human behavior is simple to understand and/or modify. Obtaining immediate feedback of results on an enriched job is a form of instant reward related to behavior on the job. The primary technique suggested by Skinner is organizational behavior modification.

Organizational behavior modification (OBM) is *the application of Skinner's reinforcement theory to organizational change efforts.* OBM rests on two fundamental concepts: (1) people act in ways they find most personally rewarding, and (2) behavior can be shaped and determined by controlling the rewards. In OBM, rewards are termed *reinforcers* because the goal is to stimulate continuation of the rewarded behavior. Which reinforcers actually work in motivating people is determined by a manager's trial and error and experience. What is successful with one employee may not work with another because needs and wants differ. Praise is used most frequently because it is most readily available. It becomes less effective whenever it becomes predictable or is continuously applied. Money is also

organizational behavior modification (OBM)

used, as are public or private letters of commendation, time off, and increased status.

In OBM, punishment is rejected as a reinforcer because it suppresses the undesired behavior while at the same time stimulating anger, hostility, aggression, and rebellion. And at times, it is difficult to identify the punishment. In one instance, placing prisoners in solitary confinement on bread and water turned out to be a high-status symbol and led to repetition of offenses. When the bread and water was changed to baby food, the status symbol disappeared, leading to a significant reduction in the number of undesirable acts. When undesired behavior is not rewarded, it tends to disappear over time.

In reinforcing desired behavior in a positive fashion, it is important to allocate the rewards soon after the behavior occurs so that the person perceives a clear and immediate linkage. Fast and accurate feedback of information to the performer in itself constitutes a reinforcer.

Organizational behavior modification has been used successfully in a number of organizations to improve performance. In one firm, positive reinforcement was used to reduce absenteeism.[15] Each day an employee came to work on time, he or she received a playing card. At the end of the week, the highest poker hand received $20. Over a three-month period, the absenteeism rate of the experimental group decreased 18 percent, whereas that of a control group actually increased. In their use of OBM, Michigan Bell Telephone identified specific desired behaviors such as the following: (1) service promptness in answering calls, (2) shortness of time taken to give information, (3) use of proper references in handling the call, and (4) attendance.[16] Praise and recognition were the dominant reinforcers. The results were an improvement in attendance by 50 percent and above standard productivity and efficiency levels.

The Emery Air Freight OBM program is one of the biggest success stories to date.[17] It used the simple reinforcers of information feedback and praise to condition employee behavior. In responding to customer questions about service and schedules within a standard ninety-minute period, performance moved from 30 percent of the standard to 90 percent within a few days. Employees were provided with feedback charts through which they could monitor their own performance. Employees who did not achieve the desired results were reminded of the goal and then praised for their honesty. This 90 percent achievement remained stable for over three years. As a result of the application of OBM, estimated savings to Emery Air Freight were placed at $650,000 per year.

If the manager desires to use OBM, the following actions are necessary:

- Identifying the desired performance in specific terms, for example, improving attendance rates or answering questions within one hour.
- Identifying the rewards that will reinforce the desired behavior, for example, praise, money, time off.
- Making the reward a direct consequence of the behavior.
- Selecting the optimum reinforcement schedule.

Despite the successes achieved by behavior modification, it has been criticized as being a manipulative and autocratic approach to the management of people. People are conditioned to change their behavior in the direction required by management and the organization. Some critics argue that OBM is not consistent with the theories of such behavioral scientists as Maslow, Argyris, and McGregor. The assumption underlying these theories is that people are motivated by their own internal needs and are capable of a degree of self-control. On the other hand, OBM assumes that the causes of human behavior are in the environment and therefore external to the individual.

**PEOPLExpress
FLY SMART** In 1981, as the international airline industry was entering the most turbulent period in its history, People Express Airlines was born. Since then, deregulation has brought increased competition, two recessions have occurred, and the air traffic controllers' strike of August 1981 threatened to bring the entire industry to its knees. The price wars that resulted sent Braniff and Continental running for shelter under the bankruptcy laws. In Great Britain, Sir Freddy Laker's Skytrain was placed in liquidation. But the upstart People Express, operating out of Newark Airport, close to New York City but distinctly second rate, showed unprecedented growth and profitability. In fact, while other airlines' stocks plummeted in 1983, the market value of People Express's shot up to $360 million in total value. Eastern Airlines, with ten times as many planes, was valued at only $217 million, and Piedmont, a "healthy" airline four times as big as People Express, was valued at $370 million.

The company's formula for success is simple: "Keep costs and prices below those of competitors." One way People Express does this is by flying used planes, some bought at fire sale prices. For example, People purchased twenty of Braniff's planes when that carrier went under. And the company's aircraft fly an average of thirteen and a half hours a day, twice the industry average. People also flies out of second-rate airports—Newark instead of LaGuardia and West Palm Beach instead of Miami, for example—because landing fees and other costs are lower at those airports. Many People executives do their own paperwork—and therefore keep it to a minimum. It is not unusual to receive correspondence from the company in a twice-used envelope. People's cost per seat mile is barely half that of most other carriers. And because the low cost allows lower fares, People flies its planes an average of 80 percent full.

The main reason for low cost at People Express, though, is not cheap airports, cheap planes, or the lack of executive secretaries. "You don't keep costs down by counting pencils and paper clips," says Leroy Martin, a People Express general manager. "You have to squeeze massive productivity out of people and planes."

Labor costs at People Express are low. Donald Burr, president and CEO, says the organization is filled with young people "having a blast." Pilots earn under $40,000 their first year, less than some airlines pay senior ticket agents. There is no union at People, even for pilots. All employees switch jobs when necessary—pilots work the ticket counter at times, and ticket agents load baggage.

Every employee is required to buy a hundred shares of stock, with company financing available. Many of the early participants in this program have shares valued above $50,000. Burr explains that the people work hard

A modern success story is that of People Express Airlines.   Kirk Williamson

because stock ownership "gives them a sense that they have a significant stake in the entity, a piece of the rock." Even top executives, from Chairman Burr on down, have filled in as dispatchers, schedulers, and baggage handlers.

Burr sees air travel as a commodity product like "steel, tennis balls, and dead chickens." He shuns such usual frills as hot meals and free magazines for passengers, but he does emphasize one frill for the company. "To be a winner," he claims, "you have to have the ultimate frill—nice people."

"Fly smart" is the slogan at People Express. In today's nerve-racking world of deregulation, People Express is doing just that.[14]

MOTIVATION IN PRACTICE

There is little agreement about what motivates people to work. Managers must nevertheless make explicit decisions about how to achieve greater worker productivity. People Express uses a wide variety of approaches to "squeeze massive productivity out of people and planes." Discussed below are a number of ideas that relate to the practical aspect of motivation.

The Role of Money as a Motivator

There has been much discussion about whether pay motivates. Remember from our description of motivation theories that Herzberg classified pay as a satisfier, not a motivator. If any of the other theories we discussed are valid, however, pay can certainly be a motivator. First, pay helps to satisfy the lower-order needs and perhaps even esteem needs. Second, since most workers value pay highly, expectancy theory would suggest that pay can motivate if it is tied directly to performance. Third, if an increase in pay immediately follows a certain kind of behavior, reinforcement theory says that the behavior will be repeated. Properly used, pay can provide substantial motivation.

Several factors influence how pay works as a motivator. The major determining factor is how closely pay is tied to performance. If pay is not connected to performance, it will not be a motivator. Promising everyone a 10 percent, across-the-board raise probably will not motivate anyone. They may be happy, but they may not necessarily be more productive. A bonus for work already performed also does not motivate. Bonuses should be offered only for improved or increased performance in the future.

Another consideration is the degree of trust the workers have in the company. Suppose a company pays piece rates and constantly changes the rates when workers increase production. After a while, they think, "What is the use?" and do only the minimum necessary to keep their jobs. The Lincoln Electric Company, featured in Chapter 9, has a very successful piece-rate system. Lincoln's piece rates are almost never changed except for inflation adjustments. Some rates have been the same for over twenty years. Lincoln workers trust the system. Worker productivity there is about twice the industry average. At People Express, managers try to maintain the trust of workers by being more "down to earth"—doing without private secretaries, serving as baggage handlers when required, and so forth.

Finally, the use of money as a motivator must be compatible with the organizational culture that exists within the firm.[18] In much of U.S. industry, pay has been seen mainly as a reward for performance rather than as a motivator. If workers have the attitude that putting forth extra effort in order to get more money is demeaning or otherwise inappropriate, the effectiveness of money as a motivator will be decreased. On the other hand, if the company's culture condones the use of piece rates, the effectiveness of money as a motivator is enhanced.

Employee Performance and Equity

Employee perceptions of equity have a major impact on performance. Every person wishes to be treated fairly. In the work environment, perceptions of equity tend to be strongly related to three factors:

1. The amount of compensation and other benefits received in relation to the effort, education, and training required to do the job and the adversity of working conditions.
2. The fairness of pay and rewards compared to those of other employees.
3. The comparison of pay, rewards, and working conditions now in existence with those that existed for the same workers in the past.

If any of these comparisons results in a feeling of inequity, it is likely that workers will become demotivated.

An example of this occurred in GM's Lordstown plant, which for some years had manufactured Chevrolet Impalas. When the Vega model was introduced in 1970, the plant was automated to a much higher degree than it had been, resulting in an increased rate of production; however, the work force was not cut. Later, a new management team drastically reduced the work force while holding production constant. Although the workers were not overtaxed, there was a perceived inequity. Workers felt that it was wrong for GM to require a smaller number of workers to produce the same number of cars as before. The tremendous labor problems that ensued played a large part in the decision to discontinue manufacture of the Vega.[19]

The Self-Fulfilling Prophecy

A manager's expectations have a significant influence on employee motivation and performance. According to J. Sterling Livingston,

- A manager's expectations of employees and the way he or she treats them largely determine their performance and career progress.
- A unique characteristic of superior managers is their ability to create high performance expectations that subordinates fulfill.
- Less effective managers fail to develop similar expectations, and, as a consequence, the productivity of their subordinates suffers.
- Subordinates, more often than not, appear to do what they believe they are expected to do.[20]

High performance expectations tend to be *self-fulfilling prophecies*. A manager communicates expectations through both verbal and nonverbal means. The manager's facial expressions, eye contact, body posture, or tone of voice can indicate high approval and high expectations or the reverse.

Numerous studies support the notion of the self-fulfilling prophecy. In one such study, eighteen elementary school teachers were informed that about 20 percent of their students were "intellectual bloomers." The teachers were told that these youngsters would achieve remarkable progress during the school year. In actuality, the 20 percent sample of students was chosen at random and did not differ in intelligence or abilities from the remainder of the students in the classes. The only variable was the teachers' expectations of the group of intellectual bloomers. The students actually achieved significantly greater progress during the school year. Thus, the teachers' expectations of the students became a self-fulfilling prophecy.

Similar results have been achieved by managers. More often than not, if managers have high expectations of their employees, the employees' performance will meet those expectations. For example, the high expectations of the manager of a large computer center at a major university substantially changed the life and work of a janitor. The manager believed that George Johnson, a janitor with limited formal education, had the potential to become a computer operator. The computer center manager had high expectations and believed that George could learn the new job. After several months of training, George Johnson did become a successful computer operator and ultimately progressed to the point of providing training to others. This illustrates how the expectations of one person (in this case, the manager of the computer center) can have a significant impact on the actions of another.

Many businesses have not developed effective managers rapidly enough to meet the needs of their organization. As a consequence, organizations are not developing their most valuable resource—talented young men and women. In fact, the self-fulfilling prophecy seems to have the greatest potential impact on younger employees and managers. By failing to create high expectations and provide for the training and development of their personnel, firms are experiencing high costs due to excessive employee turnover. Also, managers who fail to communicate high expectations may significantly damage the attitudes and career aspirations of younger personnel.

Managers in every organization who are interested in high productivity must meet the challenge of encouraging the development of managers who will treat their employees in ways that contribute to high performance and career development and personal satisfaction. Effective managers who have high expectations of subordinates tend to build the employees' self-confidence and develop their performance capabilities. By contrast, ineffective managers tend to create a climate of negative or low expectations of subordinates. And as a result, the employees' level of motivation and performance will be lower, and their self-esteem or self-image as well as their careers may be severely damaged.[21]

Job Design

Is it possible to enhance employee motivation, improve job satisfaction, and maximize production all at the same time? This question poses a significant challenge for managers. Increasingly, America's more highly educated work force has expectations for a job that not only provides for their basic needs but also allows them to achieve satisfaction of such needs as achievement, growth, recognition, and self-fulfillment. Another important challenge is to increase the productivity of American workers by finding ways to "unlock the potential that exists in the overwhelming majority of our workforce."[22]

As was discussed in Chapter 1, the productivity of the U.S. work force is higher than that for any other industrialized nation. During the past decade, however, there has been a decline in the productivity growth rate in the United States compared to most other industrialized nations. In addition, one study found a "subtle but substantial decrease in job satisfaction among factory workers, clerical personnel, and millions of other people who in the final analysis do the productive work in our complex organization."[23]

On the other hand, J. Richard Hackman and Greg R. Oldham contend that it is possible to achieve an improvement in the quality of work life and also to increase or maximize worker productivity.[24] They challenge several traditionally held assumptions such as these:

• The basic nature of work is fixed and cannot be changed.

• Technology and work processes determine job design.

• All management can do is properly select and train personnel.

Job design is concerned with the specific tasks to be performed, the methods used in performing the task, and how the job relates to other work in the organization. In their book, *Work Redesign,* Hackman and Oldham assert that if managers wish to create a climate for a high level of motivation, reliable feedback on performance must be provided; there must be a sense that the worker is accountable for specific results and a feeling that the job has meaning beyond pay.[25] Workers get more satisfaction from completing a "whole and identifiable piece of work" than from producing indistinguishable pieces. Because of this, job design becomes an important concept in creating a motivational climate for today's work force.

Technology constraints on job design include the type of equipment and tools, as well as the particular work layout and methods used in producing the product or services. Technology may make job redesign difficult and perhaps expensive though not impossible. For example, adapting or redesigning the assembly-line production of automobiles or electronic components may not be technically or economically feasible.[26]

Economic factors affect job design. The question must be asked, "Are sufficient resources available to the organization should the firm wish to redesign some or all of its jobs?" While we may suggest ways to redesign jobs to improve output and the level of worker satisfaction, the cost may be prohibitive. A manager must continually balance the benefits of job design with the costs.

Job design is also affected by government requirements or regulations. Management may wish to design a job in a way that might increase worker performance but be in violation of labor laws or environmental or safety standards. Some proponents of work redesign have even urged the federal government to legislate changes in work design.

If a company has a union, job design can be affected by the philosophy, policies, and strategies of the union. Typically, the contract between the company and the union specifies and defines the types of jobs and the duties and responsibilities of workers. Unions traditionally have been opposed to many work redesign experiments. They perceive them to be attempts by management to "squeeze more work out of the worker" without any increase in wages. Also, unions may view job redesign as a threat to their power and position with the workers. One reason that People Express has such flexibility in job design is that the company has no union.

Important considerations for job design are the abilities, attitudes, and motivation of personnel within the organization. Obviously, the design of particular jobs depends on the ability or training of present or potential employees. It would be ridiculous to design a job that would be considerably more complex than the ability level of employees available for the positions. The ability and willingness of employees to be trained can limit job redesign.

Finally, management philosophy, objectives, and strategies may determine the degree of job redesign possible. Top management must be committed to the concept of job redesign. Job redesign may allow employees to gain greater authority to determine how their jobs are performed and how the worker is managed. Thus, managers who identify with Theory X assumptions would likely have difficulty with job redesign.

Job Enrichment

In the past two decades, there has been considerable interest in and application of job enrichment in a wide variety of organizations. Strongly advocated by Frederick Herzberg, **job enrichment** refers to *basic changes in the content and level of responsibility of a job so as to provide greater challenge to the worker.* The individual is provided with an opportunity to derive a feeling of greater achievement, recognition, responsibility, and personal growth in performing the job. Although job enrichment programs have not always achieved positive results, such programs have demonstrated improvements in job performance and in the level of satisfaction of personnel in many organizations.

job enrichment

AT&T, Polaroid, Texas Instruments, Monsanto, Weyerhaeuser, General Motors, Corning Glass, and many other firms have achieved excellent results after implementing job enrichment programs. In most instances productivity and job satisfaction increased, accompanied by reduction in employee turnover and absenteeism.[27]

According to Herzberg, there are a number of principles applicable for implementing job enrichment:

1. *Increasing job demands:* Changing the job in such a way as to increase the level of difficulty and responsibility of the job.
2. *Increasing a worker's accountability:* Allowing more individual control and authority over the work while retaining accountability of the manager.
3. *Providing work scheduling freedom:* Within limits, allowing individual workers to schedule their own work.

Recognition is often a major factor associated with motivation.

Alan Carey/The Image Works

4. *Providing feedback:* Making timely periodic reports on performance to employees (directly to the worker rather than to the supervisor).

5. *Providing new learning experiences:* Work situations should encourage opportunities for new experiences and personal growth of the individual.[28]

Job Enlargement

job enlargement

Many people have attempted to differentiate between job enrichment and job enlargement. **Job enlargement** is *the changes in the scope of a job so as to provide greater variety to the worker.* Job enlargement is said to provide a horizontal expansion of duties. For example, instead of knowing how to operate only one machine, a person is taught to operate two or even three, but no higher level of responsibility is provided. The fact that People Express ticket agents may handle freight and do other similar tasks is job enlargement. On the other hand, job enrichment entails providing a person with additional responsibilities. There may be other tasks to perform, but responsibility is given with the tasks. For instance, the worker may be given the responsibility of scheduling the three machines. Increased responsibility means providing the worker with increased freedom to do the job—make decisions and exercise more self-control over the work.

Quality Circles

quality circles (QCs)

Another technique that has been shown to be effective in enhancing motivation and achieving improved quality and productivity in several hundred U.S. companies is a concept known as quality circles.[29] In most firms, **quality circles (QCs)** are *small groups of employees who get together on company time to develop ways to improve the quality and quantity of work.*[30]

At Xerox's Reprographics Technology Group, QCs have been established that involve horizontal councils of people on the same level from different departments and vertical work-study groups from different levels within a department. This prevents the QC from considering improvements in only one department, therefore requiring the consideration of problems and universal solutions for the company as a whole. General Motors has implemented various forms of QCs in over ninety of its plants worldwide. One particularly successful QC in a Dayton, Ohio, plant implemented a process developed in Britain known as the sociotechnical system—a method of integrating workers' ideas for improving jobs with technical requirements set by engineers. This allowed the laborers who carried out the detailed plans of the engineers to add their own suggestions for time- or motion-saving techniques (or human considerations) to the process. At Shaklee Corporation's plant in Norman, Oklahoma, employees working in teams have achieved the same volume of production at approximately 40 percent of the previous labor costs. One QC at a Westinghouse plant is responsible for a $22,000 cost savings to the company because the workers devised the scheme that one employee reports to work fifteen minutes ahead of the shift in order to activate wire-bonding machines, thus preventing the remaining employees on the shift from being idle until the equipment could be readied.[31]

At an Iowa plant of Butler Manufacturing Company, work teams were allowed to set their own production goals. The man-hours required per building unit have been reduced by 30 to 35 percent during the first two years as compared with production in two older plants of the company. Many current business-related periodicals tell numerous success stories when employees are encouraged to work together to improve the quality and quantity of the company. Quality circles encourage workers' energy and creativity to solve the company's—and the workers'—problems.

Theory Z

William Ouchi, in his book *Theory Z: How American Business Can Meet the Japanese Challenge,* and Anthony Athos and Richard Pascale in *The Art of Japanese Management* describe management practices in a number of progressive U.S. companies that are similar to those that successful Japanese firms have been utilizing for years.[32] Ouchi identifies Hewlett-Packard, IBM, Procter & Gamble, and Eastman Kodak as Theory Z organizations. **Theory Z** is *the belief that a high degree of mutual responsibility, loyalty, and consideration between companies and their employees will result in higher productivity and improved employee welfare.* Type Z companies tend to practice a system of lifetime employment and avoid layoffs. The companies usually enjoy low employee turnover, low absenteeism, and high employee morale. The workers are more involved in their jobs with the company, a factor that leads to increased productivity and performance. Theory Z companies tend to develop their own traditions, ideals, and culture and foster somewhat of a "family environment." This "family" or culture within the organization tends to bond its members—employees and managers— thereby facilitating decision making and communications within the company. All of this has much in common with Japanese patterns and practices. Companies in the United States have not necessarily imitated Japanese practices but have developed their own management style through the recognition of the types of employees who make up today's U.S. work force. Nissan hopes to develop a Theory Z–type organization at its Tennessee plant.

Theory Z

While U.S. managers obviously can learn a great deal from the Japanese, the support for Theory Z has not been unanimous. A study of managers from five developed countries found that successful managers favor an achievement orientation, interaction, and risk taking. Less successful managers emphasize the family type of culture, which is central to Theory Z. It was also found that Japanese managers emphasize ordinary motivational ideas, like the use of advancement, money, and challenging assignments to motivate workers.[33]

SUMMARY

Motivation is defined as the willingness to put forth effort in the pursuit of goals. In order to learn how to create an environment conducive to a high level of employee motivation, managers must develop a more complete understanding of the philosophies of human nature. Douglas McGregor believed that managers usually attempt to motivate employees by one of two basic approaches. Theory X is the traditional view of management; it suggests that managers are required to coerce, control, or threaten employees in order to motivate them. Theory Y is a view of management whereby a manager basically believes people are capable of being responsible and mature. Another researcher, Chris Argyris, emphasized the importance of the process of maturity.

The theories of Maslow, Herzberg, McClelland, Vroom, and Skinner are helpful to managers because they attempt to provide a more complete appreciation of basic human needs and the reasons for human behavior. Maslow's hierarchy of needs is a widely accepted theory, which supports the idea that people are motivated by unsatisfied needs. According to Maslow, a person's needs are arranged in priority from the basic physiological to the complex self-actualization needs. The key point for managers to accept is that needs that are fairly well satisfied do not motivate behavior. Herzberg's motivation-hygiene theory classifies human needs into two categories—hygiene factors and motivators. The hygiene factors correspond to the lower-level needs on Maslow's hierarchy, and the motivators represent upper-level needs. Herzberg contends that despite the fact that most managers and organizations concentrate on satisfying the hygiene needs, this action does not motivate employees. He feels firms should direct more attention to the motivators and to enriched or more challenging jobs, but at the same time firms should not forget to be concerned about the hygiene needs. McClelland's theory stresses that there are certain needs that are learned. He argues that each person's need for achievement, power, and affiliation affects his or her behavior in the work environment.

The needs approach to motivation as developed by Maslow and Herzberg does not adequately explain individual differences in the way people behave in accomplishing goals. Victor Vroom's expectancy theory of motivation attempts to explain behavior in terms of an individual's goals, choices, and the expectations of achieving the goals. Employees are motivated by what they expect in terms of rewards as a result of their behavior. B. F. Skinner contends that behavior can be controlled and shaped by reinforcing desired behavior. The primary approach suggested by Skinner is organizational behavior modification (OBM), which has been successfully applied in a number of organizations. Under this approach, people act in the way they find most rewarding, and by controlling rewards, people's behavior can be directed and/or modified.

In addition to the major theories of motivation, managers should develop an understanding of the role of money as a motivator and the importance of equity between an employee's performance and the pay received. Managers should also be aware that their expectations have a significant influence on employee motivation and performance.

Job design is concerned with the specific tasks to be performed, the methods used in performing the tasks, and the relation of the job to others in the organization. Job enrichment refers to the basic changes in the content and level of responsibility of a job so as to provide greater challenge to the worker. Job enlargement is the changes in the scope of a job so as to provide greater variety to the worker.

Another technique that has been shown to be effective in enhancing motivation and achieving improved quality and productivity in several hundred U.S. companies is a concept known as quality circles. In most firms, quality circles are small groups of employees who get together on company time to develop ways to improve the quality and quantity of work.

Ouchi identifies Hewlett-Packard, IBM, Procter and Gamble, and Eastman Kodak as Theory Z organizations. Theory Z is the belief that a high degree of mutual responsibility, loyalty, and consideration between companies and their employees will result in higher productivity and improved employee welfare. Type Z companies tend to practice a system of lifetime employment, low turnover, low absenteeism, and high employee morale.

REVIEW QUESTIONS

1. How would you define motivation?
2. Compare and contrast McGregor's Theory X and Theory Y. What are some examples of managerial practices that are consistent with a Theory Y philosophy of human nature?

3. What is Argyris's maturation theory? How does it apply to motivation?

4. Relate Herzberg's theory of motivation to the theory developed by Maslow.

5. Describe McClelland's theory of human motives. How does it relate to motivation, and what are the basic characteristics of individuals described by the theory?

6. What is expectancy theory, and how can managers use it in the motivation process? Provide examples.

7. Briefly describe organizational behavior modification.

8. What is the role of money as a motivator?

How important is the issue of equity of pay in terms of motivation? Explain.

9. What is meant by job enrichment, and how does it differ from job enlargement? How would you apply job enrichment? Give an example.

10. What is the notion of the "self-fulfilling prophecy"? How is it related to management and motivation?

11. What are quality circles, and how successful have they been in improving the quality and quantity of work?

12. What characterizes Theory Z–type companies?

EXERCISES

1. Interview three managers—for example, a bank president, a college dean, and a local retailer. Ask these managers to describe their approach to creating a climate for motivation within their organization. Compare their comments with the concepts on motivation presented in this chapter.

2. Using expectancy theory as a model, describe when money would be a motivator.

CASE STUDY

The New Analyst

Harry Neal had been employed with Trimark Data Systems, Inc. (TDS) for five years and had progressed to his current position of senior programmer analyst. He was generally pleased with the company and thoroughly enjoyed the creative demands of his job.

One Saturday afternoon during a golf game with his friend and coworker Randy Dean, Harry discovered that his department had hired a recent State University graduate as a programmer analyst. Harry became upset when he learned that the new man's starting salary was only $30 a month lower than his own. Although Harry was a good-natured fellow, he was bewildered. He was upset because he felt that he was being treated unfairly.

The following Monday morning, Harry confronted Dave Edwards, the personnel director, and asked if what he had heard was true. Dave apologetically admitted that it was and attempted to explain the company's situation: "Harry, the market for programmer analysts is very tight, and in order for the company to attract qualified prospects, we have to offer a premium starting salary. We desperately needed another analyst, and this was the only way we could get one."

Harry asked Dave if his salary would be adjusted accordingly. Dave answered, "Your salary will be reevaluated at the regular time. You're doing a great job, though, and I'm sure the boss will recommend a raise." Harry thanked Dave for his time but left the office shaking his head and wondering about his future with TDS.

QUESTIONS

1. Do you feel that Dave's explanation was satisfactory? Discuss.

2. What is likely to be the impact of this incident on Harry's motivation to work?

3. What action do you think the company should have taken with regard to Harry? Explain.

CASE STUDY

A Birthday Present for Kathy

Bob Rosen could hardly wait to get back to work Monday morning. He was excited about his chance of getting a large bonus. Bob is a machine operator with Ram Manufacturing Company, a Wichita, Kansas, maker of electric motors. He operates an armature winding machine. The machine winds copper wire onto metal cores to make the rotating elements for electric motors.

Ram pays machine operators on a graduated piece-rate basis. Operators are paid a certain amount for each part made, plus a bonus. A worker who produces 10 percent above standard for a certain month receives a 10 percent additional bonus. For 20 percent above standard, the bonus is 20 percent. Bob realized that he had a good chance of earning a 20 percent bonus that month. That would be $287.

Bob had a special use for the extra money. His wife's birthday was just three weeks away. He was hoping to get her a new Chevrolet Citation. He had already saved $450, but the down payment on the Citation was $700. The bonus would enable him to buy the car.

Bob arrived at work at seven o'clock that morning, although his shift did not begin until eight. He went to his work station and checked the supply of blank cores and copper wire. Finding that only one spool of wire was on hand, he asked the fork truck driver to bring another. Then he asked the operator who was working the graveyard shift, "Sam, do you mind if I grease the machine while you work?"

"No," Sam said, "that won't bother me a bit."

After greasing the machine, Bob stood and watched Sam work. He thought of ways to simplify the motions involved in loading, winding, and unloading the armatures. As Bob took over the machine after the eight o'clock whistle, he thought, "I hope I can pull this off. I know Kathy will be happy not to be grounded while I'm at work."

QUESTIONS

1. Explain the advantages and disadvantages of a graduated piece-rate pay system such as that at Ram.

2. Explain Bob's high level of motivation in terms of needs theory, reinforcement theory, and expectancy theory.

NOTES

1. This article is a composite from a number of published accounts, among them: "From Tennessee to Tokyo," *Newsweek* (August 9, 1982): 59; "A Tale of Two Worlds in Tennessee," *U.S. News & World Report* (December 20, 1982): 84–85; "The Japanese Style Is Catching on in Tennessee," *Washington Post* (July 25, 1982): 91; "Truckabout Datsuns Invade Detroit's Back-yard," *Economist* (November 8, 1980): 69–70; "Nissan's Truck Plant: People and Robots under One Roof," *Iron Age* (September 15, 1982): 29–33; James V. Higgins, "Runyon Puts Smryrna on the Map," *Detroit News* (February 3, 1982): 6C.

2. Douglas McGregory, *The Human Side of Enterprise* (New York: McGraw-Hill, 1960).

3. Chris Argyris, *Personality and Organization* (New York: Harper, 1957).

4. Abraham Maslow, *Motivation and Personality* (New York: Harper, 1954).

5. Clayton P. Alderfer, "A Critique of Salancik and Pfeffer's Examination of Need-Satisfaction Theories," *Administration Science Quarterly* 22 (December 1977): 658–672.

6. Frederick Herzberg, *Work and the Nature of Man* (Cleveland: World, 1966).

7. S. M. Klein and R. R. Ritti, *Understanding Organizational Behavior* (Boston: Kent Publishing Co., 1984), p. 257.

8. D. C. McClelland and David H. Burnham, "Power Is the Great Motivator," *Harvard Business Review* 54 (March–April 1976):103.

9. David R. Hampton, Charles E. Summer, and Ross A. Webber, *Organizational Behavior and the Practice of Management* (Glenview, Ill.: Scott, Foresman, 1978), pp. 11–15.

10. M. J. Stahl, "Achievement Power and Managerial Motivation: Selecting Managerial Talent with the Job Choice Exercise," *Personnel Psychology* (Winter 1983): 786.

11. Victor Vroom, *Work and Motivation* (New York: Wiley, 1964).

12. C. W. Kennedy, J. A. Fossum, and B. J. White, "An Empirical Comparison of Within-Subjects and Between-Subjects Expectancy Theory Models," *Organizational Behavior and Human Performance* (August 1983): 124.

13. B. F. Skinner, *Beyond Freedom and Dignity* (New York: Knopf, 1971).

14. "Full Trade in the Sky," *Economist* (June 4, 1983): 14; "People Power," *Forbes* (April 25, 1983): 170; Peter Nulty, "A Champ of Cheap Airlines," *Fortune* (May 22, 1982): 127–128; "Real PEOPLE, Real Profits," *Newsweek* (April 4, 1983): 16; "Icarus Rebounds," *Economist* (August 13, 1983): 59; Henry Lefes, "People Express Slashes Its Way into Market with 'Cheaper Than Driving' Fares," *Air Transport World* (June 1981): 26–27; "Is People Express Stock Flying Too High?" *Business Week* (May 30, 1983): 79–82; "Let the People Fly Smart," *Economist* (April 16, 1983): 77.

15. Ed Pedalino and Victor U. Gamboa, "Behavior Modification and Absenteeism," *Journal of Applied Psychology* 59 (December 1974): 694–698.

16. W. Clay Hamner and Ellen P. Hamner, "Behavior Modification on the Bottom Line," *Organizational Dynamics* 4 (Spring 1976): 12.

17. "At Emery Air Freight: Positive Reinforcement Boosts Performance," *Organizational Dynamics* 1 (Autumn 1973): 41–50.

18. L. L. Cummings, "Compensation, Culture, and Motivation: A Systems Perspective," *Organizational Dynamics* (Winter 1984): 43.

19. Klein and Ritti, p. 265–266.

20. J. Sterlington Livingston, "Pygmalion in Management," *Harvard Business Review* (July–August 1969).

21. John L. Single, "The Power of Expectations: Productivity and the Self-Fulfilling Prophecy," *Management World* (November 1980): 19, 37–38.

22. Robert H. Guest, "Review of Work Redesign," *Harvard Business Review* (January–February 1981): 46–47, 52.

23. Ibid., p. 46.

24. Ibid.

25. J. Richard Hackman and Greg R. Oldham, *Work Redesign* (Reading, Mass.: Addison-Wesley, 1980).

26. John F. Runcie, "By Days I Make the Cars," *Harvard Business Review* (May–June 1980): 106–115.

27. See "Case Studies in the Humanization of Work," in *Work in America: Report of Special Task Force to the Secretary of Health, Education and Welfare* (Cambridge, Mass.: MIT Press, 1973), appendix, pp. 188–200.

28. Frederick Herzberg, "One More Time: How Do You Motivate Employees?" *Harvard Business Review* 22, no. 2 (Winter 1979).

29. "Will the Slide Kill Quality Circles?" *Business Week* (January 11, 1982): 108–109.

30. "The New Industrial Revolution," *Business Week* (May 11, 1981): 85–98.

31. "The Workers Know Best," *Time* (January 28, 1980): 65.

32. William Ouchi, *Theory Z: How American Business Can Meet the Japanese Challenge* (Reading, Mass.: Addison-Wesley, 1981); and Anthony Athos and Richard Pascale, *The Art of Japanese Management: Applications for American Executives* (New York: Simon & Schuster, 1981).

33. A. Howard et al., "Motivation and Values Among Japanese and American Managers," *Personnel Psychology* (Winter 1983): 883, 897.

REFERENCES

Armstrong, J. "How to Motivate." *Management Today* 12 (February 1977): 60–63.

Berry, L. E. "Motivation Management." *Journal of Systems Management* 30 (April 1979): 30–32.

Cook, C. W. "Guidelines for Managing Motivation." *Business Horizons* 23 (April 1980): 61–69.

Cummings, L. L. "Compensation, Culture, and Motivation: A Systems Perspective." *Organizational Dynamics* (Winter 1984): 33–44.

Gallagher, W. E., Jr., and H. J. Einhorn. "Motivation Theory and Job Design." *Journal of Business* 49 (July 1976): 358–373.

Gayle, J. B., and F. R. Searle. "Maslow, Motivation, and the Manager." *Management World* 9 (September 1980): 18–20.

Giblin, E. J. "Motivating Employees: A Closer Look." *Personnel Journal* 55 (April 1976): 68–71.

Hackman, J. R. "Is Job Enrichment Just a Fad?" *Harvard Business Review* 53 (September 1975): 129–138.

Hatuany, N., and V. Puick. "Japanese Management Practices and Productivity." *Organizational Dynamics* 9 (Spring 1981): 4–21.

Howard, A. et al. "Motivation and Values among Japanese and American Managers." *Personnel Psychology* (Winter 1983): 883–898.

Kennedy, C. W., J. A. Fossum, and B. J. White. "An

Empirical Comparison of Within-Subjects and Between-Subjects Expectancy Theory Models." *Organizational Behavior and Human Performance* (August 1983): 124–143.

Klein, S. M., and R. R. Ritti. *Understanding Organizational Behavior.* Boston: Kent Publishing Co., 1984.

Klimoski, R. J., and N. J. Hayes. "Leader Behavior and Subordinate Motivation." *Personnel Psychology* 33 (Autumn 1980): 543–555.

McClelland, D. C., and D. H. Burnham. "Power Is the Great Motivator." *Harvard Business Review* 54 (March 1976): 100–110.

Miller, William B. "Motivation Techniques: Does One Work Best?" *Management Review* (February 1981): 47–52.

Neider, L. L. "Experimental Field Investigation Utilizing an Expectancy Theory View of Participation." *Organizational Behavior and Human Performance* 26 (December 1980): 425–442.

Odiorne, G. S. "Uneasy Look at Motivation Theory." *Training and Development Journal* 34 (June 1980): 106–112.

Ouchi, William G. "Organizational Paragrams: A Commentary on Japanese Management and Theory Z Organizations." *Organizational Dynamics* 9 (Spring 1981): 36–42.

———. "Theory Z Corporations." *Industry Week* (May 4, 1981): 49–51.

Peters, Thomas J. "Putting Excellence into Management." *Business Week* (July 21, 1980): 196–205.

Pinder, C. C. "Concerning the Application of Human Motivation Theories in Organizational Settings." *Academy of Management Review* 2 (July 1977): 384–397.

Quick, J. C. "Dyadic Goal Setting within Organizations: Rolemaking and Motivational Considerations." *Academy of Management Review* 4 (July 1979): 377–380.

Rehder, R. R. "What American and Japanese Managers Are Learning about Each Other." *Business Horizons* 24 (March–April 1981): 63–70.

Rosenthal, Robert. "The Pygmalion Effect Lives." *Psychology Today* (September 1973): 56–60.

Runcie, John F. " 'By Days I Make the Cars.' " *Harvard Business Review* (May–June 1980): 106–115.

Schmitt, N., and L. Son. "Evaluation of Valence Models of Motivation to Pursue Various Post High School Alternatives." *Organizational Behavior and Human Performance* 27 (February 1981): 135–150.

Speigel, D. "How Not to Motivate." *Supervisory Management* 22 (November 1977): 41–45.

Stahl, M. J. "Achievement Power and Managerial Motivation: Selecting Managerial Talent with the Job Choice Exercise." *Personnel Psychology* (Winter 1983): 775–790.

Trautman, L. J. et al. "Managing People: Choosing the Right Motivator." *Mortgage Banker* 40 (August 1980): 34–37.

leadership
autocratic leader
participative leader
democratic leader

trait approach to
   leadership
initiating structure
consideration

managerial grid
path-goal theory
leadership continuum

LEARNING OBJECTIVES

After completing this chapter you should be able to

1. Define leadership and state the importance of good leadership in an organization.
2. Describe the trait approach to the study of leadership.
3. Identify and describe the major leadership theories that focus on the search for an appropriate style.
4. Describe the leadership theories of Fiedler and Hersey and Blanchard.
5. Identify and describe factors that affect the choice of a leadership style.

11

Leadership

CHAPTER OUTLINE

In the corporate turnaround story of the century, the mammoth Wickes Companies, a marketer of building products, went from a $258 million loss in 1982 to a modest profit in the 1983–1984 fiscal year. Most authorities give the credit to one man, Sanford Sigoloff. When Sigoloff took over the chairmanship of Wickes in 1982, the company had lost more than $400 million in just fifteen months. Money was flowing out, shelves and showrooms in thousands of Wickes stores were bare or stocked with inferior goods, and customers were staying away in droves.

Sanford Sigoloff—"Flash Gordon" or "Ming the Merciless," depending on whom you ask—had earned his reputation turning around disabled companies. In Wickes, the fifty-two-year-old former nuclear physicist faced his greatest challenge ever. He accepted what he called "a very, very tough challenge" because "I couldn't resist it. How many times in a lifetime do you get the opportunity to put your stamp on a business of this magnitude in the American system?" The Sigoloff stamp means total commitment throughout the organization. Sigoloff expects fourteen-hour days out of his corporate staff. Almost the entire financial department at Wickes quit when he told them this. Many other employees left involuntarily; as he fired nearly a quarter of Wickes's 40,000-member work force. The managers who chose and were permitted to remain with Wickes were supplemented with Sigoloff lieutenants who had worked with him in the past.

Sigoloff practices a team approach to problem solving. He demands and gets not only personal loyalty from top executives but their help in making difficult decisions. The frequent trips he and his senior managers make to farflung stores and offices served to encourage and inform workers and managers at every level.

Early in his turnaround effort at Wickes, Sigoloff chose to file for protection under Chapter 11 of the U.S. Bankruptcy Code. This staved off creditors and gave time to make necessary changes. But it also discouraged employees and customers, many of whom knew that most companies never successfully emerge from Chapter 11. Sigoloff had to convince all of them that Wickes would emerge. "We developed an efficient nomenclature," explains Sigoloff, "a way for top management to communicate with middle management and with creditors." The "efficient nomenclature" involves the use of charts, graphs, and tables to simplify presentations inside and outside the organization.

Simultaneously with his efforts inside the company to refurbish stores and restore optimism, Sigoloff launched a national TV ad campaign, with the serious-looking chairman in front of the camera personally guaranteeing Wickes's products and services. "There are a lot of tough decisions that have to be made to ensure this company's survival," Mr. Sigoloff says. "It isn't a game for the faint-hearted." Whatever anyone thinks of Sigoloff's management and financial decisions, no one considers him faint-hearted.[1]

Sigoloff is recognized worldwide as an effective leader. Because of his leadership, Wickes Companies and two other companies he previously saved continue in operation, and thousands of jobs have been saved.

What does it take to be a good leader, and what is the most effective leadership style? These questions have perplexed and challenged managers for generations. Literally thousands of research studies concerning leadership have been conducted to provide greater insight into these questions. Such studies of leaders and the leadership process have not yielded any set of traits or qualities that are consistently related to effective leadership. The basic conclusion that can be drawn from these studies is that there is *no one* most effective leadership style. What we do know is that effective leadership is absolutely essential to the survival and overall growth of every organization.

As we noted at the beginning of Chapter 1, 50 percent of all new businesses fail within the first two years. Despite high salaries and excellent opportunities in large corporations, there continues to be a shortage of competent managers who are effective leaders. The lack of capable leadership is not just confined to business organizations but has also been felt in government, churches, education, and all other types of organizations. The problem is not a lack of people who want to be leaders or managers but rather a scarcity of skilled people who are capable of performing effectively in leadership positions. The primary challenge of leadership or management is to guide an organization toward the accomplishment of its objectives. The leader achieves this by influencing and encouraging employees of the organization to attain the highest level of performance possible within the limitation of available resources, skills, and technology.

Wickes is only one of many large businesses that have made successful turnarounds as a result of a change in leadership. Although we do not have all the answers, a more complete knowledge of the skills, attitudes, and values that are related to effective leadership would greatly improve our ability to select, train, and develop more effective managers.

In this chapter, we will first define leadership and identify four basic leadership styles. Next, the trait approach to leadership will be described. This will be followed by a discussion of the search for an appropriate leadership style. We will then present some modern contingency theories of leadership. The chapter ends with a discussion of factors that affect the choice of an appropriate leadership style.

LEADERSHIP DEFINED

Leadership is *the ability of getting others to do what the leader wants them to do.* Leadership is closely associated with management but is not the

leadership

same. A good manager is a good leader, but a good leader may not necessarily be an effective manager. Sigoloff's success at Wickes has often been credited to good leadership only. But he was clearly an effective manager as well as a good leader.

A person can have the title of manager but have very little influence over the behavior and actions of others. On the other hand, an individual might not carry the title of manager but be an important informal leader exercising considerable influence over the behavior of others in the work group.

BASIC LEADERSHIP STYLES

autocratic leader

participative leader

democratic leader

Four basic leadership styles have been identified: autocratic, participative, democratic, and laissez-faire. An **autocratic leader** is *a person who tells subordinates what to do and expects to be obeyed without question*. This style is typical of a person who accepts McGregor's Theory X assumptions, described in Chapter 10. A **participative leader** is *a person who involves subordinates in decision making but may retain the final authority*. A **democratic leader** is *a person who tries to do what the majority of subordinates desire*. Participative and democratic leaders tend to be those who make Theory Y assumptions. The laissez-faire leader is uninvolved in the work of the unit. It is difficult to defend this leadership style unless the leader is supervising expert and well-motivated specialists, such as scientists. In fact, practically every leader who has attained recognition for effectiveness—from political leader Mahatma Gandhi in India to business leader Sanford Sigoloff at Wickes—has done so by being deeply involved and active.

THE TRAIT APPROACH TO LEADERSHIP

trait approach to leadership

The leader has always occupied a strong and central role in traditional management theory. Most of the early research on leadership attempted to (1) compare the traits of people who became leaders with those who remain as followers and (2) identify characteristics and traits possessed by effective leaders. The **trait approach to leadership** is *the evaluation and selection of leaders based on their physical, mental, and psychological characteristics*. Research studies comparing the traits of leaders and nonleaders have found that leaders tend to be somewhat taller, more outgoing, more self-confident, and more intelligent than nonleaders. But a specific combination of traits has not been found that can differentiate leaders or potential leaders from followers. Clearly it is difficult to identify a leader from an initial impression.

Considerable research has been conducted to compare the traits of effective and ineffective leaders. Traits such as aggressiveness, ambition, decisiveness, dominance, initiative, intelligence, physical characteristics (looks, height, and weight), self-assurance, and other factors were studied to determine if they were related to effective leadership. The major question was, "Could such traits differentiate effective from ineffective leaders?" Perhaps the underlying assumption of some trait research has been that leaders are born, not made. Although research has demonstrated that this is not the case, some people still believe there are certain inborn or

TABLE 11-1 Ghiselli's Managerial Traits

Traits	Importance Value[a]
Supervisory ability (A)	100
Occupational achievement (M)	76
Intelligence (A)	64
Self-actualization (M)	63
Self-assurance (P)	62
Decisiveness (P)	61
Lack of need for security (M)	54
Working-class affinity (P)	47
Initiative (A)	34
Lack of need for high financial reward (M)	20
Need for power (M)	10
Maturity (P)	5
Masculinity-femininity (P)	0

Source: James F. Gavin, "A Test of Ghiselli's Theory of Managerial Traits," *Journal of Business Research* (February 1976):46. Reprinted by permission.

Note: A = ability trait; P = personality trait; M = motivational trait.

[a]100 = very important; 0 = plays no part in managerial talent

acquired traits that make a person a good leader. Research has clearly not shown that physical traits can distinguish effective from ineffective leaders.

The trait approach to the study of leadership is not dead, however. Edwin Ghiselli has continued to conduct research in an effort to identify personality and motivational traits related to effective leadership.[2] Ghiselli identified thirteen trait factors. Subsequent research studies of these trait factors have ranked these in order of significance, as illustrated in Table 11-1. The six most significant traits are defined as follows:

The leader has always occupied a strong and central role in traditional management theory.

Robert Eckert/Stock, Boston Inc.

1. *Supervisory ability:* The performance of the basic functions of management, including planning, organizing, influencing, and controlling the work of others.
2. *Need for occupational achievement:* The seeking of responsibility and the desire for success.
3. *Intelligence:* Creative and verbal ability, including judgment, reasoning, and thinking capacity.
4. *Decisiveness:* Ability to make decisions and solve problems capably and competently.
5. *Self-assurance:* Extent to which the individual views himself or herself as capable of coping with problems.
6. *Initiative:* Ability to act independently and develop courses of action not readily apparent to other people. Self-starter—able to find new or innovative ways of doing things.

Notably absent from the list of significant traits is gender. Although the overwhelming majority of managers are males, most research has concluded that this may be because of sex role stereotyping. In fact, some researchers believe that there are no significant differences at all in leadership behavior between the sexes.[3]

In spite of the contributions of Ghiselli, the trait approach to the study of leadership has left many unanswered questions concerning what is required for effective leadership. This has led to a continuing search for an appropriate leadership style.

THE SEARCH FOR AN APPROPRIATE STYLE

Dissatisfaction with the trait approach caused most leadership researchers to focus attention on how leaders should behave as opposed to traits or characteristics they possess. Several of the resulting theories and studies are discussed below. Some of these suggest a particular style for all situations, and others reflect the more reasonable proposition that leadership style must vary.

Likert's Systems of Management

Rensis Likert, former director of the Institute for Social Research at the University of Michigan, developed a leadership theory that posited a continuum of styles ranging from autocratic to participative. Likert's systems of management are as follows: System I, Exploitative Autocratic; System II, Benevolent Autocratic; System III, Consultative; and System IV, Participative Team. Only the last style was deemed best in the long run for all situations.[4]

System I—Exploitative Autocratic

Managers make all decisions. They decide what is to be done, who will do it, and how and when it is to be accomplished. Failure to complete work as assigned results in threats or punishment. Under this system, management exhibits little confidence or trust in employees. A typical managerial response with this system is, "You do it my way or you're fired." According to Likert, there is a low level of trust and confidence between management and employees.

System II—Benevolent Autocratic

Managers still make the decisions, but employees have some degree of freedom and flexibility in performing their jobs so long as they conform to specific procedures. Under this system, managers take a very paternalistic attitude—"I'll take care of you if you perform well." With System II, there is a fairly low level of trust between management and the employees, which causes employees to use caution when dealing with management.

System III—Consultative

Managers consult with employees prior to establishing the goals and making decisions about the work. Employees have a considerable degree of freedom in making their own decisions as to how to accomplish the work.

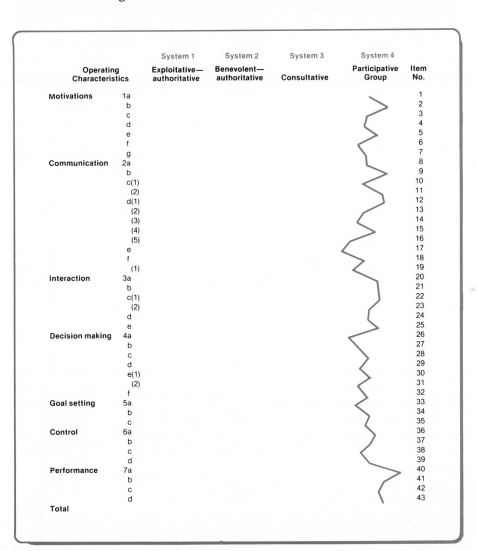

Figure 11–1

Likert Chart— Management Systems

Source: Rensis Likert. *The Human Organization* (New York: McGraw-Hill, 1967). © 1967 by McGraw-Hill Book Company. Used with permission.

Note: Management system used by the most productive plant (Plant L) of a well-managed company, as seen by middle- and upper-level managers.

A manager using System III might say to an employee, "Charlie, I'd like your opinion on this before I make the decision." Management tends to rely on rewards as opposed to punishments to motivate employees. Also, the level of trust between the employees and management is fairly high. This creates a climate in which employees feel relatively free to discuss openly work-related matters with management.

System IV—Participative Team

This is Likert's recommended system or style of management. The emphasis of System IV is on a group participative role with full involvement of the employees in the process of establishing goals and making job-related decisions. Employees feel free to discuss matters with their manager, who displays supportive rather than condescending or threatening behavior. It is contended that an entire organization should be designed along System IV lines, with work being performed by a series of overlapping groups. The leader provides a link between the group and other units at higher levels in the organization. This concept is often referred to as the linking-pin

Figure 11–2 Sample of Questions on Likert Scale Relating to Communications Within the Organization
Source: Rensis Likert, *The Human Organization* (New York: McGraw-Hill, 1967). © 1967 by McGraw-Hill Book Company. Used with permission.

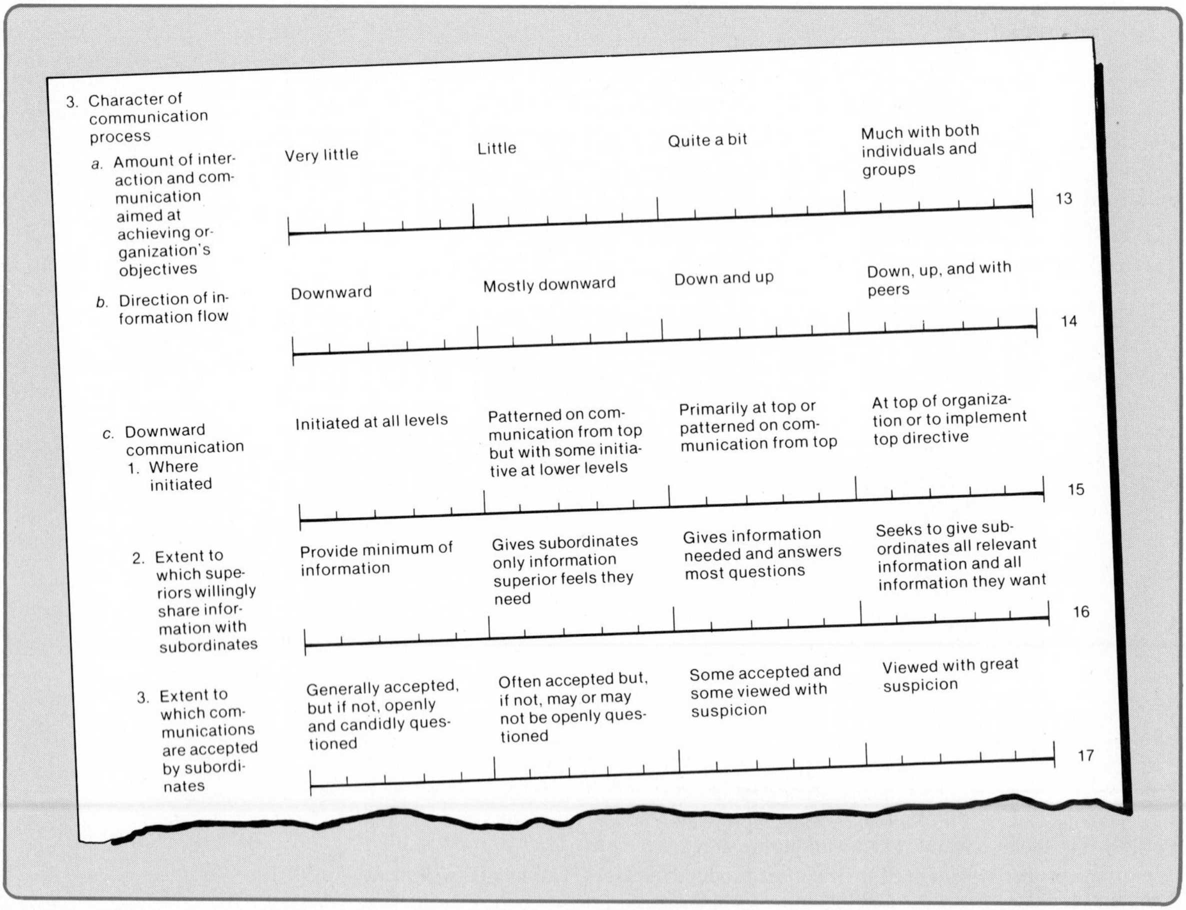

theory. Decision making is widespread throughout the enterprise, with the power of knowledge usually taking precedence over the power of authority.

Measurement of the type of style in the Likert framework is usually accomplished by having the employees assess the organizational culture and management system on a Likert scale. A profile showing the management system existing within an organization is developed through this survey of opinion (Figure 11–1). For example, when the question, "Extent to which superiors are willing to share information with subordinates?" is asked, the employee can answer on the continuum from "provide minimum information" all the way to "seeks to give subordinates all relevant information and all information they want" (see question 3C2 in Figure 11–2). It has been found that the positions on these scales can be significantly altered through organizational and management development programs, which will be discussed in Chapter 13.

Ohio State Leadership Studies

Beginning in 1945, researchers in the Bureau of Business Research at Ohio State University made a series of in-depth studies of the behavior of leaders in a wide variety of organizations. The key concern of the Ohio State leadership studies was the leader's behavior in directing the efforts of others toward group goals. After a considerable number of studies had been completed, two important dimensions of leader behavior were identified: **initiating structure**—*the extent to which leaders establish goals and structure their roles and the roles of subordinates toward the attainment of the goals,* and **consideration**—*the extent to which leaders have relationships with subordinates characterized by mutual trust, respect, and consideration of employees' ideas and feelings.*

initiating structure

consideration

Initiating structure and consideration were identified as separate and distinct dimensions of leadership behavior. As illustrated in Figure 11–3, there are four basic leadership styles representing different combinations of leadership behavior. A manager can be high in both consideration and initiating structure, low in both, or high in one and low in the other. Although there are two important elements of leadership behavior, the *one* most effective combination that meets the needs of all situations was not suggested by the Ohio State model. Rather, the combination or appropriate level of initiating structure and consideration was determined by the demands of the situation.

Among the many situational variables that must be related to leadership behavior are the following:

- Expectations of the led.
- Degree of task structuring imposed by technology.
- Pressures of schedules and time.
- Degrees of interpersonal contact possible between leader and the led.
- Degree of influence of the leader outside of the group.
- Congruency of style with that of one's superior.

The following observations can be made with regard to the type of leadership styles proposed in the Ohio State model:

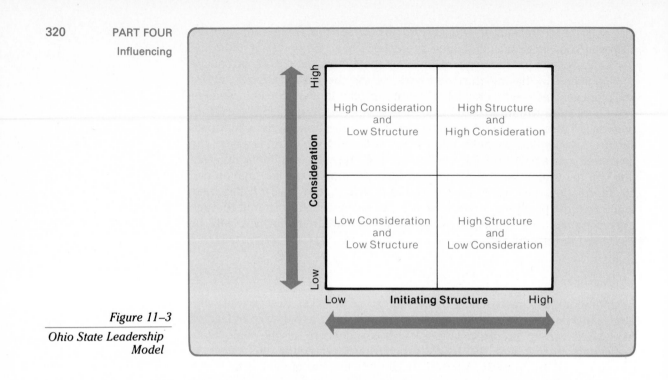

Figure 11–3

Ohio State Leadership Model

- If a group expects and wants authoritarian leadership behavior, it is more likely to be satisfied with that type of leadership.
- If group members have less authoritarian expectations, a leader who strongly emphasizes initiating structure will be resented.
- If the work situation is highly structured by technology and the pressures of time, the supervisor who is high in consideration is more likely to meet with success as measured by absenteeism, turnover, and grievances.
- If task structuring precludes individual and group self-actualization, it will be useless to look for motivation from this source.
- When subordinates have little contact with their supervisor, they tend to prefer a more autocratic style.
- If employees must work and interact continuously, they usually want the superior to be high in consideration.

Managerial Grid

managerial grid

One of the most widely known leadership theories is that based on the managerial grid.[5] The **managerial grid** is *a two-dimensional matrix developed by Robert Blake and Jane Mouton that shows concern for people on the vertical axis and concern for production on the horizontal axis.* The managerial grid is illustrated in Figure 11–4. The two dimensions of the 9×9 grid are labeled "concern for people" and "concern for production." A score of one indicates low concern, and a score of nine shows a high concern. The grid depicts five major leadership styles representing the degree of concern for "people" and "production."

- 1,1 *Impoverished Management:* The manager has little concern for either people or production.

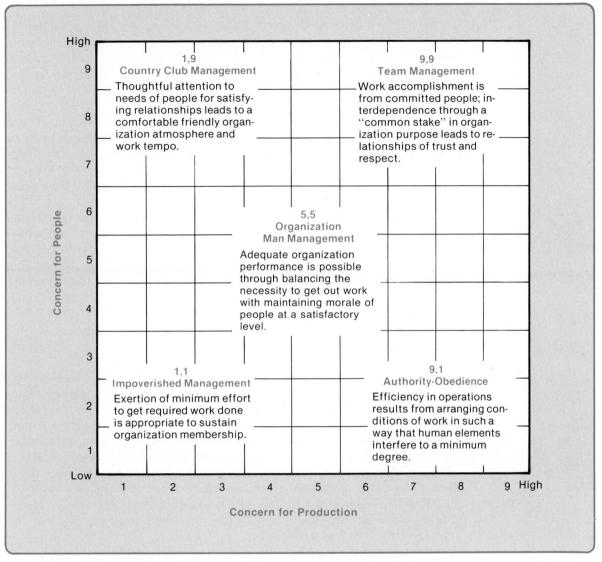

Figure 11–4 Blake and Mouton's Managerial Grid® Source: The Managerial Grid from *The Managerial Grid III,* by Robert R. Blake and Jane Srygley Mouton. Houston: Gulf Publishing Company, Copyright © 1985, page 12. Reproduced by permission.

- 9,1 *Authority-Obedience:* The manager stresses operating efficiently through controls in situations where human elements cannot interfere.
- 1,9 *Country Club Management:* The manager is thoughtful, comfortable, and friendly, and has little concern for output.
- 5,5 *Organization Man Management:* The manager attempts to balance and trade off concern from work in exchange for a satisfactory level of morale—a compromiser.
- 9,9 *Team Management:* The manager seeks high output through committed people, achieved through mutual trust, respect, and a realization of interdependence.[6]

According to Blake and Mouton, the first four styles listed are not the most effective leadership styles. They strongly suggest that only the 9,9 position of maximum concern for both output and people is the most effective. They argue that using the 9,9 team approach will result in improved performance, lower employee turnover and absenteeism, and greater employee satisfaction. The use of job enrichment and subordinate participation in managerial decision making contributes to this 9,9 situation where both the organization and its members are accorded maximum and equal concern. The managerial grid concept has been introduced to many managers throughout the world since its development in the early 1960s and has influenced the management philosophies and practices of many of them. Blake and Mouton have conducted grid training seminars around the world.

To some degree Sanford Sigoloff's behavior at Wickes reflects an understanding of the managerial grid. While necessarily most concerned about getting Wickes's employees to produce, Sigoloff still took time to visit individual stores, chatting with clerks and store managers alike, making them all feel special. This attitude of a dual concern for production and people was adopted by Sigoloff lieutenants, as well as by other managers at Wickes.

Path-Goal Theory of Leadership

path-goal theory

Robert House developed what he termed the path-goal theory of leadership.[7] This approach to leadership is also closely related to the expectancy theory of motivation discussed in Chapter 10. **Path-goal theory** is *the proposition that managers can facilitate job performance by showing employees how their performance directly affects their receiving desired rewards.* In other words, a manager's behavior causes or contributes to employee satisfaction and acceptance of the manager if it increases goal attainment by employees. According to the path-goal approach, effective job performance results if the manager clearly defines the job, provides training for the employee, assists the employee in performing the job effectively, and rewards the employee for effective performance.

Four distinct leadership behaviors are associated with the path-goal approach:

- *Directive:* The manager tells the subordinate what to do and when to do it (no employee participation in decision making).
- *Supportive:* The manager is friendly with and shows interest in employees.
- *Participative:* The manager seeks suggestions and involves employees in decision making.
- *Achievement oriented:* The manager establishes challenging goals and demonstrates confidence in employees in achieving these goals.

Although this may appear similar to Rensis Likert's four systems, Likert felt that only System IV was appropriate. Following the path-goal theory, a manager may use all four of the behaviors in different situations. For instance, a manager may use directive behavior when supervising an inexperienced employee and supportive behavior when supervising a well-trained, experienced worker aware of the goals to be attained. The primary focus of the path-goal approach is on how managers can increase employee motivation and job satisfaction by clarifying performance goals and the path to achieve the goals.[8]

The Leadership Continuum

The **leadership continuum** is *the graphical representation developed by Robert Tannenbaum and Warren H. Schmidt showing the trade-off between a manager's use of authority and the freedom that subordinates experience as leadership style varies from boss centered to subordinate centered.* Tannenbaum and Schmidt described a series of factors that they thought influenced a manager's selection of the most appropriate leadership style. Their approach advocated a continuum of leadership behavior supporting the notion that choosing an effective leadership style depends on the demands of the situation. As illustrated in Figure 11–5, leadership behavior ranges from boss centered to subordinate centered, which is similar in concept to the other dimensions of leadership behavior discussed. Tannenbaum and Schmidt emphasized that a manager should give careful consideration to the following factors before selecting a leadership style:

leadership continuum

- *Characteristics of the manager:* Background, education, experience, values, knowledge, goals, and expectations
- *Characteristics of the employees:* Background, education, experience, knowledge, goals, values, and expectations
- *Requirements of the situation:* Size, complexity, goals, structure, and climate of the organization, as well as the impact of technology, time pressure, and nature of the work

Figure 11–5 Continuum of Leadership Behavior   Source: Reprinted by permission of the *Harvard Business Review.* Exhibit from "How to Choose a Leadership Pattern" by Robert Tannenbaum and Warren H. Schmidt (May/June 1973). Copyright © 1973 by the President and Fellows of Harvard College. All rights reserved.

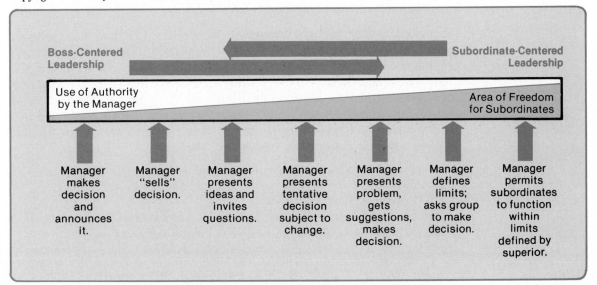

According to the Tannenbaum and Schmidt leadership continuum, a manager may engage in a more participative leadership style when subordinates

- Seek independence and freedom of action.
- Understand and are committed to the goals of the organization.
- Are well educated and experienced in performing the jobs.
- Seek responsibility for decision making.
- Expect a participative style of leadership.

If the above conditions do not exist, managers may need to adopt a more autocratic or "boss-centered" leadership style. Thus, in essence, managers must be able to diagnose the situations confronting them and then attempt to choose a leadership style that will improve their chances for effectiveness. The most effective leaders are neither task centered nor people centered; rather, they are flexible enough to select a leadership style that fits their needs, as well as the needs of their subordinates and the situation.

When Sigoloff first took over at Wickes, the situation demanded that his leadership style be boss centered. The company was failing, and no one would have expected him to give subordinates a free rein. Also, his recognized knowledge of what is needed to save a failing company marked him as the one who should determine what to do. Later, as he learned the capabilities of subordinates and as they learned from him, he could relinquish some authority.

MODERN SITUATIONAL THEORIES

Several of the leadership theories previously discussed are situational in nature. But two modern theories go beyond the proposition that leadership style should vary and attempt to define specific factors that determine the appropriate style. These are: Fiedler's contingency leadership model and Hersey and Blanchard's situational leadership model.

Fiedler's Contingency Leadership Model

The contingency theory developed by Fred E. Fiedler has received considerable recognition as a situational approach to leadership.[9] Fiedler's contingency leadership model suggests that there is no one most effective style that is appropriate to every situation. He says that there are a number of styles that may be effective depending on the situation. The framework is made up of eight significantly different situations and two basic types of leadership orientations. Three major elements are said to determine whether a given situation is favorable to a leader. These are:

- *Leader-member relations:* The degree to which the leader feels accepted by subordinates. The atmosphere may be friendly or unfriendly, relaxed or tense, and threatening or supportive.
- *Task structure:* Clearly defined goals, decisions, and solutions to problems.
- *Position power of the leader:* The degree of influence over rewards and punishments, as well as by his or her official authority.

The concept of leader-member relations is similar to the consideration or relationship behavior concepts, while task structure and position power

TABLE 11–2   Framework of Fiedler's Contingency Leadership Model

Situation	Degree of Favorableness of Situation to Leader	Leader-Member Relations	Task Structure	Position Power of Leader
1	Favorable	Good	Structured	High
2	Favorable	Good	Structured	Low
3	Favorable	Good	Unstructured	High
4	Moderately Favorable	Good	Unstructured	Low
5	Moderately Favorable	Poor	Structured	High
6	Moderately Favorable	Poor	Structured	Low
7	Moderately Favorable	Poor	Unstructured	High
8	Unfavorable	Poor	Unstructured	Low

Source: Edwin B. Flippo and Gary M. Munsinger, *Management,* 5th ed. (Newton, Mass.: Allyn and Bacon, 1982), p. 342.

are closely related to initiating structure or task behavior as discussed previously. By mixing these three elements, eight situations can be identified in Table 11–2.

These eight situations vary in accordance with the degree of favorableness of a situation to a leader—which is the leader's influence and control over the group. A leader has maximum influence in situation 1 and very little in situation 8. Research evidence indicates that a task-oriented, controlling leader will be most effective when the situations are either very favorable or easy (1, 2, and 3) or very difficult (see Table 11–2).[10] The more permissive, considerate leader performs more effectively in the intermediate situations, which are moderately favorable to the leader (4, 5, 6, and 7). Another way to illustrate Fiedler's framework is seen in Figure 11–6. The task-oriented style of leader is more effective in situations 1, 2, 3, and 8

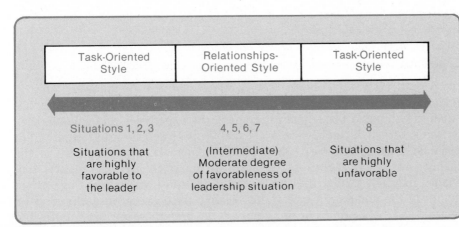

Figure 11–6

Appropriateness of Leadership Styles to Situation

Source: Adapted from Edwin B. Flippo and Gary M. Munsinger, *Management,* 5th ed. (Newton, Mass.: Allyn and Bacon, 1982), p. 342.

while the relationship-oriented style is more effective in situations 4, 5, 6, and 7. As demonstrated by Fiedler's theory, the most effective leadership style is contingent on many situational factors.

Using the Fiedler framework, Sigoloff's situation at Wickes should probably be placed in category 1, suggesting a task-oriented style. Leader-member relations were good because of Sigoloff's established reputation and a desire of employees to see their jobs saved. The task structure was clearly defined in terms of goals (become profitable) and solutions (cut costs). As chairman of the board and chief executive officer, answerable to no one, Sigoloff had extremely high positive power.

Hersey and Blanchard's Situational Leadership Theory

Paul Hersey and Kenneth Blanchard have developed a situational leadership theory that has attracted considerable attention on the part of managers.[11] Hersey and Blanchard's situational leadership theory is based on the notion that the most effective leadership style varies according to the level of maturity of the followers and demands of the situation. Their model uses two dimensions of leadership behavior—task and relationship. These are similar to the classifications used in the leadership models developed by Ohio State and the managerial grid. Hersey and Blanchard argue that an effective leader is one who can diagnose the demands of the situation and the level of maturity of the followers and use a leadership style that is appropriate. Their theory is based on a relationship between these factors:

1. The amount of task behavior the leader exhibits (providing direction and emphasis on getting the job done).
2. The amount of relationship behavior the leader provides (consideration of people, level of emotional support for people).
3. The level of task-relevant maturity followers exhibit toward the specific goal, task, or function that the leader wants accomplished.

The key concept of their leadership theory is the level of task-relevant maturity of the followers. Maturity is not defined as age or psychological stability. The maturity level of the followers is defined as:

• *A desire for achievement*—level of achievement motivation based on the need to set high but attainable goals.
• *The willingness and ability to accept responsibility.*
• *Education and/or experience and skills* relevant to the particular task.

A leader should consider the level of maturity of followers only in relation to the work or job to be performed. Certainly employees are "mature" on some tasks when they have the experience and skills as well as the desire to achieve and are capable of assuming responsibility. For example, Dianne Crawford, an accountant, may be very "mature" in the manner in which she prepares accurate quarterly IRS tax reports, but Dianne may not exhibit the same level of maturity when preparing written audits of the company's operations. Dianne needs very little direction on task-related behavior from her manager in preparing the tax reports but may require considerably closer supervision and direction over the preparation and writing of audits. Dianne may not have the skills and/or motivation to prepare audits, but with proper training, direction, and encouragement from her manager she can assume greater responsibility in this area.

Hersey and Blanchard argue that leadership style and effectiveness can be measured, and they have designed an instrument for this purpose—the Leader Effectiveness & Adaptability Description (LEAD). The LEAD provides feedback on leadership style and the effectiveness of the individual completing the instrument.

As illustrated in Figure 11–7, the appropriate leadership style used by a manager varies according to the maturity level (represented by M1 through M4) of the followers. There are four distinct leadership styles that

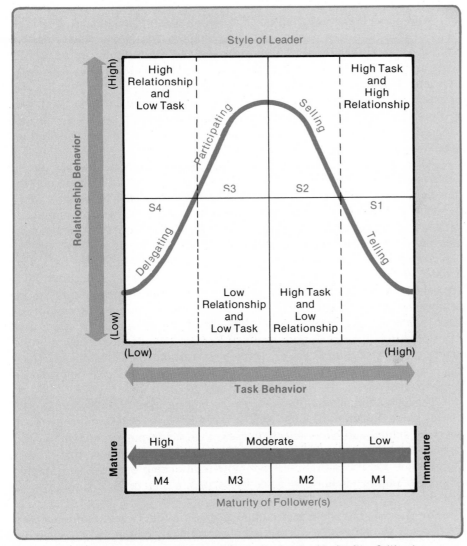

Figure 11–7

Hersey and Blanchard's Situational Leadership Theory

Source: Paul Hersey and Kenneth Blanchard. Center for Leadership Studies. California American University, 1977. Used with permission.

are appropriate given different levels of maturity. As the task-relevant maturity level of followers increases, the manager should reduce task behavior and increase relationship behavior. These are illustrated by the classifications of the styles as:

S1—Telling	High task
	Low relationship
S2—Selling	High task
	High relationship
S3—Participating	High relationship
	Low task
S4—Delegating	Low relationship
	Low task

With the S1 (Telling) high-task, low-relationship leadership style, the leader uses one-way communication, defines the goals and roles of employees, and tells them what, how, when, and where to do the work. This style is very appropriate when dealing with subordinates who lack task-relevant maturity. For example, in supervising a group of relatively new, inexperienced employees, a high level of task-directed behavior and low-relationship behavior may be an appropriate leadership approach. Inexperienced employees need to be told what to do and how to accomplish their jobs.

As employees learn their jobs, the manager begins to use an S2 leadership style. There still is a need for a high level of task behavior since the employees do not yet have the experience or skills to assume more responsibility, but the manager provides a higher level of emotional support—high-relationship behavior. The manager encourages the employees and demonstrates greater trust and confidence in them.

As we move toward the S3 leadership style, the employee begins to exhibit an increase in task-relevant maturity. As employees become more experienced and skilled, as well as more achievement motivated and more willing to assume responsibility, the leader should reduce the amount of task behavior but continue the high level of emotional support and consideration. A continuation of a high level of relationship behavior is the manager's way of reinforcing the employees' responsible performance. Thus, S3—high-relationship and low-task behavior—becomes the appropriate leadership style.

The S4 leadership style represents the highest level of follower maturity. In this stage, the employees possess a very high level of task maturity. They are very skilled and experienced, possess high achievement motivation, and are capable of exercising self-control. Thus, the leadership style that is most appropriate for this situation is S4—low relationship and low task. At this point the employees no longer need or expect a high level of supportive or task behavior from their leader.

We should not conclude from this discussion that Hersey and Blanchard consider it simple to determine the appropriate leadership style. The ability to diagnose the maturity level of the followers, as well as the specific needs of the situation, is complex. The leader must have insight into the abilities, needs, demands, and expectations of followers and be aware that these can and do change over time. Also, managers must recognize that they must adapt or change their style of leadership whenever there is a change in the level of maturity of followers for whatever reason—change in jobs, personal or family problems, or change in complexity of present job due perhaps to new technology. For example, Bill Woodall, the sales manager, has been using an S4 leadership style in supervising John Chriswell, a normally highly productive sales representative. But suppose that John's pending divorce has recently been adversely affecting his performance. In this situation, Bill might increase both the level of task and relationship behavior in order to provide John with the direction, support, and confidence he may need to cope with his problems and improve his performance.

In summary, Hersey and Blanchard's theory provides a useful and understandable framework for situational leadership. In essence, their model suggests that there is *no one* best leadership style that meets the needs of all situations. Rather, a manager's leadership style must be adaptable and flexible enough to meet the changing needs of employees and situations. The effective manager is one who can change styles as employees develop and change or as required by the situation.

In a 1982 study, Blake and Mouton pitted their proposition against the Hersey and Blanchard situational theory. They found that the professional managers they surveyed consistently chose the 9,9 style rather than varying their styles as Hersey and Blanchard advocate.[13]

IBM Means Service

"Years ago we ran an ad that said simply, *'IBM means service.'* I have often thought it was our very best ad. It stated clearly just exactly what we stand for. *We want to give the best customer service of any company in the world.*" So wrote Thomas J. Watson, Jr., shortly after he succeeded his father as chairman of International Business Machines Corporation.

This service orientation permeates every level at IBM. It is the practice to answer every customer complaint within twenty-four hours. The customer orientation is enforced through incentives for keeping customers and disincentives for losing them. For example, if a customer terminates a lease within a year after equipment is installed, the account representative responsible for that customer must give up salary and bonus to make up for the company's loss. Sales representatives receive fifteen months of basic sales training. Customer satisfaction is formally surveyed once a month, and quarterly employee attitude surveys are largely concerned with how well customers are being served.

There is much more to the IBM tradition than customer service, however. Tom Watson, Jr., touts "our respect for the individual as the company's first principle." The senior Thomas Watson started an open door policy in the 1920s and a $1 a year country club for all employees. IBM offers a wide range of other employee benefits, among them, lifetime employment, day care centers, and recreational facilities. During the Great Depression, IBM avoided layoffs by making parts for inventory and storing them.

But IBM demands a lot of its people, too. The traditional gray suit and white shirt is a reflection of the senior Mr. Watson's demand for "tasteful" dress. Sales representatives operate under a quota system, and quotas are increased each year or sales territories are cut. New employees are closely supervised and graded according to how well they meet frequently modified goals.

Watson is famous for having used "almost every kind of fanfare" to create enthusiasm. According to a recent *Wall Street Journal* article:

> Achievement is followed by immediate rewards. Insiders say that the most cherished of these isn't money, it's having your name and quota on the bulletin board with a notation saying, "100%." It's having a party thrown for you at your branch because you have satisfied a prickly customer. It's a steady flow of letters of commendation.

And almost everyone is eligible for some kind of award. There is a Gold Circle for the top 10 percent of IBM's sales representatives. But 80 percent are eligible for the One Hundred Percent Club. In fact, sales quotas are engineered so that more than two-thirds of the sales representatives make their quotas.

Contrary to popular opinion, IBM has seldom been the first to market new technology—waiting on its personal computer, for example, until others were well established in that market. The IBM 360 and 370 mainframes stayed on the market for years after other manufacturers had more advanced technology. IBM chose to leave those machines in use as long as they were making money for the company.

Still, IBM traditionally has promoted internal competition among new product ideas. R&D managers were encouraged to encroach on one another's turf and to come up with multiple solutions to the same problems. Then they had the opportunity to sell their solutions to the sales force through performance "shoot-outs," where demonstrations compared the actual working hardware and software, not just product descriptions.

The authority structure at IBM is strong. Every employee gets an annual performance plan with specific written goals. Meeting or exceeding the plan results in promotions and raises.

IBM has begun to market its computers through retailers like Computerland and Sears, reducing its control over customer service. The company has moved into joint ventures with the Japanese, buying 12 percent of Intel Corporation. In a major departure from past strategies, IBM encourages customers to buy rather than lease, further deemphasizing IBM's responsibility for its products.

IBM has begun to emphasize price more than in the past. At the high end of its line, the company cut prices on its 3081 super computer a month after Amdahl began to market a similar product and quickly sold fifty to Amdahl's biggest customer, AT&T. IBM now gives special prices to customers that sign volume purchase commitments. IBM has priced its PC and PC, Jr. (Peanut) personal computers near the prices competitors charge for similar units.[12]

FACTORS AFFECTING CHOICE OF LEADERSHIP STYLE

The discussion may seem to imply that managers merely decide which leadership style to use, sometimes changing styles to adapt to different situations. For instance, the situation IBM faces now is vastly different from that it faced at the turn of the century. Even when we know the situation, the appropriate leadership style may not be obvious, but there are factors that help the leader decide which style to use in a given case. There are also certain constraints. The following discussion concentrates on the practical aspects of choosing a leadership style.

Factors Related to the Manager

Self-knowledge is important to effective leadership. Leaders have different abilities and goals; they also have had different experiences. Through those experiences, they develop basic beliefs about people. Some think that people must be threatened to make them work. Others believe in encouraging workers and rewarding them for performance. Although managers should be flexible in the choice of a leadership style, they usually perform better if they use a style consistent with their personal beliefs. The manager's professional and technical competence also affects leadership style. Not only are competent managers more confident, but workers are also less likely to challenge or question them. This would seem to allow the manager to be more autocratic. In fact, it permits the managers more flexibility in leadership styles. Thus, a leader like Thomas Watson, Sr., at IBM could be a gentle, supportive manager in certain situations and a stern disciplinarian in others.

Factors Related to the Workers

Characteristics of subordinates must also be taken into account when deciding on leadership style. One important consideration is the work ethic of subordinates. Some workers feel that work is, in and of itself, satisfying, pleasurable, and fulfilling. Such workers are easy to lead. Others see work as an unpleasant way to get money. Perhaps rewards and punishments are the only effective motivators for these workers.

Workers' attitudes toward authority must also be considered. Some believe that the job of the manager is to tell them what to do. They do not want to help make decisions. Others wish to make all the decisions; they resist any exercise of authority by the leader.

The maturity level of the subordinates influences leadership style. Some workers are mature in the way they approach their work. They exercise initiative not only in doing their job but also in self-development. Others may have to be watched quite closely to obtain even minimum performance. Workers may handle one aspect of their job maturely yet be quite immature in other aspects.

Another factor is the experience level and skill of subordinates. The leadership style used with a trainee will be different from that used with an experienced craftsperson. A more directive style may prove best for the trainee, while the craftsperson may need no direction at all.

For some employees an autocratic style will work best. This may be particularly true in extremely favorable or extremely unfavorable situations. Studies have shown, however, that workers generally respond more favorably to a participative approach. This appears to be true for subordinates exhibiting a very wide range of characteristics.[14] Even at companies like

There are numerous factors that can affect the choice of an appropriate leadership style. Arthur Grace/Stock, Boston Inc.

IBM with a strong authority structure, workers tend to be more highly motivated if they take part in the decision-making process.

Factors Related to the Situation

Many situational factors affect the supervisor's leadership style. Some of the major situational factors are described below.

1. *Number of people in the work group.* Managers can give more individualized attention in smaller work groups. As group size increases, management by exception may tend to be used.

2. *Kinds of tasks.* Jobs involving simple repetition may permit the manager to be more autocratic. Workers with creative or complex jobs require more freedom.

3. *Situational stress.* Managers often shift to a more autocratic style when the going gets tough. The firm may be in financial difficulties, and the manager may be experiencing unusual pressure to increase output. This was the case at Wickes Companies when Sigoloff took over. The supervisor should be careful in changing leadership styles and should not do so as a reflex action.

4. *Objectives of the unit.* The specific objectives the manager is expected to accomplish affect leadership style. If the only objective is to get the job done immediately, the use of strong authority may be justified, even though it may make workers unhappy. When there is an important rush project, subordinates are more likely to accept simply being told what to do.

5. *Whether or not the company has a union.* Union workers often do not want to participate in management. They may believe that supervisors should supervise and workers should work. Managers in nonunion firms are able to adopt a wider range of leadership styles. Being able to maintain nonunion status has been a major strength of IBM management.

6. *Leadership style of the manager's boss.* Managers tend to lead as they are led. If the boss is autocratic, managers may lean toward this leadership style. The example set by Thomas Watson, Sr., still guides managers throughout that large organization.

7. *Relationship of the manager with subordinates.* If the relationship is one of mutual respect, the manager will usually let workers take part in managing themselves. Workers, too, are likely to contribute more when they are respected and liked by their supervisor. Because of a careful selection process at IBM, employees tend to be "a cut above average" and thus can be given extra responsibility.

After reading the preceding list, your first reaction might be to throw up your hands in despair. You might say, "I want to know exactly what leadership style to use." There is no absolute answer. We question those who say there is. In the 1980s, organizations are moving toward flatter, more decentralized structures. This has increased, not decreased, the need for interdependence, collaboration, and communication—for flexibility in leadership style.[15] In a recent "critical review" of contingency leadership theories, Graeff found that for situational leadership to be effective, the leader must come to two conclusions: First, the leader must be flexible in behavior; patterns of habit must be broken. Second, the subordinate must be recognized as a major situational determinant. This involves not only careful observation of behavior but the ability to interpret that behavior in a meaningful way.[16]

The best we can suggest is that you thoroughly evaluate yourself, your subordinates, and the situation and then choose an appropriate style. The style you use may change as you deal with various members of your work group and with a certain member at various times. The choice of a leadership style is truly situational.

SUMMARY

Effective leadership is essential to the survival and growth of every organization. A leader is someone who can get others to do what he or she wants them to do. But what is required to be an effective manager and what is the most effective leadership style? These questions have been of concern to managers for generations and have been the subject of thousands of research studies. Despite volumes of leadership research, no simple list of traits or characteristics has been identified that is consistently related to effective leadership. In fact, the basic conclusion of these studies is that there is no one most effective leadership style.

Three basic theories of leadership were discussed in this chapter: trait, appropriate style, and modern situational. The early studies of leadership attempted to identify the traits and characteristics of effective leaders. Traits relating to physical characteristics, personality, or intelligence were studied to determine if they were related to effective leadership. For the most part, research has not shown that traits alone can distinguish effective from ineffective leaders. Despite these findings, the trait approach to the study of leadership has continued. Edwin Ghiselli has identified six traits/characteristics that his extensive research indicates are related to effective leadership. These include supervisory ability, need for occupational achievement, intelligence, decisiveness, self-assurance, and initiative.

Dissatisfaction with the trait approach caused most researchers to focus attention on the actual behavior and actions of leaders. Rensis Likert developed a leadership theory that posited a continuum of styles ranging from autocratic to participative. In the Ohio State leadership studies, two dimensions of leader behavior—initiating structure and consideration—were identified. Robert R. Blake and Jane S. Mouton developed a two-dimensional managerial grid labeled "concern for people" and "concern for production." Robert House developed the path-goal theory of leadership, which concluded that managers can facilitate job performance by showing employees how their performance directly affects their receiving desired rewards. Robert Tannenbaum and Warren H.

Schmidt described a series of factors that they thought influenced a manager's selection of the most appropriate leadership style.

Two modern leadership theories go beyond the proposition that leadership style should vary and attempt to define specific factors that determine the appropriate style. In Fred Fiedler's theory, the degree of favorableness or unfavorableness of the leader-member relations, task structure, and position power of the leader determine the style of leadership that is most effective. Finally, Hersey and Blanchard's theory is based on the notion that the most effective leadership style varies according to the level of maturity of the followers and the demands of the situation. Their theory offers four basic styles or combinations of task and relationship behavior of the leader. If the leader is dealing with highly mature followers, the appropriate leadership style might be low emphasis on both relationships and task behavior.

REVIEW QUESTIONS

1. Define leadership. Why is it an important subject?

2. What is the distinction between management and leadership? Is it possible to be a good leader but an ineffective manager? Explain.

3. List several significant traits identified by the research of Edwin Ghiselli as being important for effective leadership.

4. What are the four basic styles or systems of management identified by Rensis Likert? Explain each.

5. What were the Ohio State leadership studies? What basic dimensions of leadership behavior were identified? What were some of the factors that determined the most effective style of leadership?

6. Describe the five leadership styles presented in the managerial grid. Which style is recommended as most effective by Blake and Mouton?

7. What basic conclusion can be derived from the Tannenbaum and Schmidt leadership continuum? What factors should be considered before choosing a leadership style?

8. What is the basic contention of Fiedler's theory of leadership? In what situations are task-centered leaders most effective? People-centered leaders?

9. Briefly explain Hersey and Blanchard's leadership theory. What is the key concept of their theory?

10. Describe the factors that affect the choice of a leadership style.

EXERCISE

Assume you are a newly appointed manager over the following types of workers. What leadership style would you suggest? Defend your response in view of the leadership theories you have studied.

a. New, untrained machine operator

b. Skilled, highly motivated mechanic

c. Research scientist

d. Tenured full professor at a major state university.

A Cause for Dismissal

Dwayne Bandy groggily reached for the phone as it rang for about the tenth time. The voice on the other end said, "This is Joe Davis, with the sheriff's patrol. I just found your Center Street store unlocked."

Immediately wide awake, Dwayne asked, "Has it been broken into? What does it look like?"

Officer Davis told Dwayne that the store seemed to have been left open, that there was no sign of a forced entry. Dwayne asked him to keep an eye on the store. "I'll be there in ten minutes," he said.

Dwayne was the Dallas-area supervisor for Quik-Stop, a chain of convenience stores. There were seven Quik-Stop stores in Dallas, and Dwayne had full responsibility for managing them. Each store operated with only one person on duty at a time. Although several of the stores stayed open all night, the Center Street store was open only from 6:00 A.M. to 10:00 P.M.

After finding that nothing seemed to be missing, Dwayne thought about what he should do. The company had a policy that anyone leaving a store unlocked is fired on the spot. Bill Catron worked the night shift at the Center Street store and was responsible for locking up. Dwayne decided to wait until the next day when Bill reported to work before deciding what to do.

As Dwayne drove up to the Center Street store the next day at 2:30 P.M., he saw Bill at work inside the U-shaped counter. There were no customers in the store at the moment so Dwayne decided to get it over with. "Hello, Bill," Dwayne said, "I need to talk to you."

Obviously concerned, Bill said, "What's wrong, Dwayne? You look worried."

"You left the store open last night and you know what the company policy is," Dwayne said.

Bill was very upset. "I really need this job," Bill exclaimed. "With the new baby and all the medical expenses we have had this winter, I sure can't stand to be out of a job."

"You knew about the policy, though, Bill," said Dwayne.

"Yes, I did, Dwayne," said Bill, "and I really don't have any excuse. If you don't fire me, though, I promise you that I'll be the best store manager you've got."

While Bill waited on a customer, Dwayne called his boss at the home office in Houston. With the boss's approval, Dwayne decided not to fire Bill.

QUESTIONS

1. Discuss Dwayne's leadership style in terms of the managerial grid.
2. Evaluate the action Dwayne took. Take particular note of how the events in the case might affect other store managers.

A Natural-Born Leader

"Phil is a natural-born leader," said Jim Hollis, the plant manager, as he looked out over the factory floor from the production manager's office.

"Yes," said the production manager. "I believe those carpenters would follow him off the end of the earth."

Phil Granger is the carpentry supervisor in the shipping department at the Jacobs Castings Company. He is a big man, six-foot-four, 240 pounds. He has a booming voice. His size and the steel-blue sternness of his eyes belie a gentle spirit. He avoids confrontations and is known to be patient and lenient with subordinates. Phil and his crew of six make wooden boxes for packaging the several hundred custom-made castings that Jacobs ships every day. The work requires little skill, but it is vital to the plant.

Before Phil took over, the carpentry division was a bottleneck. Shipments were often delayed for days because the carpentry work just did not seem to get done. Turnover in the department had been high. The carpenters seemed to have more personal problems than other workers in the plant.

When Phil took over, everything seemed to change almost immediately. The work was caught up within a few days, and castings no longer had to wait for more than a day to be shipped. The carpenters also seemed happier. During the first two months that Phil was in charge, there was not a single complaint and only one day was lost because of absenteeism.

As Phil sketched the boxes to be made the next morning, he thought, "I sure would like to go home a little early today, but I want the others to know I'm trying as hard as they are. Anyway, I need to finish these sketches so I'll have time to help with the boxes in the morning. I also want to check with Brad about his new baby before he leaves today. Since I took him around and showed him how our work affected the rest of the plant, he sure has done a great job."

QUESTIONS

1. Is Phil a natural-born leader? Explain.
2. What do you believe accounts for the success of the carpentry division? Defend your answer.

NOTES

1. Roger Skrentny, "Sandy Sigoloff: The Man Who Threw Wickes a Life Raft," *California Business* (February 1983): 18–23; Mark Liff, "Ming Shows Wickes Cos. No Mercy," *Advertising Age* (January 23, 1984): M-27-28; "On the Comeback Trail," *Time* (March 12, 1984): 52–53; and Jennifer Fendleton, "Sigoloff Finds Star Status Is Hard Work," *Advertising Age* (September 19, 1983): 47.

2. Edwin Ghiselli, *Explorations in Managerial Talent* (Pacific Palisades, Calif.: Goodyear, 1971).

3. R. W. Rice, D. Instone, and J. Adams, "Leader Sex, Leader Success, and Leadership Process: Two Field Studies," *Journal of Applied Psychology* (February 1984): 27.

4. Rensis Likert, *The Human Organization* (New York: McGraw-Hill, 1967).

5. Robert R. Blake and Jane S. Mouton, *The New Managerial Grid* (Houston: Gulf Publishing, 1978): 11.

6. Ibid.

7. Robert House, "A Path-Goal Theory of Leadership Effectiveness," *Administrative Science Quarterly* 16 (September 1971): 321–338.

8. Alan C. Filley, Robert House, and Steven Kerr, *Managerial Process and Organizational Behavior* (Glenview, Ill.: Scott, Foresman, 1976): 256–260.

9. Fred E. Fiedler, *A Theory of Leadership Effectiveness* (New York: McGraw-Hill 1967).

10. Ibid.

11. See Paul Hersey and Kenneth Blanchard, "So You Want to Know Your Leadership Style?" *Training and Development Journal* (February 1974): 22–32. This article contains the Leader Adaptability and Style Inventory (LASI), an instrument that can be used to examine leadership behavior, style adaptability, and effectiveness. Since this article, the LASI has been renamed as the Leader Effectiveness and Adaptability Description (LEAD). Information, LEAD inventories, and training materials may be obtained from the Center for Leadership Studies, 17253 Caminito Canasto, Rancho Bernardo, San Diego, California 92127.

12. Peter D. Petre, "Meet the Mean, Lean New IBM," *Fortune* 107 (June 13, 1983): 69–82; Thomas J. Watson, Jr., *A Business and Its Beliefs: The Ideas That Helped to Build IBM* (New York: McGraw-Hill, 1963); Thomas J. Peters and Robert H. Waterman, Jr., *In Search of Excellence: Lessons from America's Best Run Companies* (New York: Harper & Row Publishers, 1982); and a number of articles from *The Wall Street Journal.*

13. Robert R. Blake and Jane S. Mouton, p. 282.

14. M. E. Heilman, H. A. Hornstein, J. H. Cage, and J. K. Herschdag, "Reactions to Prescribed Leader Behavior as a Function of Role Perspective: The Case of The Vroom-Yetton Model," *Journal of Applied Psychology* (February 1984): 50.

15. R. Lippitt, "The Changing Leader-Follower Rela-

tionships of the 1980s," *Journal of Applied Behavioral Science* 18 (March 1982): 396.

16. C. L. Graeff, "The Situational Leadership Theory: A Critical View," *Academy of Management Review* (April 1983): 290.

REFERENCES

Blake, R. B., and J. S. Mouton. "Theory and Research for Developing a Science of Leadership." *Journal of Applied Behavioral Science* 18 (March 1982): 275–291.

Burke, W. W. "Leadership: Is There One Best Approach?" *Management Review* 69 (November 1980): 54–56.

Butler, Mark C., and Allan P. Jones. "Perceived Leader Behavior, Individual Characteristics, and Injury Occurrence in Hazardous Work Environments." *Journal of Applied Psychology* 64, no. 3 (June 1979): 299–304.

Carbone, T. C. "Theory X and Theory Y Revisited." *Managerial Planning* 29 (May–June 1981): 24–27.

Fiedler, F. E. "Job Engineering for Effective Leadership: A New Approach." *Management Review* 66 (September 1977): 29–31.

————, and Linda Mahar. "The Effectiveness of Contingency Model Training: A Review of the Validation of Leader Match." *Personnel Psychology* 32, no. 1 (Spring 1979): 45–62.

Fox, W. M. "Limits to the Use of Consultative-Participative Management." *California Management Review* 20 (Winter 1977): 17–22.

Graeff, C. L. "The Situational Leadership Theory: A Critical View." *Academy of Management Review* (April 1983): 285–291.

Green, S. G., and D. M. Nebeker. "Effects of Situational Factors and Leadership Style on Leader Behavior." *Organizational Behavior and Human Performance* 19 (August 1977): 368–377.

Greene, Charles N. "Questions of Causation in the Path-Goal Theory of Leadership." *Academy of Management Journal* 22, no. 1 (March 1979): 22–41.

Griffin, R. W. "Relationships among Individual, Task Design and Leader Behavior Variables." *Academy of Management Journal* 23 (December 1980): 665–683.

Heilman, M. E., H. A. Hornstein, J. H. Cage, and J. K. Herschdag. "Reactions to Prescribed Leader Behavior as a Function of Role Perspective: The Case of The Vroom-Yetton Model." *Journal of Applied Psychology* (February 1984): 50–60.

Himes, G. K. "Management Leadership Styles." *Supervision* 42 (November 1980): 9–11.

Katz, R. "Influence of Group Conflict on Leadership Effectiveness." *Organizational Behavior and Human Performance* 20 (December 1977): 265–286.

Klimoski, R. J., and N. J. Hayes. "Leadership Behavior and Subordinate Motivation." *Personnel Psychology* 33 (Autumn 1980): 543–545.

Leister, A. et al. "Validation of Contingency Model Leadership Training: Leader Match." *Academy of Management Journal* 20 (September 1977): 464–470.

Likert, R. "Management Styles and the Human Component." *Management Review* 66 (October 1977): 23–28.

Lippitt, R. "The Changing Leader-Follower Relationships of the 1980s." *Journal of Applied Behavioral Science* 18 (March 1982): 395–403.

Miner, Frederick C., Jr. "A Comparative Analysis of Three Diverse Group Decision Making Approaches." *Academy of Management Journal* 22, no. 1 (March 1979): 81–93.

Peters, Thomas J. "Leadership: Sad Facts and Silver Linings." *Harvard Business Review* 57, no. 6 (November–December 1979): 164–172.

Rice, R. W., D. Instone, and J. Adams. "Leader Sex, Leader Success, and Leadership Process: Two Field Studies." *Journal of Applied Psychology* (February 1984): 12–31.

Schriesheim, C. A., and J. F. Schriesheim. "Test of the Path-Goal Theory of Leadership and Some Suggested Direction for Future Research." *Personnel Psychology* 33 (Summer 1980): 368–370.

Sinetar, M. "Developing Leadership Potential." *Personnel Journal* 60 (March 1981): 193–196.

Zeleznik, A. "Managers and Leaders: Are They Different?" *Harvard Business Review* 55 (May 1977): 67–68.

Zierden, William E. "Leading through the Follower's Point of View." *Organization Dynamics* 8, no. 4 (Spring 1980): 27–46.

KEY TERMS

communication

source (sender)

communication
  channels

formal communication
  channels

informal
  communication
  channels

open-door policy

grievance procedure

ombudsperson

timing

information overload

information filtering

perception set

empathy

body language

LEARNING OBJECTIVES

After completing this chapter you should be able to

1. Describe the basic components of the communication process and state what should be communicated to workers.
2. Explain the basic forms of organizational channels of communication.
3. Identify the barriers that can cause breakdowns in communication.
4. Describe the facilitators available to improve communication.
5. Describe the effect of new technologies on the communication process.

12

Communications

*Corporate
Communications
at
Holiday
Corporation*

HOLIDAY
CORPORATION

When Holiday Inns appointed Jerry Daly vice-president of corporate communications in 1984, the company was continuing a tradition of emphasis on communicating with its people. President Michael D. Rose says, "We believe strongly that the greatest future productivity gain will come from and through our people." It is a rare company that has a department devoted entirely to communications, let alone one headed by a vice-president.

In 1972, Holiday Inns established the Holiday Inn University (HIU). "Our university is more than a training center for employees of the Holiday Inns system," says a senior executive. "It is also a communication center and a meeting place for international visitors. It provides the framework, not only to teach the necessary job skills, but also instills pride and commitment in all of our people regarding their contribution to Holiday Inns' success."

Each year the company (renamed Holiday Corporation in 1985) conducts a climate survey. Each employee is asked to give impressions about the company, its future, and the part he or she plays in that future. Survey results are taken seriously and frequently form the basis for managerial changes.

Holiday Corporation is a large, complex company. The Holiday Corporation hotel system has 1,696 hotels, with 310,450 rooms in 49 countries. The size and complexity of the organization heightened the challenge stated by Roy E. Winegardner, chairman of the board: "We will promote a climate of enthusiasm, teamwork, and challenge, which attracts, motivates, and retains superior personnel and rewards superior performance." Mr. Winegardner recognizes the importance of communications. He says, "We will maintain integrity in both our internal and external relationships, fostering respect for the individual and open, two-way communications."[1]

Perhaps the worst criticism that managers can receive from their peers, superiors, and subordinates is that they cannot communicate effectively. The emphasis that Holiday Corporation places on training managers in communication skills helps to avoid this criticism. A similar concern for communication was expressed by Marvin F. Gade, executive vice-president for Kimberly-Clark Corporation: "Unless an individual is capable of clear and timely communication with deputies, peers, and principals, he or she is nearly totally ineffective."

In a previous chapter, management was defined as the accomplishment of objectives through the efforts of other people. In order for employees to achieve the goals identified by the manager, they must have a clear understanding of those goals. A statement by a frustrated manager such as, "You did what you thought I meant very effectively. Unfortunately, that was not what I wanted you to do," reveals that effective communication did not take place.

Effective communication should not be considered an end in itself but a means of achieving company goals. The statement by chairman Roy Winegardner relating to communication, motivation, and performance at Holiday Corporation is a recognition of this.

The main encouraging feature of communication is that it is a learned quality. Individuals who truly desire to improve their ability to communicate can improve by giving proper attention to the task.

The chapter begins with a discussion of the communication process. Next, the various channels of communication will be presented. Concentration will then be placed on items that can cause a breakdown in communication. Then, factors that can assist or facilitate the communication process will be presented. Finally, the effect of new technologies on the communication process will be discussed.

THE COMMUNICATION PROCESS

Communication is *the transfer of information, ideas, understanding, or feelings between people.* In an organization, communication provides the means by which the objectives of the firm may be accomplished. The manner in which plans are to be implemented and actions coordinated to achieve a particular goal must be communicated to the individuals who must accomplish the task. In fact, it has been estimated that managers

communication

Ken Robert Buck/Stock, Boston Inc.

Communication is the transfer of information, ideas, understanding, or feelings between people.

spend a large portion of their time communicating—approximately 75 percent. Communication provides the means by which members of the firm may be stimulated to accomplish organizational plans willingly and enthusiastically.

Figure 12–1   The Communication Process   Source: Adapted from H. Joseph Reitz, *Behavior in Organizations* (Homewood, Ill.: Irwin, 1977), p. 342. Copyright © 1977 by Richard D. Irwin, Inc. Used with permission.

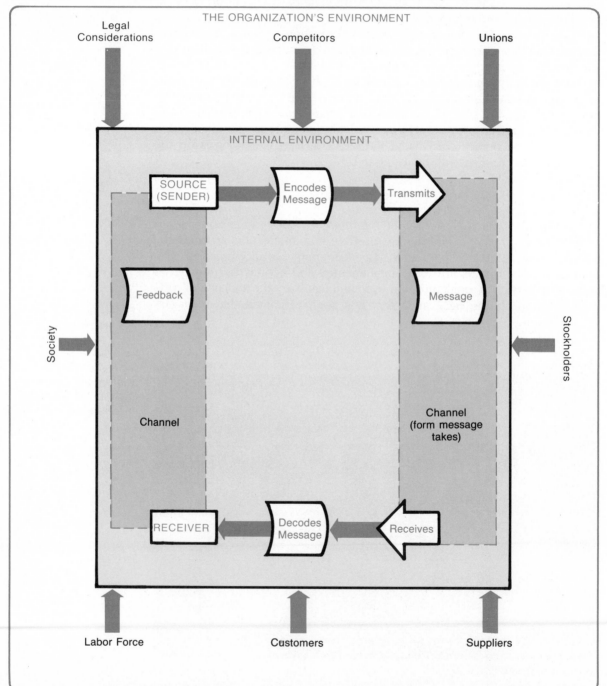

Communication must always take place between two or more people. Shouting for help on a desert island is not communication; similarly, if the professor lectures and no one listens or understands, there is no communication. The basic elements of the communication process are shown in Figure 12–1. Each step in the sequence is critical to success. The **source (sender)** is *the person who has an idea or message to communicate to another person or persons.* A problem that often affects the communication process is that each of us has different backgrounds, experiences, and goals. As the first step in the communication process, a sender must encode the message or idea into a set of symbols that the receiver will understand. Words on this page are symbols to you as a reader. The sound of a car's horn on a busy freeway may mean that an accident appears likely. Thus, the blast of the horn becomes a symbol of danger.

source (sender)

When communication is attempted, messages are transmitted through such means as speaking, writing, acting, and drawing. A number of channels may be used to transmit any message. Words can be communicated orally through such methods as face to face conversations, telephone conversations, radio, and television. Books, articles, and letters can serve as written channels. The senses of touch, smell, and taste are nonverbal channels (although for a blind person reading braille, touch is a verbal channel). Much meaningful communication takes place without a word being spoken.

Continuing to the lower part of Figure 12–1, the receiver of the message must decode it by converting the symbols into meaning. Like senders, receivers have diverse backgrounds, experiences, and aspirations. Communication is effective to the extent that the receiver's decoding matches the sender's encoding. Based on the meaning transmitted, the receiver will act in response to the communication. This action can be to ignore the message, perform some task, store the information for future use, or something else. Feedback is provided so that the sender will know if the message was accurately received and the proper action taken. At Holiday Corporation, the annual climate survey provides feedback from employees to determine if the company has communicated the desired image to them.

WHAT SHOULD BE COMMUNICATED?

Some managers limit their communication with subordinates to the issuance of orders. But communication should take on a much larger scope. As W. D. Johnson, vice-president of personnel for Baxter-Travenol Labs, Inc., stated, "Every day it becomes dramatically apparent that communication with employees is a critical requirement of good management." Behavior scientists have demonstrated that motivation of workers is impossible without effective communication.

Research has also underscored the need for subordinates to be heard and understood by their supervisors. The 1980s are likely to be years of continued organizational budget tightening. Heightened competition over already-scarce resources can be expected at all levels. The responsibility to maintain a good communication climate clearly falls to management.[2]

Determining the specific topics to be communicated is often difficult. The manager who believes that everything is suitable for transmission will not only clog the channels with insignificant trivia but may harm operations by releasing harmful information. The National Association of Manufacturers has suggested that the following should be communicated:

1. Information about the company—its operations, products, and prospects.
2. Information about company policies and practices related to personnel and their jobs, such as vacations, seniority, and pay systems.
3. Information about specific situations that arise in the company, such as a change in management or a change in plant layout.
4. Information about the general economic system in which the company and its employees operate.

Within these broad areas, many specific details must be considered. For example, management should inform its employees of the company's products, believing that their understanding will inspire interest, loyalty, and cooperation. But on the other hand, disclosure of future product plans may jeopardize the company's future in a highly competitive industry. In matters more closely related to the employee's interests, such as seniority and pay, the tendency is toward providing all information that could possibly be desired.

To sustain employee cooperation in the pursuit of organizational goals, the needs of the employee must be considered. Employees want to know such things as the following:

• Their standing in relation to the official, formal authority structure.
• Their standing in relation to the informal organization with respect to individual status, power, acceptance, and so forth.
• Events that have bearing on their own and the company's future economic security.
• Operational information that will enable them to develop pride in the job.

Holiday Corporation's concern for the last item is shown by the senior executive's comment that Holiday Inn University is a communication center that "instills pride and commitment."

CHANNELS OF COMMUNICATION

communication channels

formal communication channels

informal communication channels

Organizations provide many channels for communication. **Communication channels** are *the means by which information is transmitted.* Communication channels may be classified as formal and informal. **Formal communication channels** are *those communication channels that are officially recognized by the organization.* Instructions and information are passed downward along these channels, and information flows upward. Information also travels through informal channels. **Informal communication channels** are *ways of transmitting information within an organization that bypass formal channels.*

Formal Downward Channels

Many managers emphasize the importance of the downward channels of communication. They are aware of the necessity for conveying upper management's orders and viewpoints to subordinates although perhaps unaware of how subordinates will perceive the communicated information.

It is believed that the logic of these orders will stimulate desired action. Some of the various channels available to carry the information downward are examined next.

Chain of Command

Orders and information can be given personally or in written fashion and transmitted from one level to another. This is the most frequently used channel and is appropriate on either an individual or a group basis.

The most common way in which communication flows downward is face-to-face interaction. Therefore, the subordinate, whether manager or worker, should become a good listener. Body language, voice tones, and other nonverbal signals are important. The junior person can usually ask questions to clarify the message. That person might hesitate to ask too many questions for fear of looking foolish, but failing to ask questions and then taking the wrong action will look even more foolish.

Written documents also provide a major means of downward communication through the chain of command. Letters and memoranda should be written with consideration for how they will be understood. Incorrect interpretations are frequent, however. Lower and middle managers may not have originated the confusing communication, but they can help subordinates understand any from upper management. The directive may require some translation into the language of subordinates.

Written communications should be used for matters that are extremely important to either the manager personally or the company. Relatively permanent information such as policies, procedures, and rules usually should be written. Also, managers should write communications that they suspect might otherwise be misunderstood.

Posters and Bulletin Boards

Information of concern to company employees is often communicated on posters and bulletin boards. Some workers may not read them, however. This is especially true when the posters or bulletins are not kept current. Information often remains on the board long after its usefulness has passed. Thus, this channel may be useful only as a supplementary device.

The House Organ

Many firms have company newsletters or newspapers, often referred to as house organs. The one at Holiday Corporation is called *Up Front,* suggesting a desire to communicate honestly. In addition, most large Holiday Inns have a management newsletter prepared locally. A great deal of information regarding the organization can be communicated in this way. Information about new products, how well the company is doing, and even policies is often contained in the newsletter. Readership is increased if some space is allocated to personal items of interest to employees. For instance, scores of the company bowling team or an award to a long-term employee might be mentioned.

Letters and Pay Inserts

Direct mail may be used when top management wants to communicate matters of importance. Since the letter is sent directly to the employee from the company, there is a reasonable chance that it will be read. Inserting a letter with the paycheck may also encourage readership. It at least ensures that each worker receives a copy. Typically, the worker is in a good mood because it is payday. Such letters also help to interest spouses of employees in company matters.

Employee Handbooks and Pamphlets

Handbooks frequently are used during the hiring and orientation process as an introduction to the organization. Too often, however, they are unread even when the firm demands a signed statement that the employee is acquainted with their contents. When special systems are being introduced, such as a pension plan or a job evaluation system, concise, well-illustrated pamphlets are often prepared to facilitate understanding and stimulate acceptance.

Annual Reports

Annual reports are increasingly written not only for the Holiday Corporation stockholders but also for the employees. A worker may be able to obtain information about the firm in this way. Information about new plants, new products, and company finances is often included. Holiday Corporation's annual reports always include a letter from the chief executive officer discussing the company's plans for the coming year and invariably mentioning the importance of employees to those plans. Every manager should review the annual report, even if it is not routinely distributed.

Loudspeaker Systems

The loudspeaker system is used not only for paging purposes but also to make announcements while they are "hot." Such systems can also be misused, as in the case of a certain company president who sent his greetings from his cool vacation place in the mountains to the hot, sweaty workers on the production floor.

*Like
a Good
Neighbor* State Farm has been the country's largest automobile insurer since 1942. Today, the company offers life, health, and fire coverage, in addition to automobile insurance, and has about 40 million policyholders represented by nearly 16,000 State Farm agents. The company employs more than 30,000 people in facilities throughout the United States and Canada, including 25 regional offices and corporate headquarters in Bloomington, Illinois. When the company was started in 1922, it had just one employee, the founder, George Mecherle, who claimed, "I reckon if I can sell one policy I can sell a million." He surely did not sell a million, but the company he founded has issued many times that number. As State Farm grew, the job of management became more and more complex.

The first concern of State Farm executives is the policyholders, who also are the company's owners since it is a mutual company rather than the more usual stock company. The devotion to policyholders was stated in the 1922 motto: "Service, Satisfaction, Safety, and Savings." Today the slogan is, "Like a good neighbor, State Farm is there." State Farm president,

Edward Rust, spells out the philosophy more clearly: "In every transaction, every encounter, every contact with the people we serve, we must do our best to see that the public's needs and wants are best served—first served." His predecessor, Adlai Rust, put it this way: "Whenever we serve ourselves but not our customer, we will in time serve no one. Whenever we put first the sure performance of our duty to the policyholders, we will surely succeed." In keeping with this philosophy, State Farm has been a leader in promoting plain talk, a trend toward writing legal documents, including insurance policies, in understandable language. Since there are no stockholders, profits in excess of the company's financial needs are paid out to policyholders in the form of dividends.

The second group State Farm executives must manage is the thousands of agents who stand between the company and its policyholders. Turnover among the agents is extremely low. And well it should be—they earn the highest average income in the industry. They are required to sell only State Farm policies. In exchange, though, they are given significant autonomy; an agent can pay small claims without checking with the company, for example.

The final group that must be managed, and the one toward which most companies direct their primary attention, is the internal work force. Aside from tight financial controls and constant pressure to live up to the "good neighbor" slogan, the company tries to promote a family feeling among its employees. Each one of them can expect a card and a rose on his or her birthday. "It sounds hokey, doesn't it," says one employee, "but the family feeling does exist."

The family feeling is reinforced by a better-than-average pay among major insurance companies, along with a full range of benefits. The company also provides excellent working conditions, informal management, and open communications. For example, at State Farm's largest regional office, in Jacksonville, Florida, when the work area recently became crowded, more space was added. Most of the workers and managers alike do their jobs in large, open areas with partitions installed only to separate the various divisions. The building is surrounded with neatly trimmed grass and shrubbery. Parking is ample, and the facility is located next to an interstate highway exit, providing easy access from every direction. In the entrance area is a rack with dozens of cards describing the many benefits available to State Farm workers and answering most of the common questions they have.[3]

Formal Upward Channels

Advocates of participative management have emphasized the establishment of upward channels of communication. This is necessary not only to determine if subordinates have understood the information that was sent downward but also to satisfy the need of subordinates to be involved. A communication effectiveness survey of thousands of employees showed that only half believed that significant upward communication was present. The others saw little chance of discussion or dialogue with upper management.[4] One purpose of the annual survey at Holiday Corporation is to locate such communication failures. An upward flow of information is also necessary if management is to coordinate the various activities of the organization. There are many channels from which to choose for the upward flow of information.

Open-Door Policy

An **open-door policy** is *an established guideline that allows workers to bypass immediate supervisors concerning substantive matters without fear of reprisal.* Managers are encouraged to create an environment in which subordinates will feel free to come to them with problems and recommendations. An open-door policy can go a long way toward reducing tension among subordinates and improving trust.

It is important that employees know of the open-door policy and believe management is sincere about it. One example of an effort to communicate commitment to an open-door policy occurred at Cabot Corporation's Satellite Division Plant. To test the plant manager's office heating unit, the maintenance man requested that the door be kept shut all of one day. The plant manager prepared a handwritten sign for the door. The sign read, "This door is closed because the heating unit is being worked on." The plant manager wanted to make sure that employees would not assume that the door was closed to keep them out.

The advantages of an open-door policy are well known, but the disadvantages should also be recognized. Managers often feel insecure when they know that subordinates can take complaints directly to upper managers. Often the first time a supervisor knows of a problem is when an upset upper manager calls. Also, an open-door policy may cost management time. Feeling obligated to stop work anytime a worker shows up at the door may make it hard to complete administrative tasks.

State Farm Insurance has a long-standing open-door policy. As at many other organizations, employees at State Farm are asked to work with their immediate supervisors to resolve problems. But they are assured that they can communicate with any manager in the company, right up to the president, on a confidential basis and with no fear of reprisals.

Suggestion Systems

Many companies have formal suggestion systems. Some have suggestion boxes. Others have "beneficial suggestion" forms that workers are encouraged to complete. At State Farm, the suggestion system is given a name, "Discovery." Employees whose suggestions are implemented are allowed to select gifts from the Discovery catalog.

When a suggestion system is used, every suggestion should receive careful consideration. Workers should be promptly informed of the results of the decision on each suggestion.

Questionnaires

Anonymous questionnaires sometimes are given to workers in an attempt to identify problem areas within the organization. The Holiday Corporation climate survey is an example. The survey includes every employee, right down to the maids and janitors, and attempts to identify both positive and negative perceptions regarding the company.

When a large number of workers rate the firm low in a given area, management should search for solutions. For instance, if a significant number of workers indicated dissatisfaction with pay, investigation is certainly warranted. Pay may actually be too low, or the workers may just be unaware of what other firms are paying. Whatever the case, the company should take some action, or workers' faith in the use of questionnaires may be lost.

The Grievance Procedure

A systematic process that permits employees to complain about matters affecting them is referred to as a grievance procedure. The **grievance procedure** is *a mechanism that gives subordinates the opportunity of carrying appeals beyond their immediate supervisors.* Most unions have negotiated formal grievance procedures. State Farm, although not unionized, has a written grievance procedure. This is the exception rather than the rule, however. One study showed that only 11 percent of a large group of nonunion firms had any kind of formal procedure for handling worker complaints.[5] When employees do not have avenues to voice their complaints, even small gripes may grow into major problems. Some managers believe that formal grievance procedures weaken their authority. Others see the grievance procedure as a way of keeping minor problems from becoming serious.

grievance procedure

Ombudsperson

The ombudsperson provides a means of resolving grievances in nonunion organizations. Ombudspersons have been used for some time in Europe, and the practice is becoming more popular in the United States. Ombudspersons act as top management's eyes and ears. An **ombudsperson** is *a complaint officer with access to top management who hears employee complaints, investigates, and sometimes recommends appropriate action.* Because of their access to top management, ombudspersons can often resolve problems swiftly. In many cases, the ombudsperson simply helps employees find people who can solve their problems. Sometimes ombudspersons recommend specific action to managers.

ombudsperson

Special Meetings

Special employee meetings to discuss particular company policies or procedures are sometimes scheduled by management to obtain employee feedback. The keystone of teamwork in the Pitney Bowes Company, for example, is monthly departmental meetings of all employees. In addition, a central employee council of thirteen employee representatives meets with top executives on a monthly basis. Employees on this main council are elected for two-year terms and devote time to investigating company problems and improving communication processes.

Exit Interviews

Informal Communication Channels

Informal communication channels are not included in the formal organization structure. If a manager has a problem that is affected by another department, the two managers involved may get together over coffee. When managers are at the same organizational level, such communication is known as

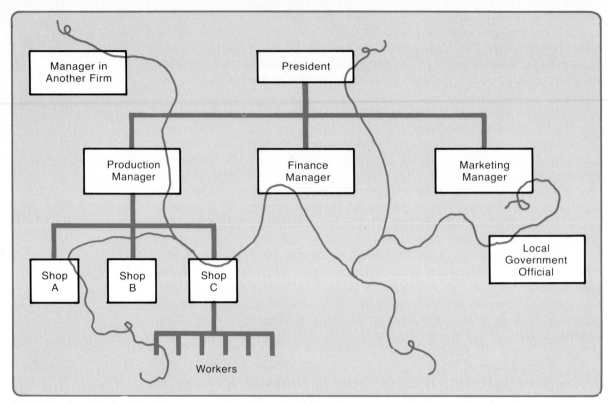

Figure 12–2   The Grapevine

lateral communication. This form of communication benefits from established personal relationships. Mutual trust must first develop, and this often takes time. But effective lateral communication can improve the productivity of both departments. Some companies provide for lateral communication as part of the formal organizational structure.

Another type of informal channel that bypasses the formal chain of command is diagonal communication. In diagonal communication, information is exchanged with those higher or lower in the organization but not directly in the formal chain of command. Again, this is not an automatic process. Trust must first develop. Care must be taken in using diagonal communication because immediate superiors might take offense. Used effectively, diagonal communication can be an important information source for the manager.

The grapevine is the informal communication system that exists in an organization but may extend beyond it. The grapevine does not respect formal lines of authority and often extends throughout an organization; however, it does get much of its information from the formal organization. It usually transmits this information more rapidly than the formal system although sometimes not as accurately. Employees generally rate the grapevine as one of the primary sources of current information.[6] A much simplified representation of the grapevine is shown in Figure 12–2.

The grapevine has four basic characteristics. First, it transmits information in every direction throughout the organization. Information on the grapevine can go down, up, laterally, and diagonally, all at the same time. It can connect organizational units that have very indirect formal relationships. Second, the grapevine transmits information rapidly. It is not restricted by any formal policies and procedures. The chain of command does not have to be followed. Once a message gets into the grapevine, it can move almost instantaneously to any point in the organization. Third, the grapevine is selective in who receives the information. Some people are tuned in to it and others are not. There are certain persons to whom even gossips do not talk. Consequently some managers are not even aware of the grapevine. Finally, the grapevine extends beyond the formal organization. Considerable communication about the firm occurs off the job. Workers may be at a party and pass on or receive information about the company. Note that Figure 12–2 shows the grapevine connecting to a manager in another company, as well as a government official. There are usually hundreds or even thousands of such connections.

Managers should not ignore the grapevine because it cannot be eliminated. Wise managers attempt to remain tuned in to the grapevine. Not only will they obtain useful information, but they will be able to replace incorrect messages with accurate information. The rack of information cards about company benefits mentioned in the State Farm story is designed to ensure that workers do not have to depend on the grapevine for such vital information. Undoubtedly cards on certain topics were developed after managers learned through the grapevine that there was confusion about those topics. The grapevine is a very important part of the communication process, even for enlightened companies like State Farm that try to make the formal communication system as effective as possible.

BARRIERS TO COMMUNICATION

Effective communication means that the receiver correctly interprets the message of the sender. Often this is not the case due to various breakdowns that can occur in communication. A survey of 32,000 employees in 26 organizations showed that only half of the employees thought that the organization's communications were accurate and candid, and two-thirds felt it to be incomplete.[7] If a manager tells an employee to "produce a few more parts" and the employee makes two but the manager wanted two hundred, a breakdown in communication certainly took place. If managers are to develop their communication ability, the manner in which communication breakdowns can occur must be fully understood.

As seen in Figure 12–3, successful management decisions must pass through the bottleneck, or barriers of communication, if organizational goals are to be achieved. If the barriers are excessive, communication may be reduced to the point where the firm's objectives cannot be achieved. Barriers may be classified as technical, language, or psychological. Each of these is discussed below.

Technical Barriers

Environmental barriers to communication are referred to as technical breakdowns. Timing, information overload, and cultural differences are three such barriers.

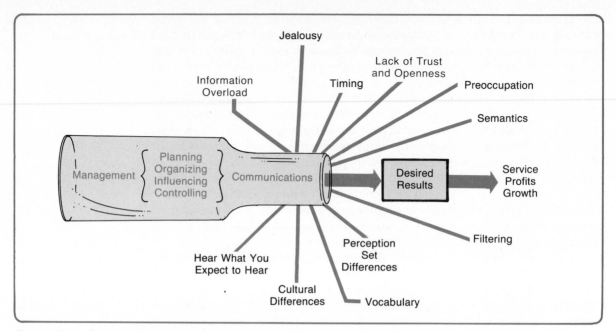

Figure 12–3 Successful Management Decisions Must Pass Through the "Bottleneck" or Barriers to Communications Prior to Achieving Desired Results

Timing

timing

The *determination of when a message should be communicated* is referred to as **timing**. It is often quite important for a manager to determine the most appropriate time to transmit a message. For instance, a manager who must reprimand a worker for excessive tardiness would likely want to speak with the worker as soon as possible after the event occurred. The worker would likely have forgotten the event if, say, six months passed before the reprimand was made.

Information Overload

information overload

With the many channels and media available, as well as the changed philosophy toward a greater sharing of information, it is little wonder that information overload occurs. **Information overload** is *a condition that exists when an individual is presented with too much information in too short a time.* A person can absorb only so many facts and figures at a time. When excessive information is provided, a major breakdown in communication can occur.

As a professor, one of the authors experienced information overload in a classroom. The course was a statistics class that met one day a week for four hours. For the first hour, students were eager to take notes. Progressing toward the fourth hour, few students could tell another person what the instructor had said. Information overload had occurred. Some students have discovered that their grades suffer when they attempt to take all of their classes in the morning on Monday, Wednesday, and Friday. By the end of the last class, many of the students have no idea what the teacher has said, and their grades suffer.

Cultural Differences

Cultural differences can also cause a breakdown in communication. In the United States, time is a highly valuable commodity, and a deadline suggests urgency. But in the Middle East, giving another person a deadline is considered rude, and the deadline is likely to be ignored. If a client is kept waiting in the outer office for thirty minutes in the United States, the delay may mean that a person has low status. In Latin America, a thirty-minute wait is common. If a contract offer has not been acted on in this country over a period of several months or a year, an American might conclude that the other party has lost interest. In Japan, long delays mean no slackening of interest, and delay is often a negotiation tactic known to be effective in dealing with impatient Americans.

Americans conduct most business at an interpersonal interval of from five to eight feet; a distance of one to three feet suggests more personal or intimate undertakings. The normal business distance in Latin America is closer to the personal distance of the United States. Thus, we observe the highly interesting communication difficulties of a back-pedaling North American as his or her Latin American counterpart presses ever closer. Regarding status symbols, a manager's office in the United States that is spacious, well furnished, and located on the top floor conveys meanings of high prestige. In the Middle East, size and decor of office mean little or nothing, and in France, the manager is likely to be located in the midst of subordinates in order to control them.

Language Barriers

Language problems can result from the vocabulary used and from different meanings being applied to the same word (semantics).

Vocabulary

A manager must understand the type of audience being addressed. Statisticians, skilled mechanics, and ditch diggers have different vocabulary sets. Words that the statistician might fully understand have little meaning to ditch diggers, and vice-versa. Breakdowns in communication often occur when the sender does not tailor the message to match the knowledge base of the receiver. This problem is most severe when someone deliberately uses fancy words just to seem more knowledgeable.

Certain words are part of practically every person's vocabulary. Figure 12–4 illustrates these as the common vocabulary base. We have arbitrarily shown these as having difficulty levels from 0–4 on a scale of 10. If we speak using words of level 4 or less, both the statistician and the ditch digger will understand. As we progress above this base level, more and more people will be unable to comprehend the message. If the statistician uses words above the scale of 6, communication with the skilled mechanic is lost. Naturally, there will be times when higher-level words must be used to communicate a technical concept, but if managers can concentrate their messages in the common vocabulary base, they have a much better chance of being understood.

Two systems for measurement of reading ease are the fog index developed by the late Robert Gunning and the Flesch system developed by

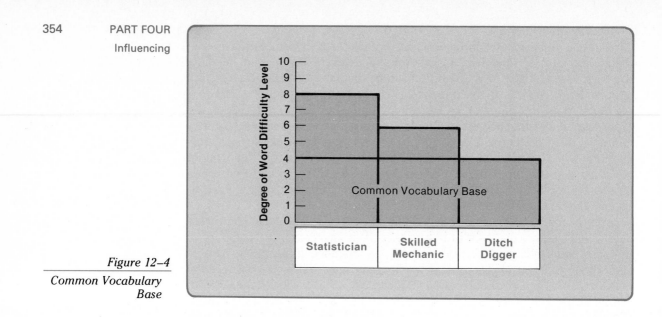

Figure 12–4

Common Vocabulary Base

Rudolph Flesch. The purpose of the fog index is to determine the reading level of a manuscript. Assume that you wish to evaluate something you have written using the fog index. A score of 10 would mean that tenth graders can understand what you write.[8] The Flesch system helps you determine whether your writing is interesting to read. Of course, there is more to communication than can be revealed by counting syllables and sentence lengths. Each communicator must have a clear and coherent grasp of the idea he or she hopes to transmit. The Flesch and Gunning indexes merely aid the writer in keeping the audience in mind. The efforts that State Farm has made in developing "plain talk" insurance policies are based on this principle.

Semantics

When a sender sends words to which a receiver attaches different meanings than those intended by the sender, a semantic—or meaning of words—communication breakdown has occurred. A major difficulty with the English language is that multiple meanings may be attached to a word, for instance, the word *charge*. A manager may place an employee *in charge* of a section. The company *charges* for its services. A person gets a *charge* out of a humorous story. When two individuals attach different meanings to a word, a breakdown in communication can occur.

The use of jargon can also create a barrier to communication. Virtually every industry develops certain jargon that is used in everyday business. The statistician, computer programmer, typist, or ditch digger likely develops expressions peculiar to his or her specific profession. When speaking to an individual not associated with the trade jargon, a breakdown in communication may occur. It is likely for this reason that many firms provide new personnel with a list and definition of terms associated with the particular industry.

Psychological Barriers

Although technical factors and semantic differences are credited with causing breakdowns in communication, psychological barriers tend to be the major reasons for miscommunication and communication breakdowns. These include various forms of distortion and problems involving interpersonal relationships.

Information Filtering

Information filtering refers to *the process by which a message is altered through the elimination of certain data as the communication moves from person to person in the organization.* Managers often discover that information that has been provided them by subordinates has been filtered. As subordinates contribute information to superiors, they know that it will be used for at least two purposes: (1) to aid management in controlling and directing the firm (and therefore the worker) and (2) to evaluate the worth of their performance. Managers at all levels are tempted to filter information as it progresses up the chain of command. Even the president may filter information before it goes to the board of directors.

information filtering

Because the data have been filtered, an incorrect impression of the true situation may occur. There have been many managerial attempts to reduce both the number and thickness of the authority filters that clog organization communication channels. It should be apparent that decentralization reduces the number of levels of authority within the organization. One organization reduced the number of managerial levels from eight to four, with a consequent speeding up of the communication process. Such reorganizations are drastic and require considerable efforts in the area of retraining and establishing realistic control standards.

A consultant can serve as a means of reducing communication filters. In one company, there was a steady decrease in productivity for no reason that could be identified by management. The consultant systematically interviewed all employees over a six-month period. The results of these many interviews indicated strong feelings on the part of many employees that work standards were too high, that older employees resented the high wage scales of the new employees, and that temporary transfers to new jobs to avoid layoff were widely resented. In each case, management had felt that it had communicated effectively its intent to the employees.

Lack of Trust and Openness

Openness and trust on the part of managers and employees must exist if orderly changes in the organization are to occur. When employees feel that openness and trust do not exist, barriers to communication are present. The open-door policy at State Farm can be effective only if workers believe the company's promise of confidentiality and lack of reprisals when they bypass the chain of command.

If employees perceive the manager as being open and receptive to ideas, feedback is encouraged. Managers need this feedback to do their job, as was illustrated in Figure 12–1. On the other hand, if managers give the impression that their orders should never be questioned, communication tends to be stifled.

One of the major factors in the success of Japanese businesses is said to be that managers trust not only their workers but also their peers and superiors. As a result, a simpler organizational structure than in the United States is possible. Toyota, for example, has only six levels of management between a factory worker and the chief executive; Ford Motor Company has eleven. These many layers cause high overhead and much red tape. Japanese firms assume that personnel at all levels are trustworthy, and they do not have to employ highly paid executives to review the work of other highly paid executives.[9]

Jealousy

It is perhaps a difficult lesson for a manager to learn, but everyone may not be pleased by successful performance. Competency and effective performance may actually be viewed as a threat to the security of peers and superiors. Individuals may attempt to minimize the accomplishments of another person because they are jealous. If the jealous person is able to gain the attention of upper management, there is a possibility that when you attempt to communicate, a "less receptive ear" may be present. Because of jealousy, the effectiveness of the communication may be reduced.

Preoccupation

Some people are so preoccupied with themselves they may listen in such a way that they hear little or none of the message. Preoccupation may cause a person to respond in a certain rather predictable manner even though it is an inappropriate response. A New York columnist tells the story of attending a party at a well-known socialite's home. The socialite was famous for being so preoccupied with making a favorable impression on her guests that she did not listen to what the guests said. The columnist decided to play a trick on the socialite, so he deliberately came late to one of her parties. As he entered, he gave this explanation of being late: "I'm sorry to be late, but I killed my wife this evening and had a difficult time stuffing her body into the trunk of my car." The charming hostess beamed and said, "Well, darling, the important thing is that you have arrived; now the party can really begin."

We Hear What We Expect to Hear

Like preoccupation, most of us are often conditioned in the communication process to hear what we expect to hear, not what is actually said. Because of past experiences, we have developed a concept of what will be said. At times we hear what we want to hear. An employee who has been reprimanded quite a few times by a certain supervisor may even interpret a compliment by the manager as a negative statement.

Perception Set Differences

perception set

A **perception set** is *a fixed tendency to interpret information in a certain way.* Differences in past experiences, educational background, emotions, values, and beliefs—to name just a few—affect each person's perception of a message or of words. The word *management,* for example, may provoke an entirely different image in the minds of two persons, one of whom's parents have been managers while the other's have been labor union organizers. Perception set differences even affect the meanings of words like *chair, pencil,* and *hat,* which represent tangible objects. The impact is clearly much greater for such terms as *liberal* and *conservative.*

CHAPTER 12   357
Communications

FACILITATORS TO COMMUNICATION

Once it is recognized that breakdowns in communication can occur, a manager is in a position to work toward improving communication ability. The major factor that should be remembered is that communication is learned. If persons truly desire to improve their communication ability, there are means available to assist in this undertaking. Empathy, listening, reading skills, observation, word choice, body language, actions, and transactional analysis will be discussed as facilitators to communication in the following sections.

Empathy

You have likely heard the expression, "I see where you are coming from." When statements such as that are made, empathy is being expressed. **Empathy** is *the ability to identify with the various feelings and thoughts of another person.* It does not mean that you necessarily agree with the other person, but while you are with the individual, you can appreciate why that person speaks and acts in a certain way. If a person is bitter, you are able to relate to this bitterness; if scared, you understand this fear.

empathy

Taken in its broadest meaning, an empathetic person is communicating. For this reason managers should take the time to understand as much as possible about the people whom they must work with daily. With this information, the manager is in a much better position to understand why people act as they do. The manager may not agree with the individual, but if the time is taken to understand the reason for certain action, problems may more easily be resolved.

Listening

One of the most effective tools managers have at their disposal to facilitate communication is the ability to listen. A person who is constantly talking is not listening or learning. Listening assists a manager in discovering problems and determining solutions to problems.

Communication cannot take place unless messages are received and understood by the other party. It has been observed that the average speaking speed is 120 words per minute. One is able to listen more than four times as rapidly. The question therefore arises, What does the listener do with the free time that results from this difference in speeds?

At least three types of listening have been identified: marginal, evaluative, and projective. The speed of listening provides the opportunity for marginal listening, a dangerous type that can lead to misunderstanding of and even insult to the speaker. For instance, most of us have experienced a situation where we have been speaking to someone, but we know that the person's mind is a million miles away. The individual may occasionally hear some words, but the majority of the message was not understood.

Evaluative listening requires the second party to allocate full attention to the speaker. The excess time is devoted to evaluating and judging the nature of the remarks heard. Often we are forming rebuttal remarks while the sender is still speaking, thus moving into a type of marginal listening. As soon as the sender says something that is not accepted, communication ceases and the receiver begins to develop a response in his or her own mind. Thoughts such as, "This person does not know what he is talking about. I was in Vietnam and I know the way it was," can significantly reduce, or even eliminate, the communication process. Instead of one idea being transmitted and held by two people, we often end up with two ideas, neither of which is really communicated to the other. If the listener allocated too much time to disapproving or approving of what is heard, it is doubtful whether he or she has the time to understand fully. This is particularly true when the remarks are loaded with emotion or concern over the security and status of the receiver.

Active or nonevaluative listening holds the greatest potential for effective communication. Listeners fully utilize their time by attempting to project themselves into the position of the speaker and understand what is being said from the speaker's viewpoint. We should first listen without evaluation. After feeling that we understand what has been said, we can then evaluate what has been said. Rogers suggested a rule to be followed to ensure some degree of projective listening: "Each person can speak for himself only *after* he has related the ideas and feelings of the previous speaker accurately and to that speaker's satisfaction."[10] There is no need to agree with the statements, but there is a need to understand them as the speaker intended. Only in this way is it possible to frame a reply that will actually respond to the speaker's remarks. Effective listening is empathic listening. It requires an ability to listen for feeling as well as for words. The person attempts to place himself or herself in the "shoes of the other person."

Reading Skills

Reading skills have received great attention in our society. The amount of written material a manager must cover has increased significantly, and some attempt should first be made to consolidate and reduce it. However, the ability to read rapidly and with understanding is an essential communication skill, particularly in larger organizations. It has been found that reading speeds can be doubled and tripled with little or no loss in comprehension.

Observation

As in the case of listening, there are too few attempts to increase skill in observation outside of training for law enforcement. Most of us have heard reports where there were many witnesses to a traffic accident. When the police arrived and questioned the witnesses, there were many different versions to what actually occurred. "The blue car went through the stop light," said one witness. "No, that is not correct," said another. "The light was green." Most people miss a great deal by not carefully observing important elements in the environment. It was mentioned earlier that some managers are very adept at assessing the general atmosphere of an organization by merely strolling through its workplaces. Observation of furnishings, housekeeping, dress of personnel, and activities can convey much information. Using our powers of observation to supplement listening and reading will add immeasurably to our understanding of what is actually transpiring.

Word Choice

There is a certain threshold of words that virtually everyone can understand. Managers who desire to communicate effectively must make certain that the choice of the words transmitted by the sender is in the vocabulary set of the receiver. Generally, simple or common words provide the best means through which communication is accomplished. This is the basis of State Farm's "plain talk" insurance policies.

Body Language

Most subordinates do not have to be told when their boss is displeased with them. A frown or arms crossed and not smiling may communicate this message clearly. **Body language** is defined as *a nonverbal method of communication in which physical actions such as motions, gestures, and facial expressions convey thoughts and emotions.*

body language

Appreciation of the importance of understanding of body language in the communication process is also quite important for a manager. All people—managers, superiors, and subordinates—give off unintentional signals that can provide significant insight into the exact meaning that a person is attempting to communicate. The manager particularly must be constantly aware of the signals that he or she is presenting. Employees grasp at these small symbols to determine what the "boss" means. A frown, even though the words were positive in nature, may be taken wrong. A sarcastic smile when "you did a good job" was mentioned will not likely be interpreted to mean that the worker actually did a good job. A blank stare may mean to the employee that the manager is not interested.

A manager must also be aware of the signals that a subordinate may be giving off. Sweaty hands or nail biting in the presence of the supervisor may mean that the worker feels ill at ease. Managers need to recognize these signs and be prepared to adjust their action.

Most nonverbal signals are given subconsciously. Hence it takes more effort to change the traditional signals. Such signals may be particularly hard to change for women. In today's corporate environment, women have risen from the level of secretaries, but studies show that unconscious communications with their male counterparts still tend to say that their status is lower than for male managers in similar positions.[11]

Actions

The manager must also recognize that one communicates by what one does or does not do. If a person comes to work one day and finds his desk moved from a location in a private office to one in an open area, communication of a sort has taken place. If no verbal explanation accompanies the action, people with interpret it their own way; the missing symbol or signal will be supplied by the observer. And despite any verbal statement to the contrary, such a move will likely be interpreted as a demotion for the person.

In one company, management had introduced a change in procedure for a small crew of employees. The new method was timed, and piece rates were established. None of the personnel produced more than half of the standard amount and were therefore on a time-wage basis rather than piece rates. They all filed grievances protesting the unfairness of the standard. Management tried everything it could think of to correct the problem, from all-day time studies to providing each employee with a private instructor in the new method. A check on similar jobs in other companies revealed that the standard was in line. Thus, management concluded that a concerted work restriction was involved.

The next move was one of communication by *action*. An engineer was sent to the production department, and he proceeded to measure various angles and spaces on the floor. He volunteered no information to the group. Finally, one man's curiosity got the best of him, and he asked the engineer what he was doing. The engineer indicated that management wanted to see if there was sufficient room to locate certain machinery that could do the work of this crew. He continued about his business of measuring. The next day, all work crew members were producing amounts well above the established standard.

Transactional Analysis

With transactional analysis (TA) there are three ego states that are constantly present and at work within each individual: the Parent, the Adult, and the Child.[12] The manner in which individual ego states interact can have a significant effect upon interpersonal relations and an organization's effectiveness.

Parent

The Parent ego state may take on the characteristic of being either the Nurturing or the Negative Parent. When the Nurturing Parent dominates, the person gives praise and recognition, comfort in time of distress, and reassurance in time of need. Statements such as "you have done a good job" or "I am certain the problem will work out all right" might be associated with the Nurturing Parent. The Negative Parent is overcontrolling, suffocating, critical, and oppressive. Comments such as "women should be seen and not heard" or "be careful, you can hurt yourself with the knife" might be associated with the Negative Parent. When the Negative Parent dominates, the person tends to lecture, believes that his or her moral standard is best for everyone, and often will not accept other ideas.

Child

The Child may take on the characteristics of the Natural Child, the Little Professor, or the Adaptive Child. The Natural Child is spontaneous, impulsive, untrained, expressive, self-centered, affectionate, and curious.

The Little Professor tends to be intuitive, manipulative, and creative. The Adaptive Child tends to react in a way determined by parental figures.

Adult

A person who tends to evaluate the situation and attempts to make decisions based on information and facts is in the Adult ego state. No emotions are involved, and the individual tends to function like a computer, with all decisions based on logic.

The interaction of ego states can have a significant impact on behavior in organizations. The manager must recognize that a person will not always be in the Adult state and make decisions based entirely on logic. In fact, the greatest amount of creativity is associated with the Child. Also, the manager will be able to recognize when communication is impossible. For instance, the manager who is in the Adult state may attempt to speak to the Adult of the employee. The Child state of the employee returns the conversation to the Parent of the manager. The following conversation is given to illustrate such a communication problem.

Manager: This task needs to be completed today.

Employee: Why are you always pushing me to work harder?

Communication has broken down because the employee is not addressing the problem that the manager was attempting to communicate.

Managers should also be aware of the ego state that they themselves are speaking from. If the state is properly interpreted, managers will recognize and possibly change their actions. Should you recognize that you are in one state and an employee is in a state that precludes effective communication, it may be best to postpone discussion. For instance, if the manager is in the Child state and the employee is in the Adult state, communication may be postponed. The employee who is in the Adult state is serious about work at this time and may misinterpret joking remarks.

Applying TA concepts on a broad basis may prove valuable in producing desired organizational change. As individuals in a firm learn to analyze their own social interactions, better communication and greater organizational effectiveness can occur.

EFFECTS OF NEW TECHNOLOGIES

As a consequence of the electronic revolution, communication methods in today's organizations are rapidly changing. Information processing is becoming more and more automated. Word processors, microcomputers, minicomputers, and mainframe computers are common equipment. New developments in telecommunication and video technology have also contributed to changes. One reason for the electonics explosion is the tumbling cost of technology. The insurance industry in particular has become dependent on computers. The typical State Farm regional office has its own mainframe with many terminals. The regional systems are tied together with State Farm's central computer in a massive network that provides for virtually instantaneous communication throughout the company. At some offices, State Farm has introduced a computer-controlled robot, which delivers and picks up mail.

Read Brugger/The Picture Cube

As a consequence of the electronics revolution, communication methods in today's organizations are rapidly changing.

Company video, or "private television," has had its ups and downs since the late 1960s. Now, though, the problems caused by lack of standardization and compatibility between components have largely been overcome. With the advent of the videocassette in 1972, video has become an inexpensive alternative for communication. Increasing numbers of managers are turning to this medium for information dissemination.[13] Since many persons are accustomed to, and even prefer, getting information through television, more emphasis is being placed on using video for transmitting corporate information. This medium "puts the face behind the memo."[14] Private television breaks through communication barriers and delivers the message straight, with no editing by intermediate managers and less chance of misunderstanding.

Converging technologies in data and word processing, voice and data communications, networking, electronic mail, and computer graphics have made communications more effective and efficient. Large data bases within management information systems (MIS) have speeded up data processing and information flows.[15] Communication networks connect various office machines together, making possible instantaneous electronic transfers of messages, images, and data. Contrasted with traditional communication processes, these devices are fast and convenient, and they integrate a variety of communication tasks. "Information democracy"—equal access to information by all organizational members—is arriving as larger numbers of on-line terminals are installed in corporations.[16]

A new development, combining video and computer and telecommunication technologies, is teleconferencing. Uses of teleconferencing run from the simple speakerphone to satellite-transmitted video.[17] The middle part of this spectrum, audiographics, combines graphics-oriented visual displays with vocal teleconferencing facilities to provide the opportunity for multisite dialogues.[18]

As computer hardware and software become more sophisticated, the machines are becoming more cost-effective and user friendly. Fewer skills are required to use the latest systems, facilitating their adoption.

A new technology on the horizon is artificial intelligence (AI). AI computers have been developed to think and learn somewhat as human beings do. Expert systems are computers that can draw highly specialized conclusions from huge stores of data, much like the human brain does. Scientists predict their increasing use in routine management tasks.[19]

SUMMARY

Communication is the transfer of information, ideas, understanding, or feelings between people. The source (sender) is the person who has an idea or message to communicate to another person or persons. When communication is attempted, messages are transmitted through such means as speaking, writing, acting, and drawing. A number of channels may be used to transmit the message. The receiver of the message must decode it by converting the symbols into meaning. Communication effectiveness is determined to the extent that the receiver's decoding matches the sender's encoding.

There are numerous channels of communication through which a manager transmits information. Downward channels provide means through which management's orders and viewpoints are transmitted to subordinates. Upward channels provide means through which subordinates can communicate with their superiors. Informal communication channels are ways of transmitting information within an organization that bypass formal channels.

Effective communication often is not achieved because of various breakdowns that can affect the communication process. Barriers may cause communication to be reduced to the point that the firm's objectives cannot be achieved. Barriers may

be classified as technical, language, or psychological. Technical barriers include improper timing, communication overload, and cultural differences. Language barriers result when different meanings are applied to the same word. Psychological barriers include various forms of distortion and problems involving interpersonal relationships.

Although there are many barriers to communication, there are means available to eliminate or reduce these breakdowns. The use of empathy and the development of good listening skills can facilitate the communication process. In addition, reading and observation skills as well as making better choices of words can aid the manager in better communication with employees. Studying transactional analysis and developing the ability to read body language have been used to improve a manager's ability to communicate.

As a consequence of the electronic revolution, communication methods in today's organizations are rapidly changing. Information processing is becoming more and more automated with the use of word processors, microcomputers, minicomputers, and mainframe computers, as well as new developments in telecommunication and video technology. One reason for the electronics explosion is the tumbling cost of the technology.

1. Define communication. Describe the basic communication process.

2. Distinguish by definition between formal and informal channels of communication. Provide examples of both types of channels of communication.

3. What is meant by the phrase *barriers to communication?* Distinguish among technical, language, and psychological barriers.

4. List the topics that have been identified as facilitators to communication.

5. Explain how empathy may be used to assist a person to become a better listener.

6. What is transactional analysis? How can it be used as a facilitator?

7. What has been the effect of new technologies on the communication process?

EXERCISES

1. Over a twenty-four-hour period, identify factors and situations that created barriers to communication. Attempt to secure at least one example of each of the barriers to communication identified in this text. What facilitators of communication could have been used to reduce these barriers to effective communication?

2. This is an exercise regarding observation skills. With one of your classmates, go to the window and observe what is occurring outside for ten seconds. Each of you will now write down what you saw. After completing the list, compare your list with your partner's list. Compare the differences.

CASE STUDY

A Failure to Communicate

"Could you come to my office for a minute, Bob?" asked Terry Geech, the plant manager. "Sure, be right there," said Bob Glemson. Bob was the plant's quality control director. He had been with the company for four years. After completing his degree in mechanical engineering, he worked as a production supervisor and then as maintenance manager, prior to promotion to his present job. Bob thought he knew what the call was about.

"Your letter of resignation catches me by surprise," began Terry. "I know that Wilson Products will be getting a good man, but we sure need you here, too." "I thought about it a lot," said Bob, "but there just doesn't seem to be a future for me here." "Why do you say that?" asked Terry. "Well," replied Bob, "the next position above mine is yours. With you only thirty-nine, I don't think it's likely that you'll be leaving soon."

"The fact is that I am leaving soon," said Terry. "That's why it's even more of a shock to know that you are resigning. I think I'll be moving to the corporate offices in June of next year. Besides, the company has several plants that are larger than this one. We need good people in those plants from time to time, both in quality control and in general management."

"Well, I heard about an opening in the Cincinnati plant last year," said Bob, "but by the time I checked, the job had already been filled. We never know about job opportunities in the other plants until we read about them in the company paper."

"All this is beside the point now. What would it take to get you to change your mind?" asked Terry. "I don't think I can change my mind now," replied Bob. "I've already signed a contract with Wilson."

1. Evaluate the communication system at this company.
2. What actions might have prevented Bob's resignation?

CASE STUDY

A Management Trainee in Trouble

Miriam Impson went to work with Centurian Electric Company two weeks after she graduated from Michigan State University. Centurian, though relatively unknown to the general public, is one of the nation's largest manufacturers of electric transformers and generators. The company is headquartered in Detroit, with branch offices in a number of cities. Miriam was one of two hundred management trainees Centurian hired that year and one of fifteen trainees who were to be prepared for branch office management.

During the preliminary two weeks of training at corporate headquarters in Detroit, Miriam learned that she was to develop competence in the following areas: shipping and receiving, inventory control, purchasing, personnel, production, order service, and outside sales. In addition to on-the-job experience in these areas, the branch manager trainees were to return to Detroit four times a year for a week of classroom instruction. During that time, they were also expected to compare notes and review individual progress with members of upper management.

Miriam was assigned to the Indianapolis branch and was placed under the direct supervision of Jerry Mundy, the branch manager. Mr. Mundy, fifty-eight, had been with Centurian for thirty-seven years, having joined the company at the end of World War II. He had not attended college but had worked his way up and believed this way of making it into management provided better training than the company's one-year rotation program. After Miriam's arrival she was assigned to perform a number of jobs in the branch but not according to the planned program. She was asked to fill in as needed and found herself doing mostly clerical work. In the first three months, she never got out of shipping and receiving.

When Miriam returned to headquarters for the first one-week training session, she discussed her problem with the coordinator of management training and development, James Simpson. Mr. Simpson assured Miriam that he would check into the matter and attempt to make sure that she was properly prepared for her future management job.

When Miriam returned to the branch, Mr. Mundy reprimanded her for "putting him on report." The conversation proceeded as follows:

Mr. Mundy: "Miriam, you work for me. At least as long as you are at this branch. If you have anything negative to say, you should say it to me, not to Simpson. Why did you do that?"

Miriam: "I don't know. I guess I was just frustrated with the training I've received."

Mr. Mundy: "You're just like a lot of young college graduates. You think your degree should entitle you to special treatment. Well, I'm sorry. But in my book it doesn't mean a thing."

Miriam: "I understand. What do you want me to do now?"

Mr. Mundy: "Go back to work and don't cause any more trouble."

QUESTIONS

1. What do you believe Miriam should do now?
2. Was Miriam out of order in talking with Mr. Simpson? Should Mr. Simpson have contacted Mr. Mundy? Explain your answer.

3. Discuss how communications might have broken down, if you believe they did, between Mr. Mundy and the headquarter's staff.

NOTES

1. This story is a composite from a number of sources, including: *Holiday Inns, Inc. 1983 Annual Report;* "Holiday Inns Woos Budget Travelers," *Business Week* (December 26, 1983): 34; Barbara Etorre, "Leisure," *Forbes* (January 2, 1984): 235–236; numerous company press releases; and articles in *The Wall Street Journal.*

2. M. L. Fahs, "Communication Strategies for Anticipating and Managing Conflict," *Personnel Administrator* (October 1982): 28–34.

3. Lisa Grose, "The Hook," *Forbes* (November 8, 1982): 110–111; John R. Dorfman, "Insurance," *Forbes* (January 3, 1983): 80–82; "1983, A Great Year in All Lines," *Reflector* (February 1984): 4–8; "200 Leading Property/Casualty Companies and Groups," *Best's Review—Property/Casualty* (June 1983): 12–14; "Allocation of Assets," *Best's Review—Property/Casualty* (October 1983): 10; "1983 Report to Policyholders," State Farm Mutual Automobile Insurance Company.

4. R. Foltz and R. D'Aprix, "Survey Shows Communication Problems," *Personnel Administrator* (February 1983): 8.

5. Wilson G. Scott, *The Management of Conflict: Appeal Systems in Organizations* (Homewood, Ill.: Richard D. Irwin, 1977): 56–80.

6. Foltz and D'Aprix, "Survey."

7. Ibid.

8. Robert Gunning, "How to Improve Your Writing," *Factory Management and Maintenance* 110 (June 1952): 134.

9. "Trust: The New Ingredient in Management," *Business Week* (July 6, 1981): 104.

10. Carl R. Rogers and F. J. Roethlisberger, "Barriers and Gateways to Communication," *Harvard Business Review* 30 (July–August 1952): 48.

11. L. R. Cohen, "Minimizing Communication Breakdown between Male and Female Managers," *Personnel Administrator* (October 1982): 57–58.

12. For an expanded coverage of transactional analysis, see Thomas A. Harris, *I'm O.K.—You're O.K.* (New York: Harper, 1969).

13. J. M. Brush and D. P. Brush, "Companies Tune in to Video," *Management World* (January 1984): 25.

14. Ibid.

15. P. F. Calise and M. Locke, "Office Automation: Who's in Control?" *Management World* (March 1984): 17.

16. Z. K. Quible and R. A. Ankerman, "Office Connections," *Management World* (December 1983): 31.

17. Ibid.

18. L. G. A. Graham, "Audiographics for Sound Teleconferencing," *Computer World* (September 28, 1983): 63.

19. "Artificial Intelligence Is Here," *Business Week* (July 9, 1984): 54.

REFERENCES

Allen, T. H. "Communication Networks: The Hidden Organizational Chart." *Personnel Administrator* 21 (September 1976): 31–35.

"Artificial Intelligence Is Here." *Business Week* (July 9, 1984): 54.

Brush, J. M., and D. P. Brush. "Companies Tune in to Video." *Management World* (January 1984): 25.

Calise, P. F., and M. Locke. "Office Automation: Who's in Control?" *Management World* (March 1984): 17.

Davis, Keith. "Cut Those Rumors Down to Size." *Supervisory Management* 20 (June 1975): 2–6.

Deutsch, A. R. "Does Your Company Practice Affirmative Action in Its Communication?" *Harvard Business Review* 54 (November–December 1976): 16.

Donath, Bob. "Corporate Communications." *Industrial Marketing* 65 (July 1980): 52–53.

Ewing, David W., and Pamela M. Banks. "Listening and Responding to Employees' Concerns." *Harvard Business Review* 58 (January–February 1980): 101–114.

Foltz, Roy G. "Internal Communications, Give Them Facts." *Public Relations Journal* 36 (October 1980): 25.

Gildea, Joyce A., and Myron Emanuel. "Internal Communications: The Impact on Productivity." *Public Relations Journal* 36 (February 1980): 8–12.

Graham, L. G. A. "Audiographics for Sound Teleconferencing." *Computer World* (September 28, 1983): 63.

Hargreaves, J. "Six Keys to Good Communications." *International Management* 31 (December 1976): 54–56.

Huseman, R. C. "Managing Change through Communication." *Personnel Journal* 57 (January 1978): 20–25.

Kikoski, John F. "Communication: Understanding It, Improving It." *Personnel Journal* 59 (February 1980): 126.

Laing, G. J. "Communication and Its Constraints on the Structure of Organizations." *Omega* 8 (1980): 287–301.

Leavitt, Harold J. *Managerial Psychology.* 2d ed. Chicago: University of Chicago Press, 1964.

Levine, Edward. "Let's Talk: Breaking Down Barriers to

Effective Communication." *Supervisory Management* 25 (August 1980): 3–12.

Lewis, Carl B. "How to Make Internal Communication Work." *Public Relations Journal* 36 (February 1980): 14–17.

McMaster, J. B. "Getting the Word to the Top." *Management Review* 68 (February 1979): 62–65.

Miles, James M. "How to Establish a Good Industrial Relations Climate." *Management Review* 67 (August 1980): 42–44.

Muchinsky, P. M. "Organizational Communication: Relationships to Organizational Climate and Job Satisfaction." *Academy of Management Journal* 20 (December 1977): 592–607.

Quible, Z. K., and R. A. Ankerman. "Office Connections." *Management World* (December 1983): 31.

Roberts, Karlene H., and Charles A. O'Reilly III. "Failures in Upward Communication in Organizations: Three Possible Culprits." *Academy of Management Journal* 17 (June 1974): 205–215.

Schlachtmeyer, Albert, and F. Halperin. "Criteria-Based Planning for Employee Communication." *Personnel Administrator* 24 (August 1979): 77–81.

Schuler, Randall S. "Effective Use of Communication to Minimize Employee Stress." *Personnel Administrator* 22 (June 1979): 40–44.

Tavernier, Gerard. "Improving Managerial Productivity: The Key Ingredient Is One-on-One Communication." *Management Review* 70 (February 1981): 13–16.

LEARNING OBJECTIVES

After completing this chapter you should be able to

1. Explain the concept of corporate culture and describe the factors that determine it.

2. Describe a participative climate and identify the values and limitations of participation.

3. Identify and describe the change sequence and relate sources of resistance to change and the approaches that can be used in reducing resistance to change.

4. Describe the organizational development techniques that are available to implement change.

5. Explain the causes of stress management and executive burnout.

6. Define conflict and list the various techniques for dealing with it.

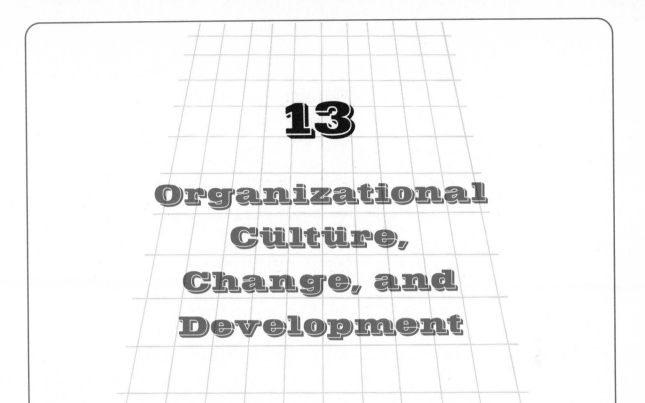

13

Organizational Culture, Change, and Development

IBM was featured as an excellently managed company in the landmark book *In Search of Excellence* published in 1982. The authors credited IBM's corporate culture with much of the company's success. The main elements of that culture are a service orientation, conservative dress, incentive-type compensation, internal competition among employees, and new ideas. Most of these principles have been reasonably constant for several decades, having grown out of the personal philosophies of Thomas J. Watson, who became president of IBM in 1914.

IBM purposely initiated radical change in the early 1980s. Writing about the "lean, mean new IBM," *Fortune* reports,

Competitors have felt the ground tremble. Their nemesis from Armonk [Armonk, New York, where IBM is headquartered] has revolutionized the way it does business, from grand strategy to the finest tactical detail, and has emerged a tougher opponent than ever before. IBM now speeds products to market faster than in the past, attacks its rivals with unprecedented price cuts and outraces competitors to emerging new businesses. . . . To its old motto "Think," IBM seems to have appended the word "Differently."

Since 1981, IBM has started fourteen new companies that can more or less independently seek opportunities in such areas as robotics, medical technology, and communications equipment.

Finally, the company's dependency on people has been changed somewhat by the $10 billion sunk into plant and equipment since 1977. John Opel, IBM's chairman and chief executive, says, "Dominance may be a very transitory thing." By changing its culture rather than clinging to tradition, IBM has improved its chances of remaining number one. *Fortune* magazine concludes, "When a dominant company's advantage wanes, seemingly perilous, tradition-shattering change can be the course of least risk."[1]

The corporate culture at IBM, like that at many other companies, springs in large measure from the philosophy of a strong chief executive. Until recently most people believed that the environment within a company was a constraint that managers had to contend with. It is recognized today, however, that not only can companies change their cultures but they *must* change in order to survive. In fact, it has been found that when extensive organizational change is necessary in response to change in the environment, the best means of change are culture centered rather than technology centered.

IBM logo reproduced courtesy of International Business Machines Corporation.

This chapter first defines corporate culture and then identifies factors that determine it. Various types of cultures are then described. A model of the change sequence is presented next. Sources of resistance to change and approaches to reducing it follow. Organizational development techniques for implementing cultural change from an organizational viewpoint are then described. Next, stress management and executive burnout are discussed. We end the chapter with a presentation on conflict management.

CORPORATE CULTURE DEFINED

Corporate culture is *the system of shared values, beliefs, and habits within an organization that interacts with formal structure to produce behavioral norms.*[2] According to Howard M. Schwartz, vice-president of Management Analysis Center, Inc., a leader in corporate culture consulting, "Culture gives people a sense of how to behave and what they ought to be doing."[3] It is similar in concept to meteorological climate. Just as the weather is described by such variables as temperature, humidity, and precipitation, organizational culture is composed of such factors as friendliness, supportiveness, and risk taking. For instance, just as the weather of the southwestern United States may be described as "warm and pleasant," the employees may characterize their organization as being "open and supportive." Such perceptions are gradually formed for each individual over a period of time as the person performs assigned activities under the general guidance of a superior and a set of organizational policies. The culture exisiting within a firm has an impact on the employees' degree of satisfaction with the job, as well as on the level and quality of their performance. The assessment of how good or poor the organization's culture is may differ for each employee. One person may perceive the environment as bad, and another may see the same environment as good. An employee may actually leave an organization in the hope of finding a more compatible culture.

Writing in 1967, Antony Jay stated, "It has been known for some time that corporations are social institutions with customs and taboos, status groups and pecking orders, and many sociologists and social scientists have studied and written about them as such. But they are also political institutions, autocratic and democratic, peaceful and warlike, liberal and paternalistic."[4] What Jay was writing about, although the term had not then achieved broad usage, was corporate culture, as we have defined it. In the early 1980s, several best-selling books on corporate culture appeared, including *In Search of Excellence, Theory Z: How American Business Can Meet the Japanese Challenge,* and *Corporate Culture.*[5] In 1981, Harvard University introduced its first course on corporate culture.

corporate culture

FACTORS THAT DETERMINE CORPORATE CULTURE

The previous three chapters concentrated on the topics of motivation, leadership, and communication. These topics were presented prior to a discussion of corporate culture because of the impact they can have on a firm's psychological environment. We will now identify typical factors that affect corporate culture, among them work groups, organizational charac-

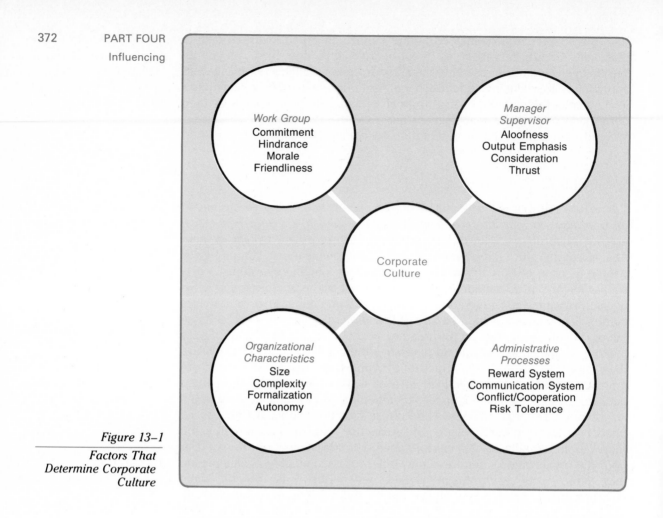

Figure 13–1

Factors That Determine Corporate Culture

teristics, supervision, and administration.[6] These factors are shown in Figure 13–1. As you can see, it would be difficult to discuss these topics without a good understanding of the concepts of motivation, leadership, and communication.

Let us consider each of the factors shown in Figure 13–1. The nature of the immediate work group will affect one's perception of the quality of culture. Commitment refers to whether this group is just going through the motions of work. If people are just going through the motions, it is difficult for a particular individual to obtain high levels of output and satisfaction. Hindrance is concerned with the degree to which a great deal of busywork of doubtful value is given to the group. Morale and friendliness within the group are factors with which most readers are familiar.

The leadership style of the immediate supervisor will have a considerable effect on the culture of the group, and vice-versa. If the manager is aloof and distant in dealing with subordinates, this attitude will have an impact. If the supervisor is always pushing for output, this alters the environment. Thrust refers to supervisory behavior characterized by personally working hard and setting an example. Consideration is a leadership characteristic.

Organizational characteristics may also affect the type of culture.

Organizations vary on such attributes as size and complexity. Large organizations tend toward higher degrees of specialization and greater impersonalization. Labor unions often find that large firms are easier to organize than smaller ones because smaller firms tend to be closer and have more informal relationships between employees and management. Complex organizations tend to employ a greater number of professionals and specialists, which alters the general approach to solving problems. Organizations also vary in the degree to which they write things down and attempt to program behavior through rules, procedures, and regulations. They can also be distinguished on the basis of the degree of decentralization of decision-making authority, which affects the degree of autonomy and freedom of personnel within the organization.

Corporate culture can be affected by administrative processes. Firms that can develop a direct link between performance and rewards tend to create cultures conducive to achievement. Communication systems that are open and free-flowing tend to promote participation and creative atmospheres. The general attitudes that exist toward the handling of risk and the tolerance of conflict will, in turn, have considerable impact on the type of teamwork effected. They also affect the amount of organizational innovation and creativity.

From these sixteen factors organization members will develop a subjective impression of "what kind of place this is to work for." This general impression will have some impact on performance, satisfaction, creativity, and commitment to the organization.

TYPES OF CULTURES

At times an organization must alter its culture in order to survive. *Fortune* magazine concluded that this was necessary for IBM when the computer industry changed so drastically in the early 1980s.

What are the types of corporate culture that a firm may wish to emulate, and why should one particular culture prove superior to another? In terms of the openness and the degree of participation allowed, most behavioralists advocate an open and participative culture. This type of culture is characterized by such attributes as these:

- Trust in subordinates
- Openness in communications
- Considerate and supportive leadership
- Group problem solving
- Worker autonomy
- Information sharing
- High output goals

Some behavioralists contend that this culture is the only viable one for all situations.

The opposite of the open and participative culture is a closed and autocratic one. It, too, may be characterized by high output goals. But such goals are more likely to be declared and imposed on the organization by autocratic and threatening leaders. There is greater rigidity in this culture,

At times an organization must alter its culture in order to survive. M.E. Warren/Photo Researchers

resulting from strict adherence to the formal chain of command, shorter spans of management, and stricter individual accountability. The emphasis is on the individual rather than teamwork. Employee reactions are often characterized by going through the motions and doing as they are told.

Despite criticism of traditional organizational cultures by behavioralists, a more participative philosophy may not always work. In one instance involving the packaging of the product of low-priced china, low productivity of the work group was caused by excessive and unnecessary interaction between employees during working hours. Management found that the threat of termination did not prevent the unproductive talking because these low-skilled and low-paid employees were eligible for government subsidy programs. Management resolved the problem by redesigning the space allocated to the china packaging process. Cubicles constructed of soundproofing material were built for each worker. The cubicles virtually eliminated the unproductive conversation between workers. As a result, productivity increased substantially, and employee turnover was reduced. The total cost was $3,200, which was recovered during the first three weeks.[7]

From the story at the beginning of the chapter, it is clear that the culture at IBM is neither purely open and participatory nor closed and autocratic. Although IBM employees are expected to dress conservatively and otherwise follow company rules, new ideas are encouraged and rewarded through incentive compensation.

THE PARTICIPATIVE CULTURE

The prevailing managerial approach in most organizations has been one characterized as being highly structured. Consequently, most attempts to alter organizational culture have been directed toward creating a more open and participative culture. The theme of participation developed by McGregor, Herzberg, and Maslow, among others, relates primarily to self-actualization, motivator factors, consultative and democratic leadership, job enrichment, and management by objectives. All of the companies identified in *In Search of Excellence* as having favorable corporate cultures evidenced a participative environment.

Values of Participation

The possible values of involving more people in the decision-making process within a firm relate primarily to productivity and morale. Increased productivity can result from the stimulation of ideas and from the encouragement of greater effort and cooperation. Psychologically involved employees will often respond to shared problems with innovative suggestions and unusual efforts.

Open and participative cultures are often used to improve the levels of morale and satisfaction. Specific values in the area include:

- Increased acceptability of management's ideas.
- Increased cooperation with members of management and staff.
- Reduced turnover.
- Reduced absenteeism.
- Reduced complaints and grievances.
- Greater acceptance of changes.
- Improved attitudes toward the job and the organization.

In general, the development of greater employee participation appears to have a direct and immediate effect on employee morale. Employees take a greater interest in the job and the organization. They tend to accept, and sometimes initiate, changes not only because of their understanding of the necessity for change but also because their fear or insecurity has been reduced by knowing more about the change. Thus, even though a credibility gap may exist for practicing managers in the area of productivity, most experience and research indicate a positive relationship between employee participation and measures of morale, turnover, and absenteeism. However, there has been little evidence presented that would suggest a positive relationship exists between job satisfaction and productivity. If productivity is not harmed by participation, it would appear that these supplementary values would make a program worthwhile. If productivity is actually decreased, then serious decisions will have to be made concerning management's philosophy of organizational and human values.

Limitations of Participation

Despite the values of a participative approach to management, there are some limitations. There are certain prerequisites to and limitations on greater employee participation in decision making. The requirements for greater participation in decision making are (1) sufficient time; (2) adequate ability and interest on the part of the participants; and (3) restrictions generated by the present structure and system.

If immediate decisions are required, time cannot be spared for group participation. Because of rapid changes in the computer industry, IBM managers often find it difficult to take the time to involve workers in decisions. The manager decides what to do and issues the order accordingly. Should management decide to switch from a practice of autocracy to one of increased participation, some time for adjustment on the part of both parties will be required. Participation calls for some measure of ability to govern oneself instead of leaning on others. In addition, it requires time for the subordinate to learn to handle this new-found freedom and time for the supervisor to learn to trust the subordinate.

Whether greater involvement in decision making can be developed largely depends on the ability and interest of the participants, both subordinates and managers. This is not an easy concept to implement. Obviously, if the subordinate has neither knowledge of nor interest in a subject, there is little need to consult that person. As organizations and technology become increasingly complex and as management becomes more professionalized, it is likely that employee participation will become more characterized by cooperation seeking or information gathering. It should also be noted that not all employees are equally desirous of participation. Managers must face the fact that some workers, it is hoped just a few, do not seek more responsibility and greater involvement in their job.

Finally, as indicated in Figure 13–2, the area of job freedom left to the individual may be quite restricted, but can be expanded. An individual's task is governed by management directives, organizational policies and procedures, the union contract, relations with the union steward, staff

Figure 13–2

Limits to Participative Freedom

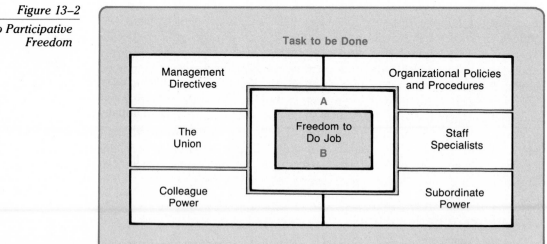

Source: Edwin B. Flippo and Gary M. Munsinger, *Management,* 5th ed. (Boston: Allyn and Bacon, 1982), p. 360.

specialists, and the degree to which one can obtain the cooperation of subordinates. The greater the area in the Freedom to Do Job section, the greater the degree of participative freedom that is available. In the illustration, *A* would have more freedom to accomplish the job than *B*.

THE CHANGE SEQUENCE

Whether the intended change is from a less participative to a more participative corporate culture or along some other dimension, the process tends to follow a certain pattern. The sequence of events needed to bring about change in an organization is shown in Figure 13–3. Management must first recognize a need for change. Then the specific change method(s) must be chosen. Finally, the following steps are carried out: (1) unfreezing the status quo, (2) moving to the new condition, and (3) refreezing to create a new status quo.

Recognizing the Need for Change

Perhaps the most important question to ask regarding the subject of change is, "Is this change necessary?" There are some who unwisely believe that changes should be made merely for the sake of change. Managers who make a change merely to satisfy a personal desire may create a disruptive effect on their section. When one of the authors was working as a consultant for a manufacturing firm, he inadvertently noticed a note on the desk of a new vice-president who had been brought in from the outside to attempt to improve the performance of a division that was doing poorly. The note said, "Do not make any major changes for three months." The new executive obviously wanted to be aware of the total situation before changes were made. If he began to make changes immediately, inappropriate changes could be made and an entire division could be further damaged. Organizations and people desire some degree of stability in order to accomplish their assigned tasks. But there are times when changes are necessary and failure to deal effectively with them can have a disastrous effect.

A number of major companies, particularly in the fast-moving computer industry, have found cultural change not only feasible but necessary. One expert writes about Apple Computer, "Things have changed since its salad days before IBM entered the market in August 1981 (when IBM became an Apple competitor by introducing its personal computer, a time when Apple was seen as a kind of playground for ambitious and idealistic computer wizards)."[8] There are rumblings among some Apple staffers that the company is becoming regimented and is losing its entrepreneurial soul. Apple is noted for a corporate culture that emphasizes blue jeans and tennis shoes, video games outside the executive offices, free thinking, and a flexible organizational structure. On the other hand, IBM traditionally has emphasized white shirts and gray suits and conservative thinking. But, as we have seen, IBM is changing too. That company's new strategy appears to be aimed at becoming more like Apple—while Apple is becoming more like IBM. Other companies have accomplished broad-scale cultural change include American Telephone and Telegraph, Pepsico, Chase Manhattan, and Twentieth Century Fox.[9]

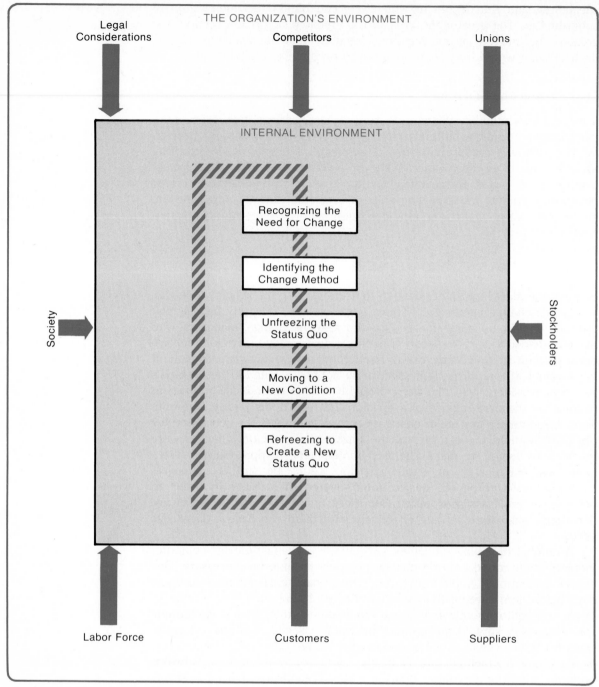

Figure 13–3   The Change Sequence

Donaldson and Lorsch argue that all companies must change their cultures or die, though the change may be revolutionary or evolutionary.[10] There are five possible reasons for imposing rapid cultural change:

1. If your company has strong values that don't fit a changing environment.
2. If the industry is very competitive and moves with lightning speed.
3. If your company is mediocre or worse.
4. If the company is about to join the ranks of the very largest companies.
5. If it's smaller, but growing rapidly.[11]

Coors "Coors is now more than ready to take on Miller and Busch. We're wiser, we are tougher, and better prepared. We can leap tall buildings at a single bound." When Coors's sales vice-president, Fred Vierra, made this statement, it may have sounded a bit overconfident. But a few years earlier the Adolph Coors Company had seemed unconquerable. Through 1970, Coors sold its beer only in eleven southwestern states. The company sold just one kind of beer, an unpasteurized brew that was the favorite of such notables as Gerald Ford, Henry Kissinger, Paul Newman, and Clint Eastwood. In states surrounding Coors's territory, college students willingly paid twice the list price for Coors six-packs smuggled in by their classmates. For some reason—the "Rocky Mountain spring water" Coors used to make its beer, the lack of pasteurization or preservatives, or the intentional restriction of supply—a mystique surrounded the product. Because of this intense demand, Coors spent only a fraction of what other brewers spent on advertising.

The Coors Mystique

Because Coors beer had to be transported in refrigerated trucks, distribution costs were high, but the company made up for the cost through efficient production. All Coors beer is made at the company's huge Golden, Colorado, brewery, a showcase of efficiency. Coors owns its own barley fields and container plants, and supplies its breweries with gas from its own gas wells. The chairman and chief executive officer, Bill Coors, said, "Our top management thrust is on engineering and production . . . we're production oriented. Nobody knows more about production that I do." When sales doubled between 1968 and 1973, this low-cost structure produced large profits. There seemed to be no end to it. "You could have sold Coors beer in Glad bags," said the Coors marketing chief.

The company's management philosophy is credited with much of its success. Employees are encouraged to address top executives by their first names. Outdoor adventures, such as skiing trips and outdoor survival schools, as well as golf and other sports, are subsidized by the company. There are no formal lines of authority. Even the chief executive responsibilities are split: Bill handles technical matters, and Joe is largely concerned with finance and administration.

The situation has changed markedly since the mid-1970s. Coors broke out of its eleven-state area and now distributes its beer in twenty-six states. Because of a company policy of requiring employees to take lie detector tests, the company's brewery workers walked out in April 1977. A week later the AFL-CIO announced a nationwide boycott of the company's beer. The Coors family, which still controls the majority of the common stock, would not budge and eventually broke the strike. A decertification election was held in 1978, and 71 percent of the union members voted to oust the union. But the Coors image was tarnished. Not only had union-sponsored hate campaigns marked the company "unfair to labor" in general, but Coors management was criticized for the low percentages of various minority groups in the work force. During the same time period, Anheuser-Busch and Miller were fighting it out for the number one position and wherever Coors had moved beyond its initial eleven-state territory, it was a target of intense competition.

In response to the attacks and a slowing growth rate, Coors introduced Coors Lite in 1978 and began experimenting with a number of other brands. That same year, Coors quadrupled its advertising budget and soon began to consider placing a second brewery on the East Coast to try to reduce its huge transportation costs. The declining fortunes of the company provoked Bill Coors to a more pessimistic perspective: "There will be fewer than ten brewers in the United States in ten years. I don't say we have to be number one, but we do have to stay in the top five to survive."[12]

Identifying the Change Method

Management has at its disposal numerous organizational development methods or techniques. Specific techniques discussed later in this chapter are survey feedback, team building, sensitivity training, management by objectives, job enrichment, and the grid approach. The technique chosen should meet the needs of the organization in reacting to the external environment and the identification of the type of culture that will provide for the greatest productivity in the organization.

Unfreezing the Status Quo

If individuals are to change their present attitudes, current beliefs must be altered or unfrozen.[13] Resistance to change must be eliminated or reduced if a change is to be effective. Once resistance to change has been reduced, the manager is in a position to implement the desired change. Sources of resistance to change and approaches to reduce resistance to change are discussed later in the chapter.

Unfreezing in the change process generates self-doubt and provides a means of remedying the situation. Employees must be made to feel that ineffectiveness is undesirable, but it can be remedied. If organization members are to be receptive to change, they must feel that they can change.

Moving to a New Condition

The initiation of a change can come from an order, a recommendation, or a self-directed impetus. A manager with authority can command that a change be made and enforce its implementation by threats, punishments, and close supervision. If this path of implementing change is taken, the manager will likely find that the change must be constantly monitored. Change is more permanent and substantial if a person truly wants and feels a need to change.

The most effective approach to initiate change is for a two-way relationship to exist between the person who is attempting to implement the change and the person(s) who will be changed. Rather than a one-way flow of commands or recommendations, the person implementing the change should make suggestions, and the changees should be encouraged to contribute and participate. Those initiating the change should be responsive to suggestion, either by reformulating the change or by providing explanations as to why the suggestions cannot be incorporated.

Refreezing to Create a New Status Quo

If a person changes to a new set of work habits for a week and then reverts to former practices, the change has not been effective. Too often changes that are introduced do not stick. If the change is to be permanent, changees must be convinced that it is in their own and the organization's best interest. One of the best ways to accomplish this is to collect objective evidence of the success of the change. A manager who sees production increase because of a change in leadership style has obtained excellent evidence of the success of the change. People should have feelings of competence and pleasure in using the new behavior. But the change will be completely accepted only if the reward system of the organization is geared to the new form of behavior. If a university states that all its faculty must begin to publish articles and there is no reward attached to publishing, it is likely that few faculty members could be motivated to make this change. An employee's job may be substantially enriched in terms of content and self-supervision, but if the change is not accomplished by properly enriched pay and status symbols, dissatisfaction is likely to result. People tend to repeat behavior that they find rewarding.

SOURCES OF RESISTANCE TO CHANGE

A change may cause some loss to the person who is affected by it. Attachments to old and familiar habits, places, and people must be given up. When the Coors union was voted out by its members the 29 percent who wanted to keep the union undoubtedly had to make severe adjustments. Even those in favor of the change faced a new situation. In major and unexpected changes, employees often experience daze, shock, recoil, and turmoil.[14] Some of the many sources of resistance to change are looked at next.

Insecurity

Once people have operated in a particular environment for a long time, they begin to feel comfortable. A change of environment often brings about uncertainty; they do not know exactly what to expect. The feeling of insecurity surrounded virtually all of us as we made the transition from high school to college. The same sense of insecurity continues as the move is made from undergraduate to graduate work or when individuals move from one job to another or to a new city. It is perhaps because of such feelings of insecurity that some people seemingly become perpetual students.

Possible Social Loss

A change has the potential to bring about social losses. As was discussed in Chapter 8, the informal work group may be extremely powerful. If change causes individuals in the group to be transferred, the power of the group is likely diminished. A change may cause established status symbols to be destroyed, or an individual of lower status may even be awarded a high-status symbol. In the Coors example, union stewards, accorded high status before decertification, suddenly became just regular workers.

The impact that a change can have on the social environment was vividly illustrated when one of the authors was doing a consulting job for a regional medical center. The hospital had been a small, local, 100-bed hospital, but because industry was moving rapidly into the area, the board of directors had decided to expand the hospital to 300 beds. In one department all personnel reported directly to the department head, and a close rapport had developed among the members. On a rotating shift, staff members would have to work the evening and night shift, but they still maintained close contact with the other department members.

Because of the great increase in work load, the work force was expanded, and a decision was made to have three shifts with a shift supervisor for each shift. The department head now had only three people reporting directly to him, and it was believed that the work could be performed much more efficiently. But the social loss was drastic. Subordinates no longer had a close relationship with the department head; some, because they were on a different shift, rarely saw the department head. This created a tremendous social loss to several long-term employees and resulted in over 50 percent of the personnel quitting in six months.

Economic Losses

Technology may be introduced that can produce the same amount of output with fewer personnel. While most companies make an honest attempt to transfer or retain employees who have been affected by the change, the fear of being laid off remains. When the computer was first introduced, the number of clerical personnel needed was often drastically reduced. The computer firms attempted to lessen this fear by claiming that the number of jobs had actually increased through the use of the computer. This explanation did not help the employee who was capable only of accomplishing the clerical work. To this individual a major economic loss had occurred.

Inconvenience

Even if no social or economic loss were associated with a change, any change represents a new way of doing things. As such, new procedures and techniques may have to be learned. Physical and mental energy must be expended (for some people this is not an enjoyable task). This was the case for all of the Coors employees, whether they had favored decertification or not. When a new telephone system was installed at a university, initially there were many complaints. The new system meant that time and effort had to be expended. It took approximately one year for the system to be accepted by a majority of the university personnel.

Resentment of Control

As a whole, Americans are very independent. When employees are told that a change must take place, they are made to realize that they do not have control over their destiny. Although the change may be for the better, a certain amount of resentment may develop. IBM's Tom Watson was convinced that conservative dress by employees would help to sustain the company's image and, indirectly, increase profitability. Some within the company, however, resent being told how to dress. This might be true even for persons who normally dress conservatively.

Unanticipated Repercussions

Because the organization is a system, a change in one part is likely to have unforeseen repercussions in another portion. For example, a newly enriched job is likely to demand a change in supervisory behavior. Supervisors may resist this change in behavior although initially they support the concept of job enrichment. At Coors, though management was successful in eliminating the union, the company has since been subjected to union-sponsored hate campaigns.

Union Opposition

Labor union representatives are often accused of opposing any change suggested by management. Employees are often more comfortable with a fighting union than they are with one inclined to cooperate with management on changes designed to promote organizational interest. There are indications, however, that the old adversarial relationship is being replaced by a more cooperative one between companies and unions. Sometimes joint collaboration is occurring with regard to improving productivity and enhancing the quality of work life. Recent surveys have indicated that many rank-and-file workers want something more from their jobs and their unions than wages, benefits, and job security.[15] Perhaps this changing attitude had a large part in the union's being ousted by Coors union workers.

APPROACHES TO REDUCING RESISTANCE TO CHANGE

Change is often necessary despite resistance that might arise. One of the authors, while working as a personnel administrator for a large insurance company, observed that an anticipated change in computers brought about considerable employee resistance. Management of the company had announced that a new computer system with greatly increased capacity would be installed in about six months. The new computer would cause substantial changes in many of the clerical jobs being performed by office personnel. Uncertain as to what to expect from the change in computer systems, numerous employees began expressing fear and concern about the impact of the change.

Before management took any action, the employees caused a rather severe slowdown in work flow in the office. Customer and agent complaints rose substantially during the six-week period after the announced change. Management took action to correct the situation by holding a series of small group meetings to explain the new computer system and how it would affect each job and each work group. While there would be several major changes in job functions affecting some individuals and work groups, management made a commitment to all employees that no one would be dismissed as a result of the installation of the new computer. The company would provide retraining programs to increase the affected employees' skills, thereby improving their adaptability to the new system.

Provide Information in Advance

Whenever possible, the manager should provide the reasons for the change, its nature, planned timing, and the possible impact on the organization and its personnel. Withholding information that could seriously affect the lives and futures of particular individuals, such as keeping secret the planned closure of a plant in order to preserve the work-force level until the last possible moment, should be avoided if possible. The firm that gains a reputation for such actions will have difficulty making future changes. There are occasions when competitive survival requires that information be closely held until shortly before introduction. In these cases, the information should be provided on an *as required* basis.

Encourage Participation

When possible, subordinate participation should be encouraged in establishing the change. A person who is involved in implementing change procedures will likely be more supportive of the change. It will be recalled from Chapter 10 that Theory Y assumes that abilities are widespread in the population. Thus, many valuable ideas may be gained by permitting employees a degree of participation in implementing the change. A company that has gained a reputation for participative management is Xerox Corporation. David T. Kearns, president, said to his employees, "I pledge to you that management of this company at all levels will listen to you and put your ideas to work."[16]

Guarantee against Loss

To promote acceptance of technological changes, some organizations guarantee no layoffs as a result of such changes. In cases of a change in methods and output standard, employees are often guaranteed retention of their present level of earnings during the learning period. At Coors, workers were made aware after the union was gone that wages would continue to exceed those paid in unionized plants by competitors.

Make Only Necessary Changes

Changes should be made only when the situation demands, not because of a whim on the part of a manager. A manager who gains a reputation for making change for the sake of making change will discover that any change, whether beneficial or not, will receive only minimum acceptance.

Attempt to Maintain Useful Customs and Informal Relationships

As was mentioned in Chapter 8, the informal work group has real value from the standpoint of interpersonal understanding and cooperation. When possible, changes should be made to coincide with the culture of the personnel within the organization. When safety shoes were first introduced, few would wear them willingly because of their appearance. When they were redesigned to resemble dress shoes, resistance faded. The granting of fictional rank to civilian consultants who are to work with military personnel makes their integration into ongoing operations more understandable and acceptable. A staff expert who wants a change introduced may find it advisable to have the announcement made by a line executive with some sharing of the credit. Changes that go against established customs and informal norms will likely experience resistance and a minimum chance of acceptance.

Build Trust

If a manager has obtained a reputation for providing reliable and timely information to employees in the past, the explanation as to why a change is to be made will likely be more believable. The change may still be resisted, but if the manager is trusted by the employees, problems will be minimized. On the other hand, managers who have gained a reputation for providing incomplete or inaccurate information will often have difficulty convincing employees that a proposed change is good for them. Both IBM and Coors management have tended to maintain open communication with employees and to honor the commitments made to them. Undoubtedly, the resulting trust played a large part in the two companies' successful change efforts.

Provide Counseling

At times some form of nonthreatening discussion and counseling may not only prevent rebellion but have some chance of stimulating voluntary adaptation. Nondirective counseling has been used effectively in many change situations. The approach rests on a fundamental belief that people have the ability to solve their problems with the aid of a sympathetic listener. The role of a counselor is one of understanding rather than of passing judgment. This requires a somewhat permissive, friendly atmosphere, with actions and statements that exhibit continuing interest but not judgment. In most instances, managers with authority are unable to establish this type of atmosphere. Successful nondirective counseling must usually be undertaken by staff psychologists. What the manager can do is to permit some subordinate ventilation of feelings, particularly those of frustration and anger. Just talking about the "good old days" will assist in the transition process. Discovering that others have similar feelings and doubts will often make the transition less painful; "misery loves company."

Allow for Negotiation

Resistance to change can be reduced by the process of negotiation. Negotiation is the primary method used by labor unions to effect modification of proposed managerial changes. For example, in return for accepting many changes in work rules, a West Coast employer at one time provided a $29 million benefit fund to aid longshoremen through early retirement and a type of annual wage guarantee. In 1984, when wage reductions were necessary at Eastern Airlines, President Frank Borman agreed to give employees company stock in exchange for the cuts.

ORGANIZATIONAL DEVELOPMENT

One Monday morning, employees of a midwestern railroad company arrived at their office at the usual time. They tried the door and were surprised to find it locked. A notice was attached to the corridor wall, which read that effective immediately that office of the company had been eliminated. The rooms were empty, and all equipment had been moved to a more central office 600 miles away. No one was laid off, but if an employee wished to retain employment, he or she would have to be on the train the next afternoon headed for the consolidated central office. Should an employee wish to resign, personal effects on his or her desk would be mailed back. Over the preceding weekend, moving vans had cleared the local office of all equipment and had transported it to the new office.

The change may be technically justified, assuming that the railroad is in serious financial difficulties. The manner of introducing the change is, however, subject to criticism. The company's approach was to make the change an accomplished fact, utilizing the power of the "new" status quo. Rapidity of execution was, they felt, the only answer to resistance that could never be overcome anyway.

We will describe several change efforts that affect the entire organization and are referred to as organizational development (OD). The organizational development movement has been strongly advocated by such researchers as Chris Argyris and Warren Bennis. **Organizational development (OD)** *is a planned and systematic attempt to change the organization, typically to a more behavioral environment.* OD education and training strategies are designed to develop a more open, real, and compatible environment regardless of existing differences in personalities, culture, or technologies.[17]

organizational development (OD)

The Survey Feedback Method

The method of basing organizational change efforts on the systematic collection and measurement of subordinate attitudes by anonymous questionnaires is referred to as the **survey feedback method**. The three basic steps in the process are shown in Figure 13–4. First, data are collected from members of the organization by a consultant. Surveys are typically either the objective multiple-choice type (see Figure 13–5) or a scaled

survey feedback method

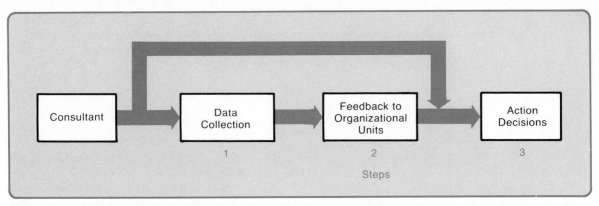

Figure 13–4   The Survey Feedback Method   Source: Adapted from Michael E. McGill, *Organization Development for Operating Managers.* (New York: AMACOM, a division of American Management Associations, 1977).

answer to suggest agreement or disagreement with a particular question (see Figure 13–6). Normally, anonymously answered questionnaires are used. If we are to obtain truthful information concerning attitudes, the employee must feel comfortable, secure, and confident in responding.

In the second step, the results of the study are presented to concerned organizational units. In the final step, the data are analyzed and decisions are made. Some means by which the data may be compared and analyzed include:

• Scores for the entire organization now and in the past.
• Scores for each department now and in the past.
• Scores by organizational level.

Figure 13–5

Examples of Multiple-Choice Responses to Survey Questions

Why did you decide to do what you are now doing?

a. Desire to aid or assist others
b. Influenced by another person or situation
c. Always wanted to be in this vocation
d. Lack of opportunity or interest in other vocational fields
e. Opportunities provided by this vocation
f. Personal satisfaction from doing this work

What do you like least about your job?

a. Nothing
b. Pay
c. Supervisor relations
d. Problems with fellow workers
e. Facilities
f. Paperwork and reports

Considering all aspects of your job, evaluate your compensation with regard to your contributions to the needs of the organization. Circle the number that best describes how you feel.

Pay too Low		Pay Low		Pay Average		Pay Above Average		Pay Too High	
1	2	3	4	5	6	7	8	9	10

What are your feelings about overtime work requirements? Circle the number that best indicates how you feel.

Unnecessary			Necessary on Occasion				Necessary		
1	2	3	4	5	6	7	8	9	10

Figure 13–6

Examples of Scaled Responses to Survey Questions

Source: R. Wayne Mondy and Robert M. Noe, III, *Personnel: The Management of Human Resources,* 2nd ed. (Newton, Mass.: Allyn and Bacon, 1984), p. 584.

- Scores by seniority.
- Relative scores on each question.
- Scores for each question for each category of personnel cited above.

The decisions are directed at improving relationships in the organization. This is accomplished by revealing problem areas and dealing with them through straightforward discussions.

Team Building

team building

One of the major techniques in the arsenal of the organizational development consultant is **team building,** *a conscious effort to develop effective work groups throughout the organization.*[18] The focus of team building is the development of effective management teams. These work groups focus on solving actual problems in building efficient management teams. The team-building process begins when the team leader defines a problem that requires organizational change. Next, the group analyzes the problem to determine the underlying causes of the problem. These factors may be related to such areas as communication, role clarifications, leadership styles, organizational structure, and interpersonal frictions. The next step is to propose alternative solutions and then select the most appropriate one. Through this process, the participants are likely to be committed to the solution. Interpersonal support and trust develops. The overall improvement in the interpersonal support and trust of group members enhances the implementation of the change.[19] The concept of the quality circle, imported from Japan, is a modern example of team building.

Sensitivity Training

sensitivity training

An organizational development (OD) technique that uses leaderless discussion groups is referred to as **sensitivity training** (also called T-group training or laboratory training). The general goal of sensitivity training is to develop awareness of and sensitivity to oneself and others. More specifically, the goals of sensitivity training include the following:

- Increased openness with others.
- Greater concern for needs of others.
- Increased tolerance for individual differences.
- Less ethnic prejudice.
- Awareness and understanding of group processes.
- Enhanced listening skills.
- Greater appreciation of the complexities of behaving competently.
- Establishment of more realistic personal standards of behavior.

Sensitivity training is not widely used in business today as an OD technique.[20] It has been labeled "psychotherapy" rather than proper business training. Leaders of T-groups have been criticized as having an insufficient background in psychology. Detractors have suggested that individual defense mechanisms that have been built up to preserve the personality over a period of years may be destroyed with little help being provided in replacing them with more satisfactory behavioral patterns. It is contended that one cannot exist without ego defense mechanisms.

Also, in business organizations, managers frequently must make unpleasant decisions that work to the detriment of particular individuals and groups. Excessive empathy and sympathy will not necessarily lead to a reversal of the decision and may exact an excessively high emotional cost for the decision maker. Many business organizations have internal environments characterized by competition and autocratic leadership. The power structure may not be compatible with openness and trust. In some instances, an effective manager must practice diplomacy by telling only part of the truth or perhaps even telling different stories to two different persons or groups. Truth is not always conducive to effective interpersonal and group relations. Sensitivity training would also tend to ignore organizational values that are derived from aggressiveness, initiative, and the charismatic appeals of a particular leader.

Management by Objectives

In Chapter 4, we described management by objectives as a systematic approach that facilitates achievement of results by directing efforts toward attainable goals. MBO is a philosophy of management that encourages managers to plan for the future. Because MBO emphasizes participative management approaches, it has been called a philosophy of management. Within this broader context, MBO becomes an important method of organizational development. The participation of individuals in setting goals and the emphasis on self-control promote not only individual development but also development for the entire organization.

Job Enrichment

The deliberate restructuring of a job to make it more challenging, meaningful, and interesting is referred to as job enrichment. As we suggested in Chapter 10, the individual is provided with an opportunity to derive greater achievement, recognition, responsibility, and personal growth in performing the job. IBM demands a great deal of its employees and rewards them with recognition. The top 10 percent of sales representatives are given membership in the Gold Circle, and quotas are set so that over two-thirds are eligible for the One Hundred Percent Club.

The Grid Approach to OD

One of the best-known predesigned OD programs is the managerial grid by Robert Blake and Jane Mouton. As we discussed in Chapter 11, Blake and Mouton suggest that the most effective leadership style is that which stresses maximum concern for both output and people. The managerial grid provides a systematic approach for analyzing managerial styles and assisting the organization in moving to the best style.

CHANGE AGENTS

change agent

The person who is responsible for ensuring that the planned change in OD is properly implemented is referred to as a **change agent**. This individual(s) may be either an external or an internal consultant(s). Change agents have knowledge in the OD techniques previously described and use this knowledge to assist organizational change.

When an organization first attempts to change, outside consultants are often used. An outside expert may bring more objectivity to a situation and be better able to obtain acceptance by and trust from organizational members. With time, internal consultants may move into the role of a change agent.

MANAGEMENT DEVELOPMENT

management development programs (MDP)

Organizational development techniques are designed to change the entire organization. **Management development programs (MDP)** are *formal efforts to improve the skills and attitudes of present and prospective managers.* Managers learn more effective approaches to managing people and other resources. With MDP, specific areas that have been identified as possible organizational weaknesses are included in the program. Some of these areas might relate to leadership style, motivation approaches, or communication effectiveness.

The training programs may be administrated by either in-house or external personnel. An illustration of a management development program that was utilized by a major independent telephone company is provided in Figure 13–7. The intent of MDP is not only to learn new methods and techniques but to develop an inquisitive thought process. Too often personnel within a firm become so accustomed to performing the same task day after day that they forget how to think. A properly designed management development program places a person in a frame of mind to analyze problems and is often used to provide the foundation for a change to occur.

I. **Management Development Program Title:**
"Improving Group Effectiveness and Team Building"

II. **Objectives:**
(1) To identify the reasons for group formation
(2) To understand the types of groups and their attributes
(3) To discover the implications of research on group dynamics
(4) To acquire an understanding as to forces in intra- and inter-group processes
(5) To learn the characteristics of teamwork and ways to achieve it
(6) To provide experience in analyzing and diagnosing work group dimensions
(7) To acquire an appreciation for various team-building techniques

III. **Description and Evaluation:**
The course is designed to provide greater understanding of, and ability to work with and through, groups. Special emphasis is given to understanding the various need levels of groups and what can be done to appeal more effectively to those levels. Actual practice in team-building techniques is given, as well as experience in analyzing work groups. Evaluation is made of the major contingencies affecting groups. Observing group behavior through various media is a portion of the course content.

IV. **Size of Class:**
The class should have a maximum enrollment of 20 participants so as to allow the group process to be seen in action in the group itself, yet small enough to allow for active participation.

V. **Assignment of Instructor:**
The instructor allocates an equal amount of time to lecture and active class discussion with approximately one-third of the time devoted to various media presentations and group involvement. The course is designed for a two- or three-day session.

VI. **Enrollment Requirements:**
Middle- and upper-level managerial experience desired

Figure 13–7

*Course Content for a
Management
Development Program*

STRESS MANAGEMENT

A by-product of some change is the stress that can develop in workers. **Stress** is defined as *the nonspecific response of the body to any demands made on it.* Over a period of time or under intense conditions, stress can take its toll on the wear and tear of one's body. A vast array of ailments ranging from lower back pains to headaches to coronary problems and cancer are considered to be by-products of stress. If stress is strong enough and permitted to last long enough, it can damage both mental and physical health. Unmanaged coping with stress can create anxiety, depression, paranoia, and other mental difficulties for the individual. The cost and pain of stress are enormous. Stress-related absenteeism, illness, and premature death have been estimated to cost U.S. industry between $20 billion and $50 billion each year.[21]

stress

Exercise is a major means of controlling stress.

David Burnett/Contact–Woodfin Camp Associates

Managers are beginning to realize that effective stress management is important to them, their employees, and the organization. Job-related stress can be as disruptive, and as costly, to the corporation as any accident that occurs to an employee. In fact, many employee accidents are considered to be stress related.

It is important for managers to recognize employee behavior patterns that may suggest stress overload. Some of these patterns are:

- Working late more than usual or the opposite, increased tardiness or absenteeism
- Difficulty in making decisions
- Increases in the number of careless mistakes
- Missing deadlines or forgetting appointments
- Problems interacting and getting along with others
- Focusing on mistakes and personal failure[22]

Naturally, all behavioral change is not stress related, but astute managers can be made alert to changes in employee patterns. A normally productive worker becomes sloppy and productivity decreases. Or a normally friendly worker becomes irritable and short-tempered.

There is that old saying that goes like this: "An ounce of prevention is worth a pound of cure." It is certainly that way in stress management. Firms can do much to reduce stressful conditions. For instance, if management finally recognizes that the organizational culture produces considerable stress, efforts can be made to change the culture. Perhaps the culture would move toward a more open and less threatening one where workers can do their jobs without fear. Another means of reducing stress might be to redesign jobs or change the work-flow schedule. Stressful conditions might be eliminated through this procedure. Also, the physical environment might be changed. Perhaps the noise level is excessive. Ear plugs might be furnished or the noise level reduced.

One rapidly growing area of stress reduction is the development of company physical fitness programs for employees. Xerox Corporation has eight in-house physical fitness laboratories at locations across the United States. A program is designed to help each individual feel and look better. It also helps them build their self-concept. The Xerox Executive Fitness Program emphasizes four areas: (1) cardiovascular fitness, (2) flexibility, (3) relaxation by means of biofeedback, and (4) weight conditioning. Similar programs are expected to increase dramatically in the future. Firms are beginning to see how stress-related problems affect the profitability of the organization.[23]

EXECUTIVE BURNOUT

Although closely related to stress, executive burnout is somewhat different. **Executive burnout** has been defined as *"someone in a state of fatigue or frustration brought about by devotion to a cause, way of life, or relationship that failed to produce the expected reward."*[24] Burnout is said to affect approximately 10 percent of managers and executives.[25] A major problem associated with burnout is that it is extremely contagious. Executives who become burnout victims are likely to become cynical, negativistic, and pessimistic. They are literally ready to explode. An entire work group can be quickly turned into a collection of burnouts.[26] Therefore, it is extremely important for burnout symptoms to be recognized. One burnout victim can affect many people.

executive burnout

Some of the symptoms of burnout include: (1) chronic fatigue; (2) anger at those making demands; (3) self-criticism for putting up with the demands; (4) cynicism, negativism, and irritability; (5) a sense of being besieged; and (6) a hair-trigger display of emotions.[27] Other symptoms might include recurring health problems, such as ulcers, back pain, and frequent headaches. The burnout victim is often unable to maintain an even keel emotionally. Unwarranted hostility may occur in completely inappropriate situations.

Burnout often occurs among talented, achievement-oriented workers. Many of these people are business executives. Perhaps they have set their standards too high and then refuse to admit that the goals cannot be achieved. Sometimes the organization itself designs situations that are capable of causing burnout. Giving a manager a job to do and then making it virtually impossible to accomplish provides an example. Burnout is the "consequence of a work situation in which the person gets the feeling he's butting his head against the wall day after day, year after year."[28]

The problem can be corrected. Some firms are arranging full-time counselors on staff to help employees who are experiencing burnout. Seminars are being given to help managers to help their workers overcome the problem. Some firms are granting disability leaves until the worker recovers.

Firms can also take measures to prevent burnout among employees. For example, workers should not be permitted to work too much overtime, even on critical problems. Often the best person is always called upon in times of crisis. These are the people likely to burn out. Another method might be to rotate employees who are working on stressful jobs. Moving people to a new project may help. Some firms are starting physical exercise programs and counseling programs. Breaks in the business routines are helpful.[29] The job at hand should not overshadow all other aspects of living.

MANAGEMENT OF CONFLICT

conflict **Conflict** refers to *antagonism or opposition between or among persons.* When individuals are brought together in a highly structured environment, a potential for major disagreements exists. Conflict may result from a difference in opinion about how to accomplish a goal or a disagreement as to what is the proper goal. At times, conflict occurs because of unclear authority. A manager may not have a clearly defined role within the firm. Also, roles may overlap, a situation that has the potential to create considerable conflict among employees.

Some degree of conflict is unavoidable in any organization. There may even be an optimum level of conflict that should be permitted for the good of the organization. Too little conflict may lead to mediocrity, apathy, and, at times, destruction. The Penn Central Railroad went quietly into bankruptcy some years ago when its board of directors offered no challenging questions to management. If former President Nixon had not surrounded himself with "yes men," the events of Watergate might not have occurred. Certainly the conflict surrounding the civil rights movement led to social decisions in keeping with the long-run interests of the United States.

Interpersonal Conflict Management

There are numerous techniques for dealing with conflict between two or more individuals. They range from the use of force by a superior over a subordinate to the problem-solving approach. Possible ways of dealing with interpersonal conflict management are discussed below.

Force

When force is used in the resolution of conflict, official authority may compel one party to accept a solution. The old expression, "He may not be right, but he's still the boss," applies in this instance. The party to whom the decision is directed may not agree with the results, but must accept the directive if he or she wishes to stay within the organization. The union at Coors attempted to use force, though unsuccessfully, in the form of a strike to resolve the conflict with the company.

Withdrawal

A solution that some individuals use in resolving conflict is to withdraw from or avoid the person with whom the conflict exists. Conflict is reduced, but the original cause remains. For example, suppose you see a person with whom you do not want to speak approaching you. You withdraw by walking around the block to avoid speaking to the person.

Smoothing

When smoothing is used, a manager attempts to provide a semblance of peaceful cooperation by presenting an image that "we're one big happy family." With this approach, problems are rarely permitted to come to the surface, but the potential for conflict remains.

Compromise

Neither party gets all it wants when compromise is used. This is the most typical way of dealing with labor-management conflict. For example, management may offer to increase wages by 8 percent, while the union may be seeking a 12 percent pay hike. A compromise figure of a 10 percent pay increase may result in a reasonable settlement of the conflict.

Mediation and Arbitration

Both arbitration and mediation call for outside neutral parties to enter the situation to assist in resolving the conflict. **Arbitration** is *a process in which a dispute between two parties is submitted to a third party to make a binding decision.* Arbitration is frequently used in union-management grievance conflicts. The arbitrator is given the authority to act as a judge. The decision rendered is usually final because both union and management agree in advance that it will be.

arbitration

Mediation is *a process in which a third party enters a dispute between two parties for the purpose of assisting them in reaching an agreement.* A mediator can only suggest, recommend, and attempt to keep the two parties talking in hopes of reaching a solution.

mediation

Superinordinate Goals

At times, a goal may be encountered that supersedes the conflict of two opposing factions. If the firm is in danger of going out of business, both union and management have been known to put aside minor conflict and work toward the common goal of survival. There have been instances where union members have taken a decrease in pay and benefits in order to assist in the survival of the firm. For example, union members and management at Chrysler and General Motors and other firms have cooperatively worked together to ensure the survival of their firms. Chrysler and General Motors, responding to major financial crises, have experienced significant reductions and changes in their management ranks, as well as reductions in the work force, wages, and benefits.

Problem Solving

A recommended approach to conflict management is problem solving. As usually practiced, problem solving is characterized by an open and trusting exchange of views and facts. A person realizes that conflict is caused by relationships among people and is not within the person. With the problem-solving approach, an individual can disagree with your ideas and still remain your friend. It is a healthy approach that recognizes that one person is rarely completely right and the other person completely wrong. Granting a concession is not seen as a sign of weakness. Neither party feels that it has to win every battle to maintain self-respect.

A certain amount of conflict is healthy in the problem-solving approach. If a difference of opinion exists between two individuals and they openly discuss their difficulties, a superior solution often results. With problem solving, a person is encouraged to bring difficulties into the open without fear of reprisal. When this occurs, a situation that initially appeared to be a major problem may evolve into only a minor one, which is easily resolved.

Structural Conflict Management

Conflict can also be managed by changing procedures, organizational structure, physical layout, or expanding resources. These methods for resolving conflict are discussed next.

Procedural Changes

Conflict can occur because a procedure is illogically sequenced. When a credit manager and a sales manager were both about to be fired because of an irreconcilable personality conflict, it was discovered that the processing of credit applications too late in the procedure was the cause of the difficulty. The credit manager was forced to cancel too many deals already made. When the credit check was placed earlier in the procedure, most of the conflict disappeared. In another instance, the personnel director and the production manager were in continuous disagreement. At times the conflict came to blows. Then it is was discovered that the production manager was not being permitted to view the applicants at an early stage of the hiring sequence and make comments regarding an applicant. When the procedure was changed, many of the difficulties were resolved.

Organizational Structure Changes

Some degree of conflict is often desirable. For example, this is the case where a quality control department must oversee the work of the production department. Conflict between quality control and production can probably be minimized if the quality control director reports to the production manager. In this case, however, quality control loses its independence. This is why the quality control director typically reports to someone high in the organization, often even the president. The resulting potential conflict is justified by the quality improvement that results from such a structure.

In other cases, conflict between departments is unplanned and undesirable. In some firms, sales and distribution are in separate departments, each reporting to a senior general manager. This division often creates conflict when sales expects quick response to customer requests for special services. In an effort to keep costs down, the distribution department wants to make deliveries in full trucks and at scheduled intervals. To resolve this kind of conflict, it may be desirable to combine the two departments under a marketing manager who is a specialist in sales and distribution. The marketing manager can ensure that the organization's needs take priority over the preferences of sales and distribution personnel.

Physical Layout Changes

Changes in the design of the physical workplaces have been used effectively to reduce or eliminate conflict. Office space can be designed either to force interaction or to make it difficult. Personnel can use desks as barriers and buffers. Some offices have dividers to separate workers. However, if a manager desires to stimulate a problem-solving atmosphere, a more open office arrangement may be permitted. When known antagonists are seated in conference directly across from each other, the amount of conflict increases. When they are seated side by side, the conflict tends to decrease.

A detrimental conflict involving physical layout existed between two groups of workers in a truck assembly plant. Working at different phases on the assembly line, the two groups came into conflict because both had to obtain parts from the same shelving unit. Each group would deliberately rearrange the other group's supply of parts, which sometimes resulted in fights. The conflict was resolved by moving the shelving unit between the two groups so as to set up a barrier between each work group. Thus, each group had its own supply area or "territory." As a result of this change, mistakes were reduced by 50 percent within two days.[30]

SUMMARY

Corporate culture is the system of shared values, beliefs, and habits within an organization that interacts with formal structure to produce behavioral norms. The culture existing within a firm has an impact on the employees' degree of satisfaction with the job, as well as on the level and quality of their performance. A number of factors affect corporate culture, among them work groups, organizational characteristics, supervision, and administration. The culture advocated by most behavioralists is the open and/or participative climate, which is characterized by such attributes as trust in subordinates, openness in communication, considerate and supportive leadership, group problem solving, worker autonomy, information sharing, and the establishment of high output goals.

The sequence of events needed to bring about change in an organization begins with management's recognizing a need for change. Next the change method to be used is identified. The next steps consist of unfreezing the status quo, moving to a new level, and freezing to create the new status quo.

A change may cause some loss to the person who is affected by it and thus generate resistance. Some of the possible sources of resistance to change include insecurity, possible social loss, economic losses, inconvenience, resentment of control, unanticipated repercussions, and union opposition. Approaches that may be used to reduce resistance to change include providing information in advance, encouraging participation, guaranteeing against loss, providing counseling, making only necessary changes, attempting to maintain useful customs and informal relationships, building trust, and allowing for negotiation.

Change efforts that affect the entire organization are referred to as organizational development (OD). OD is a planned and systematic attempt to change the organization, typically to a more behavioral environment. Some of the OD techniques available include the survey feedback method, team building, sensitivity training, management by objectives, job enrichment, and the grid approach. The person who is responsible for ensuring that the planned change in OD is properly implemented is referred to as a change agent.

Whereas organizational development techniques are designed to change the entire organization, management development programs are specifically tailored to benefit managers. Some of the areas for development might include leadership style, motivation approaches, and communication effectiveness.

Stress management and executive burnout are

of increasing concern to modern managers. Stress is the nonspecific response of the body to any demands made upon it. A person experiencing executive burnout is someone in a state of fatigue or frustration brought about by devotion to a cause, way of life, or relationship that failed to produce the desired reward. There are numerous ways to identify and treat both stress and executive burnout.

Conflict refers to antagonism or opposition between or among persons. Conflict management may be classified as interpersonal or structural. Interpersonal conflict management deals with conflict between two or more individuals. Structural conflict management is concerned with changing the structures and processes that can have an effect on behavior.

REVIEW QUESTIONS

1. Define corporate culture. What are the factors that interact to determine the type of corporate culture that exists in a firm?
2. Identify the values and limitations of a participative climate.
3. List and describe the change sequence discussed in the text.
4. What are the sources of resistance to change as described in the text?

5. Describe the approaches that may be used in reducing resistance to change.
6. Define each of the following terms:
   a. Organizational development
   b. Team building
   c. Sensitivity training
7. Define and distinguish stress and burnout.
8. What are the various means whereby conflict can be reduced? Briefly describe each.

EXERCISES

1. Identify the major changes that have occurred in your life during the past year. How did you react to these changes?
2. Assume that you are the president of a college or a university and you would like to make the following changes:
   a. Students must be professionally attired at all times.
   b. Faculty members must be at their office by 8:00 A.M.

   c. All single students must live in the dormitory.

   Assuming that all of the above-mentioned changes are made for a logical reason, what type of resistance to these changes could you expect? How could you possibly overcome some of the resistance to these changes?

CASE STUDY

A Change in Environment

Until one year ago Wayne, Don, and Robert had been supervisors with a small chain of thirty-nine grocery stores. Each supervisor had responsibility for thirteen stores and reported directly to the company president. All three supervisors worked well together, and there was a constant exchange of information, which was quite useful in coordinating the activities of the stores. Each supervisor had specific strengths that were useful in helping the others. Wayne coordinated the deployment of the part-time help at all thirty-nine stores. Don monitored the inventories, and Robert interviewed prospective new employees prior to sending them to Wayne and Don for review. It was a complete team effort directed toward getting the job done.

One year later a completely different environment existed at the chain. The president, wishing to relieve himself of many daily details, decided to promote Robert to vice-president. Another supervisor, Phillip, was hired for Robert's position. Robert had a completely different idea of how the activities of the supervisors should be conducted. Under Robert's leadership each supervisor was now responsible for the activities at only his stores. If a problem occurred, the supervisor was to discuss it with Robert, and he would provide the solution. When either Wayne, Don, or Phillip attempted to solve problems on his own, he was reprimanded by Robert. After a few "chewing outs" Wayne, Don, and Phillip decided not to fight the system and did as Robert wanted; they rarely saw each other any more. If Don had a problem at his stores that caused him to work all night, that was not any concern of Wayne or Phillip.

The only problem with the new system was that efficiency dropped drastically. For instance, Wayne was a good coordinator of part-time help. He had the type of personality that could talk a person into coming to work at 5:00 P.M. on Saturday when the individual had a date at 6:00 P.M. Wayne's stores remained well staffed with part-time help, but the others suffered. Many times the part-time help did not show up and either Don or Phillip had to act as the replacement if the store manager could not be convinced to work overtime. On the other hand, Wayne's inventory control suffered because Don was best qualified in this area.

Robert accused the three supervisors of working against him and threatened them with dismissal if operations did not get better. Wayne, Don, and Phillip felt that they could not be productive in this environment and found other positions. When the president discovered what had occurred, Robert was fired. It took the president six months to get the operations back to the level of efficiency that it had achieved previously.

QUESTIONS

1. What different organizational environment was created as a result of promoting Robert to vice-president?
2. How do you feel that this situation could have been avoided? Discuss the possibility of the use of the participative approach in this instance.

CASE STUDY

Rumors at Duncan Electric

Donna Garcia is a supervisor for Duncan Electric Corporation, a manufacturer of high-quality electrical parts. Donna had been with the firm for five years and had a reputation for having one of the best teams in the plant. Donna had picked the majority of these employees and was proud of the reputation they had achieved. But a problem was now brewing that had the potential of destroying her department.

For weeks, rumors of a substantial reduction in personnel at Duncan Electric have been circulating. Donna has not received any confirmation from the corporate office regarding the reduction. The rumors, all claiming to be from reliable sources, range from minor reductions to a large-scale reduction in personnel. Every day someone claims to have the inside story, and every day the story changes. Donna, who has a reputation for leveling with her people, successfully discounted the rumors for awhile. But as the doubts began to grow, work output began to suffer.

Her employees were now spending time trying to verify the latest rumor. Speculation increased to the point where the best-qualified employees were starting to shop around.

The action by these employees does not make sense unless there is to be a very large-scale layoff. Donna was convinced that a minor layoff was the worst that could possibly happen, and she was demoralized to see things falling apart for no good reason.

On Friday, Bob Phillips and Henry Barham, two of the most skilled employees in the department, told Donna that they had taken a job with a competitor. This situation was what she had feared the most; the most qualified workers would leave and the least qualified workers would remain. Instead of having one of the best departments at Duncan Electric, she may now have the worst.

QUESTIONS

1. To what extent have the rumors of the anticipated change in the work force damaged the morale of the employees?
2. What should management do to reduce the fear of the anticipated change?
3. What should Donna do in a situation like this?

NOTES

1. This story is a composite of a number of published accounts, including: Peter D. Petre, "Meet the Mean, Lean New IBM," *Fortune* 107 (June 13, 1983): 69–82; Thomas J. Watson, Jr., *A Business and Its Beliefs: The Ideas That Helped to Build IBM* (New York: McGraw-Hill, 1963); Thomas J. Peters and Robert H. Waterman, Jr., *In Search of Excellence: Lessons from America's Best Run Companies* (New York: Harper & Row Publishers, 1982); and a number of articles from *The Wall Street Journal*.

2. Arthur Sharplin, *Strategic Management* (New York: McGraw-Hill, 1985), p. 102.

3. "Corporate Culture: The Hard to Change Values That Spell Success or Failure," *Business Week* (October 27, 1980): 148–160.

4. Antony Jay, *Management and Machiavelli* (New York: Holt, Rinehart and Winston, 1967).

5. Peters and Waterman, *In Search of Excellence;* William G. Ouchi, *Theory Z: How American Business Can Meet the Japanese Challenge* (New York: Avon Books, 1982); Terrence E. Deal and Allan A. Kennedy, *Corporate Culture* (Reading, Mass.: Addison-Wesley, 1981).

6. Many of the factors were taken from the Organizational Climate Description Questionnaire generated by Halpin and Croft as described in Andrew W. Halpin, *Theory and Research in Administration* (New York: Macmillan, 1966), chap. 4. Another widely used measure is that of Litwin and Stringer found in G. Litwin and R. Stringer, *Motivation and Organizational Climate* (Cambridge: Harvard University Press, 1968).

7. H. Kenneth Bobele and Peter J. Buchanan, "Building a More Productive Environment," *Management World* 1 (January 1979): 8.

8. Petre, "Meet the Lean, Mean New IBM," pp. 69–82.

9. "Corporate Culture."

10. Gordon Donaldson and Jay Lorsch, *Decision Making at the Top* (New York: Basic Books, 1983).

11. Bro Uttal, "The Corporate Culture Vultures," *Fortune* (October 17, 1983): 66–72.

12. *Coors Pride* (Golden, Colo.: Adolph Coors Company, Corporate Communications Department, 1982); Robert Reed, "Coors Charts Path over a Rocky Road to Growth," *Advertising Age* (July 11, 1983): 4; Robert F. Hartley, "Coors: A Mystique Tarnished through Lack of Marketing Orientation," in *Marketing Mistakes,* 2d ed. (Columbus, Ohio: Grid Publishing, 1981): 151–165; "Coors' Bitter Brew," *Financial World* (April 30, 1983): 31–32; and numerous articles from *The Wall Street Journal*.

13. Kurt Lewin, *Field Theory and Social Science* (New York: Harper, 1964), chaps. 9, 10.

14. Ralph G. Huschowitz, "The Human Aspects of Managing Transition," *Personnel* 51 (May–June 1974): 13.

15. "The New Industrial Relations," *Business Week* (May 11, 1981): 98.

16. Ibid.

17. Portions of the following discussion were adapted from R. Wayne Mondy and Robert M. Noe III, *Personnel: The Management of Human Resources,* 2d ed. (Newton, Mass.: Allyn and Bacon, 1984) pp. 224–240.

18. Edgar F. Huse, *Organization Development and Change* (St. Paul, Minn.: West, 1975): 230.

19. Michael A. Hitt, R. Dennis Middlemist, and Robert Q. Mathis, *Effective Management* (St. Paul, Minn.: West, 1979) pp. 462–464.

20. For a detailed review of one hundred research studies on sensitivity training, see P. B. Smith, "Control Studies on the Outcome of Sensitivity Training," *Psychological Bulletin* (July 1975): 597–622.

21. Oliver L. Niehouse and Karen B. Massoni, "Stress—An Inevitable Part of Change," *Advanced Management Journal* 44 (Spring 1979): 17.

22. John M. Ivancevich and Michael T. Matteson, *Stress and Work: A Managerial Perspective* (Glenview, Ill.: Scott, Foresman, 1980) p. 208.

23. Mondy and Noe, *Personnel,* pp. 371–372.

24. Herbert J. Freudenberger, *Burnout: The High Cost of High Achievement* (Garden City, N.Y.: Anchor Press, Doubleday, 1980), p. 13.

25. Beverly Norman, "Career Burnout," *Black Enterprises* 11 (July 1981): 46.

26. Cary Cherniss, "Job Burnout: Growing Worry for Workers, Bosses," *U.S. News and World Report* (February 27, 1980): 72.

27. Harry Levinson, "When Executives Burn Out," *Harvard Business Review* 59 (May–June 1981): 76.

28. Freudenberger, *Burnout,* pp. 17–18.

29. Levinson, "When Executives Burn Out," pp. 78–81.

30. H. Kenneth Bobele and Peter J. Buchanan, "Building a More Productive Environment," *Management World* 8 (January 1979): 8.

REFERENCES

Allen, R. F., and S. Silverzweig. "Changing Community and Organization Cultures." *Training and Development Journal* 31 (July 1977): 28–34.

Baird, John E., Jr. "Supervisory and Managerial Training through Communication by Objectives." *Personnel Administrator* 26 (July 1981): 28–32.

Baysinger, Rebecca T., and Richard W. Woodman. "The Use of Management by Objectives in Management Training Programs." *Personnel Administrator* 25 (February 1981): 83–86.

Bensahel, J. G. "How to Overcome Resistance to Change." *International Management* 32 (September 1977): 66–67.

Biggart, N. W. "Creative-Destructive Process of Organizational Change: The Case of the Post Office." *Administrative Science Quarterly* 22 (September 1977): 410–426.

Bobele, H. Kenneth, and Peter J. Buchanan. "Building a More Productive Environment." *Management World* 8 (January 1979): 8.

Carlson, H. C. "Organizational Research and Organizational Change." *Personnel* 54 (July 1977): 11–22.

Cherniss, Cary. "Job Burnout: Growing Worry for Workers, Bosses." *U.S. News and World Report* (February 27, 1980): 72.

"Corporate Culture: The Hard to Change Values That Spell Success or Failure." *Business Week* (October 27, 1980): 148–160.

Davis, L. E. "Individuals and the Organization." *California Management Review* 22 (Spring 1980): 5–14.

Deal, Terrence E., and Allan A. Kennedy. *Corporate Culture.* Reading, Mass.: Addison-Wesley, 1981.

Donaldson, Gordon, and Jay Lorsch. *Decision Making at the Top.* New York: Basic Books, 1983.

Freudenberger, Herbert J. *Burnout: The High Cost of High Achievement.* Garden City, N.Y.: Anchor Press, Doubleday, 1980, p. 13.

Gordon, G. G., and B. E. Goldberg. "Is There a Climate for Success?" *Management Review* 66 (May 1977): 37–44.

Greiner, Larry E. "Evolution and Revolution as Organizations Grow." *Harvard Business Review* 50 (July 1971): 37–46.

Hellriegel, Don, and John W. Slocum, Jr., "Organizational Climate: Measures, Research, and Contingencies." *Academy of Management Journal* 17 (June 1974): 255–280.

Hitt, Michael A., R. Dennis Middlemist, and Robert Q. Mathis. *Effective Management.* St. Paul, Minn.: West, 1979.

Howe, R. J. et al. "Introducing Innovation through Organizational Development." *Management Review* 67 (February 1978): 52–56.

Huschowitz, Ralph G. "The Human Aspects of Managing Transition." *Personnel* 51 (May–June 1974): 13.

Huse, Edgar F. *Organization Development and Change.* St. Paul, Minn.: West, 1975.

Ivancevich, John M., and Michael T. Matteson. *Stress and Work: A Managerial Perspective.* Glenview, Ill.: Scott, Foresman, 1980.

Jay, Antony. *Management and Machiavelli.* New York: Holt, Rinehart and Winston, 1967.

Jennings, Eugene E. "How to Develop Your Management Talent Internally." *Personnel Administrator* 26 (July 1981): 20–23.

Kelly, Joe, and Kamiran Khozan. "Participative Management: Can It Work?" *Business Horizons* (August 1980): 74–79.

Levinson, Harry. "When Executives Burn Out." *Harvard Business Review* 59 (May–June 1981): 76.

Lewin, Kurt. *Field Theory and Social Science.* New York: Harper, 1964.

Margerison, Charles, and Colin New. "Management Development by Intercompany Consortiums." *Personnel Management* 12 (November 1980): 42–45.

Miles, James M. "How to Establish a Good Industrial

Relations Climate." *Management Review* 67 (August 1980): 42–44.

Miller, Danny, and Peter H. Friesen. "Momentum and Revaluations in Organizational Adaptation." *Academy of Management Journal* 23 (December 1980): 591–614.

Mintzberg, Henry. "Organizational Design: Fashion or Fit?" *Harvard Business Review* 59 (January–February 1981): 103–116.

Monat, Jonathan S. "A Perspective on the Evaluation of Training and Development Programs." *Personnel Administrator* 26 (July 1981): 47–52.

Mondy, R. Wayne, and Robert M. Noe III. *Personnel: The Management of Human Resources,* 2d ed. Newton, Mass.: Allyn and Bacon, 1984.

"The New Industrial Relations." *Business Week* (May 11, 1981): 98.

Niehouse, Oliver L., and Karen B. Massoni. "Stress—An Inevitable Part of Change." *Advanced Management Journal* 44 (Spring 1979): 17.

Norman, Beverly. "Career Burnout." *Black Enterprises* 11 (July 1981): 46.

Olivas, Louis. "Using Assessment Centers for Individual and Organizational Development." *Personnel* 57 (May–June 1980): 63–67.

THE ORGANIZATIONAL CLIMATE AT LINCOLN ELECTRIC

Lincoln Electric Company is the world's largest manufacturer of welding machines and electrodes with 2,600 employees in two U.S. factories near Cleveland, Ohio, and approximately 600 in three factories located in other countries. Lincoln's market share is more than 40 percent of the U.S. market for arc-welding equipment and supplies.

A HISTORICAL SKETCH

In 1895, after being "frozen out" of the depression-ravaged Elliott-Lincoln company, John C. Lincoln obtained his second patent and began to manufacture an improved motor. He began business with $200 he had earned redesigning a motor for young Herbert Henry Dow, who later found The Dow Chemical Company.

In 1906, Lincoln incorporated and moved from a one-room, fourth-floor factory to a new three-story building erected in east Cleveland. He expanded his work force to 30 and sales grew to over $50,000 a year. John Lincoln preferred being an engineer and inventor rather than a manager, though, and it was left to another Lincoln to manage the company through its years of success.

In 1907, after a bout with typhoid fever forced him from Ohio State in his senior year, James F. Lincoln, John's younger brother, joined the fledgling company. In 1914, with the company still small and determined to improve its financial condition, he became the active head of the firm, with the titles of general manager and vice-president. John Lincoln remained president of the company for some years, but he became more involved in other business ventures and in his work as an inventor.

One of James Lincoln's early actions as head of the firm was to ask the employees to elect representatives to a committee to advise him on company operations. The advisory board has met with the chief executive officer twice monthly since that time. The first year the advisory board was in existence, working hours were reduced from fifty-five per week—then standard—to fifty hours a week. In 1915, the company gave each employee a paid-up life insurance policy. In 1918, an employee bonus plan was attempted but was not continued, although the idea was to resurface and become the backbone of the Lincoln Management System.

The Lincoln Electric Employees' Association was formed in 1919 to provide health benefits and social activities. This organization continues today and has assumed several additional functions over the years. By 1923, a piecework pay system was in effect, employees got two-week paid vacations each year, and wages were adjusted for changes in the Consumer Price Index. Approximately 30 percent of Lincoln's stock was set aside for key employees in 1914 when James F. Lincoln became general manager, and a stock purchase plan for all employees was begun in 1925.

The board of directors voted to start a suggestion system in 1929. The program is still in effect, but cash awards, a part of the early program, were discontinued several years ago. Now, suggestions are rewarded by additional performance appraisal "points," which affect year-end bonuses. The legendary Lincoln bonus plan was proposed by the advisory board and accepted on a trial basis by James Lincoln in 1934. The first annual bonus amounted to about 25 percent of wages. There has been a bonus every year since then. The bonus plan has been a cornerstone of the Lincoln Management System and recent bonuses have approximated annual wages.

James F. Lincoln died in 1965 and there was some concern, even among employees, that the Lincoln system would fall into disarray, that profits would decline, and that year-end bonuses might be discontinued. Quite the contrary, seventeen years after Lincoln's death, the company appears stronger than ever. Each year since 1965, except for the recession years 1982 and 1983, has seen higher profits and bonuses. Employee morale and productivity remain high; employee turnover is almost nonexistent except for retirements, and Lincoln's market share is stable.

COMPANY PHILOSOPHY

James F. Lincoln was the son of a Congregational minister, and Christian principles were at the center of his business philosophy. While Christian principles have served as important guidelines for business operations, there is no indication that the company has attempted to evangelize its employees or customers—or the general public for that matter. The current board chairman, Mr. Irrgang, and the President, Mr. Willis, do not even mention the Christian gospel in their recent speeches and interviews. The company motto, "The actual is limited, the possible is immense," is prominently displayed, but there is no display of religious slogans and there is no company chapel.

Attitude toward the Customer

James Lincoln saw the customer's needs as the raison d'être for every company. "When any company has achieved success so that it is attractive as an investment," he wrote, "all money usually needed for expansion is supplied by the customer in retained earnings. It is obvious that the customer's interests, not the stockholder's, should come first" (Lincoln, 1961, p. 119). In 1947 he said, "Care should be taken . . . not to rivet attention on profit. Between 'How much do I get?' and 'How do I make this better, cheaper, more useful?' the difference is fundamental and decisive." Lincoln's goal, often stated, is "to build a better and better product at a lower and lower price." It is obvious, James Lincoln said, "that the customer's interests should be the first goal of industry." (p. 117)

Attitude toward Stockholders

Stockholders are given last priority at Lincoln. This is a continuation of James Lincoln's philosophy: "The last group to be considered is the stockholders who own stock because they think it will be more profitable than investing money in any other way" (p. 38). Concerning division of the largess produced by incentive management, Lincoln writes, "The absentee stockholders also will get his share, even if undeserved, out of the greatly increased profit that the efficiency produces."

Attitude toward Unionism

There has never been a serious effort to organize Lincoln employees. While James Lincoln criticized the labor movement for "selfishly attempting to better its position at the expense of the people it must serve" (p. 18), he still had kind words for union members. He excused abuses of union power as "the natural reactions of human beings to the abuses to which management has subjected them" (p. 76). Lincoln's idea of the correct relationship between workers and managers is shown by this comment: "Labor and management are properly not warring camps; they are parts of one organization in which they must and should cooperate fully and happily" (p. 72).

Beliefs and Assumptions about Employees

If fulfilling customer needs is the desired goal of business, then employee performance and productivity are the means by which this goal can best be achieved. It is the Lincoln attitude toward employees, reflected in the following quotations (all taken from Lincoln, 1961):

> The greatest fear of the worker, which is the same as the greatest fear of the industrialist in operating a company, is lack of income. . . . The industrial manager is very conscious of his company's need of uninterrupted income. He is completely oblivious, evidently, of the fact that the worker has the same need (p. 36).

> He is just as eager as any manager is to be part of a team that is properly organized and working for the advancement of our economy. . . . He has no desire to make profits for those who do not hold up their end in production, as is true of absentee stockholders and inactive people in the company (p. 75).

> If money is to be used as an incentive, the program must provide that what is paid to the worker is what he has earned. The earnings of each must be in accordance with accomplishment (p. 98).

> Status is of great importance in all human relationships. The greatest incentive that money has, usually, is that it is a symbol of success. . . . The resulting status is the real incentive. . . . Money alone can be an incentive to the miser only (p. 92).

> There must be complete honesty and understanding between the hourly worker and management if high efficiency is to be obtained (p. 39).

George E. Willis, president, dispels the impression that Lincoln management is "soft" management. "We care about one another around here, but we are quite autocratic. When managers tell workers to do something, they expect it to be done."

ORGANIZATIONAL STRUCTURE

Lincoln has never had a formal organization chart. The objective of this policy is to ensure maximum flexibility. An open-door policy is practiced throughout the company and personnel are encouraged to take problems to the person most capable of resolving them. Perhaps because of the quality and enthusiasm of the Lincoln work force, routine supervision is almost nonexistent. A typical production foreman, for example, supervises as many as 100 workers, a span-of-control which does not allow more than infrequent worker-supervisor interaction. Position titles and traditional flows of authority do imply something of an organization structure, however. For example, the vice-president, sales, and the vice-president, electrode division, report to the president, as do various staff assistants such as the personnel director and the director of purchasing. From such implied relationships, it has been determined that production workers have two or, at most, three levels of supervision between themselves and the president.

PERSONNEL POLICIES

Recruitment and Selection

Every job opening at Lincoln is advertised internally on company bulletin boards, and any employee can apply for any job so advertised. External hiring is done only for entry level positions. Selection for these jobs is done on the basis of personal interviews—there is no aptitude or psychological testing. In 1979, out of about 3500 applicants interviewed by the personnel department fewer than 300 were hired. Final selection is made by the supervisor who has the job opening.

Job Security and Compensation

After one year, employees are guaranteed thirty hours per week and promised that they will not be discharged except for misconduct. There has been no layoff at Lincoln since 1949.

Insofar as possible, base wage rates are translated into piece rates. Practically all production workers and many others—for example, some fork truck drivers—are paid by piece rate. Once established, piece rates are never changed unless a substantive change in the way a job is done results from a source other than the worker doing the job. In December of each year, a portion of annual profits is distributed to employees as bonuses. Incentive bonuses since 1934 have averaged about the same as annual wages and somewhat more than after-tax profits. For example, the average bonus for 1981 was about $17,600. Even for the recession years 1982 and 1983, bonuses averaged over $10,000 each year.

Training and Education

Production workers are given a short period of on-the-job training and then placed on a piecework pay system. Lincoln does not pay for off-site education. The idea behind this latter policy is that everyone cannot take advantage of such a program and it is unfair to expend company funds for an advantage to which there is unequal access. Sales personnel are given on-the-job training in the plant followed by a period of work and training at one of the regional sales offices.

Fringe Benefits and Executive Perquisites

A medical plan and a company-paid retirement program have been in effect for many years. A plant cafeteria, operated on a break-even basis, serves meals at about 60 percent of usual costs. An employee association, to which the company does not contribute, provides disability insurance and organizes social and athletic activities. An employee stock ownership program, instituted in about 1925, and regular stock purchases have resulted in employee ownership of about 50 percent of Lincoln's stock.

As to executive perquisites, there are none—crowded, austere offices, no executive washrooms or lunchrooms, and no reserved parking spaces. Even the company president pays for his own meals and eats in the cafeteria.

FINANCIAL MANAGEMENT

James F. Lincoln felt strongly that financing for company growth should come from within the company—through initial cash investment by the founders, through retention of earnings, and through stock purchases by those who work in the firm. The company uses a minimum of debt in its capital structure. There is no borrowing at all, with the debt being limited to current payables. Even the new $20,000,000 plant in Mentor, Ohio was financed totally from earnings.

The unusual pricing policy at Lincoln is succinctly stated by President Willis: ". . . at all times price on the basis of cost and at all times keep pressure on our costs." This policy resulted in Lincoln's price for the most popular welding electrode then in use going from 16 cents a pound in 1929 to 4.7 cents in 1938. More recently the SA-200 welder, Lincoln's largest selling portable machine, decreased in price from 1958 through 1965. According to Dr. C. Jackson Grayson of the American Productivity Center in Houston, Texas, Lincoln's prices in general have increased only one-fifth as fast as the Consumer Price Index since 1934. This has resulted in a welding products market in which Lincoln is the undisputed price leader for the products it manufactures. Not even the major Japanese manufacturers, such as Nippon Steel for welding electrodes and Osaka Transformer for welding machines, have been able to penetrate this market.

WORKER PERFORMANCE AND ATTITUDES

Exceptional worker performance at Lincoln is a matter of record. The typical Lincoln employee earns about twice as much as other factory workers in the Cleveland area. Yet the labor cost per sales dollar at Lincoln, currently 23.5 cents, is well below industry averages.

Annual sales per Lincoln production employee is approximately $157,000. An observer at the factory quickly sees why this figure is so high. Each worker is proceeding busily and thoughtfully about his task. There is no idle chatter. Most workers take no coffee breaks. Many operate several machines and make a substantial component unaided. The supervisors, some with as many as 100 subordinates, are busy with planning and recordkeeping duties with hardly a glance at the people they supervise. The manufacturing procedures appear efficient—no unnecessary steps, no wasted motions, no wasted materials. Finished components move smoothly to subsequent work on hand.

Worker turnover at Lincoln is practically nonexistent except for retirements and departures by new employees.

In an effort to gain greater insight into company practices and the attitudes and perceptions of employees, a series of interviews were conducted. The following are excerpts from interviews with employees at Lincoln by the casewriter.

- *Ed Sanderson, a twenty-three-year-old high school graduate who had been with Lincoln for four years as a machine operator.*
  Q. Roughly, what were your earnings last year including your bonus?
  A. $37,000.
  Q. What have you done with the money since you have been here?
  A. Well, we've lived pretty well and we've bought a condominium.
  Q. Have you paid for the condo?
  A. No, but I could!
  Q. Are you paid on a piece-rate basis?
  A. My gang is. There are nine of us who make the bare electrodes and the whole gang gets paid on how many electrodes we make.
  Q. Why do you think Lincoln employees produce more than workers in other plants?
  A. That's the way the company is set up. The more you put out the more you are going to make.

Q. Do you think it's the piece rate and bonus together?
A. I don't think people would work here if they didn't know that they would be rewarded at the end of the year.
Q. Do you think Lincoln employees will ever join a union?
A. No! We don't have a union shop and I don't think I could work in a union shop.

- *Betty Stewart, a fifty-two-year-old high school graduate with Lincoln for thirteen years and who was working as a cost accounting clerk.*
  Q. What jobs have you held here besides the one you have now?
  A. I worked in payroll for a while and then came into cost accounting.
  Q. How much did you earn last year?
  A. Roughly $20,000, but I was off several weeks because of back surgery.
  Q. You weren't paid while you were off for back surgery?
  A. No.
  Q. Did the Employees' Association help out?
  A. Yes. The company doesn't furnish that, though. We pay $6 a month into the Employees' Association. I think my check from them was $105.00 a week.
  Q. How did you get your job at Lincoln?
  A. I was bored silly where I was working and I had heard that Lincoln kept their people busy. So I applied and got the job.

- *Roger Lewis, twenty-three-year-old Purdue graduate in mechanical engineering, who had been in the Lincoln sales program for fifteen months.*
  Q. How did you get your job at Lincoln?
  A. I saw that Lincoln was interviewing on campus at Purdue and I went by. I later came to Cleveland for a plant tour and was offered a job.
  Q. Do you think Lincoln salesmen work harder than those in other companies?
  A. Yes. I don't think there are many salesmen for other companies who are putting in fifty- to sixty-hour weeks. Everybody here works harder. You can go out in the plant or you can go upstairs and there's nobody sitting around.
  Q. Why do you think Lincoln employees have such high productivity?
  A. Piecework has a lot to do with it. Lincoln is smaller than many plants, too; you can stand in one place and see the materials come in one side and the product go out the other. You feel a part of the company. The chance to get ahead is important, too. They have a strict policy of promoting from within; you know you have a chance. I think in a lot of other places you may not get as fair a shake as you do here. The sales offices are on a smaller scale, too. I like that. I tell someone that we have two people in the Baltimore office and they say, "You've got to be kidding." It's smaller and more personal. Pay is the most important thing. I have heard that this is the highest paying factory in the world.

- *Joe Trahan, fifty-eight-year-old high school graduate, had been with Lincoln thirty-nine years and was employed as a working supervisor in the tool room.*
  Q. Roughly, what was your pay last year and how much was your bonus?
  A. Around $55,000; salary, bonus, stock dividends. My bonus was about $23,000.
  Q. What do you think of the executives at Lincoln?
  A. They're really top notch.
  Q. Why do you think you produce more than people in similar jobs?
  A. We are on the incentive system. Everything we do we try to improve to make a better product with a minimum of outlay. We try to improve the bonus.

Q. Tell me something about Mr. James Lincoln, who died in 1965.

A. You are talking about Jimmy, Sr. He always strolled through the shop in his shirt sleeves. Big fellow. Always looked distinguished. Gray hair. Friendly sort of guy. I was a member of the advisory board one year. He was there each time.

QUESTIONS

1. Describe Lincoln Electric's management philosophy, especially with regards to the motivation and leadership of the firm's work force.

2. The typical Lincoln employee earns about twice as much as other factory workers, yet labor costs are well below industry averages. Why? How can this be explained?

3. What are the major factors contributing to the high employee productivity at Lincoln Electric? Discuss.

4. What can other companies learn from Lincoln Electric's experience? Why haven't other firms applied the Lincoln philosophy and approach?

5. Would you want to work for Lincoln Electric? Explain your response.

REFERENCES

Lincoln, James F. *Incentive Management.* Cleveland, Ohio: Lincoln Electric Company, 1951.

Lincoln, James F. *A New Approach to Industrial Economics.* New York: Devin-Adair Company, 1961.

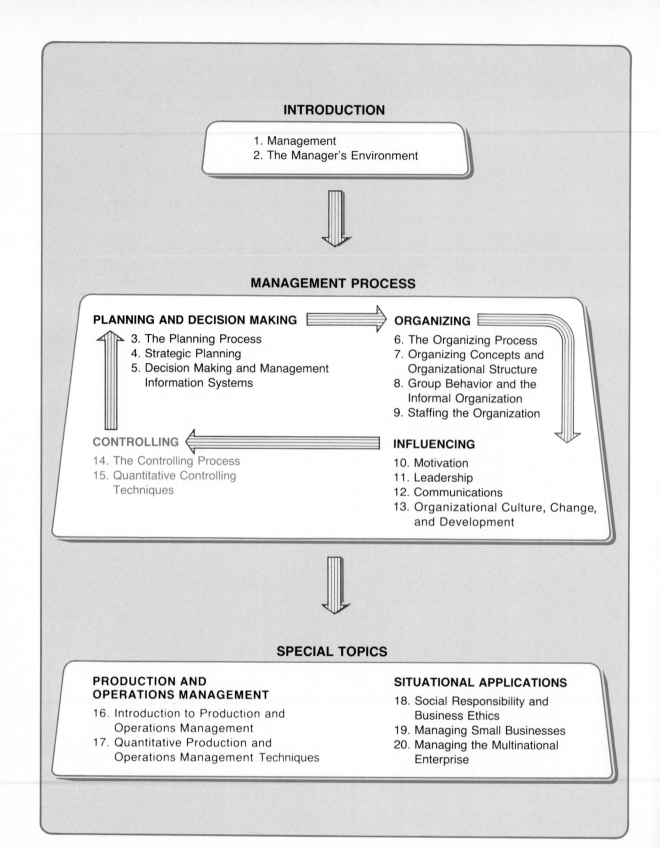

INTRODUCTION

1. Management
2. The Manager's Environment

MANAGEMENT PROCESS

PLANNING AND DECISION MAKING

3. The Planning Process
4. Strategic Planning
5. Decision Making and Management
   Information Systems

ORGANIZING

6. The Organizing Process
7. Organizing Concepts and
   Organizational Structure
8. Group Behavior and the
   Informal Organization
9. Staffing the Organization

CONTROLLING

14. The Controlling Process
15. Quantitative Controlling
    Techniques

INFLUENCING

10. Motivation
11. Leadership
12. Communications
13. Organizational Culture, Change,
    and Development

SPECIAL TOPICS

**PRODUCTION AND
OPERATIONS MANAGEMENT**

16. Introduction to Production and
    Operations Management
17. Quantitative Production and
    Operations Management Techniques

SITUATIONAL APPLICATIONS

18. Social Responsibility and
    Business Ethics
19. Managing Small Businesses
20. Managing the Multinational
    Enterprise

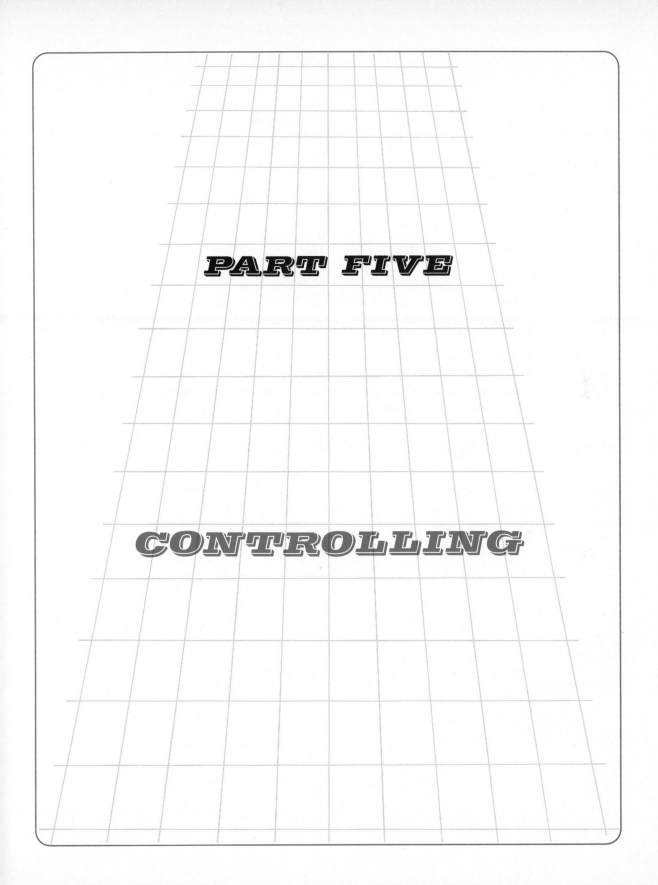

PART FIVE

CONTROLLING

LEARNING OBJECTIVES

After completing this chapter you should be able to

1. Define controlling and describe the control process.
2. Describe the most frequent types of standards and explain control tolerances.
3. Relate controlling to the business system.
4. Describe and identify the characteristics of strategic control points.
5. Relate the reasons for negative reactions to controls and describe ways of overcoming negative reactions to controls.
6. Explain the importance of disciplinary action and describe what is meant by the concept of progressive discipline.

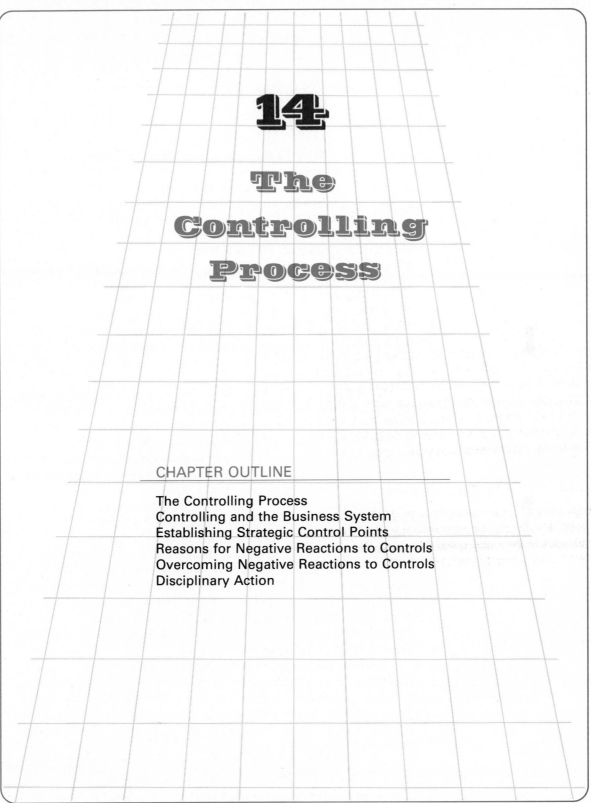

14

The Controlling Process

*Disciplined
Management
at 7-Eleven*

Through its 7-Eleven Stores Division, The Southland Corporation operates more than 10,000 convenience stores throughout the world, most of them in the United States. For more than twenty years, the company's revenues and earnings have grown, recently exceeding $8 billion and $131 million, respectively, per year. Fifteen and 20 percent yearly gains have not been unusual for Southland.

The 7-Eleven organization is well known for its system of tight control and disciplined management. The efficiency of the company's control system may be a reflection of the personality of the founder, Joe C. Thompson. His sister wrote, "The biggest influence on Joe's life, I believe, was discipline." Even competitors give the company good marks. The president of a rival convenience store chain said, "I think it has to be said that Southland is one of the great retailing stories of our time."

To make sure its small, 2,400-square-foot stores are successful, Southland extensively studies potential sites and uses computer programs to forecast a proposed store's sales for the first five years. A store that does not measure up to standards is often closed. John Thompson, son of the founder and now chairman, says that when stores look like losers, "we would rather close them than take our licks."

7-Eleven has been a leader in the computerization of store operations. Five automated distribution centers supply 7-Eleven stores in the United States. Specially designed trucks deliver prepriced items, along computer-designed routes, to individual stores. Careful analysis is made of which items sell best in which stores. Even shelf location is the subject of careful computerized evaluation. When trends change, items that no longer sell well are replaced by others, which are being continually tested in a few strategically located stores. A product that appears to be a rapid seller is tried nationwide.

Because of the limited floor space and wide array of merchandise, inventories must be tightly controlled. Using central computers in Dallas, Southland is able to determine which items to stock and what prices to charge. In addition, it is possible to analyze the operations of each store in the system in terms of profitability, inventory turnover, and so forth.

The ability of The Southland Corporation to respond to changing conditions is illustrated by the company's experience with gasoline

A typical 7-Eleven store.

Jerry Howard/Positive Images

marketing. In 1972, only 200 7-Eleven stores sold gasoline, but in the mid-1970s, when gasoline prices skyrocketed due to the Arab oil embargo, the self-service pumps at 7-Eleven stores became very popular. The company began to relocate a few of their stores from the traditional midblock location to corners, a proved marketing technique for gasoline stations but not for convenience stores. The corner locations produced 50 percent extra sales. Of the several thousand stores added since the mid-1970s, almost all sell gasoline and almost all are on corners. Although gasoline produces a very small profit margin for 7-Eleven, gasoline customers must come inside to pay, and many make purchases other than gasoline.[1]

As the 7-Eleven story illustrates, the control function is a vital part of the management process. A properly designed control system alerts the manager to the existence of potential problems and helps him or her to take corrective actions. At first, one might think that properly performing the functions of planning, organizing, and influencing would eliminate the need for controlling. Nothing could be further from the truth. First, it is impossible to anticipate every situation; consequently the organization must be ready to respond to unexpected changes. Consider what might happen if 7-Eleven were not ready to change product selection and prices in response to customer preferences. Even when we can identify the events that are likely, we are not certain what the future holds, so some adjustment is always necessary. An effective control system provides for these adjustments.

This chapter first describes the controlling process. Next, three types of controls are discussed. Then procedures for establishing strategic control points are described, followed by a discussion of the reasons why controls often produce negative reactions and a description of how these negative reactions may be overcome. Finally, disciplinary action as a means of controlling employee behavior is described.

THE CONTROLLING PROCESS

controlling **Controlling** is *the process of comparing actual performance with standards and taking any necessary corrective action.* The control process has three steps: (1) establish standards, (2) evaluate performance, and (3) take corrective action. Figure 14–1 illustrates these steps. Notice that like the other management functions, the controlling function is subject to environmental influences. For example, in 1984, 7-Eleven stores were picketed by fundamentalist Christian groups opposed to the distribution of *Penthouse* and *Playboy* magazines. This effort by members of the public undoubtedly caused some 7-Eleven customers to start shopping elsewhere. It was also of concern to the stockholders because of the probable impact on sales and profits. Southland's controlling process has to be carried out in the context of these and other external forces and must produce the proper responses. The phases of the controlling process at Southland are the same as in any other organization.

Establish Standards

standards We must know what is expected before the control process can be implemented. **Standards** are *established levels of quality or quantity used to guide performance.* For example, a shaft might have a standard diameter, and the machinist might try to cut the shaft to that size. Standards are sometimes viewed as goals. Wherever possible, standards should be expressed numerically, to reduce subjectivity, which tends to depersonalize the control process.[2] The most frequently used types of standards are listed and described below.

1. *Time standards:* Time standards state the length of time it should take to make a certain product or perform a certain service. An airline pilot has a standard time span in which to make a certain trip. Most organizations have a standard lunch time.
2. *Productivity standards:* These standards are based on the amount of product or service produced during a set time period. For instance, a productivity standard might be to produce 10 units per hour or to serve 150 customers per hour in a Wendy's restaurant.
3. *Cost standards:* These standards are based on the cost associated with producing the goods or service. For example, the material cost might be $10 per unit. Cost standards are usually set in the expense budget for the supervisor's unit. At 7-Eleven, strict quality standards are observed in selecting which brands of products to stock. Because of limited shelf space, 7-Eleven carries only the best-selling one or two brands of any particular item.

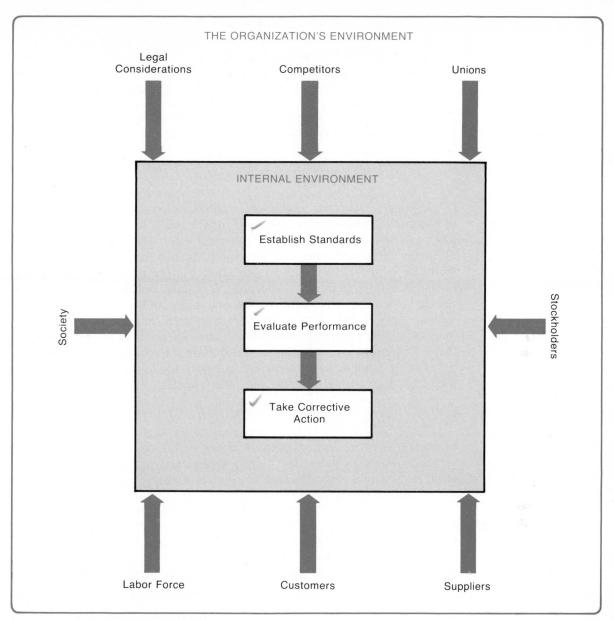

Figure 14–1   The Controlling Process

4. *Quality standards:* These are based on the level of perfection desired. For instance, no more than a certain percentage of impurities may be allowed in a chemical, or a valve may have to hold pressure for ten minutes in order to pass inspection.

5. *Behavioral standards:* These are based on the type of behavior desired of workers in the organization. Expressing these standards precisely is difficult. The convenience store industry, in particular, imposes strict standards of behavior on store managers and clerks. Workers in 7-Eleven stores are required to wear standard clothing, be neat, and treat customers courteously. Employees who violate behavioral standards are often subject to disciplinary action, the topic of a later section of this chapter.

Figure 14–2

*Standards and Control
Tolerances*

Standards	Tolerances
3.1″ shaft diameter	±0.05″
Perfect attendance	Two absences per month
8:00 A.M. starting time	Five minutes late
One minute waiting time	Fifteen seconds more
Clear polished surface	Two visible defects

control tolerances

Although standards are clear, control tolerances also need to be established. **Control tolerances** are *specifications of how much deviation will be permitted before corrective action is taken.* For instance, a standard of quality for a particular part may be 3.1 inches (see Figure 14–2), but a tolerance of ±0.05 inch may be permitted. If a part is produced within the range of 3.05 to 3.15, it is accepted. If it falls outside this range, it is rejected. As another example, a company might allow only two unexcused absences per month. A standard workday might be eight hours, but most managers have a certain tolerance of lateness, perhaps five minutes, that they will permit. Whether the standard relates to a product, a service, or behavior, it is important to communicate both the standard and the control tolerances to workers. If this is done, many workers will control themselves.

Evaluate Performance

Evaluating performance consists of checking for deviation from standard and determining if those deviations exceed control tolerances. Evaluation requires accurate measurement of what is taking place and an effective means of comparison with standards.

When the process being controlled is a mechanical one, measurement and comparison may be quite simple. For example, a quality control inspector may use a micrometer or other instrument to measure a part. Table 14–1 illustrates a checklist that a tire inspector for a major manufacturer uses. The inspector need only glance at the checklist after measuring the tire to see if a deviation from standard exceeds control tolerances.

Other processes, especially behavioral ones, are more difficult to measure. The courtesy with which a 7-Eleven employee serves customers

TABLE 14–1   QC Tread Checklist

	Standard	*Minimum*	*Maximum*	*Actual*
Width	22.15″	22.0″	22.3″	22.1″
Length	72.25″	72.0″	72.5″	72.1″
Thickness	.845″	.82″	.87″	.85″
Weight	8.7#	8.6#	8.8#	8.7#
Number of visible defects	0	0	2	0

is an example. When one of the authors was a young navy personnel officer, he reprimanded a clerk for working too slowly. The leading chief petty officer showed the young officer that, although the clerk appeared to be working slowly, he was actually doing more than his share. Managers should be careful to measure accurately before taking corrective action.

Take Corrective Action

The manager must consider what action to take to correct performance when deviations occur. Often the real cause of the deviation must be found before corrective action can be taken. Assume that the number of allowable defects produced by a certain machine exceeds standard. The cause may be a faulty machine or a careless operator. Clearly the proper corrective action depends on which one is the case.

Not all deviations from standard justify corrective action, and in some cases, personal judgment is necessary. Suppose that a worker is fifteen minutes late for work (a deviation from the standard), but you realize the lateness was unavoidable. You may decide to take no action, even though a deviation occurred. In this case, the standard is to be on time.

Corrective action may be either immediate or permanent. Immediate corrective action is often aimed at correcting *symptoms*. Permanent corrective action corrects the *cause* of the symptoms or problem. Most frequently corrective action is of the immediate type; it is done right away to correct the situation. For example, a particular project is a week behind schedule. If the delay is not corrected, other projects will be seriously affected. The first problem is not to worry about who caused the difficulty but to get the project back on schedule. Depending on the authority of the manager, the following corrective actions may be ordered: (1) overtime hours may be authorized; (2) additional workers and equipment may be assigned; (3) a full-time director may be assigned to push the project through; (4) an extra effort may be asked from all employees; or (5) if all these fail, the schedule may have to be readjusted, requiring changes all along the line.

After the degree of urgency has been diminished, attention can be devoted to more permanent corrective action. Just how and why did events stray from their planned course? What can be done to prevent a recurrence of this type of difficulty? Many managers fail at this phase. Too often they find themselves "putting out daily fires," and they never discover the actual cause of the problem. For instance, managers may find themselves constantly having to interview and hire new people to replace those who are leaving the firm. A manager may be working twelve hours a day attempting to locate new employees. But the high turnover problem is not solved merely by employing new workers. Managers must take some type of corrective action after they have determined what has caused the high turnover. A supervisor may be extremely difficult to work with, or the pay scale may not be competitive for the area. Whatever the problem, it must be identified and corrected, or the high turnover problem is likely to continue. Permanent corrective action must be taken for the sake of future economical and effective operations.

As illustrated by the project that was not on schedule, the manager may discover various fundamental causes for the difficulty. The schedule may not have been met because of a continuing difficulty in one department. Or it may be discovered that not only was this particular project in trouble, but most of the other projects in this company are behind schedule. In the first example, investigation may reveal that poor equipment in the one department is the major source of trouble. Thus, basic corrective actions would be to provide new or improved equipment or new or improved management. The project that initially experienced the difficulty will not likely be helped by this action; however, future projects should be improved. If most of the projects in a firm are usually behind schedule, an even more serious type of basic corrective action may be demanded: perhaps a drastic overhaul of general control procedures, or even reorganization of the entire company.

CONTROLLING AND THE BUSINESS SYSTEM

Recall from Chapter 2 that the business system was illustrated by the following simple diagram:

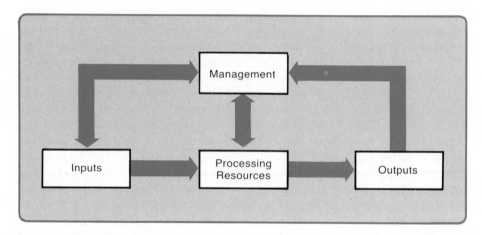

Controlling efforts by management may concentrate on inputs, the process itself, or outputs.

Controlling Inputs

With input controls, an attempt is made to monitor the resources—material and personnel—that come into the organization for the purpose of ensuring that they can be used effectively to achieve organizational objectives.

Material Controls

The material resources an organization requires must meet specified quality standards and be available when needed by the firm. If Ethan Allen, a major furniture manufacturer, purchased low-quality wood with which to manufacture furniture, the company could not maintain its reputation for producing excellent furniture. Statistical sampling (discussed in greater detail in Chapter 15) is often used to assist in material control. With statistical sampling, a portion of the items received into the firm are checked to estimate the quality of the entire lot. For instance, 5 percent of the lumber Ethan Allen receives might be examined. In many cases, failure of even a small percentage of the incoming items could create difficulty. Components for commercial aircraft engines are an example. Statistical sampling is not typically used in such situations. Rather, each item is inspected individually.

Personnel Selection Controls

If a firm is to maintain stability or growth, it continually needs new workers because of such factors as deaths, retirements, loss of employees to other organizations, and the firm's growth. In order to obtain new people capable of sustaining the organization, certain controls must be established regarding the selection of individuals. Skill requirements of each job must be determined, and new employees should meet or exceed these skills before being employed.

Controlling the Process

Overseeing the actual process of producing goods and services offers an opportunity to correct problems before outputs have been affected. Most of a typical supervisor's time is spent overseeing the process. Effective supervisors usually become familiar with the sights and sounds of the workplace and can often tell when something unusual is occurring. A wide range of possible signals is available to the supervisor. A noisy bearing on a bolt machine might warn the supervisor that the machine will begin to make defective bolts. Before a single faulty bolt has been produced, the bearing can be replaced.

Perhaps the most important aspect of this kind of control is observation and correction of employee behavior. A 7-Eleven store supervisor might observe an individual store manager's failing to put excess cash into the "drop safe" (to keep the cash exposed to potential theft at a minimum). Before this has caused any problem, the supervisor can correct the store manager's behavior. In fact, this is such a serious violation in the convenience store business that it often prompts disciplinary action (discussed later in this chapter). An observant supervisor often notices a worker looking around or behaving carelessly and takes action before output has been affected.

Observing workers, managers, and machines in the process of doing the organization's work is a tool of management at every level. A senior manager might observe a junior one cursing or otherwise behaving inappropriately and stop the misbehavior before it affects morale or productivity.

Controlling Outputs

The ultimate purpose of controlling focuses on the quality and quantity of outputs produced. In fact, most people think of controlling as simply checking what has occurred and taking corrective action. In the business system, this consists of quality and quantity controls, financial controls, and evaluation of employee performance based on output.

Quality and Quantity Controls

The purpose of quality control is to ensure that a certain level of excellence is attained. Quality has received renewed emphasis as Americans have become convinced that foreign manufacturers typically produce better automobiles, stereos, bicycles, and other products. Quality control must also be concerned with the costs of increasing quality. Therefore it is important for the quality necessary to meet company objectives to be determined in the planning stage. The Southland Corporation makes many of the items sold at 7-Eleven stores. The octane of the gasoline Southland makes at its Louisiana refinery is an indicator of quality; however, producing only 100 octane fuel would be prohibitively expensive so the company ensures that its gasoline is of at least standard quality in terms of octane. A similar situation exists in the manufacture of ice cream and yogurt by Southland's dairy products division. Trade-offs are necessary between the quality level one might prefer and the cost of achieving that level.

A common approach to evaluating quality is to seek comparison with other organizations or subunits. Figure 14–3 shows how three shift crews compare in terms of the acceptable parts they produce. The supervisor for shift 3 probably feels that that shift is deficient in comparison to the other two and should take corrective action.

Productivity is normally thought of in terms of the quality of output. Most companies expect a certain amount of production from each individual or organizational unit, often expressed in terms of a quota. Sales quotas specify the amount of sales an individual, district, or region is expected to meet. Production quotas specify the amount or number of an item that needs to be produced. Control of quotas at every level is important if the

Figure 14–3

Monthly Quality Comparison Report, by Shifts

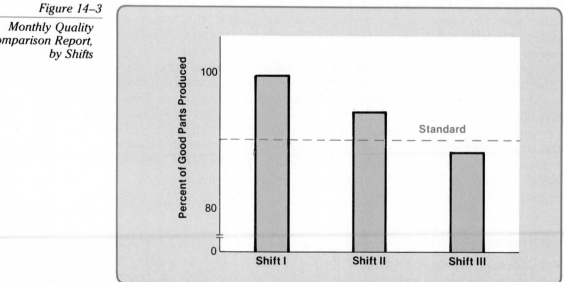

organization is to achieve its objectives. When a 7-Eleven store does not live up to sales expectations, it is closed. This is only done, of course, after a good deal of effort has been expended to bring the store up to standard.

Financial Controls

The ultimate output that most companies desire is net profit. The quality and quantity of goods and services is often seen as a means to this end. Financial statements provide valuable information with regard to whether a company, department, or unit is effectively using its financial resources. Intelligent interpretation of financial data provides an excellent means by which management can control its financial welfare.

Budgetary controls (discussed in the next chapter) also offer a way of ensuring that the company is performing well financially. Plans are made for certain levels of revenues and expenses. If at any time the company is not on track toward achieving those levels, a good budgeting system will initiate corrective action.

In order to analyze financial position, a firm would likely begin with ratio analysis. Financial ratio analysis provides management with a basis for comparing current to past performance. In addition, financial ratios can

TABLE 14–2   Summary of Financial Ratio Analysis

Category of Ratio	Name of Ratio	Formula for Calculation	Meaning and Definition of Ratio
Liquidity	Current ratio	$\dfrac{\text{current assets}}{\text{current liabilities}}$	Measures ability to meet debts when due—short-term liquidity
	Quick ratio	$\dfrac{\text{current assets-inventory}}{\text{current liabilities}}$	Measures ability to meet debts when due—very short-term liquidity
Leverage	Debt to total assets	$\dfrac{\text{total debt}}{\text{total assets}}$	Measures percentage of total funds that have been provided by creditors (debt = total assets − equity)
	Times interest earned	$\dfrac{\text{profit before tax} + \text{interest charges}}{\text{interest charges}}$	Measures the extent to which interest charges are covered by gross income
Profitability	Return on sales (net profit margin)	$\dfrac{\text{net income}}{\text{sales revenue}}$	Measures percent of profit earned on each dollar of sales
	Return on total assets	$\dfrac{\text{net income (AT)}}{\text{total assets}}$	Measures the return on total investment of a firm
	Return on equity	$\dfrac{\text{net income (AT)}}{\text{stockholder equity}}$	Measures rate of return on stockholders' investment
	Earnings per share	$\dfrac{\text{net income (AT)}}{\text{number of common shares outstanding}}$	Measures profit earned for each share of common stock
Activity	Total asset turnover	$\dfrac{\text{revenues}}{\text{total assets}}$	Measures effectiveness of assets in generating revenues
	Collection period	$\dfrac{\text{receivables}}{\text{revenues per day}}$	Measures amount of credit extended to customers
	Inventory turnover	$\dfrac{\text{sales}}{\text{inventory}}$	Measures number of times inventory is used to generate sales

be compared not only to past trends within the company but also to other divisions within the company and to other firms in the industry. If the ratios are not in line with acceptable standards, the manager is in a position to make corrections. There are four basic types of ratios:

- *Liquidity ratios* measure a firm's ability to meet its current obligations.
- *Leverage ratios* measure whether a firm has effectively used outside financing.
- *Activity ratios* measure how efficiently the firm is utilizing its resources.
- *Profitability ratios* measure the overall operating efficiency and profitability of the firm.

Names of ratios, the formula for their calculation, and the meaning and definition of the ratios may be seen in Table 14–2.

Evaluation of Employee Performance

Given a particular task to be accomplished, we would all likely perform at different levels of efficiency. One manager may be quite proficient in planning techniques and another in communication skills. But if we are to improve, we must know our deficiencies and determine what can be done to overcome these obstacles. An effective employee performance system is a means of control whereby individuals learn of their strengths and weaknesses and are told what should be done to overcome deficiencies. Collaborative approaches to performance appraisal done in a realistic, objective manner help subordinates grow and become more effective employees.[3] Employee performance evaluation systems that give each worker the same rating do not benefit the individual who is a superior performer nor do they assist the substandard worker who desires to improve.

The Challenge of Control

 Managing "the Chase," as the Chase Manhattan Bank is often called, is a truly monumental task. Chase is a global financial institution with more than 300 branches, 50 major subsidiaries, and 6,000 correspondent banks. The company's $80 billion in assets exceeds the gross national product of over half the nations of the world. After a spurt of growth from 1961 to 1967, the Chase was almost equal in assets to the largest U.S. bank, Bank of America, and the third largest, Citicorp. Beginning in the mid-1970s, the bank fell on hard times. The petrodollars that flowed into Arab coffers after the oil embargo of 1973 had swelled Chase's assets. Loan officers had hurriedly invested the cash in real estate investment trusts. But real estate values plummeted during that period, and Chase lost much of its money. "By the time we realized what was happening, it was out of control," one manager remarked. The bank had to write off over $500 million in real estate loans in the late 1970s. To prevent a recurrence, David Rockefeller, then president, restructured management and imposed a system of tight internal controls. A revised "mission statement" stressed growth through lending to top-rated borrowers.

Even after the new management system was in place, the Chase lost hundreds of millions in dealings with a government securities broker, Drysdale Government Securities, Inc., and through energy-related loans made in cooperation with the now-defunct Penn Square Bank in Oklahoma. By 1982, the company was less than two-thirds as large as either of its major competitors.

Some believe that the controls themselves fostered management misjudgments. "We've become a bank of internal salesmen," one official says. Another remarks, "If we try to do something innovative, we must knock ourselves out to get it through internally." George Champion, who served as chairman from 1961 to 1969, though, thinks the controls still are not tight enough. "Nothing like that happened when I was chairman," he says. "We knew what was going on in every department. I went through all of the departments to see and observe for myself. If any loan was $500 million or over, I took it to the board after studying it personally."

The ten officers who were responsible for the Drysdale and Penn Square loans were pushed out, and controls were tightened. Chase president Thomas Labrecque says that before doing anything new and different, managers must provide procedural documentation, and chairman Willard Butcher says managers are told to "put in an accounting memo that describes everything you do. No product or change can be made without filing a memo." One vice-president is quoted by *Forbes* magazine as saying, "Who the hell cares?" This attitude points up the challenge the Chase faces: how can the company impose the controls necessary to avoid debacles like those of the recent past and yet keep its people caring?[4]

ESTABLISHING STRATEGIC CONTROL POINTS

Management is concerned with controlling the business system, consisting of inputs, processes, and outputs. A frequent problem is determining what part of the system to monitor. Ideally, every resource, processing activity, and output should be measured, reported, and compared to a predetermined standard. This can be extremely costly and time-consuming. Imagine how complex this would be for a company like the Chase with its hundreds of branches and thousands of employees. A manager must determine what activity to measure and when to measure it. *Critical points selected for monitoring in the process of producing goods or services* are called **strategic control points**.

strategic control points

Strategic control points should have a number of basic characteristics. First, they should be established to regulate key operations or events. If a difficulty occurs at a strategic control point, the entire operation may grind to a halt. For instance, if the word processing manager for a Chase Manhattan branch does not have control of the type and quality of equipment purchased, inaccurate and untimely information may be sent to depositors. The problem created by poor-quality equipment may have a detrimental impact on the sales of the company even though the word processing personnel and sales force are of exceptional quality.

A second important characteristic of strategic control points is that they must be set up so that problems can be identified before serious damage occurs. If the control point is properly located, action can be taken to stop or alter a defective process before major harm is done. Testing for defects early in the process typically cuts costs and improves both

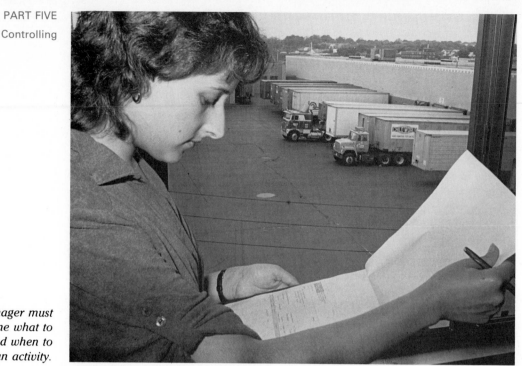

A manager must determine what to measure and when to measure an activity.

Richard Wood/The Picture Cube

production and quality.[5] It does little good to discover that a million defective parts have been produced. The control point should be located so deviations can be quickly identified and corrections made.

In the early days of one of the authors' careers, he had the opportunity to observe how the improper selection of strategic control points virtually caused a major tire manufacturer to be forced to cease operation. In the manufacture of a tire, four basic phases are required (see Figure 14–4). The mixing department must obtain the proper blend of rubber for the type of tire that is being produced. The tread is then shaped with specific attention being given to length, width, and thickness. The next phase, building, entails placing the various components such as the tread, steel belting, and white walls together. In the molding department, the tires are heated and shaped into final form.

A major problem occurred that forced the tire company to reevaluate the entire control procedure. The old system of control consisted only of inspecting tires after they had been molded. Because there was already a large investment in a tire at this stage, a tire would have to have a major defect before it would be rejected. Recognition of the deficiency in the control process occurred when the tire manufacturing firm received an order for several million dollars from a company that purchased tires and sold them at retail outlets under a different brand name. The retail chain, after careful inspection of the tires, rejected the order and demanded that the entire batch be redone. The tire manufacturing firm nearly went out of business because of this decision. Due to the large investment tied up in rejected inventory, the firm had to go heavily into debt to remake the order.

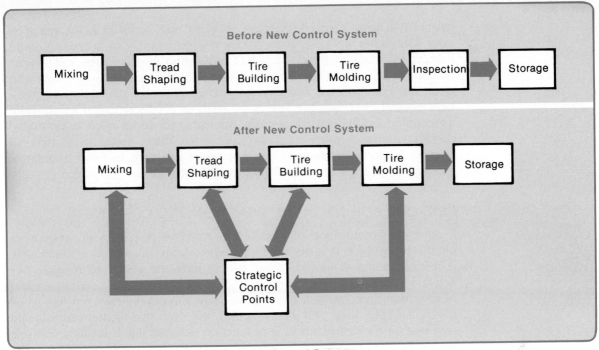

Figure 14–4   *Example of Placement of Strategic Control Points*

After this experience, major changes were made in the control process. A separate quality control department, reporting directly to the president, was established. Quality control inspectors were hired and given authority to stop operations, even over the advice of the production superintendent, if they felt it was needed to maintain high quality. Strategic control points were located in the four major departments (see Figure 14–4). If a problem occurred in the mixing department, it would be discovered before the tire progressed through the other stages. Because of this intensive effort to improve quality, the firm was able to survive and prosper.

A third consideration is that the choice of strategic control points should indicate the level of performance for a broad spectrum of key events. At times, this comprehensiveness conflicts with the need for proper timing. Net profit, for example, is a comprehensive strategic control point, indicating the progress of the entire enterprise. Yet if one waits until the regular accounting period to obtain this figure, one loses control of the immediate future. It does little good to recognize that you are now bankrupt; you need to have accounting figures ahead of time so that corrective action may be taken.

Economy is the fourth consideration in the choice of proper control points. With computer and management information systems available, there is a strong temptation to demand every conceivable bit of information. But there is only a limited amount of information that an executive can effectively use. If every bit of information is available to the executive, critical information may be lost in the masses of data. Simply stated, "You can't see the forest for the trees."

Finally, the selection of various strategic control points should be balanced. If only credit losses are watched and controlled, for example, sales may suffer because of an overly stringent policy in accepting credit risks. If sales are emphasized out of proportion, credit losses will mount. Overemphasis on sales was the problem with the managers at Chase who made the Penn Square and Drysdale loans. There is a tendency to place tight control over tangible functions, such as production and sales, while maintaining limited control over the intangible functions such as personnel development and other staff services. This often leads to a state of imbalance where production line executives are held to exact standards, and staff executives are seemingly given blank checks.

REASONS FOR NEGATIVE REACTIONS TO CONTROLS

Despite the importance of controls to effective management, employees often view controls in a negative way. When the term *controls* is mentioned, it reminds some of us that other people have the power to regulate our activities. There is a natural resistance to controls because a certain amount of individual freedom has been taken away. Employees may not like to be controlled, but they will likely accept the fact that some controls are necessary if the organization is to function successfully. It is when controls are established that are inappropriate, unattainable, unpredictable, uncontrolled, or contradictory that major negative resistance is encountered.[6]

Inappropriate Controls

Often controls are not related to the goals of the organization. If the wrong thing is being controlled, this will not contribute to doing the right thing efficiently. After Chase lost millions in real estate investment trusts, David Rockefeller imposed tight internal controls. He failed, however, to place adequate controls on Chase's dealing with Drysdale Government Securities and Penn Square Bank. At that time, the risk of losses from real estate trusts had already been corrected, but the concentration on controlling real estate dealings apparently caused Chase to neglect other high-risk areas.

Unattainable Standards

Employees realize when a standard is unrealistic. When unattainable controls are established, it may actually cause some employees to work below their capabilities. For instance, suppose that you are a machine operator and had been producing effectively at a standard of twenty units an hour. If management arbitrarily increased the standard to forty units, you may feel that the standard is unattainable. Productivity may actually be lowered below the original twenty units.

Unpredictable Standards

When the control system is unpredictable and constantly changed, much frustration and resentment of the control process can result. For instance, if a production manager is told that he or she should strive to achieve maximum output and, once this high output level has been achieved, told that quality is more important, resentment to the control process can result. The production manager could not predict what standard he or she was to be evaluated on. The managers at Chase probably thought they were doing the right thing by attempting to increase loan volume through lower-quality loans. Later, however, the attention of the bank was on loan quality rather than volume.

No Control over the Situation

A frustrating encounter that can occur to anyone is to be reprimanded for something you cannot control. Suppose, for instance, that a manager is told that she will be evaluated regarding the profit and loss of her department, but she does not have the authority to hire and fire employees. Frustration becomes extremely high in instances such as this and can work to the detriment of the entire control system.

Contradictory Standards

At times, various controls may be established that do not complement each other. It may appear to the manager that if one standard is achieved, it would be impossible to accomplish the other. For instance, it might appear to some managers that high quality and maximum output are contradictory in nature. To a marketing manager, a control system that stresses both increased sales and reducing the advertising expenditure rate may appear contradictory.

OVERCOMING NEGATIVE REACTIONS TO CONTROLS

Although people may be inclined to resist controls, there are means that a manager can use to assist in reducing negative reactions. Some of the reasons discussed below may appear obvious, but the ineffectiveness of some control systems makes it clear that they are not always practiced.

Justifiable

If employees believe that there is a need for a particular control system, compliance is much easier to obtain. For instance, the firm may have to increase the quality of its product in order to obtain future contracts. These contracts will mean not only profit for the firm but job stability for the employees. A control system will have higher acceptability if the reason for the control appears justifiable to those who must comply.

Understandable

Employees who know exactly what is expected of them with regard to a control system tend to exhibit less resistance. For instance, a statement by a manager that quality should increase does not clearly convey what is expected. A requirement that the number of defects should decrease by 10 percent is precise and understandable. When workers do not understand what is expected of them, frustration and resentment can occur.

Realistic

A realistic control system is one that permits the organization to achieve its goals and is also obtainable by the employees who work within the control system. For example, at times it may appear that controls are established merely to harass the worker. Excessive standards that are higher than needed to accomplish the purpose of the organization are not only expensive but may well be resisted by company employees. Although Chase may desire to have zero loan losses in the future, such an expectation is unrealistic. Banks typically have to decide what degree of risk is acceptable.

Timely

For a control system to be effective, information regarding deviations needs to be communicated to employees as quickly as practical. It does little good to tell workers that their performance was below standard three weeks ago. If a problem is to be corrected, it must receive immediate attention. At Chase, the managers who were fired for making bad loans years earlier would probably have appreciated knowing what the standards were before they made the loans.

Accurate

Nothing could be worse than to have a control system that provides inaccurate information. If information feedback has proved incorrect in the past, it may be difficult to convince individuals that their effort is below standards. If workers consistently find errors made by supervisors, belief in their ideas may be questioned. An employee who receives a low performance evaluation may have reason to suspect the evaluation is inaccurate even if it is not.

DISCIPLINARY ACTION

Although employees are carefully selected, they sometimes behave in ways that appear to be unacceptable.

> John Phillip, a machine operator for Boeing Aircraft, was not wearing safety glasses when his supervisor came to his work area. A company directive required all personnel to wear the glasses when working in that plant location.
>
> Jodi Haun, an accounts receivable specialist for Southeast Utilities, has arrived one hour late for work four times this week, and it is only Thursday. She has never called in to explain the reason for being late.
>
> Betty Garcia, an airline hostess for Eastern Airlines, has been advised that the public relations office has received several passenger complaints regarding her attitude and performance on the plane.

In all three instances, a potential for disciplinary action exists; however, because the details of each circumstance are not known, a person cannot readily determine if disciplinary action is actually required. But if a control system does not exist to identify problems when they occur, potential problems will go unrecognized. The purpose of establishing controls is to determine if deviations have taken place regarding a particular standard. It follows that a natural by-product of controls is disciplinary action.

Figure 14–5   *The Disciplinary Action Process*   Source: Adapted from R. Wayne Mondy and Robert M. Noe, III, *Personnel: The Management of Human Resources,* 2nd ed. (Newton, Mass.: Allyn and Bacon, 1984), p. 524.

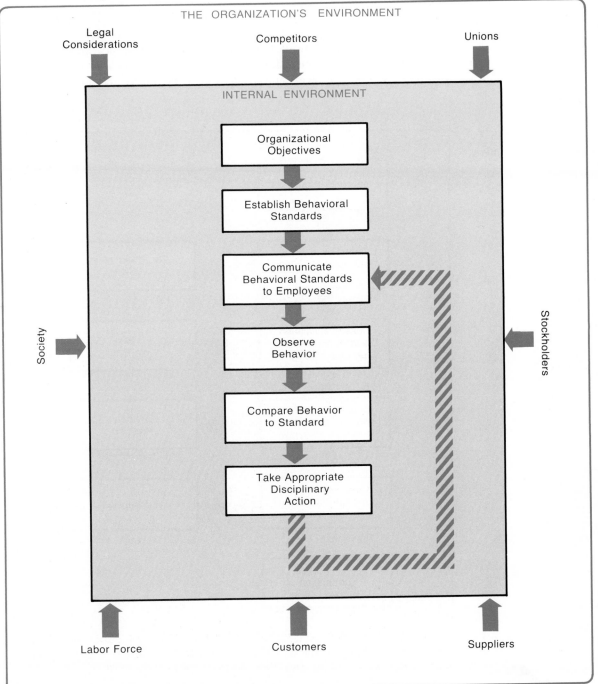

Disciplinary action is *action taken to correct unacceptable behavior.* Many of the problems a manager faces relate to disciplinary actions. Approximately half of all grievance cases appealed to an impartial arbitrator by labor unions involve disciplinary action, and management's decisions are overturned in approximately half of these cases. It is evident from the statistics that managers are not applying disciplinary action in a generally accepted manner.

The disciplinary action process is shown in Figure 14–5. The process begins with gaining a clear understanding of organizational objectives. Behavioral standards should be created to facilitate accomplishment of these objectives, and they should be clearly communicated to employees. Behavior is then observed and compared to standards. No difficulty exists

Figure 14–6

Progressive Discipline

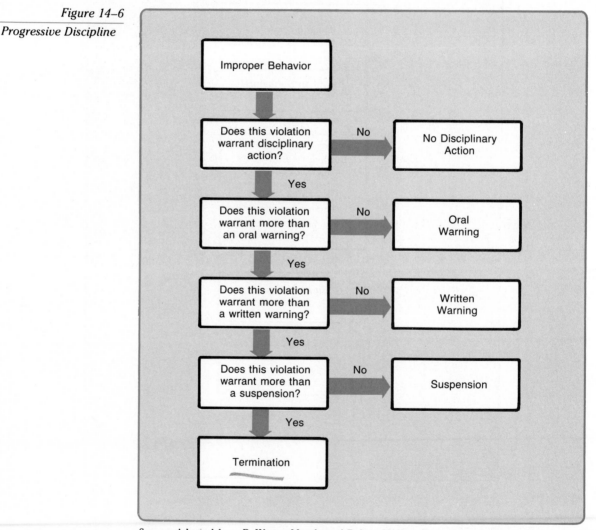

Source: Adapted from R. Wayne Mondy and Robert M. Noe, III. *Personnel: The Management of Human Resources,* 2nd ed. (Newton, Mass.: Allyn and Bacon, 1984), p. 526.

if behavior is in line with standards; however, disciplinary action *may* be needed when deviations exist. Once disciplinary action has been taken, it serves to reinforce the importance of the standard to other employees.

A modern concept of discipline is known as progressive discipline, illustrated in Figure 14–6. The idea of **progressive discipline** is *an approach to imposing disciplinary action designed to ensure that the minimum penalty appropriate to the offense is imposed and involves answering a series of questions about the severity of the offense.* As you progress down the list of questions, disciplinary action gets progressively more severe. Also notice that the mere fact that a violation has occurred does not mean that disciplinary action must be taken. Managers may use their discretion and decide that no action should be taken. On the other hand, fighting on the job may result in automatic suspension. When the violation is serious, as was considered to be the case with several Chase loan officers, and the answers to all of the questions are "yes," the person is fired. An extension of the progressive discipline concept is called *no-fault attendance control.* Under this procedure, workers and supervisors together decide the maximum allowable absences and the penalties to be assessed.[7]

progressive discipline

Managers should keep in mind that the main purpose of disciplinary action is not to punish or eliminate employees but to improve their contribution to the organization. Rehabilitation achieves this goal more often than termination. Managers have identified guides to assist in handling disciplinary cases, whether or not the detailed process of progressive discipline is practiced.

• The manager should exhibit the attitude of assuming that all employees desire to conform to reasonable organizational requirements. One should not appear to invite trouble.
• The act, rather than the person, should be condemned.
• Although the act may be the basis for penalty, a model of future desired behavior should be communicated.
• Reasonable promptness is important so that the employee can connect the penalty to the violation.
• A managerial listening role is highly essential to (1) effect greater understanding of the reasons for the act and (2) prevent hasty decisions that may lead to unjustified penalties.
• Negative disciplinary action should be administered in private so that the employee can save face among colleagues.
• Definite, but tactful, follow-up should occur to determine the degree of success of the conditioning effort.
• Consistency and flexibility, though apparently contradictory, are both desirable elements of a superior's style of disciplining.

SUMMARY

Controlling is the process of comparing actual performance with established standards and taking any necessary corrective action. The control process has three steps: establish standards, evaluate performance, and take corrective action. In an organization, the most important means by which performance can be compared to standard relate to time, productivity, cost, quality, and behavior. Controlling efforts by management may concentrate on inputs, the process itself, or outputs. Controlling inputs may take place as resources enter the organization. Controlling the process offers an opportunity to correct problems before outputs have been affected. The ultimate purpose of controlling focuses on the quality of output produced. At all times, a manager must determine what to measure and when to measure an activity. These critical areas are referred to as strategic control points.

Managers must understand that employees may react negatively to controls. Some of these negative reactions are a result of inappropriate controls, unattainable standards, unpredictable standards, no control over the situation, and contradictory standards. Negative reactions to controls may be overcome. Controls that are justifiable, understandable, realistic, timely, and accurate will likely receive the least resistance.

A natural by-product of controls is disciplinary action, action taken to correct unacceptable behavior. Progressive discipline is an approach to improving disciplinary action designed to ensure that the minimum penalty appropriate to the offense is imposed; it involves answering a series of questions about the severity of the offense. Although difficulties can arise through the use of disciplinary action, guidelines to handling disciplinary cases can help to avoid such problems.

REVIEW QUESTIONS

1. Define controlling. What are the steps in the control process?
2. What are the most frequently used types of standards? Briefly discuss each.
3. What are specific means of controlling inputs and outputs? Briefly describe each.
4. What factors should a manager consider in establishing strategic control points?
5. List and describe the reasons for negative reactions to controls. What are the ways of overcoming negative reactions to controls?
6. Define disciplinary action and progressive discipline. What guidelines should a manager follow when disciplinary action must be taken?

EXERCISES

1. Develop a plan for obtaining an A in this course. What type of control measures must you develop to accomplish this goal?
2. What types of controls do you believe the following types of businesses and managers must have to ensure that they accomplish their objectives?

a. Small convenience store
b. College or university
c. Firm that manufactures a high-quality hand calculator
d. Insurance agency
e. Automobile repair shop

CASE STUDY

Flextime

Kathy Collier is a supervisor of a government office in Washington, D.C. Morale in her office has been quite low recently. The workers have gone back to an 8:00 A.M. to 4:30 P.M. work schedule after having been on flextime for nearly two years.

When the directive came down allowing Kathy to place her office on flextime, she spelled out the rules carefully to her people. Each person was to work during the core period from 10:00 A.M. to 2:30 P.M.; however, they could work the rest of the eight-hour day at any time between 6:00 A.M. and 6:00 P.M. Kathy felt her workers were honest and well motivated, so she did not bother to set up any system of control.

Everything went along well for a long time. Morale improved, and all the work seemed to get done. In November 1985, however, an auditor from the General Accounting Office investigated and found that Kathy's workers were averaging seven hours a day. Two employees had been working only during the core period for more than two months. When Kathy's department manager reviewed the auditor's report, Kathy was told to return the office to regular working hours. Kathy was upset and disappointed with her people. She had trusted them and felt they had let her down.

QUESTIONS

1. What type of controls should Kathy have used to prevent the problem: initial, overseeing, or post-controls? Explain your answer.
2. Should Kathy be disappointed with her people? Why or why not?

CASE STUDY

Differing Philosophies

Collins and Bradford (C&B) is a manufacturing company with sales of approximately $250 million. C&B employs twelve college-trained accountants at its headquarters. These positions are divided among financial accounting, cost accounting, accounts payable, and auditing. Tom Brown came to work at C&B in the financial accounting department. He had a B.B.A. from a major university and two years of previous work experience in accounting. He caught on quickly, did a good job, and was well liked by his supervisor and fellow employees. After eleven months, a position became available in the cost accounting department that offered Tom a higher salary and an opportunity to develop professionally in another area.

After three months in the cost accounting department, it became apparent to Tom that he and his supervisor, Ed Blake, could not work together. Tom disagreed with Ed's training techniques and Ed's philosophy on how certain problems should be handled. It also became evident that they had a severe personality conflict. After a full month of deliberation on what to do, Tom decided to go to John Collins, Ed's supervisor, and ask for a transfer. He explained that he wanted to remain at C&B but that neither he nor the cost department was benefiting from his being in his present position.

Ed and John had been friends and working associates for years, and John's initial reaction was to blame Tom for the bad situation. He surveyed the other accounting positions and did not see any openings coming up in the near future. John felt that he had three alternatives—to create an additional accounting position in another department and transfer Tom, to work with Ed and Tom to reconcile the problems, or to terminate Tom.

QUESTIONS

1. What might have caused the conflict between Tom and Ed? How can this type of conflict be controlled so as not to affect adversely a firm's operations?

2. What action should John take? Is he limited to the three alternatives mentioned at the end of the case?

3. If you were Tom Brown, what would you do?

NOTES

1. This story is a composite taken from a number of published sources, including: Shawn Tully, "Look Who's a Champ of Gasoline Marketing," *Fortune* (November 1, 1982): 149–154; Mitchell Gordon, "A Matter of Convenience: Southland's Sprawling 7-Eleven Chain Rings Up Fresh Gains," *Barrons* (December 6, 1982): 43–47; Tom Bayer, "7-Eleven Takes Steps to Move beyond Image," *Advertising Age* (December 7, 1981): 77–78; "From Super to Merely Excellent," *Financial World* (October 1, 1980): 22–23; "Southland's Risky Plunge into Refining," *Business Week* (April 11, 1983): 33.

2. S. M. Klein and R. R. Ritti, *Understanding Organizational Behavior* (Boston: Kent Publishing Co., 1984), p. 509.

3. R. L. Taylor and R. A. Zawachi, "Trends in Performance Appraisal: Guidelines for Managers," *Personnel Administrator* 29, no. 3 (March 1984): 71.

4. Priscilla S. Mayer, "Burdens of the Past," *Forbes* (July 18, 1983): 32–34; Adam Smith, "How Banks Got into Such Trouble," *Esquire* (January 1983): 14–16; "History of Chase 1799–1982," *Chase News* (March 1982): 2–8; David Blake, "Banks on the Brink," *New Statesman* (January 7, 1983): 18–19; Richard B. Miller, "Chase Manhattan—The Rockefeller Years," *Bankers Magazine* (March–April 1981): 54–64.

5. Jon Turino, "Test Strategies That Cut Manufacturing Costs," *SAM Advanced Management Journal* 49, no. 1 (Winter 1984): 53.

6. Robert N. Anthony and Regina E. Herzlinger, *Management Control in Non-Profit Organizations* (Homewood, Ill.: Irwin, 1975), pp. 222–226.

7. D. Olson and R. Bangs, "No-Fault Attendance Control: A Real World Application," *Personnel Administrator* 29, no. 6 (June 1984): 54.

REFERENCES

Buffa, Elwood S. *Modern Production-Operations Management.* 6th ed. New York: Wiley, 1980.

Camillus, John C. "Six Approaches to Preventive Management Control." *Financial Executive* 48 (December 1980): 28–31.

Chase, Richard B., and Nicholas J. Aquilano. *Production and Operations Management: A Life Cycle Approach.* Homewood, Ill.: Irwin, 1981.

Dalton, Dan R., and William D. Todor. "Win, Lose, Draw: The Grievance Process in Practice." *Personnel Administrator* 26 (March 1981): 25–29.

DeWelt, R. L. "Control: Key to Making Financial Strategy Work." *Management Review* 66 (March 1977): 18–25.

Flamholtz, Eric. "Organizational Control System as a Managerial Tool." *California Management Review* 22 (Winter 1979): 50–59.

Gannon, John S. "How to Handle Discipline within the New National Labor Relations Board Requirements." *Personnel Administrator* 26 (March 1981): 43–47.

Gitman, Lawrence J. *Principles of Managerial Finance.* 2d ed. New York: Harper, 1979.

Hayhurst, B. "Proposal for a Corporate Control System." *Management International Review* 16 (1976): 93–103.

Horovitz, J. H. "Strategic Control: A New Task for Top Management." *Long Range Planning* 12 (June 1979): 2–7.

Klein, S. M., and R. R. Ritti. *Understanding Organizational Behavior.* Boston: Kent Publishing Co., 1984.

Lippert, F. G. "Quality Indicators." *Supervision* (March 1984): 16–17.

Lissy, William E. "Necessity of Proof to Support Disciplinary Action." *Supervision* 40 (June 1978): 13.

Machin, John L., and Lyn S. Wilson. "Closing the Gap between Planning and Control." *Long Range Planning* 12 (April 1979): 16–32.

Mondy, R. Wayne, and Robert M. Noe III. *Personnel: The Management of Human Resources,* 2nd ed. Newton, Mass.: Allyn and Bacon, 1984.

Nelson, E. G., and J. L. Machin. "Management Control: Systems Thinking Applied to Development of a Framework for Empirical Studies." *Journal of Management Studies* (October 1976): 274–287.

Olson, D., and R. Bangs. "No-Fault Attendance Control: A Real World Application." *Personnel Administrator* 29, no. 6 (June 1984): 53–56.

Ouchi, W. G. "Relationship between Organizational Structure and Organizational Control." *Administrative Science Quarterly* 22, no. 1 (March 1981): 95–113.

Pingpank, Jeffery C., and Thomas B. Mooney. "Wrongful Discharge: A New Danger for Employers." *Personnel Administrator* 26 (March 1981): 31–35.

Schroeder, Roger G. *Operations Management: Decision Making in the Operations Function.* New York: McGraw-Hill, 1981.

Solomon, Ezra, and John J. Pringle. *An Introduction to Financial Management.* Santa Monica, Calif.: Goodyear, 1980.

Swann, James P., Jr. "Formal Grievance Procedures in Non-Union Plants." *Personnel Administrator* 26 (August 1981): 66–70.

Taylor, R. L., and R. A. Zawachi. "Trends in Performance Appraisal: Guidelines for Managers." *Personnel Administrator* 29, no. 3 (March 1984): 71–80.

Turino, Jon. "Test Strategies That Cut Manufacturing Costs." *SAM Advanced Management Journal* 49, no. 1 (Winter 1984): 42–53.

budget	inventory	ABC inventory method
capital budget	economic order	just-in-time inventory
operating budget	quantity (EOQ)	method (JIT)
quality	ordering costs	PERT
acceptance sampling	carrying costs	CPM
control chart		

LEARNING OBJECTIVES

After completing this chapter you should be able to

1. Define various types of budgets and identify the benefits and limitations of budgets.
2. Explain quality control and state the usefulness of control charts.
3. Describe the importance of inventory control and explain various methods of inventory control.
4. Explain network models and describe how PERT can assist in both planning and control.

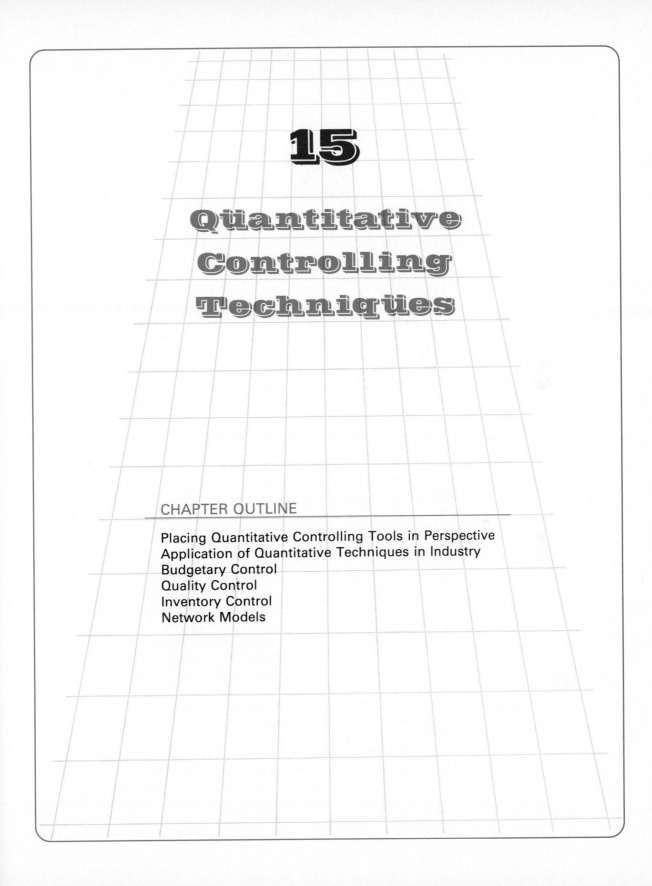

15

Quantitative Controlling Techniques

CHAPTER OUTLINE

Placing Quantitative Controlling Tools in Perspective
Application of Quantitative Techniques in Industry
Budgetary Control
Quality Control
Inventory Control
Network Models

A thirty-five-year veteran autoworker at General Motor's Pontiac engine plant number 18 in Detroit describes how it was in the old days when he found a tool was going bad. "I'd tell the supervisor and he'd say 'Leave it for the second shift.' The second shift would leave it for the third shift, and the third shift would leave it for me in the morning. Then my supervisor would say, 'Leave it for the weekend.' Well, now we've got only the day shift left. And if we don't do better, there just ain't gonna be no day shift."

Today worker participation and training are the rule rather than the exception at plant 18. Workers and union officials recently even helped design a new production line. Years earlier, that would have been left to the process engineers. Every worker takes a four-week course and leaves with a magnifying glass to help see defects in the tools, a pocket calculator, and a good understanding of statistical controls. With many new quantitative controls in effect, workers find frequent uses for what they have learned.

The output of the plant shows the changes that have occurred. Pontiac struggled for years to improve the quality of its engines. Now improvements happen every day. Plant 18 had trouble with threads on the connecting rod bolts it bought from four suppliers. As it turned out, practically all the defective bolts came from one supplier. When that supplier was dropped, the failures stopped. A certain camshaft gear has to be accurate within a few ten-thousandths of an inch. If the gear does not meet the standard, the engine has to be pulled and the gear replaced at a cost of over $1,000. It was discovered that checking three successive gears once an hour kept the boring from getting out of kilter. Failures dropped from thirty-eight engines requiring the costly repair job one year, to six the next, to none in the most recent year.

What accounts for the change? The main factor is Dr. W. Edwards Deming, the eighty-three-year-old statistician who is given credit for much of Japan's manufacturing preeminence and for whom two of that country's national productivity prizes are named. Deming was invited to the Pontiac plant after general manager William Hogland saw an NBC documentary, "If Japan Can . . . Why Can't We?" Deming was then already back in the United States at Nashua Corporation. Hogland invited him to come to plant 18.

Hogland had no idea what a difference Deming would make. "His message shook the foundations of our approach to quality," says Hogland. Workers and managers alike at plant 18 view Deming—who looks more like Charles de Gaulle than Albert Einstein—with awe.

Many have memorized his "14 points to improve quality." A few of his points follow:

- Don't rely on mass inspection.
- Drive out fear by encouraging open, two-way communications.
- Teach statistical techniques. The rudiments can be learned in five-day crash courses.
- Make maximum use of the statistical knowledge and talent in your company.

The new concern for quantitative controls applies not only to product quality but to costs as well. Thus, budgeting has taken on a new importance at plant 18.

Deming claims that a company can improve quality best by controlling its purchasing system. "Work with fewer vendors," he says. "First, find one good supplier; then you can look for more." Deming continues, "Insist on evidence of quality through control charts from every vendor. . . . Without the charts, neither the vendor nor the buyer can prove that quality levels are constant—day after day, lot after lot—or what his costs are."

Just as the system worked in Japan, so it is working at plant 18. James Harbour, an auto industry consultant, writes, "The Pontiac engine plants are a superb example of what can be accomplished when you decide that quality and productivity go hand in hand."[1]

In the last chapter we discussed the controlling process. Today, this process uses many quantitative techniques. The Deming system provides an excellent example of a properly implemented quantitative control system. In fact, statistical control systems are credited with causing the turnaround of plant 18. The control systems that are imposed must support and encourage employees rather than constrain them.

In this chapter, we first place the quantitative tools available to management in proper perspective. Then, the applications of quantitative techniques in industry will be described. Next, we will discuss budgetary control. The latter sections of the chapter are devoted to quality control, inventory control, and networking techniques. Some of the tools mentioned below have their primary application in production and operations management, the subjects of Chapters 16 and 17.

PLACING QUANTITATIVE CONTROLLING TOOLS IN PERSPECTIVE

Numerous quantitative techniques are available to managers. The techniques have application in every area of management, and especially in planning and controlling. Our emphasis on quantitative tools should not be taken to mean that a manager is always expected to know the detailed mathematics of each approach. James F. Olson, manager, corporate strategic planning for General Mills, Inc., reinforced the authors' philosophy with regard to quantitative tools when he stated, "I would urge students to become as familiar as possible with all techniques but to remain enough detached from them to allow clear thinking to take place." A manager should at least have an appreciation of the following: the tools available, the situation for which the tools are designed, and how the tools are used in business.

An apparent misconception has evolved among students of management regarding the use of quantitative techniques: that these tools cannot be used without complete knowledge of and skill in the quantitative techniques. *This need not be the case.* Prudent managers want to utilize their resources to the maximum extent. Thus, a manager must be capable of recognizing what tools are applicable and when they should be used. Once the manager has made this determination, a mathematician, statistician, or computer specialist can perform the actual calculation. These individuals are trained to implement a quantitative technique once the manager has made the decision as to which tool is appropriate and identified the factors that should be considered in the problem. In many cases specialists like W. Edwards Deming are available to help in deciding which tools to use. But managers must still use their personal judgment once a mathematical answer has been obtained. As D. F. Eckdahl, senior vice-president, engineering and manufacturing, of NCR Corporation stated: "Since no mathematical model can satisfactorily emulate all aspects of most decision problems, it is essential that sound judgment is exercised in evaluating mathematical models rather than unquestioning reliance on simple quantitative results."

After all factors affecting a decision are considered, a manager must still exercise sound judgment in deciding whether to use solutions that have been derived from the use of quantitative techniques.

APPLICATION OF QUANTITATIVE TECHNIQUES IN INDUSTRY

Many companies make extensive use of various quantitative tools. The need may be different for each firm, but the fact remains that the tools are being used. This was vividly illustrated when the authors surveyed a sample of major firms in the United States as to which primary quantitative tools they used (Table 15–1). Each surveyed firm had a minimum of $250 million in annual sales. As you might imagine, their use of the quantitative tools apparently depended on the nature of the business and the specific desires of management.

TABLE 15–1   Use of Quantitative Techniques

Primary Product of Firm	Primary Quantitative Techniques Used
Vehicle components and assemblies	Inventory control models Economic modeling
Railroad transportation	Discounted cash flow techniques PERT, CPM Simulation
Pharmaceuticals, proprietary remedies, confections, cosmetics and toiletries	Simulation

Primary Product of Firm	Primary Quantitative Techniques Used
Petroleum	Simulation Mathematical programming Discounted cash flow techniques Probability theory (Bayesian statistics, payoff and risk analysis)
Construction, engineering, and real estate development	Simulation Mathematical programming PERT, CPM
Tires and tubes	Inventory control models Discounted cash flow techniques
Automobile accessories	Simulation Probability theory (Bayesian statistics, payoff and risk analysis) Inventory control models
Industrial and agriculture products	Inventory control models
Petroleum products	PERT, CPM Discounted cash flow techniques
Building products	Simulation Probability theory (Bayesian statistics, payoff and risk analysis) Inventory control models Discounted cash flow techniques
Steel	Inventory control models Mathematical programming Discounted cash flow techniques
Building products	Inventory control models PERT, CPM
Electrical equipment	Inventory control models PERT, CPM
Paper products	Discounted cash flow techniques Simulation Mathematical programming
Computers	PERT, CPM Simulation
Natural gas	Discounted cash flow techniques
Toiletries and grooming aids	Inventory control models Discounted cash flow techniques Simulation
Aircraft	Discounted cash flow techniques PERT, CPM
Computers	Discounted cash flow techniques Simulation
Tires	Inventory control models Discounted cash flow techniques
Heating and refrigeration equipment	Inventory control models Discounted cash flow techniques
Construction and engineering	PERT, CPM
Engines and trucks	Inventory control models Discounted cash flow techniques Mathematical programming
Petroleum	Discounted cash flow techniques
Catalog order and retail department store	Inventory control models Simulation
Beverages and food concentrates	Discounted cash flow techniques

budget

BUDGETARY CONTROL

The most basic and widely used quantitative controlling technique is the budget. A **budget** is *a statement of planned allocation of resources expressed in financial or numerical terms.* Budgetary control is concerned with the comparison of actual to planned expenditures. Most areas of operations in a business enterprise—marketing, production, materials, labor, manufacturing expense, capital expenditures, and cash—have budgets. The operating budget for Pontiac's plant 18 includes specific allowances for every major activity in making engines.

Types of Budgets

capital budget

Often the budget is the most important document a manager uses in planning and controlling operations. There are basically two broad categories of budgets: capital budgets and operating budgets. A **capital budget** is *a statement of planned expenditures of funds for facilities and equipment.* The machines that will be required to make engines at plant 18 must be designed and even ordered years in advance. The capital budget therefore typically extends over several years. When it is first known that a new or replacement machine will be needed, the capital budget is modified to include the expected expenditure.

operating budget

An **operating budget** is *a statement of the planned income and expenses of a business or subunit.* The expenditures for material and labor expected to be made at plant 18 during a given year are included in the plant's operating budget. There are also allowances for utilities, maintenance, and all other recurring expense items. For a subunit of a large organization, like plant 18, the "income" the subunit can expect is just an allocation of funds from headquarters.

An Illustration of Budgetary Control

The use of a budget as a control device is relatively simple. Assume that Figure 15–1 shows the monthly budget for the cylinder block boring department. The major expense items include direct labor (such as wages for the unit's boring machine operators), indirect labor (the department

Figure 15–1

Department Operating Budget: Cylinder Block Boring Department Budget, January 13

Item	Budget	Actual	Over	Under
Direct labor	$10,000	$10,800	$800	
Indirect labor	1,800	1,800		
Operating supplies	1,250	1,500	$250	
Maintenance	1,800	1,400		$400
Miscellaneous expense (telephone)	190	150		40
Total	$15,040	$15,650	Over $610	

Charles Gupton/Stock, Boston Inc.

*Budgetary control is
concerned with the
comparison of actual to
planned expenditures.*

manager's salary), operating supplies (grinding disks), maintenance expenses (repair of machines), and miscellaneous expenses. Actual expenditures are compared with budgeted or planned expenditures in Figure 15–1. In this department, actual exceeded budgeted expenditures for direct labor and operating supplies by $800 and $250, respectively. Actual spending for maintenance and miscellaneous was under the budgeted amount by $440. Budgetary control enables the manager to identify significant deviations in actual versus budgeted or planned expenses and to take corrective action when necessary. For example, the $800 over budgeted expenses for the wages of boring machine operators may have been caused by the necessity to pay overtime wages. The need for overtime may have resulted from ineffective work scheduling or the sudden appearance of a rush job. This situation, if it occurred in several successive periods, may cause the manager to take actions such as requesting additional personnel or improving the scheduling of work to correct the problem. Clearly budgeting control is a useful tool for managers at virtually every level of an organization.

Benefits of the Budgeting Process

The fact that virtually every type of organization—profit or nonprofit— operates within the framework of budgets attests to their benefits. Budgeting is significant as a part of both the planning and controlling processes. Budgets are widely used by managers to plan, monitor, and control various activities and operations at every level of an organization. There are several important advantages for preparing and using budgets. Some of the benefits of the budgeting process are:

1. *Provides standards against which actual performance can be measured.* Budgets are a quantified plan that allows management to measure and control performance objectively. If, for instance, a department knows that the budgeted expenditure for supplies is $1,000 per month, the manager is in a position to monitor and control the expenses for supplies.

2. *Provides managers with additional insight into actual organizational goals.* Monetary allocation of funds as opposed to merely lip-service more often than not is the true test of a firm's dedication to a particular goal. For instance, suppose that two firms of relatively equal size had a stated policy of hiring minority personnel, but Firm A allocates $100,000 to minority programs and Firm B budgets $10,000. A manager from Firm A likely realizes that a much stronger commitment to minority hiring is expressed by Firm A as opposed to Firm B.

3. *Tends to be a positive influence on the motivation of personnel.* People typically like to know what is expected of them, and budgets clarify specific performance standards.

4. *Causes managers to divert some of their attention from current to future operations.* To some extent, a budget forces managers to anticipate and forecast changes in the external environment. For example, an increase in transportation costs created by higher-priced petroleum might force the firm to seek an alternative transportation or distribution system.

5. *Improves top management's ability to coordinate the overall operation of the organization.* Budgets are blueprints of the company's plans for the coming year and greatly aid top management in coordinating the operations/activities of each division or department.

6. *Enables management to recognize and/or anticipate problems in time to take the necessary corrective action.* For example, if production costs are substantially ahead of the budgeted amount, management will be alerted to make changes that may realign actual costs with the budget. This use of budgeting at Pontiac is enhanced by the existence of supporting controls. Not only are overall departmental costs monitored, but the costs of individual activities are isolated and controlled. Long before departmental expenditures are out of control, corrective action can begin.

7. *Facilitates communications throughout the organization.* The budget significantly improves management's ability to communicate the objectives, plans, and standards of performance important to the organization. Budgets are especially helpful to lower-level managers by letting them know how their operations relate to other units or departments within the organization. Also, budgets tend to pinpoint managers' responsibility and improve their understanding of the goals of the organization. This process usually results in increased morale and commitment on the part of managers.

8. *Helps managers recognize when change is needed.* The budgeting process requires managers to review carefully and critically the company's operations to determine if the firm's resources are being allocated to the *right* activities and programs. The budgeting process causes management to focus on such questions as: What products appear to have the greatest demand? What markets appear to offer the best potential? What business are we in? Which business(es) should we be in?[2]

Limitations of the Budgeting Process

Although numerous benefits can be attributed to the use of budgets, potential problems may also arise. If the budgetary process is to achieve its maximum effectiveness, these difficulties must be recognized and an attempt made to reduce the potential damaging side-effects associated with the use of budgets. Some of the major problems are:

• The attitude by some, that all funds allocated in a budget must be spent, may actually work against the intent of the budgetary process. Some managers have learned from experience that if they do not spend the funds that have been budgeted, their budget will be reduced the following year. Managers have found that they can actually hurt their department because of a conscientious cost-effectiveness approach. A manager who operates in this type of environment may make an extraordinary effort to spend extra funds for reasons that may be marginal at best. Undoubtedly this kind of attitude existed at plant 18 in the "old days" described by the thirty-five-year veteran autoworker.

• A budget may be so restrictive that supervisors are permitted little discretion in managing their resources. The actual amount that can be spent for each item may be specified, and funds cannot be transferred from one account to another. This has sometimes resulted in some unusual situations. There may be funds for typewriter paper but no money available for typewriter ribbons.

• Budgets may be used to evaluate the performance of a manager as opposed to evaluating the actual results that the individual has accomplished. If this philosophy is prevalent within the firm, a poor manager may be recognized as superior because he or she met the budget, but a good manager may be reprimanded for failure to follow the exact budgetary guidelines. With this corporate philosophy, the amount of risk a manager will be willing to take may be severely reduced. Managers may spend a majority of their time ensuring that they are in compliance with the budget when their time might be best spent in developing new or innovative ideas.

Zero Base Budgeting

Zero base budgeting (ZBB), originally developed by Texas Instruments, received widespread recognition when Jimmy Carter implemented the system when he was governor of Georgia. In 1977, President Carter required that ZBB be used in preparing budgets in the executive branch of the federal government. ZBB requires management to take a fresh look at all programs and activities each year rather than merely building on last year's budget. In other words, last year's budget allocations are not considered as a basis for this year's budget. Each program, or "decision package," must be justified on the basis of a cost-benefit analysis. There are three main features of zero base budgeting:

1. The activities of individual departments are divided into *decision packages*. Each decision package provides information so that management can compare costs and benefits of the program or activity.

2. Each decision package is evaluated and ranked in the order of decreasing importance to the organization. Priorities are established for all programs and activities. Each of these is evaluated by top management to arrive at a final ranking.

3. Resources are allocated according to the final rankings of the programs by top management. As a rule, decisions to allocate resources for high-priority items will be made rather quickly, whereas greater analysis or scrutiny will be given lower-priority programs or activities.[4]

ZBB is not a panacea for solving all problems associated with the budgeting process. Organizations may experience problems in implementing ZBB. Most managers are reluctant to admit that all of their activities are not of the highest priority or to submit their programs to close scrutiny. However, ZBB does establish a system whereby an organization's resources are allocated to the higher-priority programs. Under this system, programs of lower priority are reduced or eliminated. Thus, the benefits of zero base budgeting appear to outweigh the costs.[5]

QUALITY CONTROL

Quality is likely to be in the vocabulary of the majority of Americans. When a buyer states that he got a "lemon," the immediate impression is that the product purchased was of inferior quality. Quality of a product is the combination of several factors such as form, dimension, composition, and color. For a particular product, all of these factors may have to be considered with regard to quality.

quality   But what exactly is meant by the term *quality?* **Quality** is *the degree of excellence of a product or service.* The purpose of quality control is to make sure a product or service is likely to serve the purposes for which it is intended. Standards are ultimately derived from the company's objectives. If the company wishes to gain a reputation for high-quality products, standards will have to be high. The company must have a very rigid quality control program in order to meet these high standards. Increased quality generally results in higher costs and allows higher prices. Therefore, some

Quality is the degree of excellence of a product or service.

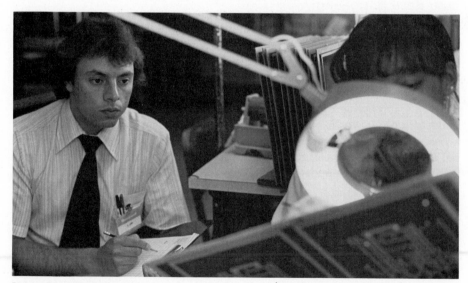

Richard Wood/The Picture Cube

firms may sell to a market segment that desires lower prices and will accept lower quality. Certain standards remain, but they are not as rigid as with the high-quality-oriented company.

There are numerous ways to maintain quality of a product. A company could make the decision to have a 100 percent inspection of all items manufactured. But, even with a total inspection program, some defects will not be discovered. When you insert the human element into a quality control environment, mistakes will occasionally be made. Some items that are good may be rejected, and other items that are bad will be accepted.

In many instances it is impossible to have a 100 percent inspection. For instance, if the standard for the life of a light bulb were 200 hours, you would have to burn the light for the assigned number of hours to determine if it met standards. Naturally, you would have no product to sell in this situation. Tire manufacturing companies set standards for their tires in order that they will be capable of being driven a certain number of miles. If each tire were placed on a machine and run the assigned number of miles to determine if it can meet standards, there would be no product to market. In still other instances, the cost to inspect each item to determine if it conforms to standard is prohibitive. If each nail in a keg were inspected separately, the cost to inspect might be higher than the price of the nails.

The technique that is available to overcome the above deficiencies is known as statistical quality control. In statistical quality control, a portion of the total number of items is inspected. For instance, five out of one hundred items may be selected and an estimate made as to the characteristics of the other ninety-five. Some degree of error exists. For instance, if out of one hundred items only five are defective (this amount of error may be perfectly acceptable), it is conceivable that all five defectives might be selected, and the entire lot would be rejected. On the other hand, there might be only five good parts out of the one hundred parts manufactured. These five good parts might be the ones drawn, and the batch would be accepted. With sampling there is risk, but the benefits of sampling are far superior to other procedures in many instances. Recall that it was possible to eliminate gear failures at plant 18 by inspecting just three gears each hour.

Acceptance Sampling

Acceptance sampling is *the inspection of a portion of the output or input of a process to determine acceptability.* Assume that it has been statistically determined that taking a sample of fifteen items from each batch of one hundred and limiting defective units to two will result in the desired quality. If two or more items are defective, the entire lot is rejected. When a lot is rejected, every item in that batch may be inspected. Or the lot may be returned to the supplier and the supplier required to straighten out the problem. Through this kind of sampling, plant 18 was able to identify the supplier of defective connecting rod bolts.

There are two basic approaches to sampling: sampling by variables and sampling by attributes. Both are appropriate for use but under different circumstances.

acceptance sampling

Sampling by Variables

A plan developed for variable sampling consists of determining how closely an item conforms to an established standard. In essence, degrees of goodness and degrees of badness are permitted. For instance, a stereo speaker is designed to project a certain tone quality. All speakers will not project precisely the same tone quality. Some speakers will have quality that is above the established standard, and some will have tone quality that is below standard. The variance does not necessarily mean that the speaker will be rejected. Only when the quality is outside a certain established limit will it be rejected.

Sampling by Attributes

With sampling by variables, degrees of conformity are considered; with attribute sampling, the item is either acceptable or unacceptable. The product is either good or bad; there are no degrees of conformity to consider. At plant 18 an engine block that has a hole in the side of any cylinder is rejected.

Control Charts

control chart   A **control chart** is *a graphic record of how closely samples of a product or service conform to standards over time.* The chart is used with both variable and attribute sampling, although the statistical procedure for developing the charts is different. In both instances, the standard is determined (Figure 15–2). A variable sampling plan in the manufacture of tire treads might have standards that test thickness, weight, length, and width. If the average thickness of a certain tire thread is expected to be 0.87 inch, this becomes the standard.

Once the standard has been established, the manager must determine the amount of deviation that will be acceptable. The maximum level that will be allowed is referred to as the *upper control limit* (UCL), and the minimum level is called the *lower control limit* (LCL). In the tire tread example, the UCL might be 0.89 inch and the LCL might be 0.84 inch. If a

Figure 15–2

Example of Control Chart

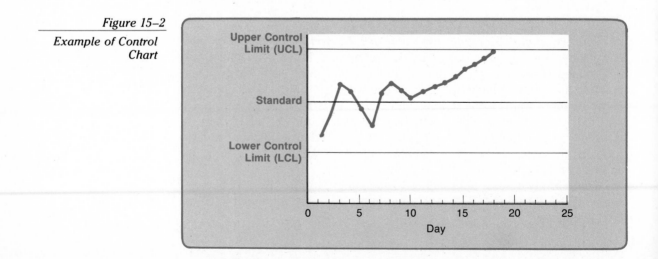

thickness of a tread being evaluated falls within the two extremes, it will be accepted. If it falls outside the limit, it will be rejected.

Another benefit that accrues through the use of control charts is that potential problems may be recognized prior to their actual occurrence. Figure 15–2 shows that from day 10 until day 17, the quality of the product progressively worsened. Although the item is still within the limits of acceptability, if the problem is not corrected, the process may soon go above the upper control limit. When managers see this pattern developing, they are in a position to take corrective action.

From the Garage to the Fortune 500

Steve Jobs and Steve Wozniak, founders of Apple Computer Company, took six months to design their first computer and forty hours to build it. Their first "factory" was Jobs's garage. Today Apple's MacIntosh factory in Cupertino, California, produces a personal computer every twenty-seven seconds, and the MacIntosh is only one of a number of computers Apple makes. To keep pace with rapid technological change, Apple's research and development spending has exceeded $60 million a year.

The only people Jobs and Wozniak had to supervise in 1976 were themselves. Today their company employs thousands, and Jobs and Wozniak must be concerned not only with managing them but with managing the company's complex relationships with hundreds of suppliers, customers, creditors, and other publics.

Apple's two founders were the innovators and were way ahead of the competition in 1976. By 1984, many small competitors—Osborne, Atari, PET, and dozens of others—had been joined by giants like IBM and AT&T. As late as 1981 Apple still retained 40 percent of the personal computer market, but by 1984 the figure was less than 25 percent, and Apple was distinctly number two, behind IBM.

Financing the early operation was simple. Jobs sold his Volkswagen and Wozniak his programmable calculator to raise money to finance the first few computers they made. Apple is now publicly held. Its early stock issues were gobbled up at steadily increasing prices. Recently Apple's stock price has moved up and down with each new report of an innovation or the birth or demise of a competitor. The price changes in Apple's stock for a single day might be enough to purchase hundreds of Volkswagens or thousands of programmable calculators, and debt and equity issues have to be timed to take advantage of movements in the financial markets.

The first Apple computers were sold in kit form to electronics buffs. But now, because of their low cost, small size, and ease of use, personal computers find thousands of applications. They are used to make charts and graphs for boardroom presentations and to monitor oil drilling and seismographic testing. It is a rare small business today that does not have at least one computer, and practically no big business is without them. Students use microcomputers to help them with mathematics, spelling, and science and even to write term papers.

There have been many other changes. Only word-of-mouth advertising was used for the early computers Apple sold, but the new MacIntosh, Lisa, and Apple IIC were each the object of multimillion dollar ad campaigns. Even so, it was impossible to match IBM's $40 million marketing effort for its PC Jr. The small, informal organization that Jobs and Wozniak favored has become significantly more structured. With sales at a billion dollars a year, a worldwide distribution system, and several factories, Apple in 1983 became the youngest company to enter the ranks of the Fortune 500.

The early success, based as it was on the introduction of a revolutionary new product, seems long ago. As new products come along every month, with only incremental differences among them, it has become harder to find an innovation that is truly remarkable and will produce rapidly growing sales for an extended period of time. Apple's president, John Sculley, a former Pepsi-Cola marketing executive, has plotted the course for the future: "Our top management team has been developing a comprehensive product line strategy designed to keep Apple positioned as the technology-marketing leader in the fast growing personal computer industry."[5]

How Much Quality?

The objective of a manager cannot be simply to maximize quality. Through an understanding of the objectives of the firm, a manager establishes standards and levels of quality in line with these goals. They realize that as quality increases, costs go up. Quality represents a cost. There is an optimum level of quality for each product consistent with maximizing profits. For example, Steve Jobs would like to claim that Apple computers have zero defects. Approaching this goal would require 100 percent inspection at every step in the production process. Apple managers, working in conjunction with statistical and accounting personnel, must determine the level of quality that is cost justified. The quality level that is appropriate is primarily determined by top management. Supervisors monitor the quality on a day-to-day basis to ensure that the stated level of quality is being maintained.

U.S. industry has been criticized for not matching competition, especially the Japanese, in the quality of its output. A recent *Harvard Business Review* article revealed that U.S. room air-conditioning assembly lines produced eighty times (not 80 percent more but eighty times) as many defects as those in Japan.[6] The result has been that U.S. manufacturers are now more and more willing to pay the costs that quality entails in order to remain competitive with foreign producers. And consumers, with the alternative of buying quality products from abroad, now demand a higher level of quality. For example, the trucks made at Ford Motor Company's Louisville, Kentucky, assembly plant once had the lowest quality rating of all U.S.-made Ford vehicles. Because Ford was willing to invest in statistical controls, a tougher inspection system, and tighter standards for vendors, the Ranger trucks made there today get Ford's highest quality rating.[7]

INVENTORY CONTROL

inventory   **Inventory** refers to *the goods or materials available for use by a business.* Concern with inventory is almost continuous. You hear that a car dealer has excessive inventory and will offer you a special deal to get you to buy a car. A furniture dealer provides a similar offer. Although there may be a bit of sales promotion in these offerings, inventory does represent a cost that must be controlled. A product in inventory constitutes an idle but valuable resource. The Purchasing Management's Association says that total inventory carrying costs exceed 25 percent of the inventory value each year, and one expert estimates that they run between 30 and 36 percent.[8]

General Motors's inventory is valued at $9 billion and Ford's at $5 billion.[9] Suppose that these car manufacturers keep $1 million in extra inventory for one year. At a 14 percent interest rate, they would lose $140,000 because the extra inventory represents cars not sold. (If they were sold, the sales revenue could be drawing interest in a bank.) Much of the resources of some major companies are in inventory, so failure to control inventories can mean the difference between profit and loss. As Christmas 1984 approached, Atari, an Apple competitor, had 600,000 personal computers in stock. To avoid having to carry this inventory after Christmas, the company reduced prices of the units by 30 percent.

Purposes of Inventory

One of the major purposes of inventory is that it permits relative independence of operations between two activities. For instance, if Machine A makes a product that will be used in a later stage by Machine B and Machine A breaks down, Machine B will have to cease operation unless inventory of the product has been previously built up.

Inventories also provide for continuous operations when demand for the product is not consistent. Electric razors are sold primarily during the Christmas holiday season, but a manufacturer of electric razors typically keeps production going through the entire year. Stability is ensured in that a skilled work force can be maintained and equipment usage can be kept at an optimal level.

Another purpose of inventory is to be capable of filling orders when they are received, thereby maintaining customer satisfaction. If orders arrived on a constant basis, there would be no need to maintain inventory. But if five orders come in this month and a hundred are processed next month, a company might be hard pressed to fill the hundred requests unless an inventory had been maintained. Companies like Apple Computers must ensure that they have inventories on hand to ship to retailers. They also have to be concerned with the inventories retailers carry. Distribution contracts between Apple and computer stores require the stores to keep a minimum quantity of products on hand.

Economic Order Quantity (EOQ) Method of Inventory Control

The **economic order quantity (EOQ)** method of inventory control is *a procedure for balancing ordering costs and carrying costs so as to minimize total inventory costs.* **Ordering costs** are *administrative, clerical, and other expenses incurred in initially obtaining inventory items and placing them in storage.* **Carrying costs** are *the expenses associated with maintaining and storing the products before they are sold or used.* Taxes, insurance, interest

*economic order
quantity (EOQ)*

ordering costs

carrying costs

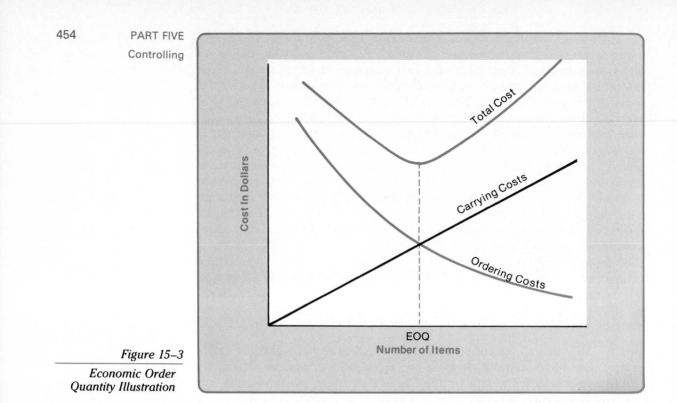

Figure 15–3

Economic Order
Quantity Illustration

on capital invested, storage, electricity, and spoilage are some of the items associated with carrying costs. The purchase price is the price of the product multiplied by the number of items ordered. Thus, the total cost associated with a particular order follows the following general formula:

Total cost = Ordering cost + carrying cost + purchase cost.

The task of the manager is to purchase in amounts that will minimize total cost (economic order quantity, EOQ). If you order less frequently, ordering costs will go down, but carrying costs go up. If you submit frequent orders, ordering costs go up but carrying costs are reduced. This balancing process is graphically presented in Figure 15–3. The optimum number of items to order at any one time is at the lowest point on the total cost curve. The lowest point is where carrying costs and ordering costs intersect.

In order to determine the EOQ, calculus is used in the development of the mathematical model. Again, the manager does not have to be a quantitative wizard to determine EOQ. A manager, however, must be capable of identifying two primary costs: carrying *(C)* and ordering *(O)*. Through the power of calculus, an EOQ formula is then determined from the total cost equation. The basic equation for EOQ is presented below:

$$\text{EOQ} = \sqrt{\frac{2\left(\begin{array}{c}\text{ordering}\\\text{cost}\end{array}\right)\left(\begin{array}{c}\text{annual}\\\text{demand}\end{array}\right)}{\text{carrying costs}}} = \sqrt{\frac{2(O) \times (D)}{C}}.$$

If we assume that annual demand is 1,000 units, carrying cost is $2 per unit, and ordering cost is $4, we will determine that optimum number to order is 63.25, or 63 when rounded to the nearest unit. We cannot choose another order quantity that would lower the total cost.

The model described is one of the simplest to develop. The sophistication level of the model depends on the actual need of the company and the demands of the environment. The manager must be capable of realizing when inventory control procedures may be useful and must identify what costs may be associated with the problem. Then specialists such as accountants and mathematicians are called upon to assist in the development of the model. The manager provides the guidelines and ensures that necessary output is received.

ABC Inventory Method

Sometimes it is impractical to monitor every item in inventory with the same degree of intensity. In such cases it is useful to categorize the items of inventory according to the degree of control needed. The **ABC inventory** *ABC inventory method* **method** is *the classification of inventory items for control purposes into three categories according to unit costs and number of items kept on hand.* The usual categories are:

- A—Small number of items but high unit cost
- B—Moderate number of medium-cost items
- C—Large number of low-cost items

A manager using the ABC classification is able to develop a sophisticated system to monitor Category A items. Items in the category might include automobiles, machinery, and tractors. Category B items would have a less sophisticated inventory control system. Category C items might not even be controlled if the cost associated with monitoring the items would be prohibitive, as may be the case for pencils and paper. Through the ABC method, a manager is capable of monitoring inventory in an optimum manner.

Just-in-Time Inventory Method

The Japanese success in cutting manufacturing costs is partly attributed to their use of the **just-in-time inventory method (JIT)**. This is *the practice* *just-in-time inventory* *of having inputs to the production process delivered precisely when they are* *method (JIT)* *needed and assigning responsibility to suppliers for keeping inventories to a minimum.* The Japanese have shown how the responsibility for keeping inventories to a minimum can be assigned to suppliers. Traditionally, U.S. factories have attempted to manage and build inventories internally. More and more, however, they are using the just-in-time method. One expert even suggests that the use of this method can result in "zero" inventory.[10] Zero inventory might seem unrealistic, but there is no doubt that JIT can reduce inventory considerably.

U.S. automobile manufacturers have led the way in adopting JIT. At GM's Buick City plant in Flint, Michigan, a number of suppliers have been encouraged to place their facilities within walking distance of the assembly line. They are doing so because Buick has given them complete responsibility for quality, inventory, and delivery of the items they supply.[11] Attempting to spring back from its near collapse in 1980, Chrysler too has adopted JIT. "In the past," says Chrysler's production control chief, "suppliers paid very little attention to inventory. Now they have to: inventory costs so much. Automakers may not be able to afford suppliers who do not control inventory."[12]

Automobile makers are not alone in efforts to improve inventory control. Woolworth's Department Stores has adopted a computerized system of inventory control called visual electronic ordering (VEO). Under VEO, the

TABLE 15–2 Uses of PERT or CPM

Company	Uses
Bendix Corporation	Plant construction Project work
Carrier Corporation	Plant construction Government projects
Kimberly-Clark	Control of major projects Systems design
The Signal Companies, Inc.	Petroleum process unit construction Industrial building construction
Southern Railway	Major plant construction project Installation of new MIS system at major railroad yards Time schedule for preparing five-year plan
3M Company	Construction projects Introduction of new products Marketing plans
Oscar Mayer & Company	Plant construction New product development and production start-up Allocation of craft personnel
The Southland Corporation	Facility construction Establishment of a new operation
Glidden Division, SCM Corporation	Plant construction
Lear Siegler	New product development Major program control (particularly government contracts)
Procter & Gamble Company	Facilities construction New product introduction
Kellogg Company	New product development Construction project control Forecasting New plant construction
Crown Zellerbach	Construction Most capital projects Planning inputs
J. Ray McDermott & Co., Inc.	Plant construction
Kaiser Steel Corporation	Construction of new facilities

variety chain is able to order just what it needs and program delivery just as old stock is likely to sell out.[13] Paragon Industries, a six-store home center chain headquartered in Fresno, California, has a similar system in effect.[14]

NETWORK MODELS

The number of separate tasks that must be accomplished to build a skyscraper or a dam across a river are almost impossible to conceive for the average person. We are often fascinated at how the construction manager in charge of a project of this magnitude is able to coordinate all the tasks and arrive at a finished product. When the project is nonrecurrent, large, complex, and involves multiple organizations, the manager needs a tool that will assist in coordinating this complicated network of interdependencies. He or she needs to be able to think through the project in its entirety and see where resources can be shifted or rescheduled to ensure that the project is completed within the time and cost constraints.

The primary techniques available to accomplish these tasks are program evaluation and review technique (PERT) and critical path method (CPM). PERT was developed to assist in the rapid development of the Polaris submarine program. During approximately the same time period (1957–1958), researchers for E. I. DuPont de Nemours and Company and computer specialists from what was the Remington Rand's Univac division combined their talents to develop a method to schedule and control all activities involved in constructing chemical plants. The result of their effort was a network model termed *critical path method.*

Both PERT and CPM have received widespread acceptance since their beginning. One major advantage of each of these techniques is the ease with which they can be computerized. The uses to which some firms have put the techniques are listed in Table 15–2. PERT and CPM are used primarily for construction projects, but some firms, such as 3M Company, use the techniques to assist in the development of new products. Firms that do major construction work for the government are required by contract to use PERT. Because of the similarity of PERT and CPM, only PERT will be discussed in detail.

PERT

PERT (program evaluation and review technique) is *a planning and control technique that involves the display of a complex project as a network of events and activities with three time estimates used to calculate the expected time for each activity.* An event is the beginning or completion of a step. It does not consume time or resources. An event is represented by a circle or node, as shown below:

PERT

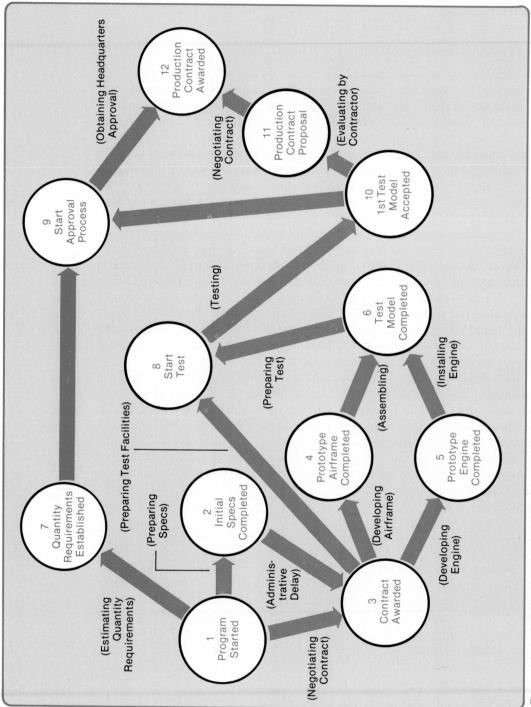

Figure 15–4 *PERT Network with Activities and Events*

An activity is a time-consuming element of the program. It is represented by an arrow:

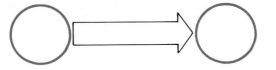

In order to assist in the understanding of PERT, a project will be developed. The project entails obtaining a production contract award for an aircraft. The principal steps to be taken by a project manager in this problem are described below.

1. Define the objective of the project and specify the factors (time, cost) that must be considered as the variables to be controlled—for instance, how quickly the project must be completed or how much money is allocated for completion of the project.
2. List all of the significant activities that must be performed for the project objectives to be achieved. These are as follows:

   Preparing specifications
   Establishing quantity requirements
   Negotiating contract
   Preparing test facilities
   Developing airframe
   Developing engine
   Assembling airframe
   Installing engine
   Preparing test
   Testing
   Obtaining headquarter's approval
   Evaluating by contractor
   Negotiating contract
3. Develop a statement of the relationship among project activities. The order in which each task is to be accomplished is also specified. A PERT network is then developed through this information (see Figure 15–4). As may be seen, the prototype airframe and the prototype engine must be completed before the test model is completed.
4. Determine the expected times that will be required to complete each activity. PERT requires that three time estimates be provided.

   Optimistic Time—If everything goes right and nothing goes wrong, the project can be completed in this amount of time.
   Most likely time—The most realistic completion time for the activity.
   Pessimistic time—If everything goes wrong and nothing goes right, the project will be completed in this amount of time.

   The expected time for the completion of each activity may be seen in Figure 15–5. For instance, the optimistic time for the activity "developing airframe" is thirty-six weeks, the pessimistic time is fifty-six weeks, and the most likely time is forty weeks. Inserting these figures into the expected time formula, we determine that forty-two weeks is the expected time to complete the activity. Expected time is then computed by applying the three time estimates to the following formula:

$$\text{Expected time (te)} = \frac{\text{Optimistic time} + 4\ (\text{most likely time}) + \text{pessimistic time}}{6}$$

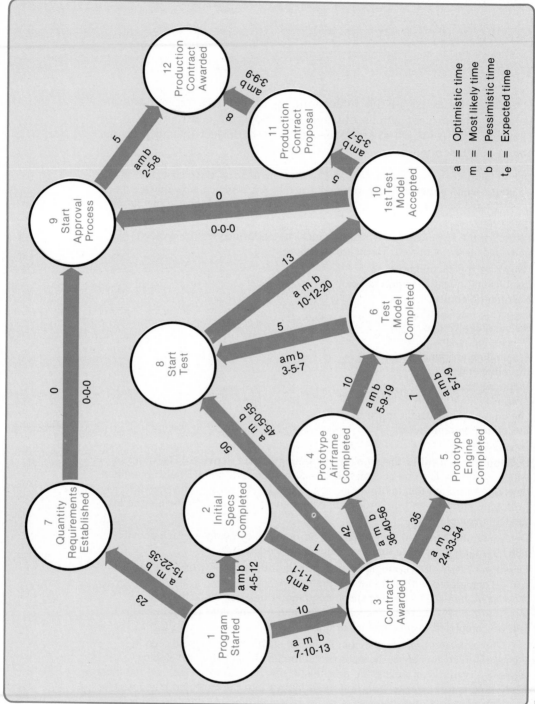

Figure 15–5   Expected Times to Complete Each Activity

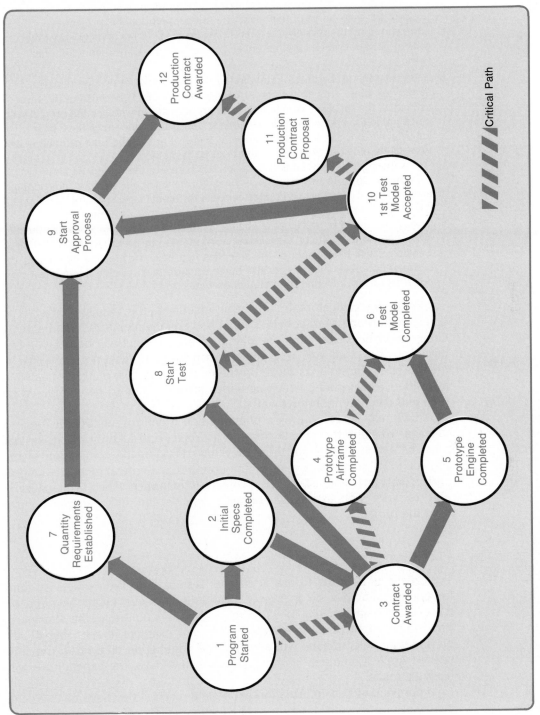

Critical Path

Figure 15–6   Critical Path for Project

461

5. Determine the critical path, that is, the longest path from start to finish of the project. (The actual work of the manager terminates once the three time estimates have been obtained.) Numerous computer programs are available to perform the mechanics of this task. The critical path for this project is represented by the broken line seen in Figure 15–6. If any activity along the critical path is a week late, the entire project will be delayed an additional week.

6. Determine the probability of completing the entire project or a particular activity on time. This in itself is a major feature of PERT. Because of the three estimates, the manager is able to obtain an estimate of whether the project will be completed on schedule. The optimistic and pessimistic times have been determined to assist in this operation. If there were but one time estimate—the most likely time—probabilities could not be computed.

A manager usually finds it beneficial to compare the optimistic and pessimistic times to the most likely time. For instance, the activity "developing engine" would likely cause greater concern to the manager than the activity "developing airframe." The difference between the optimistic time and pessimistic time for "developing engine" is thirty weeks (54 − 24) while the difference for the activity "developing airframe" is but twenty weeks (56 − 36). A manager will likely monitor the activities that have the greatest difference between optimistic and pessimistic times because they provide the greatest potential for not meeting the completion date.

Once the critical path has been identified, the manager is able to quickly determine what activities must be carefully monitored. If an activity along the critical path slips one day, the entire project will be delayed one day. Activities that are not on the critical path may not have to be monitored as carefully as those on the critical path. The manager is also in a position to determine which activities are not likely to be completed on time and carefully monitor them.

PERT may serve both as a planning and a control function. It *forces* a manager to think thoroughly through a project and identify the tasks that must be accomplished and how they interrelate in the completion of the project. PERT serves as a control function in that a critical path (the longest path from start to finish of the project) is identified. Thus, a manager is able to work with extremely complex projects and still maintain control over the project.

PERT/Cost

Typically it is possible to use additional resources to reduce activity time for certain activities on a project. Additional workers might be hired or more equipment brought in. Although expenses would rise, the shortened time frame might justify the added costs. For example, if spending $1,000 on additional electricians will advance the completion date of an urgently needed Apple Computer factory by even a few days, the expenditure will likely be made.

Improvements in information processing capabilities have enabled the inclusion of cost consideration in PERT analysis. The purpose of PERT/cost is to reduce the entire project completion time by a certain amount at the least cost. Reducing completion time might be especially important to a company that faces costly penalties for being late with a project. Also, there may be fixed costs for every day of the project. Therefore, it might be cost-effective to use additional resources to shorten the project time. The PERT/cost technique helps identify the least expensive method of shortening the entire project.

Critical Path Method

CPM (critical path method) is *a planning and control technique that involves the display of a complex project as a network with one time estimate used for each step in the project.* The developers of CPM were dealing with projects for which the time and cost of tasks (activities) required to complete the project were known. In CPM the points or nodes of the CPM network represent activities rather than events. Also, there is but one time estimate in CPM because it was designed to accommodate situations in which sets of standardized activities were required for the completion of a complex project. Time for completion of a task was relatively easy to determine accurately. Because there was but one time estimate, probabilities of completing the project on time were not available. With these minor exceptions, PERT and CPM provide for accomplishment of similar functions.

CPM

SUMMARY

Numerous quantitative techniques are available to managers. The techniques have application in every area of management and especially in the planning and control functions. Managers do not have to know the detailed mathematics of each approach, but they should be aware of the tools (techniques) available, the situations for which the tools are designed, and how the tools are used in business.

The most basic and widely used quantitative controlling technique is the budget. A budget is a statement of planned allocation of resources expressed in financial or numerical terms. There are basically two broad categories of budgets: capital and operating. A capital budget is a statement of planned expenditures of funds for facilities and equipment. An operating budget is a statement of the planned income and expenses of a business or subunit.

Quality is the degree of excellence of a product or service. The purpose of quality control is to make sure a product or service is likely to serve the purpose for which it is intended. With statistical quality control, a portion of the total number of items is inspected. Acceptance sampling is the inspection of a portion of the output or input of a

process to determine acceptability. There are two basic types of acceptance sampling plans: sampling by variable and sampling by attributes. Variable sampling determines how closely an item conforms to an established standard. With sampling by attributes, the item is either acceptable or unacceptable. A control chart is a graphic record of how closely samples of a product or service conform to standards over time.

Inventory refers to the goods or materials available for use by a business. One of the major purposes of inventory is that it permits relative independence of operation between two activities. Inventories also provide for continuous operations when demand for the product is not consistent. Another purpose of inventory is to enable orders to be filled when they are received. The economic order quantity (EOQ) method of inventory control is a procedure for balancing ordering costs and carrying costs so as to minimize total inventory costs. With the ABC method of inventory control, inventory is categorized according to the degree of control needed. The just-in-time inventory method is the practice of having inputs to the production process delivered precisely when they are needed and assigning responsibility to suppliers for keeping inventories to a minimum.

When the project is nonrecurrent, large, complex, and involves multiple organizations, the manager needs a tool that will assist in coordinating this complicated network of interdependencies. The primary techniques available to organize and coordinate this type of project are program evaluation and review technique (PERT) and the critical path method (CPM).

REVIEW QUESTIONS

1. What information should a manager have an appreciation of with regard to quantitative tools?
2. Define a budget. What are the two broad categories of budgets?
3. What are the benefits and limitations of budgets?
4. What is zero base budgeting?
5. Define quality control. What is the purpose of quality control?
6. What are the two basic types of acceptance sampling plans? How are control charts used?
7. Explain the purposes of inventory. What is the economic order quantity (EOQ) method of inventory control?
8. Distinguish between PERT and CPM.

EXERCISES

1. Assume that ordering costs are $6.00 per order, carrying costs are $1.50 per unit per year, and the annual demand is 1,000 units. What would be the economic order quantity (EOQ) for this situation?
2. Assume that you are responsible for monitoring inventory control for the following types of firms:
   a. Fancy restaurant
   b. Automobile dealership
   c. Bookstore
   Using the ABC method of inventory control, identify inventory items that would be in each class.
3. Develop a small PERT network for a task with which you are very familiar. The task that is chosen should have at least two people performing different tasks at the same time.

CASE STUDY

Pooling Our Knowledge

"This is the third batch of sticks we've gotten back from Brunswick this quarter," said Jerry Hodges, "and it's been different problems each time." Jerry and his shop manager, John Kenner, were looking over the checklist of defects Brunswick had provided with the returned pool sticks. The sticks had been made by Jerry's company, Hodges' Woodworks. Brunswick is a major manufacturer of recreation equipment of all kinds, and Hodges had contracted to provide the company 5,000 pool sticks per month during 1985.

The defects in the 200 sticks in the returned batch ranged from misaligned leather tips on two of the sticks to four thread defects where the sticks screwed together in the middle, to an incomplete covering of varnish on the wood sections of four others. Altogether sixteen faults were noted in the batch.

"The costs are just too high to inspect every piece of every stick," said Jerry. "Yeah, I know," replied John, "but it's not as expensive as having to rework an entire batch. Anyway, Brunswick uses 100 percent inspection. Why shouldn't we?"

Jerry replied, "We may have to do that. But if the number of defectives is below 2 percent, Brunswick will accept the batch. Let's see if we can figure out a cheaper way to accomplish that."

The manufacturing process for pool sticks is complex. The wood parts are cut from solid maple and machined to shape on numerically controlled lathes. Then they are drilled and shaped on other machines to fit plastic, metal, and rubber parts purchased from other manufacturers. After being assembled, the pool cues are varnished in batches of twenty with a spray gun. Because of the small volume, most of the assembly work is done by hand.

After some discussion, John and Jerry determined that, except for the varnish problem, all of the defects in the present batch resulted from parts purchased from others. "Obviously," said Jerry, "we should do the same thing to our suppliers that Brunswick is doing to us: check the parts when we get them, and return them if they are defective."

QUESTIONS

1. What techniques are available to help Hodges' Woodworks get the defective rate down below 2 percent?
2. Should the company attempt to prevent any defective cue sticks at all from leaving the factory? Explain.

CASE STUDY

A Problem of Inventory Control

As supervisor of ten stores in a convenience store chain, Martha Young is responsible for their general operation. Each of these small stores has a day manager and two assistant managers who work the evening and midnight shifts. These "managers" are not really managers because they have no subordinates reporting directly to them. The day manager is typically the senior person and has chosen the day shift.

Mark McCall is the day manager of one of the stores that Martha supervises. Mark has been at the store for three months and sales have been increasing steadily. Mark maintains his store in good order, and the first two monthly inventory checks have been satisfactory. But as Martha reads the inventory report for this month, she becomes quite disturbed. Inventory is $1,000 short for the previous month (anything over $200 is considered out of the ordinary).

Martha realizes that this report is extremely serious. Other managers have been terminated for inventory shortages of this amount. She liked Mark, but something must be done to keep this situation from occurring in the future. Martha sits down and reviews the situation regarding the store. The following points come to mind:

- The store is located close to a school. When Mark took control of the store, school was not in session. There might be some shoplifting occurring.
- One of the assistant managers has been with the store for only one month. There is a possibility that there could be internal theft.
- The other assistant manager broke up with his girlfriend last month. There is a possibility that he has not been paying close attention to his job.

QUESTIONS

1. What type of controls, if any, should Martha instigate?
2. If the inventory is short next month, what do you think Martha should do?

NOTES

1. This story is a composite from a number of sources, including: "Dr. Deming Shows Pontiac the Way," *Fortune* (April 18, 1983): 19–36; and Daniel W. Gottlieb, "Purchasing's Part in the Push for Quality," *Purchasing* (September 10, 1981): 75–78.

2. Robert N. Anthony and Regina E. Herzlinger, *Management Control in Non-Profit Organizations* (Homewood, Ill.: Irwin, 1975), pp. 222–226.

3. James A. F. Stoner, *Management* (Englewood Cliffs, N.J.: Prentice-Hall, 1978), pp. 600–677.

4. Gordon Shillinglaw, *Managerial Cost Accounting: Analysis and Control,* 4th ed. (Homewood, Ill.: Irwin, 1977), pp. 142–143.

5. Gregory S. Blundell, "Personal Computers in the Eighties," *Byte* (January 1983): 166–182; Jay Cocks, "The Updated Book of Jobs," *Time* (January 3, 1983): 25–27; Otto Friedrich, "The Computer Moves In," *Time* (January 3, 1983): 14–24; Stephen Kindel and Anne Field, "Bringing Home the Computer," *Forbes* (August 2, 1982): 61–66; Peter Nulty, "Apple's Bid to Stay in the Big Time," *Fortune* (February 7, 1983): 36–41; "The Coming Shake Out in Personal Computers," *Business Week* (November 22, 1982): 72–75; and numerous articles from *The Wall Street Journal.*

6. David A. Garvin, "Quality on the Line," *Harvard Business Review* (September–October 1983): 67.

7. Jeremy Main, "Ford's Drive for Quality," *Fortune* (April 18, 1983): 62.

8. William E. Dollar, "The Zero Inventory Concept," *Purchasing* (September 29, 1983): 43.

9. "U.S. Auto-Makers Adopt Just-in-Time Methods," *Iron Age* (July 5, 1982): 15–17.

10. Dollar, "Zero Inventory Concept," p. 43.

11. "Buick City Places Suppliers in Backyard," *Purchasing* (November 10, 1983): 15.

12. "U.S. Auto-Makers," p. 15.

13. "Woolworth's Wanding Is Made to Order," *Chain Store Age Executive* (April 1984): 52.

14. "Paragon Tracks Inventory with Customized System," *Chain Store Age* (April 1984): 59.

REFERENCES

Backes, Robert W. "Cycle Counting—A Better Way for Achieving Accurate Inventory Records." *Production and Inventory Management* 21 (Second Quarter 1980): 36–44.

Brennan, J. M. "Up Your Inventory Control." *Journal of Systems Management* 28 (January 1977): 39–45.

"Buick City Places Suppliers in Backyard." *Purchasing* (November 10, 1983): 15.

Chase, Richard B., and Nicholas J. Aquilano. *Production and Operations Management: A Life Cycle Approach.* 2d ed. Homewood, Ill.: Irwin, 1981.

Dollar, William E. "The Zero Inventory Concept." *Purchasing* (September 29, 1983): 43.

Garvin, David A. "Quality on the Line." *Harvard Business Review* (September–October 1983): 67.

Gullapelli, S. M. "Simulating a Cash Budget for a Small Manufacturer." *Management Accounting* 61 (November 1979): 25–29.

Hostage, G. M. "Quality Control in a Service Business." *Harvard Business Review* 53 (July–August 1975): 98–106.

Main, Jeremy. "Ford's Drive for Quality," *Fortune* (April 18, 1983): 62.

Mittelstaedt, Arthur H., and Henry A. Berger. "The Critical Path Method: A Management Tool for Recreation." *Parks and Recreation* 7 (July 1972): 14–16.

"Paragon Tracks Inventory with Customized System." *Chain Store Age* (April 1984): 59.

Plossl, G. W., and W. Evert Welch. *The Role of Top Management in the Control of Inventory.* Reston, Va.: Reston Publishing, 1979.

Reuter, Vincent G. "ABC Method of Inventory Control." *Journal of Systems Management* 27 (November 1976): 26–33.

Schenner, Roger W. *Productions Operations Management.* Chicago: Science Research Associates, 1981.

Shillinglaw, Gordon. *Managerial Cost Accounting: Analysis and Control.* 4th ed. Homewood, Ill.: Irwin, 1977).

Smith, Martin R. "A 10-point Guide to Making Quality Control Management Effective." *Management Review* 64 (April 1975): 52–54.

Solomon, S. L. "Building Modelers: Teaching the Art of Simulation." *Interfaces* 10 (April 1980): 65–72.

"U.S. Auto-Makers Adopt Just-in-Time Methods." *Iron Age* (July 5, 1982): 15–17.

Wiley, J. M. "Just Enough Queuing Theory." *Datamation* 23 (February 1977): 87.

"Woolworth's Wanding Is Made to Order." *Chain Store Age Executive* (April 1984): 52.

HIWASSE HOMES, INC.

For several years, Mr. Roger Thomas had been interested in the growth and development of the mobile home industry. Thomas was impressed by the operation of a successful mobile home manufacturing plant located in the area. Thomas had been engaged in the hardware and lumber business for several years in Hiwasse, Arkansas, population 425, located in the extreme northwestern corner of Arkansas. The hardware and lumber company was a very successful operation, and Thomas had earned the reputation as a capable businessman.

However, Thomas was seeking new business opportunities and believed that the bright prospects for the mobile home industry would continue, since mobile homes had become a primary housing alternative for low-income families and families interested in weekend or vacation homes. Because of the economic and demographic characteristics of Arkansas and the surrounding states, as well as the absence of any major mobile home producers, Thomas was reasonably certain that the mobile home manufacturing business provided an exceptional business opportunity. Since Thomas had no prior experience in the mobile home business, and in an effort to gain more information concerning the feasibility of establishing a mobile home manufacturing plant, he contacted a former professor at a nearby university to discuss his plans. He asked the professor if, as a class project, a graduate class could conduct a feasibility study of his proposed entry into the mobile home business. The professor liked the idea and made arrangements for the study to be conducted by a team of eight graduate business administration students.

CONCLUSIONS OF THE STUDY

The consultants recommended northwestern Arkansas as a very favorable region for the establishment of a mobile home manufacturing plant. This conclusion was based on three primary factors.

The Market

The present and future market for mobile homes will be expanding considerably from all indications. National mobile home demand is expected to reach 650,000 units within five years, a 10 percent annual growth rate. Potential demand in the four-state region of Arkansas, Oklahoma, Missouri, and Kansas is predicted to increase by 60 percent during the next five years. The region does appear vulnerable to additional firms entering the regional area at this time.

Nature and Extent of Competition

Competition in the mobile home industry is essentially based on product quality, price, and service by dealers. There are thirty-eight mobile home plants in the four-state region, and three additional ones are scheduled for construction during the current year. The market is a sellers' market in this region and is expected to remain as such for several more years. It is estimated that demand for mobile homes will exceed the supply of mobile homes by approximately 4,000 units next year in the four-state region.

While the market for mobile homes is expected to increase substantially during the next several years, in order to be financially successful, a prospective firm must develop and implement sound production, personnel, and finance plans. Specifically, the successful entry and operation of a new mobile home manufacturing plant depends upon:

- An efficient plan layout and process flow designed to minimize production delays and idle time while maintaining product quality;
- Producing a low- to moderate-priced unit to meet market demand in the regional market;
- Selection and retention of key personnel; and
- The determination of and procurement of adequate financing.

RECOMMENDATIONS

The following recommendations were made by the consultants:

- Construction of a mobile home plant in northwest Arkansas.
- A plant with an output of four units a day, reached by the beginning of the sixth month of operation.
  a. A plant size necessary to accommodate the recommended production (325 ft. by 100 ft.).
  b. The recommended plant layout combined with the suggested process flow designed to provide maximum efficiency.
- The plant should produce and market an inexpensive 12 ft. by 60 ft. mobile home that is currently the largest selling line. The plant should have the flexibility to produce other size units including modular homes.
- The personnel required for the manufacturing facility consists of fifty production workers, two office/clerical people, and four managers.
- The capital required to establish the proposed plant is $320,000, which includes $75,000 for working capital and initial operational contingencies.

In their closing comments in the study, the consultants noted that, while it was relatively easy to enter the mobile home business, failure rates have been substantial. The consultants stated that the probabilities of success seem to be primarily dependent upon: financial strength (particularly during the first several months of operation and especially during recessionary periods), managerial expertise and ability (especially in selecting key personnel), production and technical expertise, and the ability to establish an effective dealer network.

SUBSEQUENT MOVES

After reviewing the conclusions and recommendations of the feasibility study, Mr. Thomas and a group of investors were very encouraged about prospects for the mobile home plant. Mr. Thomas and several investors were able to arrange the necessary financing, and construction of the plant began on December 1. Hiwasse was organized with a financial structure consisting of $61,250 of capital supplied by selling 12,500 shares of common stock at $4.90 per share, and loans from the Small Business Administration and a local bank totalling $300,000. The plant was to be located in Gravett, Arkansas, a town with a population of 600.

The top management of Hiwasse consisted of:

- An eight-member board of directors consisted of several prominent local community leaders including an M.D., lawyer, banker, and leading retailer. Mr. Thomas controlled 51 percent of Hiwasse's stock and was chairman of the board and chief executive officer. Hiwasse's general manager was also on the board.
- Mr. Roger Thomas, chairman of the board and president, held a bachelor's and master's degree in business administration and had more than ten years of successful experience in the hardware and lumber business.
- Mr. Dick Johnson, the thirty-nine-year-old general manager, was a high school

graduate, had eight years' experience as a production superintendent at a large mobile home company noted for producing high-quality/high-priced units. His overall responsibilities will include planning, directing, and controlling production operations. In addition, he is to coordinate production plans with the sales manager.

- Mr. Bill Melton, sales manager, was thirty-six years old and a college graduate with a major in marketing. He was Dick Johnson's brother-in-law and had previous experience as a mobile home sales representative with the same company as Johnson had been with prior to joining Hiwasse.
- Mr. Graham Richards, purchasing manager, was twenty-eight years old and an industrial management graduate of Kansas State. Although he had no experience in the manufacture of mobile homes, he had been a production supervisor in a nearby garments manufacturing plant.

Stockholders, the board, top management at Hiwasse, as well as many people in the small town of Gravett, were encouraged and excited about the prospects for a successful manufacturing plant. The company would provide needed jobs and be an asset to the community. The major goals of Hiwasse, according to Mr. Thomas, were:

- profit—achieve return on stockholder investment of 25 percent per year after the first year of operation
- provide needed jobs for area residents and thus increased economic prosperity
- produce an inexpensive mobile home, but of higher quality than those of competitors within the price range.

One week prior to the start of production operations, Mr. Thomas sent a letter to each stockholder. The following are excerpts from this letter.

The building is nearing completion and most of the equipment has been installed. Most of the hand tools and portable power tools have been received including the bulk of the stapling and nailing equipment. . . .

To date, materials have been ordered for the first ten units; the specialty items, or items that are fabricated, have been ordered for the second ten units. Many of the materials have been received with more to be received soon. Production is scheduled to start next week with approximately fifteen new production employees beginning work at that time. The first unit should be finished within five days of the starting of production. Workers will be added as needed each week for the first six or eight weeks. . . .

At the present time we have two sales representatives on the road starting to establish our dealer network. To date, the response from the dealers has been approximately 75 percent favorable. We anticipate no problems in marketing the first twenty units scheduled for production. We have firm orders for five units now.

Despite top management's optimism, the company began experiencing serious difficulties by the end of the first month of operation. The following is a summary of several board of directors' meetings held during the first few months after Hiwasse began production operations on December 1 relating to some of their problems.

January 19 Board Meeting

Mr. Thomas, the president, and the general manager, Mr. Dick Johnson, presented a summary of activities during the building of the plant and initial production operations. It was reported that the company has a cash flow problem due primarily to a lack of sales. There have been only two firm sales of mobile homes, although the company has several pending orders. Finished goods inventory currently is $92,500 (twenty unsold mobile homes).

The company is currently experiencing some production and management problems that should be resolved within the next two weeks. Prior to adjourning, the board set a goal of $55,000 worth of mobile home sales during the next two weeks.

February 2 Board Meeting

Mr. Thomas reported that ten mobile home units at $5,100 each had been sold to a dealer in Tulsa with a promised delivery date of March 1. To date, Hiwasse only received money from the sale of two mobile homes totalling $10,500. Several deliveries have been made for which money has not yet been received. The company's sales, production, and internal problems were again discussed at length. President Thomas stated that he thought that part of the company's difficulties were due to errors in judgment by General Manager Johnson and, in Thomas's opinion, inadequate performance by Johnson and the sales force. Thomas stated that Johnson had decided that Hiwasse should produce a higher-quality/higher-priced mobile home. After considerable discussion, no definite decisions were reached by the board.

February 15 Board Meeting

President Thomas reported that it was necessary to temporarily lay off twenty production employees at the end of the week. As cash flow improves, these workers will be recalled. The company has a signed order from a dealer in Joplin, Missouri, for ten units at $7,150 each. However, Hiwasse had to sign a repurchase agreement for any units remaining unsold after ninety days, and for any units sold they have to pay the dealer a rebate of $200 per unit plus a 5 percent discount on net cost.

The company currently has a finished goods inventory of mobile homes of $150,000–$170,000. The company's sales, production, and internal conflicts were again discussed at length. President Thomas asked that the board void Dick Johnson's employment contract and that he himself, at least until the company's financial position is more favorable, assume the duties of general manager in addition to his duties as president. The board declined to act on Mr. Thomas's request.

March 10 Special Board Meeting

All board members except Mr. Thomas signed the following statement, which was being placed in the board minutes.

> We, the undersigned shareholders and directors of Hiwasse Homes, Inc., wish to place the following comments and observations on the record of the minutes of the special meeting of March 10.
>
> We are of the opinion that the decision of Roger Thomas to terminate contractual relations with the "management team" (specifically Dick Johnson and Bill Melton) is not well founded. These people were personally selected by Mr. Thomas and were represented to us by Mr. Thomas as being the best qualified people available in the field for management of the corporation. We do not agree that they are not competent in this capacity and that they have failed to perform satisfactorily at this time.
>
> We are further of the opinion that the board of directors has not been kept fully informed at regular meetings as to the performance or lack of performance of the executive and supervisory personnel. Nor have we been supplied with a regular, comprehensive presentation of the financial condition of the firm. We have not been apprised of the creation and current status of liabilities in the form of loans and accounts payable, which we feel are policy matters subject to the approval and review by the board of directors as a

whole. We recognize that Roger Thomas, by virtue of the capital structure of the corporation, probably has the ability, at a regularly constituted annual meeting, to establish a board of directors, the majority of whom would be of his (Thomas's) own choosing. Therefore, in the event of the realignment of the board of directors as outlined above, we feel that the success or failure of the corporation will rest squarely upon Mr. Thomas rather than upon the undersigned who feel that they have not been permitted to function as a board of directors would ordinarily do.

We are most hopeful that the policies of Mr. Thomas, and consequently the direction the corporation takes, will be successful, both for the sake of those investors who placed their faith in Mr. Thomas and for the economic benefit of the community as a whole. We do not wish to harass or deter the progress of the firm and are hopeful of the problems being resolved by Mr. Thomas and extend to him our sincere wish for his success in this effort.

In other action for consideration by the board, Mr. Thomas reported that there were several firms that might be interested in purchasing a portion or possibly all of the stock of Hiwasse Homes. The board authorized Thomas to pursue any such possibilities immediately.

The board authorized Mr. Thomas to fire Mr. Bill Melton for failure to adequately perform as sales manager. Mr. Dick Johnson offered to resign from the company and requested that he be granted one week's paid vacation. A board member moved that Hiwasse regretfully accept Johnson's resignation and grant him fifteen days of paid vacation. The motion was approved unanimously with Johnson's resignation effective on March 25.

HIWASSE DISCONTINUES OPERATIONS

It was a typical hot August day in northwestern Arkansas as Mr. Thomas made final preparations for closing Hiwasse Homes. Hiwasse Homes was bankrupt after only nine months of operation. Mr. Thomas, the founder and president of Hiwasse, was very disappointed to see his dreams and two years of planning and hard work end in the failure of the business.

From mid-March to the final closing of the plant on August 1, Hiwasse continued to experience financial and operational problems. After the departure of Johnson, Mr. Thomas assumed almost total responsibility for plant operations. The plant continued to produce mobile homes with an average output of one per day but experienced considerable difficulty selling its finished products. During the first six months of operation, Hiwasse sustained a net loss of over $81,000.

QUESTIONS

1. If you were Mr. Thomas and had just reviewed the conclusions and recommendations of the feasibility study, would you have entered the mobile home manufacturing business?

2. What were Mr. Thomas's basic objectives in starting Hiwasse Homes? Did he have standards of performance for his new business?

3. What types of initial controls did Mr. Thomas use in beginning Hiwasse? Specifically, comment on controls in the areas of material, personnel selection, and capital.

4. Despite considerable planning and a detailed feasibility study, Hiwasse Homes failed just a few months after it began operations. Why? What were the primary reasons for the failure of Hiwasse?

This case was written by Robert E. Holmes of James Madison University and R. Dean Lewis formerly of Sam Houston State University. Reprinted with permission.

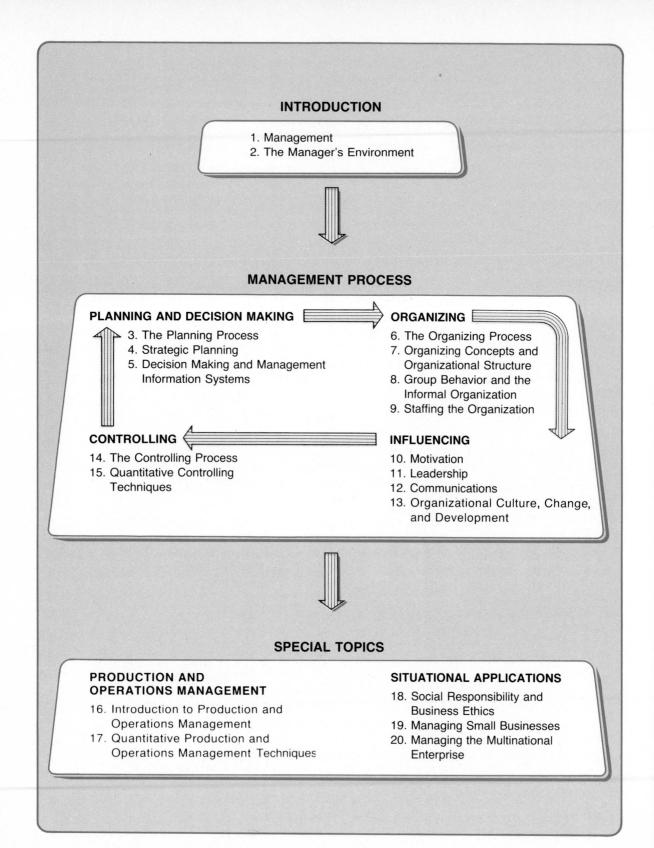

INTRODUCTION

1. Management
2. The Manager's Environment

MANAGEMENT PROCESS

PLANNING AND DECISION MAKING

3. The Planning Process
4. Strategic Planning
5. Decision Making and Management Information Systems

ORGANIZING

6. The Organizing Process
7. Organizing Concepts and Organizational Structure
8. Group Behavior and the Informal Organization
9. Staffing the Organization

CONTROLLING

14. The Controlling Process
15. Quantitative Controlling Techniques

INFLUENCING

10. Motivation
11. Leadership
12. Communications
13. Organizational Culture, Change, and Development

SPECIAL TOPICS

PRODUCTION AND OPERATIONS MANAGEMENT

16. Introduction to Production and Operations Management
17. Quantitative Production and Operations Management Techniques

SITUATIONAL APPLICATIONS

18. Social Responsibility and Business Ethics
19. Managing Small Businesses
20. Managing the Multinational Enterprise

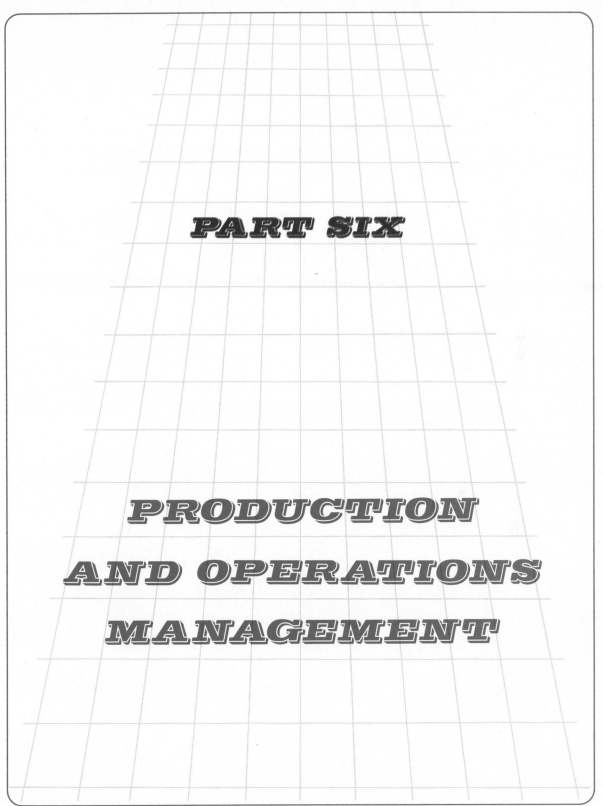

PART SIX

PRODUCTION AND OPERATIONS MANAGEMENT

KEY TERMS

production and operations management
flow process chart
operation chart
worker-machine chart
time study
predetermined time standards
work sampling
process layout
product layout
maintenance
preventive maintenance
learning curve
flexible manufacturing system (FMS)

LEARNING OBJECTIVES

After completing this chapter you should be able to

1. Identify and describe some of the graphic techniques used in production and operations methods analysis.
2. Explain the primary labor measurement methods.
3. State the basic approaches to arranging physical facilities.
4. Explain the concepts of maintenance control and learning curve.
5. Describe the major trends regarding factories of the future.

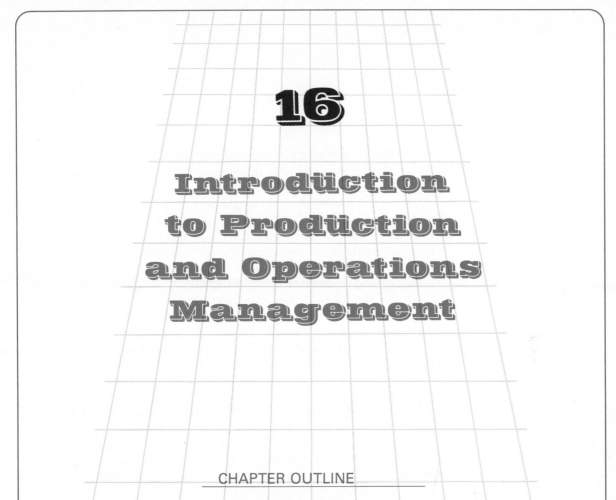

16

Introduction to Production and Operations Management

CHAPTER OUTLINE

Graphic Methods
Principles of Motion Economy
Work Measurement
Site Selection
Physical Facility Layout
Maintenance Control
Learning Curves
Factories of the Future

The farm machinery industry was failing in the early 1980s. Massey Ferguson was threatening bankruptcy. International Harvester, the giant of the business, was in such dismal shape that it headed *Fortune* magazine's 1984 list of least-admired American companies. But Deere & Company, maker of the green tractors familiar to most Americans, was spending millions of dollars to adopt the latest in manufacturing technologies. This was especially the case at Deere's complex of factories in Waterloo, Iowa, where the company had undertaken a major capital development program that produced the following new or modernized facilities: Product Engineering Center, Engine Works, Component Works, and Tractor Works.

The Product Engineering Center was greatly expanded. At this facility, research and development is conducted on farm machinery and engines, transmissions, and other components. In the expansion, emphasis was upon more sophisticated research and testing facilities for computer-based engineering and upon improving research capabilities in the area of farm equipment electronics.

Even more important changes were instituted at three of Deere's factories: the Component Works, an Engine Works, and a Tractor Works, the last two of which were built on so-called greenfield sites (sites in outlying rural areas). The Tractor Works is viewed by many as one of the most modern among U.S. factories—it has received design awards for its computer integration from the prestigious Society of Manufacturing Engineers. The Component Works also features a wide range of manufacturing innovations.

The Component Works, among the largest of the firm's factories, houses one of the world's largest and most efficient flexible manufacturing systems (FMS). This computer-controlled system is a network of 16 separate machining centers that automatically load and use approximately 1,000 different tools. Covering an area the size of a football field, the FMS is able to automatically machine a large variety of castings, such as transmission cases, in random sequence. More than a dozen of these large castings move about within this system simultaneously. The parts move from operation to operation on computer-directed carriers.

This FMS is seen as unique for its ability to perform so many functions automatically on very large parts. The system enables the company to introduce new or redesigned parts into manufacturing rapidly with very little cost for retooling. It thus permits the company to respond quickly to a changing market with new products or to act swiftly to meet demands from companies who come to Deere as a supplier of original equipment components.

The massive technology update at Waterloo, coupled with similar capital programs at other Deere factories, is designed to assure that the company will maintain a firm grip on its position as the industry's low-cost manufacturer. Not only does Deere have a distinct advantage over its traditional competitors, but the company can compete on a price and delivery basis with so-called short-liners— companies that make only one or two farm implements and do so on a high-volume, low-cost basis. A Milwaukee stock analyst who specializes in equipment makers says Deere & Company has "some of the most up-to-date manufacturing facilities in the world—in any industry." When one considers what *any industry* includes today, that is truly remarkable.[1]

Only a few years ago, production management was taught exclusively as it related to a factory environment like that of John Deere. Today the expanded field of production and operations management (POM) applies to all organizations, including hospitals, schools, and government agencies. **Production and operations management** is *the application of objective, especially quantitative, techniques to the design and operation of any system that transforms inputs into desired outputs.* Most POM techniques are equally applicable to both factory and service industries.

production and operations management

In this chapter, we will first discuss a number of traditional techniques: graphic methods, principles of motion economy, work measurement, site selection, physical facility layout, maintenance control, and learning curves. This will be followed by a brief look at the factory of the future with emphasis on robotics and flexible manufacturing systems.

GRAPHIC METHODS

Several graphic techniques have been developed to assist in production and operations methods analysis. The techniques in and of themselves do not improve the way a task is done; instead, they permit a person with an inquiring mind and knowledge of the subject to improve the production process. Several of these techniques will next be discussed.

Flow Process Chart

A **flow process chart** is *an illustration of the activities involved in an entire process showing the sequence in which they are performed.* Standard symbols have been developed to serve as a type of shorthand in recording activities. The symbols used in a flow process chart to depict the flow of a job are as follows:

flow process chart

 Operation   ☐ Inspection   ▽ Storage

 Transportation   D Delay

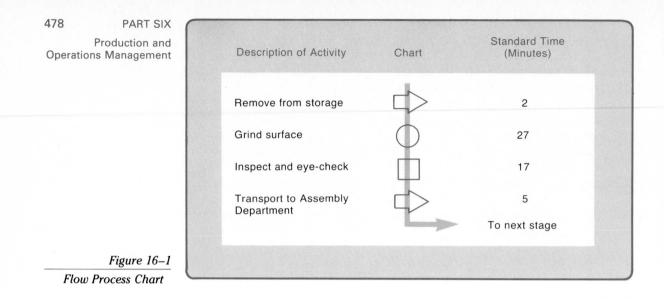

Description of Activity	Chart	Standard Time (Minutes)
Remove from storage		2
Grind surface		27
Inspect and eye-check		17
Transport to Assembly Department		5
	To next stage	

Figure 16–1

Flow Process Chart

Each task to be accomplished is identified, along with the time it will take. A manager can then study the sequence of tasks to determine if there is a better way to accomplish the job. Assume that Figure 16–1 is the flow process chart for a cylinder head (the top part of a gasoline engine), which is to be ground and inspected prior to assembly onto a John Deere tractor engine. Only the activities related to the grinding department are shown.

Operation Chart

operation chart

The **operation chart** is *a chart showing an operator's activities while performing one operation in a process.* It might show the motions of the left hand and right hand of an operator. Its use is essential when the time from start to finish of an operation (cycle time) is fairly short. Operations are usually broken down into smaller categories than those used with a flow process chart. A major benefit of an operations chart is that it permits a manager to view a task to see if it is being completed in an optimum way.

Worker-Machine Chart

worker-machine chart

These charts are beneficial when both a worker and a machine are used to perform a particular task. A **worker-machine chart** is *a chart showing if there is excessive idle time associated with either the worker or the machine.* An idle worker may be assigned an additional machine to control. On the other hand, if the machine is expensive and needs to be kept operating a majority of the time, it may be worth the cost of an additional worker to help operate the machine even though the idle time of the worker goes up.

A worker-machine chart is illustrated in Figure 16–2. Notice that if only Machine 1 were used, the operator would be idle about one-third of each cycle. When Machine 2 is added, however, one or the other of the machines is idle much of the time.

Subject Charted __Milling slot in regulator clamp__   Chart No. ____807____
Drawing No. __J-1492__   Part No. __J-1492-1__   Chart of Method __Proposed__
Chart Begins __Loading mchs. for milling__   Charted By __C. A. Anderson__
Chart Ends __Unloading milled clamps__   Date __8-27__   Sheet _1_ of _1_

ELEMENT DESCRIPTION	OPERATOR	B.&S. Hor. Mill MACHINE 1	B.&S. Hor. Mill MACHINE 2
Stop machine #1	.0004		
Return table mch. #1 5 inches	.0010	Unloading .0024	
Loosen vise remove part and lay aside (mch. #1)	.0010		Mill Slot .0040
Pick up part and tighten vise mch. #1	.0018		
Start machine #1	.0004	Loading .0032	
Advance table and engage feed mch. #1	.0010		Idle
Walk to machine #2	.0011		
Stop machine #2	.0004		
Return table machine #2 5 inches	.0010	Mill Slot .0040	Unloading .0024
Loosen vise remove part and lay aside (mch. #2)	.0010		
Pick up part and tighten vise mch. #2	.00.8		
Start machine #2	.0004		Loading .0032
Advance table and engage feed mch. #2	.0010	Idle	
Walk to machine #1	.0011		

Idle man time per cycle	.0000	Idle hours machine #1	.0038
Working man time per cycle	.0134	Productive hours mch. #1	.0096
Man-hours per cycle	.0134	Machine #1 cycle time	.0134

Idle hours machine #2	.0038
Productive hours mch. #2	.0096
Machine #2 cycle time	.0134

Figure 16–2

Man and Machine Process Chart for Milling Machine Operation

Source: Benjamin W. Niebel, *Motion and Time Study,* 7th ed. (Homewood, Ill.: Richard D. Irwin, Inc., 1982), p. 136.

Activity Chart

In both manufacturing and the service industry, efficient accomplishment of objectives requires the use of teams. An activity chart is useful for this purpose and is quite similar to the worker-machine chart. An activity chart can show the interaction of members of the group in performing a task. For example, in a hospital the activities of a surgical team in performing an emergency operation must be carefully controlled. If any member of the team fails to act correctly at the right time, the results could be disastrous. An activity chart allows the actions of each team member to be graphically displayed in relation to those of other members.

TABLE 16-1 Principles of Motion Economy

Use of the Human Body	Arrangement of the Workplace	Design of Tools and Equipment
1. The two hands should begin as well as complete their motions at the same time.	9. There should be a definite and fixed place for all tools and materials.	18. Two or more tools should be combined whenever possible.
2. The two hands should not be idle at the same time except during rest periods.	10. Tools, materials, and controls should be located close in and directly in front of the operator.	19. Tools and materials should be prepositioned whenever possible.
3. Motions of the arms should be made in opposite and symmetrical directions and should be made simultaneously.	11. Gravity feedbins and containers should be used to deliver materials close to the point of use.	20. Where each finger performs some specific movement, such as in typewriting, the load should be distributed in accordance with the inherent capacities of the fingers.
4. Hand motions should be confined to the lowest classification with which it is possible to perform the work satisfactorily.	12. Drop deliveries should be used whenever possible.	21. Handles, such as those used on cranks and large screwdrivers, should be designed to permit as much of the surface of the hand to come in contact with the handle as possible. This is particularly true when considerable force is exerted in using the handle. For light assembly work the screwdriver handle should be so shaped that it is smaller at the bottom than at the top.
5. Momentum should be employed to assist the worker whenever possible, and it should be reduced to a minimum if it must be overcome by muscular effort.	13. Materials and tools should be located to permit the best sequence of motions.	
6. Smooth continuous motions of the hands are preferable to zigzag motions or straight-line motions involving sudden and sharp changes in direction.	14. Provisions should be made for adequate conditions for seeing. Good illumination is the first requirement for satisfactory visual perception.	22. Levers, crossbars, and handwheels should be located in such positions that the operator can manipulate them with the least change in body position and with the greatest mechanical advantage.
7. Ballistic movements are faster, easier, and more accurate than restricted (fixation) or "controlled" movements.	15. The height of the workplace and the chair could preferably be arranged so that alternate sitting and standing at work are easily possible.	
8. Rhythm is essential to the smooth and automatic performance of an operation, and the work should be arranged to permit easy and natural rhythm whenever possible.	16. A chair of the type and height to permit good posture should be provided for every worker.	
	17. The hands should be relieved of all work that can be done more advantageously by a jig, a fixture, or a foot-operated device.	

Source: R. M. Barnes, *Motion and Time Study: Design and Measurement of Work*, 6th ed. (New York: Wiley, 1968).

PRINCIPLES OF MOTION ECONOMY

The principles of motion economy presented in Table 16-1 are useful in improving efficiency and reducing fatigue. They relate to principles concerning the use of the human body, arrangement of the workplace, and design of tools and equipment. The principles have been extremely beneficial in job design. In its traditional operations, John Deere has used these principles extensively. The completion of the new highly automated factory in Waterloo in no way diminishes the importance of motion economy. In fact, since advanced machines will make one worker's output much higher than previously, efficient movements might make an even greater difference.

WORK MEASUREMENT

The most critical factor in the production process is labor. If management is to manage labor resources effectively, there must be some way of

*Graphic techniques as-
sist in production and
operations methods
analysis.*

David Aronson/Stock, Boston Inc.

measuring their use. Labor standards specify the amount of time necessary
to perform a certain task. Standards are used to set up incentive plans and
to compare the performance of individuals performing similar tasks. They
are also used in preparation of bids on contracts and for estimating
completion dates. There are three primary labor measurement methods:
time studies, the use of predetermined time standards, and work sampling.

Time Studies

Time study is *the systematic measurement and analysis of the time required*   *time study*
to do work. The most common approach to time study is patterned after
that developed by Frederick W. Taylor in 1881. Under this procedure, a
stopwatch is used to measure one worker's performance, and then the
results become a standard for all workers. The following steps are normally
included in a time study effort:

1. Describe the task to be performed.
2. Break the task down into a number of simple elements.
3. Measure the time required to perform each element and note operator
   performance. (This should be done over a number of work cycles.)
4. Compute the average time required to do the total task according to the
   following formula:

$$\text{Average performance} = \frac{\text{Times recorded to perform all elements}}{\text{Number of cycles observed}}$$

5. Compute the normal time. The normal time is determined by computing a
   performance rating that is the percentage of reasonable working speed at which

the observed worker is judged to be working. The formula for normal time is as follows:

$$\text{Normal time} = (\text{Average performance time}) \times (\text{Rating factor}).$$

Although the Society for the Advancement of Management provides benchmarks for a wide range of work elements, performance rating is still a very subjective task.

6. Calculate the standard time according to the following formula:

$$\text{Standard time} = \frac{\text{Normal time}}{1 - \text{Allowance fraction}}.$$

The allowance fraction adjusts for personal needs, unavoidable work delays, and worker fatigue, among other variables. Suppose, for example, that an average performance time of five minutes was determined for painting a John Deere tractor wheel hub and that the time study analyst felt that the worker was moving at 90 percent of normal speed. Assume further that the work method department of the firm has a standard allowance for this kind of work of 15 percent. The standard time is computed as follows:

$$\text{Normal time} = (\text{Performance time}) \times (\text{Performance rating})$$
$$= (5.0) \times (.9) = 4.5 \text{ minutes.}$$

$$\text{Standard time} = \frac{\text{normal time}}{1 - \text{allowance}}$$
$$= \frac{4.5}{1 - .15}$$
$$= \frac{4.5}{.85}$$
$$= 5.3 \text{ minutes.}$$

Although the worker is moving at only 90 percent of normal speed, standard time can still be computed.

Predetermined Time Standards

*predetermined time
standards*

An alternative to the measurement of actual times required to do work is the use of **predetermined time standards.** These are *established estimates of the time that should be required to perform minute elements of work.* In order to estimate how long a certain task will take, the time factors for each element are added together.

The most widely known approach to using predetermined time standards was developed by Frank and Lillian Gilbreth and is called methods time measurement (MTM). The Gilbreths called the basic work elements *therbligs* (notice that if you reverse the last two letters of the Gilbreths' name and then spell it backward you get *therblig*). Therbligs included such activities as select, grasp, position, assemble, reach, hold, rest, and inspect. Time values for various therbligs are available from the MTM Association for Standards and Research.

The use of predetermined time standards has several advantages. First, the standards may be established in a laboratory environment and not disturb normal production activities. Second, the standard can be known before a task is done, and this knowledge can aid in planning. Finally, the method is widely accepted by unions in setting standards, perhaps because the association that sets the standards is independent of management.

Work Sampling

A way of measuring work that does not use a stopwatch is called **work sampling**. This is *the observation of a worker or workers at random times to determine the proportion of their time that is being spent on various tasks*. A detailed procedure for work sampling was developed by L. Tippet in the 1930s. Statistical sampling techniques are used to determine the number of observations needed to obtain the degree of reliability desired.

work sampling

Suppose that we wish to determine how much of a typist's time is involved in the preparation of correspondence. If we observe the typist at one hundred random selected times and find that correspondence is being prepared thirty of those times, we can estimate that the typist works on correspondence 30 percent of the time.

SITE SELECTION

Every firm has its own criteria for choosing a particular site for locating a new facility. In addition to consideration of the costs associated with purchasing and building on a new site, many other factors must be evaluated. These factors include the supply of skilled labor, union activities, quality of life, and state and local policies. For many reasons, a site that may be completely satisfactory for one company may be totally unacceptable for another.

A number of mathematical and computer-based techniques have been developed to assist in determining where to locate a physical facility. The most commonly used approach is to develop a set of criteria and rate each location on how well it meets the criteria. An example of this procedure is illustrated in Table 16–2. In this case, the most important factor for site selection is availability of skilled labor, so this factor is assigned a maximum score of 30. Availability of raw materials, with a maximum score of 20, is the next most important criterion. Third is access to transportation, with a top score of 15. In the example, three sites have been proposed and rated on each of the criteria. The total score for site 2 is significantly above the others, although it ranks lowest on access to transportation. Often there are many more factors than are shown in this simple illustration. For example, John Deere's decision to build its $500 million complex in Waterloo was affected by tax considerations, energy costs, and proximity to suppliers.

TABLE 16–2 Plant Location Scoring Model

	Maximum Score	Site 1	Site 2	Site 3
Availability of skilled labor	30	18	25	15
Availability of raw materials	20	12	18	10
Access to transportation	15	10	5	10
Total score		40	48	35

The assembly line is an excellent example of a product layout.   Owen Franken/Stock, Boston Inc.

PHYSICAL FACILITY LAYOUT

Management must determine the most effective way to lay out the physical facilities for virtually any type of operation. In a factory environment, management might be concerned with the best placement for lathes and punch presses. Offices, desks, and typewriters might be of concern in an administrative setting. And in a hospital, the locations of operating rooms, laboratories, and nursing stations have a major impact on efficiency. The overriding goal of physical facility layout is to maximize efficiency and effectiveness. There are two basic approaches to arranging physical facilities: process and product.

Process Layouts

process layout   A wide variety of products or services can be handled simultaneously when the process layout is used. A **process layout** is *an arrangement of the processing components according to the function they perform.* A typical example of the use of the process layout is the job shop that produces different products, each by a different sequence of operations. The product

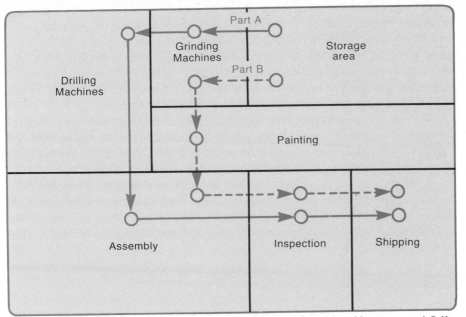

Figure 16–3

A Process Layout

Source: Ralph M. Stair, Jr. and Barry Render, *Production and Operations Management: A Self-Correcting Approach.* (Boston: Allyn and Bacon, Inc., 1980), p. 279.

is typically one at a time or in batches (see Figure 16–3). The batch moves from one department to another in a particular sequence.

A common example of the process layout is found in a hospital. Patients come to the hospital with a wide variety of problems. Depending on their ailment, they are routed through various departments—admissions, lab, X-ray, and so on. When the process layout is used, the goal is to arrange departments or work centers in the most economical manner.

In most situations, an attempt is made to minimize material handling cost. For example, the huge machinery centers at John Deere need to be reasonably close to the departments that send items there for machining.

A major advantage of the process layout is that it provides for flexibility in equipment and labor assignments and often for efficient use of machines. If one machine breaks down, for example, the entire process may not have to be stopped. Work can simply be rerouted. Another advantage is that the process layout permits the economic manufacture of goods and services in small batches. It also permits a wide variety of outputs in different sizes and forms.

A disadvantage of the process layout is that it allows less specialized use of equipment and labor. Also, the items being processed require additional handling since they must be moved to each process point. Finally, labor skill requirements are high, inventories must be large, and scheduling and coordination may present major problems.

Product Layout

A production arrangement that entails moving a product down an assembly line or conveyor and through a series of work stations until completed is *product layout*   called a **product layout**. Automobiles, television sets, and soft drinks are produced in this manner. Tractor assembly at John Deere is arranged along a product layout. When the product layout is used, the goal is to create a smooth, continuous flow along the assembly line with a minimum of idle time at each work station. Essentially the product layout presents a balancing problem. Output capacity at each work station needs to be balanced so that it is nearly the same as the following one.

The main advantage of a product layout is that cost per unit of production is usually lower. This is partly because automated and specialized equipment is used. Also, material handling is lower, inventories are reduced at each work station, and workers can usually be more quickly trained.

Product layouts have weaknesses too. First, assembly lines typically require a large investment. Recall that John Deere's new facility cost $500 million. Second, a breakdown at one point on the assembly line causes the entire line to stop. Finally, assembly lines are not set up to handle a wide variety of products.

MAINTENANCE CONTROL

When the organization is highly mechanized and complex, the breakdown of even one machine can have severe effects. Workers may be idle, and in some instances the plant may have to be closed. Consider what happens if the air-conditioning system in a large, modern office building fails or if the central computer at General Motors is out of order for even a day.

maintenance   **Maintenance** is *the sum of all activities involved in keeping a production system in working order.* In most organizations, maintenance represents a significant part of total costs. *Routine inspection and other efforts aimed at*

Figure 16–4

Preventive versus Breakdown Maintenance Costs

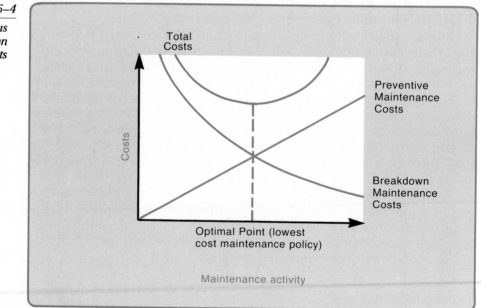

Source: Ralph M. Stair, Jr. and Barry Render, *Production and Operations Management: A Self-Correcting Approach.* (Boston: Allyn and Bacon, Inc., 1980), p. 350.

keeping equipment and facilities in good working order are referred to as **preventive maintenance**. If a company is not willing to bear the costs of preventive maintenance, breakdowns tend to occur. Such breakdowns typically must be repaired on an emergency or priority basis, often at considerable expense. The purpose of preventive maintenance is to identify potential problems and make changes or repairs before breakdowns occur. For example, keeping a machine well oiled is a better alternative than replacing the machine because a bearing failure causes it to break down.

preventive maintenance

A balance must be struck between preventive and breakdown maintenance. Notice in Figure 16–4 that as preventive costs rise, breakdown maintenance costs fall. The intersection of these two costs curves represents the lowest maintenance costs. Putting more and more money into preventive maintenance will reduce the number of breakdowns. Beyond this point, though, the firm will be better off waiting for breakdowns to occur and repairing them when they do. Of course, this approach would not be taken for the new machining centers at John Deere because their continuous operation is so vital to the rest of the factory.

LEARNING CURVES

The **learning curve** is *a graphical representation of the decreasing time required to do a particular task as that task is repeated by a certain person.* Essentially the more times a person does a particular job, the easier the task becomes. Two basic principles are involved. First, the more times a task is accomplished, the less time it will take. Assume, for example, that a technician has just begun assembling a number of identical small components. If she needs twenty minutes to complete the first unit, by the time she has done four units, the time may be down to fifteen minutes. Second, the amount of time saved completing each unit normally decreases. The technician just mentioned has decreased the time required by five minutes in making just four units. That many additional repetitions may be needed to shave just one more minute off the time. This kind of relationship is shown in Figure 16–5. Notice that the time required approaches a minimum no matter how long the operation is continued.

learning curve

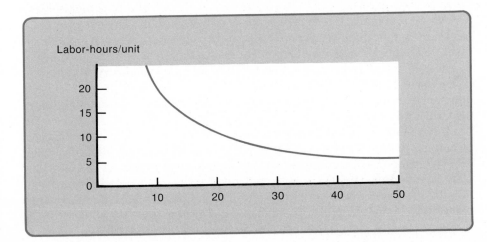

Figure 16–5

Learning Curve

A mathematical relationship can be developed to determine how long it takes to produce any unit as a function of how many units have been produced before it. The consequences of learning curve analysis are far reaching. For instance, failure to consider the learning curve effect can result in running out of inventory and raw materials because the units produced are taking less and less time to finish. Also, considering the learning curve effect helps in labor planning and scheduling. Otherwise managers may schedule more time than is necessary for a project, resulting in idle workers.

FACTORIES OF THE FUTURE

It is difficult to say what the future holds for manufacturers, but a number of trends are evident. Two of these trends are robotization and the use of flexible manufacturing systems. These innovations in manufacturing create significant challenges for the human resources manager.[2] Concern for the impact of technology on the human element has resulted in an entirely new area of study, called ergonomics, biotechnology, or human factors engineering. Although ergonomics grew out of a concern for the human element, the result has been to facilitate the trend toward robotization rather than slow it. Although much has been written in these areas, we will limit the discussion to the two major trends mentioned.

Robotics in the Factory

Fortune magazine describes a Japanese plant where robots make parts for other robots:

> In Fanuc Ltd.'s cavernous, bumblebee-yellow buildings in a pine forest near Mount Fuji, automatic machining centers and robots typically toil unattended through the night, with only subdued blue warning lights flashing as unmanned delivery carts move like ghostly messengers through the eerie semi-darkness.[3]

The Japanese have been leaders in the use of robots. Because of this, they have become the lowest-cost producer of automobiles, certain machine parts, electronic items, and as the quotation illustrates, of robots themselves. Now more and more, U.S. factories are employing robots. The use of robots has improved productivity at Ford Motor Company's thirty-year-old assembly plant in Wayne, Michigan, by 25 percent over a four-year period.[4] In addition to being installed in large numbers in the automobile industry, robots are being used in shipbuilding and furniture production and in warehouses, unmanned transportation, medical centers, firefighting, coal mining, waste disposal, and even skyscraper window washing.[5]

It has been predicted that machines will soon become a standard aspect of automation and have profound impact on manufacturing methods.[6] One recent advance has been the use of vision-controlled robots. At the Chrysler plant in Windsor, Ontario, vision-controlled robots can detect even small defects in car doors before they are fitted into an auto body. Vision-controlled robots can adjust to changing circumstances.

Because of Japanese competition and the 1981–1982 recession, General

Electric decided to robotize its diesel electric locomotive plant in Erie, Pennsylvania. The plant is now able to turn out 800 locomotives a year, one-third more than previously, with 20 percent fewer workers. In one area, five workers do what seventy did before. They can machine a 2,500 pound motor frame in 16 hours, compared to 16 days before.[7]

GENERAL ELECTRIC "Here in this old northeastern U.S. industrial community, we are giving an aging industrial complex 'an electronic heart transplant' that will make it a world-class facility, competitive with the Japanese, Germans, or anyone else in the world." Thus Carl Schlemmer, a General Electric vice-president, described GE's efforts to install flexible manufacturing systems at its diesel electric locomotive factory in Pennsylvania. It has taken five years and costs $316 million, but Duane Shull, modernization program chief, said that productivity has tripled and capacity can now be expanded by 100 percent. Production time for the heaviest motor frame has been reduced from sixteen days to sixteen hours.

The impact on employees has been no less remarkable than the technological innovations. All 7,500 employees at the Erie, Pennsylvania, plant were required to attend communications sessions. Some continued in the training center as instructors. Others received special training in operating and servicing the 300 numerically controlled machines in the plant.

One flexible manufacturing system machines ten different locomotive components ranging from a small gearbox weighing only 150 pounds to large castings weighing more than a ton and containing as many as 140 machined surfaces. As a casting or welded frame enters the machining process, it is turned over to the central computer. This executive computer then orders the automatic transporter to take the piece to its first machining station. The executive computer loads the proper program into the individual machine computer. The central computer shuffles the pieces among the various machines to make sure each machine is used efficiently. "Not a single nonrobotic hand will work on the frames until the computer is satisfied with the work and summons a human to take them away," said James Baker, who is in charge of technical systems at GE. The central computer also keeps track of tool life so that tools can be replaced before they wear out and create defects. Some of the machines change their own tooling between jobs. On others, a robot situated nearby makes the tool changes. As modern as this may sound, a GE engineer points out that the technology in the plant is at least two years old because of the necessary construction time.

FMS has the potential for solving the traditional conflict between marketing and production. Through flexible manufacturing, an endless variety of product designs can be manufactured without losing the benefits of mass production. The flexible manufacturing effort at the Erie plant is as much designed to serve the people and employees in the area as to increase profitability. James Baker said, "It is an old American business that decided a while back that it wanted to stay in Erie, that declined to be run out of business by Hitachi or the French or anyone else, and that the way to stay world-class competitive was not to whine or procrastinate or wait for better times and high volume, but to produce the world-class best locomotive at a competitive price. That determination led inevitably to the type of automation that is in progress today."[8]

Flexible Manufacturing Systems

One of the advantages of the product or assembly-line layout is that costs per unit are lowered. But a weakness is that large numbers have to be produced to achieve economy of scale. Since 75 percent of all machined parts produced today are in batches of fifty or fewer, the assembly-line method of manufacturing is not always best.[9]

flexible manufacturing system (FMS)

This need for producing small batches of items, coupled with the capabilities of modern robots, has led to the development of the **flexible manufacturing system (FMS).** This is *a numerically controlled production arrangement that can be programmed to do a wide variety of tasks and to change from one task to another in a routine manner.* General Electric uses FMS to make 2,000 different versions of its basic electric meter on one group of machines. In the past, a complete new setup would have been required for each version. The numerically controlled indexers of John Deere's new plant, which hold up to sixty-nine different tools, are another example of FMS. Since the same machines can be easily changed from making one item to making another, small batch processing is tending to replace the old inflexible assembly line.

A major problem with changing to new methods of making new and existing products and to new items has been that workers experience significant learning curve effects. Thus, it often takes months, and sometimes years, to reach an acceptable level of efficiency. With FMS, the learning curve is eliminated except as it relates to the programming of the machines.

FMS has also diminished the requirement for economies of scale. Once a factory is converted to FMS, it is not necessary to produce thousands or even hundreds of units to achieve low costs. Break-even points tend to be lowered.

SUMMARY

Several graphic techniques have been developed to assist in production and operations method analysis. A flow process chart is an illustration of the activities involved in an entire process showing the sequence in which they are performed. The operation chart shows an operator's activities while performing one operation in a process. Through studying worker-machine charts, a manager is able to determine if there is excessive idle time associated with either the worker or the machine. An activity chart is useful to show the interaction of members of the group in performing a task. Principles of motion economy relate to the principles concerning the use of the human body, arrangement of the workplace, and design of tools and equipment.

There are three primary labor measurement methods: time studies, the use of predetermined time standards, and work sampling. Time study is the systematic measurement and analysis of the time required to do work. Predetermined time standards are established estimates of the time that should be required to perform minute elements of work. A way of measuring work that does not use a stopwatch is called work sampling.

A number of mathematical and computer-based techniques have been developed to assist in determining where to locate a physical facility; however, the most commonly used approach is to develop a set of criteria and rate each location on how well it meets the criteria.

There are two basic approaches to arranging

physical facilities: process and product. A process layout is an arrangement of the processing components according to the function they perform. A production arrangement that entails moving a product down an assembly line or conveyor and through a series of work stations until completed is called a product layout.

Maintenance is the sum of all activities involved in keeping a production system in working order. Routine inspection and costs associated with keeping the equipment in good working order are referred to as preventive maintenance. A balance must be struck between preventive and breakdown maintenance.

The learning curve is a graphical representation of the decreasing time required to do a particular task as that task is repeated by a certain person. This concept has two basic principles. First, the more times a task is accomplished, the less time it will take. Second, the amount of time saved completing each unit normally decreases.

It is difficult to say what the future holds for manufacturers; however, a number of trends are evident. Two of these trends are robotization and flexible manufacturing systems. In addition to being installed in large numbers in the automobile industry, robots are being used in a wide variety of other activities. The need for producing small batches of items, coupled with the capabilities of modern robots, has led to the development of flexible manufacturing systems. These are numerically controlled production arrangements that can be programmed to do a wide variety of tasks and to change from one task to another in a routine manner.

REVIEW QUESTIONS

1. Define each of the following terms:
   a. Flow process chart
   b. Operation chart
   c. Worker-machine chart
   d. Activity chart
2. Distinguish by definition and example between time studies and work sampling.
3. When would a manager use a process layout? A product layout? Explain your answer.
4. Regarding maintenance control, when would the firm be better off waiting for breakdowns to occur and repairing them when they do?
5. What are the basic assumptions associated with the learning curve?
6. Describe some trends of the future regarding manufacturing.

EXERCISES

1. Assume that you are considering locating the following types of manufacturing facilities. What factors would you foresee as being important with regard to determining whether or not the site is satisfactory?
   a. High-tech production facility
   b. Paperboard plant
   c. Bread and cookie plant
2. Describe how the learning curve would be associated with the following activities:
   a. Managing an automobile assembly plant
   b. Writing term papers
   c. Studying

CASE STUDY

The New Continuous-Feed System

Louise McGowen was worried as she approached the training director's office. She is the supervisor of six punch press operators at Keller-Globe, a maker of sheet metal parts for the industrial refrigeration industry. She had just learned that her punch presses would soon be replaced with a continuous-feed system that would double the speed of operations. She was thinking about how the workers might feel about the new system when the training director, Bill Taylor, opened the door and said, "Come on in, Lou. I've been looking forward to seeing you."

After a few pleasantries, Lou told Bill of her concerns. "The operators really know their jobs now. But this continuous-feed system is a whole new ballgame. And,

I'm concerned, too, about how the workers will feel about it. The new presses are going to run faster. They may think that their job is going to be harder."

Bill replied, "After talking with the plant engineer and the production manager, I have made up a tentative training schedule that might make you feel a little better. I think we first have to let the workers know why this change is necessary. You know that both of our competitors changed to this new system last year. After that, we will teach your people to operate the new presses."

"Who's going to do the teaching?" Lou asked. "I haven't even seen the new system."

"Well, Lou," said Bill, "the manufacturer has arranged for you to visit a plant with a similar system. They'll also ship one of the punch presses in early so your workers can learn to operate it."

"Will the factory give us any other training help?" Lou asked.

"Yes, I have asked them to send a trainer down as soon as the first press is set up. He will conduct some classroom sessions and then work with your people on the new machine."

After further discussion about details, Lou thanked Bill and headed back to the production department. She was confident that the new presses would be a real benefit to her section and that her workers could easily learn the skills required.

QUESTIONS

1. If you were Lou, how would you break the news to your workers?
2. Discuss how the new continuous-feed system is likely to be a benefit or a detriment to Lou's subordinates.

CASE STUDY

A Busy Shut-Down

Cecil Ross is the maintenance supervisor for Devcon Products Company, a Knoxville, Tennessee, producer of plastic pipe and fittings. In early December he was told by the plant manager to make plans to refurbish the number 3 extruding machine. This was to be done the weekend of January 9 and 10.

The extruding machine is a vital part of Devcon's operations. Cecil had been keeping a checklist of needed repairs, but the machine had not been shut down for a single day since July.

Cecil stayed on the job late that evening to inspect the machine and to update his checklist. He also checked the spare parts room and the tool room and made up an order for additional parts and tools that would be needed for the job.

The next day, Cecil held a meeting with his maintenance workers so that they would be prepared. Over the next several days, he looked at each individual repair item and prepared a written task assignment schedule. He assigned each task to the worker he considered most competent to do it.

Cecil knew that after the machine was shut down, he would find some unexpected defects. Also, some of the jobs would not go exactly as planned. So he decided to use his best worker, Breece Gimler, as a utility man. Breece would handle unexpected repairs and help the other workers when needed.

When the crew returned from the Christmas holidays, Cecil gave each a list of their repair tasks for the machine. On January 7, he held a final meeting to prepare for the shutdown. Cecil worked some extra hours that weekend. Because he had planned well, the machine was back on line in good repair on Monday morning.

QUESTIONS

1. Describe how the plant manager might decide how frequently to shut down the number 3 extruding machine.

2. Explain why the period just after Christmas might be a usual time to shut down heavy machinery.

3. What techniques described in this chapter might have been used in planning for the shutdown?

NOTES

1. This story is a composite from a number of sources, including: Jill Bettner and Lisa Gross, "Planting Deep and Wide at John Deere," *Forbes* (March 14, 1983): 119–122; Somerby Dowst, "Computer Is Strategy Tool for Deere & Co.," *Purchasing* (February 9, 1984): 45–51; "Lesson in Strategy: Deere Plows Straight Ahead While Harvester Comes a Cropper," *Los Angeles Times,* August 8, 1982; and Gene Bylinsky, "The Race to the Automatic Factory," *Fortune* (February 21, 1983): 52–64.

2. Edward M. Knod, Jr., Jerry L. Wall, John P. Daniels, Hugh M. Shane, and Theodore A. Wernimont, "Robotics: Challenges for the Human Resources Manager," *Business Horizons* (March–April 1984): 38–46.

3. Gene Bylinsky, "The Race to the Automatic Factory," *Fortune* (February 21, 1983): 54.

4. "High Tech: Blessing or Curse," *U.S. News & World Report* (January 16, 1984): 39.

5. Sara Kiesler, "New Technology in the Work Place," *Public Relations Journal* (December 1983): 12.

6. "Machines That Can See: Here Comes a New Generation," *Business Week* (January 9, 1984): 118.

7. "High Tech," p. 42.

8. Anderson Ashburn, "GE Puts FMS in an Aging Plant," *American Machinist* (May 1983): 104–105; John Holusha, "The New Allure of Manufacturing," *New York Times,* December 18, 1983, sec. 3, p. 1; "The Factory of the Future," *Newsweek* (September 6, 1982): 69; B. H. LeCerf, "GE Pumps New Life into an Aging Factory," *Iron Age* (May 20, 1983): 74–77.

9. Bylinsky, "Race," p. 53.

REFERENCES

Adam, N., and J. Surkis. "Comparison of Capacity Planning Techniques in a Job Shop Control System." *Management Science* 23 (May 1977): 1011–1015.

Buffa, Elwood S. *Modern Production/Operations Management.* 6th ed. New York: Wiley, 1980.

Bylinsky, Gene. "The Race to the Automatic Factory." *Fortune* (February 21, 1983): 52–64.

Chase, Richard B., and Nicholas J. Aquilano. *Production and Operations Management: A Life Cycle Approach.* Homewood, Ill.: Irwin, 1981.

Clay, M. J. "Evaluating the Production Function." *Journal of Accountancy* 148 (May 1977): 82.

Cummings, L. L. "Needed Research in Production/ Operations Management: A Behavioral Perspective." *Academy of Management Review* (July 1977): 500–504.

Green, T. B. "Why Are Organizations Reluctant to Use Management Science/Operations Research? An Empirical Approach." *Interfaces* 7 (August 1976): 59–62.

Harwood, G. G., and R. H. Hermanson. "Lease or Buy Decisions." *Journal of Accountancy* 147 (September 1976): 83–87.

"High Tech: Blessing or Curse." *U.S. News & World Report* (January 16, 1984): 39–42.

Kiesler, Sara. "New Technology in the Work Place." *Public Relations Journal* (December 1983): 12.

Knod, Edward M., Jr., Jerry L. Wall, John P. Daniels, Hugh M. Shane, and Theodore A. Wernimont. "Robotics: Challenges for the Human Resources Manager." *Business Horizons* (March–April 1984): 38–46.

Lebell, D., and O. J. Krasner. "Selecting Environmental Forecasting Techniques from Business Planning Re- quirements." *Academy of Management Journal* 20 (July 1977): 373–383.

"Linear Programming Discovery." *Science* (November 30, 1979): 1022.

"Machines That Can See: Here Comes a New Generation." *Business Week* (January 9, 1984): 118.

Miller, L. W. "Using Linear Programming to Derive Planning Horizons for a Production Smoothing Problem." *Management Science* 25 (December 1979): 1217– 1231.

Morey, R. "Operations Management in Selected Non- manufacturing Organizations." *Academy of Management Journal* 19 (March 1976): 120–124.

Petry, Glen H. "Effective Use of Capital Budgeting Tools." *Business Horizons* 18 (October 1975): 57–65.

Remick, Carl. "Robots: New Faces on the Production Line." *Management Review* 68 (May 1979): 27.

Robinson, S. M. "Characterization of Stability in Linear Programming." *Operations Research* 25 (May 1977): 435–447.

Schmenner, Roger. *Production/Operations Management: Concepts and Situations.* Chicago: Science Research Associates, 1981.

Solomon, Eyra, and John J. Pringle. *An Introduction to Financial Management.* Santa Monica, Calif.: Goodyear, 1980.

Sprague, L. G., and C. R. Sprague. "Management Science?" *Interfaces* 6 (November 1976): 57–62.

Thomapoulis, Nick T. *Applied Forecasting Methods.* Englewood Cliffs, N.J.: Prentice-Hall, 1980.

KEY TERMS

payback method	objective function	moving average
break-even analysis	constraint function	exponential smoothing
fixed costs	long-run trend	regression analysis
variable costs	cyclical variation	time series analysis
discounted cash flow	seasonal variations	waiting line theory
technique	random variations	simulation
linear programming		

LEARNING OBJECTIVES

After completing this chapter you should be able to

1. Explain some of the basic financial models that are especially useful in production and operations management.
2. Describe linear programming and state some of the uses of linear programming.
3. Explain the need for forecasting and describe some of the forecasting techniques.
4. Define waiting line or queuing theory and state when it is useful in solving business problems.
5. Describe simulation and explain how simulation may be used in business.

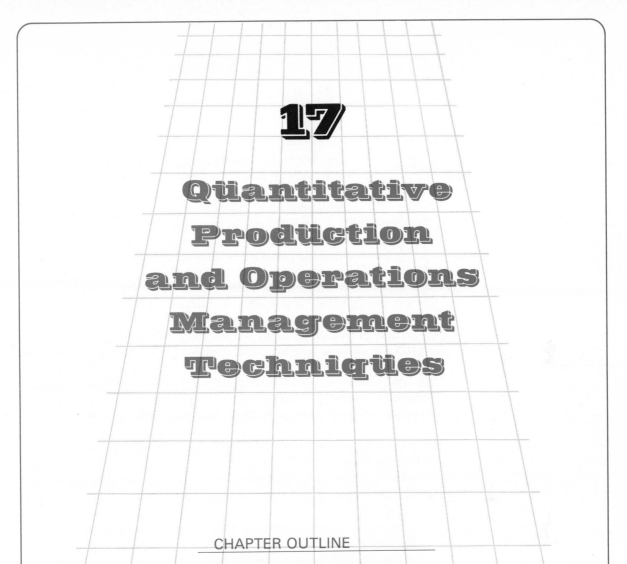

17

Quantitative Production and Operations Management Techniques

"Our fully integrated operations insure exacting control over every phase of engineering, testing, production—everything right down to final inspection," reads the annual report of Briggs and Stratton Corporation (B&S), the dominant U.S. manufacturer of small gasoline engines. B&S is effective in managing its production system; the company has been continuously profitable, through recessions and upswings, for decades. With profits of $39.4 million on sales of $636 million, Briggs and Stratton recently ranked 442d in sales but 167th in total return to investors on the Fortune 500 list. *Fortune* magazine calls B&S "an American company Honda can't mow down."

There is something particularly striking about Briggs and Stratton in today's world of robotized and flexible manufacturing systems; the company relies mainly on "the most flexible manufacturing system of all—the human being." Says executive vice-president Vern J. Socks, "We will consider automation wherever possible, practical, and economical; but if you are talking about one of those unmanned factories, you'll never see our operation all automated like that." *Fortune* magazine says much of the machinery in Briggs and Stratton's Wauwatosa, Wisconsin, factory is so old it "looks like the industrial exhibit at the Smithsonian Institution," but continues that the factory "towers as a stronghold of human skill, agility—and high productivity."

Simply managing its operation complex, let alone maintaining its status as the world's lowest-cost producer of small engines, is a monumental task. A typical Briggs and Stratton engine has more than 500 parts, and almost everything—engine castings, starters, alternators, ignition coils, and carburetors, to name a few parts—is made in the B&S factory. The company proudly claims, "A Briggs and Stratton engine is Briggs and Stratton throughout."

Complicating the production management process is the company policy that engines are manufactured only to specific customer orders and according to individual specifications. Production is leveled through incentive discount plans to encourage customers to buy during the off-season and contracts with customers who agree to buy evenly throughout the year. Still, B&S must stay on top of every aspect of factory operations. Unlike most other manufacturing concerns that use components supplied by subcontractors, B&S must absorb any drops in quantities demanded in-house. The company also cannot close down a small factory here and there and thus minimize the impact of slowdowns. All 3 million square feet of Briggs and Stratton's gasoline engine manufacturing facilities are located in the Milwaukee area, two-thirds of it in the Wauwatosa plant.

One thing Briggs and Stratton does not have to worry about is the motivation of its work force. A formal employee participation program reinforces quality control. A piecework incentive system motivates workers to be punctual and to produce as much as they can. And managers spend most of their time maintaining communications with workers, not supervising them.

There are some clouds on the horizon. Japan's Honda motor company has entered the U.S. market for small engines as a supplier to the Snapper power equipment unit of Fuqua Industries, Inc. Snapper has already taken part of the recreational generator business and claims that lawn mowers and generators will become its third major line behind autos and motorcycles. B&S chief executive Frederick P. Stratton, Jr., grandson of one of the founders, says, "The real battle over the next five years is with the Japanese. I hate to admit it, but Japan has set a new standard for quality." Far from throwing in the towel, Briggs and Stratton has quadrupled its advertising budget and introduced a number of product innovations, making its engines look better and run quieter and longer. CEO Stratton says that the company's advertising, along with its "clean balance sheet, modern plant, and new product commitment," will keep it winning. He continues, "We are not going to let the Japanese take this market from us."[1]

Briggs and Stratton is well known for its effective production and operations management (POM). We tend to identify the quantitative POM techniques with highly automated companies. In fact, companies like Briggs and Stratton, which operate labor-intensive factories, have just as much need for these methods.

Chapter 16 provided an introduction to production and operations management. In this chapter, more sophisticated quantitative techniques are described. First, we will discuss techniques for production planning. Then, waiting line/queuing theory will be described. The final section of the chapter is devoted to a discussion of simulation as it relates to production and operations management.

PRODUCTION PLANNING TECHNIQUES

In this section, several techniques are presented that have been used effectively for business planning in production and operations management. Our emphasis on planning should not be taken to mean that the techniques are reserved solely for the planning function. POM techniques are useful to some degree in each of the management functions.

Financial Models

One of the most valuable tools for a business planner is financial modeling. This is especially true in making capital investment decisions, an aspect of production and operations management. Briggs and Stratton would not have been able to establish its record of profitability without the use of financial models to help determine when new and different machines were necessary. Factors relating to profit and loss are so vital to the growth and even survival of a firm that it is advantageous for any planner to understand the techniques that are available. In this section, several basic financial approaches will be discussed.

Payback Method

payback method

The most common and easiest method of financial analysis is called the **payback method**—*the method by which investments are ranked according to payback period, the time it takes an investment to pay back the initial capital in profits.* For example, if the initial investment is $1,000 and the return is $200 per year, the payback period is five years.

Although easy to understand, the payback method has major limitations. First, returns after the payback period are not considered. In the example, the investment might keep returning $200 for five more years. Second, the time value of money is not considered. A dollar today is not the same as a dollar ten years from now. To overcome the inaccuracy of this approach, many companies use it in a very conservative manner. For example, Lincoln Electric Company, the world's largest maker of arc welding products, has a maximum payback period for new projects of only two years. Thus, if a machine will not pay for itself during the first two years of operations, Lincoln will not buy it.

Break-even Analysis

break-even analysis

An approach used to determine the amount of a particular product that must be sold if the firm is to generate enough revenue to cover costs is **break-even analysis**. Fixed and variable costs and total revenue are charted according to the number of units produced in order to determine the point at which revenue and costs are equal and the operation begins to make money. In order to progress in a break-even study, you must be capable of identifying the following items:

1. Fixed costs.
2. Variable costs.
3. Price of the item.

fixed costs

variable costs

Fixed costs are *costs that do not change with the level of output.* Items that normally are considered fixed are the salaries of top management, rent, property taxes, and other similar expenses. **Variable costs** are *costs that are directly related to changes in output.* Items that might be included as variable costs are direct materials and labor expenses used in manufacturing a particular product. The fact that Briggs and Stratton has delayed using robotized machinery tends to give it a higher percentage of variable costs as opposed to fixed costs. This is because labor tends to be a variable cost.

The distinction between fixed and variable costs is not always as clear-cut as we would like them to be. Often there is a gray area in which some costs can at times be considered either fixed or variable. This should not deter you from understanding and appreciating the concept.

Let us next work a break-even problem to gain a better understanding

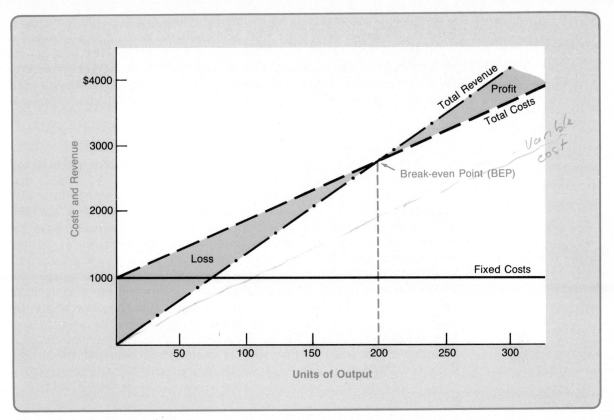

Figure 17–1 Break-even Analysis

of the concept. Suppose that a product is priced at $15, the variable cost is $10 per unit, and total fixed costs are $1,000. Using the following formula to determine the break-even point (BEP) in units of output we have:

$$\text{Break-even point in amounts} = \frac{\text{Total fixed costs}}{\text{Price} - \text{Variable cost}} = \frac{\$1,000}{\$15 - \$10} = 200.$$

Thus, according to break-even analysis, we would have to sell 200 units before we could begin making a profit.

We next show how to use break-even analysis through a graphical illustration. As seen in Figure 17–1, the vertical axis is designated as cost and revenue, and the horizontal axis shows the units of output.

Since it is assumed that our $1,000 fixed costs do not change, they are placed on the graph as a straight line. Our $10 variable costs change with the level of production, and the cost line slopes upward. The variable cost line is drawn starting at the point where fixed costs intercept the vertical axis. The resulting line is total cost. Next, our total revenue line is drawn showing the total amount of revenue (price times number of units sold) at all possible combinations of production. When the total revenue line intersects the total cost line, the break-even point of 200 units has been reached.

How reliable is this one point in space? Would you bet your firm's survival on its accuracy? Likely not, but its benefits are substantial if used with full appreciation of the weaknesses of the technique. If you drew a bead on the break-even point with a shotgun and fired, the pattern of the shots would spread out around the break-even point. This is about as accurate as you might expect because of the nature of identifying correctly fixed and variable costs. But the break-even analysis has been used effectively because it forces a manager to plan. An individual who plans is in a position to make better decisions than a nonplanner.

Discounted Cash Flow

Remember that one of the disadvantages of the payback method was that a dollar earned today does not have the same value as a dollar that will be earned one year from today. This is because if you invest this dollar today, a year later it will be worth the dollar plus interest. Thus, the time value of money becomes quite important in business planning. Take for example the signing of a superstar professional athlete for over $1 million. We are often awed by these large amounts and wonder how a team can afford to stay in business by paying these salaries. But the managers of these clubs are usually business people and understand the time value of money. This was vividly illustrated in the signing of Tony Dorsett by the Dallas Cowboys, described in the article in Figure 17–2. As you can see, even though the contract was in excess of $1 million, this amount was paid back in one year when the time value of money was considered. The signing

Figure 17–2

Time Value of Money Example

Touchdown Tony: What Price Glory?

Dorsett: *Sound Investment.*

There's really no need to feel sorry for the Tony Dorsetts of this world, but things aren't quite as rich as they seem. Headlines suggest that Dorsett's five-year Cowboy contract calls for $1.1–$1.2 million. A million dollars or so over five years is worth more than $200,000 a year? Right? Not really.

We checked with a well known local sports executive, who prefers to remain anonymous. Aided by his accountant, our executive gave us this "hypothetical" example of a Dor-

sett-like, million-dollar, superstar contract.

A five-year contract calls for a salary beginning the first year at $40,000, and increases by $20,000 each year until it reaches $120,000 in year five. Total salary over five years: $400,000.

Next, the contract adds $600,000 in deferred payments. The first payment begins 10 years after the contract is signed and payments continue at $20,000 a year for the next 30 years.

The trick here is a financial principle money wizards call "net present value." Ordinary folks call it common sense. Because the salary payments are spread over five years the superstar forfeits the right to earn interest from the beginning on the entire $400,000. He thus loses the interest he needs to cover the declining value of his dollar (the inflation pinch). In effect, that delay makes the

$400,000 he eventually will receive in salary worth only $312,120 in today's money. Applying the same logic to the deferred payments, one finds the $600,000 spread out over 30 years worth only $104,291 in today's money. Total value of the million dollar contract: $414,411 in today's dollars.

Now, let's assume that a player such as Dorsett could draw 7,900 fans for each 1977 home game, not too far-fetched if you note the season ticket boom tony has triggered. The Cowboys' take from 7,900 extra tickets at 11 home games would be about $414,000. Invest that money at eight percent for 40 years and it will grow to nine million dollars. In today's dollars that would be $414,411, fully repaying the Cowboys for the "million dollar" contract. Meaning that Touchdown Tony would pay for himself — in just one season. Hypothetical, of course.

"Touchdown Tony: What Price Glory," *D Magazine,* August 16, 1977. Copyright © 1977, Dallas Southwest Media Corporation. Reprinted with permission.

TABLE 17–1   Uses of Discounted Cash Flow Techniques

Company	Uses
AMF Inc.	Evaluation of strategic alternatives
Bendix Corporation	Plant expansion Machinery purchase
Carrier Corporation	Plant expansion Major capital expenditures
Crown Zellerbach	Make or buy decisions Lease or buy decisions Plant expansion decisions Alternative courses of action
Glidden Division, SCM Corporation	Capital expenditure request model—corporate- wide Capital investment analysis system New product planning
Inland Steel Company	Capital investment decisions Lease or buy Repair or replace
Kellogg Company	Project justification and decision making Justification of new technologies All capital expenditures
Kimberly-Clark	Maintenance analysis Project evaluation Lease/buy decisions
Lear Siegler, Inc.	Capital equipment purchases Plant expansion Make or buy
Oscar Mayer & Co.	All major economic analyses Investment analysis Investment risk analysis
Procter & Gamble Company	New product decisions Evaluation of capital appropriations Evaluation of engineering alternatives
The Signal Companies, Inc.	All major capital investment decisions (new plants, equipment) Lease vs. purchase Acquisitions
Southern Railroads	Investment decisions RR rate and pricing decisions Merger and acquisition analysis
The Southland Corp.	Building decisions
3M Company	Investment analysis Decisions for capital expenditures Make or buy and lease and buy

of a superstar or placing an order for new equipment have the same implications—the decision should take into consideration the time value of money.

In business planning the discounted cash flow technique is used extensively. The **discounted cash flow technique** is *a way of valuing an investment that uses an interest or discount rate to calculate the present value of the income the investment is expected to produce.* Table 17–1 shows a wide diversity of firms that are deeply involved in the use of

discounted cash flow technique

TABLE 17–2 Purchase Decision

	Savings per Year		Present Value		
Year	Machine A	Machine B	of $1	Machine A	Machine B
1	$50,000	$60,000	0.870	$43,500	$52,200
2	50,000	60,000	.756	37,800	45,360
3	50,000	60,000	.658	32,900	39,480
4	50,000	60,000	.572	28,600	34,320
5	50,000		.497	24,850	
6	50,000		.432	21,600	
7	50,000		.376	18,800	
				208,050	171,360
		Less cost of equipment		200,000	150,000
		Net discounted cash flow		8,050	21,360
		Difference in net discounted cash flow		└─$13,310─┘	

Note: Machine A costs $200,000; Machine B costs $150,000.

discounted cash flow techniques for solving business problems, but most are capital investment decisions. Taking into consideration the time value of money can mean the difference between a firm's achieving a profit or loss.

Assume that the vice-president of production for Briggs and Stratton must decide which of two machines should be purchased. One piece of equipment costs $200,000 and is capable of providing a savings of $50,000 a year over the next seven years. The other machine costs $150,000 but will generate $60,000 in savings over the next four years. If we assume an interest rate of 15 percent, let us see what choice should be made. Referring to Table 17–2, notice that the net discounted cash flow (the amount saved) for Machine B is $21,360 while that for Machine A is only $8,050, a difference of $13,310. Therefore, Machine B is clearly the better choice even though the total amount of cash saved over a seven-year period is greater for Machine A. When time value of money is taken into consideration, decisions should be evaluated much more thoroughly.

Make/Buy Decisions

When a make/buy planning decision is considered by a manager, he or she is concerned with evaluating the benefits of making the product *in-house* or going *outside* to another manufacturer. A prime factor that a manager should consider relates to whether the manufacturing costs in-house are lower than the cost to go outside. But this is not the only factor to consider. The manager must also ask whether the space that will be used to manufacture the product in-house could be used more advantageously. If the space could be used more effectively (make more money) through manufacturing other products, the decision might be made to produce the product outside the firm. At Briggs and Stratton, the decision to make engine parts in-house was based on a number of factors. The company gets advertising benefits out of being able to say, "A Briggs and Stratton engine is Briggs and Stratton throughout." Also, B&S would have to find other uses for much of its 3 million square feet of manufacturing space if it bought parts outside.

Purchase/Lease Decisions

Another financial alternative that many business people are considering is whether to purchase or lease equipment. Such a decision is called a purchase/lease decision. Realistically, at times it is better to purchase and at other times it becomes more advantageous to lease. The answer may be derived through evaluating the time value of money. If a manager were to purchase the equipment, such items as interest expense, depreciation, and salvage value must be evaluated to come up with a net discounted cash flow value. However, if a firm were to lease the equipment, only the lease payment could be used with regard to tax savings in computing a net discounted cash flow value. Under the leasing arrangement, there is no salvage value, and although leasing may be attractive at times, the decision should certainly be evaluated as to which decision would be better for the firm.

Linear Programming

Linear programming is *a mathematical technique that attempts to allocate limited resources among competing demands in an optimum way.* Resources to be allocated usually include machinery, people, money, time, warehouse space, and raw materials. All linear problems attempt to maximize or minimize some quantity that is typically profit or cost, respectively. As Table 17–3 shows, linear programming is used for a variety of reasons in industry, but its use depends on the nature of the needs of the firm. Summarizing the uses presented in Table 17–3 and other uses, linear programming has been used effectively in industry to solve these and other types of problems:

linear programming

- Locations and closures of plants, warehouses, and retail stores.
- Product scheduling.
- Distribution planning between factory and warehouse.
- Product mix problems.
- Determination of optimal use of transportation facilities.
- Strategic and tactical planning.
- Blending problems.

Linear programming has many uses in the business world, especially for manufacturing companies like Briggs and Stratton. The manager must be able to define two basic areas: the objective and constraint functions. The **objective function** is *a mathematical expression of what the decision maker is attempting to maximize or minimize.* For example, assume that we must help Barry Williams, the production manager for Ampex Corporation, to determine the optimum number of tables and chairs to manufacture in order to maximize profits. We first must determine the contribution to profit of both items. Barry has determined that chairs will contribute $5 (selling price of $11 minus cost of $6) and tables will contribute $7 (selling price of $17 minus cost of $10). The objective function would be stated as:

objective function

$$\text{Maximize} = \$5 \text{ (chair)} + \$7 \text{ (table)}.$$

TABLE 17–3   Uses of Linear Programming

Company	Uses
Bendix Corporation	Minimizing transportation costs for truck fleet Production scheduling
Glidden Division, SCM Corporation	Product formulation Analysis of competitors' products Capacity planning (long range)
Inland Steel Company	Evaluating energy impact of facility and policy decisions Allocating products to certain production facilities
Kaiser Steel Corporation	Proportioning of raw materials to satisfy quantitative constraints
Kellogg Company	Analyzing production capacity for budgets Long-range production planning Minimizing transportation costs for finished products
Kimberly-Clark	Distribution planning between multiple production locations New plant location-distribution cost comparison
Lear Siegler Inc.	Work flow Transportation analysis
Oscar Mayer & Co.	Product formulation Identifying new plant locations Design of distribution transportation systems
Procter & Gamble Company	Allocations of material to suppliers and to manufacturing plants Warehouse and plant site selection Production planning
3M Company	Selection of manufacturing facility for new product

constraint function

Once the objective function has been identified, the manager must determine the constraint function. A **constraint function** is *a mathematical statement of a restriction or limitation involved in a linear programming problem.* If the resources of personnel, material, and equipment were unlimited, there would be no need for linear programming. But since this is unlikely, managers must know what restrictions are placed on their ability to make decisions. For instance, Barry knows that there will be only sixty hours available in the machine shop to work on either tables or chairs. Also, there are only forty-eight hours available in the paint shop. If it takes four hours to machine a chair and two hours to machine a table and two hours to paint a chair and four hours to paint a table, we come up with the following constraint equations for Barry:

$$4 \text{ (chair)} + 2 \text{ (table)} \leq 60 \text{ (machine shop constraint).}$$
$$2 \text{ (chair)} + 4 \text{ (table)} \leq 48 \text{ (paint shop constraint).}$$

Notice the inequality signs ($\leq$) in both equations. We are merely stating that the maximum amount of time in either the machine or paint shop does

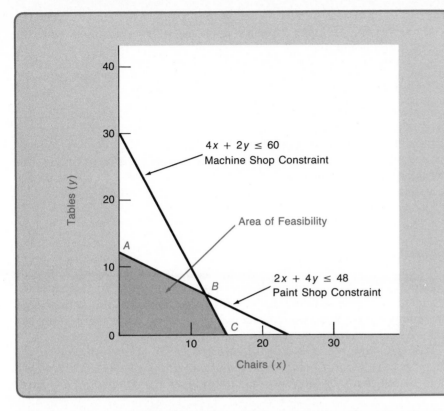

Figure 17–3

*Linear Programming
Example*

not have to be used. The inequality could also go the other direction ($\geq$), which means that a minimum amount of time must be used. Once the objective and constraint functions have been identified, the manager may turn the problem over to the analyst.

We will next use the graphical solution to linear programming to determine the optimum number of tables and chairs that Barry should produce. We have plotted the two constraints in Figure 17–3. Since the inequality signs are less than or equal to ($\leq$), our area of feasibility, where we could have a potential solution, is the shaded area. A characteristic of linear programming is that optimum solutions can occur only at extreme points. We have three in this problem (Points A, B, and C). Next, we must read from the graph to determine the solution points. They would be:

$$\text{Point A:}\quad 0 \text{ chairs, } 12 \text{ tables}$$
$$\text{Point B:}\quad 12 \text{ chairs, } 6 \text{ tables}$$
$$\text{Point C:}\quad 15 \text{ chairs, } 0 \text{ tables}$$

When these values are substituted into the objective function, we can see that if we wish to maximize profits, six tables and twelve chairs should be produced, and a maximum profit of \$102 will be achieved.

$$\text{Point A:}\quad 0 \,(5) + 12 \,(7) = \$\ 84$$
$$\text{Point B:}\quad 12 \,(5) + \ 6 \,(7) = \$102$$
$$\text{Point C:}\quad 15 \,(5) + \ 0 \,(7) = \$\ 75$$

In using linear programming, the manager's job is to develop the constraint and objective functions. The manager is the individual who is closest to the problem and best capable of providing this information. The actual mechanics of linear programming are often performed with the assistance of a computer.

Forecasting

An effective business planner must be capable of estimating with a certain degree of accuracy what will occur in the future. Naturally, we can never be completely correct in projecting the future, but a high *batting average* in accomplishing this task often separates the successful from the less successful manager. In this section, we concentrate on some of the forecasting techniques that have proved beneficial to business planners.

Terminology

A general overview of terminology used in forecasting will first be presented and is illustrated in Figure 17–4. An attempt to estimate the demand for a firm's product is referred to as demand forecasting. Four basic components must be considered in demand forecasting: long-run trend, cyclical variations, seasonal variations, and random variations.

long-run trend

The **long-run trend** is *a projection of the long-run estimate of the demand for the product being evaluated.* Long-run projections are typically said to be five years or more into the future. Like the demand for the small

Figure 17–4

Forecasting

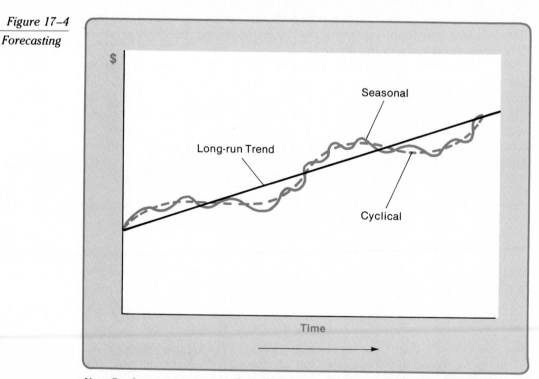

Note: Random patterns are not shown because we do not know when they will occur.

engines that Briggs and Stratton makes, the trend we have shown is an increasing one.

A business planner needs more than just a long-run trend. **Cyclical variation** is *a reasonably predictable movement about the trend line that occurs over a regular period of more than a year.* A business recession may cause sales to go down or, on the other hand, demand may be above the trend line in a recovery period. A common view of cyclical variations is greater than one year but fewer than five, with the typical cyclical span being three years. Cyclical consideration is important because of the severe peaks and valleys associated with the demand for some products. Many of the products that use B&S engines tend to be discretionary ones like lawn mowers and garden tillers. During recessions, customers tend to delay purchases of such conveniences. Thus, B&S can reasonably expect a substantial cyclical component in its product demand. Although there is a trend for increased demand for the product, a firm may currently be in a valley in the business cycle, which may affect production, inventory, and labor requirements. *cyclical variation*

A business person often needs to evaluate demand patterns in a shorter time frame than cyclical. **Seasonal variations** are *reasonably predictable changes in demand that occur over a period of a year.* During a twelve-month period the demand for many products fluctuates drastically. Electric shaver sales are concentrated heavily in the holiday seasons; swimsuits are sold in the spring. At Briggs and Stratton, demand tends to be highest in winter as makers of products using gasoline engines prepare for their spring peak. B&S management expends a great deal of effort at smoothing out seasonal variations. Knowledge of these seasonal demand patterns is important to the business planner because of production, inventory, and labor requirements. *seasonal variations*

Finally, random demand patterns are the ones that accelerate the early retirement of many business planners. **Random variations** are *variations for which there is no pattern.* By definition, they occur for reasons that the business manager cannot anticipate, even with the most sophisticated forecasting techniques. A concern at Briggs and Stratton is the unpredictability of Japanese competition. *random variations*

With this brief discussion of forecasting terminology, we can now consider some specific tools available to business forecasters. It should be remembered that forecasting tools are especially needed in the factory environment. It is important to forecast sales adequately because production forecasts, labor forecasts, material forecasts, and cash forecasts depend on the projection of sales. The following discussion should not be considered all-encompassing but is presented to give the students of management an appreciation of some of the tools that are available.

Moving Averages

A technique of smoothing the effects of random variation by averaging specified time periods is referred to as a **moving average.** Since business people do not have to make a business decision based on a random occurrence that may never again happen, they have attempted to remove the effect of this one-time occurrence through moving averages. In Table 17–4, the different time periods are averaged to get both a three-month *moving average*

TABLE 17–4   Moving Average Example

Month	Actual Demand	Three Month Moving Average	Five Month Moving Average
1	3,000	—	—
2	2,350	2,767	—
3	2,950	2,758	3,075
4	2,975	3,342	3,025
5	4,100	3,275	3,065
6	2,750	3,133	3,548
7	2,550	2,533	2,980
8	2,300	2,683	2,915
9	3,200	3,092	3,035
10	3,775	3,442	—
11	3,350	—	—

moving average and a five-month moving average. The greater the number of months that are averaged, the less effect the random variations will have on the random estimation. The moving average is expressed mathematically as follows:

$$\text{Moving average} = \frac{\text{Demand in previous } n \text{ periods}}{n},$$

where n is the number of periods in the moving average. To compute a three-month moving average, periods 1, 2, and 3 are averaged. This calculation provides the first figure for the three-month moving average. To get the next month's estimate, the first month is dropped and the fourth month is added and again averaged. Through the use of moving averages, the effects of random variation are reduced, and the demand estimate is smoothed.

Exponential Smoothing

One of the major difficulties associated with moving averages is that a large amount of historical data must be used. *A forecasting technique that uses a smoothing constant and recent actual and forecasted demand to estimate future demand* is referred to as **exponential smoothing**. When the exponential smoothing technique is applied, the manager needs only three types of data:

exponential smoothing

1. The forecast from the previous period.
2. The actual demand that resulted from this forecasted period.
3. A smoothing constant (between 0 and 1).

While the first two pieces of data are relatively easy to obtain, determining the smoothing constant requires that managers personally identify what they believe is a good response rate. This smoothing constant depends to a large extent on the past demand for the product. If it has been relatively stable, the smoothing constant will likely be small. If the product is experiencing rapid growth, the manager may wish to have a large smoothing constant to ensure that the firm is keeping up with the actual demand.

Let us envision how exponential smoothing might be helpful through considering two products; one has a stable demand (Briggs and Stratton lawn mower engines), and the other has experienced a rapidly increasing demand (engines for three-wheelers). A low smoothing constant (perhaps 0.05) might be chosen for the lawn mower and a high smoothing constant (0.50) for the three-wheeler engine. Let us assume that in both instances the previous forecast was 1,000 units and actual demand was 2,000 units. Two greatly different projections for future demand result:

New forecast = Past forecast
           + Smoothing constant(Actual demand − Past forecast)
New forecast (Stable product) = 1,000 + 0.05 (2,000 − 1,000)
                              = <u>1,050</u> units of forecasted demand

New forecast (Rapid growth product) = 1,000 + 0.5 (2,000 − 1,000)
                                  = <u>1,500</u> units of forecasted demand.

If the demand for the product has been relatively stable, there is no reason to believe that a rapid surge in sales will occur through other than perhaps random fluctuation. When a high smoothing constant is chosen, however, the manager realizes that demand shifts rapidly and requires swift action in order for the business to be competitive. The identification of the proper smoothing constant represents the major difficulty in working exponential smoothing problems.

Regression Analysis

With the increased use of high-speed computers and sophisticated statistical packages, managers have at their disposal a useful tool for forecasting: regression analysis. Its use has obtained respectability in accomplishing many forecasting functions, ranging from estimating product demand to development of profiles of successful versus less successful employees within a particular firm.[2]

Regression analysis is *a mathematical technique used to predict one item (known as the dependent variable) through knowledge of other items (known as the independent variables).* Your task as a manager would be first to determine what you would like to predict and then to identify the independent variables to determine if they actually are capable of predicting a particular outcome. Suppose, for instance, a manager would like to determine the relationship that advertising and size of the sales force has on company sales. The basic equation that would develop is as follows:

regression analysis

Y (company sales)   = Advertising (X_1) + Sales force size (X_2)
(dependent variable)   (independent variable(s))

If there does exist a relationship, the equation that might result is:

$$Y = 2 (X_1) + 4 (X_2).$$

Interpreted, the manager would determine that for each added dollar spent on adding to the sales force, total sales would increase by four dollars. However, for every dollar spent on advertising, total sales would increase by only two dollars. The manager might use this model to assist in developing a marketing plan to achieve the greatest company sales.

TABLE 17–5 Engine Sales	
Year	Engines Sold (000s)
1978	74
1979	79
1980	80
1981	90
1982	105
1983	142
1984	122

Naturally, the manager must determine the reliability of the model, but we do not wish to take away from the enjoyment of a statistics class to learn the detailed mechanics associated with regression analysis.

Time Series Analysis

time series analysis   **Time series analysis** is *a variation of regression analysis in which the independent variable is expressed in units of time.* It is an analysis of past demand or sales to find a trend over time. We can then project this trend into the future. For instance, we might like to project the demand for 12 horsepower and larger Briggs and Stratton engines for 1985. In order to accomplish this, we would need the engine sales for previous years, as shown in Table 17–5. With a series of data over time, the computations can be simplified by transforming the values of the X variable (time) to simpler numbers that add up to zero. In this case, we can designate 1978 as year -3, 1979 as year -2, and so on to year 1984 as $+3$. Given these data, the prudent manager turns the work over to the analyst, and the following equation is given to the manager (the 98.86 represents a constant that results from the calculation of the regression equation):

$$Y \text{ (engine sales)} = 98.86 + 10.54X.$$

The year for which we wish to project sales, 1985, is designated year $+4$. Substituting $+4$ for X and solving for Y gives the following result:

$$Y = 98.86 + 10.54(4) = 141.02.$$

Thus, the estimated number of 12 horsepower and larger engines that B&S will sell in 1985 is 141,020. As with the previous illustration, the manager must study the accompanying statistics to determine the reliability of the model.

WAITING LINE/QUEUING THEORY

Friday is payday, and you want to get to the bank to cash your check in time to do some shopping before the stores close. You know the main bank is closed, but the one-window drive-in bank is still open. As you pull into the drive-in bank lane, your heart sinks; there are ten cars ahead of you,

A waiting line may take the form of people waiting for service.   Barbara Alper/Stock, Boston Inc.

and the line does not appear to be moving very fast. Banks and other organizations that serve the public can partly avoid such customer dissatisfaction by applying waiting line/queuing theory to their operation.

A. K. Erland, a Danish mathematician, originated waiting line or queuing theory in the early 1900s as he studied the problem of telephone traffic. His theory was used extensively in World War II and has become a useful tool of production and operations management. **Waiting line theory** is *a production and operations management tool that attempts to determine the optimum rate of flow-through service points by balancing the costs of making customers wait against the costs of serving them more rapidly.* Most waiting line problems attempt to answer the question of what is the ideal level of service. A waiting line may take the form of people or parts of machines waiting for service. The three basic components of a queuing theory problem are arrivals, service facilities, and actual waiting time. Queuing theory helps in making decisions that balance desirable service costs with waiting line costs. In the bank illustration, the service facility was the bank's drive-in window, and the people who want service are all the car drivers who want banking service. The problem that exists is that all customers do not require the same type of service (some may want merely to cash a check and others want to deposit an entire week's receipts) and customers do not arrive at regular intervals (at times it has appeared that everyone arrives at

waiting line theory

TABLE 17–6   Uses of Waiting Line/Queuing Theory

Company	Uses
Bendix Corporation	Maintenance Skilled trades study
Kimberly-Clark	Process systems layout Process design capacities of component units
Southern Railroads	Shop assembly line procedures Scheduling locomotive maintenance
Oscar Mayer & Company	Production line balancing Plant design problems Production scheduling
The Southland Corporation	EDP system
Glidden Division, SCM Corporation	Queuing theory developing industrial engineering standards Line balancing developing industrial engineering standards
Proctor & Gamble Company	Design of communication facilities Design of manufacturing facilities
Crown Zellerbach	Maintenance evaluation
Kaiser Steel Corporation	Hot Metal Delivery System Study

once and you are a second too late). The solution of a waiting line problem via simulation involves a trade-off or balance of costs. If the line is constantly too long, some customers may get angry and change banks; this results in lower deposits and lost revenue for the bank. But there is another cost that must be considered. It also costs to add another drive-in window and pay the salary of another teller. From a managerial standpoint, waiting line theory assists the manager in determining if it is worth the additional investment to add the new drive-in window.

Another illustration of a waiting line problem that virtually everyone has seen relates to the number of checkout counters at a grocery store. How many should be kept open at a given time? Customers may get quite angry if they have to wait an excessive amount of time to be checked out. But it also costs the store if checkers are behind the cash registers with nothing to do. Again, a balance must be achieved. When the store was built, a waiting line problem should also have been considered. The store developer must consider how many checkout counters to install initially. Every checkout counter costs money because store space is valuable. However, if insufficient counters are included, lost revenue may result.

Businesses have found that waiting line or queuing theory can assist in the solution of a variety of problems. As may be seen in Table 17–6, the uses are quite widespread but differ depending on the specific needs of the firm. A major petroleum firm uses queuing theory to determine if it needs to construct additional docking facilities. A ship delayed in unloading costs the firm a certain amount per day. The ship cannot make money for the firm if it is not transporting petroleum. But constructing additional docks is also expensive. Again, a balance must be achieved.

The mathematics of waiting line problems is often quite complicated. But as with the other quantitative tools, this should not keep the manager from using the approach. He or she must first recognize that queuing theory is appropriate to solve the problems and be able to identify the costs that are involved in the balancing process. At this point the quantitative expert may be brought in to accomplish the mathematical manipulation.

Vehicle
Replacement
at Phillips

With $15 billion in sales, Phillips Petroleum Company is the nation's eighteenth largest industrial firm. Phillips uses a wide range of quantitative approaches to manage its farflung enterprises. Engineers and geologists at Phillips forecast oil well production and evaluate the profitability of proposed drilling sites using a computer system called MANTIS. Robert Hite, senior evaluation specialist, says this system allows the company to have quick answers to the basic exploration question: to drill or not to drill. Hite says, "With MANTIS I enter new data and get immediate results based on the updated information. These improvements in turnaround time are vital when you consider that we may evaluate up to 2,000 proposed drill sites in a year."

Phillips also uses quantitative techniques in managing its fleet of 3,800 tractor-trailer rigs and 1,500 passenger cars. Deciding when to replace such a large number of vehicles is a monumental task. To assist in making this decision, Phillips uses a computer-based discounted cash flow (DCF) model. It is assumed that the decision to replace or retain equipment can only be made at certain points in time. These points are represented by nodes on a chart. The present value of expenses between nodes is calculated using various cycle times. Then the optimum replacement cycle time is identified as the one that minimizes total expenses.

The model includes variables for maintenance, operating expenses (fuel, oil, salaries), and road use taxes. Even investment tax credits saved or lost and variations in predicted salvage values are considered. The vehicles are divided into groups according to age, odometer mileage, and function. Then the model is applied to a representative vehicle within each group. The replacement period is set to minimize the expected costs of the representative vehicle and those purchased to replace it over a twenty-year period into the future. The present value of expenses beyond twenty years is negligible, assuming any reasonable discount rate. Phillips's managers emphasize that the program is only a tool. The final decision is still made with due regard for considerations that are not included in the model, such as safety and driver comfort and morale. The program applies to individual vehicles but has also been used for fleets of small refinery vehicles during transitions to a more advanced design. It has also been applied to a number of lease-versus-buy studies.

More recently, Phillips has begun to consider using a similar model to decide when to replace industrial machinery. In this case, hours would replace mileage as one of the variables. Phillips's analyst, Richard Wadell, says, "It seems certain that this program will continue to receive heavy use. It has been very valuable in reducing the agony of some highly complex and highly visible decisions."[4]

In front of a radarscope in the western United States sits a young officer with his eyes fixed on the scope. He is controlling an air force fighter jet whose target is a Soviet bomber flying toward San Francisco. The conversation is progressing in the following manner:

Young controller: "Tango Papa zero one, this is Ringdove. You have a Russian bomber in your 12 o'clock position closing fast. Looks as if its target is San Francisco."

Fighter pilot: "Roger, Ringdove. I have a visual and am going in for the kill. Ringdove, Ringdove, my engine just flamed out. I am bailing out."

Will San Francisco be destroyed? Will the fighter pilot be saved? These

TABLE 17–7   Uses of Simulation Techniques

Company	Primary Uses
Bendix Corporation	Inventory control Production scheduling
Carrier Corporation	Energy modeling
Crown Zellerbach	Inventory control Production planning
Glidden Division, SCM Corporation	Price-profit analysis Production scheduling Capacity analysis system
Inland Container Company	Determine the impact of the number of pugh ladles on hot metal distribution Evaluate productivity effect of additional pollution control equipment
Kaiser Steel Corporation	Hot strip mill production rates under different conditions
Kimberly-Clark	Plant layout Inventory control Process system design
Lear Siegler, Inc.	Projecting results based on assumptions tied to math models to project economic impact on sales volumes, profits, and cash flow
Oscar Mayer & Company	Product layout within an order filling cooler Economic analysis of alternate hog cutting methods Plant design problems
Procter & Gamble Company	Design of manufacturing facilities Design of communication facilities Understanding of chemical processes
The Southland Corporation	Analysis of operations EDP teleprocessing system Distribution center layout Vehicle delivery programs
Southern Railway	Calculation of locomotive fuel requirements
3M Company	Distribution system Inventory control

and other types of problems occurred daily to one of the authors when he was an air force aircraft controller. The Soviet bomber was on the radar screen, but a real bomber was not attacking San Francisco. The pilot who bailed out was merely in another room simulating the problem. The purpose of this exercise was to train the young controller for possible real-life situations. A fighter pilot would hate to have to bail out and lose the plane in order for the controller to be trained. It was much better to simulate the occurrence, representing the real-life situation as much as possible. Businesses, as well as the military, have found simulation a valuable tool to assist in the planning and decision-making process.

We will define **simulation** as *the use of computers to assist in performing experiments on a model of a real system.*[3] A model is an abstraction of the real world. Thus, a simulation model represents a real world situation through mathematical logic in an attempt to predict what will occur in an actual situation. Its uses are many and widespread. The MANTIS system at Phillips is a good example of simulation.

As may be observed in Table 17–7, firms are using simulation for a variety of reasons ranging from "economic analysis of alternate hog cutting methods" by Oscar Mayer & Company to the calculation of locomotive fuel requirements by Southern Railway. In all instances simulation assists the manager by permitting him or her to ask many *what if* questions without having to make the decision in the real world.

A major factor that should be realized is that simulation transcends the boundaries of many of the other quantitative techniques that have been and will be discussed. As such, it is not a separate quantitative tool; rather it is a procedure that has been used effectively in conjunction with other mathematical tools such as inventory control, quality control, waiting line theory, and mathematical modeling. At Phillips, simulation of vehicle maintenance is combined with discounted cash flow techniques and even intuitive judgments about drive comfort. When a manager operates in an uncertain environment, simulation may be considered.

Simulation is a quantitative approach that many students of management often shy away from because they believe it is too sophisticated for them to use. They apparently believe that they must know computer programming and how to operate the computer to use simulation. This certainly need not be the case, for many firms have their own in-house programmers capable of interpreting the needs of the user and developing the necessary computer programs.

On the other hand, this does not mean that managers have nothing to do. They must be capable of clearly defining the problem that needs solving and identifying the factors that may be associated with the problem. The general steps associated with developing a simulation model are presented in Figure 17–5. Once the problem has been identified, a simulation model is developed and run. The results are analyzed and then if the manager again desires to ask other *what if* questions regarding the problem, they can be asked. The manager is in a position to ask many questions regarding the other factors that could affect the problem.

Assume for a moment that you are employed by Oscar Mayer and you are attempting to determine the optimum manner to cut up a hog to maximize profits. The problem has not been defined, but what are some of

simulation

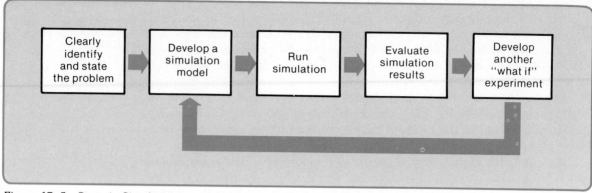

Figure 17–5   Steps in Simulation

the possible factors that could affect obtaining optimum results? Perhaps the manager desires to determine whether to automate a production line or hire additional workers. What happens as the size of the hogs varies? The hog-cutting methods may have to be changed. Through simulation a person is once again able to see that there is more than one way to skin a hog!

Railroads also have found simulation quite beneficial. Have you ever wondered why more trains don't arrive at the same time on a single track? Trains are different lengths and weights; they travel at different speeds and typically must share a common track to get from one place to another. At times there are two or more tracks that the cars could travel, but the majority of the time there is only one. Simulation provides the manager with the ability to recognize the many variables that are involved and ask questions regarding solutions to the problem.

Procter & Gamble Company also utilizes simulation to assist in solving some unusual problems. Gary O. Walla, management science manager for Procter & Gamble Company, provides the following example of how they use simulation.

Pulp forms the basic raw ingredient for manufacturing paper and can be made in a variety of grades that are dependent on the chemical processing and the blend of wood species. Procter & Gamble refines pulp from trees, and they use simulation to aid in the design of a woodyard, assuring maximum operating efficiency with a minimum of capital investment.

A woodyard serves as a surge area for wood arriving from various sources by unscheduled railcars and trucks. The wood is in the form of short and long logs and must be stored until used in the pulp mill. Naturally, railcars require different unloading equipment than trucks and the simulation helps determine the optimum number of unloading stations for both. Additionally, different equipment is needed to handle long logs than short logs for both railcars and trucks. After long logs are unloaded, they are cut into short logs before they can be stored, an operation that requires other special equipment. Finally, the operation of the pulp mill needs a constant feed of a well-controlled blend of wood species to be efficient. Wood must be stockpiled sufficiently to assure a constant feed regardless of the weather, which can bring the tree cutting operations to a standstill for a couple of weeks, or equipment failures in the woodyard. In net, the simulation of the flow of materials through the woodyard helps size equipment and stockpiles of logs to assure constant availability of the proper wood species for input to the pulp mill.

Examples of how simulation has been used effectively in business are extensive. Its use is expected to receive additional attention by managers in the future. As the risk of making a particular decision increases, managers will need to evaluate many options prior to making a commitment to allocate resources. Simulation provides an excellent tool for evaluating alternatives and finding solutions to problems.

PRODUCTION AND OPERATIONS MANAGEMENT: A WRAP-UP

The production and operations management topics discussed in this and the previous chapter were provided to help students gain further insight into the tools available to managers. These techniques are not the only ones that managers have at their disposal; a course in statistics should dispel this notion. But managers should always remember that these are but tools to be used, just like a calculator or a piece of machinery. They need not know the inner workings of either; experts do that. A manager's primary concern is the end result. Thus, managers need to be able to select the correct tool that will solve the problem at hand and not become overly concerned with the details of each technique. In this way, the production and operations tools become a valuable part of a manager's repertoire of knowledge.

SUMMARY

One of the most valuable tools for a business planner is financial modeling. The most commonly used and easiest method of financial analysis is called the payback method. When the payback method is used, investments are ranked according to the time it takes an investment to pay back in profits the initial capital. An approach used to determine the amount of a particular product that must be sold if the firm is to generate enough revenue to cover costs is break-even analysis. The discounted cash flow technique is a way of valuing an investment that uses an interest or discount rate to calculate the present value of the income the investment is expected to produce.

Linear programming is a mathematical technique that attempts to allocate limited resources among competing demands in an optimum way. An attempt to estimate the demand for a firm's products is referred to as demand forecasting. The long-run trend is a projection of the long-run estimate of the demand for the product being evaluated. Cyclical variation is a reasonably predictable movement about the trend line that occurs over a regular period of more than a year. Seasonal variation is reasonably predictable changes in demand that occur over a period of a year. Random variations are variations for which there is no pattern.

A technique for smoothing the effects of random variation is through the use of moving averages. When the exponential smoothing technique is applied, the manager needs only three types of data: the forecast from the previous period, the actual demand that resulted from this forecasted period, and a smoothing constant. A regression analysis is a mathematical technique used to predict one item (known as the dependent variable) through knowledge of other items (known as the independent variables). With times series analysis, the independent variable is expressed in units of time.

A waiting line may take the form of people or parts waiting for service. The three basic components of a queuing theory (waiting line) problem are arrivals, service facilities, and actual waiting time. Queuing theory helps in making decisions that balance desirable service costs with waiting line costs.

Simulation is defined as the use of computers to assist in performing experiments on a model of a real system. Simulation transcends the boundaries of many of the other quantitative techniques. It is not a separate quantitative tool; rather it is a procedure that has been used effectively in conjunction with other mathematical tools, such as inventory control, quality control, waiting line theory, and mathematical modeling.

REVIEW QUESTIONS

1. What are the costs involved in a break-even analysis? Define each.
2. Why might a manager want to use the discounted cash flow technique of evaluating investment decisions as opposed to the payback method?
3. Define linear programming. List five types of problems that might benefit from the use of linear programming.
4. What are the four basic components of demand forecasting? Define each.
5. Distinguish by definition among moving averages, exponential smoothing, regression analysis, and time series analysis.
6. When would a waiting line or queuing theory technique be used? What are the three basic components of a queuing theory problem?
7. What is meant by the statement, "Simulation transcends the boundaries of many of the other quantitative techniques"?

EXERCISES

1. How might the discounted cash flow technique be used in the following instances?
   a. Purchase of a major league ballplayer
   b. Purchase of a fleet of trucks
   c. Decision by you to purchase or lease your business automobile
   d. A decision as to whether to go to college or go to work after completing high school

2. Think of five different types of businesses. How could the following quantitative planning techniques be useful in their operations?
   a. Moving averages
   b. Exponential smoothing
   c. Time series analysis
   d. Regression analysis

CASE STUDY

Exponential Smoothing

Larry Smiler is the production manager for a firm that manufactures high-quality watches. His job is to maintain a smooth flow of production of these watches. In order to determine what levels of output to produce, Larry relies heavily on sales forecasts. If he produces too many watches, inventory will increase, and this can be extremely costly to a company in the quality watch business. Should inventory become excessive, workers may have to be laid off or terminated. On the other hand, if too few watches are produced, the sales force gets extremely unhappy since orders cannot be filled. Larry is aware of exponential smoothing and decides to use it to assist him in estimating next month's demand. He realizes that last month's sales forecast was for 10,000 watches, but actual demand for watches during the month was 12,000. Larry also realizes that demand changes rapidly, so he decides to use a 0.5 smoothing constant.

QUESTIONS

1. What is the forecasted demand for next month?
2. If demand were relatively constant, what size smoothing constant would you recommend that Larry use?

CASE STUDY

Break-Even Analysis

Phyllis Stevens, a junior management major at Midwestern State University, has been elected promotional manager for the Society for the Advancement of Management (SAM), a professional organization of which she is a member. She is thinking of recommending that SAM sell miniature flags of the university to the student body. Students can take these flags to football games and wave them to cheer their team on to victory. (The team is expected to have a winning season.)

Phyllis is aware of break-even analysis, so she develops some cost figures for producing the flags. She estimates that the fixed cost for the project will be $200. The flags will be made by members, and she estimates that the variable cost to make each flag is $0.50. They will sell them for $1.

QUESTIONS

1. How many flags must the organization sell in order to break even?
2. How many flags must the group sell to make a profit of $100?
3. If Phyllis thinks that the maximum number of flags that the group can sell is 500, do you feel that SAM should take on the project? Discuss.

NOTES

1. This story is a composite from a number of sources, including: "Where Robots Can't Yet Compete," *Fortune* (February 21, 1983): 64; Gwen Kinkhead, "An American Company Honda Can't Mow Down," *Fortune* (July 28, 1980): 54–55; "Briggs & Stratton's New Hard Sell," *Business Week* (February 14, 1983): 45–46; Briggs and Stratton Corporation, *Annual Report, 1983.*

2. R. Wayne Mondy and Frank N. Edens, "An Empirical Test of the Decision to Participate Model," *Journal of Management* 2 (1977): 11–16.

3. Richard B. Chase and Nicholas J. Aquilano, *Production and Operations Management: A Life Cycle Approach,* rev. ed. (Homewood, Ill.: Irwin, 1977), p. 269.

4. Richard Wadell, "A Model for Equipment Replacement Decisions and Policies," *Interfaces* 13, no. 4 (August 1983): 1–7; "Application Development System Improves Oil Forecasting," *Infosystems* 29, no. 12 (December 1962): 56; Grover Heiman, "Making the Best Use of Money and Manpower," *Nation's Business* 71 (August 1983): 48–50; *Moody's Industrial Manual* (1984), 2: 4226–4231.

REFERENCES

Backes, Robert W. "Cycle Counting—A Better Way for Achieving Accurate Inventory Records." *Production and Inventory Management* 21 (Second Quarter 1980): 36–44.

Buffa, Elwood S. *Modern Productions Operations Management.* 6th ed. New York: Wiley, 1980.

Chase, Richard B., and Nicholas J. Aquilano. *Production and Operations Management: A Life Cycle Approach.* Rev. ed. Homewood, Ill.: Irwin, 1981.

Green, T. B. "Why are Organizations Reluctant to Use Management Science/Operations Research? An Empirical Approach." *Interfaces* 7 (August 1976): 59–62.

Gullapelli, S. M. "Simulating a Cash Budget for a Small Manufacturer." *Management Accounting* 61 (November 1979): 25–29.

Harwood, G. G., and R. H. Hermanson. "Lease or Buy Decisions." *Journal of Accountancy* 147 (September 1976): 83–87.

Lebell, D., and O. J. Krasner. "Selecting Environmental Forecasting Techniques from Business Planning Requirements." *Academy of Management Journal* 20 (July 1977): 373–383.

"Linear Programming Discovery." *Science* (November 30, 1979): 1022.

Miller, L. W. "Using Linear Programming to Derive Planning Horizons for a Production Smoothing Problem." *Management Science* 25 (December 1979): 1217–1231.

Morey, R. "Operations Management in Selected Non-manufacturing Organizations." *Academy of Management Journal* 19 (March 1976): 120–124.

Petry, Glenn H. "Effective Use of Capital Budgeting Tools." *Business Horizons* 18 (October 1975): 57–65.

Robinson, S. M. "Characterization of Stability in Linear Programming." *Operations Research* 25 (May 1977): 435–447.

Solomon, Eyra, and John J. Pringle. *An Introduction to Financial Management.* Santa Monica, Calif.: Goodyear, 1980.

Solomon, S. L. "Building Modelers: Teaching the Art of Simulation." *Interfaces* 10 (April 1980): 65–72.

Thomapoulis, Nick T. *Applied Forecasting Methods.* Englewood Cliffs, N.J.: Prentice-Hall, 1980.

Wiley, J. M. "Just Enough Queuing Theory." *Datamation* 23 (February 1977): 87.

ATLAS AIRCRAFT

OBSERVATIONS

"It's sure too bad about Willis, Ball, and Conrad," Bob Harris said to George Mathews, who was stirring his coffee when Bob joined him on a Friday afternoon break. George shook his head in apparent disbelief at the news. The three managers mentioned had just been fired as a result of a disastrous bid on a proposal they had worked on. Mathews then asked, "What do you suppose really went wrong on that bid?" It was now Harris's turn to shake his head. "We'll probably never know the whole story," he said. "Oh sure, somebody has to be responsible for goofs, but it really shakes you up to think of those guys, all of them with over twenty years here, and all at once out on their butts!" Nodding his head in agreement, George said, "Boy, we really gotta watch what the hell we're doing from now on!"

BACKGROUND

Atlas had been a successful airframe manufacturer—one of the five largest—for forty years. The firm took pride in the fact that 85 percent of its managers were engineers. This feeling seemed to stem from the idea that such a manager could better cope with the technical aspects of airplane manufacture than could a nonengineer manager.

TROUBLE

The Cargo Plane

About one year prior to the above conversation, Atlas had submitted a bid on a giant cargo plane for the U.S. Air Force. At the time of the bid, the engineering was not yet complete on the internal materials-handling equipment that would be used to load a wide variety of cargoes. Cargoes would range from heavy tanks or trucks to the bulk-loading of small, irregularly shaped packages. To ensure submission of the bid on time, the Atlas executive committee insisted on getting a "safe but competitive" price from engineering on the loading system.

Atlas was awarded the contract on the cargo plane, but the estimated costs on the loading system were nowhere near the actual costs. The additional R&D needed to make the loading system operational and efficient ran to about $160,000, compared to the $20,000 estimate. Also, the production costs of the system were over $135,000 per plane, in contrast to the $27,000 per unit estimate. These increased costs amounted to nearly $1.5 million for the twelve-plane contract, and the air force admitted only $600,000 for additional billing on this system. This meant that Atlas' potential profit on the contract was reduced by nearly $1 million.

Henry Murphy, the president, was furious at this result, which he blamed on poor engineering and on irresponsibility on the part of those who put the loading-system estimate together. In order to shake up the entire management and to force the managers and staff to accept responsibility, Murphy insisted on seeing "some

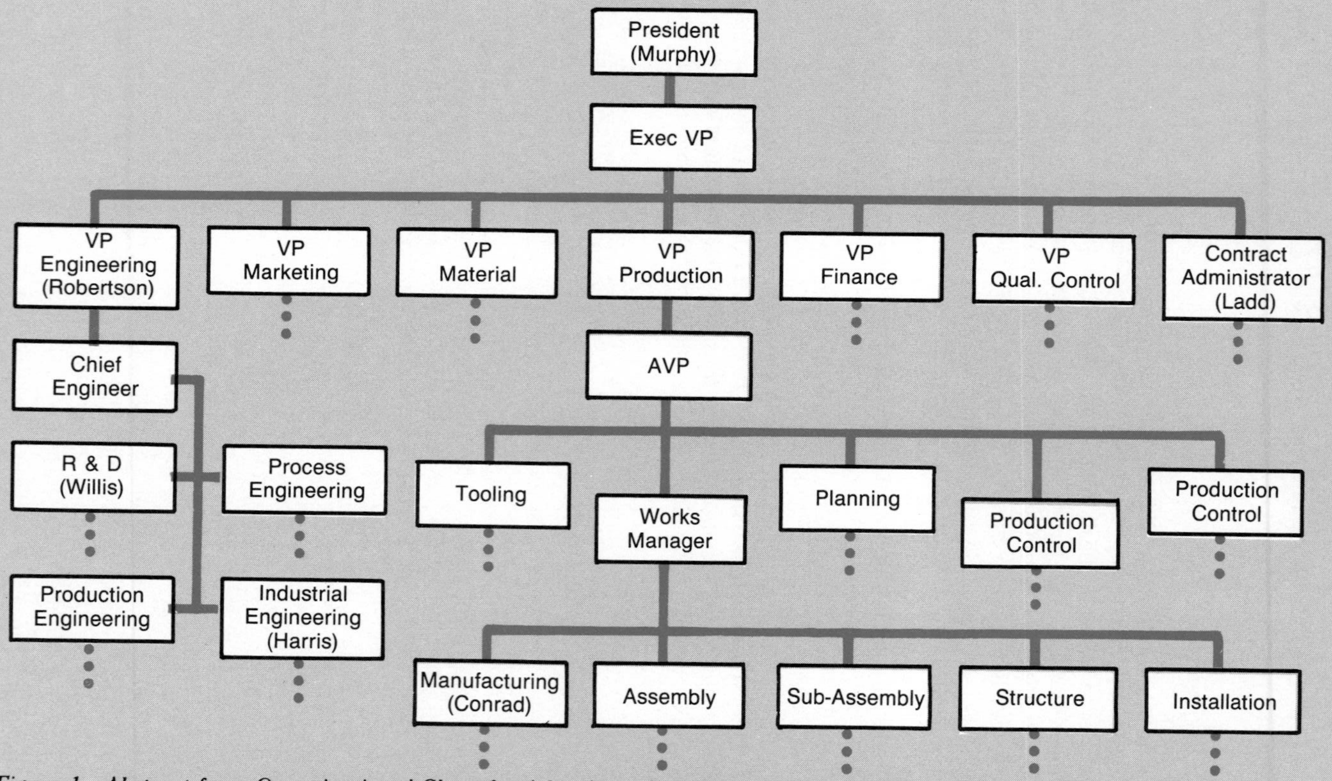

Figure 1   Abstract from Organizational Chart for Atlas Aircraft, at Beginning of Case Time Period

heads roll." Consequently, the chief of R&D was fired, along with the chief of production engineering and the manager of manufacturing.

Murphy was correct in expecting management to be shaken, but the event did not seem to be followed by any noticeable improvement in decision making. The organizational chart for Atlas Aircraft may be seen in Figure 1.

The Fighter Plane

It has been the practice among U.S. planemakers for a prime contractor* to subcontract 40 percent to 60 percent of the contract value to other manufacturers. In keeping with this practice, Atlas prepared plans and requested proposals for various subcontracts on a new fighter plane—the NFX-3. The total amount of electronic gear on this sophisticated plane was considerably greater than had appeared on any previous Atlas plane. The electronics manufacturers who commonly subcontracted for Atlas were not able to handle the physical volume required by the NFX-3 schedule. Consequently, Atlas was forced to seek new electronics manufacturers for this purpose. The usual "Requests for Bids" were sent out, and several companies responded with proposals. After correspondence regarding specifications and costs, Atlas dispatched some electronics engineers and production coordinators to evaluate physically the potentialities of the interested electronics firms. Out of the five firms evaluated, the team determined that two of the five were fully qualified as subcontractors and wrote their report to that effect. They had found that both firms were currently in production of sophisticated army and navy electronics and that their production lines were not "contaminated" with civilian consumer items. The investigation suggested a highly satisfactory on-time delivery record.

After the scheduling was completed and all subcontracts had been let for the NFX-3, the manufacturing and the assembly operations were begun. These, and the subcontracting and purchasing deliveries, were closely observed and checked with the PERT charts. The first deliveries of the electronic equipment from the two new subcontractors were due in the 38th week of the NFX-3 schedule. Delivery from Firm A came in, a few days early, while Firm B's delivery missed the deadline. Following the PERT schedule, Production Control had checked with Firm B two weeks before the scheduled delivery. Production Control was told that some purchased component parts had been unacceptable and had been returned to the maker, who had promised immediate replacement. Since the PERT dates for these items included some slack, the delay seemed to be relatively minor, and quickly correctible, with rush work on the part of Firm B.

Unfortunately, Week 42 went by with still no delivery from Firm B. Now, things began looking serious; by Week 44, additional equipment would have to be installed, which could go in only after the gear from Firm B had been installed. This meant that a real possibility existed that a line-stoppage would occur unless the delayed electronics arrived almost immediately.

An electonics engineer and a production planner were dispatched to Firm B to get an actual look at the situation and to try to devise means to accelerate deliveries.

The subsequent report was grim; according to the troubleshooters, Firm B's production line was very primitive, and an educated guess would put earliest delivery at around Week 58!

Murphy really blew his top. As after the loading-system fiasco, he thought that

---

*Holder of the airplane contract from the customer.

drastic action was necessary. Therefore, the senior electronics engineer and the production control chief were fired. Again, the reason was to inspire the remaining managers and staff to approach the decision making more seriously and to accept responsibility more completely.

A couple of days later, George Whyte, board chairman of Atlas, called Murphy. "I hear that heads have rolled again," he said. "I'm afraid so," replied Murphy, as the weight in his stomach seemed to get heavier. "You may have good reason to be afraid," said Whyte, "if this action doesn't start bringing in some answers. I hope that you haven't lost control."

The Swing-Wing

In the following year, nearly all production seemed to slow, although almost imperceptibly. Schedules became more difficult to maintain; new development, bids, and proposals seemed excruciatingly slow. Several times, requests for extensions in bidding deadlines were forwarded by Atlas because of behind-schedule conditions. Investigations into the reasons for such delays seemed to always suggest a nearly unanimous feeling among managers that the increasingly complex technology in nearly every aspect of airframe design and manufacture seemed to require greater precision and certainly in decision making. This, of course, would require more research, more data, and more time to come up with optimum decisions and their implementing plans.

Since *time* was one thing which Atlas surely could not spare, the only solution occurring to top management was an increase in the number of managers and staff experts to get the work out.

The resulting organizational structure turned out to have nearly one manager or staff person for each three hourly workers at Atlas. This is in contrast to the two-year earlier proportion of one manager/staff member to each 3.46 hourly workers (at the start of this case history). This can be seen as an increase of almost one-seventh in administrative salaries.

In the meantime, the air force was soliciting bids for a swing-wing fighter. Atlas was very eager to get such a contract. In fact, overhead expenses were so high that new contracts seemed imperative to maintain an acceptable cash flow.

As the swing-wing bid deadline approached, no proposal from Atlas had been finalized. The president called in his top-level people and asked, "Why the delay?" All reasons suggested were centered on new technology and the need for more data. Murphy emphasized the need for a timely bid and suggested an all-out effort.

Five days before the deadline, the bid was still not finished, and the need for more data was again insisted on. Through political contacts, Murphy was able to get a two-week extension on the deadline, but at the cost of some strained friendships. Upon receiving the extension, Murphy put out the word that the proposal *must* be ready, this time.

Three days before the extended deadline, President Murphy received a copy of a report sent to Contracts Administration by the group responsible for the proposal figures. The third paragraph caught his eye; it read:

3. The production technology for the swing-wing hinge is in flux at this time. It is necessary to combine great strength with optimum weight. There are two or three firms which might be able to make the hinges with a forging-press. The tooling for this may run to $180,000, but we have no firm commitment as to the cost of tooling, the unit cost, or delivery schedule.

There are several firms interested in the carbon filament technique, but time has not permitted the necessary stress-analyses to determine optimum size and weight. Here, the cost of tooling is estimated at from $40,000 to $115,000.

If neither of these processes is available and appropriate, we can hang the hinges from 8" titanium stock. The tooling here would probably be below $20,000, but there is a great waste in scrap, from which there is little salvage.

If we are able to get a forging for the hinges, we can produce the hinges for about $17,000 (direct cost) per plane. If we could seek a manufacturer to produce them from carbon-filament, we can expect about $29,000 per plane. If neither of these techniques is available, we shall have to machine them from titanium plate, at about $48,000 per set.

After a very deep sigh, Murphy murmured to himself, "What the hell kind of a proposal is this?"

A few minutes later, Murphy rang his secretary and told her, "Cancel all of my appointments. Get hold of Ladd* and Robertson†—tell them to cancel *their* appointments and to plan to spend the next forty-eight hours with me, to get this proposal finalized."

Shortly thereafter, Chairman Whyte called Murphy, "How's the proposal?" Murphy explained the situation as briefly as possible. Whyte responded with, "You'd better meet that deadline!"

Hanging up, Murphy heaved another sigh, as his ulcers burned, then sat motionless for five minutes. "Where did I go wrong?" he thought. "What have I solved?" He then phoned a nationally known management consulting firm and talked with one of the partners. "We seem to have lost our capability for making decisions," Murphy said. "Can you help me?"

QUESTION
What would you do in this situation?

*Contract administrator.
†VP, engineering.

The case history was written by Edgar A. Wiley, Professor of Management Emeritus, California State University, Fullerton, as the basis for class discussion. Names and incidents have been disguised at the request of the participants. Presented at a Case Workshop and distributed by the Intercollegiate Case Clearing House, Soldiers Field Road, Boston, Mass. 02136. All rights reserved to the contributor. Copyright 1975. Used with permission.

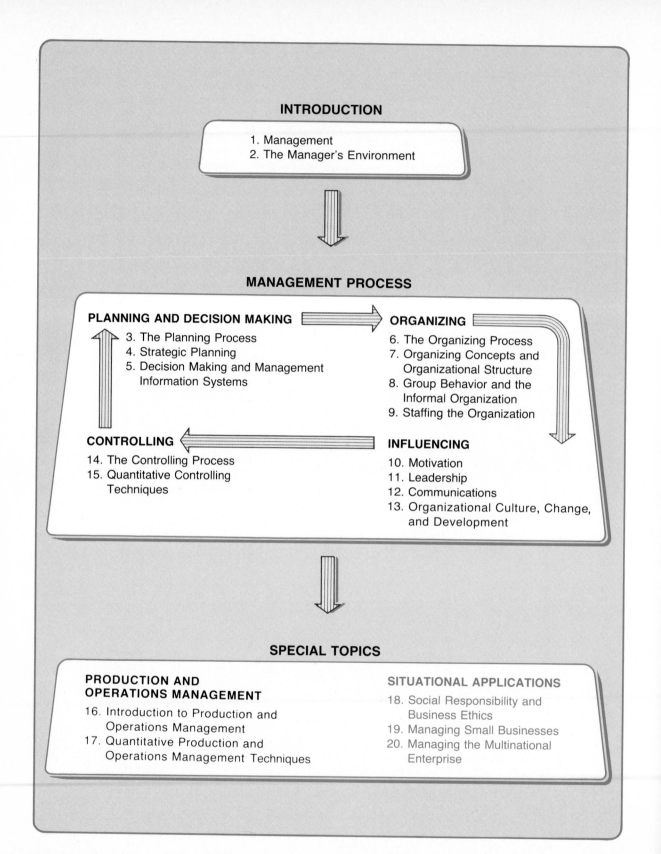

INTRODUCTION

1. Management
2. The Manager's Environment

MANAGEMENT PROCESS

PLANNING AND DECISION MAKING

3. The Planning Process
4. Strategic Planning
5. Decision Making and Management Information Systems

ORGANIZING

6. The Organizing Process
7. Organizing Concepts and Organizational Structure
8. Group Behavior and the Informal Organization
9. Staffing the Organization

CONTROLLING

14. The Controlling Process
15. Quantitative Controlling Techniques

INFLUENCING

10. Motivation
11. Leadership
12. Communications
13. Organizational Culture, Change, and Development

SPECIAL TOPICS

PRODUCTION AND OPERATIONS MANAGEMENT

16. Introduction to Production and Operations Management
17. Quantitative Production and Operations Management Techniques

SITUATIONAL APPLICATIONS

18. Social Responsibility and Business Ethics
19. Managing Small Businesses
20. Managing the Multinational Enterprise

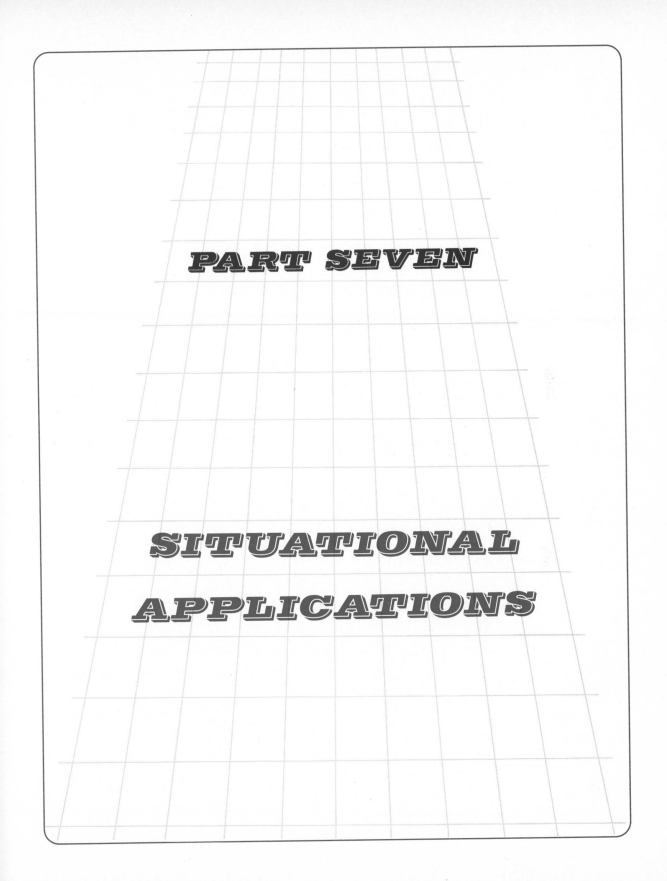

PART SEVEN

SITUATIONAL APPLICATIONS

social responsibility

social contract

iron law of
responsibility

organizational
constituency

organizational
stakeholder

political action
committees (PACs)

ethics

Type I ethics

Type II ethics

business ethics

social audit

LEARNING OBJECTIVES

After completing this chapter you should be able to

1. Describe the concept of social responsibility.
2. Explain what is meant by the social contract.
3. State the trends that are occurring regarding social responsibility.
4. Explain the concepts of ethics.
5. Define business ethics and describe why it is important for an industry and/or company to establish ethical codes of behavior.

18

Social Responsibility and Business Ethics

CHAPTER OUTLINE

Johnson & Johnson

FAMILY OF COMPANIES

Cyanide is a deadly poison. Even a minute amount can cause instant death. The substance found its way into a few bottles of Extra-Strength Tylenol capsules in Chicago in September 1982. The results were disastrous: seven people died. With more than 30 million bottles on store shelves all over the world and many millions more in home medicine cabinets, the fatalities raised an unthinkable spectre: If just 1 percent of the bottles were poisoned, thousands might die.

Tylenol is manufactured by McNeil Consumer Products, a subsidiary of Johnson & Johnson Pharmaceuticals, a $5.4 billion health care giant. "Are you sure this isn't a hoax?" asked Arthur Quitty, a member of J&J's executive committee, when the news first broke. As the story hit the international news wires, calls began to come in from television and radio stations, pharmacies, doctors, poison control centers, and hundreds of panic-stricken consumers. In the confusion of those first hours, thousands reported suspected poisoning. Practically all of the reports turned out to be false. "It looked like the plague," recalls McNeil's chief, David Collins.

Within hours, J&J had determined that the cyanide was probably placed in the capsules after they left the McNeil plant. Nevertheless, the plant was closed. An investigation quickly revealed that all of the poisoned Tylenol capsules had been purchased on Chicago's West Side, and all seemed to have come from one lot. J&J had every reason to believe that the danger could be eliminated by recalling that one lot from the relatively few retailers to whom it had gone.

But the company's credo was written for all to see at J&J's red brick headquarters. It declared that J&J's "first responsibility" is to those who "use our products and services." Chairman James Burke prepared to recall all Extra-Strength Tylenol capsules. Burke says the FBI opposed the recall "because it would say to whomever did this, 'Hey, I'm winning. I can bring a major corporation to its knees.'" And the Food and Drug Administration argued, "It might cause more public anxiety than it would relieve." Still, the campaign to get back $100 million worth of Extra-Strength Tylenol capsules was initiated immediately. At its own expense, the company took out advertisements, sent thousands of letters to doctors and pharmacists, and orchestrated a major media campaign. The company took no chance that anyone else would be harmed. In an omission that many found remarkable for a major corporation, J&J spent almost no effort in publicizing a defense or disclaiming responsibility. But no expense was spared in protecting the public.

Within weeks, the fear subsided, and J&J recaptured 95 percent of its earlier market share for nonaspirin, extrastrength pain reliever. But the near monopoly that J&J had was broken, and several other drug manufacturers began national promotion of similar products.

Although the company suffered tens of millions of dollars in losses, J&J's reputation was not hurt. In a recent *Fortune* magazine survey, the company was among the top five U.S. "most admired corporations." In the area of community and environmental responsibility, J&J ranked number one.[1]

Johnson & Johnson's positive image clearly springs in large measure from its handling of the Tylenol scare. There seems to be general agreement that J&J did as much as it should have done. Most questions of corporate social responsibility are not so clear-cut. There are no simple right or wrong answers. Rather, management must juggle the claims of various groups. It must produce profits for stockholders, preserve jobs for employees, comply with government regulations, and provide a product to consumers at a price they will pay.

In this chapter, we will examine a number of basic issues of social responsibility and business ethics. First, the concept of corporate social responsibility will be discussed. This will be followed by an analysis of the social contract that exists between the organization and other elements of society. Then, traditional and modern views concerning the social responsibilities of business will be described. The next three sections of the chapter will discuss the business-government interface, present a model of ethics, and address the specific topic of business ethics. The last topic covered in the chapter is the social audit, whereby companies can evaluate their social performance.

CORPORATE SOCIAL RESPONSIBILITY

When a corporation behaves as if it had a conscience, it is said to be socially responsible. **Social responsibility** is the *implied, enforced, or felt obligation of managers, acting in their official capacities, to serve or protect the interests of groups other than themselves.* When Johnson & Johnson chose to protect the public interest by destroying millions of containers of Tylenol, the company surely suffered, at least in the short-run.

social responsibility

Many companies develop patterns of concern for moral issues. This is done through policy statements, practices over time, and the leadership of morally strong individuals. Some companies have programs of community involvement for their employees and managers. They cooperate with fund drives such as United Way. Open door policies, grievance procedures, and employee benefit programs often stem as much from a desire to do what is right as from a concern for productivity and avoidance of strife. In fact, some argue that a corporation itself can have a conscience.[2] Certainly most Americans believe that J&J does because of the way it handled the Tylenol issue.

A survey of 232 large corporations revealed that approximately two-thirds have definite policies regarding social responsibilities and special

Many companies develop patterns of concern for moral issues.

Larry Lawfer/The Picture Cube

organizational units to deal with these areas.[3] The most common unit is headed by a vice-president reporting to the chief executive officer or president. It appears that the larger the number of stockholders for a corporation, the more committed management is to a sense of social responsibility. Allied Chemical, for example, has set up the Environment Service Department concerned with air and water pollution control, occupational health, and product safety. The manager of that department reports directly to the company president. Koppers Company established two committees of outside directors, one concerned with the environment and the other with human resources. At least twice a year, Koppers' management will account to these two committees concerning efforts in this regard.

Other companies feel that the responsibility cannot be segmented and compartmentalized. When Coca-Cola's treatment of migrant fieldworkers was brought forcefully to the company's attention, a special project was established at the direction of the president of Coca-Cola's food division. Expenditures on housing, education, and health services for migrant workers have now been integrated into the company's regular activities.

Economic and social values at times can be coaligned even in the short run. In a recent year, Dow Chemical invested $20 million in pollution control equipment. The yearly cost to run the equipment was $10.5 million. Dow claims to have recovered its costs by way of reduced corrosion on cooling towers and the saving of valuable chemicals previously pumped out as waste. In three years' time, over $6 million was saved in recovery of these wasted chemicals alone. Although this attempt at a Michigan plant was quite successful, Dow still has serious air and water pollution problems to be solved in other plants it owns.

Business Week has given awards for private company efforts in the two major areas of improving the physical environment and developing human resources. The process of selecting companies for these awards has brought

to light many examples of specific company actions in these two fields. CHAPTER 18 533
Among these are the following:

Social Responsibility and
Business Ethics

- An educational program to combat drug abuse.
- Provision of seed money to minority suppliers.
- Urban rehabilitation.
- Loans to construct low-cost housing.
- Provision of managerial training to minority groups.
- Establishment of manufacturing plants in ghetto areas.

International Business Machines Corporation located a new plant in the Bedford-Stuyvesant neighborhood of Brooklyn several years ago. After a financially disastrous beginning, the facility became profitable within two years. The plant probably could have been immediately profitable if located elsewhere, but the decision to build the plant in Brooklyn was affected by a felt responsibility for providing jobs in an area that probably had the largest concentration of hard-core unemployed in the United States.

Most Americans would not have predicted the kind of socially responsible actions described above. During the 1970s and into the 1980s, managers and the corporations they worked for were subjected to considerable criticism and received low levels of approval from the public. Hardly a week passed without news headlines of corporate bribery, illegal political contributions, or price-fixing practices. The public's mistrust of business and business executives is exemplified by surveys of public opinion indicating a decline in the public's confidence in business. In one study, over 50 percent of the respondents believed that the "bad" features of the U.S. business system either equal or outweigh the "good."[4] Another survey indicated that public confidence in the executives who manage major corporations had declined drastically, from 55 percent to 16 percent, in just ten years. In another survey, 87 percent of those interviewed agreed that most business people are more interested in profits than in serving the public's needs, and 53 percent felt that many major companies should be dismantled.

Other surveys have revealed that the public's estimate of the profits of business is considerably out of line with reality. For example, the public's estimate of the level of after-tax profits per dollar of sales for the typical business is between twenty-five and thirty cents; the actual amount was about four cents in 1984.

Socially responsible decision makers within corporations consider both the economic and social impact of their decisions and the firm's operations on the various groups in society. Noted authority Keith Davis believes that in meeting its responsibilities to society, a firm must be concerned with more than narrow technical and legal requirements.[5] It should recognize that an obligation exists to protect and enhance the interests and welfare of not only the corporation but also those of society.

In today's environment, business organizations are being expected to assume broader and more diverse responsibilities to the various groups within society. There is little doubt that an increasing amount of attention is being directed to the social responsibilities of business firms. Critics argue that there is more lip-service than action, more public relations programs than concrete social responsibility activities. Nevertheless, social responsibility is an area in which the modern business firm must develop a stance, accompanied by appropriate policies and activities. Social responsibility can be understood in terms of the social contract that exists between a firm and its environment.

THE SOCIAL CONTRACT

social contract   In a sense, organizations and society enter into a contract. This **social contract** is the *set of rules and assumptions about behavior patterns among the various elements of society.* Much of the social contract is embedded in the customs of society. For example, society has come to expect companies to do more than the law requires to integrate minorities into the work force. When a company like Johnson & Johnson behaves in an especially commendable way, its actions tend to increase the expectations society has concerning other companies.

Some of the "contract provisions" result from practices between parties. Like a legal contract, the social contract often involves a quid pro quo (something for something) exchange. One party to the contract behaves in a certain way and expects a predictable pattern of behavior from the other. For example, a relationship of trust may have developed between a

Figure 18–1

The Social Contract

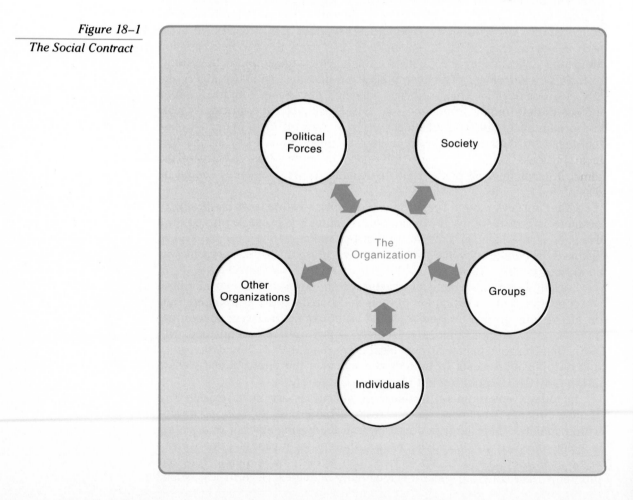

manufacturer and the community in which it operates. Because of this, each may inform the other well in advance of any planned action that might cause harm, such as the closing of the plant by the company or the imposition of a new dumping regulation by the community.

The social contract concerns relationships with individuals, government, other organizations, and society in general. This is illustrated in Figure 18–1. Let us consider these relationships individually.

Obligations to Individuals

Individuals often find healthy outlets for their energies through joining organizations. From the church, they expect guidance, ministerial services, and fellowship, and they devote time and money to its sustenance. From their employers, they expect a fair day's pay for a fair day's work—and perhaps much more. Many expect to be paid for time off to vote, perform jury service, and so forth. Clubs and associations provide opportunities for fellowship and for community service. Customers expect to be catered to. To some degree, most of our society still subscribes to the notion that the customer is king. To the extent that these expectations are acknowledged as responsibilities by the organization, they become part of the social contract.

Obligations to Other Organizations

Managers must be concerned with relationships involving other organizations like their own—such as competitors—and vastly differing ones. Commercial businesses are expected to compete with one another on an honorable basis, without subterfuge or reckless unconcern for their mutual rights. Charities such as the United Way expect support from businesses, often including the loaning of executives and help with annual fund drives. At the same time, such institutions are expected to come hat in hand, requesting rather than demanding assistance.

In keeping with the traditional view of social responsibility discussed earlier in this chapter, some companies view the social contract as severely limited by the company's own interest. For example, FMC Corporation, a major diversified manufacturer, has firm policies about how it will direct its contributions. The basic criteria FMC applies are that contributions help areas around company facilities or where its employees live and that gifts must improve the corporation's business environment.[6] For example, FMC might contribute to a business college in an area where it has a plant, but it would not make gifts to distant universities.

Obligations to Government

Government is an important party to the social contract for every kind of organization. Under the auspices of government, companies have a license to do business, along with patent rights, trademarks, and so forth. Churches are often incorporated under state laws and given nonprofit status. Many quasi-governmental agencies, such as the Federal Depository Insurance

Corporation, regional planning commissions, and levee boards, have been given special missions by government.

In addition, organizations are expected to recognize the need for order rather than anarchy and to accept some government intervention in organizational affairs. For example, the law no longer gives the Occupational Safety and Health Administration (OSHA) inspector the right to come into an organization without permission, but it is usual for the organization to accept such visits. Johnson & Johnson must deal with the Food and Drug Administration (FDA) on a daily basis. In the case at the beginning of the chapter, J&J went well beyond what the FDA requires.

Obligations to Society in General

Traditionally, the responsibility of the business firm has been to produce and distribute goods and services in return for a profit. Businesses have performed this function effectively. Largely as the result of our economic system and the important contributions of business firms, the United States enjoys one of the highest overall standards of living in the world. Rising standards of living in the United States have enabled a high percentage of the population to have their basic needs for food, clothing, shelter, health, and education reasonably well satisfied. Businesses can take pride in these accomplishments because they had a great deal to do with making the higher standards of living possible.

Business has been able to make significant contributions to the rising living standards primarily because of the manner in which the free enterprise economic system operates. The profit motive provides incentive to business to produce products and services efficiently. Business firms try to improve the quality of their products and services, reduce costs and prices, and thereby attract more customers. By earning profits, the successful firm pays taxes to the government and makes donations to provide financial support for charitable causes. Because of the efficient operations of business firms, an ever-increasing number of people have increasing means and leisure time.

Businesses operate by public consent with the basic purpose of satisfying the needs of society. Despite significant improvements in standards of living in recent years, society has begun expecting—even demanding—more of all of its institutions, particularly large business firms. Goals, values, and attitudes in society are changing to reflect a greater concern for improvements in the quality of life. An indication of these concerns would include such goals as the following:[7]

- Eliminating poverty and providing quality health care.
- Preserving the environment by reducing the level of pollution.
- Providing a sufficient number of jobs and career opportunities for all members of society.
- Improving the quality of working life of employees.
- Providing safe, livable communities with good housing and efficient transportation.

As responsible corporate citizens, businesses should follow the spirit of laws as well as the letter. Many companies that created huge hazardous

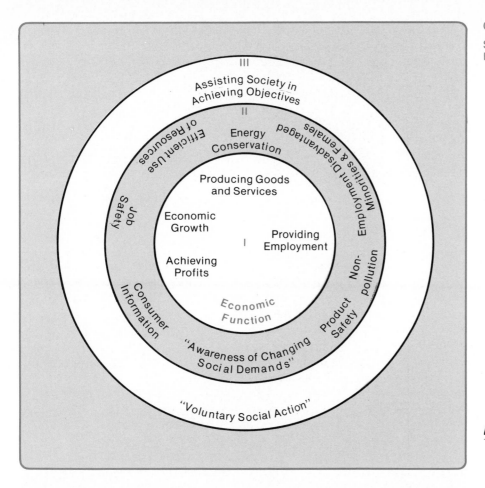

Figure 18–2

*Primary Roles of
Business*

waste dumps throughout the country now defend themselves by saying that the dumps were legal when created. In fact, the laws and regulations controlling hazardous waste dumping were designed to protect the public health. The dumping of certain concentrations of certain substances was prohibited. In many cases, such as the notorious Love Canal case involving Hooker Chemical, dangerous but unregulated substances and harmful (though legal) concentrations of other substances were dumped over an extended period of years. The result is that the public health in those areas has been endangered. It is clear that society now considers this unacceptable.

Many believe that protecting the public is simply a matter of "managerial self-interest."[8] If this were true, as Sir Thomas More said, "Common sense would make us good, and greed would make us saintly." It is a clear consensus today in the United States that corporate strategists must consider other groups, even when doing so conflicts with managerial self-interest or with the interests of stockholders.

As the discussion indicates, society's expectations of business have broadened considerably in recent years to encompass more than the traditional economic function. This is illustrated in Figure 18–2. Inner circle I represents the traditional economic functions of business. The economic function is the primary responsibility of businesses to society. In

As responsible corporate citizens, business people should follow the spirit of the law as well as the letter.

Ellis Herwig/The Picture Cube

performing the economic function, businesses produce needed goods and services, provide employment, contribute to economic growth, and earn a profit. Level II represents the responsibility of business to perform the economic functions with an awareness of changing social goals, values, and demands. Management must be aware of such concerns as the efficient utilization of resources, the reduction of environmental pollution, the employment and development of disadvantaged minorities and females, and the provision of safe products and a safe working environment. The actions of Hershey Chocolate Company following the Three Mile Island (TMI) nuclear incident provide an example of Level II concern. Located near the nuclear plant, Hershey immediately instituted a careful testing program for milk received from within seventy-five miles of TMI and isolated all milk coming from within ten miles. A Hershey executive said, "While we have no indication of anything wrong with any product, if we are going to err, we want to err on the safe side."[9]

In Level III, the outer circle is concerned with the corporation's responsibility for assisting society in achieving such broad goals as the elimination of poverty and urban decay through a partnership of business, government agencies, and other private institutions. Although the responsibilities in Level III are not primary obligations of business, business has shown increasing interest in voluntary social action programs. In its handling of the Tylenol incident, J&J went beyond simply carrying out economic functions with "an awareness of changing social goals, values, and demands." This is an example of Level III concern.

Union Carbide at Bhopal

On the night of December 3, 1984, a misty, white cloud of gas weaved its way through the streets and alleys of the central Indian city of Bhopal. As the gaseous tentacles reached into the city's crowded shanties, where some of India's poorest citizens lived, there was panic and confusion. At least 1700 died, according to Indian government estimates. One survivor said, "It was like breathing fire." An estimated 200,000 others suffered injuries ranging from skin inflammation and temporary blindness to severe lung damage. The gas was methyl isocyanate (MIC), a highly volatile, toxic chemical intermediate used in the production of various pesticides. The MIC had escaped from a storage tank at the Bhopal plant of Union Carbide India Limited (UCIL), a subsidiary of The U.S. company, Union Carbide Corporation (UCC). (At the time of the incident, UCC owned 50.9% of the stock of UCIL. The remaining 49.1% was widely held by the Indian public.)

UCIL's operations in India began in 1934, when the company opened a battery plant in Calcutta. Over the years the company diversified into heavy and fine chemicals and a wide range of industrial products, eventually operating fifteen plants in eight locations. In 1969, UCIL began production at a pesticide plant at Bhopal. Initially UCIL's investment in Bhopal was small, only $1 million, and the process was simple. Concentrated pesticide powder was imported, diluted, and packaged for sale. Use of the product resulted in significant gains in India's agricultural output.

Because the Indian government was interested in increasing the technology base of the Indian economy, it encouraged the Bhopal plant to upgrade its operations from the mere formulation and packaging of pesticide.

Accordingly, the plant began to manufacture pesticide using imported MIC and, ultimately, to manufacture and store MIC itself. The Indian government also encouraged the employment of Indian nationals at the plant. Employees of UCC, the U.S. company, provided technical information for the design of the plant and were involved in the plant start-up. Later, UCC continued to provide safety audits and other services to UCIL. Meanwhile Indian employees of UCIL were trained in plant operations, both in India and at UCC locations in the U.S. At the time of the incident, the Bhopal plant was run entirely by employees of the Indian company.

The Bhopal facility was originally designed to produce over 6,000 tons of pesticide a year. Profits of several million dollars were predicted by 1984. Several factors kept these expectations from being realized. First, an economic recession made farmers more cost conscious and caused them to search for less expensive alternatives to the plant's products. Second, a large number of small-scale producers were able to undersell the company because they were exempt from excise and sales taxes. Finally, a new generation of low cost pesticides was becoming available. With sales collapsing, the Bhopal plant became a money loser in 1981. The prediction for 1984 was for a loss of $4 million based on 1,000 tons of output, one-fifth of capacity.

Press accounts have charged that in the face of these difficulties, extensive cost-cutting began. According to these accounts, the staff at the MIC plant was cut from twelve operators on a shift to six; the maintenance team was reduced in size; job entrance requirements were lowered and some training programs eliminated; some jobs which had previously required college science degrees were filled by high school graduates. Accounts have charged that in a number of instances, faulty safety devices remained unrepaired for weeks; and that because a refrigeration unit, designed to keep the methyl isocyanate cool, continued to malfunction, it was shut down. Press accounts have also charged that on the night of the tragedy, the response of operating personnel was delayed, almost casual. In fact, it has been charged, one worker stopped to take a tea break before attempting to correct the malfunction, so that by the time the seriousness of the problem was recognized, it was too late.

Shortly after the incident occurred, the chairman of UCIL flew from UCIL headquarters in Bombay to Bhopal, taking medicines and medical equipment along. Later he directed UCIL to send in additional equipment, and he pledged 10 million rupees ($830,000) in emergency aid. Warren Anderson, chairman of UCC, the parent company, also flew to Bhopal within days of the accident. In public statements, he said he hoped that a negotiated settlement of compensation to victims could be speedily arranged, in order to prevent long, drawn-out litigation. In the meantime, he arranged for medical specialists to be flown to India at UCC's expense, and he pledged, separately from UCIL, $1 million in emergency relief funds.

Mr. Anderson also sent a team of UCC experts to Bhopal to help secure the plant and investigate the causes of the incident. Indian authorities, who were conducting their own investigation, restricted access to the plant, but the UCC team was admitted to the plant site on December 7. The team first assisted in the conversion of remaining quantities of MIC into finished pesticide, then turned its attention to the technical causes of the emission. UCC suspended the manufacture of MIC until results of the team's investigation became available, and existing inventories of MIC at UCC and its subsidiaries were converted into other compounds.

The team's report was completed and made public in March of 1985. The report concluded that the emission had been triggered when a large quantity of water, which reacts violently with MIC, had been introduced, "inadvertently or deliberately," into an MIC storage tank. The report confirmed that a number of safety systems had been out of operation at the plant, in violation of standard operating procedures. Anderson said that neither he nor others at UCC headquarters had been aware of the violations and that had they been, the situation would not have been allowed to continue. The report did not speculate on the human failures, if any, that led to the incident. According to Anderson, the Indian authorities had not allowed the UCC team sufficient access to the personnel involved to draw conclusions in that area. The Indian authorities' own report was presumably to address such matters but, as of April 10, had not been made public.

In the immediate aftermath of the incident, a number of American tort lawyers flew to Bhopal to recruit clients among the Indian victims. The lawyers' aim was to sue UCC in U.S. courts, rather than UCIL or UCC in Indian courts, because damage awards—and lawyers' compensation—are generally considerably higher in the U.S. than in India. Damages sought in these suits totaled in the hundreds of billions of dollars, considerably in excess of the total assets of UCC. Early in 1985, the Indian government issued an ordinance providing that the Indian government had "exclusive right" to represent Bhopal claimants, but the legislation also provided that claimants could choose their own lawyers to be "associated" with the government's efforts. On April 8, the Indian government filed suit against UCC in a U.S. court, but indicated it was still willing to negotiate.

Following the incident, a crisis management team and a special senior management committee were formed at UCC to coordinate the parent corporation's response. These groups were directly responsible to the UCC chairman, who began devoting the bulk of his time to issues arising from the incident. Day-to-day business activities of the corporation were supervised by UCC's president. Prior to the incident, UCC had enjoyed a reputation as a company with an excellent safety record and an international reputation for good corporate citizenship.[10]

CHANGING VALUES TOWARD SOCIAL RESPONSIBILITY

Numerous associations and groups of respected business leaders including the American Management Association and the Committee for Economic Development have encouraged corporations and managers to become involved in socially responsible activities. These groups have stressed such programs as providing better jobs and promotion opportunities to minorities and women; financial support for education; financial and managerial support for improving health and medical care; a safer working environment; leadership and financial support for urban renewal; and means to reduce environmental pollution.

The major arguments for the acceptance of social responsibility by business are summarized below:

1. People expect businesses and other institutions to be socially responsible.
2. It is in the best interest of the business to pursue socially responsible programs.
3. It improves the image of the firm.
4. Business should be involved in social projects because it has the resources.
5. Corporations must be concerned about society's interests and needs because society, in effect, sanctions business operations.
6. If the business is not responsive to society's needs, the public will press for more governmental regulation requiring more socially responsible behavior.
7. Socially responsible actions may increase profits in the long run.

iron law of responsibility

Keith Davis summarizes these arguments with what he terms the **iron law of responsibility**. The law states that "*in the long-run, those who do not use power in a manner in which society considers responsible will tend to lose it.*" Thus, if business firms are to retain their social power and role, they must be responsive to society's needs.[11]

The Traditional View of Social Responsibility

In 1776, Adam Smith published *The Wealth of Nations,* which has sometimes been called the "Capitalist Manifesto." Smith described a system where individuals and businesses pursued their own self-interests and government played a limited role. This system became the model for capitalism in the United States. Adam Smith wrote:

> [An individual or business] generally, indeed, neither intends to promote the public interest, nor knows how much he is promoting it. . . . He intends only his own gains, and he is in this, as in many other cases, led by an invisible hand to promote an end which was no part of his intention, nor is it always the worse for society that it was no part of it. By pursuing his own interest he frequently promotes that of the society more effectively than when he really intends to promote it.[12]

This idea—that capitalism allows the serving of the public interest by individuals and businesses who seek maximization of satisfaction or profit—is the foundation of the U.S. economic system. Traditionally, companies were not expected to serve social goals, except indirectly. For example, until the mid-1930s it was illegal for a U.S. corporation to make charitable contributions. This was based on a precedent set in an 1883 lawsuit in Great Britain, *Hutton* v. *West Cork Railway Corporation.* The court in that case ruled that the corporation should be concerned only with the equitable distribution of its earnings to its owners. This could not include corporate philanthropy.[13]

In 1935 the Federal Revenue Act made provisions for tax deductibility of corporate charitable contributions. Under that revision, corporations could deduct up to 5 percent of net income for charitable purposes. By 1953, the right of businesses to make extensive charitable gifts was clearly established. That year, in *A. P. Smith Manufacturing Company* v. *Barlow, et al.,* the New Jersey Supreme Court concluded that business support of higher education is in society's best interest.[14]

Nobel laureate economist Milton Friedman called the idea of corporate social responsibility a "fundamentally subversive doctrine." Friedman said, "There is one and only one social responsibility of business—to use its resources and engage in activities designed to increase its profits so long as it stays within the rules of the game, which is to say engages in open and free competition without deception or fraud."[15]

Friedman's statement is often quoted as an example of a radical view. Far from being a radical, however, Dr. Friedman simply subscribes to the idea that, in the long run, the public interests are served by individuals and businesses pursuing their own best interests, primarily financial well-being, through participation in a relatively free economy. Friedman sets a rather high standard, suggesting that businesses should operate within the "rules of the game," practicing neither deception nor fraud. The rules of the game obviously include international, national, and other laws, as well as accepted ethical practices. How many corporations actually are willing to tell the absolute truth in their advertisements and to engage in open and fair competition, avoiding collusion, price fixing, and so forth? The general public would be greatly surprised if STP Corporation were to admit that the lubricating oil additive has no real value, as has been shown.[16]

Many who oppose Friedman would place on business managers the burden of using corporate resources, including both money and time, for social motives. Yet much of the corporate giving that occurred in the United States came from fortunes amassed by individuals who blatantly violated the Friedman principles of free enterprise.[17] This is why many of today's great universities and charitable foundations bear the names of persons like Daniel Drew, John D. Rockefeller, J. P. Morgan, Cornelius Vanderbilt, and Andrew Carnegie. Noted author Matthew Josephson called these men the "robber barons."[18]

There is evidence that few subscribe to Friedman's hard-line views. Let us look at how values concerning social responsibility are changing.

The Recent Trend Concerning Social Responsibility

More and more U.S. corporate executives see themselves as legitimate servants of a variety of constituencies. In a political sense, constituency means a body of citizens or voters that is entitled to elect a representative to a legislative or other public body. An **organizational constituency** is *any identifiable group that organizational managers either have or acknowledge a responsibility to represent.* The intention of political constituents is that they will be represented by the person they elect. Unlike political constituents, those of corporate managers may or may not have the power to elect those managers.

organizational constituency

For some executives, the common shareholder is only one of many constituencies to be served—and not even the primary one. For example, at Lincoln Electric Company, the world's largest producer of arc welding products, corporate executives see the customer as their primary constituency. Employees are in second place, with stockholders only a distant third. James Lincoln, the company's founder and president until his death in 1965, said, "The last group to be considered is the stockholders, who own stock because they think it will be more profitable than investing money in any other way."[19]

Every business or other organization has a large number of stakeholders,

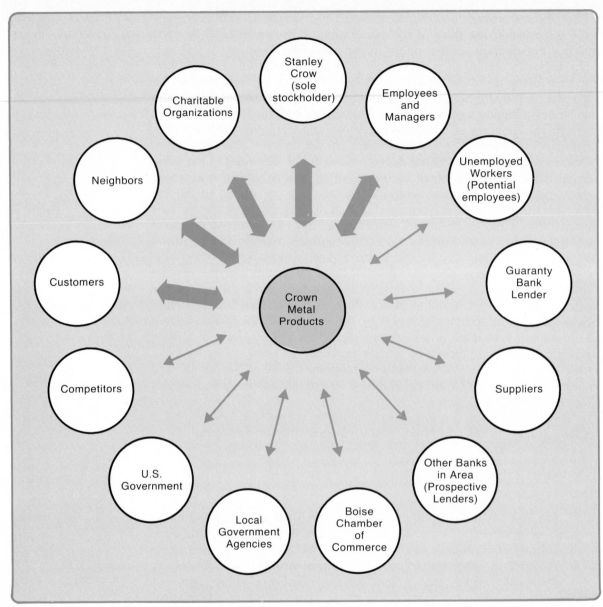

Figure 18–3   Stakeholders of Crown Metal Products

organizational stakeholder

some of which are recognized as constituents and some of which are not. An **organizational stakeholder** is *an individual or group whose interests are affected by organizational activities.* Remember that although the interests of all stakeholders are affected by the corporation, managers may not acknowledge any responsibility to them. A few of the stakeholders identified for Crown Metal Products, a small manufacturer of metal furniture near Boise, Idaho, are shown in Figure 18–3. The stakeholders that Crown management views as constituencies are identified by bold arrows.

The actions of many corporate executives are not designed to serve simply the common shareholder's interests. For example, a number of corporate managements have recently placed large amounts of company stock in employee stock ownership trusts for the purpose of avoiding takeover attempts that were clearly in the interest of common shareholders. This benefited the employees, of course, but it also helped the managers keep their jobs. Major companies that have recently taken these kind of actions to avoid takeovers include Walt Disney Production, and Martin-Marietta Corporation. Other companies make gifts of company resources, often cash, to universities, churches, clubs, and so forth, knowing that any possible benefit to shareholders is remote. Some authorities suggest that members of the public should be placed on the boards of directors of major corporations to protect the interests of nonowner stakeholders.[20]

Representing such a diversity of interests requires answering questions such as the following: During an economic downturn, should employees be afforded continuous employment even when this is not in the long-term best interest of the owners of the corporation and does not accord with their preferences? Should managers be concerned about whether suppliers receive a reasonable profit on the items purchased from them, or should management simply buy the best inputs at the lowest price possible?

THE BUSINESS-GOVERNMENT INTERFACE

The general public is justifiably concerned about the influence of business firms and other private organizations on government. But most managers express greater concern for the pervasive involvement of government in business activities. One prominent law school dean, Thomas Erlich of Stanford University, complained that the increasing "legal pollution" in the United States unduly constrains business.[21]

John Dunlop, dean of the Faculty of Arts and Sciences at Harvard University and U.S. secretary of labor in 1975 and 1976, said, "The past decade has seen a vast expansion in the scope and detail of government regulation of business decisions, beyond those of the New Deal era, beyond regulating the public utility industry, and beyond temporary periods of wage and price controls."[22] A Harvard University researcher estimates that regulation may cost U.S. business as much as $100 billion per year.[23] The great historian Alfred Chandler indicates that the problem is more severe in the United States than in other countries.[24] Crawford Greenwalt, former chairman of the board at DuPont, asks, "Why is it that my American colleagues and I are constantly being taken to court—made to stand trial—for activities that our counterparts in Britain and other parts of Europe are knighted or given peerages or comparable honors for?"[25]

Taking a more balanced view, George Shultz, U.S. secretary of state in the Reagan administration, acknowledges that "government seems to be an opponent, not a friend or even a neutral referee."[26] He also suggests that the issue looks different from the government's side. Shultz says that businesses can serve their political interests by doing their homework better and by "looking beyond the very narrow interests of the individual company or industry and offering some connection between what the businessman wants and the broader public interest."[27]

The recent trend has been toward lessening regulation and reducing government interference with business and private activities. The airline, trucking, and banking industries are now largely deregulated. It is noteworthy that deregulated industries themselves tend to be the most vehement opponents of deregulation. After companies have adapted to a regulated environment, they apparently are not sure they will be able to compete in a freely competitive one.

Recently there has been fear that political contributions are likely to subvert governmental processes by causing elected officials to serve the interests of those groups that make the contributions rather than those of their constituents. This is especially true for contributions made by PACs, *political action committees*. **Political action committees (PACs)** are *tax-favored organizations formed by special interest groups to accept contributions and influence governmental action.* The growth of PACs has afforded an avenue whereby corporations contribute hundreds of millions of dollars to political candidates. Much of the money is obviously aimed at serving the special interests of those corporations. Billions in subsidies and price supports were approved for the dairy industry and even the tobacco industry in 1983 after PACs representing those industries made large contributions to key legislators.

political action committees (PACs)

A MODEL OF ETHICS

Closely related to social responsibility, but not identical to it, is the concept of ethics. **Ethics** is *the discipline dealing with what is good and bad or right and wrong or with moral duty and obligation.* Each of us must make ethical (or unethical) decisions every day. Should we tell the clerk that we have received too much change? What should we do if the professor makes a mistake in our favor in calculating our grade?

ethics

A model of ethics is presented in Figure 18–4. It can be seen that ethics consist mainly of two relationships, indicated by arrows in the figure. A person or organization is ethical if these relationships are strong and positive. There are a number of sources that one might use to determine what is right or wrong, good or bad, moral or immoral behavior. These include the Bible, the Koran, and a number of other holy books. They also include that "still small voice" that many refer to as conscience. Millions believe that conscience is a gift of God or the voice of God. Others see it as a developed response based on internalization of societal mores.

Another source of ethical guidance is the behavior and advice of what psychologists call "significant others"—our parents, friends, role models,

Figure 18–4

A Model of Ethics

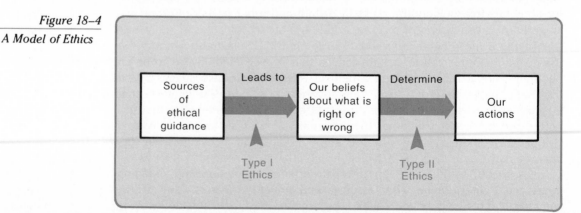

and members of our churches, clubs, and associations. For organized professionals especially, there are often codes of ethics that proscribe behavior. Any type of act sufficiently hurtful to others is often prohibited by law. Thus enacted laws offer guides to ethical behavior. If a certain behavior is illegal, most would consider it to be unethical. There are exceptions, of course. For example, through the 1950s, laws in most southern states relegated black persons to sit in the backs of buses (and otherwise assign them an inferior status). Today many consider it to have been highly moral for Martin Luther King, Jr., to have opposed such laws and, in fact, to have disobeyed them.

Notice in Figure 18–4 that the sources of ethical guidance should lead to appropriate beliefs or convictions about what is right and wrong. Most would agree that persons have a responsibility to avail themselves of these sources of ethical guidance. In short, individuals should care about what is right and wrong and not just be concerned with what is expedient. *The strength of the relationship between what an individual or an organization believes to be moral and correct and what available sources of guidance suggest is morally correct* is **Type I ethics**. For example, suppose a student believes it is acceptable to copy another student's exam paper despite the fact that almost everyone condemns this practice. This student is unethical in a Type I sense.

Type I ethics

Simply having strong beliefs about what is right and wrong and basing them on the proper sources does not make one ethical. Figure 18–4 illustrates that behavior should conform with what we believe about right and wrong. **Type II ethics** is *the strength of the relationship between what one believes and how one behaves.* Generally a person is not considered ethical unless possessed of both types of ethics. Everyone would agree that to do what one believes is wrong is unethical. For example, if a student knows that it is wrong to look on another's examination answer sheet while taking a test and does so anyway, the student has been unethical in a Type II sense. If a business manager knows that it is wrong to damage the environment yet dumps poisonous waste in a nearby stream, this behavior is unethical also.

Type II ethics

BUSINESS ETHICS

One can usually provoke a lively discussion by simply mentioning the words *business ethics.* **Business ethics** is *the application of ethical principles to business relationships and activities.* Reading the newspapers or watching the evening news provides ample illustrations of illegal and/or unethical practices of individuals within large corporations. Particularly ethical practices seldom make the news. When Southland Corporation executives were accused of bribing New York tax officials in 1984, the story made every major newspaper. That company's support of Olympic athletes was barely noted.

business ethics

Deciding what is ethical is often difficult. The following are examples of activities usually perceived as unethical:

• Padding expense accounts to obtain reimbursement for questionable business expenses.

• Divulging confidential information or trade secrets.

• Using company property and/or materials for one's own personal use.

- Giving or receiving gifts in return for favors.
- Firing an employee for whistle-blowing.
- Terminating employment without giving sufficient notice.
- Stealing from the company.
- Receiving or offering kickbacks.

Many industries and individual companies have formal, written codes of ethics that provide specific guidelines for managers and other employees. The key question in this regard is whether individuals within organizations are truly governed by the code of ethics or simply give lip-service to the guidelines. Another issue is whether the company or industry enforces the code if individuals or companies violate it. In any event, these codes of ethics define or clarify the ethical issues and allow the individual to make the final decision.

Many companies have developed specific codes of ethics. Eastman Kodak and Texas Instruments provide excellent examples. Kodak's SPICE concept provides guidelines for company practices (see Figure 18–5) and as such is dynamic and flexible. Kodak intends for SPICE to reflect the needs in the marketplace and to anticipate legal changes. Kodak communicates this concept to its employees in meetings and discussion groups by members of management.

Texas Instruments published a handbook entitled "Ethics in the Business of T.I."[28] The company's overall philosophy of business can be summarized as follows:

> It is fundamental to TI's philosophy that good ethics and good business are synonymous when viewed from moral, legal and practical standpoints. The trust and respect of all people—fellow workers, customers, consumers, stockholders, government employees, elected officials, suppliers, competitors, neighbors, friends, the press, and the general public—are assets that cannot be purchased. They must be earned. This is why all of the business of TI must be conducted according to the highest ethical standards.

In the handbook, TI has statements establishing guidelines for ethical decision making in business. Areas covered include: truthfulness in advertising, gifts and entertainment, improper use of corporate assets, political contributions, payments in connection with business transactions, conflicts of interest, trade secrets and proprietary information, and other matters.

There are advantages for organizations to form industry associations to develop and promote improved codes of ethics. It is difficult for a single firm to pioneer ethical practices if its competitors undercut them by taking advantage of unethical shortcuts. For example, U.S. companies must comply with the Foreign Corrupt Practices Act of 1977 with respect to bribes of foreign government officials or business executives. Obviously this law does not prevent foreign competitors from bribing government or business officials to achieve business.[29] Perhaps the best hope would be for the major multinational enterprises to agree jointly to such a prohibition. When codes are not voluntarily followed, a society usually resorts to specific laws and penalties. In the case of international bribes, there is no international law. Should the United States declare the practice illegal, its multinational companies may find it difficult to compete with firms based in nations that

Throughout the history of Eastman Kodak Company, the principal factor in its growth has been the conviction that fulfilling customer needs and desires is the only road to corporate success. Such clichés as "share of the market," when used to explain performance, gloss over the fact that the consumer is supreme in a free economy and that all ingredients contributing to corporate success rest ultimately with him.

Kodak recognizes that it has to meet many responsibilities to assure successful operations. Our concern for Shareowners, the Public Interest, Customers, and Employees has come to be known throughout the Kodak organization as the "SPICE" concept.

A review for management of each element in the SPICE concept reveals how its combined approaches to influencing business operations apply to the company's growth and success.

Shareowners

Currently there are more than 222,000 shareowners of Eastman Kodak Company—an increase from 210,000 a year ago and from fewer than 121,000 in 1960. Kodak investors now own more than 161,000,000 common shares. These figures indicate that investors expect continued good performance from Kodak.

Men, women, and institutions have used their savings to invest in Kodak, and the Company has a primary obligation to satisfy their fair interests. Their judgment of Kodak and their confidence in the Company rest on the prospects of dividends and growth from their investments. In response to shareowners' interest in the Company, it is necessary to produce profits and provide an adequate return on investment. Today, the shareowners' judgment also is based increasingly on the ability of Kodak to meet its responsibilities to employees and the public interest.

In this respect, the concern of investors and employees should be parallel, serving each other for mutual benefit.

Public Interest

Our corporate social responsibility may take diverse forms, but in essence it reflects concern for the well-being of the communities and countries in which Kodak carries on its activities. Examples of Kodak's activities in the public interest can be found in the improvement of communities through special training programs to upgrade the disadvantaged; clean air and water (healthful environment) programs, aid to education and numerous other projects for civic betterment. This concern also is reflected in Kodak's encouragement of employee participation in civic, community, political, and other similar individual pursuits. It is exhibited, too, in the constant, substantial research and development efforts to produce new and improved products and services. Although often overlooked, corporate profits are essential to finance public interest projects. Kodak's 114,000 people are, of course, members of the public that renders judgment of performance in the public interest. While this judgment of accomplishment obviously varies among Kodakers, collectively it will have a substantial influence on public opinion about the Company.

Customers

Kodak must sell products and services—and continue to sell them in volume. Only satisfied customers will come back again and again. Thus, customer satisfaction is both a short- and long-term goal. To reach this objective, the Company must produce and offer—at fair prices—high-quality products and services containing the features and capabilities that customers desire. This requires all the inventive genius we can muster in research and development leading to new and improved products and services; better ideas and greater efficiency in production, purchasing, distribution, marketing, and every other area of the Company's activities. This also means continued attention to the informative quality and scope of advertising and promotion; better exercise of personal and collective skills and capabilities; improved training programs for product users and for Kodak people as well as for our intermediate customers, the dealers and distributors. *(continued)*

Figure 18–5 SPICE Concept Guides Kodak Business Practices Used with permission from Eastman Kodak Company.

Figure 18–5   (continued)

Employees

Each Kodak man and woman is likely to judge the Company's overall performance in a different way; perhaps in terms of wages and salaries, opportunity for advancement, or direct and indirect benefits such as the Wage Dividend, hospital and medical care benefits, and work environment. There are also intangibles that he may consider, such as pride in the Company, opportunity through his job to make contributions to improving products or services and personal recognition for his accomplishments. The interests of Kodak people, Kodak shareowners, and Kodak customers are not mutually exclusive as one might initially be inclined to believe. During the past 10 years, 31,000 Kodak people have shown their faith in the future of the Company by deferring $146,000,000 in Wage Dividend payments for investment in the Savings and Investment Plan. Their interests merge with those of other shareowners in renewed appreciation for achieving profits and growth.

This, then, is a summary of the SPICE concept. It emphasizes that concern for shareowners, public interest, customers, and employees must motivate any successful business. Companies that are dedicated to satisfying the fair needs of these elements to the exclusion of all others are indispensable for the continued health of our society and the survival of the free enterprise system.

do not disapprove. In this case, a voluntary code adopted by the leading firms of the world is likely to be the most effective method of handling the situation.

The concern for ethics in business appears to be increasing. According to one researcher, "Business behavior is more ethical than it was in 1961, but the expectations of a better educated and ethically sensitized public have risen more rapidly than the behavior." The study also found that respondents thought that they were more ethical than the average manager and that their department and company were more ethical than others. The respondents suggested that a written code of ethics would help to improve business practices.[30]

Apparently the use of formalized corporate codes of ethics is increasing in U.S. businesses. A 1980 survey of 611 companies found that 77 percent of the firms had a code of conduct. Ninety-seven percent of the largest companies (those with $400 million or more in sales) had corporate codes of conduct.

THE SOCIAL AUDIT

Many firms acknowledge their responsibilities to various segments of society, and some even set specific objectives in social areas. Over the last two decades or so, a number of organizations and individuals have recommended that firms measure the degree to which they contribute to the welfare of various elements of society and to that of society as a whole.

social audit   When this effort is formalized, it is called a **social audit**. This is *a systematic assessment of a company's activities in terms of social impact.* Despite the efforts of the American Institute of Certified Public Accountants and a number of management societies, it has not been possible to apply the rigor of financial auditing in social areas. There are a number of possible reasons for this failure:

1. The company may not have specific objectives in social areas.
2. Specific criteria or units of measurement may not be agreed upon.
3. It may be difficult to determine how an action today might affect society's interests tomorrow.
4. The business system, which previously has focused on economic variables, may not have control points or measurement techniques appropriate to measuring social variables.
5. Auditing implies the collection of complete, objective, and accurate data, not usually available in social areas.

Although few companies have ever attempted to conduct a rigorous social audit, most make efforts to respond to the public's desire to know how they are doing in social areas. A survey of the annual reports of 500 large companies in the United States showed that over 90 percent of them contained social responsibility disclosures.[31] Four possible types of audits are currently being utilized: (1) a simple inventory of activities, (2) compilation of socially relevant expenditures, (3) specific program management, and (4) determination of social impact. The inventory is generally the place where one would start. It would consist of a simple listing of activities undertaken by the firm over and above what is required. For example, firms have itemized the following types of social activities: (1) minority employment and training, (2) support of minority enterprises, (3) pollution control, (4) corporate giving, (5) involvement in selected community projects by firm executives, and (6) a hard-core unemployed program. The ideal social audit would involve determination of the true *benefits* to society of any socially oriented business activity.

SUMMARY

When a corporation behaves as if it had a conscience, it is said to be socially responsible. Social responsibility is the implied, enforced, or felt obligation of managers, acting in their official capacities, to serve or protect the interests of groups other than themselves. Social responsibility can be understood in terms of the social contract that exists between a firm and its environment. This social contract is the set of rules and assumptions about behavior patterns among the various elements of society.

Values are changing with regard to social responsibility. The iron law of responsibility states that "in the long run, those who do not use power in a manner in which society considers responsible will tend to lose it." Traditionally, however, companies were not expected to have social goals, except indirectly. Recently, more and more U.S. corporate executives see themselves as legitimate servants of a variety of constituencies. An organizational constituency is any identifiable group that organizational managers either have or acknowledge a responsibility to represent.

Most managers express great concern for the pervasive involvement of government in business activities. There has been a trend toward lessening regulation and reducing government interference with business and private activities. Also, however, there has been fear that political contributors are likely to subvert governmental processes by causing elected officials to serve the interests of political action committees rather than those of their constituents.

Ethics is the discipline dealing with what is good and bad or right and wrong or with moral duty and obligation. The strength of the relationship between what an individual or an organization believes to be moral and correct and what available sources of guidance suggest is morally correct is Type I ethics. Type II ethics is the strength of the relationship between what one believes and the way one behaves. Generally a person is not considered ethical unless possessed of both types of ethics. Business ethics is the application of ethical principles to business relationships and activities.

A social audit is a systematic assessment of a company's activities in terms of their social impact.

Although few companies have ever attempted to conduct a rigorous social audit, most make efforts to respond to the public's desire to know how they are doing in social areas. Four possible types of audits are currently being utilized: (1) a simple inventory of activities, (2) a compilation of socially relevant expenditures, (3) specific program management, and (4) determination of social impact.

REVIEW QUESTIONS

1. Define social responsibility. In general, how is U.S. business viewed by the general public?
2. What is the social contract? Describe the various relationships involved with the social contract.
3. Contrast the traditional view of social responsibility to the recent trend concerning social responsibility.
4. What are political action committees?
5. What are ethics? Distinguish between Type I and Type II ethics.
6. Are the ethics of business and its managers changing? Discuss.
7. What is the purpose of the social audit?

EXERCISES

1. Visit two local companies that have formal codes of ethics. Compare the codes of ethics with our discussion of ethics in this chapter.
2. Select what you consider to be a local social or environmental problem—such as water or air pollution. Make a list of the groups or businesses within the community that are concerned about the problem. Analyze the impact of the problem on the various segments of the community. Develop a proposal for solving the problem giving consideration to the benefits and costs of your solution.

CASE STUDY

Firing Tom Serinsky

As Norman Blankenship came into the mine office at Consolidation Coal Company's Rowland mine, near Clear Creek, West Virginia, he told the mine dispatcher not to tell anyone of his presence. Norman was the general superintendent over the Rowland operation. He had been with Consolidation for over twenty-three years, having started out as a coal digger.

Norman had heard that one of his section bosses, Tom Serinsky, had been sleeping on the job. Tom had been hired two months earlier and assigned to the Rowland mine by the regional personnel office. He went to work as section boss, working the midnight to 8:00 A.M. shift. Because of his age and experience, he was the senior person in the mine on his shift.

Norman took one of the battery-operated jeeps used to transport personnel and supplies in and out of the mine and proceeded to the area where Tom was assigned. Upon arriving, he saw Tom lying on an emergency stretcher. Norman stopped his jeep a few yards away from where Tom was sleeping and approached him. "Hey, you asleep?" Norman asked. Tom awakened with a start and said, "No, I wasn't sleeping."

Norman waited a moment for Tom to collect his senses and then said, "I could tell that you were sleeping. But that's beside the point. You weren't at your work station. You know that I have no choice but to fire you." After Tom had left, Norman called his mine foreman, who had accompanied him to the dispatcher's office, and asked him to complete the remainder of Tom's shift.

The next morning, Norman had the mine personnel officer officially terminate Tom. As part of the standard procedure, the mine personnel officer notified the regional personnel director that Tom had been fired and the reasons for firing him. The regional personnel director asked the personnel officer to get Norman on the line. When he did so, Norman was told, "You know that Tom is the brother-in-law of our regional vice-president, Eustus Frederick?" "No, I didn't know that," replied Norman, "but it doesn't matter. The rules are clear. I wouldn't care if he was the regional vice-president's son."

The next day, the regional personnel director showed up at the mine just as Norman was getting ready to make a routine tour of the mine. "I guess you know what I'm here for," said the personnel director. "Yeah, you're here to take away my authority," replied Norman. "No, I'm just here to investigate," said the personnel director.

When Norman returned to the mine office after his tour, the personnel director had finished his interviews. He told Norman, "I think we're going to have to put Tom back to work. If we decide to do that, can you let him work for you?" "No, absolutely not," said Norman. "In fact, if he works here, I go." A week later, Norman learned that Tom had gone to work as section boss at another Consolidation coal mine in the region.

QUESTIONS

1. What would you do now if you were Norman?
2. Do you believe the personnel director handled the matter in an ethical manner? Explain.

CASE STUDY

The Hiring of a Friend's Daughter

Marcie Sweeney had recently graduated from college with a degree in general business. Marcie was quite bright, although her grades might lead a person to think otherwise. She had thoroughly enjoyed school—dating, tennis, swimming, and similar stimulating academic events. When she graduated from the university, she had not found a job. Her dad was extremely upset when he discovered this, and he took it on himself to see that Marcie became employed.

Her father, Allen Sweeney, was executive vice-president of a medium-sized manufacturing firm. One of the people he contacted in seeking employment for Marcie was Bill Garbo, the president of another firm in the area. Mr. Sweeney purchased many of his firm's supplies from Garbo's company. On telling Bill his problem, Allen was told to send Marcie to his office for an interview. Marcie did as instructed by her father and was surprised that before she left that day she had a job in the accounting department. Marcie may have been lazy but she certainly was not stupid. She realized that this job was obtained because of the hope of future business from her father's company. Although the work was not challenging, it paid better than the other jobs in the accounting department.

It did not take long for the employees in the department to discover the reason she had been hired—Marcie told them. When a difficult job was assigned to Marcie, she normally got one of the other employees to do it, inferring that Mr. Garbo would be pleased with them by helping her out. She developed a pattern of coming in late, taking long lunch breaks, and leaving early. When the department manager attempted to reprimand her for these unorthodox activities, Marcie would bring up the close relationship that her father had with the president of this firm. The department manager was at his limit when he asked for your help.

QUESTIONS

1. From an ethical standpoint, how would you evaluate the merits of Mr. Garbo employing Marcie? Discuss.

2. Now that she is employed, how would you suggest that the situation be resolved?

3. Do you feel that a firm should have policies regarding such practices? Discuss.

NOTES

1. This story is a composite taken from a number of published sources, including: Thomas Moore, "The Fight to Save Tylenol," *Fortune* (November 29, 1982): 44–49; Michelle Osborn, "Tylenol Crisis Tests Public Relations Staff," *Editor & Publisher* (October 23, 1982): 15; "Salvaging Tylenol," *Dun's Business Month* (November 1982): 14–19; "The Battering of a Best-Selling Brand," *Fortune* (November 1, 1982): 7; "A Death Blow for Tylenol?" *Business Week* (October 18, 1982): 151; Nancy Giges, "Tylenol Tablets Lead Rebound," *Advertising Age* (December 13, 1982): 1; Nancy J. Perry, "America's Most Admired Corporations," *Fortune* (January 9, 1984): 50–56; and numerous articles from *The Wall Street Journal.*

2. Kenneth E. Goodpaster and John B. Matthews, Jr., "Can a Corporation Have a Conscience?" *Harvard Business Review* 60, no. 1 (January–February 1982): 132–141.

3. Vernon M. Buehler and Y. K. Shetty, "Managerial Response to Social Responsibility Challenge." *Academy of Management Journal* 19 (March 1976): 69.

4. Thomas Benham, "The Factual Foundation," in Clarence H. Danhof and James C. Worthy, eds., *Crisis in Confidence* II: *Corporate America* (Springfield, Ill.: Sagamon State University, 1975), pp. 21–53.

5. Keith Davis, "The Case for and against Business Assumption of Social Responsibilities," *Academy of Management Journal* (June 1973): 39.

6. Louis F. Boone and David L. Kurtz, *Principles of Management,* 2d ed. (New York: Random House, 1984), p. 547.

7. Adapted from the Committee for Economic Development and from Sandra L. Holmes, "Corporate Social Performance and Present Areas of Commitment," *Academy of Management Journal* 20 (1977): 435.

8. William J. Byron, "In Defense of Social Responsibility," *Journal of Economics and Business* 34, no. 2 (1982): 190.

9. Dennis Montgomery, "Candy Firm Monitoring Atomic Risk," *Detroit News,* April 2, 1979, pp. 3A, 6A.

10. Sailesh Kottary, "Whose Life Is It Anyway?" *Illustrated Weekly of India,* December 30, 1984, pp. 6–9; "Pesticide Plant Started as a Showpiece But Ran into Troubles," *New York Times,* February 3, 1985, p. 8; Stuart Diamond, "The Disaster in Bhopal," *New York Times,* January 28, 30, 31, February 3, 1985; Rajendra Prabhu, "Flaws Revealed in Bhopal Plant," *Hindustan Times,* January 5, 1985, pp. 1, 8; "CBI Team to Probe All

Aspects," *Times of India,* December 4, 1984, pp. 1, 12; "India's Night of Death," *Time* (December 17, 1984): 22–31; various articles from *The Wall Street Journal;* Union Carbide Corporation statements and press releases.

11. See Davis, "Case For and Against," p. 36.

12. Adam Smith, *The Wealth of Nations* (New York: Modern Library, originally published in 1776), p. 423.

13. Daniel Wren, *The Evolution of Management Thought,* 2d ed. (New York: Wiley, 1979), p. 109.

14. Ibid., p. 453.

15. Milton Friedman, *Capitalism and Freedom* (Chicago: University of Chicago Press, 1962), p. 133; also see Theodore Leavitt, "The Dangers of Social Responsibility," *Harvard Business Review* 36, no. 5 (September–October 1958).

16. Robert F. Hartley, *Marketing Mistakes,* 2d ed. (Columbus, Ohio: Grid Publishing, 1981).

17. See Mathew Josephson, *The Robber Barons* (New York: Harcourt Brace Jovanovich, 1934), and Ida Tarbell, *History of Standard Oil* (New York: Harper and Row, 1905).

18. Josephson, *Robber Barons.*

19. James F. Lincoln, *A New Approach to Industrial Economics* (New York: Devin Adair Co., 1961), pp. 38, 122.

20. Thomas M. Jones and Leonard D. Goldberg, "Governing the Large Corporation: More Arguments for Public Directors," *Academy of Management Review* 7, no. 4 (October 1982): 603–605.

21. "Complaints about Lawyers." *U.S. News and World Report,* July 21, 1978, p. 44.

22. John T. Dunlop et al., "Business and Public Policy," *Harvard Business Review* (November–December 1979): 82.

23. Ronald J. Fox, "Breaking the Regulatory Deadlock," *Harvard Business Review* (September–October 1981): 98.

24. Dunlop et al., "Business," p. 82.

25. Ibid.

26. Ibid., p. 93.

27. Ibid.

28. Texas Instruments, "Ethics in the Business of T.I." (Dallas, 1977).

29. Bernard J. White and B. Ruth Montgomery, "Corporate Codes of Conduct," *California Management Review* 22, no. 2 (Winter 1980): 80.

30. Steven N. Brenner and Earl A. Molander, "Is the

Ethics of Business Changing?" *Harvard Business Review* (January–February 1977): 60.

31. *Social Responsibility Disclosure: 1977 Survey of* *Fortune 500 Annual Reports,* Ernst and Ernst, 1300 Union Commerce Building, Cleveland, Ohio 44115.

REFERENCES

Armandi, B. R., and F. Tuzzolino, "Need Hierarchy Framework for Assessing Corporation Social Responsibility." *Academy of Management Review* 6 (January 1981): 21–28.

Boone, Louis F., and David L. Keirtz. *Principles of Management.* 2d ed. New York: Random House, 1984.

Byron, William J. "In Defense of Social Responsibility." *Journal of Economics and Business* 34, no. 2 (1982): 189–192.

Carroll, Archie E. "A Three-Dimensional Conceptual Model of Corporate Performance." *Academy of Management Review* 4, no. 4 (October 1979): 497–505.

Clutterbuck, D. "Blowing the Whistle on Corporate Misconduct." *International Management* 35 (January 1980): 14–16.

"Complaints about Lawyers." *U.S. News and World Report* (July 21, 1978): 44.

Dhir, K. "American Corporate System." *Management International Review* 19 (1979): 13–20.

Drory, Amos, and Uri M. Gluskinos. "Machiavellianism and Leadership." *Journal of Applied Psychology* 64, no. 1 (February 1980): 81–86.

Dunlop, John T. et al. "Business and Public Policy." *Harvard Business Review* (November–December 1979): 85–102.

Fombrum, Charles, and W. Graham Astley. "Beyond Corporate Strategy." *Journal of Business Strategy* 3, no. 4 (Spring 1983): 47–54.

Fox, J. Ronald. "Breaking the Regulatory Deadlock." *Harvard Business Review* 59, no. 5 (September–October 1981): 97–105.

Friedman, Hershey H., and Linda W. Friedman. "Ethics: Everybody's Business." *Collegiate News and Views* 35, no. 2 (Winter 1981–1982): 11–13.

Friedman, Milton. *Capitalism and Freedom.* Chicago: University of Chicago Press, 1962.

Goodpaster, Kenneth E., and John B. Matthews, Jr. "Can a Corporation Have a Conscience?" *Harvard Business Review* 60, no. 1 (January–February 1982): 132–141.

Greenough, William Croan. "Keeping Corporate Governance in the Private Sector." *Business Horizons* 23, no. 1 (February 1980): 71–81.

Grunig, James E. "A New Measure of Public Opinions on Corporate Social Responsibility." *Academy of Management Journal* 22, no. 4 (December 1979): 738–764.

Hartley, Robert F. *Marketing Mistakes.* 2d ed. Columbus, Ohio: Grid Publishing, 1981.

Henderson, H. "Changing Corporate-Social Contract in the 1980s: Creative Opportunities for Consumer Affairs Professionals." *Public Relations Quarterly* 24 (Winter 1979): 7–14.

Hipp, H. "Business Ethics and Society's Future." *National Underwriter* (September 14, 1979): 7–14.

"How Business Treats Its Environment." *Business and Society Review* 33 (Spring 1980): 56–65.

Jones, T. M. "Corporate Social Responsibility Revisited, Redefined." *California Management Review* 22 (Spring 1980): 59–67.

Jones, Thomas M., and Leonard D. Goldberg. "Governing the Large Corporation: More Arguments for Public Directors." *Academy of Management Review* 7, no. 4 (October 1982): 603–611.

Josephson, Mathew. *The Robber Barons.* New York: Harcourt Brace Jovanovich, 1934.

Leavitt, Theodore. "The Dangers of Social Responsibility." *Harvard Business Review* 36, no. 5 (September–October 1958): 41–50.

Lincoln, James F. *A New Approach to Industrial Economics.* New York: Devin Adair Co., 1961.

Lippin, P. "When Business and the Community Cooperate." *Administrative Management* 42 (February 1981): 34–35.

Marusi, A. R. "Balancing Power through Public Accountability." *Public Relations Journal* 35 (May 1979): 24–26.

"Privacy Issue Arouses Concern about Ethics in Marketing Research." *Sales and Marketing Management* (December 8, 1980): 88–89.

Reich, Robert B. "Why the U.S. Needs an Industrial Policy." *Harvard Business Review* 60, no. 1 (January–February 1982): 74–81.

Rosen, G. R. "Can the Corporation Survive." *Dun's Review* 114 (August 1979): 40–42.

Shapiro, I. S. "Accountability and Power: Whither Corporate Governance in a Free Society?" *Management Review* 69 (February 1980): 29–31.

Smith, Adam. *The Wealth of Nations.* New York: Modern Library, originally published in 1776.

Sonnenfeld, Jeffrey, and Paul R. Lawrence. "Why Do Companies Succumb to Price Fixing?" *Harvard Business Review* 56, no. 4 (July–August 1978): 145–156.

Tarbell, Ida. *History of Standard Oil.* New York: Harper & Row, 1905.

Waters, James A. "Catch 20.5: Corporate Morality as an Organizational Phenomenon." *Organizational Dynamics* 6, no. 4 (Spring 1978): 3–19.

White, B. J., and B. R. Montgomery. "Corporate Codes of Conduct." *California Management Review* 22 (Winter 1980): 80–87.

Wren, Daniel. *The Evolution of Management Thought.* 2d ed. New York: Wiley, 1979.

Small Business Act   entrepreneur   Small Business
small business   nepotism   Institute

LEARNING OBJECTIVES

After completing this chapter you should be able to

1. Describe what is meant by a small business and identify why some people want to have their own business.
2. Describe some of the factors affecting the management of a small business.
3. State some of the pitfalls to starting a small business.
4. Describe the types of assistance available to small businesses from the U.S. Small Business Administration.

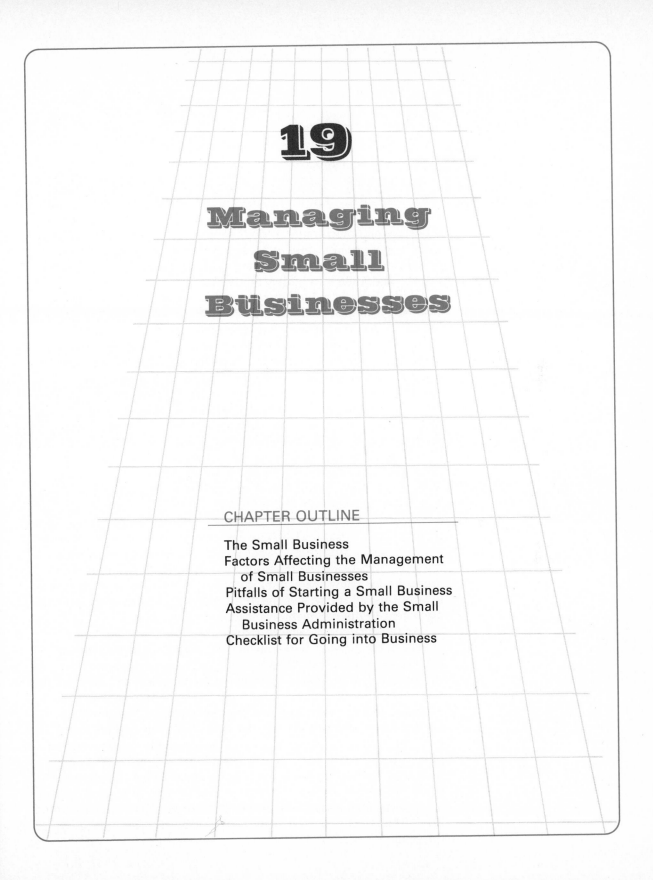

19

Managing Small Businesses

WALL DRUG

The sign says "Free Ice Water, Wall Drug Store." But if you take the exit to the little town of Wall, near the Badlands of South Dakota, you will find a lot more than a drugstore and much more to do than drink ice water. In fact, Wall Drug is more than a store, it's a service station, a place of amusement, a family entertainment center, a gallery of South Dakota history, and a western heritage museum.

With about $5 million in sales and as many as 200 employees, Wall Drug Company may be the most widely known small business in the world. A series of Wall Drug Company case studies have appeared in a dozen or more management texts. The Wall Drug case has been taught to thousands of university students, from Harvard and Stanford to Millsaps College in Jackson, Mississippi. The company takes out small ads in such unlikely places as the *Village Voice* (in New York City) and the *International Herald Tribune.* Articles about Wall Drug have appeared in the *New York Times, Redbook* magazine, *Time,* and *Readers Digest.* Posters that mimic the Wall Drug Company signs along the highways in South Dakota have been seen in Manhattan's Greenwich Village, all over Europe, and along jungle trails in Korea and Vietnam—placed in those last spots by U.S. servicemen from South Dakota.

As unlikely a site as Wall is for a $5 million business, it was even more unlikely in 1931. That year, Ted Hustead and his wife, Dorothy, bought a small drugstore in what was then a desolate crossroads town of 300 people. The Husteads eked out a living from the small drugstore for a few years, until Dorothy had the most important idea in Wall Drug's history: she and Ted would begin placing eye-catching signs next to the two highways leading to Wall.

As the customers came to sample the "free ice water," they bought other items as well—medicines, combs, and facial tissues. Shelves were no sooner filled than they were empty again. The Husteads began to expand their line of merchandise and increase the size of the store every few years. Until 1971, the Husteads remained cautious, adding inventories and floor space only when the funds to pay for them were in sight. By that time, Wall Drug included a gasoline station, a coffee shop, an art gallery, and a hodgepodge of other attractions. In 1972, the Husteads borrowed $250,000 to build what they called "the Mall," and sales jumped 20 percent the next year. The mall is patterned after the main street of a typical western town, with small shop buildings constructed of native timber and old brick. The street surface is made of rock hauled from the nearby Cheyenne River.

As Wall Drug expanded, so did the work force. The Husteads' son, Bill, was old enough to start working in 1951. The work force has never been stable because the business is so seasonal. South Dakota winters do not encourage tourism. Bill comments, "I really think there isn't anything more difficult than running a business with 20 to 30 employees in the winter and . . . 180 to 200 in the summer. It's kind of exciting and fun for the first twenty-five years, but after thirty years you begin to think it's a tough racket."

Ted Hustead is over eighty, but he still exercises authority. A caller who asks for the public affairs department is likely to hear Ted's rasping voice. The third generation of Husteads began to be heard when Bill's son Rick joined the store in 1980.

Some have asked about expanding such a successful operation to other towns. Bill's answer: "We will try to diversify within our own community." The Husteads have several hundred acres near the interstate highway. That is as far away as they have any thought of doing business. Among the possibilities are a motel and a modified drugstore. With pride in his voice, Bill indicates that Wall Drug is much more than a job to him. He says, "The place is so crazy, so different—it's the largest drugstore in the world. It may get in the *Guinness Book of Records* as the only drugstore with a church in it."[1]

Wall Drug is hardly a typical small business. To begin with, $5 million in sales is not small by most standards. Also, most small businesses are unknown outside of the cities or towns in which they are located. But in many ways Wall Drug Company is a classic small business. Family owned, the company was started on a shoestring and struggled for some years. It not only provided income, however meager, to the founders, but guaranteed employment for them and their offspring. Wall Drug did not follow any permanent grand plan. There was no corporate headquarters to set down policies and furnish funds for growth, no teams of consultants to keep the manager from going astray. Knowing how much was at stake and how uncertain the future, the Husteads were financially conservative. Small businesses in general have much in common with their larger counterparts, but there is much that differs.

In this chapter, we will define and describe the role of small businesses in our society, discuss the reasons why people want to own a small business, the factors affecting the management of small businesses, the pitfalls or problems of small businesses, and the types of assistance available to small business owners. At times in the chapter, readers might think the authors are being unduly pessimistic with regard to recommending that individuals start their own small businesses. This is certainly not the case. But individuals should be fully aware of the difficulties they may encounter if a decision is made to start a small business. Successfully starting and continuing profitable operations of a small business requires knowledge and application of the basic fundamentals of business and management. The potential small business owner should be aware of the pitfalls or possible causes of failure, as well as the types of assistance available to help avoid becoming part of the failure statistics.

THE SMALL BUSINESS

Every year thousands of individuals, motivated by a desire to be their own boss, to earn a better income, and to realize the American dream, launch a new business venture. These individuals, often referred to as entrepreneurs, have been essential to the growth and vitality of the American free enterprise system. In fact, the number of new business incorporations nearly doubled from 1974 to 1983 when over 600,000 were started.[2]

Entrepreneurs develop or recognize new products or business opportunities, secure the necessary capital, and organize and operate the business. Most people who start their own business get a great deal of satisfaction from owning and managing their own firm. Wall Drug clearly has given Ted and Dorothy Hustead great pleasure.

Small Business Act

Believing that the development of the small business is vital to the success of the U.S. economic system, Congress passed the **Small Business Act** in 1953. This act *set up the Small Business Administration (SBA) and specified the support that the federal government would provide to small businesses.* The intent of the act is summarized below:

> It is the declared policy of the Congress that the Government should aid, counsel, assist and protect, insofar as is possible, the interests of small business concerns in order to preserve free competitive enterprise . . . to maintain and strengthen the overall economy of the nation.[3]

Even with the assistance provided by the U.S. government, the failure rate of small businesses is extremely high. Statistics reveal that 50 percent of all new businesses fail within the first two years of operation, and 70 percent fail within five years. According to Dun and Bradstreet, most businesses fail because of ineffective management. However, in spite of high failure rates, a large number of people each year decide to challenge the odds.

Beginning and managing one's own business continues to be a prime motivator for many people. According to Peter Drucker, most of the new small business persons come from big companies like General Electric, Mount Sinai Hospital, and Bank of America. Typically they have spent eight or ten years as trainees or middle managers and do not see early promotion ahead.[4] There are approximately 14 million businesses in the United States, including nearly 3 million corporations; almost 97 percent of these are classified as small businesses. As shown in Figure 19–1, approximately 75 percent of all business establishments in the United States have nine or fewer employees. Small businesses provide income to millions of families in the United States.

Peter Drucker says that 20 million new jobs have been created in the last decade, while the Fortune 500 companies have lost 4 million or 5 million. He says that most of the 20 million additional jobs are in small businesses. Drucker continues, "They absorbed all of the post-World War II babies and they absorbed the millions of women who entered the job market."[5]

Women especially are setting up their own businesses. The Small Business Administration (SBA) reports that the number of self-employed women increased by 35 percent in a recent five-year period to more than 2.3 million. Men still outnumber women in small businesses, but the number of self-employed men increased by only 12 percent during the same period.

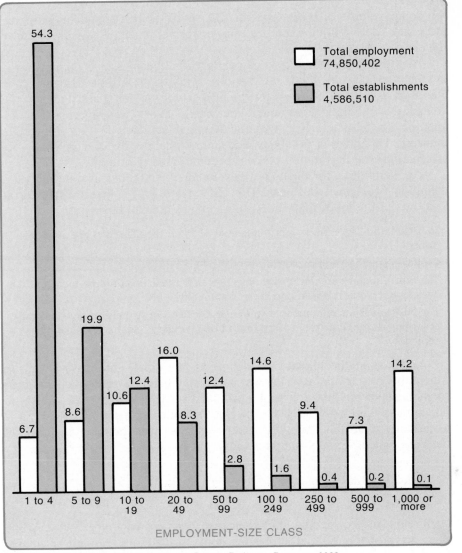

Source: U.S. Department of Commerce, County Business Patterns, 1983.

Figure 19–1

*Percentage
Distribution of
Employment and
Establishments, by
Employment Size
Class*

What Is a Small Business?

Almost every large corporation began as a small business. Thousands of
small businesses are so successful that they become a big business. For
example, in the mid-1970s, Steven Jobs and Steve Wozniak began making
personal computers in Wozniak's garage. From this meager beginning, Apple
Computer Company evolved in just ten years into the second leading U.S.
personal computer maker. Jobs and Wozniak's success story proves once
again that the American dream of developing a successful small business
can be realized.

   There is no commonly agreed-on definition of what constitutes a small
business. The Small Business Act of 1953 defines a **small business** as *one
that is independently owned and operated and not dominant in its field.*[7]
Under the act, the Small Business Administration (SBA) was empowered to

small business

set more specific criteria in conjunction with the number of employees and the dollar volume of business. The SBA has established guidelines for the purpose of determining who may receive special financial assistance under the act.

The flexibility of the SBA in classifying small businesses is demonstrated by the fact that in 1966, the nation's sixty-third largest company was identified as a small business for the purpose of providing assistance to the company in obtaining government contracts. The firm was American Motors, and the key characteristic was its marginal standing in the automobile industry. Though this company had approximately 28,000 employees, its sales comprised less than 4 percent of total industry output.

The Committee for Economic Development (CED) has also developed a definition of a small business. The CED stated that a firm must meet at least two of the following criteria to qualify as a small business:

- Management of the firm is independent. Most often the managers are also the owners.
- Capital is supplied and ownership is held by an individual or small group.
- The firm's primary area of operations is local. Markets need not be local, but the owners and workers are in one home community.
- The business is small compared to the largest firms in its field. This would vary according to the industry. A large firm in one industry might seem small in another.[8]

As noted in the above CED definition, the small enterprise is one in which the owner-operator knows personally the key personnel. In most small businesses, this key group would ordinarily not exceed twelve to fifteen people. Regardless of the specific definition of a small business, it is a certainty that this category makes up the overwhelming majority of business establishments in this country.

Why Some People Want to Have Their Own Business

Many thousands of people start their own business each year. Why? While there are probably dozens of reasons, some of the more common ones may be seen in Figure 19–2 and are discussed below.

1. A strong desire to be one's own boss—to be independent, able to set one's own direction, relying on one's own talents, skills, and hard work.
2. The opportunity to work at something enjoyable instead of settling for, perhaps, a more secure job in a large organization.
3. Achieving a goal of financial success and desire for and expectations of future profits and wealth. Earning a profit is a primary motivator for wanting to own a business.
4. An ego identification with their business. Most small business owners have a close identification with their business and demonstrate a pride of ownership. The business often represents an extension of themselves and their ideals and values. Or a business may allow a family to maintain a historic tradition of ownership of a particular business firm. For example, the owners of a large Southwest U.S. bakery firm continually stress that their bread is "baked with family pride."
5. A strong motivation for recognition and prestige. A business owner may gain

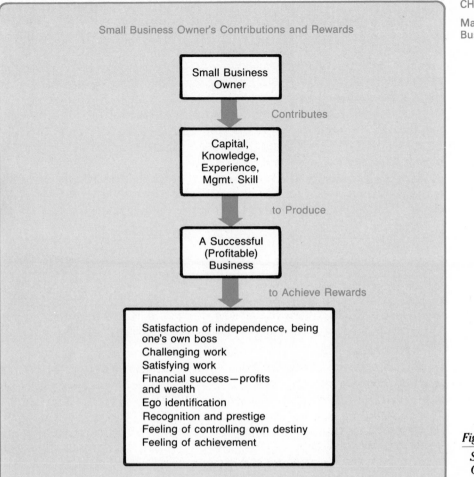

Small Business Owner's Contributions and Rewards

Small Business
Owner

Contributes

Capital,
Knowledge,
Experience,
Mgmt. Skill

to Produce

A Successful
(Profitable)
Business

to Achieve Rewards

Satisfaction of independence, being
one's own boss
Challenging work
Satisfying work
Financial success—profits
and wealth
Ego identification
Recognition and prestige
Feeling of controlling own destiny
Feeling of achievement

Figure 19–2

*Small Business
Owner's Contributions
and Rewards*

considerable prestige or status from owning and operating a small business. A small business gives the owner a base of power in the community and an opportunity for political and economic influence.

6. A feeling they are controlling their own destiny. To many individuals, controlling their own firm is tremendously rewarding.

7. A desire for achievement. One of the most prevalent characteristics of the entrepreneur is a strong drive for achievement. Most studies of the motives of individuals who own their own firm indicate that they are achievers—they prefer to set their own goals and like to control their future.

Many are surprised at how strong these motives can be. For example, it must have taken a lot for Ted and Dorothy Hustead to open any business, let alone a drugstore in a desolate town in South Dakota.

FACTORS AFFECTING THE MANAGEMENT OF SMALL BUSINESSES

The small business enterprise offers unique challenges and opportunities— and considerable difficulties—that differ from those encountered by large

There are many reasons why some people want to have their own business.

Donald Dietz/Stock, Boston Inc.

businesses. In fact, a number of factors may have a greater impact on small businesses than on large companies; a large firm usually has the resources to weather adverse conditions. Several factors affecting the management of small businesses are discussed below.

Economic Environment

Unlike the large corporation, the small business can concentrate on a restricted economic market in one locale or in one segment of an industry. But this condition is a two-edged sword. If economic conditions become depressed in one portion of the industry, the small business may suffer severely, whereas the large, diversified firm may be capable of relying on other segments of the firm to offset the adverse conditions. However, in some situations the small business may be able to choose a more favorable economic environment in which to operate.

In numerous instances, a small business may find itself in competition with a large enterprise. When it does, it often will seek to protect itself by serving a particular market segment. The situation exists for a small grocery store competing for sales against the major chains such as Safeway and Kroger. Because of the volume sales of the giants, the small stores may find it very difficult to engage in strong price competition. Factors such as staying open late, offering shorter service lines, and allowing customers to charge their purchases frequently provide the means for the small business to survive.

The flexibility of being small is somewhat offset by weaker power because of limited resources. On occasion, a major customer can take advantage of the small company by insisting on excessively favorable terms in price, quality, or delivery. It is difficult to push around a supplier larger than the small firm itself. Small businesses often find it more difficult to secure adequate financing from institutional lenders because of their size. Lenders are aware that the small business has less depth in management. They are also aware of the statistics with respect to small business failure—one of the major reasons for the establishment of special loans under the Small Business Act of 1953. However, many small businesses are able to secure a loan simply on the basis of the owner's personal reputation.

Unlike many large enterprises, the small business is typically unable to exert a major influence on the economic environment. There is usually little doubt that the small firm is involved in a highly competitive free enterprise system. In this environment, the small business that is able to maintain lower operational costs will be the most profitable and have the greatest chances of remaining in business.

Political and Legal Environment— Government Regulation

It would seem that the political and legal environment for small businesses would be no different from that of large enterprises. One could also contend that this aspect of the environment would be considerably simpler for the small business since it is unlikely to be subject to prosecution under such laws as the Sherman Antitrust Act or the Employees Retirement Income Security Act. Since about 75 percent of the small businesses employ nine or fewer people, some federal laws, such as the Civil Rights Act, do not apply to them.

There are, however, many laws that apply equally to small and large enterprises and that require considerable expertise and resources. Though the effort is burdensome, the large enterprise can utilize its staff of specialists and larger capital resources to meet legal and/or administrative requirements. The small business, on the other hand, often has few, if any, staff experts and may experience difficulty in complying with government regulations. For example, a firm with fifty or sixty employees may be required to complete as many as seventy-five to eighty government report forms a year. One expert estimates that as much as one-quarter of a small business proprietor's time can be spent on government regulatory paperwork.[9]

The severity of the problem of complying with government regulation is illustrated by the results of a recent survey of several thousand small businesses. Five of the top eight problems cited by respondents referred to government regulation, taxes, and paperwork. The study reports, "Of the eight highest ranked problems, labor quality is probably the only one that cannot be directly or indirectly linked to government action."[10]

As a tangible example of this problem, the Occupational Safety and Health Act applies to all firms with one or more employees (in addition to the owner). Basically, the approach in this revolutionary law is one of setting comprehensive and specific standards, regulating company practices and workplaces, and enforcing by citations and fines. Standards governing physical conditions and work practices are published in a voluminous *Federal Register.* Some have stated that if small businesses are required to adhere rigorously to these detailed specifications, many would be forced into bankruptcy. However, considering the millions of business establishments as compared with the hundreds of OSHA inspectors, the odds of receiving a surprise inspection are quite low.

Another major factor that must be considered is that of ecology. Many small firms have been charged with excessively polluting sewer systems, waterways, and the air. Prevailing winds can carry animal and waste odors generated from hog and cattle feedlots as far as two miles. Small laundries that bleach blue jeans have added blue water and sludge to municipal sewer systems. Most small businesses operate on thin margins and have reduced their operating costs by pouring wastes into available streams, air, land, and sewers. This, combined with the lack of expert staff and alternative production facilities, makes coping with new ecological demands a critical problem.

In a few instances, the owner-manager of a small business has found means to cope with environmental problems and to do so at a profit. For example, animal waste solids from feedlots have been collected, sterilized, and sold as organic fertilizer or converted to gas to be used to heat a home. Some laundry managers who were forced to buy a special tank truck to remove excessive sludge have expanded into the septic tank drainage business. The pressing necessity for ecological cleanup applies to both small and large enterprises.

Social Environment

The small business typically has fewer problems in coping with the social environment than does the large corporation. First, the small firm typically has only one community with which to deal. Also, the small firm's manager, being part of the local community, is better able to understand its customs and mores than is the manager of a large corporation. Customers in the community may patronize the business because they know the owners. A small grocery store may find that some of its customers will pay a higher price for their groceries because they know and trust the owner. The citizens of Wall, South Dakota, know that much of that community's growth has resulted from the success of Wall Drug Store. There is a tendency, therefore, to encourage and support the Husteads in any change they decide to make.

Owner-Entrepreneur

The key individual in most small businesses is the owner. Because of the nature of the factors in establishing small businesses, the small business owner is often referred to as an entrepreneur. An **entepreneur** is *a person who organizes, manages, and assumes responsibility for a business or other enterprise*. In fact, the small business is a natural haven for the entrepreneur. The entrepreneur is a unique person whose major characteristic is the ability to create an ongoing enterprise where none existed before. Ted and Dorothy Hustead did this in 1931 just as the Great Depression was beginning. It has been suggested that an entrepreneurial person strongly feels that security cannot be found in working for others in a well-structured situation. For such a person, security is found only in working for oneself with minimum external constraints.

entrepreneur

Entrepreneurs desire to control their own destiny and have a tremendous need for independence. There is a constant drive to remove all restrictions and threatening figures. Any other person in the small firm who appears to aspire for power will be quickly removed. It is for this reason that some small businesses fail when their owners die or retire; no one has been developed to take their place.

This yearning for security by independence demands a great deal of self-confidence. An entrepreneur finds it exceedingly difficult to accept leadership from others. Such a person often makes a relatively poor member of a large enterprise. In addition, entrepreneurs have little fear of failure; they seek risks eagerly. Venturesomeness is almost an obsession; their level of activity is steadily high. Entrepreneurs are ardent believers in a truly competitive system and take great joy in winning.

The management style of the entrepreneur does not fit well into structured and orderly organizations. The classic entrepreneur shows great reluctance to formalize structure and processes. Entrepreneurial leadership is primarily based on charisma. Such leaders have a high level of mobility. They tend to be organization starters rather than organization builders. They move from one deal to another, rationalizing their move in the name of profit. They have few qualms about severing relationships with people or with organizations. They would rather leave intolerable situations than stay and resolve problems. The entrepreneurial personality provides a highly dynamic and innovative element in our economic system.

Objectives

The objectives of a small business are typically no different from those of a large enterprise, although the priorities that the owner may place on them may be different. As we discussed in Chapter 3, the major objectives that a firm may have are survival, profit, service, and growth.

For a small business, survival of the enterprise is often most crucial and difficult to attain. A significant percentage of new business ventures fail in the first year of existence. Earning a profit is essential to long-term business survival. But a newly formed small business must be prepared financially and psychologically not to earn a profit during the early phases of operation. The profit objective provides incentive to assume business risks, and without the profit motive, few people would start their own business. It is apparent that the survival objective constantly haunts the small business. Because of its very nature, the small business is limited, short on capital, subject to competitive destruction, and often operates on a hand-to-mouth existence. With respect to the service objective, the typical small business is highly customer oriented. Whereas the large enterprise can manipulate and control products and markets with its vast resources, the small firm must be attuned to specific customer wishes and requirements. In this way it can gain a unique market niche.

The small business has the advantage of specialization by concentrating on a limited number of services. Though real estate agents often concentrate on a particular type of property, such as residential or commercial, one particular agency carved out a niche by concentrating solely on providing faculty housing in a city that contained a major university. A retail supermarket may develop special excellence in providing unusually good meat products. One small pharmaceutical company prospered in competition with larger firms by concentrating on the needs of one type of medical specialty—the ophthalmologic surgeon. The large enterprise must also adapt to customer requirements, but such adaptions are not usually as specific or as rapid.

Another basic objective of most small businesses is growth. However, there are certain limitations to growth that must be considered. Unlimited growth cannot be an objective of the small business if:

1. The owner-manager seeks to retain direct and personal control of the firm.
2. The firm wishes to remain in certain selected products or services.
3. Management wants the firm to remain highly flexible.
4. The owner does not value growth.

The personal values and stage of life of the owner of a small business have a significant effect on the goal of growth. Still, it is a rare firm, small or large, that does not prefer growth over stability or decline.

Technology

Technology exerts a significant impact on the types of products and services provided by small business firms. These products and services tend to possess characteristics that distinguish them from those of larger enterprises. These characteristics include the following:

- The technology needed to create these products and services is characterized by shorter processing cycles. This enables promptness of service and does not require extensive investment in facilities.
- The demand for products and services of many small businesses tends to show greater seasonal variations.
- Small businesses are often in a better position to produce higher-quality products than are larger firms.
- The technology used to produce the products and services tends to be relatively stable. The small firm does not have the resources to be constantly bringing out new products as markets for old products disappear.

Because of these technological characteristics, there will always be a place for small business to provide products and services uniquely adapted to their capabilities. With over 70 percent of small businesses being engaged in retailing, wholesaling, and services, it has been suggested that the most commonly needed technology is that of dealing directly with customers. Because customers are not completely controllable, this would demand greater flexibility and freedom. For example, Wall Drug can easily modify its mix of products, add a new attraction, or change the services offered in response to customer preferences.

Many small businesses were started because of one technological innovation by its owner. As the owner begins to deal with the day-to-day operations of the business, there often is not sufficient time to devote to continued research and development. The reason that caused the small business to be created may also be the cause of its failure. Should the competition develop a superior product, the small business may find itself in severe difficulties.

Organizational Structure

The major characteristics of small business organizational structure are: (1) an emphasis on informality, (2) the critical importance of the owner and/or manager, and (3) the necessity for increased departmentalization with growth. Small firms tend to operate in a somewhat informal manner. The small size permits it; the need for flexibility demands it. High degrees of formalization, in terms of organizational charts, job descriptions, and procedures, do not encourage creativity and change. The large organization must formalize in order to effect coordination and control.

Because of the size of the small business, its owner and/or operator is of critical importance. There has been a tendency for operators of successful small firms to remain in the position for long periods of time—sometimes as many as twenty to forty years. In large enterprises, a president remains for a much shorter period, typically fewer than ten years. Heads of small businesses almost always wear two or more hats—they must perform several important functions. Not only do they manage the total enterprise but almost always perform a second or third function, frequently the finance function. In some small manufacturing firms, owners personally handle the big bread-and-butter sales, placing themselves in competition with subordinate sales representatives. If a labor union is present, the owner-manager often handles the negotiations personally. If the owner has an engineering degree, he or she may be the firm's only machine maintenance person. Management problems have to wait until the machine is back in operation.

As the small business grows, the variety, number, and complexity of functions and relationships increase. The typical span of control in the small firm ranges from four to seven subordinates, whereas in the large company it ranges from five to over eleven. Thus, in the small business, communication distances are short and personal contacts frequent.

Not only do the typical small business manager and virtually all personnel wear two or more hats, they are expected to perform many activities that would normally be handled by a staff of experts in a large organization. For example, there may be only six people in a small business. One day all six may be sales personnel, the next day they may spend seeking financing, and the next day they all may be on the production line. The limited number of different departments and specialization of personnel enables the small business to operate with speed and flexibility.

There also tend to be fewer rigid or formal rules to follow in small firms. Employees may leave assigned workplaces without permission, have more flexible starting and quitting times, and have a more flexible dress code. The climate of the organization is more personalized. Names are more important than time clock numbers. It is likely that there are neither time clocks nor codified rule books. When instances calling for disciplinary action do arise, there is more individualized handling of the case. The less rigid scheduling of tasks permits greater degrees of interaction among employees.

The nature of the job assignment combined with the friendly climate that can be developed in a small business leads to greater employee identification with the enterprise. There is an excitement in being in on things, of having personal contact with managers and customers. Individual impact on the total organization is greater, and one can see what has been personally accomplished. Absence rates are often significantly lower in the small firm. There is considerably less likelihood that an organized labor union will be present.

Personnel

There are many noneconomic reasons for a person to prefer to work in a small business. While work in a large organization is often highly specialized, the typical task assignments in the small firm offer variety, challenge, and greater degree of self-control. This is why many recent graduates are beginning to seek jobs with small businesses. At times, an employee has an opportunity to carry a job through from the original idea to its introduction into the market. Experience is gained at an accelerated pace. Such opportunities provided by a small business are very important to many people.

Although there are exceptions, larger organizations usually pay their employees higher salaries than do most small businesses. Most small firms have a tendency to view salary as an expense rather than the employee as an asset. If the owner of a small business had to choose between a $25,000 accountant and one costing $35,000, the odds are heavily in favor of the former. If the owner were choosing between a $25,000 piece of machinery and one costing $35,000, considerably more deliberation would go into the decision. The owner may be aware that the more expensive machine might have certain advantages over the less expensive one, which would make the additional expenditure worthwhile.

nepotism

A type of employee that is sometimes characteristic of small firms is a member of the owner-manager's family. *The practice of hiring one's own relatives* is known as **nepotism**. In the past this has been the son or son-in-law of the owner. One writer states that the most lethal of all deadly triangles in small businesses is where all three—father, son, and son-in-law—are key people in the enterprise. More recently, a number of daughters of successful small business owners have gone to work in the family business.

Using family members has some advantages to the concern. Identification with the business should be great, thereby leading to increased effort and dedication. In addition, family members may constitute sources for funds to finance the enterprise. Bringing the son or daughter into the firm enables retention of control by the family in the years ahead. This may be a reason that Ted and Dorothy Hustead encouraged Bill, their son, to join the firm. However, if a firm rigidly follows a policy of nepotism in its hiring or promotion practices, competent nonfamily personnel may leave the firm because they see little opportunity for advancement.

Employing family members can cause a number of interpersonal problems. Family quarrels can and do spill over into the everyday operations of the firm. In one instance, the introduction of the son initially caused few problems in a small hardware business. As the firm prospered, the standard of living of the son's family exceeded that of the daughter and her husband. The daughter brought pressure on the father to bring the son-in-law into the firm. After this was done, head-on competition began to develop between the son and the son-in-law as the daughter used the firm to increase her family status. Ultimately the father was forced to dissolve the firm because of family warfare. This story is typical of many arising out of family-owned small businesses.

PITFALLS OF STARTING A SMALL BUSINESS

A person who desires to start a small business should be aware of a number of limitations or pitfalls. Dun and Bradstreet has prepared a list of potential problems that small businesses often encounter.[12] Most of the problems relate to ineffective management. An awareness and understanding of the possible pitfalls discussed below should be of value to the small business manager.

Lack of Experience in the Business

A study reported in the *American Journal of Small Businesses* shows that small business managers themselves rate "lack of management expertise" as the primary cause of failure.[13] A good rule of thumb is: "You don't enter a business that you know nothing about." Much more experience is needed than merely a knowledge of the product or service that will be provided. Experience relates also to areas such as purchasing, marketing, and finance. Many small businesses fail because of lack of balanced experience. The old adage "Build a better mousetrap and the world will beat a path to your door" is not necessarily so when discussing small business. For instance, an engineer who has a tremendous idea for a new product will likely discover that the statement is incorrect. Before the product can be manufactured, capital must be available to secure parts required to produce the item. The engineer must determine what quantities and quality levels are needed. Once the item has been manufactured, it must be marketed. A certain amount of personal selling is necessary. Thus, in order to go into business for oneself, a person should ask if he or she has the package of experience that is necessary to operate the business on a sound basis.

Sarah Putnam/The Picture Cube

There are numerous pitfalls to consider before starting a small business.

Lack of Capital

A good idea does not guarantee success of a small business. A person should evaluate carefully the amount of capital required to start and maintain a business. Often these calculations are much too low, and a person can fail before the business has opened. For instance, an individual decided to take over the operation of a small convenience store. All expenses were carefully calculated: salaries, rent, utilities, and advertising. The only thing that was forgotten was that additional inventory had to be purchased for the successful operation of the business because the previous owner had reduced inventory to a very low level prior to selling the store. The new owner was not aware of this and did not have funds to purchase the inventory required. The store was never opened. The study mentioned above revealed that "undercapitalization, overextension" was considered by the small business managers surveyed to be the fourth leading cause of failure.[14] Although Wall Drug had been profitable for many years, the Husteads had to borrow the $250,000 needed to build the Mall.

Lack of Adequate Inventory Management

Inventory represents a debt for management; it ties up funds that could be used for other purposes. Inventory mismanagement may be thought of as a double-edged sword. If a person attempts to get by on minimum inventory, customers may begin shopping at other locations because all of the items that are wanted are not available. On the other hand, if excessive inventory is carried, funds cannot be used for other purposes. Also, if the items cannot be sold, they represent a complete loss for the business.

Another major factor related to inventory mismanagement is internal theft. Often the greatest number of thefts are committed by in-house personnel. Managers of small businesses often become so closely involved with their personnel that they never believe that they would steal. There have been numerous instances where the employee was making more than the owner because of internal theft. An inventory control system should be established to discover shortages before they become excessive.

Excessive Capital Investment in Fixed Assets

Fixed assets such as buildings and equipment cannot be converted into cash easily, if at all. Sales may be increasing so the owner decides to purchase additional equipment. Additional personnel are then hired to use the equipment. If a decline in sales is experienced, payment on the equipment may prove difficult. The business may be forced into bankruptcy even though it had an excellent chance for success. The small business owner must consider this factor much more carefully than do large established firms.

Location is important

SHARPCO

Singing the Small-Business Blues

"There seems to be a conspiracy out there to keep me from making money and to increase my stress level," said James Sharplin. James is the sole owner of Sharpco, Inc., a small company that manufactures steel items for heavy equipment and rebuilds the heavy tracks and related components for crawler tractors or "dozers."

James went on to explain the elements of the "conspiracy." "The workers," he said, "try to get as much pay as they can for doing as little as possible. Customers want us to repair their equipment for less than our costs. Then they bring it back a year later, expecting warranty work. Half of the customers try to pay a little late—and if I don't hound them, they'll pay a lot late, or not at all. Suppliers try to give us inferior merchandise at premium prices—everything from paint that doesn't cover to steel that has flaws.

"And government! I'd swear half of my time is spent filling out forms, worrying about income taxes, trying to keep a worker I fired for stealing from collecting unemployment compensation, meeting with the fire marshal to explain why we don't have a fire extinguisher on every column—it just goes on and on. Sometimes I think even the equipment is involved in the conspiracy. Yesterday I was just getting ready to load a rush job on a customer's truck, and the crane broke down. Mother used to say, 'If it's not one thing, it's another.' I've become convinced that it's five or six others."

After getting all of that out of his system, James remarked that things were really much better than he had ever expected. Only twelve years before that he had left an 8-to-5 job with a local Caterpillar dealer to start his own business. Sharpco was started on a shoestring. With the help of two brothers, James built a small metal building and opened up shop with just a set of tools and two welding machines.

At first, James and his crew of two did repair work for local equipment owners and steel fabrication for a few construction firms. The company was profitable, though, and over the years James bought more machinery, hired more workers, and expanded the building several times. By 1984, sales were consistently exceeding $1 million a year, and profits after James's $30,000 salary were averaging $60,000 a year.

In 1985, James was able to move the business into a new 30,000-square-foot facility on the interstate highway. The new plant had been built from the ground up, according to James's specifications. "It seems almost like a dream," said James. "I'm still hemmed in by the conspiracy I was talking about, but I really am my own boss. And now I have a place of business that I can really be proud of. In fact, there's not a tractor dealer in town, and certainly not a welding shop, that has a place as nice as this one."

James mentioned a number of other advantages of having his own business: two of his nephews work at Sharpco; he had been able to help one of his brothers out of a bind by lending him a few thousand dollars; James's nine-year-old daughter often comes to the office and spends the whole day with her father; Sharpco has a company-paid medical plan; and there is a copy machine, all kinds of tools and equipment, and even a computer available for James to borrow for personal use.

Summing up, James said, "I reckon I work a lot more hours than if I worked for someone else, but I say what those hours are. I think people respect me, more than they would if I worked for somebody else. If I had stayed with the Caterpillar dealer, I'd be lucky to be making $30,000 a year by now. Here I am, practically a millionaire in just twelve years, with a plant that will last me until I retire—if I ever decide to retire." James settled into his leather upholstered chair behind the Chippendale desk he had bought for his new office. "I don't suppose I really have much reason to gripe," he said.

Lack of a Good Location

A large percentage of small businesses are retail store operations. As such, a major factor that should be considered is the selection of the proper location. Low rent in the wrong location may be high; high rent in the right location may be low. Factors that should be considered might be the following:

• *Population.* What is the traffic volume surrounding the store? Are the types of customers who will potentially purchase the product located within the trading area? For instance, approximately 70 percent of all convenience store customers reside within one mile of the store.

- *Accessibility.* Do cars have to cross traffic to get to the location? How fast is the traffic generally moving past the location?
- *Competition.* Are there a large number of similar types of businesses in the marketing area? The question that must be answered is, "How will the competition affect the proposed location?"
- *Economic stability.* The site must be considered not only for its current location potential but also for future potential considerations. The anticipated move of a large supermarket across the street may have a detrimental effect on some businesses.

Poor Credit Policies

One sure way to make a sale is to give credit. But small business owners have discovered that one of the fastest ways to go out of business is to give excessive credit. In many instances, credit is granted based on whether or not the owner "likes" a person. The owner has not determined if the individual is a poor credit risk. An owner may find that sales are increasing but there is little cash inflow. Because the owner may feel uncomfortable in asking people to pay their debts, the debt owed by the customer may not be collected.

Small business managers are becoming aware of the need for proper collection policies. This interest is reflected in the recent high attendance at SBA accounts receivable and credit management seminars.

The Owner Taking Too Much Cash Out of the Business

Money that is spent by the owner cannot be used to make the business grow. When a small business is just starting to develop, it is likely that a major problem relates to securing sufficient capital. If the owner takes too much cash out of the business to maintain a high life-style, growth may be stymied. Sacrifices must be made at first to enjoy future success.

Unplanned Expansions

If one store is doing fine, there may be the temptation to add an additional store and do twice as well. This growth by acquisition has often caused major problems for owners of small businesses. When rapid expansions occur, difficulties are often experienced. The manager will likely discover that running two locations is much more difficult than one. He or she may not be accustomed to delegating authority, and this must be done if there is more than one location. If the owner has been making all the decisions, efficiency may drop when additional locations are involved.

Wrong Attitudes

Let's face it; starting a business is difficult. There is a good possibility of failure. It is certainly not a nine-to-five job where you can leave the problems of the job behind at quitting time. If a business is to be successful, it will take a lot of hard work. It has been said that "success is 10 percent inspiration and 90 percent perspiration." The responsibilities of the business will likely mean that many outside interests will have to be reduced. When an outside activity is considered, the question that must be raised is, "Can I afford it?" The answer is not merely in terms of money. Personal decisions may need to be made in light of how they will affect the business. If the owner decides to go fishing, this decision could even affect the business. Sacrifices will be necessary, but to see a business survive and grow is worth the effort. The business is yours and you are answerable to no one but yourself.

ASSISTANCE PROVIDED BY THE SMALL BUSINESS ADMINISTRATION

Given the pitfalls, where can a small business owner obtain assistance? The Small Business Act of 1953 created the Small Business Administration (SBA) to provide assistance to prospective, new, and established small businesses. The SBA provides financial assistance, management training, and counseling and helps small firms obtain government contracts. The types of assistance provided by the SBA are discussed below.

Financial Assistance

The SBA offers a variety of programs of financial assistance for small businesses that need money and cannot borrow it on reasonable terms from conventional lenders. The SBA, individually or working with a local financial institution, may make or guarantee loans for small businesses. The typical practice is for the SBA to guarantee up to 90 percent of a loan that a bank or other lender agrees to make to a small business. The SBA is permitted to make direct loans to small businesses only if local financial institutions are unable or unwilling to provide the funds. SBA loans may be used for these purposes:

- Business construction, expansion, or conversion.
- Purchase of machinery, equipment, facilities, supplies, or materials.
- Working capital.

Procurement Assistance

Each year the U.S. government purchases billions of dollars worth of goods and services from thousands of businesses in the United States. In recent years, about one third of the total government purchases have been from small businesses. The SBA provides procurement assistance and counseling to small businesses on how to obtain government contracts. Specific services offered by the SBA include counseling on how to prepare bids and obtain contracts, help in getting the name of the business placed on the bidders' lists, and advice on research and development projects and new technology.

TABLE 19–1 Free SBA Publications

Financial Management and Analysis

The ABC's of Borrowing
What Is the Best Selling Price?
Keep Pointed toward Profit
Basic Budgets for Profit Planning
Pricing for Small Manufacturers
Cash Flow in a Small Plant
Credit and Collections
Attacking Business Decision Problems with Breakeven
   Analysis
A Venture Capital Primer for Small Business
Accounting Services for Small Service Firms
Analyze Your Records to Reduce Costs
Profit by Your Wholesalers' Services
Steps in Meeting Your Tax Obligations
Getting the Facts for Income Tax Reporting
Budgeting in a Small Business Firm
Sound Cash Management and Borrowing
Keeping Records in Small Business
Check List for Profit Watching
Simple Breakeven Analysis for Small Stores
Profit Pricing and Costing for Services

Planning

Locating or Relocating Your Business
Problems in Managing a Family-Owned Business
The Equipment Replacement Decision
Finding a New Product for Your Company
Business Plan for Small Manufacturers
Business Plan for Small Construction Firms
Business Life Insurance
Planning and Goal Setting for Small Business
Fixing Production Mistakes
Setting Up a Quality Control System
Can You Make Money with Your Idea or Invention?
Can You Lease or Buy Equipment?
Can You Use a Minicomputer?
Check List for Going into Business
Factors in Considering a Shopping Center Location
Insurance Checklist for Small Business
Computers for Small Business—
   Service Bureau or Time Sharing
Business Plan for Retailers

Using a Traffic Study to Select a Retail Site
Business Plan for Small Service Firms
Store Location "Little Things" Mean a Lot
Thinking about Going into Business?

General Management and Administration

Delegating Work and Responsibility
Management Checklist for a Family Business
Preventing Retail Theft
Stock Control for Small Stores
Reducing Shoplifting Losses
Preventing Burglary and Robbery Loss
Outwitting Bad-Check Passers
Preventing Embezzlement

Marketing

Measuring Sales Force Performance
Is the Independent Sales Agent for You?
Selling Products on Consignment
Tips on Getting More for Your Marketing Dollar
Developing New Accounts
Marketing Checklist for Small Retailers
A Pricing Checklist for Small Retailers
Improving Personal Selling in Small Retail Stores
Advertising Guidelines for Small Retail Firms
Signs in Your Business
Plan Your Advertising Budget
Learning about Your Market
Do You Know the Results of Your Advertising?

Organization and Personnel

Checklist for Developing a Training Program
Pointers on Using Temporary-Help Services
Preventing Employee Pilferage
Setting Up a Pay System
Staffing Your Store
Managing Employee Benefits

Legal and Governmental Affairs

Incorporating a Small Business
Selecting the Legal Structure for Your Business
Introduction to Patents

Management Assistance

More than 90 percent of the business failures each year are due to ineffective management. To prevent business failure, an important service provided by the SBA is management assistance, which takes the form of counseling and management training. The Management and Technical Assistance Programs offer such extensive and diversified services as the following:

• Free individual counseling by retired and active business executives, university students, and other professionals.
• Courses, conferences, workshops, and problem clinics.
• Wide range of technical and management publications.

Small Business Institute

Free counseling is provided by SBA Management Assistance staff and by members of the Service Corps of Retired Executives (SCORE) and the Active Corps of Executives (ACE) and many professional organizations that offer volunteer services to small businesses. Another program that has gained considerable recognition in recent years is the counseling provided through the **Small Business Institute** (SBI) program. The SBI *uses senior and graduate students of leading business schools throughout the country to provide on-site management counseling to small businesses.* More than 450 colleges and universities have SBI programs. Supervised by a faculty member, students provide consultant services to the small business and receive academic credit for their work.

In addition to the above forms of management assistance, the SBA pays for management and technical assistance provided by professional consultants and offers short courses, conferences, and workshops for small business operators. Finally, the SBA publishes hundreds of management, technical, and marketing publications that provide valuable information to small businesses. Most of these publications are free and can be obtained from an SBA office. Table 19–1 provides a partial listing of free SBA publications.

Small business owners do not generally take advantage of the many services available from the SBA, as well as other agencies. They generally rely on easily available sources like other business people, accountants, and bankers.[15] Perhaps if they used more of the professional services, the failure rate would not be as high.

CHECKLIST FOR GOING INTO BUSINESS

A person considering starting a business should carefully and critically evaluate a number of factors. The two most important attributes that determine profitability, according to highly successful small business managers themselves, are the ability to manage cash and innovativeness.[16] The SBA has developed a comprehensive checklist of questions that assist in this evaluation process (see Table 19–2). These questions are organized under such topics as: "Before You Start," "Getting Started," and "Making It Go."

Once you have carefully answered the questions posed in Table 19–2, you have done some hard work and serious thinking. That's good! But you have probably found some things you still need to know more about or do something about.

Do all you can for yourself, but don't hesitate to ask for help from people who can tell you what you need to know. Remember, running a business takes guts! You've got to be able to decide what you need and then go after it.

Good luck!

TABLE 19–2 Checklist for Going into Business

Before You Start

How about You?
- Are you the kind of person who can get a business started and make it go?
- Think about why you want to own your own business. Do you want it badly enough to keep working long hours without knowing how much money you'll end up with?
- Have you worked in a business like the one you want to start?
- Have you worked for someone else as a foreman or manager?
- Have you had any business training in school?
- Have you saved any money?

How about the Money?
- Do you know how much money you will need to get your business started?
- Have you counted up how much money of your own you can put into the business?
- Do you know how much credit you can get from your suppliers—the people you will buy from?
- Do you know where you can borrow the rest of the money you need to start your business?
- Have you figured out what net income per year you expect to get from the business? Count your salary and your profit on the money you put into the business.
- Can you live on less than this so that you can use some of it to help your business grow?
- Have you talked to a banker about your plans?

How about a Partner?
- If you need a partner with money or know-how that you don't have, do you know someone who will fit—someone you can get along with?
- Do you know the good and bad points about going it alone, having a partner, and incorporating your business?
- Have you talked to a lawyer about it?

How about Your Customers?
- Do most businesses in your community seem to be doing well?
- Have you tried to find out whether stores like the one you want to open are doing well in your community and in the rest of the country?
- Do you know what kind of people will want to buy what you plan to sell?
- Do people like that live in the area where you want to open your store?
- Do they need a store like yours?
- If not, have you thought about opening a different kind of store or going to another neighborhood?

Getting Started

Your Building
- Have you found a good building for your store?
- Will you have enough room when your business gets bigger?
- Can you fix the building the way you want it without spending too much money?
- Can people get to it easily from parking spaces, bus stops, or their homes?
- Have you had a lawyer check the lease and zoning?

Equipment and Supplies
- Do you know just what equipment and supplies you need and how much they will cost?
- Can you save some money by buying second-hand equipment?

Your Merchandise
- Have you decided what things you will sell?
- Do you know how much or how many of each you will buy to open your store with?
- Have you found suppliers who will sell you what you need at a good price?
- Have you compared the prices and credit terms of different suppliers?

Your Records
- Have you planned a system of records that will keep track of your income and expenses, what you owe other people, and what other people owe you?
- Have you worked out a way to keep track of your inventory so that you will always have enough on hand for your customers but not more than you can sell?
- Have you figured out how to keep your payroll records and take care of tax reports and payments?
- Do you know what financial statements you should prepare?

(continued)

TABLE 19–2 *(continued)*

Getting Started

Your Records *(continued)*	• Do you know how to use these financial statements? • Do you know an accountant who will help you with your records and financial statements?
Your Store and the Law	• Do you know what licenses and permits you need? • Do you know what business laws you have to obey? • Do you know a lawyer you can go to for advice and for help with legal papers?
Protecting Your Store	• Have you made plans for protecting your store against thefts of all kinds—shoplifting, robbery, burglary, employee stealing? • Have you talked with an insurance agent about what kinds of insurance you need?
Buying a Business Someone Else Has Started	• Have you made a list of what you like and don't like about buying a business someone else has started? • Are you sure you know the real reason why the owner wants to sell the business? • Have you compared the cost of buying the business with the cost of starting a new business? • Is the stock up to date and in good condition? • Is the building in good condition? • Will the owner of the building transfer the lease to you? • Have you talked with other business people in the area to see what they think of the business? • Have you talked with the company's suppliers? • Have you talked to a lawyer about it?

Making It Go

Advertising	• Have you decided how you will advertise? (Newspapers, posters, handbills, radio, by mail?) • Do you know where to get help with your ads? • Have you watched what other stores do to get people to buy?
The Prices You Charge	• Do you know how to figure what you should charge for each item you sell? • Do you know what other stores like yours charge?
Buying	• Do you have a plan for finding out what your customers want? • Will your plan for keeping track of your inventory tell you when it is time to order more and how much to order? • Do you plan to buy most of your stock from a few suppliers rather than a little from many, so that those you buy from will want to help you succeed?
Selling	• Have you decided whether you will have salesclerks or self-service? • Do you know how to get customers to buy? • Have you thought about why you like to buy from some sales representatives while others turn you off?
Your Employees	• If you need to hire someone to help you, do you know where to look? • Do you know what kind of person you need? • Do you know how much to pay? • Do you have a plan for training your employees?
Credit for Your Customers	• Have you decided whether to let your customers buy on credit? • Do you know the good and bad points about joining a credit-card plan? • Can you tell a deadbeat from a good credit customer?

A Few Extra Questions

	• Have you figured out whether you could make more money working for someone else? • Does your family go along with your plan to start a business of your own? • Do you know where to find out about new ideas and new products?

SUMMARY

An American dream for millions of people is to own and manage their own business—"to be my own boss." This dream has been realized by many people in the nearly 14 million small businesses that exist in the United States. While the freedom to start and manage one's own business is available to everyone, each year thousands of businesses fail. In fact, statistics reveal that half of all new businesses fail within the first two years of operation and 70 percent fail within five years. Despite the grim statistics, virtually every large, successful business began as a small business. Also, it is important to note that small businesses make significant contributions to the health and vitality of our economy. The U.S. government, in an effort to provide financial and managerial assistance to small businesses, created the U.S. Small Business Administration (SBA) in 1953.

The small business enterprise offers unique challenges and opportunities—and considerable problems—that differ from those encountered by large businesses. The large firm usually has the resources to withstand adverse circumstances.

Limited resources may make it difficult for the small business to exert a major influence on the economic or political legal environment. However, in certain respects, a small business, because of its size, may be more flexible and responsive to changing conditions. For example, a small firm may be able to offer more personalized service, maintain lower operational costs, be less susceptible to some federal regulations, and often is not unionized.

The failure rates for small businesses are very high. Why do failures occur? Failures are caused primarily by ineffective management. Some of the major pitfalls or problems that small businesses often encounter include lack of experience in the business, lack of capital, lack of a good location, lack of adequate inventory management, excessive capital investment in fixed assets, poor credit practices, the owner taking too much cash out of the business, unplanned expansions, and having the wrong attitude. To help prospective, new, and established small businesses avoid and/or overcome problems that might cause failure, the SBA provides financial, procurement, and management assistance.

REVIEW QUESTIONS

1. What was the purpose of the Small Business Act of 1953?

2. What is considered to be a small business in manufacturing, retailing, and wholesaling?

3. What are the failure rates for small businesses? Why? Discuss briefly.

4. What are the basic objectives of the typical small business? Is growth always an objective of a small business? Why or why not?

5. Products and services of small businesses tend to possess characteristics that distinguish them from those of larger enterprises. Discuss any three of these characteristics.

6. What are the major characteristics of small business organizational structures?

7. What is meant by nepotism? Briefly discuss how the practice can affect a small business.

8. What is an entrepreneur? What are the major personality characteristics of entrepreneurs?

9. List and briefly discuss five of the more important pitfalls often encountered in starting a small business.

10. Review the Checklist for Going into Business. What areas covered in the checklist are most significant?

11. Briefly describe the various types of assistance available to small businesses from the U.S. Small Business Administration.

EXERCISES

1. Using Table 19–2, Checklist for Going into Business, evaluate the feasibility of starting your own restaurant specializing in steak and seafood entrees.

2. Visit three successful small businesses in your local area. Discuss with the owners-managers of each business the reasons for success of their business. Ask them if they would advise a person to begin a small business.

CASE STUDY

Billy Osbon's New Business

Billy Osbon had worked for the J. C. Penney Company for eighteen years when he decided to go into business for himself. Billy was forty-seven years old. He and his wife, Joyce, had two grown sons and another fifteen years old. Billy knew the kind of business he wanted to be in—furniture and appliances. He was the general merchandise manager for the J. C. Penney store in Charleston, West Virginia. Before Penney's had discontinued its furniture and appliances in 1983, he had managed that department in another larger Penney store.

Billy felt that he was well qualified to run his own business. He had worked for years as a commissioned salesman. As a manager, he had managed other salespersons and had been responsible for product displays, inventory turnover, credit approvals, and many other aspects of business management.

Billy and Joyce had saved nearly $10,000 in cash. Their home was nearly paid for. Billy also had 300 shares of J. C. Penney stock, valued at $52 a share.

Billy and Joyce had been actively looking for a business to buy for about three months when they learned of Garvan Appliance Company. Garvan Appliance was owned by Andrew Garvan, who was sixty-eight years old and had decided to retire. Andrew was offering his business for sale for only $25,000, although monthly sales averaged about $30,000.

The business was in a rented store in a small shopping center on the outskirts of Charleston. When Billy talked with Mr. Garvan, he found that the furniture inventory of about $80,000 was financed with a local bank and the appliance inventory was floor planned by General Electric. Under the floor planning arrangement, General Electric finances the appliances in full and charges no interest as long as the inventory is turned every ninety days. Billy knew that what he would really be purchasing with the $25,000 was a small amount of office equipment, a three-year-old delivery truck, and the company's good will.

After going over the financial statements for Garvan Appliance with his CPA, Billy decided that the business was probably a good deal. It was exactly what he and Joyce had been looking for. Joyce could keep the books and help out part time, and he could be the main salesman. Mr. Garvan had said he would stay and help four hours a day until Billy felt that he could get along without him.

QUESTIONS

1. What sources of financing do you think are available to Billy and Joyce?
2. What kinds of problems are Billy and Joyce likely to encounter in their new business venture? How would you recommend that they prepare to handle the problems which occur?

CASE STUDY

Harrison Photography Studio

The Harrison Photography Studio located in Atlanta, Georgia, has an excellent reputation for high-quality photography. The studio specializes in bridal, family, and executive portraits. In addition, the studio is very active in photographing weddings. John Harrison is the owner and manager of the studio. He started the business in his garage thirty years ago, and it has since grown to become one of the leading photography studios in Atlanta with revenues in excess of $150,000 annually and five full-time employees. Mr. Harrison has earned the reputation as a highly creative and innovative photographer.

One example of this is the fact that he was the first portrait photographer to take outdoor garden color portraits some fifteen years ago. Most of his bridal portraits and many of the individual and/or family portraits are taken in his outdoor garden studio. Because of the unique features of the studio's portraits, the studio has as much business as Mr. Harrison believes he wants. He has never advertised in any form—depending on word-of-mouth to carry his message of quality photography. Throughout the history of the business, Mr. Harrison's goal has been to be a high-quality photographer. In recent years, he has raised prices considerably but has noticed no overall decrease in revenues.

There are five key employees in the business: Mr. Harrison; his wife, Joan, who handles customers and manages the office; Mr. Harrison's son, Ken, who is also a professional photographer; Hilda, a professional spotter (touch-up work on negatives and prints); and Cathy, who performs such duties as framing pictures and working with customers. Ken, thirty-two, is one of Harrison's three sons. He is very interested in someday owning the business. Ken has had a history of instability and unpredictability, especially with regard to work. He has either quit or been fired by his father several times and has not always been a very conscientious employee. Recently, however, he seems to have taken a more responsible attitude. Mr. Harrison's other sons have never been interested in the photography business.

In recent years, Mr. Harrison has been spending less and less time in the business. Several years ago, he decided to close the studio on Mondays—which meant that the business was open from 9–5 Tuesday through Friday and from 9–noon on Saturday. Although the studio is currently operating on this schedule, Mr. Harrison, who is sixty and is interested in retiring from the business, has chosen to work a fewer number of days. His typical work week is as follows:

Wednesday: 9–5
Thursday: Plays golf
Friday: 9–5
Saturday: 9–Noon (He actually works every other Saturday)

While not at the studio, Mr. Harrison spends most of his time at his ranch located about ninety miles from Atlanta. Six years ago, he bought 150 acres of land and built a large, beautiful retirement home. He has twenty-five head of cattle on the ranch and enjoys having a garden. Mr. Harrison and his son-in-law, Bob Shroeder, have frequent discussions about the future of the Harrison Photography Studio. One of their recent conversations was as follows:

Bob: John, how are your plans for retirement coming along? Do you think that Ken is ready to take over the business?

John: I'm ready to get out now, but I don't believe that Ken can handle the business on his own yet. He is doing a good job, but if Joan and I leave the studio, I'm not sure he could make it. Ken wants to buy the business but I think that he would have a difficult time making the payments. Just the other day I was offered $300,000 for the studio property by a group of investors who want to build condominiums on the land. That's an excellent price, don't you think?

Bob: The $300,000 offer sounds good to me, especially when you consider the interest income from that amount of money. However, your annual earnings from the business are more than the interest on the $300,000.

John: I want out of the big city and the pressures of the business. However, I have been able to work two or three days a week now for two years and still earn almost what I earned when I was spending five days in the studio. Our business has declined some during the past year, but not drastically. Besides, I enjoy my golf day on Thursdays with the boys, and Joan likes to come in to Atlanta to visit friends—so I'll probably continue the two- or three-day schedule for a while longer.

QUESTIONS

1. What are the present goals of Mr. Harrison as a small business person? Have they changed over time?
2. Why has the Harrison Photography Studio been successful in the past? Do you believe its current goals ensure continued success in the future?
3. In view of what we discussed in this chapter, evaluate the effectiveness of Mr. Harrison as an owner-manager.
4. Since Mr. Harrison wants to retire, would you advise that he accept the $300,000 offer for the studio property?
5. Why do you think he does not have much confidence in his son Ken's ability to run the studio when he retires?

NOTES

1. This story is a composite from a number of sources, including: James D. Taylor, Robert L. Johnson and C. Philip Fisher, "Wall Drug Store 1983," in Arthur Sharplin, *Strategic Management* (New York: McGraw-Hill, 1985); "American Scene in South Dakota—Buffalo Burgers at Wall Drug," *Time* (August 31, 1983): 8; "Wall and Water," *Guide Post Magazine* (July 1982): 34.

2. "How New Entrepreneurs Are Changing U.S. Business," *U.S. News & World Report* (May 14, 1984): 68.

3. U.S. Congress, Reconstruction Finance Corporation Liquidation Act; Small Business Act of 1953, Public Law 163, 84th Cong., 1st sess., 1953.

4. "How New Entrepreneurs," p. 68.

5. Ibid.

6. R. D. Hisrich, and C. Brush, "The Woman Entrepreneur: Management Skills and Business Problems," *Journal of Small Business Management* 22, no. 1 (January 1984): 30.

7. U.S. Congress, Small Business Act.

8. Hal B. Pickle and Royce L. Abrahamson, *Small Business Management,* 2d ed. (New York: Wiley 1981), p. 10.

9. R. A. Peterson, "Opinions about Government Regulation of Small Business," *Journal of Small Business Management* 22, no. 1 (January 1984): 56–57.

10. Stephen G. Franklin and Jack S. Goodwin, "Problems of Small Business and Sources of Assistance: A Survey," *Journal of Small Business Management* 21 (April 1983): 9.

11. Howard J. Klein, *Stop! You're Killing the Business* (New York: Mason & Lipscomb, 1974).

12. *Pitfalls of Starting a Small Business* (New York: Dun and Bradstreet, 1980).

13. R. A. Peterson, G. Kozmetsky, and N. M. Ridgway, "Perceived Causes of Small Business Failures: A Research Note," *American Journal of Small Businesses* 8, no. 1 (July–September): 18.

14. Ibid.

15. Franklin and Goodwin, "Problems," pp. 10–11.

16. R. Chaganti and R. Chaganti, "A Profile of Profitable and Not-So-Profitable Small Businesses," *Journal of Small Business Management* 21, no. 3 (July 1983): 49

REFERENCES

Bruckman, J. C., and S. Iman. "Consulting with Small Business: A Process Model." *Journal of Small Business Management* 18 (April 1980): 41–47.

Chaganti, R., and R. Chaganti. "A Profile of Profitable and Not-So-Profitable Small Businesses." *Journal of Small Business Management* 21, no. 3 (July 1983): 43–51.

Charan, Ram, Charles W. Haber, and John Mahan. "From Entrepreneur to Professional Manager: A Set of Guidelines." *Journal of Small Business Management* 18 (January 1980): 1–10.

Clute, R. C. "How Important Is Accounting to Small Business Survival? *Journal of Commercial Bank Lending* 62 (January 1980): 24–28.

Franklin, Stephen G., and Jack S. Goodwin. "Problems of Small Business and Sources of Assistance: A Survey."

Journal of Small Business Management 21 (April 1983): 9.

Gillbreath, J. D., and N. J. Humphries. "Aggressive Contracting Strategies for Small Business Owners." *Journal of Small Business Management* 17 (October 1979): 30–36.

Hisrich, R. D. and C. Brush. "The Woman Entrepreneur: Management Skills and Business Problems." *Journal of Small Business Management* 22, no. 1 (January 1984): 30–37.

House, W. C. "Dynamic Planning for the Smaller Company—A Case History." *Long Range Plan* 12 (June 1979): 38–47.

"How New Entrepreneurs Are Changing U.S. Business." *U.S. News & World Report* (May 14, 1984): 68.

"How to Start a Sideline Business." *Business Week* (August 6, 1979): 94–95.

McKenna, J. F., and P. L. Oritt. "Small Business Growth: Making a Conscious Decision." *Advanced Management Journal* 45 (Spring 1980): 45–53.

Peterson, R. A. "Opinions about Government Regulation of Small Business." *Journal of Small Business Management* 22, no. 1 (January 1984): 56–62.

Peterson, R. A., G. Kozmetsky, and N. M. Ridgway. "Perceived Causes of Small Business Failures: A Research Note." *American Journal of Small Businesses* 8, no. 1 (July–September 1983): 15–19.

Petrof, J. V. "Small Business and Economic Development: The Case for Government Intervention." *Journal of Small Business Management* 18 (January 1980): 51–56.

Robinson, R. "Forecasting and Small Business: A Study of the Strategic Planning Process." *Journal of Small Business Management* 17 (July 1979): 19–27.

"Small Business Process a Passport to Profits." *Nation's Business* 67 (April 1979): 48.

"Study Shows Companies in Trouble Invariably Lack Planning and Control." *Management Review* 70 (February 1981): 38–39.

Timmins, S. A. "Large-Firm Forecasting Techniques Can Improve Small Business Decision-Making." *Journal of Small Business Management* 17 (July 1979): 14–18.

Walker, Gene C. "Starting a New Business—Pitfalls to Avoid." *U.S. News & World Report* (July 13, 1981): 75–76.

KEY TERMS

multinational company (MNC)

parent country
host country

less developed countries (LDC)

LEARNING OBJECTIVES

After completing this chapter you should be able to

1. Describe the characteristics of a multinational enterprise and briefly explain the history and development of multinationals.
2. Explain how the external environment, objectives, and technology affect managing international operations.
3. State how the organizational structure may change when firms are engaged in international operations.
4. Describe personnel requirements and management approaches for a multinational company.

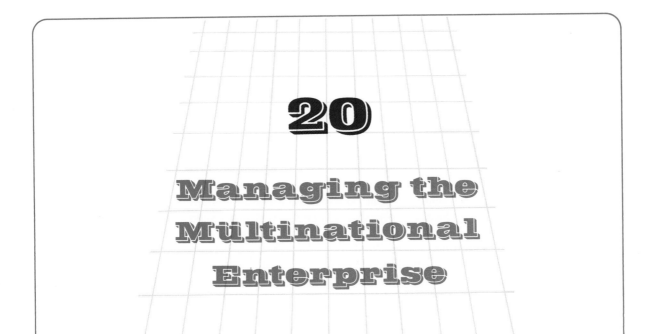

20

Managing the Multinational Enterprise

CHAPTER OUTLINE

American Motors Corporation

When the AMC Alliance was named *Motor Trend Magazine*'s "Car of the Year" in 1983, it was a compliment not only to the car but to a much broader alliance—that between the French company Renault and American Motors Corporation. Renault had purchased a small percentage of AMC's common stock in 1978 when Renault had a meager 0.14 percent of the U.S. market. Through five years of ups and downs, mostly downs, Renault had slowly increased its percentage of ownership in AMC to almost 50 percent, investing $450 million in the process.

When the alliance with Renault began, AMC seemed an unlikely choice for the famous French automaker. Renault was the sixth largest car manufacturer in the world, with plants in France and ten other countries. The company's marketing network extended to practically every country on the globe. Under France's socialist government, Renault is accustomed to being propped up whenever the need arises. American Motors Corporation, on the other hand, is by far the smallest of the big four U.S. automakers. AMC sales were sagging, the company was in the red financially, and there had not been a really successful American Motors car in over twenty years. Despite its name, American Motors was not America's favorite, and there was little sentiment for government support or concern about the company's decline.

But American Motors did have some things Renault wanted. In order to maintain its position in the world auto industry, Renault needed to sell 2.5 million cars by 1985. But the European car market grew at only 4 percent a year in the 1970s and was expected to grow even slower in the 1980s. American Motors Corporation provided Renault an entrée into the largest and fastest-growing auto market in the world. Bernard Hanon, Renault's chairman, saw another advantage, calling the United States "a fertile ground for new ideas and concepts that no car manufacturer can ignore." AMC's network of 2,000 dealers and three auto assembly plants, all operating at far below capacity, were also a major plus.

Despite its recently declining sales, AMC had solid name identification in the United States. Company executives understood the culture of the United States and offered the capability of eliminating many of the barriers foreign companies face. AMC managers were highly respected as marketers, and past failures were considered to have been for engineering and technological reasons, not because of marketing deficiencies.

The marriage was not an immediate success. There were a number of threats by U.S. lawmakers to try to prevent Renault from "taking over" an important U.S. company. Other automakers complained that the government subsidies France gave Renault would translate into an unfair advantage for American Motors. Unions complained that before long AMC cars would just be assembled in the United States, with the parts being manufactured in France, thus eliminating U.S. jobs. These objections seemed less significant after AMC lost $136.6 million in 1981, but they were still matters of concern to company executives.

At first, Renault stressed its desire to "support and not manage" its U.S. partner. After putting in $450 million in cash, however, Renault began to increase its hold over AMC management. By 1984, a French vice-president had charge of most of AMC's manufacturing and marketing activities, including research and development and quality control. All of AMC's traditional car designs have been phased out in favor of French-designed front-wheel-drive cars. The French technology has required retraining of U.S. workers. But the ingrained attitudes and abilities of U.S. workers have required some adaptation of the French cars and work methods. Because of the overwhelming success of the Alliance, Renault now controls a healthy slice of the U.S. auto market. Renault, U.S.A.'s president, Pierre Gazarian, is optimistic. "Renault has a lot of confidence in what AMC can become," he says.[1]

A company engages in international business typically because of significant opportunities beyond the home country's borders. These opportunities are usually partly offset by the well-known problems of international business: cultural differences, legal restrictions, language barriers, monetary effects, and the distances over which information and materials must travel. This is no less true for a foreign company like Renault doing business in the United States than it is for a U.S. company going abroad. The methods Renault used in taking advantage of its international marketing opportunities, while minimizing the problems of the U.S. market, are typical of those found effective by companies engaged in international business all over the world.

As recently as the 1950s and 1960s, the need for adapting business practices to different national environments was not fully appreciated. Some thought that international businesses could simply force the foreign country situation to conform to the international company's usual way of operating.[2] Today it is recognized that the challenge of engaging in multinational operations is not this simply met.

In this chapter, we begin by describing the characteristics, history, and development of multinational enterprises. Next, external environment factors confronting multinationals will be described, followed by a discussion of objectives of multinationals. Technology considerations involving multinationals will then be presented, followed by a discussion of multinational organizational structures. The last two topics of the chapter focus upon personnel and managerial problems that are unique to the multinational company.

multinational company (MNC)

A **multinational company (MNC)** is *a company that conducts a large part of its business outside the country in which it is headquartered and has a significant percentage of physical facilities and employees in other countries.* With operations in many countries, Renault is clearly an MNC. Some experts in the field of multinational enterprises believe that organizations designated as multinationals should meet the following criteria:

1. Conduct operations in at least six different countries.
2. Have at least 20 percent of the firm's assets and/or sales from business in countries other than that where the parent company is located.
3. Have and demonstrate an integrated, global managerial orientation:
   a. Resources of the enterprise are allocated without regard to national boundaries.
   b. National boundaries are merely a constraint that enters into the decision-making process; they are not part of the definition of the company itself.
   c. The firm's organizational structure cuts across national boundaries.
   d. Personnel are transferred throughout the world.
   e. Management takes on a broad, global perspective; they view the world as interrelated and interdependent.

A list of the largest twenty multinational companies is presented in Table 20–1. As shown in the table, twelve of those are based in the United States. To illustrate the impact of the multinational, a Massey-Ferguson

TABLE 20–1   The Top Twenty Multinational Companies

Company	Home Country
Exxon	USA
Royal Dutch/Shell Group	Netherlands/GB
Mobil	USA
General Motors	USA
Texaco	USA
British Petroleum	GB
Standard Oil of California	USA
Ford Motor	USA
ENI	Italy
Gulf Oil	USA
IBM	USA
Standard Oil (Indiana)	USA
Fiat	Italy
General Electric	USA
Francoise des Petroles	France
Atlantic Richfield	USA
Unilever	GB/Netherlands
Shell Oil	USA
Renault	France
Petroleos de Venezuela	Venezuela

Source: Adapted from "The Largest Industrial Companies in the World," *Fortune,* August 10, 1981, p. 205. © 1981 Time Inc. All rights reserved.

executive states, "We combine French-made transmissions, British-made engines, Mexican-made axles, and United States-made sheet metal parts to produce in Detroit a tractor for sale in Canada."

HISTORY AND DEVELOPMENT OF MULTINATIONALS

The first MNC established with a global orientation grew out of a merger in 1929 between Margarine Unie, a Dutch firm, and Lever Brothers, a British company. The company became Unilever, and it has since become one of the largest companies in the world with approximately 500 subsidiaries operating in about sixty nations. Unilever has two headquarters units, one located in Rotterdam and the other in London.

Multinationals usually operate through subsidiary companies in countries outside their home nation. Some of the names of the largest multinationals have become household words: General Motors, Ford, IBM, General Electric, and Exxon. The worldwide impact of these companies is significant. Their operations create interrelationships between countries and cultures, as well as between economic and political systems.

The economic output of MNCs contributes a significant portion of the total economic output of the world. Some economists have estimated that by the year 2000, about 200 to 300 multinationals will account for one-half of the world's total output of goods and services. In recent years, there has been a rapid growth of direct investment by multinational firms averaging about 10 percent per year. MNCs based in the United States account for more than half of this worldwide investment.

EXTERNAL ENVIRONMENT OF MULTINATIONALS

The external environment that confronts multinational enterprises is diverse and complex. The success or failure of an MNC is determined largely by how it responds to this environment. As Figure 20–1 shows, the MNC must deal with the environment not only of the parent country but of all host countries as well. The **parent country** is *the country in which the* *parent country* *headquarters of the multinational corporation is located.* The **host country** *host country* is *the country in which resides the operational unit of the multinational corporation.* A diversity of problems exists in managing a multinational. The majority of the problems can be summarized under the topics of (1) economics, (2) political-legal, and (3) social. When we add the barriers of distance and national boundaries, we can visualize an external environment characterized by great complexity, variety, and uncertainty. Such a situation requires that managers develop sophisticated skills to deal effectively with this environment.

Economic Environment

The economic environment of the various host countries is of prime importance to the management of multinational companies. A number of crucial questions must be answered, such as the following:

• What are income levels, growth trends, inflation rates, balance of payments, gross national product, and the number and nature of economic institutions?

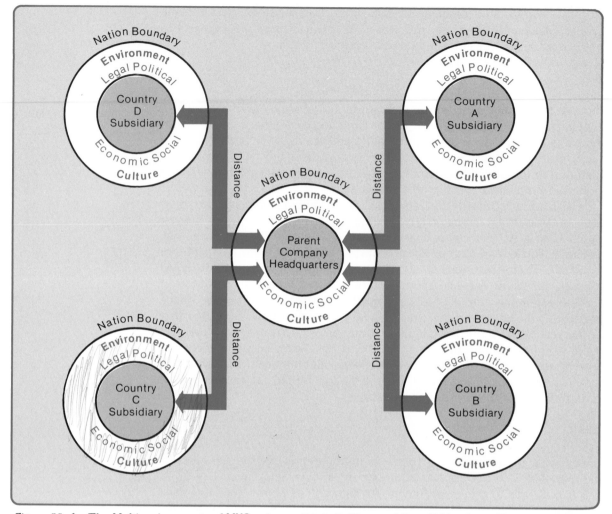

Figure 20–1   The Multienvironments of MNCs   Source: Edwin B. Flippo and Gary M. Munsinger, *Management,* 5th ed. (Newton, Mass.: Allyn and Bacon, Inc., 1982), p. 553.

- Is there a local banking and financial resource that can be tapped?
- Are there organized labor unions, economic planning agencies, and the necessary service structures for power, water, housing, communication, and the like?
- How politically stable is the country? The currency?

A major economic problem that affects multinationals is the stability of the currency of the host country. The comments of T. P. Townsend, group vice-president of Daniel International, illustrate this point: "A quick change in government direction can cause a fluctuation in the currency exchange rate and cause difficulties in repatriating profits." A multinational must be constantly aware of economic stability as reflected by the country's rate of inflation and the degree of stability of the host country's currency.

Analysis of financing decisions for the MNC is far more complicated than for a domestic firm, not only because of the exchange rate problem but for two additional reasons. First, MNCs have sources of financing not available to domestic companies. This includes the World Bank and various financing agencies set up by countries to encourage exports. For Renault, it even includes the French government. Second, doing business in foreign countries involves differing tax impacts on investment decisions. Not only is the multinational business taxed differently by its home country, but it faces diverse tax rates in the foreign country in which it does business.[4]

Generally the countries of the world are classified as either developed countries or **less developed countries (LDC)**, sometimes called developing countries. LDCs are *countries that lack modern industry and the supporting services industry requires.* The output per person is low. There is usually an unequal distribution of income, with a few very rich. France and the United States are considered developed countries; Indonesia and Nigeria are LDCs.

less developed countries (LDC)

Welcoming foreign MNCs is a common way for LDCs to start building their economies. The objective of the LDC may be to reach a level where the economy can grow on a self-sustaining basis. A substantial percentage of the MNC's total investment is located in LDCs. Often the LDC has an identity problem, which is shown in strong feelings of nationalism. Although the LDC needs the MNC to exploit its national resources, including labor, the LDC perceives the MNC as a threat to its sovereignty. When the LDC feels that it has effected sufficient transfer of skills in a particular technology, it is likely to expropriate or confiscate the business organization. The MNC must consider this risk in making investment decisions.

Experts in the field of multinational business suggest that the degree of risk is increasing. One group predicts that some LDCs will attempt to form resource-based cartels like OPEC. They also say that LDCs will make continued attempts to take over the processing and distribution of their own resources, even where cartels do not exist. Finally, it is expected that pressure will continue to renegotiate existing agreements because many LDCs are disappointed with the experiences they have had.[5]

The fact that so much of total foreign investments is in LDCs is evidence that possible returns are worth the risk. If the most important resources of a multinational are technological and managerial skills rather than property and goods, some companies can reduce the risk of expropriation or host country take-overs by one or more of the following means: (1) licensing agreements, (2) contracts to manage host country-owned installations, and (3) turnkey operations (constructing and developing the unit to the point where the key can be turned over to ownership by nationals of the host country). It is far more difficult to expropriate skills of persons than property. There are also far fewer conflicts of interests between this type of MNC and the various countries.

Political-Legal Environment

A recent study indicates that political variables are the most important constraint on multinational operations.[6] "Local laws that restrict imports and/or repatriation of profits and royalties" constitute a major political-legal barrier that confronts many multinationals according to L. R. Flandreau, vice-president, international, for Signode Corporation. The MNC must assess the stability of the existing government through careful analysis of conditions

Welcoming foreign MNCs is a common way for less developed countries to start building their economies.
Eugene Gordon/Photo Researchers

existing within the countries. Such analysis should consider competing political philosophies, how recently political independence was obtained, and the amount of social unrest and violence. The impact that violence has on the operations was highlighted by D. A. Gullette, director for administration—International Division, of A. E. Staley Manufacturing Company, when he said, "In the last few years, the incidence of terrorism in some countries has placed stress on managers, handicapping normal management and limiting the effectiveness of the person in the assignment." A Goodyear Tire and Rubber Company executive was murdered after being held hostage for six months in Guatemala. Numerous examples such as this have caused company executives to become reluctant to accept an assignment in certain countries.

Because there is no comprehensive system of international law or courts, the MNC must understand in detail the laws of each host country. The United States, England, Canada, Australia, and New Zealand have developed their legal requirements by means of English *common law.*

Judges and courts are extremely important, for they are guided by principles declared in previous cases. In most of continental Europe, Asia, and Africa, the approach is one of *civil law*. The judges play a lesser role because the legal requirements are codified. The civil servant or bureaucrat has greater power under the civil law than under the common law.

Managers of MNCs must be highly interested in:

1. Laws governing profit remission to the parent country.
2. Import and export restrictions and investment controls.
3. Degree of foreign ownership permitted.

Although the United States is a highly legalistic country and MNCs tend to carry U.S. law with them, executives must realize that other countries are different. For example, the Japanese dislike laws, lawyers, and litigation. In France, lawyers are prohibited from serving on boards of directors by codes of the legal profession. Renault officials were probably surprised to learn how many lawyers serve as directors of U.S. companies. The vastness and sheer complexity of varying legal systems throughout the world demonstrate clearly the intricate and demanding environment of the MNCs.

Social and Cultural Environment

It is apparent that the culture of one nation will differ to some extent from the cultures of all other countries. As Robert J. Sweeney, president of Murphy Oil, said, "A major problem exists because we are not citizens of the various host countries and tend to superimpose our ethics on a foreign environment." Customs, beliefs, values, and habits will vary. If the MNC is to operate in many nations, it will be required to adapt some of its managerial practices to the specific and unique expectations and situations of each nation. Attitudes will differ concerning such subjects as work, risk taking, change introduction, time, authority, and material gain. It is dangerous to assume that the attitudes within the parent country will be similar in all other countries.

Lack of cultural sensitivity has evidently limited the transfer of successful U.S. management practices to European countries.[7] In describing the process of doing business with his Soviet counterparts, a U.S. marketing executive said, "One must establish a personal relationship with the Russian businessman by toasting one another with vodka. If you don't like vodka, you are in trouble because it is offensive and appears rude to the Russian not to drink heartily and return toast for toast." Before he completed a deal in the Soviet Union, he had spent three consecutive evenings "socializing" with vodka and the Soviet businessman. He concluded, "When in Russia, one must do as the Russians do." The same is true for foreigners doing business in the United States. Renault has found it necessary to adapt to the U.S. work ethic. U.S. workers tend to prefer less direct supervision than do the French.

In some nations, authority is viewed as a natural right and is not questioned by subordinates. In other cultures, authority must be earned and is provided to those who have demonstrated their ability. In some cultures, work is good and moral; in others it is to be avoided. Building up wealth in some nations is indicative of good and approved behavior. In others, riches are to be avoided. David McClelland has discovered that the fundamental attitude toward achievement is somewhat correlated with rates of economic development. If a nation's citizens are willing to commit themselves to the accomplishment of tasks deemed worthwhile and difficult, a country will benefit economically. As previously discussed in Chapter 10, McClelland contends that the achievement motive can be taught.[8] Certainly cultural beliefs concerning one's ability to influence the future will have impact on the behavior of a country's work force. If the basic belief is one of fatalism—what will be, will be—then the importance of planning and organizing for the future is downgraded. Cultures also vary as to interclass mobility and sources of status. If there is little hope of moving up to higher classes in a society, then fatalism and an absence of a drive for achievement are likely.

In many instances, the MNC will have to adapt and conform to the requirements of the local culture. A multinational must introduce new technology and skills into a host nation's culture if economic development

What in the World Is Owens-Illinois?	A manufacturer and marketer of glass, plastic, paper, and metal packaging materials; Kimble® brand glass and plastic laboratory ware and health-care products; Libbey® glass tableware; Lily® paper and plastic convenience products; television bulbs and faceplates. We are the world's largest manufacturer of glass containers, and among the world's largest manufacturers of corrugated boxes and blow-molded plastic containers. Our consolidated sales are currently in excess of $2.6 billion, and we employ more than 84,000 individuals. We are big, diversified, and growing.
Where in the World Is Owens-Illinois?	Internationally, you'll find O-I operations in Europe, Latin America, the Middle East, South Africa, the Pacific, and the Far East. O-I is involved with more than 124 production facilities in 29 countries, manufacturing most of the items we produce domestically, and a few we don't such as flat glass and glass block. And O-I exports American products to more than 90 foreign countries.
And What Do We Do Internationally?	Owens-Illinois is enthusiastically involved with the global marketplace, and reaches international customers in one of three basic ways: through partially or wholly owned affiliates, through technical assistance and licensing agreements, and through exports.
	Each of our affiliates and licensees is an experienced manufacturer and marketer in its own respective market areas. Through our corporate headquarters in Toledo, Ohio, and our European office in Geneva, Switzerland, we can help coordinate or guide our various operations when needs extend beyond country or even international boundaries. And we can assist customers who may be facing shortages or who may be entering a foreign marketplace for the first time.
	Of course, the concept of an international marketplace doesn't mean that individual nations are losing their traditions, their local color or their identity. We recognize that international business is not simply a matter of selling the same products in different foreign

Figure 20–2 International Operations of Owens-Illinois   Used with permission of Owens-Illinois.

is to occur. Some changes proposed are revolutionary. There must be one common language and system of measurements when communicating between subsidiaries and headquarters of the MNC. English and French are the two most commonly chosen MNC languages. Despite the slowness of the United States to adapt, the metric system will be the common method of measurement.

Thus, a review of the bare outlines of differences in the economic, political-legal, and social environments of a variety of nations in the world serves to highlight the enormous complexity of the task of managing an MNC. Sophisticated and unique approaches to managing are necessary for survival and growth.

OBJECTIVES OF THE MULTINATIONAL

On first glance, the objectives of MNCs would not appear to be any different from the objectives of businesses operating exclusively within the United

locations. The people, the markets, the rules, the regulations must all be carefully considered in any given situation.

From a relatively modest beginning in 1956, O-I International Operations has expanded and diversified to the point where it now accounts for one-fourth of O-I's total sales and earnings, and employs some 32,000 individuals overseas—of whom less than 40 are U.S. citizens.

In management philosophy, O-I International Operations naturally seeks a fair return on investment, but our success is founded on long-term relationships that are mutually beneficial, rather than on short-term policies. National managers are developed not only to operate affiliates in their own countries but also to take an active part in the O-I International management team.

Working abroad carries with it responsibilities and obligations—obligations that touch people at all levels in the host countries: government, customers, the general public, employees, and partners. By meeting those obligations fairly and honestly, by exercising in our operations overseas the same good corporate citizenship which we stress in the U.S., O-I extends the benefits of the free enterprise system in the best economic, political, and social interests of both the U.S. and the host countries.

It is indeed one world, and through its International Operations, Owens-Illinois is very much a part of it.

W. F. Spengler

William F. Spengler
President and Chief Operating Officer
International Operations

States. The typical goals of survival, profit, and growth are indeed similar to companies operating in the United States. An MNC seeks to produce and distribute products and services throughout the world in return for a satisfactory return on its invested capital. It seeks to survive and grow by maintaining its technological advantages and minimizing risks. As may be seen in Figure 20–2, the objectives of Owens-Illinois illustrate the diverse goals and operations of a large multinational company.

The MNC differs from the firm that operates only within the United States because of the potential clash of its goals with the objectives of the economic and political systems of the various countries within which they operate. Some of the objectives of countries may coincide with the objectives of the MNC, and some may not. Most countries want improved standards of living for their people and such goals as a trained labor force, full employment, reasonable price stability, a favorable balance of payments, and steady economic growth.

In achieving some of these goals, there is an overlapping of interests between the MNC and the host country (as shown in Figure 20–3). For example, a new MNC in a country will usually create new jobs, thereby contributing to a higher level of employment, increased income, and economic growth. Inviting MNCs in often provides an escape route for political leaders accused of having contributed to unemployment in their countries.[9] While the MNC usually contributes to the accomplishment of such goals, it may not do so at the rate expected by the host country.

In some areas, there will be conflicts of interest. A multinational may close a plant in one country to streamline its worldwide production facilities. A company may subsidize a beginning assembly operation in Country A by underpricing component parts produced in Country B. Country B's economy in effect is required to make a sacrifice to enable the plant in Country A to get started.

If the MNC is to achieve its return-on-investment objective, some portion of subsidiary earnings must be returned to headquarters in the

Figure 20–3

Overlapping Interest of MNC and Host Countries

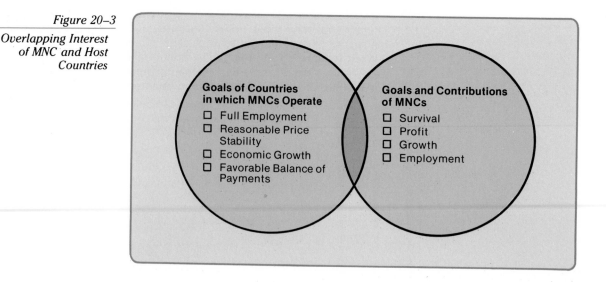

parent company. This could adversely affect the host country's balance of payments, particularly if the subsidiary unit does no exporting of its products. Funds may be shuffled among various countries so that profits are maximized in countries having the most stable political systems and the lowest tax rates.

Some of the complaints various countries have regarding multinationals are that MNCs:

- Restrict or allocate markets among subsidiaries and do not allow manufacturing subsidiaries to develop export markets.
- Are able to extract excessive profits and fees because of their monopolistic advantages.
- Enter the market by taking over existing local firms rather than developing new productive investments.
- Finance their entry mainly through local debt and maintain a majority or up to 100 percent of the equity with the parent.
- Divert local savings away from productive investments by nationals, hire away the most talented personnel, exhaust resources, and so on.
- Restrict access to modern technology by centralizing research facilities in the home country and by licensing subsidiaries to use only existing or even outmoded technologies.
- Restrict the "learning-by-doing" process by staffing key technical and managerial positions with expatriates.
- Fail to do enough in the way of training and development of personnel.
- Affront the country's social customs or frustrate the objectives of the national plan.
- Contribute to price inflation.
- Dominate key industrial sectors.
- Answer to a foreign government.[10]

A major recurring complaint about MNCs is the same as that which haunted the British empire during its heyday: MNCs are accused of colonialization. The result is said to be systematic depletion of valuable national assets of host countries with little of lasting value left behind.[11]

In response to the type of complaints noted, there have been moves toward applying restrictions on the operations of multinationals. For example, one of the guides in the Andean Common Market (Bolivia, Chile, Colombia, Ecuador, and Peru) is that 51 percent of the stock in manufacturing subsidiaries should be held by nationals of the host country within fifteen to twenty years of start-up. When the host country is extremely discontented with the MNC or needs to respond to the rising tide of nationalism, it may expropriate or confiscate the susidiaries. France gained control over its telephone system by purchasing a controlling interest from International Telephone & Telegraph Corporation of the United States and Sweden's L. M. Ericsson Group.[12] In other instances, the host country has seized the subsidiary unit without compensation, for example, the Anaconda and Kennecott Copper units in Chile and all subsidiary units in Cuba.

Although the host country has power as a result of national sovereignty, the multinational is not helpless. Its power lies in its ability to grant or withhold needed economic resources and technological knowledge. Other MNCs will observe the nature of treatment accorded by the host country, and this will affect their decision to invest in that country. Should the host country have enterprises with investments in the parent country, retaliation can be threatened. If the parent country provides foreign economic aid, this can also be used as leverage in promoting equitable treatment for the MNC subsidiary.

In most instances, the economic power of the MNC and the political power of the host country will lead to accommodations whereby both parties can achieve some of their goals. The intense emotions of national sovereignty do not always coincide with long-term national interests. The MNCs will have to alter objectives to suit minimum requirements of the host countries if operations are to be conducted in that country. If such requirements do excessive damage to global objectives, the MNC may choose to conduct its business elsewhere in the world.

Through a wide-ranging exchange of views under the auspices of the United Nations, LDC representatives have become better informed about the realities of international business.[13] Developed countries have become aware of the needs of LDCs.

The governments of twenty-four of the most highly developed noncommunist nations have developed a proposed code of ethics. Some of its provisions are as follows:

1. MNCs are not to meddle in the political processes of the countries in which they operate.
2. No bribes are permissible under any conditions.
3. No donations to political parties are proper unless national laws allow them.
4. MNCs should make full disclosure of local sales and profits, number of employees, and expenditures for research and development for major regions of the world.
5. MNCs should refrain from participating in cartels and avoid "predatory behavior toward competitors."
6. The proper amount of taxes in the countries in which they are earned should be paid. One should not seek to avoid taxes by switching money from high-tax to low-tax countries.
7. MNCs should respect the right of their employees to organize into unions.

ITT in Transition

ITT CORPORATION

ITT Corporation, formerly International Telephone and Telegraph Corporation, employs over 300,000 people, which makes it the fourth largest U.S.-based industrial employer. The company has installations in 96 countries on all seven continents. The company was founded more than 60 years ago when the Behn brothers acquired the Puerto Rican and the Cuban telephone systems and combined them. During those early years, ITT had the long-term goal of "being to the world what American Telephone and Telegraph (AT&T) is to the United States." Later, especially while the dynamic Harold Geneen was chief executive, the company expanded rapidly by acquiring hundreds of businesses of all kinds, many far removed from telecommunications. For example, ITT subsidiaries included Sheraton Hotels, Hartford Insurance, and Continental Baking. To better reflect the growing diversity, the company adopted its present name in 1983. The core business remained, however, and about one-fourth of ITT's 1983 sales came from telecommunications.

Prospects turned negative for ITT in 1983. The decision was made to refocus the company toward telephone systems and other high technology businesses. The new chief executive of ITT, Rand Araskog, announced his intention to streamline the company. Araskog also decided to place renewed emphasis on U.S. markets. By 1985 he had supervised the selling of well over sixty subsidiaries.

Traditionally, ITT was a highly centralized company and, at least under Harold Geneen, focused on short-term profitability. Each year profits and sales from each division had to be higher than the year before or managers were "called on the carpet." This created some problems with managers in some of ITT's European divisions. Many Europeans scoff at the way Americans tend to emphasize the short term, often at the expense of the long term. The company had gone into a number of joint ventures, especially in western Europe, to ease the problems of management across varying cultures. However, by 1985, efforts were being made to divest companies where ITT had less than majority ownership. In addition, ITT sold most of its French operation under the threat of nationalization by the French government. To adapt to the increasing complexity of managing in nearly a hundred countries, ITT decided to decentralize its management.

ITT faced new competition in the European market, where it had long been dominant, from its old nemesis, AT&T. AT&T was being broken up and freed from many restrictive regulations under an agreement with antitrust officials. At the same time ITT was given new freedom to compete in U.S. markets. Expanding in the U.S. market was to take time, however, and European profits were hurt by an increasingly strong dollar. Also, a new accounting rule required international companies based in the United States to value their assets in foreign countries based on current exchange rates. During 1983, ITT's common stock declined from a high of $47.75 a share to a low of $30 before recovering slightly late in the year.

ITT's decision to intensify its U.S. marketing effort placed the company in head-to-head competition with GTE Corporation and the other communications leaders, as well as AT&T. By that time, the company stock was hovering in the mid-twenties, suggesting that institutional investors, who held 44 percent of ITT's stock, had a low estimation of the company's probability of success. Sales and profits had declined from a high of $18 billion and $894 million, respectively, in 1980, to $14 billion and $675 million in 1983. 1984 sales and profits were virtually flat and analysts were predicting a 50 percent drop in earnings.

By early 1985, ITT's stock had rebounded slightly, although it was still selling at less than book value. Many were questioning ITT's plans to concentrate on the U.S. market because in a sense the United States was then a "foreign country" in the context of ITT's overall operation. On the other hand, the System 12, developed by ITT in Europe and acclaimed by many to be the world's preeminent digital communications system, was being adapted for the U.S. marketplace. Faced with continuing criticism, Araskog responded, "Our plan is to continue to sharpen the technological thrust of the company in its organization. We believe that management is best qualified to judge underlying values and realize them responsibly on behalf of our owners. . . . Our program is a viable one."[14]

Transfer of technological expertise is the primary advantage of the multinational enterprise.

Terry McKoy/The Picture Cube

TECHNOLOGY AND MULTINATIONALS

Transfer of technological expertise is the primary advantage of the multinational enterprise. Many MNCs operate in such high-technology industries as oil, tires, pharmaceuticals, electronics, and motor vehicles. There are fewer MNCs in such fields as cotton, textiles, and cement. This technological gap in other nations provides the unique opportunity for the MNC to transfer high technology from the parent country. The reverse can also be true. Through its U.S. adventure, Renault expects to tap the technology that exists in the United States.

The more important the economies of scale to be derived from a particular technology, the greater the opportunity for an MNC to transfer knowledge to other countries. If the market size of a particular country is not such that it can absorb the output of an advanced economic unit, then many nations must be interlocked. MNCs in the many small European countries started before those in the United States for just this reason. The development of the European Common Market constituted an attempt to develop a wide market area.

The situation existing within a country will dictate the nature of the technology required to accomplish work. There is obviously a wide range of environments, objectives, and technologies that would preclude any significant general statements that would apply to all multinationals. It should be noted, however, that the strength of most MNCs lies in their ability to operate highly complex technologies.

MULTINATIONAL ORGANIZATIONAL STRUCTURES

The organizational structure of a multinational firm must be designed to meet the needs of the international environment. Typically the first effort of a firm to become a multinational is the creation of an export unit in the domestic marketing department. At some point, the firm may perceive a need to locate manufacturing units abroad. After a time, these various foreign units are grouped into an international division. This is the typical structure for the U.S. multinational.

The international division becomes a centralized profit center with equal status with other major domestic divisions. It is typically headed by a vice-president and operates on a fairly autonomous basis from the domestic operations. The reasons for this approach are: (1) the necessity of obtaining managerial and technical expertise in the diverse environments of many countries and (2) the reduction of control from the often larger domestic divisions. This approach to organization has the disadvantage of decreased coordination and cohesion of the international division with the rest of the company.[15] To overcome such disadvantages, a pattern has recently developed whereby strategic plans tend to originate in the home office but are formulated using intensive communication with international divisions. Tactical planning tends to be delegated to the individual international branches.[16] To facilitate tactical planning at American Motors and to ensure consistency, Renault appointed Pierre Gazarian, a Frenchman, to head its U.S. subsidiary.

As the international division grows, it usually becomes organized on either a geographical or product base of specialization. In giant MNCs the international division is often a transitional stage in moving toward a worldwide structure that discounts the importance of national boundaries. As portrayed in Figures 20–4, 20–5, and 20–6, any such global structure requires a careful balance of three types of specialization: functional,

Figure 20–4 MNC: Global-Functional Structure   Source: Edwin Flippo and Gary M. Munsinger, *Management,* 5th ed. (Newton, Mass.: Allyn and Bacon, Inc., 1982), p. 212.

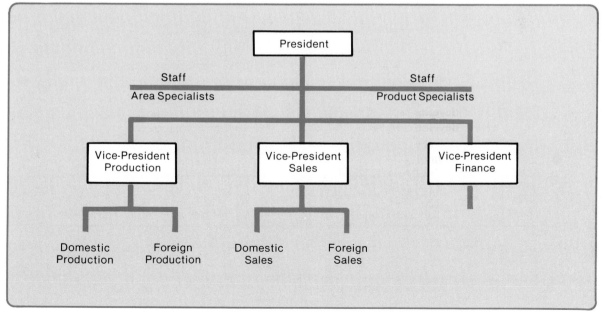

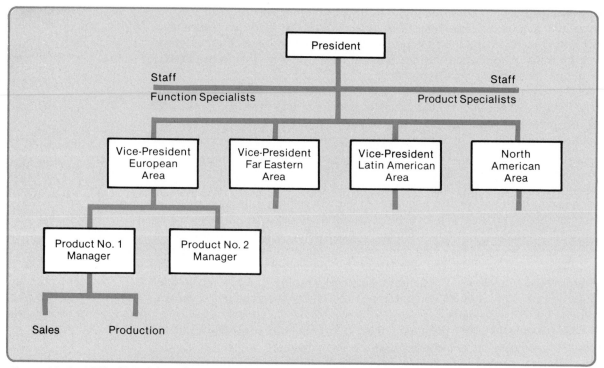

Figure 20–5 MNC: Global-Area Structure Source: Edwin B. Flippo and Gary M. Munsinger, *Management,* 5th ed. (Newton, Mass.: Allyn and Bacon, Inc., 1982), p. 213.

Figure 20–6 MNC: Global-Product Structure Source: Edwin B. Flippo and Gary M. Munsinger, *Management,* 5th ed. (Newton, Mass.: Allyn and Bacon, Inc., 1982), p. 213.

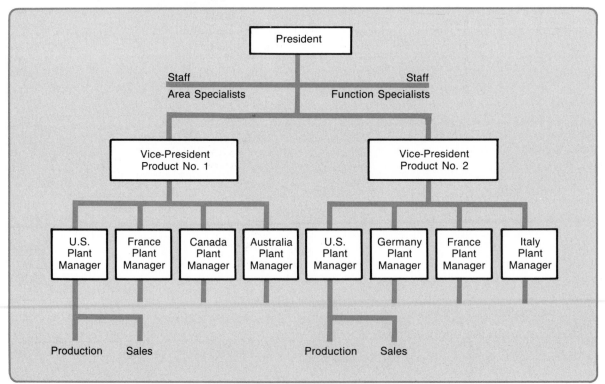

geographical, and product. When the primary base is any one of the three, the other two must be present in the form of specialized staff experts or coordinators. A clear-cut decision that is heavily in favor of any one base is usually inappropriate.

Figure 20–4 illustrates a functional organizational structure for a multinational. The executive in charge of the production function has worldwide responsibility. Together with the presidents and executives in charge of sales and finance, a small group of managers enables worldwide centralized control of the MNC to be maintained.

MNCs with widely diversified lines of products requiring a high technology to produce and distribute tend to use the area base in their global structures. This form is portrayed in Figure 20–5. During the 1960s, General Electric moved from the international division form to the global area structure. Primary responsibility for worldwide operations was assigned to the fifty to sixty general managers in charge of product divisions. International specialists, formerly in the international division, were reassigned to the various product divisions to provide aid in adapting to a multitude of national environments. To ensure that the product orientation did not dominate to the exclusion of area emphasis, four regional managers were established in Europe, Canada, Latin America, and the rest of the world. These executives were General Electric's eyes and ears in the countries assigned. They advised on the most suitable approach in each country for the product executives, identified potential partners, and aided in establishing locally oriented personnel programs. The area executive might be given line authority when a product division had not yet sufficient skill in the region or when a subsidiary unit reported to many product divisions. Though the basic emphasis is on product, the addition of the geographical concept produced a type of matrix organizational structure.

Finally, when the range of products is somewhat limited or when the product is highly standardized, MNCs tend to use the global product structure, as shown in Figure 20–6. Executives with true line authority are placed over major regions throughout the world. This type of structure is used by international oil companies (limited variety of products) and soft-drink producers (highly standardized product). As in the other instances, some supporting staff is necessary in the product and functional areas. In all forms of MNC structures, one makes sure (1) that the product is properly managed and coordinated throughout the world, (2) that the functional processes of production, sales, and finance are executed efficiently, and (3) that proper and efficient adaptations are made in response to the environments in the host country.

PERSONNEL AND MULTINATIONALS

Successful management of an MNC requires that the manager understand the needs, values, and problems of personnel in the countries where the company operates. A study of 300 managers in fourteen countries found that parent country managers had a low opinion of their subordinates' abilities to take an active role in the management process.[17] Management must recognize that no one style of leadership will be equally effective in all countries. People in the various countries have widely divergent backgrounds, education, cultures, and religions and live within a variety of social conditions and economic and political systems. Managers must consider all of these factors because they have a rather dramatic effect on the working environment.

The requirements for effective leadership of personnel in the United States, Canada, Great Britain, Australia, or many of the Western European countries differ significantly from such countries as Turkey, Mexico, Malaysia, Taiwan, Thailand, or certain African, Asian, or South American countries. Research has shown that the needs and values of people vary from nation to nation, often the result of differences in economic living standards, cultural or religious influences.

As you may recall from our discussion in Chapter 10, unsatisfied needs motivate behavior. In the United States and other highly developed countries, people's basic needs—physiological, security, and social—are fairly well satisfied. Research on the application of Maslow's hierarchy of needs theory of human behavior has shown considerable differences concerning the dominant needs of people in different countries. Thus, in some advanced countries, managers must try to satisfy the needs for esteem and self-actualization. In developing countries with lower standards of living, appeals to basic human needs may prove to be not only appropriate but the primary means for motivating desired behavior.

Types of MNC Employees

In filling key managerial, technical or professional positions abroad, multinationals can choose among three basic types of personnel: (1) parent country nationals (PCN), (2) host country nationals (HCN), and (3) third country nationals (TCN). Until the 1950s it was common for MNCs to fill foreign key posts with trusted and experienced personnel from home (PCNs). Recently stronger nationalistic feelings have led companies to alter their policies and employ more people from host countries (HCNs). Additionally, some firms have used personnel from countries other than the parent country or host country. Such personnel are known as third country nationals (TCNs); for example, one U.S.-based firm received a contract to build highways in Saudi Arabia using personnel from Turkey and Italy. Still, many companies attempt to keep parent country personnel in at least half of the identified key positions, particularly in the financial function. In general, Renault has chosen to use HCNs in its U.S. operations, although a number of PCNs have been assigned as senior managers.

Using personnel from the parent nation of the multinational ensures a greater degree of consistency and control in the firm's operations around the world. This is not without its costs because these personnel may experience considerable difficulty in understanding cultural differences. In an attitude survey of personnel in forty-nine multinationals, personnel from the host country contended that parent country personnel tended not to question orders from headquarters even when appropriate to do so.[18] This enabled them to advance their own long-term interests in the firm by getting better headquarter evaluations and facilitating repatriation at the end of their tour of duty. In addition, the common practice of frequent rotation of key personnel intensified the problem of understanding and adapting to local cultures. However, using PCNs facilitates communications with headquarters because both parties are of the same culture.

Utilizing personnel from the host country in key positions will improve the MNC's relations with the host country government. It will also enable a quicker and more accurate adaptation to requirements of the local culture. Disadvantages would include a lessened degree of central control and increased communication problems with headquarters. In addition, if the HCNs perceive that the opportunity for higher positions is blocked for ethnic reasons, they will use the MNC to gain experience so they may transfer to local national firms at higher positions.

Personnel Problems in Sending Parent Company Nationals Abroad

One of the most difficult personnel problems for the multinational is that of selecting the appropriate people to be sent on foreign assignments. Careful plans should be made to assure that selectees possess certain basic characteristics. Among these are the following:

- A real desire to work in a foreign country.
- Spouses and families who have actively encouraged the person to work overseas.
- Cultural sensitivity and flexibility.
- High degree of technical competence.
- A sense for politics.

Several surveys of overseas managers have revealed that the spouse's opinion and attitude should be considered the most important screening factor. Cultural sensitivity is also essential to avoid antagonizing host country nationals unnecessarily.

Comments from top-level executives of multinationals (see Figure 20–7) provide insight as to how their companies select managers for

Figure 20-7 How Multinational Companies Select International Managers

Daniel International Corporation	T. P. Townsend, Jr. Group Vice-President	Train and observe in a domestic position. Because of the high cost and high risk, we use only proven and tried people in our international operations.
General Electric Company	W. W. Hamilton Manager International Communications	Managers are selected internationally by the same criteria as in the United States: leadership ability, effectiveness in teaching and developing people, appropriate priority on long- and short-term goals, understanding of the business, etc. In sending a U.S. national to a foreign country or a foreign national to the United States, it is extremely important that the individual be outstanding in his field, because he will be perceived as representative of his country's best qualifications.
Signode Corporation	L. R. Flandreau Vice-President International	Selected mostly from within the company and local to the operation to be managed if possible. New hires are looked at from standpoint of marketing skills, language skills, desire for international environment, logic, personality (sensitive, flexible yet tough minded).
A. E. Staley Mfg. Co.	D. A. Gullette Director Administration International Division	With the qualities of leadership, mental and physical endurance, and a broad knowledge of parent company operations and products, we would then first screen our international managers for the skills or potential talent for these skills. Our selection process would not be limited to U.S. nationals but would also include our foreign nationals who had or could develop the necessary skills and were culturally acceptable for the new position.

international assignments. The comments of these executives suggest that managers given international assignments possess considerable understanding of the culture, history, politics, language, and business setting of the country where the operations are located.

A second major problem that confronts MNCs is the establishment of equitable compensation systems for personnel given international assignments. Typically, personnel from the parent country receive a salary plus an overseas premium of up to 50 percent plus moving expense allowances and living allowances. Personnel from the parent country of the MNC receive higher pay than personnel from the local country. This difference tends to create resentment and reduce cooperation. Many Americans have found their standard of living and social class to be considerably improved in foreign countries over what it had been in the United States. The drop in living standard when they return may make for some difficulties. An important incentive for U.S. citizens to accept assignments in foreign countries is the opportunity to exclude a portion of their income earned in the foreign country from U.S. income taxes. Internal Revenue regulations allow a U.S. citizen to exclude certain income earned while working in a foreign country provided that the individual is a resident of the foreign country for twelve months or longer. In addition to financial rewards, foreign assignments often provide career advancement opportunities.

Despite a company's intention to provide career advancement opportunities, there is still some danger that skilled managers assigned to foreign operations will come to feel that their career progress has suffered. Some managers have returned from foreign assignments to find no job available, or they are given jobs that do not utilize skills obtained during the overseas period. To solve this problem, a godfather system has been set up in companies such as Control Data Corporation.[19] Before the person leaves on assignment, a specific executive is appointed as the "godfather" to look after the person's interest while in a foreign country and to assist the executive in achieving a smooth transition on return home. A repatriation plan is worked out, including the duration of the assignment and to what job the appointee will return. Ordinarily the godfather is the person's future boss on return to the parent country. During the assignment, the individual is kept informed of major events occurring in the unit for future assignment. In this way, not only is there a logical career plan worked out, there is no feeling of being lost in the vast international shuffle of the company.

MANAGEMENT APPROACH AND MULTINATIONALS

Surveys have shown that academic research has not kept pace with internationalization of industry.[20] Much that is said concerning the appropriate management approach for international businesses must be based on common sense and informed conjecture. It seems reasonable that a successful international manager should possess the following qualities, among others:

- A knowledge of basic history, particularly in countries of old and homogeneous cultures.
- A social background in basic economics and sociological concepts as they differ from country to country.

- An interest in the host country and a willingness to learn and practice the language.
- A genuine respect for differing philosophical and ethical approaches.

The multinational company by definition is faced with a wide variety of situations: differing cultures, economic and political systems, and religions. Management must capitalize on its unique strength of being able to make worldwide decisions in the selection of markets and allocation of resources. Yet each market has different environmental constraints. Thus, multinational managers must adapt to and work with the varying cultures of a multiplicity of nations throughout the world. W. W. Hamilton, manager for international communications with General Electric, indicated the importance of the type of qualities needed by management in the international environment with the following comments:

> Leadership ability, effectiveness in teaching and developing people, appropriate priority on long- and short-term goals, and an understanding of the business. Also, a degree of self-sufficiency and willingness to understand though not necessarily adapt to local cultures and problem-solving approaches.

A Harvard University study shows that global-centered MNCs generally perform better than country-centered ones. Global-centered companies see the world marketing effort as an integrated set of activities. Country-centered ones follow the portfolio approach to their overseas subsidiaries, treating operations in each country as a separate investment. Global companies tend to think more in the long term. They are organized to achieve economy of scale.[21]

The chief executive officer of each foreign subsidiary is confronted by opposing flows of corporate uniformity and cultural fragmentation. If the officer is from the parent country, uniformity is likely to be emphasized. If the manager is from the host country, cultural adaptation may take precedence. Because of growing nationalistic tendencies in many countries, there is an increased chance that the top manager will be from the host country. In Germany, for instance, the chief executive officer must have an engineering degree to be accepted and respected. In France, graduates of the *grandes écoles* are favored. If third-country nationals are to be used as chief executive officers, varying mobilities must be considered. A married Frenchman living in Paris is almost unmovable. Most German managers are quite enthusiastic about working in other countries. The English and Scandinavians are typically willing to relocate, but they require assurance of return to their native lands.

Adaptation is not all one way. Local nationals will have to try to understand and adapt to the culture of the MNC, which inevitably requires some understanding of the culture of the parent country of the MNC. This learning, too, will require considerable effort and time. A review of literature on management practices across continents showed a trend toward similarity of management practices despite differences in managerial emphasis.[22] In dealing with headquarters executives of a U.S. MNC, the local national will have to learn to get to the point quickly. Americans are notoriously impatient with lengthy and expanded explanations. Nationals must be positive in approach and must avoid constant criticism. They must also learn to argue with the American executive but know just how far they can go.

Effective managers of multinational operations must develop a style of leadership consistent with the needs of the situation existing in the host country. The appropriate managerial style of leadership can be determined only after a careful assessment of the external environment of the host country, the type of personnel to be managed, the level of existing technology, and the specific goals and operational requirements of the company.

SUMMARY

We are now in the age of the multinational corporation (MNC). Few other developments have had the overall impact of multinationals. These firms have caused the countries of the world to become more closely related to each other. An MNC is a firm engaged in business in two or more countries. These firms typically have sales offices and sometimes manufacturing plants in many different countries. The MNCs are not only instrumental in improving the world economy and thereby standards of living of many people but also significantly affect the technology, culture, and customs of the countries in which they operate.

The multinational corporation is the type of enterprise that provides a special challenge to managers. Effectiveness in managing in an international environment requires the manager to give careful consideration to such factors as the external environment, objectives, technology, structure, personnel, and the management approach. The external environment that confronts multinational enterprises consists primarily of the economic, political-legal, and social-cultural system of the various countries in which the MNC operates. This external environment characterized by complexity, variety, and uncertainty requires that managers develop sophisticated skills to deal effectively with these conditions. Objectives of the MNC would not seem to be any different from the objectives of businesses operating exclusively within the United States. However, the MNC differs from domestic firms because of the potential clash of its goals with the objectives of the economic and political systems of the various countries within which they operate.

Technological expertise is the primary advantage of the MNC. Many MNCs operate in such high-technology industries as computers, oil, pharmaceuticals, electronics, and motor vehicles. Another major factor to be considered in managing the MNC is the organization of the firm. The organizational structure of an MNC must be designed to meet the needs of the international environment. Such a structure may differ significantly from the company's domestic operations.

Successful management of an MNC requires that the manager understand the needs, values, and problems of personnel in the countries where the company operates. Management must recognize that no one style of leadership will be equally effective in all countries. People in various countries have widely divergent backgrounds, educations, cultures, and religions and live in a variety of social conditions and economic and political systems.

Effective managers of MNCs must develop a style of leadership consistent with the needs of the situation existing in the host country. The appropriate managerial style of leadership can be determined only after careful assessment of the external environment of the host country, the type of personnel to be managed, the level of existing technology, and the specific goals and operational requirements of the company.

REVIEW QUESTIONS

1. What is a multinational corporation? List three of the major criteria used to classify multinationals.

2. List the major factors affecting the management of multinationals.

3. Describe two major economic problems that often confront multinationals.

4. Distinguish between developed and less developed countries.

5. How does the political-legal environment affect the MNC?

6. What specific types of laws or local regulations must a multinational corporation be concerned with?

7. How may the objectives of the MNC differ from domestic firms?

8. Identify five of the more typical complaints host countries have against MNCs.

9. Describe the types of personnel used by MNCs and any potential problems with these personnel.

EXERCISES

1. Assume that you have agreed to accept a position in the international division of General Electric and have been assigned to the Helsinki, Finland, office effective in sixty days. You are married and have a six-year-old daughter. What would you do to prepare yourself and your family for this assignment?

2. If you were selecting personnel to be sent on international assignments, what qualities, experience, and characteristics would you look for in prospective personnel?

CASE STUDY

The Case of the Missing Ads

When several Americans came to work as department heads at one of the largest Japanese automotive firms in the United States, they had all been reading extensively on Japanese methods. Most of them had come from a major American automotive company, and all had had long experience in the industry. Inevitably, under the pressure of business in this fast-growing organization, they turned instinctively to their accustomed Western management techniques. They looked to the Japanese nationals at the top levels of the organization to give them direction, objectives, and priorities. But nothing was forthcoming; the Japanese were waiting patiently for initiatives from them.

After a time, on the Americans' initiative, an organization chart was drawn up in an effort to settle where the authority and responsibility for decisions rested. It was a thoroughly American document, showing in neat boxes the various departments—parts, service, sales, marketing, planning, and so on—and the vertical relationships, with the Japanese president at the top and the lowest sub-department on the bottom. The Japanese, who rarely draw up organization charts (and who, if they do, invariably make them read horizontally, like a flow chart), tolerated the American version as a "when in Rome" accommodation. But the chart did not solve the problems; the organization was not functioning well, and decisions were not being made.

For example, there was the simple problem of timing the availability of advertising media for the introduction of new models each year. In the U.S. market this occurs in October; in Japan, new models are introduced in January. From the

Source: Reprinted by permission of the *Harvard Business Review.* Excerpt from "The Case of the Missing Ads" by Richard Tanner Johnson and William G. Ouchi (September/October 1974). Copyright © 1974 by the President and Fellows of Harvard College; all rights reserved.

parent company in Japan, the advertising materials consistently arrived two to three months late for the introduction of new models. Year after year, the U.S. distributors complained about the delay. The American heads of the sales and advertising departments took the problem up the chain of command and requested their Japanese president to contact Japan and straighten the matter out. The president did contact Japan—but the problem remained.

By chance, other developments in the organization provided an opportunity for overcoming the difficulty. Beginning in the early 1970s top management began to assign a Japanese "coordinator" to each American department head. The coordinators, usually promising young executives in training for international assignments, were to become acquainted with U.S. business practices. It was not long before they began observing with dismay that the American managers tended to concentrate on their functional roles and to expect coordination between functions to occur at the senior management levels—as is the practice in many U.S. companies. To the Japanese, it appeared, as one put it, "as if the various departments were separate companies, all competing against each other."

As inveterate communicators, some coordinators began to pick up problems that cropped up in one department and share them with their counterparts in other departments. In this roundabout way, the Americans learned what their colleagues were doing. Coordination between departments improved.

Soon the Japanese coordinators became aware of the difficulties typified by the late arrival of the advertising materials. True to their training in U.S. companies, the Americans were sending a report on every problem up the chain of command. Japanese top management in the United States would listen to each complaint, then send the American manager back for "more information." Translated, this meant "Come back with a proposal." Not comprehending, the Americans became increasingly impatient and frustrated. Occasionally, as in the case of the ads, the problems became so serious that the Americans insisted they be reported to Japan. The Japanese president obliged them, but the parent company remained unresponsive. The reason was simple: since Japanese organizations are unaccustomed to dealing with problems from the top down, the Tokyo organization did not know how to handle a letter from the president of the Japanese subsidiary in the United States to the president of the parent company in Japan.

Once the coordinators understood the nature of the difficulty, remedying the advertising materials lag and similar problems was easy. A coordinator would simply pick up the telephone and call somebody at his managerial level in Tokyo. In a few days an answer would come back—and in this manner the matter of the ads was resolved.

The coordinators took some time—and the American department heads a somewhat longer time—to realize that the neat boxes in the organization chart were not interacting. By U.S. standards, the Americans were doing a good job. But without American superiors to make decisions and weave the organization together, they found that their effectiveness was diminished. To bridge the gap in managerial styles, the coordinators created a shadow organization. In this manner they not only solved the coordination problem but also involved the parent organization.

QUESTIONS

1. Identify the major factors that affect U.S. managers working for this MNC.
2. Why do you believe the informal organization was so important in the solution of this problem?

Mark is Transferred Overseas

In college, Mark Hammer majored in industrial management and was considered by his teachers and peers to be one of the best all-around students to graduate from Midwest State University. Mark not only took the required courses in business, but he also acquired a minor in foreign language. The language that Mark concentrated on the most was French, and he became quite fluent in the language.

After graduation, Mark took an entry-level management training position with Tuborg International, a multinational corporation with offices and factories in thirty countries, including the United States. Mark's first assignment was in a plant in New York. His supervisors quickly identified Mark for his ability to get the job done and still maintain rapport with subordinates, peers, and superiors. In only three years, Mark had advanced from a manager trainee to the position of assistant plant superintendent.

After two years in this position, Mark was called into the superintendent's office one day and told that he had been identified as being ready for a foreign assignment. The move would mean a promotion and the location of the plant was in a small industrialized region in France. One of the reasons that Mark had been chosen for France was his knowledge of French. Mark was excited, and he wasted no time in making the necessary preparations for the new assignment.

Prior to arriving at the plant in France, Mark took considerable time to review his books in the French language. He was surprised at how quickly the use of the language came back to him. He thought that there wouldn't be any major difficulties in making the transition from the United States to France. But on arriving, Mark rapidly discovered that there were to be problems. The small industrialized community where Mark's plant was located did not speak the "pure" French that he had learned. There were many slang expressions that meant one thing to Mark but had an entirely different meaning to the employees of the plant.

While meeting with several of the employees a week after arriving, one of the workers said something to Mark that he interpreted as very uncomplimentary (in actuality, the employee had greeted him by saying a rather risqué expression but in a different tone than he had known before). All of the other employees interpreted the expression to be merely a friendly greeting. Mark's disgust was evident, and as time went by, this type of instance occurred a few more times, and the other employees began to limit their conversation with Mark. In only one month, Mark managed to virtually completely isolate himself from the workers within the plant. He became disillusioned and thought about asking to be relieved from the assignment.

QUESTIONS

1. What problems had Mark not anticipated when he took the assignment?
2. How could the company have assisted Mark to reduce the difficulties that he confronted?
3. Do you believe the situation that Mark confronted is typical of an American going to a foreign assignment? Discuss.

NOTES

1. This story is a composite taken from a number of published sources, including: "Battling for Survival," *Time* (February 1, 1982): 57; "AMC Turns to Renault for More," *New York Times,* January 29, 1984, p. F1; *American Motor Corporation, Annual Report—1981;* "France Makes Renault Its Model," *Business Week* (May 31, 1982): 48–

57; "French Automakers' Lonely Slump," *Fortune* (November 28, 1983): 121–126; and several articles from *The Wall Street Journal.*

2. Geert Hofstede, "The Cultural Relativity of Organizational Practices and Theories," *Journal of International Business Studies* 24 (Fall 1983): 75.

3. Robert W. Stevens, "Scanning the Multinational Firm," *Business Horizon* 14 (June 1971): 53.

4. Joseph D. Vinso, "Financial Planning for the Multinational Corporation with Multiple Goals," *Journal of International Business Studies* 13 (Winter 1982): 57.

5. Peter Wright, David Townsend, Jerry Kinard, and Joe Iverstine, "The Developing World to 1990: Trends and Implications for Multinational Business," *Long Range Planning* 15, no. 4 (1982): 122.

6. Hofstede, "Cultural Relativity," pp. 75–76.

7. Ibid., p. 89.

8. David D. McClelland, *The Achieving Society* (Princeton, N.J.: Van Nostrand, 1961).

9. J. O. Enitame. "Do Multinationals Create Wealth?" *International Management* 37 (January 1983): 48.

10. R. Hal Mason, "Conflicts Between Host Countries and Multinational Enterprise." Copyright (C) 1974 by the Regents of the University of California. Reprinted from *California Management Review,* volume XVII, no. 1, pp. 6 and 7, by permission of the Regents.

11. Wright et al., "Developing World," p. 119.

12. "France Seizing Control of Technical Industries," *Business Week* (May 17, 1976): 47.

13. David Morton, "Why Multinationals Are Positive Links between 'North' and 'South,'" *International Management* 37 (August 1982): 36.

14. "ITT's Big Gamble," *Business World* (October 22, 1984): 114–122; "The Troubles That Led to ITT's Dividend Shocker," *Business World* (July 23, 1984): 77; David Pauly, "ITT: A Struggling Giant," *Newsweek* (January 2, 1984): 49–50; ITT Corporation, *Annual Reports* (various issues); *Moody's Industrial Manual* (various issues); Standard & Poor's Corporation, *Standard NYSE Stock Reports* (various issues); and numerous articles from *The Wall Street Journal.*

15. L. Drake Rodman and Lee M. Caudill, "Management of Large Multinationals: Trends and Future Challenges," *Business Horizons* 19 (December, 1976): 19.

16. Narendra K. Sethi, "Strategic Planning System for Multinational Companies," *Long Range Planning* 15 (June 1982): 81–82.

17. Abdulrahman Al-Jafary and A. T. Hollingsworth, "Practices in the Arabian Gulf Region," *Journal of International Business Studies* 14 (Fall 1983): 144.

18. Yoram Zeira, "Overlooked Personnel Problems of Multinational Corporations," *Columbia Journal of World Business* 10 (Summer 1975): 96–103.

19. David M. Noer, "Integrating Foreign Service Employees to Home Organization: The Godfather Approach," *Personnel Journal* 53 (January 1974): 45–50.

20. Nancy J. Adler, "The Ostrich and the Trend," *Academy of Management Review* 8 (April 1983): 231.

21. Michael Porter, "Why Global Businesses Perform Better," *International Management* 38 (January 1983): 40.

22. Al-Jafary and Hollingsworth, "Practices," p. 144.

REFERENCES

Adler, Nancy J. "The Ostrich and the Trend." *Academy of Management Review* 8 (April 1983): 231.

Al-Jafary, Abdulrahman, and A. T. Hollingsworth. "Practices in the Arabian Gulf Region." *Journal of International Business Studies* 14 (Fall 1983): 144.

Alpander, Guvenc G. "Multinational Corporations: Home-based Affiliate Relations." *California Management Review* 20, no. 3 (Spring 1978): 47–56.

Capstick, R. "The Perils of Manufacturing Abroad." *International Management* 33 (March 1978): 43–46.

Davis, S. M. "Trends in the Organization of Multinational Corporations." *Columbia Journal of World Business* 11 (Summer 1976): 54–71.

Enitame, J. O. "Do Multinationals Create Wealth?" *International Management* 37 (January 1983): 48.

Frank, Victor H., Jr. "Living with Price Control Abroad." *Harvard Business Review* 62 (March–April 1984): 137.

Galbraith, J. K. "The Defense of the Multinational Company." *Harvard Business Review* 56 (March 1978): 83–93.

———, and A. Edstrom. "International Transfer of Managers: Some Important Policy Considerations." *Columbia Journal of World Business* 11 (Summer 1976): 100–112.

Ghymn, K. I., and T. H. Bates. "Consequences of MNC Strategic Planning: An Empirical Case Study." *Management International Review* 17 (1977): 83–91.

Herbert, Theodore T. "Strategy and Multinational Organization Structure: An Interorganizational Relationships Perspective." *Academy of Management Review* 9, no. 2 (1984): 259–271.

Hofstede, Geert. "The Cultural Relativity of Organizational Practices and Theories." *Journal of International Business Studies* 24 (Fall 1983): 75–90.

Lawrence, Paul R., Harvey F. Kolodny, and Stanley M. Davis. "The Human Side of the Matrix." *Organizational Dynamics* 6, no. 1 (Summer 1977): 43–61.

May, W. F. "Between Ideology and Interdependence." *California Management Review* 19 (Summer 1977): 88–90.

Mitchell, J., and A. Shawn. "All Multinationals Aren't the Same." *Financial World* (January 1, 1977): 36.

Morton, David. "Why Multinationals Are Positive Links between 'North' and 'South,' " *International Management* 37 (August 1982): 36.

Pohlman, R. A. "Policies of Multinational Firms: A Survey." *Business Horizons* 19 (December 1976): 14–18.

Prahalad, C. K. "Strategic Choices in Diversified MNC's." *Harvard Business Review* 54 (July 1976): 67–78.

Sethi, Narendra K. "Strategic Planning System for Multinational Companies." *Long Range Planning* 15 (June 1982): 81–82.

Sparkman, J. "Economic Interdependence and the International Corporation." *California Management Review* 20 (Fall 1977): 88–92.

Vernon, R. "Multinational Enterprises and National Governments: An Uneasy Relationship." *Columbia Journal of World Business* 11 (Summer 1976): 9–16.

Vinso, Joseph D. "Financial Planning for the Multinational Corporation with Multiple Goals." *Journal of International Business Studies* 13 (Winter 1982): 43–58.

Wright, Peter, David Townsend, Jerry Kinard, and Joe Iverstine. "The Developing World to 1990: Trends and Implications for Multinational Business." *Long Range Planning* 15, no. 4 (1982): 116–125.

Zeira, Y. "Management Development in Ethnocentric Multinational Corporations." *California Management Review* 18 (Summer 1976): 34–42.

———, and E. Harari. "Managing Third Country Nationals in Multinational Corporations." *Business Horizons* 18 (October 1977): 83–88.

MANVILLE CORPORATION

On August 26, 1982, Manville Corporation, formerly Johns-Manville, filed for protection under Chapter 11 of the bankruptcy law. This climaxed an eighty-year history during which Manville had grown to one of the largest, most prestigious U.S. industrial corporations.

The founder of what was to become Manville Corporation, Henry Ward Johns, built a sizable fortune in the late 1800s mining asbestos and inventing new uses for it. He died in 1898 of "dust pthisis pneumonitis," now called asbestosis. By the 1930s, it was clear that the problem of breathing asbestos dust was serious. Nearly fifty years later, a federal appeals court concluded, "The unpalatable facts are that in the twenties and thirties the hazards of working with asbestos were recognized." By 1930, however, Manville was the largest producer of asbestos, and new uses were being found for the product every year. It was eventually used in most automobiles, school buses, hospitals, schools, factories, and commercial facilities. Asbestos filled the bill anywhere a fireproof and permanent fibrous material was needed.

Manville successfully defended lawsuits brought by asbestos victims beginning in the 1920s. In 1934 Manville's chief lawyer wrote, "[It] is only within a comparatively recent time that asbestosis has been recognized by the medical and scientific professions as a disease—in fact [this has been] one of our principal defenses."

Manville opposed publication of information about asbestos dangers during 1934. A Manville executive wrote in 1934, "I quite agree that our interests are best served by having asbestosis receive the minimum of publicity." He was writing to another asbestos industry executive about a letter from the editor of *Asbestos*, an industry trade journal. The editor had written, "Always you have requested that for obvious reasons, we publish nothing, and, naturally your wishes have been respected."

In 1950, Manville's chief physician reported to top management that all but 4 of 708 asbestos workers he had studied had evidence of lung damage. Of the 7 who had the most severe conditions, the physician wrote, "The fibrosis of this disease is irreversible and permanent. . . . It is felt that [they] should not be told of [their] condition so that [they] can live and work in peace and the company can benefit from [their] many years experience." Efforts were made during the 1950s to clean the air breathed by Manville workers, but the dangers to users and installers of asbestos products were concealed. The physician mentioned above later told of his unsuccessful efforts to have warning labels placed on asbestos products in the early 1950s.

Until an extensive study in 1964 resulted in public awareness of the problem, Manville placed no warnings on the thousands of tons of asbestos fiber it distributed worldwide. Even after 1964, the Manville label simply stated, "Inhalation of asbestos in excessive quantities over long periods of time may be harmful." With increasing public attention, however, substitute products began to be found, and asbestos use declined precipitously after about 1975.

Asbestos had always been very profitable for Manville. It became even more profitable as competitors left the industry on discovering the disaster they had helped to create. In 1976, although asbestos fiber constituted only 12 percent of Manville's sales, it accounted for 51 percent of operating profit. As asbestos use in the United States declined by one-half and as thousands of asbestos victims began filing increasingly successful lawsuits, Manville management tried to diversify into other products. Manville bought dozens of small companies and eventually purchased the huge Olinkraft Corporation, a paper company in West Monroe, Louisiana. Nothing worked. With an entrenched and elderly management team and with the easy profits from asbestos rapidly disappearing, Manville was unable to keep net income from collapsing. Inflation-corrected earnings declined steadily from 1978 onward, to a $223 million loss in 1982.

By 1982, potential asbestos liabilities were estimated by Manville to exceed $2 billion and by others to be many times that. Through legal maneuvering, the company was able to delay payment of practically all of the asbestos judgments. The Chapter 11 filing in August 1982 stopped the asbestos lawsuits.

As receivables flowed in and debt no longer had to be paid, the company received over $300 million in extra cash. The bankruptcy filing also secured for Manville top managers a few more years of respectability, extensive corporate benefits, and half-million-dollar annual salaries.

Fifteen thousand or more asbestos victims and their families waited for the cumbersome Chapter 11 process to end, although most admitted that their claims were unlikely to be paid anyway. And each month, hundreds more discovered that they had asbestosis or, worse, mesothelioma, a rapidly growing and always fatal cancer caused by asbestos.

Manville's unrepentant lawyer-chief executive, J. A. McKinney, who had been with the company for over thirty years, disclaimed responsibility. He wrote, "There has been no cover-up. . . . Your corporation has acted honorably." In late 1983, the company began an extensive public relations and lobbying effort aimed at getting government to protect Manville and help pay for the asbestos injuries. Then Manville filed its proposed reorganization plan with the bankruptcy court. The plan provided for a surviving corporation, Manville II, which would keep the assets of the old company but be immune from asbestos lawsuits.

QUESTIONS

1. Why do you believe Manville executives chose to suppress publicity about asbestosis? Defend or oppose their action.

2. Discuss the ethics involved in J. A. McKinney's statement that the corporation has acted honorably. Should Manville have been allowed to seek protection under the U.S. bankruptcy code? Why or why not?

Glossary

ABC inventory method: The classification of inventory items for control purposes into three categories according to unit costs and number of items kept on hand. (15)

acceptance sampling: The inspection of a portion of the output or input of a process to determine acceptability. (15)

accountability: Any means of ensuring that the person who is supposed to do a task actually performs it and does so correctly. (7)

action planning: The establishment of performance objectives and standards for individuals. (3)

activity trap: The tendency described by George Odiorne of some managers and employees to become so enmeshed in carrying out activities that they lose sight of the reasons for what they are doing. (3)

arbitration: A process in which a dispute between two parties is submitted to a third party to make a binding decision. (13)

artificial intelligence (AI): The field of information technology that attempts to simulate human cognitive processes, such as learning, reasoning, problem solving, and natural language communication. (5)

authority: The right to decide, to direct others to take action, or to perform certain duties in achieving organizational goals. (7)

autocratic leader: A person who tells subordinates what to do and expects to be obeyed without question. (11)

backward integration: A company's taking control of any of the sources of its inputs, including raw materials and labor. (4)

behavioral school of management: The approach to management thought that is primarily concerned with human psychology, motivation, and leadership as distinct from simple mechanical efficiency. (1)

body language: A nonverbal method of communication in which physical actions such as motions, gestures, and facial expressions convey thoughts and emotions. (12)

brainstorming: An idea-generating technique wherein a number of persons present alternatives without regard to questions of feasibility or practicality. (5)

break-even analysis: An approach used to determine the amount of a particular product that must be sold if the firm is to generate enough revenue to cover costs. (17)

budget: A statement of planned allocation of resources expressed in financial or numerical terms. (15)

business ethics: The application of ethical principles to business relationships and activities. (18)

CPM (critical path method): A planning and control technique that involves the display of a complex project as a network with one time estimate used for each step in the project. (15)

capital budget: A statement of planned expenditures of funds for facilities and equipment. (15)

Numbers in parentheses refer to the chapters in which the terms are defined.

carrying costs: The expenses associated with maintaining and storing the products before they are sold or used. (15)

centralization: The degree to which authority is retained by higher-level managers within an organization rather than being delegated. (7)

chain of command: The line along which authority flows from the top of the organization to any individual. (7)

change agent: The person who is responsible for ensuring that the planned change in OD (organizational development) is properly implemented. (13)

classical school of management: The approach to management thought that arose mainly from efforts between 1900 and 1940 to provide a rational and scientific basis for the management of organizations. (1)

cohesiveness: The degree of attraction that the group has for each of its members. (8)

committee: A group of people assigned to work together to do something not included in their regular jobs. (7)

communication: The transfer of information, ideas, understanding, or feelings between people. (1, 12)

communication channels: The means by which information is transmitted. (12)

comparable worth: The concept that pay for a given job should be determined by the amount of skill and effort required in the performance of a job. (9)

compensation: All rewards individuals receive as a result of their employment. (9)

concentric diversification: The development of businesses related to the firm's current businesses. (4)

conceptual skill: The ability to comprehend abstract or general ideas and apply them to specific situations. (1)

conflict: Antagonism or opposition between or among persons. (13)

conglomerate diversification: The development of businesses unrelated to the firm's current businesses. (4)

consideration: The extent to which leaders have relationships with subordinates characterized by mutual trust, respect, and consideration of employees' ideas and feelings. (11)

constraint function: A mathematical statement of a restriction or limitation involved in a linear programming problem. (17)

contact chart: A diagram showing various individuals in the organization and the numbers of interactions they have with others. (8)

contingency planning: The development of different plans to be placed in effect if certain events occur. (3)

control chart: A graphic record of how closely samples of a product or service conform to standards over time. (15)

controlling: The process of comparing actual performance with standards and taking any necessary corrective action. (1, 14)

control tolerances: Specifications of how much deviation will be permitted before corrective action is taken. (14)

coordination: The process of ensuring that persons who perform interdependent activities work together in a way that contributes to overall goal attainment. (6)

corporate culture: The system of shared values, beliefs, and habits within an organization that interacts with formal structure to produce behavioral norms. (4, 13)

corporate-level strategic planning: The process of defining the overall character and purpose of the organization, the businesses it will enter and leave, and how resources will be distributed among those businesses. (4)

cyclical variation: A reasonably predictable movement about the trend line that occurs over a regular period of more than one year. (17)

decision making: The process of generating and evaluating alternatives and making choices among them. (1, 5)

decision risk: Exposure to the probability that an incorrect decision will have an adverse effect on the organization. (5)

delegation: The process of assigning responsibility along with the needed authority. (7)

Delphi technique: A formal procedure for obtaining consensus among a number of experts through the use of a series of questionnaires. (5)

democratic leader: A person who tries to do what the majority of subordinates desire. (11)

departmentation: The process of grouping related functions or major work activities into manageable units. (6)

disciplinary action: Action taken to correct unacceptable behavior. (14)

discounted cash flow technique: A way of valuing an investment that uses an interest or discount rate to calculate the present value of the income the investment is expected to produce. (17)

diversification: Increasing the variety of products or services made or sold. (4)

economic order quantity (EOQ): A procedure for balancing ordering costs and carrying costs so as to minimize total inventory costs. (15)

effectiveness: The degree to which the process produces the intended outputs. (2)

efficiency: The proportional relationships between the quality and quantity of inputs and the quality and quantity of outputs produced. (2)

empathy: The ability to identify with the various feelings and thoughts of another person. (12)

employment requisition: A form issued to activate the recruitment process; it typically includes such information as the job title, starting date, pay scale, and a brief summary of principal duties. (9)

entrepreneur: A person who organizes, manages, and assumes responsibility for a business or other enterprise. (19)

ethics: The discipline dealing with what is good and bad or right and wrong or with moral duty and obligation. (18)

executive burnout: Someone in a state of fatigue or frustration brought about by devotion to a cause, way of life, or relationship that failed to produce the expected reward. (13)

expectancy: An individual's perception of the chances or probability that a particular outcome will occur as a result of certain behavior. (10)

exponential smoothing: A forecasting technique that uses a smoothing constant and recent actual and forecasted demand to estimate future demand. (17)

fixed costs: Costs that do not change with the level of output. (17)

flexible manufacturing system (FMS): A numerically controlled production arrangement that can be programmed to do a wide variety of tasks and to change from one task to another in a routine manner. (16)

flow process chart: An illustration of the activities involved in an entire process showing the sequence in which they are performed. (16)

formal communication channels: Those communication channels that are officially recognized by the organization. (12)

forward integration: Integration toward the final users of a company's product or service. (4)

function: A type of work activity that can be identified and distinguished from other work. (1, 6)

functional authority: The right of staff specialists to issue orders in their own names in designated areas. (7)

functional-level strategic planning: The process of determining policies and procedures for relatively narrow areas of activity that are critical to the success of the organization. (4)

functional organization: A modification of the line and staff organization whereby staff departments are given authority over line personnel in narrow areas of specialization. (7)

grapevine: The informal means by which information is transmitted in an organization. (8)

grievance procedure: A mechanism that gives subordinates the opportunity of carrying appeals beyond their immediate supervisors. (12)

group: The joining of two or more people together to accomplish a desired goal. (8)

Hawthorne effect: The influence of behavioral researchers on the people they study. (1)

health: The employees' freedom from illness and their general physical and mental well-being. (9)

horizontal differentiation: The process of forming additional units at the same level in the organization. (6)

horizontal integration: Buying or taking control of competitors at the same level in the production and marketing process. (4)

host country: The country in which resides the operational unit of the multinational corporation. (20)

human relations movement: The trend that began in the 1920s and that reached its apogee in the 1940s and 1950s toward treating satisfaction of psychological needs as the primary management concern. (1)

human resources planning: The analysis of future personnel requirements. (9)

human skill: The ability to understand, motivate, and get along with other people. (1)

hypothesis: A tentative statement of the nature of the relationships that exist. (5)

influencing: The process of determining or affecting the behavior of others. (1)

informal communication channels: Ways of transmitting information within an organization that bypass formal channels. (12)

informal group: Two or more persons associated with one another in ways not prescribed by the formal organization. (8)

informal organization: The set of relationships among organizational members that are not formally prescribed. (2)

information filtering: The process by which a message is altered through the elimination of certain data as the communication moves from person to person in the organization. (12)

information overload: A condition that exists when an individual is presented with too much information in too short a time. (12)

initiating structure: The extent to which leaders establish goals and structure their roles and the roles of subordinates toward the attainment of goals. (11)

integration: The unified control of a number of successive or similar operations. (4)

inventory: The goods or materials available for use by a business. (15)

iron law of responsibility: "In the long-run, those who do not use power in a manner in which society considers responsible will tend to lose it." (18)

job analysis: The process of determining the duties and skills required for performing jobs in the organization. (9)

job description: A summary of the purpose, principal duties, and responsibilities of a job. (9)

job enlargement: The changes in the scope of a job so as to provide greater variety to the worker. (10)

job enrichment: Basic changes in the content and level of responsibility of a job so as to provide greater challenge to the worker. (10)

job specification: The statement of the minimum acceptable human qualities necessary to perform the job. (9)

just-in-time inventory method (JIT): The practice of having inputs to the production process delivered precisely when they are needed and assigning responsibility to suppliers for keeping inventories to a minimum. (15)

labor supply analysis: The process of determining the availability of needed employees. (9)

leadership: Getting others to do what the leader wants them to do. (1, 11)

leadership continuum: The graphical representation developed by Robert Tannenbaum and Warren H. Schmidt showing the trade-off between a manager's use of authority and the freedom that subordinates experience as leadership style varies from boss centered to subordinate centered. (11)

learning curve: A graphical representation of the decreasing time required to do a particular task as that task is repeated by a certain person. (16)

less developed countries (LDC): Countries that lack modern industry and the supporting services industry requires. (20)

line and staff organizations: Organizations that have direct, vertical relationships between different levels and also specialists responsible for advising and assisting other managers. (7)

linear programming: A mathematical technique that attempts to allocate limited resources among competing demands in an optimum way. (17)

line departments: Departments directly involved in accomplishing the primary purpose of the organization. (7)

line organizations: Organizations that have only direct, vertical relationships between different levels within the firm. (7)

long-run trend: A projection of the long-run estimate of the demand for the product being evaluated. (17)

maintenance: The sum of all activities involved in keeping a production system in working order. (16)

management: The process of getting things done through the efforts of other people. (1)

management by objectives (MBO): A philosophy of management that emphasizes the setting of agreed-on objectives by superior and subordinate managers and the use of these objectives as the primary basis of motivation, evaluation, and control efforts. (3)

management development programs (MDP): Formal efforts to improve the skills and attitudes of present and prospective managers. (13)

management information system (MIS): Any organized approach for obtaining information on which to base management decisions. (5)

managerial grid: A two-dimensional matrix developed by Robert Blake and Jane Mouton that shows concern for people on the vertical axis and concern for production on the horizontal axis. (11)

matrix organization: A permanent organization designed to achieve specific results by using teams of specialists from different functional areas within the organization. (7)

mediation: A process in which a third party enters a dispute between two parties for the purpose of assisting them in reaching an agreement. (13)

middle managers: Managers above the supervisory level but subordinate to the firm's most senior executives. (1)

mission: The organization's continuing purpose or reason for being. (3)

modern behaviorism: The current stage of evolution of the behavioral school of management, which gives primacy to psychological considerations but treats fulfillment of emotional need mainly as a means of achieving other, primarily economic, goals. (1)

motivation: The willingness to put forth effort in the pursuit of goals. (1, 10)

moving average: A technique of smoothing the effects of random variation by averaging specified time periods. (17)

multinational company (MNC): A company that conducts a large part of its business outside the country in which it is headquartered and has a significant percentage of physical facilities and employees in other countries. (20)

nepotism: The practice of hiring one's own relatives. (19)

nominal grouping: An approach to decision making that involves idea generation by group members, group interaction only to clarify the ideas, member rankings of ideas presented, and alternative selection by summing ranks. (5)

nonroutine decisions: Decisons designed to deal with unusual problems or situations. (5)

norm: A standard of behavior expected of informal group members. (8)

objective function: A mathematical expression of what the decision maker is attempting to maximize or minimize. (17)

objectives: The desired end results of any activity. (3)

ombudsperson: A complaint officer with access to top management who hears employee complaints, investigates, and sometimes recommends appropriate action. (12)

open system: An organization or assemblage of things that affects and is affected by outside events. (2)

open-door policy: An established guideline that allows workers to bypass immediate supervisors concerning substantive matters without fear of reprisal. (12)

operating budget: A statement of the planned income and expenses of a business or subunit. (15)

operation chart: A chart showing an operator's activities while performing one operation in a process. (16)

ordering costs: Administrative, clerical, and other expenses incurred in initially obtaining inventory items and placing them in storage. (15)

organization: Two or more people working together in a coordinated manner to achieve group results. (6)

organizational behavior modification (OBM): The application of B. F. Skinner's reinforcement theory to organizational change efforts. (10)

organizational constituency: Any identifiable group that organizational managers either have or acknowledge a responsibility to represent. (18)

organizational development (OD): A planned and systematic attempt to change the organization, typically to a more behavioral environment. (13)

organizational mission: The organization's continuing purposes—in short, what is to be accomplished for whom. (4)

organizational stakeholder: An individual or group whose interests are affected by organizational activities. (18)

organizational strategists: Those persons who spend a large portion of their time on matters of vital or far-ranging importance to the organization as a whole. (4)

organizational structure: The formal relationship among groups and individuals in the organization. (7)

organizing: The process of prescribing formal relationships among people and resources to accomplish goals. (1, 6)

orientation: A formal and informal process whereby new employees are introduced to their company, jobs, and members of the work group. (9)

parent country: The country in which the headquarters of the multinational corporation is located. (20)

participative leader: A person who involves subordinates in decision making but may retain the final authority. (11)

path-goal theory: The proposition that managers can facilitate job performance by showing employees how their performance directly affects their receiving desired rewards. (11)

payback method: The method by which investments are ranked according to payback period, the time it takes an investment to pay back the initial capital in profits. (17)

perception set: A fixed tendency to interpret information in a certain way. (12)

performance appraisal: The formal process of evaluating the activities of employees to determine how well they are performing their assigned tasks. (9)

personnel demand analysis: The determination of the numbers and types of employees needed to achieve organizational goals. (9)

PERT (program evaluation and review technique): A planning and control technique that involves the display of a complex project as a network of events and activities with three time estimates used to calculate the expected time for each activity. (15)

planning: Determining in advance what should be accomplished and how to do it. (1, 3)

plans: Statements of how objectives are to be accomplished. (3)

policy: A predetermined guide established to provide direction in decision making. (3)

political action committees (PACs): Tax-favored organizations formed by special interest groups to accept contributions and influence governmental action. (18)

politics: A network of interaction by which power is acquired, transferred, and exercised on others. (8)

power: The ability of one person to influence the behavior of another person. (8)

predetermined time standards: Established estimates of the time that should be required to perform minute elements of work. (16)

preliminary interviews: Interviews used to eliminate the obviously unqualified applicants. (9)

preventive maintenance: Routine inspection and other efforts aimed at keeping equipment and facilities in good working order. (16)

procedure: A series of steps established for the accomplishment of some specific project or endeavor. (3)

process layout: An arrangement of the processing components according to the function they perform. (16)

production and operations management: The application of objectivity, especially quantitative, techniques to the design and operation of any system that transforms inputs into desired outputs. (16)

productivity: A measure of the relationship between inputs (labor, capital, natural resources, energy, and so forth) and the ability and quantity of outputs (goods and services). (1)

product layout: A production arrangement that entails moving a product down an assembly line or conveyor and through a series of work stations until completed. (16)

product life cycle: The pattern of sales volume that all products follow and that includes the stages of introduction, growth, maturity, and decline. (4)

progressive discipline: An approach to imposing disciplinary action designed to ensure that the minimum penalty appropriate to the offense is imposed and involves answering a series of questions about the severity of the offense. (14)

project organization: A temporary organization designed to achieve specific results by using teams of specialists from different functional areas within the organization. (7)

quality: The degree of excellence of a product or service. (15)

quality circles (QCs): Small groups of employees who get together on company time to develop ways to improve the quality and quantity of work. (10)

random variations: Variations for which there is no pattern. (17)

recruitment: The encouragement of individuals with the needed skills to make application for employment with the firm. (9)

regression analysis: A mathematical technique used to predict one item (known as the dependent variable) through knowledge of other items (known as the independent variables). (17)

reinforcement theory: The idea that human behavior can be explained in terms of the previous positive or negative outcomes of that behavior. (10)

responsibility: An obligation to perform work activities. (7)

retrenchment: The reduction of the size or scope of a firm's activities. (4)

robot: An automatically controlled machine that can perform mechanical tasks. (5)

role: The total pattern of expected behavior. (8)

rule: A specific and detailed guide to action set up to direct or restrict action in a fairly narrow manner. (3)

SBU-level strategic planning: The process of determining how an SBU (Strategic Business Unit) will compete in a particular line of business. (4)

safety: The protection of employees from injuries due to work-related accidents. (9)

scalar principle: The philosophy that authority and responsibility should flow from top management downward in a clear, unbroken line. (7)

scientific management: The name given to the principles and practices that grew out of the work of Frederick Taylor and his followers and that are characterized by concern for efficiency and systematization in management. (1)

scientific method: A formal way of doing research that comprises observation of events, hypothesis formulation, experimentation, and acceptance or rejection of hypothesis. (5)

seasonal variations: Reasonably predictable changes in demand that occur over a period of a year. (17)

selection: The process of identifying those recruited individuals who will best be able to assist the firm in achieving organizational goals. (9)

sensitivity training: An organizational development (OD) technique that uses leaderless discussion groups. (13)

simulation: The use of computers to assist in performing experiments on a model of a real system. (17)

small business: One that is independently owned and operated and not dominant in its field. (19)

Small Business Act: Legislation that set up the Small Business Administration (SBA) and specified the support that the federal government would provide to small businesses. (19)

Small Business Institute: Institute that uses seniors and graduate students of leading business schools throughout the country to provide on-site management counseling to small businesses. (19)

social audit: A systematic assessment of a company's activities in terms of social impact. (18)

social contract: The set of rules and assumptions about behavior patterns among the various elements of society. (18)

social responsibility: The implied, enforced, or felt obligation of managers, acting in their official capacities, to serve or protect the interests of groups other than themselves. (18)

source (sender): The person who has an idea or message to communicate to another person or persons. (12)

span of management: The number of direct subordinates reporting to any manager. (7)

specialization of labor: The division of a complex job into simpler tasks so that a person or group may carry out only identical or related activities. (6)

staff departments: Departments that provide line people with advice and assistance in specialized areas. (7)

staffing: The process of ensuring that the organization has qualified workers available at all levels in order to achieve company objectives. (9)

staff strategic planning specialists: Specialists who assist and advise managers in strategic planning. (4)

standard operating procedures (SOP): The stable body of policies and procedures, written and unwritten, that governs an organization. (3)

standards: Established levels of quality or quantity used to guide performance. (14)

standing plans: Plans that remain roughly the same for long periods of time. (3)

status: A person's rank or position in a group. (8)

status symbol: A visible, external sign of one's social position. (8)

stockholders: The owners of a corporation. (2)

strategic business unit: Any part of a business organization that is treated separately for strategic planning purposes. (4)

strategic control points: Critical points selected for monitoring in the process of producing goods or services. (14)

strategic planning: The determination of overall organizational purposes and objectives and how they are to be achieved. (4)

strategic planning staff specialists: Specialists who assist and advise managers in strategic planning. (4)

stress: The nonspecific response of the body to any demands made on it. (13)

supervisory managers: Persons who directly oversee the efforts of those who actually perform the work. (1)

survey feedback method: The method of basing organizational change efforts on the systematic collection and measurement of subordinate attitudes by anonymous questionnaires. (13)

synergism: The potential for two or more persons working together to accomplish more than they could working separately. (8)

systems approach: The viewing of any organization or entity as an arrangement of interrelated parts that interact in ways that can be specified and to some extent predicted. (2)

team building: A conscious effort to develop effective work groups throughout the organization. (13)

technical skill: The ability to use specific knowledge, methods, or techniques in performing work. (1)

teleconferencing: The method of conducting or participating in discussions by telephone or videophone. (5)

Theory X: The traditional view of management that suggests that managers are required to coerce, control, or threaten employees in order to motivate them. (10)

Theory Y: A view of management by which a manager believes people are capable of being responsible and mature. (10)

Theory Z: The belief that a high degree of mutual responsibility, loyalty, and consideration between companies and their employees will result in higher productivity and improved employee welfare. (10)

time series analysis: A variation of regression analysis in which the independent variable is expressed in units of time. (17)

time study: The systematic measurement and analysis of the time required to do work. (16)

timing: The determination of when a message should be communicated. (12)

top managers: The organization's most senior executives. (1)

training and development (T&D): Programs designed to assist individuals, groups, and the entire organization to become more effective. (9)

trait approach to leadership: The evaluation and selection of leaders based on their physical, mental, and psychological characteristics. (11)

Type I ethics: The strength of the relationship between what an individual or an organization believes to be moral and correct and what available sources of guidance suggest is morally correct. (18)

Type II ethics: The strength of the relationship between what one believes and how one behaves. (18)

union: A group of employees who have joined together for the purpose of dealing with their employer. (2)

unity of command principle: The belief that each person should answer to only one immediate superior; each employee has only one boss. (7)

valence: The value an individual places on a specific outcome. (10)

variable costs: Costs that are directly related to changes in output. (17)

vertical differentiation: The process of creating additional levels in the organization. (6)

videotex: The remote display on a TV-type screen (cathode ray tube or CRT) of information from computer files and data bases. (5)

voice mail: Spoken messages transmitted electron- ically and stored for delivery to the recipient at a later date. (5)

waiting line theory: A production and operations management tool that attempts to determine the optimum rate of flow-through service points by balancing the costs of making customers wait against the costs of serving them more rapidly. (17)

worker-machine chart: A chart showing if there is excessive idle time associated with either the worker or the machine. (16)

work sampling: The observation of a worker or workers at random times to determine the proportion of their time that is being spent on various tasks. (16)

Index